Node.js, MongoDB and AngularJS Web Development

Developer's Library

ESSENTIAL REFERENCES FOR PROGRAMMING PROFESSIONALS

Developer's Library books are designed to provide practicing programmers with unique, high-quality references and tutorials on the programming languages and technologies they use in their daily work.

All books in the *Developer's Library* are written by expert technology practitioners who are especially skilled at organizing and presenting information in a way that's useful for other programmers.

Key titles include some of the best, most widely acclaimed books within their topic areas:

PHP & MySQL Web Development
Luke Welling & Laura Thomson
ISBN 978-0-321-83389-1

MySQL
Paul DuBois
ISBN-13: 978-0-321-83387-7

Linux Kernel Development
Robert Love
ISBN-13: 978-0-672-32946-3

Python Essential Reference
David Beazley
ISBN-13: 978-0-672-32978-4

PostgreSQL
Korry Douglas
ISBN-13: 978-0-672-32756-2

C++ Primer Plus
Stephen Prata
ISBN-13: 978-0321-77640-2

Developer's Library books are available at most retail and online bookstores, as well as by subscription from Safari Books Online at **safari.informit.com**

Developer's
Library
informit.com/devlibrary

Node.js, MongoDB and AngularJS Web Development

Brad Dayley

Addison-Wesley

Upper Saddle River, NJ • Boston • Indianapolis • San Francisco
New York • Toronto • Montreal • London • Munich • Paris • Madrid
Cape Town • Sydney • Tokyo • Singapore • Mexico City

ISBN-13: 978-0-321-99578-0
ISBN-10: 0-321-99578-3

Text printed in the United States on recycled paper at Edwards Brothers Malloy in Ann Arbor, Michigan.

First printing: June 2014

For information about buying this title in bulk quantities, or for special sales opportunities (which may include electronic versions; custom cover designs; and content particular to your business, training goals, marketing focus, or branding interests), please contact our corporate sales department at corpsales@pearsoned.com or (800) 382-3419.

For government sales inquiries, please contact governmentsales@pearsoned.com.

For questions about sales outside the U.S., please contact international@pearsoned.com.

Visit us on the Web: informit.com/aw

Library of Congress Control Number: 2014936529

Acquisitions Editor
Mark Taber

Managing Editor
Kristy Hart

Project Editor
Elaine Wiley

Copy Editor
Kitty Wilson

Indexer
Brad Herriman

Proofreader
Debbie Williams

Technical Reviewers
Russell Kloepfer
Siddhartha Singh

Cover Designer
Chuti Prasertsith

Senior Compositor
Gloria Schurick

❖

For D!

A & F

❖

Contents

Acknowledgments

I'd like to take this page to thank all those who made this title possible. First, I thank my wonderful wife for the inspiration, love, and support she gives me. I'd never make it far without you. I also want to thank my boys for the help they give me when I am writing and for making sure I still take the time to have fun.

Thanks to Mark Taber for getting this title rolling in the right direction, Russell Kloepfer and Siddhartha Singh for keeping me honest with their technical review, Kitty Wilson for turning the technical ramblings of my brain into a fine text, Tammy Graham and Laura Robbins for styling the graphics, Chuti Prasertsith for the awesome cover, and Elaine Wiley for managing the project and making sure the book is the finest quality.

About the Author

Brad Dayley is a senior software engineer with more than 20 years of experience developing enterprise applications and web interfaces. He has used JavaScript and jQuery for years and is the author of *jQuery and JavaScript Phrasebook* and *Teach Yourself jQuery and JavaScript in 24 Hours*. He has designed and implemented a wide array of applications and services, from application servers to complex Web 2.0 interfaces. He is also the author of *Python Developer's Phrasebook* and *Teach Yourself Django in 24 Hours*.

We Want to Hear from You!

As the reader of this book, *you* are our most important critic and commentator. We value your opinion and want to know what we're doing right, what we could do better, what areas you'd like to see us publish in, and any other words of wisdom you're willing to pass our way.

You can email or write directly to let us know what you did or didn't like about this book—as well as what we can do to make our books stronger.

Please note that we cannot help you with technical problems related to the topic of this book, and that due to the high volume of mail we receive, we might not be able to reply to every message.

When you write, please be sure to include this book's title and author, as well as your name and phone or email address.

Email: feedback@developers-library.info

Mail: Reader Feedback
Addison-Wesley Developer's Library
800 East 96th Street
Indianapolis, IN 46240 USA

Reader Services

Visit our website and register this book at www.informit.com/register for convenient access to any updates, downloads, or errata that might be available for this book.

Introduction

Welcome to *Node.js, MongoDB, and AngularJS Web Development.* This book is designed to catapult you into the world of using JavaScript—from the server and services to the browser client—in your web development projects. The book covers the implementation and integration of Node.js, MongoDB, and AngularJS—some of the most exciting and innovative technologies emerging in the world of web development.

This introduction covers:

- Who should read this book
- Why you should read this book
- What you will be able to achieve using this book
- What Node.js, MongoDB, and AngularJS are and why they are great technologies
- How this book is organized
- Where to find the code examples

Let's get started.

Who Should Read This Book

This book is aimed at readers who already have an understanding of the basics of HTML and have done some programming in a modern programming language. Having an understanding of JavaScript will make this book easier to digest but is not required because the book does cover the basics of JavaScript.

Why You Should Read This Book

This book will teach you how to create powerful, interactive websites and web applications—from the webserver and services on the server to the browser-based interactive web applications. The technologies covered here are all open source, and you will be able to use JavaScript for both the server-side and browser-side components.

Typical readers of this book want to master Node.js and MongoDB for the purpose of building highly scalable and high-performing websites. Typical readers will also want to leverage the innovative MVC approach of AngularJS to implement well-designed and structured webpages and web applications. Overall, Node.js, MongoDB, and AngularJS provide an easy-to-implement, fully integrated web development stack that allows you to implement amazing Web 2.0 applications.

What You Will Learn from This Book

Reading this book will enable you to build real-world, dynamic websites and web applications. Websites no longer consist of simple static content in HTML pages with integrated images and formatted text. Instead, websites have become much more dynamic, with a single page often serving as an entire site or application.

Using AngularJS technology allows you to build into your webpage logic that can communicate back to the Node.js server and obtain necessary data from the MongoDB database. The combination of Node.js, MongoDB, and AngularJS allows you to implement interactive dynamic webpages. The following are just a few of the things that you will learn while reading this book:

- How to implement a highly scalable and dynamic webserver, using Node.js and Express
- How to build server-side web services in JavaScript
- How to implement a MongoDB data store for you web applications
- How to access and interact with MongoDB from Node.js JavaScript code
- How to define static and dynamic web routes and implement server-side scripts to support them
- How to define your own custom AngularJS directives that extend the HTML language
- How to implement client-side services that can interact with the Node.js webserver
- How to build dynamic browser views that provide rich user interaction
- How to add authenticated user accounts to your website/web application
- How to add nested comment components to your webpages
- How to build an end-to-end shopping cart

What Is Node.js?

Node.js is a development framework that is based on Google's V8 JavaScript engine. You write Node.js code in JavaScript, and then V8 compiles it into machine code to be executed. You can write most—or maybe even all—of your server-side code in Node.js, including the webserver and the server-side scripts and any supporting web application functionality. The fact that the webserver and the supporting web application scripts are running together in the same server-side application allows for much tighter integration between the webserver and the scripts.

The following are just a few reasons Node.js is a great framework:

- **JavaScript end-to-end:** One of the biggest advantages of Node.js is that it allows you to write both server- and client-side scripts in JavaScript. There have always been difficulties in deciding whether to put logic in client-side scripts or server-side scripts. With Node.js you can take JavaScript written on the client and easily adapt it for the server and vice versa. An added plus is that client developers and server developers are speaking the same language.
- **Event-driven scalability:** Node.js applies a unique logic to handling web requests. Rather than having multiple threads waiting to process web requests, with Node.js they are processed on the same thread, using a basic event model. This allows Node.js webservers to scale in ways that traditional webservers can't.
- **Extensibility:** Node.js has a great following and very active development community. People are providing new modules to extend Node.js functionality all the time. Also, it is very simple to install and include new modules in Node.js; you can extend a Node.js project to include new functionality in minutes.
- **Fast implementation:** Setting up Node.js and developing in it are super easy. In only a few minutes you can install Node.js and have a working webserver.

What Is MongoDB?

MongoDB is an agile and very scalable NoSQL database. The name Mongo comes from the word "humongous," emphasizing the scalability and performance MongoDB provides. MongoDB provides great website backend storage for high-traffic websites that need to store data such as user comments, blogs, or other items because it is quickly scalable and easy to implement.

The following are some of the reasons that MongoDB really fits well in the Node.js stack:

- **Document orientation:** Because MongoDB is document oriented, data is stored in the database in a format that is very close to what you deal with in both server-side and client-side scripts. This eliminates the need to transfer data from rows to objects and back.
- **High performance:** MongoDB is one of the highest-performing databases available. Especially today, with more and more people interacting with websites, it is important to have a backend that can support heavy traffic.
- **High availability:** MongoDB's replication model makes it very easy to maintain scalability while keeping high performance.
- **High scalability:** MongoDB's structure makes it easy to scale horizontally by sharding the data across multiple servers.

- **No SQL injection:** MongoDB is not susceptible to SQL injection (that is, putting SQL statements in web forms or other input from the browser and thereby compromising database security). This is the case because objects are stored as objects, not using SQL strings.

What Is AngularJS?

AngularJS is a client-side framework developed by Google. It is written in JavaScript, with a reduced jQuery library. The theory behind AngularJS is to provide a framework that makes it easy to implement well-designed and structured webpages and applications, using an MVC framework.

AngularJS provides functionality to handle user input in the browser, manipulate data on the client side, and control how elements are displayed in the browser view. Here are some of the benefits AngularJS provides:

- **Data binding:** AngularJS has a very clean method for binding data to HTML elements, using its powerful scope mechanism.
- **Extensibility:** The AngularJS architecture allows you to easily extend almost every aspect of the language to provide your own custom implementations.
- **Clean:** AngularJS forces you to write clean, logical code.
- **Reusable code:** The combination of extensibility and clean code makes it very easy to write reusable code in AngularJS. In fact, the language often forces you to do so when creating custom services.
- **Support:** Google is investing a lot into this project, which gives it an advantage over similar initiatives that have failed.
- **Compatibility:** AngularJS is based on JavaScript and has a close relationship with jQuery. This makes it easier to begin integrating AngularJS into your environment and reuse pieces of your existing code within the structure of the AngularJS framework.

How This Book Is Organized

This book is divided into six main parts:

- Part I, "Introduction," provides an overview of the interaction between Node.js, MongoDB, and AngularJS and how these three products form a complete web development stack. Chapter 2 is a JavaScript primer that provides the basics of the JavaScript language that you need when implementing Node.js and AngularJS code.
- Part II, "Learning Node.js," covers the Node.js language platform, from installation to implementation of Node.js modules. This part gives you the basic framework you need

to implement your own custom Node.js modules as well as the webserver and server-side scripts.

- Part III, "Learning MongoDB," covers the MongoDB database, from installation to integration with Node.js applications. This part discusses how to plan your data model to fit your application needs and how to access and interact with MongoDB from your Node.js applications.
- Part IV, "Using Express to Make Life Easier," discusses the Express module for Node.js and how to leverage it as the webserver for your application. You will learn how to set up dynamic and static routes to data as well as how to implement security, caching, and other webserver basics.
- Part V, "Learning AngularJS," covers the AngularJS framework architecture and how to integrate it into your Node.js stack. This part covers creating custom HTML directives and client-side services that can be leveraged in the browser.
- Part VI, "Building Practical Web Application Components," switches gears and provides some practical real-world examples of using Node.js, MongoDB, and AngularJS end-to-end to provide authenticated user accounts, comment sections, and shopping carts for web applications. This part also covers some methods to implement Web 2.0 interactions in your web applications.

Getting the Code Examples

Throughout this book, you will find code examples in listings. The title for each listing includes a filename for the source code. To access the source code files and images used in the examples, visit:

https://github.com/bwdbooks/nodejs-mongodb-angularjs-web-development

A Final Word

I hope you enjoy learning about Node.js, MongoDB, and AngularJS as much as I have. They are great, innovative technologies that are really fun to use. Soon, you'll be able to join the many other web developers who use the Node.js-to-AngularJS web stack to build interactive websites and web applications. I also hope you enjoy this book!

1

Introducing the Node.js-to-AngularJS Stack

To get you off on the right foot, this chapter focuses on the fundamental components of the web development framework and then describes the components of the Node.js-to-AngularJS stack that is the basis for the rest of the book. The first section discusses various aspects of the general website/web application development framework, from users to backend services. The purpose of first covering the web development framework components is to help you more easily understand how the components of the Node.js-to-AngularJS stack relate to the pieces of the general framework. This should help you better see the benefits of using the Node.js-to-AngularJS stack components instead of the more traditional technologies.

Understanding the Basic Web Development Framework

To get you in the right mind-set to understand the benefits of utilizing Node.js, MongoDB, and AngularJS as your web framework, this section provides an overview of the basic components of most websites. If you are already familiar with the full web framework, then this section will be old hat, but if you only understand just the server side or client side of the web framework, then this section will give you a more complete picture.

The main components of any web framework are the user, browser, webserver, and backend services. Although websites vary greatly in terms of appearance and behavior, all have these basic components in one form or another.

This section is not intended to be in-depth, comprehensive, or technically exact but rather a very high-level perspective of the parts involved in a functional website. The components are described in a top-down manner, from user down to backend services. Then the next section discusses the Node.js-to-AngularJS stack from the bottom up, so you can get a picture of where each of the pieces fits and why. Figure 1.1 provides a basic diagram to help you visualize the components in a website/web application, which are discussed in the following sections.

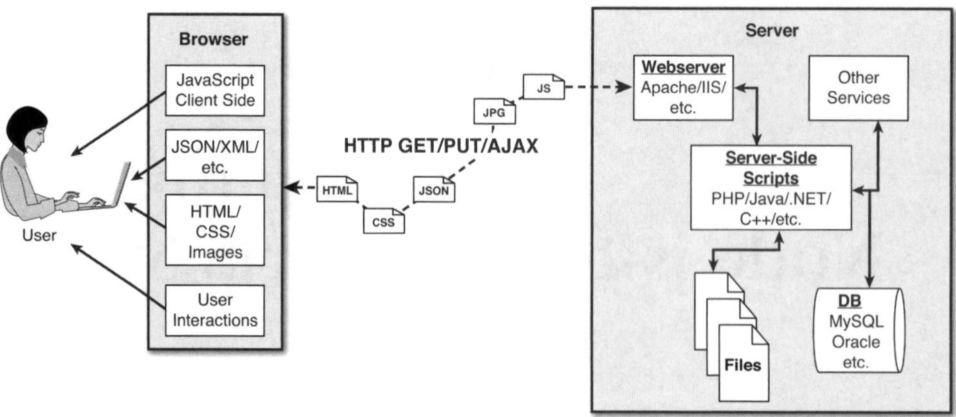

Figure 1.1 Basic diagram of the components of a basic website/web application.

Users

Users are a fundamental part of every website; they are, after all, the reason websites exist in the first place. User expectations define the requirements for developing a good website. User expectations have changed a lot over the years. In the past, users accepted the slow, cumbersome experience of the "world-wide-wait," but not today. They expect websites to behave much more quickly, like applications installed on their computers and mobile devices.

The user role in a web framework is to sit on the visual output and interaction input of webpages. That is, users view the results of the web framework processing and then provide interactions using mouse clicks, keyboard input, and swipes and taps.

The Browser

The browser plays three roles in the web framework:

- Provide communication to and from the webserver
- Interpret the data from the server and render it into the view that the user actually sees
- Handle user interaction through the keyboard, mouse, touchscreen, or other input device and take the appropriate action

Browser-to-Webserver Communication

Browser-to-webserver communication consists of a series of requests, using the HTTP and HTTPS protocols. Hypertext Transfer Protocol (HTTP) is used to define communication between the browser and the webserver. HTTP defines what types of requests can be made as well as the format of those requests and the HTTP response.

HTTPS adds an additional security layer, SSL/TLS, to ensure secure connections by requiring the webserver to provide a certificate to the browser. The user can then determine whether to accept the certificate before allowing the connection.

There are three main types of requests that a browser will make to a webserver:

- **GET:** The GET request is typically used to retrieve data from the server, such as .html files, images, or JSON data.
- **POST:** POST requests are used when sending data to the server, such as adding an item to a shopping cart or submitting a web form.
- **AJAX:** Asynchronous JavaScript and XML (AJAX) is actually just a GET or POST request that is done directly by JavaScript running in the browser. Despite the name, an AJAX request can receive XML, JSON, or raw data in the response.

Rendering the Browser View

The screen that the user actually views and interacts with is often made up of several different pieces of data retrieved from the webserver. The browser reads data from the initial URL and then renders the HTML document to build a Document Object Model (DOM). The DOM is a tree structure object with the HTML document as the root. The structure of the tree basically matches the structure of the HTML document. For example, `document` will have `html` as a child, and `html` will have `head` and `body` as children, and `body` may have `div`, `p`, or other elements as children, like this:

```
document
  + html
    + head
    + body
      + div
        + p
```

The browser interprets each DOM element and renders it to the user's screen to build the webpage view.

The browser often gets various types of data from multiple webserver requests to build a webpage. The following are the most common types of data the browser uses to render the final user view as well as define the webpage behavior:

- **HTML files:** These provide the fundamental structure of the DOM.
- **CSS files:** These define how each of the elements on the page is to be styled, in terms of font, color, borders, and spacing.
- **Client-side scripts:** These are typically JavaScript files. They can provide added functionality to a webpage, manipulate the DOM to change the look of the webpage, and provide any necessary logic required to display the page and provide functionality.
- **Media files:** Image, video, and sound files are rendered as part of the webpage.

- **Data:** Data such as XML, JSON, or raw text can be provided by the webserver as a response to an AJAX request. Rather than send a request back to the server to rebuild the webpage, new data can be retrieved via AJAX and inserted into the webpage via JavaScript.
- **HTTP headers:** HTTP defines a set of headers that the browser can use and client-side scripts to define the behavior of the webpage. For example, cookies are contained in the HTTP headers. The HTTP headers also define the type of data in the request as well as the type of data expected to be returned to the browser.

User Interaction

The user interacts with the browser via mice, keyboards, and touchscreens. A browser has an elaborate event system that captures user input events and then takes the appropriate actions. Actions vary from displaying a popup menu to loading a new document from the server to executing client-side JavaScript.

Webservers

A webserver's main focus is handling requests from browsers. As described earlier, a browser may request a document, post data, or perform an AJAX request to get data. The webserver uses HTTP headers as well as a URL to determine what action to take. This is where things get very different, depending on the webserver, configuration, and technologies used.

Most out-of-the-box webservers such as Apache and IIS are made to serve static files such as .html, .css, and media files. To handle POST requests that modify server data and AJAX requests to interact with backend services, webservers need to be extended with server-side scripts.

A *server-side script* is really anything that a webserver can execute in order to perform the task the browser is requesting. These scripts can be written in PHP, Python, C, C++, C#, Perl, Java, ... the list goes on and on. Webservers such as Apache and IIS provide mechanisms to include server-side scripts and then wire them up to specific URL locations requested by the browser. This is where having a solid webserver framework can make a big difference. It often takes quite a bit of configuration to enable various scripting languages and wire up the server-side scripts so that the webserver can route the appropriate requests to the appropriate scripts.

Server-side scripts either generate a response directly by executing their code or connect with other backend servers such as databases to obtain the necessary information and then use that information to build and send the appropriate responses.

Backend Services

Backend services are services that run behind a webserver and provide data that is used to build responses to the browser. The most common type of backend service is a database that stores information. When a request comes in from the browser that requires information from the database or other backend service, the server-side script connects to the database, retrieves the information, formats it, and then sends it back to the browser. On the other hand, when data comes in from a web request that needs to be stored in the database, the server-side script connects to the database and updates the data.

Understanding the Node.js-to-AngularJS Stack Components

With the basic structure of the web framework fresh in your mind, it is time to discuss the Node.js-to-AngularJS stack. The most common—and I believe the best—version of this stack is the Node.js-to-AngularJS stack comprised of MongoDB, Express, AngularJS, and Node.js.

In the Node.js-to-AngularJS stack, Node.js provides the fundamental platform for development. The backend services and server-side scripts are all written in Node.js. MongoDB provides the data store for the website but is accessed via a MongoDB driver Node.js module. The webserver is defined by Express, which is also a Node.js module.

The view in the browser is defined and controlled using the AngularJS framework. AngularJS is an MVC framework in which the model is made up of JSON or JavaScript objects, the view is HTML/CSS, and the controller is AngularJS JavaScript code.

Figure 1.2 provides a very basic diagram of how the Node.js to AngularJS stack fits into the basic website/web application model. The following sections describe each of these technologies and why they were chosen as part of the Node.js to AngularJS stack. Later chapters in the book will cover each of the technologies in much more detail.

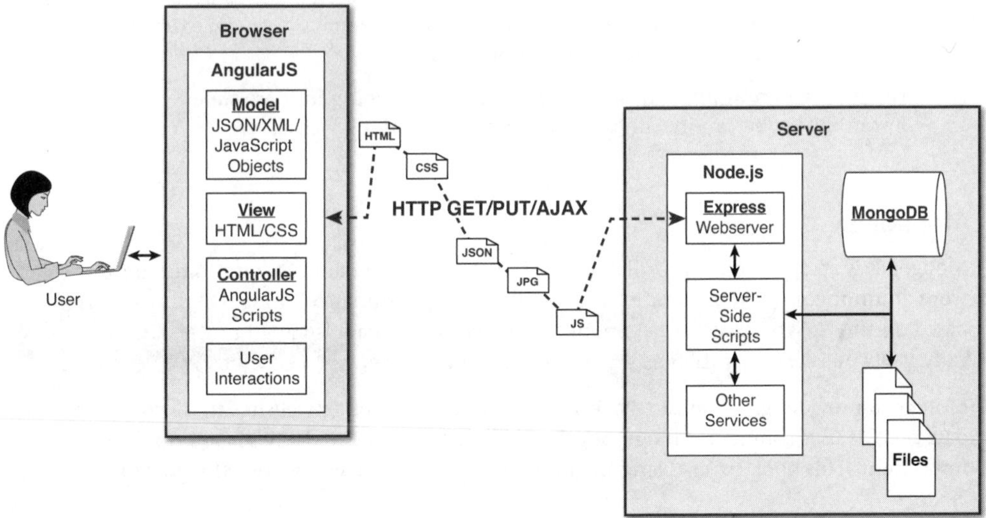

Figure 1.2 Basic diagram showing where Node.js, Express, MongoDB, and AngularJS fit in the web paradigm.

Node.js

Node.js is a development framework that is based on Google's V8 JavaScript engine and executes it.

You can write most—or maybe even all—of your server-side code in Node.js, including the webserver and the server-side scripts and any supporting web application functionality. The fact that the webserver and the supporting web application scripts are running together in the same server-side application allows for much tighter integration between the webserver and the scripts. Also, the webserver can run directly on the Node.js platform as a Node.js module, which means it's much easier than using, say, Apache for wiring up new services or server-side scripts.

The following are just a few reasons Node.js is a great framework:

- **JavaScript end-to-end:** One of the biggest advantages of Node.js is that it allows you to write both server- and client-side scripts in JavaScript. There have always been difficulties in deciding whether to put logic in client-side scripts or server-side scripts. With Node.js you can take JavaScript written on the client and easily adapt it for the server and vice versa. An added plus is that client developers and server developers are speaking the same language.
- **Event-driven scalability:** Node.js applies a unique logic to handling web requests. Rather than having multiple threads waiting to process web requests, with Node.js they are processed on the same thread, using a basic event model. This allows Node.js webservers to scale in ways that traditional webservers can't.
- **Extensibility:** Node.js has a great following and very active development community. People are providing new modules to extend Node.js functionality all the time. Also, it is very simple to install and include new modules in Node.js; you can extend a Node.js project to include new functionality in minutes.
- **Fast implementation:** Setting up Node.js and developing in it are super easy. In only a few minutes you can install Node.js and have a working webserver.

MongoDB

MongoDB is an agile and very scalable NoSQL database. The name Mongo comes from the word "humongous," emphasizing the scalability and performance MongoDB provides. It is based on the NoSQL document store model, which means data is stored in the database as basically JSON objects rather than as the traditional columns and rows of a relational database.

MongoDB provides great website backend storage for high-traffic websites that need to store data such as user comments, blogs, or other items because it is quickly scalable and easy to implement. This book covers using the MongoDB driver library to access MongoDB from Node.js.

Node.js supports a variety of database access drivers, so the data store can easily be MySQL or some other database. However, the following are some of the reasons that MongoDB really fits in the Node.js stack well:

- **Document orientation:** Because MongoDB is document oriented, data is stored in the database in a format that is very close to what you deal with in both server-side and client-side scripts. This eliminates the need to transfer data from rows to objects and back.
- **High performance:** MongoDB is one of the highest-performing databases available. Especially today, with more and more people interacting with websites, it is important to have a backend that can support heavy traffic.
- **High availability:** MongoDB's replication model makes it very easy to maintain scalability while keeping high performance.
- **High scalability:** MongoDB's structure makes it easy to scale horizontally by sharding the data across multiple servers.

Express

The Express module acts as the webserver in the Node.js-to-AngularJS stack. Because it runs in Node.js, it is easy to configure, implement, and control. The Express module extends Node.js to provide several key components for handling web requests. It allows you to implement a running webserver in Node.js with only a few lines of code.

For example, the Express module provides the ability to easily set up destination routes (URLs) for users to connect to. It also provides great functionality in terms of working with HTTP request and response objects, including things like cookies and HTTP headers.

The following is a partial list of the valuable features of Express:

- **Route management:** Express makes it easy to define routes (URL endpoints) that tie directly to the Node.js script functionality on the server.
- **Error handling:** Express provides built-in error handling for "document not found" and other errors.
- **Easy integration:** An Express server can easily be implemented behind an existing reverse proxy system, such as Nginx or Varnish. This allows you to easily integrate it into your existing secured system.
- **Cookies:** Express provides easy cookie management.
- **Session and cache management:** Express also enables session management and cache management.

AngularJS

AngularJS is a client-side framework developed by Google. It provides all the functionality needed to handle user input in the browser, manipulate data on the client side, and control how elements are displayed in the browser view. It is written in JavaScript, with a reduced jQuery library. The theory behind AngularJS is to provide a framework that makes it easy to implement web applications using the MVC framework.

Other JavaScript frameworks could be used with the Node.js platform, such as Backbone, Ember, and Meteor. However, AngularJS has the best design, feature set, and trajectory at this writing. Here are some of the benefits AngularJS provides:

- **Data binding:** AngularJS has a very clean method for binding data to HTML elements, using its powerful scope mechanism.
- **Extensibility:** The AngularJS architecture allows you to easily extend almost every aspect of the language to provide your own custom implementations.
- **Clean:** AngularJS forces you to write clean, logical code.
- **Reusable code:** The combination of extensibility and clean code makes it very easy to write reusable code in AngularJS. In fact, the language often forces you to do so when creating custom services.
- **Support:** Google is investing a lot into this project, which gives it an advantage over similar initiatives that have failed.
- **Compatibility:** AngularJS is based on JavaScript and has a close relationship with jQuery. This makes it easier to begin integrating AngularJS into your environment and reuse pieces of your existing code within the structure of the AngularJS framework.

Summary

This chapter covers the basics of the web development framework to give you a good foundation for the rest of the book. This chapter covers the basics of interaction between the webserver and browser, as well as the functionality required to make modern websites function.

This chapter also describes the Node.js-to-AngularJS stack, comprising Node.js, MongoDB, Express, and AngularJS. Node.js provides the platform for the framework, MongoDB provides the backend data store, Express provides the webserver, and AngularJS provides the client-side framework for modern web applications.

Up Next

The next chapter provides a brief primer on the JavaScript language. Because the Node.js-to-AngularJS stack is based on JavaScript, you need to be familiar with the language to be able to follow the examples in the rest of the book.

2

JavaScript Primer

Each of the components that you will be working with in this book—Node.js, MongoDB, Express, and AngularJS—is based on the JavaScript language. You'll therefore find it easy to implement and reuse code at all levels of your web development stack.

The purpose of this chapter is to familiarize you with some of the language basics of JavaScript, such as variables, functions, and objects. It is not intended as a full language guide but rather a synopsis of important syntax and idioms. If you are not familiar with JavaScript, working through this primer should enable you to understand the examples throughout the rest of the book. If you already know JavaScript well, you can either skip this chapter or review it as a refresher.

Defining Variables

You use variables in JavaScript to temporarily store and access data from your JavaScript files. Variables can point to simple data types such as numbers or strings, or they can point to more complex data types such as objects.

To define a variable in JavaScript, you use the `var` keyword and then give the variable a name, as in this example:

```
var myData;
```

You can also assign a value to the variable in the same line. For example, the following line of code creates a variable `myString` and assigns it the value `"Some Text"`:

```
var myString = "Some Text";
```

This single line does the same thing as the following two lines:

```
var myString;
myString = "Some Text";
```

After you have declared a variable, you can use its name to assign a value to the variable and access the value of the variable. For example, the following code stores a string into the myString variable and then uses it when assigning the value to the newString variable:

```
var myString = "Some Text";
var newString = myString + " Some More Text";
```

You should give variables descriptive names so you know later what data they store and can more easily use them in your programs. A variable name must begin with a letter, $, or _, and it cannot contain spaces. In addition, variable names are case sensitive, so myString is different from MyString.

Understanding JavaScript Data Types

JavaScript uses data types to determine how to handle data that is assigned to a variable. The variable type determines what operations you can perform on the variable, such as looping or executing. The following list describes the types of variables that you will most commonly work with in this book:

- **String:** This data type stores character data as a string. The character data is specified by either single or double quotes. All the data contained in the quotes will be assigned to the string variable. For example:

  ```
  var myString = 'Some Text';
  var anotherString = 'Some More Text';
  ```

- **Number:** This data type stores the data as a numerical value. Numbers are useful in counting, calculations, and comparisons. Some examples are:

  ```
  var myInteger = 1;
  var cost = 1.33;
  ```

- **Boolean:** This data type stores a single bit that is either true or false. Booleans are often used for flags. For example, you might set a variable to false at the beginning of some code and then check it on completion so see if the code execution hit a certain spot. The following examples define true and false variables:

  ```
  var yes = true;
  var no = false;
  ```

- **Array:** An indexed array is a series of separate distinct data items, all stored under a single variable name. Items in the array can be accessed by their zero-based index, using array[index]. The following is an example of creating a simple array and then accessing the first element, which is at index 0:

  ```
  var arr = ["one", "two", "three"];
  var first = arr[0];
  ```

- **Object Literal:** JavaScript supports the ability to create and use object literals. When you use an object literal, you can access values and functions in the object by using *object.property* syntax. The following example shows how to create and access properties of an object literal:

```
var obj = {"name":"Brad", "occupation":"Hacker", "age", "Unknown"};
var name = obj.name;
```

- **Null:** Sometimes you do not have a value to store in a variable either because it hasn't been created or you are no longer using it. At such a time you can set a variable to `null`. Using `null` is better than assigning a value of `0` or an empty string (`""`) because those may be valid values for the variable. By assigning `null` to a variable, you can assign no value and check against `null` inside your code, like this:

```
var newVar = null;
```

> **Note**
>
> JavaScript is a typeless language. You do not need to specify in the script what data type a variable is. The interpreter automatically figures out the correct data type for a variable. In addition, you can assign a variable of one type to a value of a different type. For example, the following code defines a string variable and then assigns it to an integer value type:

```
var id = "testID";
id = 1;
```

Using Operators

JavaScript operators allow you to alter the value of a variable. You are already familiar with the `=` operator used to assign values to variables. JavaScript provides several different operators that fall into two categories: arithmetic and assignment operators.

Arithmetic Operators

You use arithmetic operators to perform operations between variable and direct values. Table 2.1 shows a list of the arithmetic operations, along with the results that are applied.

Table 2.1 **JavaScript's arithmetic operators, with results based on y=4 initially**

Operator	Description	Examples	Resulting x
+	Addition	x=y+5	9
		x=y+"5"	"45"
		x="Four"+y+"4"	"Four44"
-	Subtraction	x=y-2	2
++	Increment	x=y++	4

Operator	Description	Examples	Resulting x
		x=++y	5
--	Decrement	x=y--	4
		x=--y	3
*	Multiplication	x=y*4	16
/	Division	x=10/y	2.5
%	Modulo (remainder of division)	x=y%3	1

Note

You can also use the + operator to add strings or to add strings and numbers together. It allows you to quickly concatenate strings as well as add numerical data to output strings. Table 2.1 shows that when you add a numerical value and a string value, the numerical value is converted to a string and then the two strings are concatenated.

Assignment Operators

You use an assignment operator to assign a value to a variable. In addition to the = operator, there are several different forms that allow you to manipulate the data as you assign a value. Table 2.2 shows a list of the assignment operations, along with the results that are applied.

Table 2.2 **JavaScript's assignment operators, with results based on x=10 initially**

Operator	Example	Equivalent Arithmetic Operators	Resulting x
=	x=5	x=5	5
+=	x+=5	x=x+5	15
-=	x-=5	x=x-5	5
*=	x*=5	x=x*5	50
/=	x/=5	x=x/5	2
%=	x%=5	x=x%5	0

Applying Comparison and Conditional Operators

Using conditionals is a way to apply logic to your applications such that certain code will be executed only under the correct conditions. You do this by applying comparison logic to variable values. The following sections describe the comparisons available in JavaScript and how to apply them in conditional statements.

Comparison Operators

A comparison operator evaluates two pieces of data and returns `true` if the evaluation is correct and `false` if the evaluation is not correct. A comparison operator compares the value on the left of the operator against the value on the right.

Table 2.3 shows a list of the comparison operators, along with some examples.

Table 2.3 **JavaScript's comparison operators, with results based on x=10 initially**

Operator	Description	Examples	Result
`==`	Equal to (value only)	`x==8`	`false`
		`x==10`	`true`
`===`	Both value and type are equal	`x===10`	`true`
		`x==="10"`	`false`
`!=`	Not equal	`x!=5`	`true`
`!==`	Both value and type are not equal	`x!=="10"`	`true`
		`x!==10`	`false`
`>`	Greater than	`x>5`	`true`
`>=`	Greater than or equal to	`x>=10`	`true`
`<`	Less than	`x<5`	`false`
`<=`	Less than or equal to	`x<=10`	`true`

You can chain together multiple comparisons by using logical operators and standard parentheses. Table 2.4 shows a list of the logical operators and how to use them to chain together comparisons.

Table 2.4 **JavaScript's comparison operators, with results based on x=10 and y=5 initially**

Operator	Description	Examples	Result
`&&`	And	`(x==10 && y==5)`	`true`
		`(x==10 && y>x)`	`false`
`||`	Or	`(x>=10 || y>x)`	`true`

<table>
<tr><th>Operator</th><th>Description</th><th>Examples</th><th>Result</th></tr>
<tr><td></td><td></td><td>(x<10 && y>x)</td><td>false</td></tr>
<tr><td>!</td><td>Not</td><td>!(x==y)</td><td>true</td></tr>
<tr><td></td><td></td><td>!(x>y)</td><td>false</td></tr>
<tr><td></td><td>Mix</td><td>(x>=10 && y<x || x==y)</td><td>true</td></tr>
<tr><td></td><td></td><td>((x<y || x>=10) && y>=5)</td><td>true</td></tr>
<tr><td></td><td></td><td>(!(x==y) && y>=10)</td><td>false</td></tr>
</table>

Using `if` Statements

An `if` statement allows you to separate code execution based on the evaluation of a comparison. The following lines of code show the conditional operators in `()` and the code to execute if the conditional evaluates to `true` in {}:

```
if(x==5){
  do_something();
}
```

In addition to only executing code within the `if` statement block, you can specify an `else` block that will be executed only if the condition is `false`. For example:

```
if(x==5){
  do_something();
} else {
  do_something_else();
}
```

You can also chain together `if` statements. To do this, add a conditional statement along with an `else` statement, as in this example:

```
if(x<5){
  do_something();
} else if(x<10) {
  do_something_else();
} else {
  do_nothing();
}
```

Implementing `switch` Statements

Another type of conditional logic is the `switch` statement. The `switch` statement allows you to evaluate an expression once and then, based on the value, execute one of many different sections of code.

The syntax for the switch statement is:

```
switch(expression){
  case value1:
    <code to execute>
    break;
  case value2:
    <code to execute>
    break;
  default:
    <code to execute if not value1 or value2>
}
```

Here is what happens: The `switch` statement evaluates the expression entirely and gets a value. The value may be a string, a number, a Boolean, or even an object. The `switch` expression is then compared to each value specified by the `case` statement. If the value matches, the code in the `case` statement is executed. If no values match, then the default code is executed.

> **Note**
>
> Typically each `case` statement includes a `break` command at the end to signal a break out of the `switch` statement. If no `break` is found, then code execution continues with the next `case` statement.

Implementing Looping

Looping is a means to execute the same segment of code multiple times. This is extremely useful when you need to repeatedly perform the same tasks on an array or set of objects.

JavaScript provides functionality to perform `for` and `while` loops. The followings sections describe how to implement loops in JavaScript.

`while` Loops

The most basic type of looping in JavaScript is the `while` loop. A `while` loop tests an expression and continues to execute the code contained in its {} brackets until the expression evaluates to `false`.

For example, the following `while` loop executes until `i` is equal to `5`:

```
var i = 1;
while (i<5){
  console.log("Iteration " + i);
  i++;
}
```

This example sends the following output to the console:

```
Iteration 1
Iteration 2
Iteration 3
Iteration 4
```

do/while Loops

Another type of `while` loop is the `do/while` loop. This is useful if you always want to execute the code in the loop at least once and the expression cannot be tested until the code has executed at least once.

For example, the following `do/while` loop executes until the `days` is equal to `Wednesday`:

```
var days = ["Monday", "Tuesday", "Wednesday", "Thursday", "Friday"];
var i=0;
do{
  var day=days[i++];
  console.log("It's " + day);
} while (day != "Wednesday");
```

This is the output at the console:

```
It's Monday
It's Tuesday
It's Wednesday
```

for Loops

A JavaScript `for` loop allows you to execute code a specific number of times by using a `for` statement that combines three statements in a single block of execution. Here's the syntax:

```
for (assignment; condition; update;){
  code to be executed;
}
```

The `for` statement uses the three statements as follows when executing the loop:

- ***assignment:*** This is executed before the loop begins and not again. It is used to initialize variables that will be used in the loop as conditionals.
- ***condition:*** This expression is evaluated before each iteration of the loop. If the expression evaluates to `true`, the loop is executed; otherwise, the `for` loop execution ends.
- ***update:*** This is executed on each iteration, after the code in the loop has executed. This is typically used to increment a counter that is used in *`condition`*.

The following example illustrates a `for` loop and the nesting of one loop inside another:

```
for (var x=1; x<=3; x++){
  for (var y=1; y<=3; y++){
    console.log(x + " X " + y + " = " + (x*y));
  }
}
```

The resulting output to the web console is:

```
1 X 1 = 1
1 X 2 = 2
1 X 3 = 3
2 X 1 = 2
2 X 2 = 4
2 X 3 = 6
3 X 1 = 3
3 X 2 = 6
3 X 3 = 9
```

`for/in` Loops

Another type of `for` loop is the `for/in` loop. The `for/in` loop executes on any data type that can be iterated. For the most part, you will use `for/in` loops on arrays and objects. The following example illustrates the syntax and behavior of the `for/in` loop on a simple array:

```
var days = ["Monday", "Tuesday", "Wednesday", "Thursday", "Friday"];
for (var idx in days){
  console.log("It's " + days[idx] + "<br>");
}
```

Notice that the variable `idx` is adjusted each iteration through the loop, from the beginning array index to the last. The resulting output is:

```
It's Monday
It's Tuesday
It's Wednesday
It's Thursday
It's Friday
```

Interrupting Loops

When you work with loops, there are times when you need to interrupt the execution of code inside the code itself, without waiting for the next iteration. There are two different ways to do this: using the `break` and `continue` keywords.

The `break` keyword stops execution of a `for` or `while` loop completely. The `continue` keyword, on the other hand, stops execution of the code inside the loop and continues on with the next iteration. Consider the following examples.

This example shows using `break` if the day is Wednesday:

```
var days = ["Monday", "Tuesday", "Wednesday", "Thursday", "Friday"];
for (var idx in days){
  if (days[idx] == "Wednesday")
    break;
  console.log("It's " + days[idx] + "<br>");
}
```

Once the value is Wednesday, loop execution stops completely:

```
It's Monday
It's Tuesday
```

This example shows using `continue` if the day is Wednesday:

```
var days = ["Monday", "Tuesday", "Wednesday", "Thursday", "Friday"];
for (var idx in days){
  if (days[idx] == "Wednesday")
    continue;
  console.log("It's " + days[idx] + "<br>");
}
```

Notice that the write is not executed for Wednesday because of the `continue` statement, but the loop execution does complete:

```
It's Monday
It's Tuesday
It's Thursday
It's Friday
```

Creating Functions

One of the most important parts of JavaScript is making code that other code can reuse. To do this, you organize your code into functions that perform specific tasks. A function is a series of code statements combined together in a single block and given a name. You can then execute the code in the block by referencing that name.

Defining Functions

You define a function by using the `function` keyword followed by a name that describes the use of the function, a list of zero or more arguments in `()`, and a block of one or more code statements in {}. For example, the following is a function definition that writes `"Hello World"` to the console:

```
function myFunction(){
  console.log("Hello World");
}
```

To execute the code in `myFunction()`, all you need to do is add the following line to the main JavaScript or inside another function:

```
myFunction();
```

Passing Variables to Functions

Frequently you need to pass specific values to functions, and the functions will use those values when executing their code. You pass values to a function in comma-delimited form. A function definition needs a list of variable names in `()` that match the number being passed in. For example, the following function accepts two arguments, *`name`* and *`city`*, and uses them to build the output string:

```
function greeting(name, city){
  console.log("Hello " + name);
  console.log(". How is the weather in " + city);
}
```

To call the `greeting()` function, you need to pass in a `name` value and a `city` value. The value can be a direct value or a previously defined variable. To illustrate this, the following code executes the `greeting()` function with a `name` variable and a direct string for `city`:

```
var name = "Brad";
greeting(name, "Florence");
```

Returning Values from Functions

Often, a function needs to return a value to the calling code. Adding a `return` keyword followed by a variable or value returns that value from the function. For example, the following code calls a function to format a string, assigns the value returned from the function to a variable, and then writes the value to the console:

```
function formatGreeting(name, city){
  var retStr = "";
  retStr += "Hello <b>" + name + "/n");
  retStr += "Welcome to " + city + "!";
return retStr;
}
var greeting = formatGreeting("Brad", "Rome");
console.log(greeting);
```

You can include more than one `return` statement in the function. When the function encounters a `return` statement, code execution of the function stops immediately. If the `return` statement contains a value to return, then that value is returned. The following example shows a function that tests the input and returns immediately if it is zero:

```
function myFunc(value){
  if (value == 0)
    return value;
  <code_to_execute_if_value_nonzero>
  return value;
}
```

Using Anonymous Functions

So far, all the examples you have seen show named functions. JavaScript also lets you create anonymous functions. These functions have the advantage of being defined directly in the parameter sets when you call other functions. Thus you do not need formal definitions.

For example, the following code defines a function `doCalc()` that accepts three parameters. The first two should be numbers, and the third is a function that will be called and passed the two numbers as arguments:

```
function doCalc(num1, num2, calcFunction){
    return calcFunction(num1, num2);
}
```

You could define a function and then pass the function name without parameters to `doCalc()`, as in this example:

```
function addFunc(n1, n2){
    return n1 + n2;
}
doCalc(5, 10, addFunc);
```

However, you also have the option to use an anonymous function directly in the call to `doCalc()`, as shown in these two statements:

```
console.log( doCalc(5, 10, function(n1, n2){ return n1 + n2; }) );
console.log( doCalc(5, 10, function(n1, n2){ return n1 * n2; }) );
```

You can probably see that the advantage of using anonymous functions is that you do not need a formal definition that will not be used anywhere else in your code. Anonymous functions, therefore, make JavaScript code more concise and readable.

Understanding Variable Scope

Once you start adding conditions, functions, and loops to your JavaScript applications, you need to understand variable scoping. Variable scoping sets out to determine the value of a specific variable name at the line of code currently being executed.

JavaScript allows you to define both a global version and a local version of a variable. The global version is defined in the main JavaScript, and local versions are defined inside functions. When you define a local version in a function, a new variable is created in memory. Within that function, you reference the local version. Outside that function, you reference the global version.

To understand variable scoping a bit better, consider the code in Listing 2.1.

Listing 2.1 **Defining global and local variables in JavaScript**

```
01 var myVar = 1;
02 function writeIt(){
03   var myVar = 2;
04   console.log("Variable = " + myVar);
05   writeMore();
06 }
07 function writeMore(){
08   console.log("Variable = " + myVar);
09 }
10 writeIt();
```

The global variable `myVar` is defined on line 1, and a local version is defined on line 3, within the `writeIt()` function. Line 4 writes `"Variable = 2"` to the console. Then in line 5, `writeMore()` is called. Since there is no local version of `myVar` defined in `writeMore()`, the value of the global `myVar` is written in line 9.

Using JavaScript Objects

JavaScript has several built-in objects, such as `Number`, `Array`, `String`, `Date`, and `Math`. Each of these built-in objects has member properties and methods. In addition to the JavaScript objects, you will find as you read this book that Node.js, MongoDB, Express, and Angular add their own built-in objects as well.

JavaScript provides a fairly nice object-oriented programming structure for you to create your own custom objects as well. Using objects rather than just a collection of functions is key to writing clean, efficient, reusable JavaScript code.

Using Object Syntax

To use objects in JavaScript effectively, you need to have an understanding of their structure and syntax. An object is really just a container to group together multiple values and, in some instances, functions. The values of an object are called properties and the values of functions are called methods.

To use a JavaScript object, you must first create an instance of the object. You create object instances by using the `new` keyword with the object constructor name. For example, to create a `Number` object, you could use the following line of code:

```
var x = new Number("5");
```

Object syntax is very straightforward: You use the object name and then a dot and then the property or method name. For example, the following lines of code get and set the `name` property of an object named `myObj`:

```
var s = myObj.name;
myObj.name = "New Name";
```

You can also get and set object methods of an object in the same manner. For example, the following lines of code call the `getName()` method and then change the method function on an object named `myObj`:

```
var name = myObj.getName();
myObj.getName = function() { return this.name; };
```

You can also create objects and assign variables and functions directly by using {} syntax. For example, the following code defines a new object and assigns values and a method function:

```
var obj = {
    name: "My Object",
    value: 7,
    getValue: function() { return this.name; };
};
```

You can also access members of a JavaScript object by using the *`object[propertyName]`* syntax. This is useful when you are using dynamic property names and when the property name must include characters that JavaScript does not support. For example, the following examples access the `"User Name"` and `"Other Name"` properties of an object name `myObj`:

```
var propName = "User Name";
var val1 = myObj[propName];
var val2 = myObj["Other Name"];
```

Creating Custom Defined Objects

As you have seen so far, using the built-in JavaScript objects has several advantages. As you begin to write code that uses more and more data, you will find yourself wanting to build your own custom objects, with specific properties and methods.

You can define JavaScript objects in a couple different ways. The simplest is the on-the-fly method: Simply create a generic object and then add properties to it as needed. For example, to create a user object and assign a first and last name as well as define a function to return them, you could use the following code:

```
var user = new Object();
user.first="Brad";
user.last="Dayley";
user.getName = function( ) { return this.first + " " + this.last; }
```

You could also accomplish the same effect through a direct assignment using the following code, where the object is enclosed in {} and the properties are defined using *property*:*value* syntax:

```
var user = {
  first: 'Brad',
  last: 'Dayley',
  getName: function( ) { return this.first + " " + this.last; }};
```

These first two options work very well for simple objects that you do not need to reuse later. A better method for reusable objects is to actually enclose an object inside its own function block. This has the advantage of allowing you to keep all the code pertaining to the object local to the object itself. For example:

```
function User(first, last){
  this.first = first;
  this.last = last;
  this.getName = function( ) { return this.first + " " + this.last; };
var user = new User("Brad", "Dayley");
```

The end result of these methods is essentially the same as if you have an object with properties that can be referenced using dot notation, as shown here:

```
console.log(user.getName());
```

Using a Prototyping Object Pattern

An even more advanced method of creating objects is using a prototyping pattern. You implement a pattern by defining the functions inside the prototype attribute of the object instead of inside the object itself. With prototyping, the functions defined in the prototype are created only once, when the JavaScript is loaded, instead of each time a new object is created.

The following example shows the prototyping syntax:

```
function UserP(first, last){
  this.first = first;
  this.last = last;
}
UserP.prototype = {
  getFullName: function(){
      return this.first + " " + this.last;
    }
};
```

Notice that you define the object UserP and then set UserP.prototype to include the getFullName() function. You can include as many functions in the prototype as you would like. Each time a new object is created, those functions will be available.

Manipulating Strings

The String object is by far the most commonly used object in JavaScript. JavaScript automatically creates a String object for you any time you define a variable that has a string data type. For example:

```
var myStr = "Teach Yourself jQuery & JavaScript in 24 Hours";
```

When you create a string, there are a few special characters that you can't add directly to the string. For those characters, JavaScript provides a set of escape codes, listed in Table 2.5.

Table 2.5 String **object escape codes**

Escape	Description	Example	Output String
\'	Single quote mark	"couldn\'t be"	couldn't be
\"	Double quote mark	"I \"think\" I \"am\""	I "think" I "am"
\\	Backslash	"one\\two\\three"	one\two\three
\n	New line	"I am\nI said"	I am I said
\r	Carriage return	"to be\ror not"	to be or not
\t	Tab	"one\ttwo\tthree"	one two three
\b	Backspace	"correctoin\b\b\bion"	correction
\f	Form feed	"Title A\fTitle B"	Title A then Title B

To determine the length of a string, you can use the length property of the String object, as in this example:

```
var numOfChars = myStr.length;
```

The String object has several functions that allow you to access and manipulate the string in various ways. The methods for string manipulation are described in Table 2.6.

Table 2.6 **Methods to manipulate** String **objects**

Method	Description
charAt(index)	Returns the character at the specified index.
charCodeAt(index)	Returns the Unicode value of the character at the specified index.

Method	Description
`concat(str1, str2, ...)`	Joins two or more strings and returns a copy of the joined strings.
`fromCharCode()`	Converts Unicode values to actual characters.
`indexOf(subString)`	Returns the position of the first occurrence of a specified `subString` value. Returns `-1` if the substring is not found.
`lastIndexOf(subString)`	Returns the position of the last occurrence of a specified `subString` value. Returns `-1` if the substring is not found.
`match(regex)`	Searches the string and returns all matches to the regular expression.
`replace(subString/regex, replacementString)`	Searches the string for a match of the substring or regular expression and replaces the matched substring with a new substring.
`search(regex)`	Searches the string, based on the regular expression, and returns the position of the first match.
`slice(start, end)`	Returns a new string that has the portion of the string between the `start` and `end` positions removed.
`split(sep, limit)`	Splits a string into an array of substrings, based on a separator character or regular expression. The optional `limit` argument defines the maximum number of splits to make, starting from the beginning.
`substr(start,length)`	Extracts the characters from a string, beginning at a specified `start` position, and through the specified `length` of characters.
`substring(from, to)`	Returns a substring of characters between the `from` and `to` index.
`toLowerCase()`	Converts the string to lowercase.
`toUpperCase()`	Converts the string to uppercase.
`valueOf()`	Returns the primitive string value.

To get you started on using the functionality provided in the `String` object, the following sections describe some of the common tasks that can be done using `String` object methods.

Combining Strings

You can combine multiple strings either by using a `+` operation or by using the `concat()` function on the first string. For example, in the following code, `sentence1` and `sentence2` will be the same:

```
var word1 = "Today ";
var word2 = "is ";
var word3 = "tomorrows\' ";
var word4 = "yesterday.";
var sentence1 = word1 + word2 + word3 + word4;
var sentence2 = word1.concat(word2, word3, word4);
```

Searching a String for a Substring

To determine whether a string is a substring of another, you can use the `indexOf()` method. For example, the following code writes the string to the console only if it contains the word `think`:

```
var myStr = "I think, therefore I am.";
if (myStr.indexOf("think") != -1){
  console.log (myStr);
}
```

Replacing a Word in a String

Another common `String` object task is replacing one substring with another. To replace a word or phrase in a string, you use the `replace()` method. The following code replaces the text `"<username>"` with the value of the variable `username`:

```
var username = "Brad";
var output = "<username> please enter your password: ";
output.replace("<username>", username);
```

Splitting a String into an Array

A very common task with strings is to split them into arrays, using a separator character. For example, the following code splits a time string into an array of its basic parts, using the `split()` method on the `":"` separator:

```
var t = "12:10:36";
var tArr = t.split(":");
var hour = tArr[0];
var minute = tArr[1];
var second = tArr[2];
```

Working with Arrays

The `Array` object provides a means of storing and handling a set of other objects. Arrays can store numbers, strings, or other JavaScript objects. There are a couple different ways to create JavaScript arrays. For example, the following statements create three identical versions of the same array:

```
var arr = ["one", "two", "three"];
var arr2 = new Array();
arr2[0] = "one";
arr2[1] = "two";
arr3[2] = "three";
var arr3 = new Array();
arr3.push("one");
arr3.push("two");
arr3.push("three");
```

The first method defines `arr` and sets the contents in a single statement, using `[]`. The second method creates the `arr2` object and then adds items to it, using direct index assignment. The third method creates the `arr3` object and then uses the best option for extending arrays: It uses the `push()` method to push items onto the array.

To determine the number of elements in an array, you can use the `length` property of the `Array` object, as in this example:

```
var numOfItems = arr.length;
```

Arrays follow a zero-based index, meaning that the first item is at index 0 and so on. For example, in the following code, the value of variable `first` will be `Monday`, and the value of variable `last` will be `Friday`:

```
var
week = ["Monday", "Tuesday", "Wednesday", "Thursday", "Friday"];
var first = w [0];
var last = week[week.length-1];
```

The `Array` object has several built-in functions that allow you to access and manipulate arrays in various ways. Table 2.7 describes the methods attached to the `Array` object that allow you to manipulate the array contents.

Table 2.7 **Methods to manipulate `Array` objects**

Method	Description
`concat(arr1, arr2, ...)`	Returns a joined copy of the array and the arrays passed as arguments.
`indexOf(value)`	Returns the first index of the value in the array or `-1` if the item is not found.
`join(separator)`	Joins all elements of an array, separated by the separator into a single string. If no separator is specified, a comma is used.
`lastIndexOf(value)`	Returns the last index of the `value` in the array or `-1` if the value is not found.
`pop()`	Removes the last element from the array and returns that element.

Method	Description
`push(item1, item2, ...)`	Adds one or more new elements to the end of an array and returns the new length.
`reverse()`	Reverses the order of all elements in the array.
`shift()`	Removes the first element of an array and returns that element.
`slice(start, end)`	Returns the elements between the `start` and `end` indexes.
`sort(sortFunction)`	Sorts the elements of the array. `sortFunction` is optional.
`splice(index, count, item1, item2...)`	At the `index` specified, removes `count` number items and then inserts at `index` any optional items passed in as arguments.
`toString()`	Returns the string form of an array.
`unshift()`	Adds new elements to the beginning of an array and returns the new length.
`valueOf()`	Returns the primitive value of an `Array` object.

To get you started using the functionality provided in the `Array` object, the following sections describe some of the common tasks that can be done using `Array` object methods.

Combining Arrays

You can combine arrays the same way that you combine `String` objects: using `+` statements or using the `concat()` method. In the following code, `arr3` ends up being the same as `arr4`:

```
var arr1 = [1,2,3];
var arr2 = ["three", "four", "five"]
var arr3 = arr1 + arr2;
var arr4 = arr1.concat(arr2);
```

> **Note**
>
> You can combine an array of numbers and an array of strings. Each item in the array will keep its own object type. However, as you use the items in the array, you need to keep track of arrays that have more than one data type so that you do not run into problems.

Iterating Through Arrays

You can iterate through an array by using a `for` or a `for/in` loop. The following code illustrates iterating through each item in the array using each method:

```
var week = ["Monday", "Tuesday", "Wednesday", "Thursday", "Friday"];
for (var i=0; i<week.length; i++){
  console.log("<li>" + week[i] + "</li>");
}
for (dayIndex in week){
  console.log("<li>" + week[dayIndex] + "</li>");
}
```

Converting an Array into a String

A very useful feature of `Array` objects is the ability to combine the elements of a string together to make a `String` object, separated by a specific separator using the `join()` method. For example, the following code joins the time components back together into the format `12:10:36`:

```
var timeArr = [12,10,36];
var timeStr = timeArr.join(":");
```

Checking Whether an Array Contains an Item

Often you will need to check whether an array contains a certain item. You can do this by using the `indexOf()` method. If the code does not find the item in the list, it returns a `-1`. The following function writes a message to the console if an item is in the `week` array:

```
function message(day){
  var week = ["Monday", "Tuesday", "Wednesday", "Thursday", "Friday"];
  if (week.indexOf(day) != -1){
    console.log("Happy " + day);
  }
}
```

Adding Items to and Removing Items from Arrays

There are several methods for adding items to and removing items from `Array` objects, using the various built-in methods. Table 2.8 shows some of the various methods used in this book.

Table 2.8 **`Array` object methods used to add and remove elements from arrays arrays shown as a progression from the beginning of the table to the end**

Statement	Value of `x`	Value of `arr`
`var arr = [1,2,3,4,5];`	`undefined`	`1,2,3,4,5`
`var x = 0;`	`0`	`1,2,3,4,5`
`x = arr.unshift("zero");`	`6 (length)`	`zero,1,2,3,4,5`
`x = arr.push(6,7,8);`	`9 (length)`	`zero,1,2,3,4,5,6,7,8`

Statement	Value of `x`	Value of `arr`
`x = arr.shift();`	`zero`	`1,2,3,4,5,6,7,8`
`x = arr.pop();`	`8`	`1,2,3,4,5,6,7`
`x = arr.splice(3,3,"four", "five","six");`	`4,5,6`	`1,2,3,four,five,six,7`
`x = arr.splice(3,1);`	`four`	`1,2,3,five,six,7`
`x = arr.splice(3);`	`five,six,7`	`1,2,3`

Adding Error Handling

An important part of JavaScript coding is adding error handling for instances where there may be problems. By default, if a code exception occurs because of a problem in your JavaScript, the script fails and does not finish loading. This is not usually the desired behavior. In fact, it is often catastrophic behavior. To prevent these types of big problems, you should wrap your code in a `try/catch` block.

`try/catch` Blocks

To prevent your code from totally bombing out, use `try/catch` blocks that can handle problems inside your code. If JavaScript encounters an error when executing code in a `try` block, it will jump down and execute the `catch` portion instead of stopping the entire script. If no error occurs, then the whole `try` block will be executed, and none of the `catch` block will be executed.

For example, the following `try/catch` block tries to assign variable `x` to a value of an undefined variable named `badVarNam`:

```
try{
    var x = badVarName;
} catch (err){
    console.log(err.name + ': "' + err.message +  '" occurred when assigning x.');
}
```

Notice that the `catch` statement accepts an `err` parameter, which is an error object. The error object provides the `message` property, which provides a description of the error. The error object also provides a `name` property that is the name of the error type that was thrown.

The code above results in an exception and the following message:

```
ReferenceError: "badVarName is not defined" occurred when assigning x.
```

Throwing Your Own Errors

You can also throw your own errors by using a `throw` statement. The following code illustrates how to add `throw` statements to a function to throw an error, even if a script error does not occur. The function `sqrRoot()` accepts a single argument `x`. It then tests `x` to verify that it is a `positive` number and returns a string with the square root of `x`. If `x` is not a positive number, then the appropriate error is thrown, and the `catch` block returns the error:

```
function sqrRoot(x) {
    try {
        if(x=="")     throw {message:"Can't Square Root Nothing"};
        if(isNaN(x)) throw {message:"Can't Square Root Strings"};
        if(x<0)       throw {message:"Sorry No Imagination"};
        return "sqrt("+x+") = " + Math.sqrt(x);
    } catch(err){
        return err.message;
    }
}
function writeIt(){
    console.log(sqrRoot("four"));
    console.log(sqrRoot(""));
    console.log(sqrRoot("4"));
    console.log(sqrRoot("-4"));
}
writeIt();
```

The following is the console output, showing the different errors that are thrown, based on input to the `sqrRoot()` function:

```
Can't Square Root Strings
Can't Square Root Nothing
sqrt(4) = 2
Sorry No Imagination
```

Using `Finally`

Another valuable tool in exception handling is the `finally` keyword. You can add this keyword to the end of a `try/catch` block. After the `try/catch` block is executed, the `finally` block is always executed, whether an error occurs and is caught or the `try` block is fully executed.

Here's an example of using a `finally` block inside a webpage:

```
function testTryCatch(value){
  try {
    if (value < 0){
      throw "too small";
    } else if (value > 10){
      throw "too big";
    }
    your_code_here
  } catch (err) {
    console.log("The number was " + err);
  } finally {
    console.log("This is always written.");
  }
}
```

Summary

Understanding JavaScript is critical to being able to work in the Node.js, MongoDB, Express, and AngularJS environments. This chapter discusses enough of the basic JavaScript language syntax for you to grasp the concepts in the rest of the book. You've learned how to create objects, how to use functions, and how to work with strings and arrays. You've also learned how to apply error handling to your scripts, which is critical in the Node.js environment.

Up Next

In the next chapter, you'll jump right into Node.js. You'll learn the basics of setting up a Node.js project, explore a few of the language idioms, and see a simple practical example.

3

Getting Started with Node.js

This chapter introduces you to the Node.js environment. Node.js is a website/application framework designed with high scalability in mind. It takes advantage of the existing JavaScript technology in the browser and flows those same concepts all the way down through the webserver into the backend services. Node.js is a great technology that is easy to implement and yet extremely scalable.

Node.js is a very modular platform, which means much of the functionality that you will use is provided by external modules rather than being inherently built into the platform. The Node.js culture is very active in creating and publishing modules for almost every imaginable need. Therefore, this chapter focuses on understanding and using the Node.js tools to build, publish, and use your own Node.js modules in applications.

Understanding Node.js

Node.js was developed in 2009 by Ryan Dahl as an answer to the frustration caused by concurrency issues, especially when dealing with web services. Google had just come out with the V8 JavaScript engine for the Chrome web browser, which was highly optimized for web traffic. Dahl created Node.js on top of V8 as a server-side environment that matches the client-side environment in the browser.

The result is an extremely scalable server-side environment that allows developers to more easily bridge the gap between client and server. Because Node.js is written in JavaScript, developers can easily navigate back and forth between client and server code and can even reuse code between the two environments.

Node.js has a great ecosystem built up, and new extensions are written all the time. The Node.js environment is extremely clean and easy to install, configure, and deploy. In only a matter of an hour or two, you can have a Node.js webserver up and running.

Who Uses Node.js?

Node.js is still fairly young, but it has quickly gained popularity among a wide variety of companies. These companies use Node.js first and foremost for scalability but also for ease of maintenance and faster development. The following are just a few of the companies using the Node.js technology:

- Yahoo!
- LinkedIn
- eBay
- *The New York Times*
- Dow Jones
- Microsoft

What Is Node.js Used For?

Node.js can be used for a wide variety of purposes. Because it is based on V8 and has highly optimized code to handle HTTP traffic, the most common use is as a webserver. However, Node.js can also be used for a variety of other web services, such as:

- Web services APIs such as REST
- Real-time multiplayer games
- Backend web services such as cross-domain, server-side requests
- Web-based applications
- Multiple-client communication such as IM

Installing Node.js

You can easily install Node.js by using an installer downloaded from the Node.js website (http://nodejs.org). The Node.js installer installs the necessary files on your PC to get you up and running. No additional configuration is necessary to start creating Node.js applications.

Looking at the Node.js Install Location

If you look at the installation location, you will see a couple executable files and the `node_modules` folder. Here's what you see in the installation location:

- **`node`:** This file starts a Node.js JavaScript engine. If you pass in a JavaScript file location, Node.js executes that script. If no target JavaScript file is specified, a script prompt allows you to execute JavaScript code directly from the console.

- **`npm`:** You use this command to manage the Node.js packages, as discussed in the next section.
- **`node_modules`:** This folder contains the installed Node.js packages. These packages act as libraries that extend the capabilities of Node.js.

Verifying Node.js Executables

You should take a minute to verify that Node.js is installed and working before moving on. To do so, open a command prompt and execute the following command to bring up a Node.js VM:

```
node
```

Next, at the Node.js prompt, execute the following to write `"Hello World"` to the screen:

```
>console.log("Hello World");
```

After you see `"Hello World"` written to the console screen, exit the console by pressing Ctrl+C in Windows or Cmd+C on a Mac.

Next, verify that the `npm` command is working by executing the following command at the command prompt:

```
npm version
```

You should see output similar to the following:

```
{ http_parser: '1.0',
node: '0.10.21',
  v8: '3.14.5.9',
ares: '1.9.0-DEV',
uv: '0.10.18',
zlib: '1.2.3',
modules: '11',
openssl: '1.0.1e',
npm: '1.3.11' }
```

Selecting a Node.js IDE

If you are planning on using an IDE for your Node.js projects, you should take a minute to configure that now as well. Most developers are particular about the IDE they use, and there will likely be a way to configure your IDE at least for JavaScript if not for Node.js directly. For example, Eclipse has some great Node.js plugins, and the WebStorm IDE by IntelliJ has some good features for Node.js built in.

You can use any editor you want to generate your Node.js web applications. In reality, all you need is a decent text editor. Almost all the code you will be generating will be .js, .json, .html, and .css. So pick the editor you feel the most comfortable using to write those types of files.

Working with Node.js Packages

One of the most powerful features of the Node.js framework is the ability to easily extend it with additional Node Packaged Modules (NPMs), using the Node Package Manager (NPM). That's right: In the Node.js world, *NPM* means two things. This book refers to the Node Packaged Modules as *modules* rather than as *NPMs* to avoid that confusion.

What Are Node Packaged Modules?

A Node Packaged Module is a packaged library that can easily be shared, reused, and installed in different projects. There are many different modules available for a variety of purposes. For example, the Mongoose module provides an ODM for MongoDB, Express extends Node's HTTP capabilities, and so on.

Node.js modules are created by various third-party organizations to provide important features that Node.js lacks out of the box. This community of contributors is very active in adding and updating modules.

Each Node Packaged Module includes a `package.json` file that defines the packages. The `package.json` file includes informational metadata such as the name, version, author, and contributors, as well as control metadata such as dependencies and other requirements that the Node Package Manager will use when performing actions such as installation and publishing.

Understanding the Node Package Registry

One of the things I love about the Node modules is that there is a managed location called the Node Package Registry where packages are registered. The registry allows you to publish your own packages in a location where others can use them as well as download packages that others have created.

The Node Package Registry is located at http://npmjs.org. From this location, you can view the newest and most popular modules as well as search for specific packages, as shown in Figure 3.1.

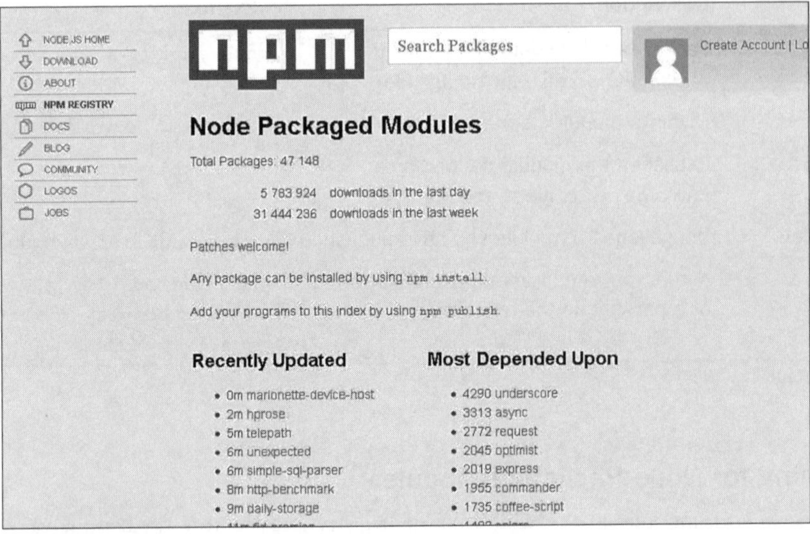

Figure 3.1 The official Node Packaged Modules website.

Using the Node Package Manager

The Node Package Manager you have already seen is a command-line utility. It allows you to find, install, remove, publish, and do a lot of other things related to Node Packaged Modules. The Node Package Manager provides a link between the Node Package Registry and your development environment.

The simplest way to really explain the Node Package Manager is to list some of the command-line options and what they do. You will be using many of these options in the rest of this chapter and throughout the book. Table 3.1 lists the Node Package Manager commands.

Table 3.1 `npm` **command-line options (with** `express` **as the package, where appropriate)**

Option	Description	Example
`search`	Finds module packages in the repository	`npm search express`

`install`	Installs a package either using a `package.json` file from the repository or from a local location	`npm install`
		`npm install express`
		`npm install express@0.1.1`
		`npm install ../tModule.tgz`

`install -g`	Installs a package in a globally accessible location	`npm install express -g`
`remove`	Removes a module	`npm remove express`

Option	Description	Example
`pack`	Packages the module defined by the `package.json` file into a .tgz file	`npm pack`
`view`	Displays module details	`npm view express`
`publish`	Publishes the module defined by a `package.json` file to the registry	`npm publish`
`unpublish`	Unpublishes a module you have published	`npm unpublish myModule`

`owner`	Allows you to add, remove, and list owners of a package in the repository	`npm add bdayley myModule`
		`npm rm bdayley myModule`
		`npm ls myModule`

Searching for Node Packaged Modules

You can search for modules in the Node Package Registry directly from the command prompt by using the `npm search <search_string>` command. For example, the following command searches for modules related to `openssl` and displays the results as shown in Figure 3.2:

```
npm search openssl
```

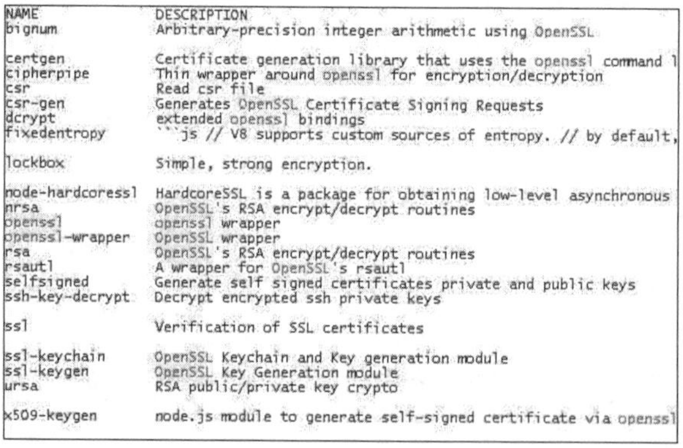

```
NAME              DESCRIPTION
bignum            Arbitrary-precision integer arithmetic using OpenSSL

certgen           Certificate generation library that uses the openssl command l
cipherpipe        Thin wrapper around openssl for encryption/decryption
csr               Read csr file
csr-gen           Generates OpenSSL Certificate Signing Requests
dcrypt            extended openssl bindings
fixedentropy      ```js // V8 supports custom sources of entropy. // by default,

lockbox           Simple, strong encryption.

node-hardcoressl  HardcoreSSL is a package for obtaining low-level asynchronous
nrsa              OpenSSL's RSA encrypt/decrypt routines
openssl           openssl wrapper
openssl-wrapper   OpenSSL wrapper
rsa               OpenSSL's RSA encrypt/decrypt routines
rsautl            A wrapper for OpenSSL's rsautl
selfsigned        Generate self signed certificates private and public keys
ssh-key-decrypt   Decrypt encrypted ssh private keys

ssl               Verification of SSL certificates

ssl-keychain      OpenSSL Keychain and Key generation module
ssl-keygen        OpenSSL Key Generation module
ursa              RSA public/private key crypto

x509-keygen       node.js module to generate self-signed certificate via openssl
```

Figure 3.2 Searching for Node.js modules from the command prompt.

Installing Node Packaged Modules

To use a Node module in your applications, it must first be installed where Node can find it. To install a Node module, use the `npm install <module_name>` command to download the Node module to your development environment and place it in the `node_modules` folder, where the `install` command is run. For example, the following command installs the `express` module:

```
npm install express
```

The output of the `npm install` command displays the HTTP requests to download the necessary files as well as the dependency hierarchy that was installed with the module. For example, Figure 3.3 shows part of the output from installing the `express` module.

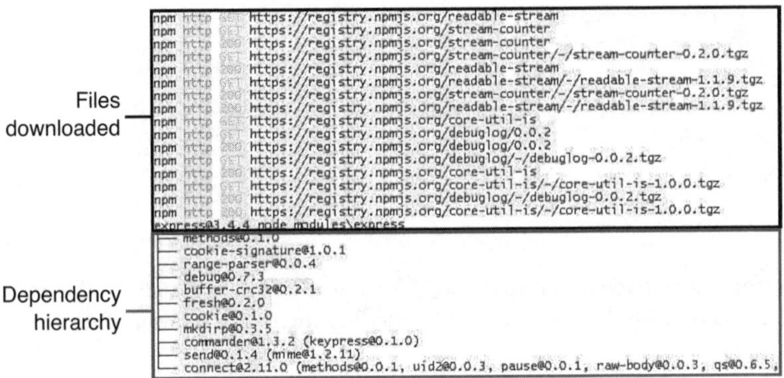

Figure 3.3 Output from installing the `express` module.

Notice that several .tgz files are downloaded, decompressed, and installed. Figure 3.3 also shows the dependency hierarchy: You can see that `express` requires the `methods`, `cookie-signature`, `range-parser`, `debug`, `buffer-crc32`, `fresh`, `cookie`, `mkdirp`, `commander`, `send`, and `connect` modules. All these modules were downloaded during the install. Notice that the version of each dependency module is listed.

Node.js has to be able to handle dependency conflicts. For example, the `express` module requires `cookie 0.1.0`, but another module may require `cookie 0.0.9`. To handle this situation, a separate copy for the cookie module is placed in each module's folder, under another `node_modules` folder.

To see how modules are stored in a hierarchy, consider the following example of how `express` looks on disk. Notice that the `cookie` and `send` modules are located under the `express` module hierarchy and that because the `send` module requires `mime`, it is located under the `send` hierarchy:

```
./
./node_modules
./node_modules/express
./node_modules/express/node_modules/cookie
./node_modules/express/node_modules/send
./node_modules/express/node_modules/send/node_modules/mime
```

Using `package.json`

All Node modules must include a `package.json` file in their root directory. `package.json` is a simple JSON text file that defines a module, including dependencies. The `package.json` file can contain a number of different directives to tell the Node Package Manager how to handle the module.

The following is an example of a `package.json` file with a name, version, description, and dependencies:

```
{
    "name": "my_module",
    "version": "0.1.0",
    "description": "a simple node.js module",
    "dependencies" : {
        "express"   :  "latest"
    }
}
```

The only required directives in the `package.json` file are name and version; the rest depend on what you would like to include. Table 3.2 describes the most common directives.

Table 3.2 **Directives used in the `package.json` file**

Directive	Description	Example
`name`	Unique name of package	`"name": "camelot"`
`preferGlobal`	Indicator that the module prefers to be installed globally	`"preferGlobal": true`
`version`	Version of the module	`"version":0.0.1`
`author`	Author of the project	`"author":"arthur@???.com"`
`description`	Text description of module	`"description":"a silly place"`
`contributors`	Additional contributors to the module	`"contributors": [ { "name":"gwen", "email":"gwen@???.com"}]`
`bin`	Binary to be installed with the project	`"bin: { "excalibur":"./bin/excalibur"}`
`scripts`	Parameters that execute console apps when launching `node`	`"scripts" { "start": "node ./bin/excalibur", "test": "echo testing"}`
`main`	The main entry point for the app, which can be a binary or a .js file	`"main":"./bin/excalibur"`

Directive	Description	Example
`repository`	The repository type and location of the package	`"repository": { "type": "git", "location": "http://???.com/c.git"}`
`keywords`	Keywords that show up in the `npm` search	`"keywords": [ "swallow", "unladen" ]`
`dependencies`	Modules and versions this module depends on; you can use the `*` and `x` wildcards	`"dependencies": { "express": "latest", "connect": "2.x.x, "cookies": "*" }`
`engines`	The version of `node` this package works with	`"engines": { "node": ">=0.6"}`

A great way to use `package.json` files is to automatically download and install the dependencies for your Node.js app. All you need to do is create a `package.json` file in the root of your project code and add the necessary dependencies to it. For example, the following `package.json` file requires the `express` module as a dependency:

```
{
    "name": "my_module",
    "version": "0.1.0",
    "dependencies" : {
        "express"   :  "latest"
    }
}
```

Then you run the following command from the root of your package, and the `express` module is automatically installed:

```
npm install
```

Notice that no module is specified in the command `npm install`. That is because `npm` looks for a `package.json` file by default. Later, as you need additional modules, all you need to do is add those to the `dependencies` directive and then run `npm install` again.

Creating a Node.js Application

Now you've learned enough about Node.js to jump into a Node.js project and get your feet wet. In this section, you will run through an example of creating your own Node Packaged Module and then use that module as a library in a Node.js application.

The code in this exercise is kept to a minimum so that you can see exactly how to create a package, publish it, and then use it again.

Creating a Node.js Packaged Module

To create a Node.js Packaged Module, you need to create the functionality in JavaScript, define the package using a `package.json` file, and then either publish it to the registry or package it for local use.

The following steps take you through the process of building a Node.js Packaged Module, using a module called `censorify` that will accept text and replace certain words with asterisks:

1. Create a project folder named `.../censorify`. This will be the root of the package.
2. Inside that folder, create a file named `censortext.js`.
3. Add the code from Listing 3.1 to `censortext.js`. Most of the code is just basic JavaScript, but note that lines 18–20 export the functions `censor()`, `addCensoredWord()`, and `getCensoredWords()`. `exports.censor` is required for Node.js applications using this module to have access to the `censor()` function as well as the other two functions.

Listing 3.1 `censortext.js`: **Node.js module code that implements a simple censor function and exports it for other modules using the package**

```
01 var censoredWords = ["sad", "bad", "mad"];
02 var customCensoredWords = [];
03 function censor(inStr) {
04   for (idx in censoredWords) {
05     inStr = inStr.replace(censoredWords[idx], "****");
06   }
07   for (idx in customCensoredWords) {
08     inStr = inStr.replace(customCensoredWords[idx], "****");
09   }
10   return inStr;
11 }
12 function addCensoredWord(word){
13   customCensoredWords.push(word);
14 }
15 function getCensoredWords(){
16   return censoredWords.concat(customCensoredWords);
17 }
18 exports.censor = censor;
19 exports.addCensoredWord = addCensoredWord;
20 exports.getCensoredWords = getCensoredWords;
```

4. You need a `package.json` file that will be used to generate the Node.js Packaged Module, so create a `package.json` file in the `.../censorify` folder. Then add contents similar to Listing 3.2. Specifically, you need to add at least the `name`, `version`, and `main` directives. The `main` directive needs to be the name of the main JavaScript module that will be loaded—in this case `censortext`. Note that the .js is not required; Node.js automatically searches for the .js extension.

Listing 3.2 `package.json`: **Package definition that defines the Node.js module**

```
{
  "author": "Brad Dayley",
  "name": "censorify",
  "version": "0.1.1",
  "description": "Censors words out of text",
  "main": "censortext",
  "dependencies": {},
  "engines": {
      "node": "*"
  }
}
```

5. Create a file named `README.md` in the `.../censorify` folder. Place in this file any readme instructions you would like.

6. Navigate to the `.../censorify` folder in a console window and execute the following command to build a local package module:

   ```
   npm pack
   ```

   The `npm pack` command creates a `censorify-0.1.1.tgz` file in the `.../censorify` folder. This is your first Node.js Packaged Module.

Publishing a Node.js Packaged Module to the NPM Registry

In the previous section, you created a local Node.js Packaged Module using the `npm pack` command. You can also publish that same module to the NPM registry at http://npmjs.org.

When modules are published to the NPM registry, they are accessible to everyone, via the `npm` utility discussed earlier. The registry therefore allows you to distribute your modules and applications to others more easily.

The following steps describe the process of publishing a module to the NPM registry. These steps assume that you have completed steps 1–5 from the previous section:

1. Create a public repository to contain the code for the module. Then push the contents of the `.../censorify` folder up to that location. In this case, I created a GitHub repository at the following location: https://github.com/bwdayley/nodebook/tree/master/ch03/censorify.

2. Create an account at https://npmjs.org/signup.

3. Use the following command from a command prompt to add the user you created to the environment:

   ```
   npm adduser
   ```

4. Type in the username, password, and email that you used to create the account in step 2.

5. Modify the `package.json` file to include the new repository information and any keywords that you want made available in the registry search, as shown in lines 7–14 in Listing 3.3:

Listing 3.3 `package.json`: **Package definition that defines the Node.js module that includes the repository and keywords information**

```
01 {
02   "author": "Brad Dayley",
03   "name": "censorify",
04   "version": "0.1.1",
05   "description": "Censors words out of text",
06   "main": "censortext",
07   "repository": {
08     "type": "git",
09     "url": "http://github.com/bwdayley/nodebook/tree/master/ch03/censorify"
10   },
11   "keywords": [
12     "censor",
13     "words"
14   ],
15   "dependencies": {},
16   "engines": {
17       "node": "*"
18   }
19 }
```

6. Publish the module using the following command from the `.../censor` folder in the console:

```
npm publish
```

Once the package has been published, you can search for it on the NPM registry and use the `npm install` command to install it into your environment.

To remove a package from the registry, make sure that you have added to the environment a user with rights to the module, using `npm adduser`, and execute the following command:

```
npm unpublish <project name>
```

For example, the following command unpublishes the `censorify` module:

```
npm unpublish censorify
```

In some instances, you will not be able to unpublish the module without using the `--force` option, which forces the removal and deletion of the module from the registry. Here's an example:

```
npm unpublish censorify --force
```

Using a Node.js Packaged Module in a Node.js Application

In the previous sections, you learned how to create and publish a Node.js module. This section provides an example of actually using a Node.js module inside your Node.js applications. Node.js makes this extremely simple. All you need to do is install the module into your application structure and then use the `require()` method to load the module.

The `require()` method accepts either an installed module name or a path to a .js file that is located on the file system. For example:

```
require("censorify")
require("./lib/utils.js")
```

The .js filename extension is optional. If it is omitted, then Node.js will search for it.

Follow these steps to see how easy this process is:

1. Create a project folder name `.../readwords`.
2. From a command prompt inside the `.../readwords` folder, use the following command to install the `censorify` module from the `censorify-0.1.1.tgz` package you created earlier:

   ```
   npm install ../censorify/censorify-0.1.1.tgz
   ```

3. Or, if you have published the `censorify` module, you can use the standard command to download and install it from the NPM registry:

   ```
   npm install censorify
   ```

4. Verify that a folder named `node_modules` should be created, along with a subfolder named `censorify`.
5. Create a file named `.../readwords/readwords.js`.
6. Add the contents shown in Listing 3.4 to your new `readwords.js` file. Notice that a `require()` call loads the `censorify` module and assigns it to the variable `censor`. Then the `censor` variable can be used to invoke the `getCensoredWords()`, `addCensoredWords()`, and `censor()` functions from the `censorify` module.

Listing 3.4 `readwords.js`: **A Node.js application that loads the `censorify` module when displaying text**

```
var censor = require("censorify");
console.log(censor.getCensoredWords());
console.log(censor.censor("Some very sad, bad and mad text."));
censor.addCensoredWord("gloomy");
console.log(censor.getCensoredWords());
console.log(censor.censor("A very gloomy day."));
```

7. Run the `readwords.js` application, using the following command, and you should get the output shown in Figure 3.4:

```
node readwords.js
```

Notice that the censored words are replaced with `****`, and that the new censored word `gloomy` is added to the `censorify` module instance `censor`.

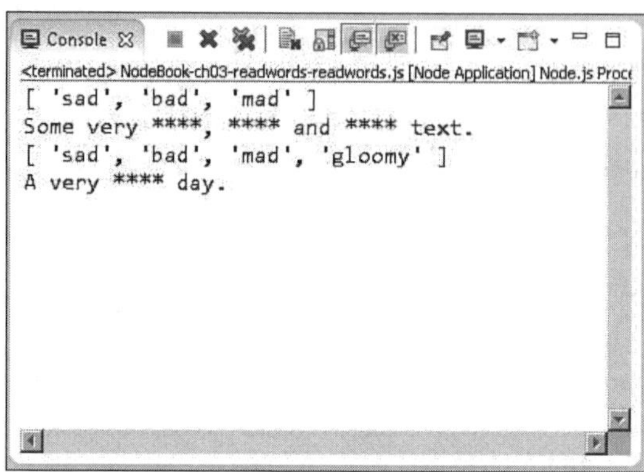

Figure 3.4 Output from executing the `readwords.js` module.

Writing Data to the Console

One of the most useful modules in Node.js is the `console` module. This module provides a lot of functionality for writing debug and information statements to the console. The `console` module allows you to control output to the console, implement time delta output, and write tracebacks and assertions to the console. This section covers using the `console` module, which you need to know how to use in later chapters of the book.

Since the `console` module is so widely used, you do not need to load it into your modules by using a `require()` statement. You simply call the console function by using `console.<function>(<parameters>)`. Table 3.3 lists the functions available in the `console` module.

Table 3.3 **Member functions of the `console` module**

Function	Description

`log([data],[...])`	Writes data output to the console. The data variable can be a string or an object that can be resolved to a string. Additional parameters can also be sent. For example:
	`console.log("There are %d items", 5);`
	`>>There are 5 items`

Function	Description
`info([data],[...])`	Same as `console.log`.
`error([data],[...])`	Same as `console.log`, but the output is also sent to `stderr`.
`warn([data],[...])`	Same as `console.error`.

`dir(obj)`	Writes out a string representation of a JavaScript object to the console. For example:
	`console.dir({name:"Brad", role:"Author"});`
	`>> { name: 'Brad', role: 'Author' }`

`time(label)`	Assigns a current timestamp with millisecond precision to the string `label`.

`timeEnd(label)`	Creates a delta between the current time and the timestamp assigned to `label` and outputs the results. For example:
	`console.time("FileWrite");`
	`f.write(data); //takes about 500ms`
	`console.timeEnd("FileWrite");`
	`>> FileWrite: 500ms`

`trace(label)`	Writes out a stack trace of the current position in code to `stderr`. For example:
	`module.trace("traceMark");`
	`>>Trace: traceMark`
	`  at Object.<anonymous> (C:\test.js:24:9)`
	`  at Module._compile (module.js:456:26)`
	`  at Object.Module._ext.js (module.js:474:10)`
	`  at Module.load (module.js:356:32)`
	`  at Function.Module._load (module.js:312:12)`
	`  at Function.Module.runMain(module.js:497:10)`
	`  at startup (node.js:119:16)`
	`  at node.js:901:3`

`assert(expression, [message])`	Writes the `message` and stack trace to the console if `expression` evaluates to `false`.

Summary

This chapter focuses on getting you up to speed on the Node.js environment. Node.js Package Modules provide functionality that Node.js does not inherently come with. You can download these modules from the NPM registry, and you can even create and publish your own. The `package.json` file provides the configuration and definition for every Node.js module.

The examples in this chapter cover creating, publishing, and installing your own Node.js Packaged Modules. You have learned how to use `npm` to package a local module as well as publish one to the NPM registry. You've also learned how to install the Node.js modules and use them in your own Node.js applications.

Up Next

The next chapter covers the event-driven nature of Node.js. You will get a chance to see how events work in the Node.js environment and how to control, manipulate, and use them in your applications.

4

Using Events, Listeners, Timers, and Callbacks in Node.js

Node.js provides scalability and performance through its powerful event-driven model. This chapter focuses on understanding the model and how it differs from traditional threading models used by most webservers. Understanding the event model is critical because it may force you to change your design thinking for your applications. However, those changes will be well worth the improvements in speed that you get by using Node.js.

This chapter also covers the different methods you use to add work to the Node.js event queue. You can add work by using event listeners or timers, or you can schedule work directly. In this chapter you'll also learn how to implement events in your own custom modules and objects.

Understanding the Node.js Event Model

Node.js applications run in a single-threaded event-driven model. Although Node.js implements a thread pool in the background to do work, the application itself doesn't have any concept of multiple threads. "Wait, what about performance and scale?" you might ask. At first a single-threaded server might seem counterintuitive, but once you understand the logic behind the Node.js event model, it all makes perfect sense.

Comparing Event Callbacks and Threaded Models

In the traditional threaded web model, a request comes to a webserver and is assigned to an available thread. The handling of work for that request continues on that thread until the request is complete and a response is sent.

Figure 4.1 illustrates the threaded model processing two requests, `GetFile` and `GetData`. The `GetFile` request opens the file, reads the contents, and then sends the data back in a response. All this occurs in order on the same thread. The `GetData` request connects to the database, queries the necessary data, and then sends the data in the response.

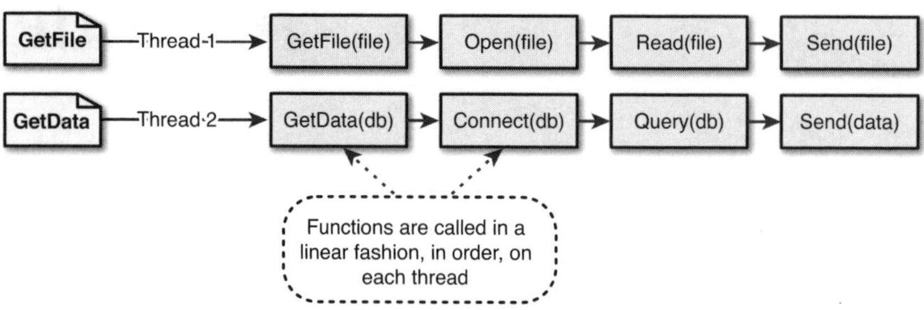

Figure 4.1 Processing two requests on individual threads, using the threaded model.

Now think about how the Node.js event model does things. Instead of executing all the work for each request on individual threads, Node.js adds work to an event queue and then has a single thread running an event loop pick it up. The event loop grabs the top item in the event queue, executes it, and then grabs the next item. When executing code that is longer lived or has blocking I/O, instead of calling the function directly, it adds the function to the event queue along with a callback that will be executed after the function completes. When all events on the Node.js event queue have been executed, the Node.js application terminates.

Figure 4.2 illustrates how Node.js handles the `GetFile` and `GetData` requests. It adds the `GetFile` and `GetData` requests to the event queue. It first picks up the `GetFile` request, executes it, and completes by adding the `Open()` callback function to the event queue. Then it picks up the `GetData` request, executes it, and completes by adding the `Connect()` callback function to the event queue. This continues until there are no callback functions to be executed. Notice in Figure 4.2 that the events for each thread don't necessarily follow a direct interleaved order. For example, the `Connect` request takes longer to complete than does the `Read` request, so `Send(file)` is called before `Query(db)`.

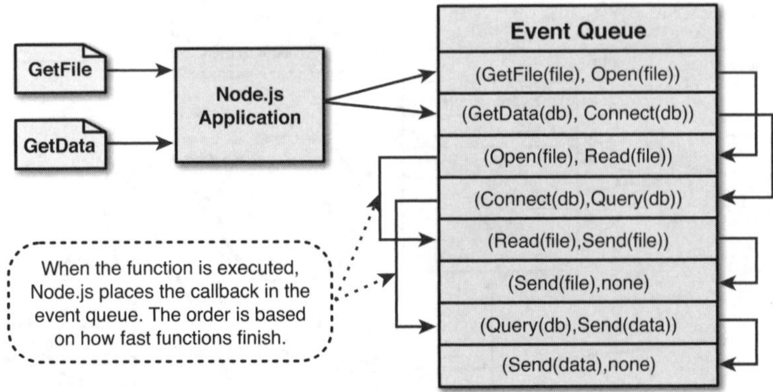

Figure 4.2 Processing two requests on a single event-driven thread, using the Node.js event model.

Blocking I/O in Node.js

The Node.js event model of using event callbacks is great until you run into the problem of functions that block on I/O. Blocking I/O stops the execution of the current thread and waits for a response before continuing. Some examples of blocking I/O are:

- Reading a file
- Querying a database
- Requesting a socket
- Accessing a remote service

Node.js uses event callbacks to avoid having to wait for blocking I/O. Therefore, any requests that perform blocking I/O are performed on a different thread in the background. Node.js implements a thread pool in the background. When an event that blocks I/O is retrieved from the event queue, Node.js retrieves a thread from the thread pool and executes the function there instead of on the main event loop thread. This prevents the blocking I/O from holding up the rest of the events in the event queue.

The function that is executed on the blocking thread can still add events back to the event queue to be processed. For example, a database query call is typically passed a callback function that parses the results and may schedule additional work on the event queue before sending a response.

Figure 4.3 illustrates the full Node.js event model, including the event queue, event loop, and thread pool. Notice that the event loop either executes the function on the event loop thread itself or, for blocking I/O, executes the function on a separate thread.

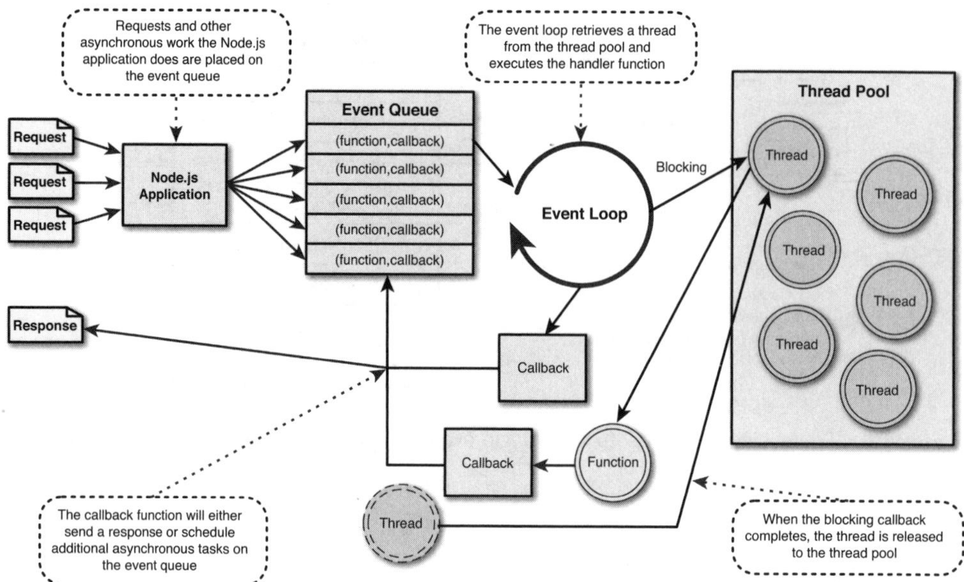

Figure 4.3 In the Node.js event model work is added as a function with callback to the event queue and then picked up on the event loop thread. The function is then executed on the event loop thread in case of non-blocking or on a separate thread in the case of blocking.

A Conversation Example

To help you understand how events work in Node.js compared to traditional threaded webservers, consider an example of having different conversations with a large group of people at a party. You are acting the part of the webserver, and the conversations represent the work necessary to process different types of web requests. Your conversations are broken up into several segments with different individuals. You end up talking to one and then another, then back to the first and then a third, back to the second, and so on.

The conversation example works well because it has many similarities to webserver processing. Some conversations end quickly (for example, a simple request for a piece of data in memory). Others are broken up in several segments that go back and forth between individuals (much like the more complex server-side conversations). Still others have long breaks while waiting for the other person to respond (like blocking I/O requests to the file system, database, or remote service).

Using the traditional webserver threading model in the conversation example sounds great at first because each thread acts like a clone of you. The threads/clones can talk back and forth with each person, and it almost seems like you can have multiple conversations simultaneously. There are two problems with this model.

The first problem is that you are limited by the number of clones. If you have only five clones, then to talk with a sixth person, one clone must completely finish its conversation. The second problem is that there is a limited number of CPUs/brains that the threads/clones must share. This means the clones sharing the same brain have to stop talking/listening while other clones are using the brain. You can see that there really isn't a very big benefit to having clones when they freeze while the other clones are using the brain.

The Node.js event model acts more similarly to a real-life conversation than does the traditional webserver model. First of all, Node.js applications run on a single thread, meaning there is only one of you—no clones. Each time a person asks you a question, you respond as soon as you can. Your interactions are completely event driven; you move naturally from one person to the next. Therefore, you can have as many conversations going on at the same time as you like and bounce between individuals. Second, your brain is always focused only on the person you are talking to since you aren't sharing it with clones.

So what happens when someone asks you a question that you have to think about for a while before responding? You can still interact with others at the party while trying to process that question in the back of your mind. That processing may impact how fast you interact with others, but you are still able to communicate with several people while processing the longer lived thought. This is similar to how Node.js handles blocking I/O requests using the background thread pool. Node.js hands blocking requests over to a thread in the thread pool so that they have minimal impact on the application-processing events.

Adding Work to the Event Queue

As you create Node.js applications and design code, you need to keep in mind the event model described in the previous section. To leverage the scalability and performance of the event model, make sure you break up work into chunks that can be performed as a series of callbacks.

When you have designed your code correctly, you can use the event model to schedule work on the event queue. In Node.js applications, you schedule work on the event queue by passing a callback function using one of these methods:

- Make a call to one of the blocking I/O library calls, such as writing to a file or connecting to a database.
- Add an event listener to a built-in event such as an `http.request` or `server.connection`.
- Create your own event emitters and add custom listeners to them.
- Using the `process.nextTick` option to schedule work to be picked up on the next cycle of the event loop.
- Use timers to schedule work to be done after a particular amount of time or at periodic intervals.

The following sections discuss implementing timers, `nextTick`, and custom events. They will give you an idea of how the event mechanism works. The blocking I/O calls and built-in events are covered in subsequent chapters.

Implementing Timers

A useful feature of Node.js and JavaScript is the ability to delay execution of code for a period of time. This can be useful for cleanup or refresh work that you do not want to always be running. You can implement three types of timers in Node.js: the timeout, interval, and immediate timers. The following sections describe each of these and how to implement them in your code.

Delaying Work with Timeouts

Timeout timers are used to delay work for a specific amount of time. When that time expires, the callback function is executed, and the timer goes away. You should use timeouts for work that needs to be performed only once.

You create timeout timers by using the `setTimeout(callback, delayMilliSeconds, [args])` method built into Node.js. When you call `setTimeout()`, the callback function is executed after `delayMilliSeconds` has expired. For example, the following executes `myFunc()` after a second:

```
setTimeout(myFunc, 1000);
```

The `setTimeout()` function returns a timer object ID, and you can pass this ID to `clearTimeout(timeoutId)` at any time before `delayMilliSeconds` expires to cancel the timeout function. For example:

```
myTimeout =  setTimeout(myFunc, 100000);
...
clearTimeout(myTimeout);
```

The code in Listing 4.1 implements a series of simple timeouts that call the `simpleTimeout()` function, which outputs the number of milliseconds since the timeout was scheduled. Notice that it doesn't matter in which order `setTimeout()` is called. The results, shown in Figure 4.4, appear in the order in which the delay expires.

Listing 4.1 `simple_timer.js`: **Implementing a series of timeouts at various intervals**

```
function simpleTimeout(consoleTimer){
  console.timeEnd(consoleTimer);
}
console.time("twoSecond");
setTimeout(simpleTimeout, 2000, "twoSecond");
console.time("oneSecond");
setTimeout(simpleTimeout, 1000, "oneSecond");
console.time("fiveSecond");
```

```
setTimeout(simpleTimeout, 5000, "fiveSecond");
console.time("50MilliSecond");
setTimeout(simpleTimeout, 50, "50MilliSecond");
```

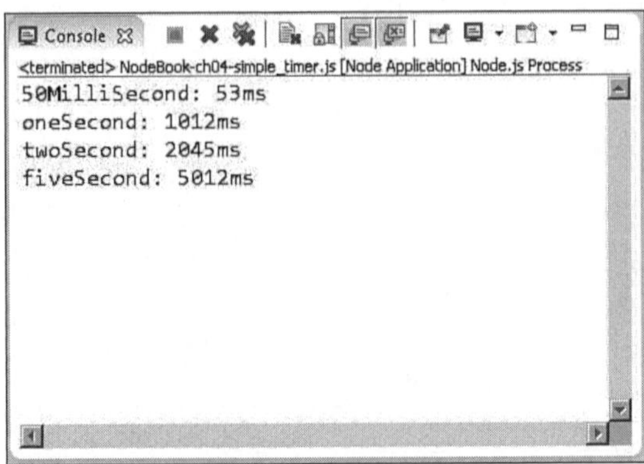

Figure 4.4 Output of the `simple_timer.js` timeout functions, executed with different delay amounts.

Performing Periodic Work with Intervals

Interval timers are used to perform work on a regular delayed interval. When the delay time expires, the callback function is executed and is then rescheduled for the delay interval again. You should use intervals for work that needs to be performed on a regular basis.

You create interval timers by using the `setInterval(callback, delayMilliSeconds, [args])` method that is built into Node.js. When you call `setInterval()`, the callback function is executed every interval after `delayMilliSeconds` has expired. For example, the following executes `myFunc()` every second:

```
setInterval(myFunc, 1000);
```

The `setInterval()` function returns a timer object ID, and you can pass this ID to `clearInterval(intervalId)` at any time before `delayMilliSeconds` expires to cancel the timeout function. For example:

```
myInterval =  setInterval(myFunc, 100000);
...
clearInterval(myInterval);
```

The code in Listing 4.2 implements a series of simple interval callbacks that update the values of the variables `x`, `y`, and `z` at different intervals. Notice that the values of `x`, `y`, and `z` are changed differently because the interval amounts are different; `x` increments twice as fast as `y`, which increments twice as fast as `z`, as shown in the output in Figure 4.5.

Listing 4.2 `simple_interval.js`: **Implementing a series of update callbacks at various intervals**

```
var x=0, y=0, z=0;
function displayValues(){
  console.log("X=%d; Y=%d; Z=%d", x, y, z);
}
function updateX(){
  x += 1;
}
function updateY(){
  y += 1;
}
function updateZ(){
  z += 1;
  displayValues();
}
setInterval(updateX, 500);
setInterval(updateY, 1000);
setInterval(updateZ, 2000);
```

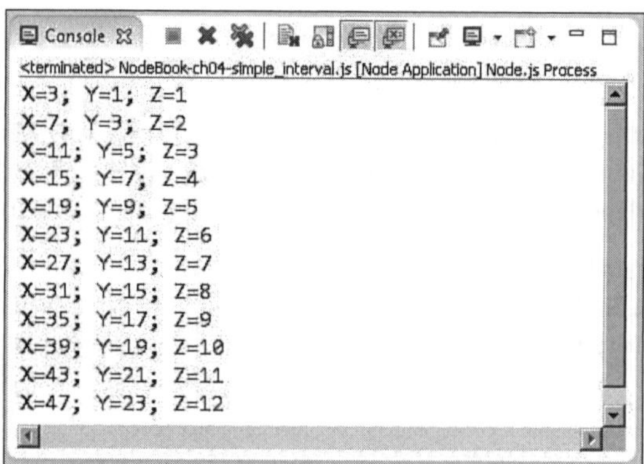

Figure 4.5 Output of `simple_interval.js` interval functions executed at different delay amounts.

Performing Immediate Work with an Immediate Timer

Immediate timers are used to perform work as soon as the I/O event callbacks begin executing but before any timeout or interval events are executed. They allow you to schedule work to be done after the current events in the event queue are completed. You should use immediate timers to yield long-running execution segments to other callbacks to prevent starving the I/O events.

You create immediate timers by using the `setImmediate(callback, [args])` method that is built into Node.js. When you call `setImmediate()`, the callback function is placed on the event queue and popped off once for each iteration through the event queue loop after I/O events have a chance to be called. For example, the following code schedules `myFunc()` to execute on the next cycle through the event queue:

```
setImmediate(myFunc(), 1000);
```

The `setImmediate()` function returns a timer object ID, and you can pass this ID to `clearImmediate(immediateId)` at any time before it is picked up from the event queue. For example:

```
myImmediate =  setImmediate(myFunc);
...
clearImmediate(myImmediate);
```

Dereferencing Timers from the Event Loop

Often you will not want timer event callbacks to continue to be scheduled when they are the only events left in the event queue. Node.js provides a very useful utility to handle this case. The `unref()` function, available in the object returned by `setInterval` and `setTimeout`, allows you to notify the event loop to not continue when these are the only events on the queue.

For example, the following code dereferences the `myInterval` interval timer:

```
myInterval = setInterval(myFunc);
myInterval.unref();
```

If for some reason you later do not want the program to terminate if the interval function is the only event left on the queue, you can use the `ref()` function to re-reference it:

```
myInterval.ref();
```

> **Warning**
>
> When using `unref()` with `setTimout` timers, a separate timer is used to wake up the event loop. Using a lot of these can have an adverse performance impact on your code, so you should create them sparingly.

Using `nextTick` to Schedule Work

A very useful method of scheduling work on the event queue is using the `process.nextTick(callback)` function. This function schedules work to be run on the next cycle of the event loop. Unlike the `setImmediate()` method, `nextTick()` executes before the I/O events are fired. This can result in starvation of the I/O events, so Node.js limits the number of `nextTick()` events that can be executed each cycle through the event queue by the value of `process.maxTickDepth`, which defaults to `1000`.

The code in Listing 4.3 illustrates the order of events when using a blocking I/O call, timers, and `nextTick()`. Notice that the blocking call `fs.stat()` is executed first, then two `setImmediate()` calls, and then two `nextTick()` calls. The output in Figure 4.6 shows that both `nextTick()` calls are executed before any of the others, then the first `setImmediate()` call, followed by the `fs.stat()` call, and then, on the next iteration through the loop, the second `setImmediate()` call.

Listing 4.3 `nexttick.js`: **Implementing a series of blocking `fs` calls, immediate timers, and `nextTick()` calls to show the order of execution**

```
var fs = require("fs");
fs.stat("nexttick.js", function(err, stats){
  if(stats) { console.log("nexttick.js Exists"); }
});
setImmediate(function(){
  console.log("Immediate Timer 1 Executed");
});
setImmediate(function(){
  console.log("Immediate Timer 2 Executed");
});
process.nextTick(function(){
  console.log("Next Tick 1 Executed");
});
process.nextTick(function(){
  console.log("Next Tick 2 Executed");
});
```

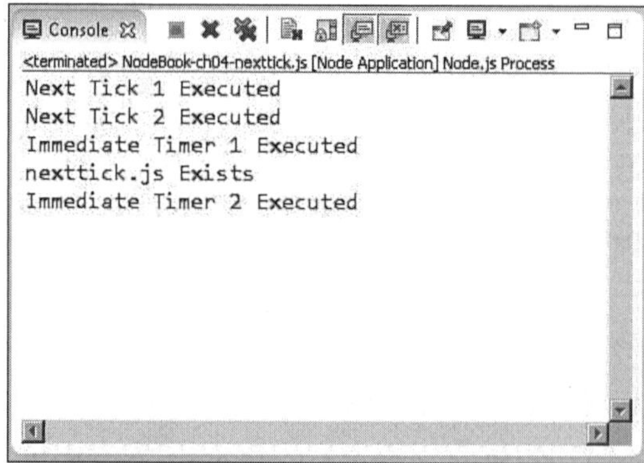

Figure 4.6 Output of `nexttick.js`, showing that the `nextTick()` calls get executed first.

Implementing Event Emitters and Listeners

In the following chapters, you have opportunities to implement a lot of the events that are built into the various Node.js modules. This section focuses on creating your own custom events as well as implementing listener callbacks that are implemented when an event is emitted.

Adding Custom Events to Your JavaScript Objects

Events are emitted using an `EventEmitter` object. This object is included in the `events` module. The `emit(eventName, [args])` function triggers the `eventName` event and includes any arguments provided. The following code snippet shows how to implement a simple event emitter:

```
var events = require('events');
var emitter = new events.EventEmitter();
emitter.emit("simpleEvent");
```

Occasionally, you will want to add events directly to your JavaScript objects. To do that, you need to inherit the `EventEmitter` functionality in your object by calling `events.EventEmitter.call(this)` in your object instantiation. You also need to add `events.EventEmitter.prototype` to your object prototyping. For example:

```
Function MyObj(){
  Events.EventEmitter.call(this);
}
MyObj.prototype.__proto__ = events.EventEmitter.prototype;
```

You can then emit events directly from instances of your object. For example:

```
var myObj = new MyObj();
myObj.emit("someEvent");
```

Adding Event Listeners to Objects

Once you have an instance of an object that will emit events, you can add listeners for the events that you care about. You add listeners to an `EventEmitter` object by using one of the following functions:

- **`.addListener(eventName, callback)`:** Attaches the `callback` function to the object's listeners. Every time the `eventName` event is triggered, the `callback` function is placed in the event queue to be executed.
- **`.on(eventName, callback)`:** Same as `.addListener()`.
- **`.once(eventName, callback)`:** Only the first time the `eventName` event is triggered, the `callback` function is placed in the event queue to be executed.

For example, to add a listener to an instance of the `MyObject EventEmitter` class defined in the previous section, you would use:

```
function myCallback(){
  . . .
}
var myObject = new MyObj();
myObject.on("someEvent", myCallback);
```

Removing Listeners from Objects

Listeners are very useful and a vital part of Node.js programming. However, they cause overhead, and you should use them only when necessary. Node.js provides several helper functions on the `EventEmitter` object that allow you to manage the listeners that are included:

- **`.listeners(eventName)`:** Returns an array of listener functions attached to the `eventName` event.
- **`.setMaxListeners(n)`:** Triggers a warning if more than `n` listeners are added to an `EventEmitter` object. The default is `10`.
- **`.removeListener(eventName, callback)`:** Removes the `callback` function from the `eventName` event of the `EventEmitter` object.

Implementing Event Listeners and Event Emitters

The code in Listing 4.4 demonstrates the process of implementing listeners and custom event emitters in Node.js. The `Account` object is extended to inherit from the `EventEmitter` class and provides two methods—`deposit` and `withdraw`—that both emit the `balanceChanged` event. Then in lines 15–31, three callback functions are implemented that are attached to the `Account` object instance `balanceChanged` event and display various forms of data.

Notice that the `checkGoal(acc, goal)` callback is implemented a bit differently than the others. This illustrates how you can pass variables into an event listener function when the event is triggered. Figure 4.7 shows the results of executing the code in Listing 4.4.

Listing 4.4 `emitter_listener.js`: **Creating a custom `EventEmitter` object and implementing three listeners that are triggered when the `balanceChanged` event is triggered**

```
01 var events = require('events');
02 function Account() {
03   this.balance = 0;
04   events.EventEmitter.call(this);
05   this.deposit = function(amount){
06     this.balance += amount;
07     this.emit('balanceChanged');
08   };
09   this.withdraw = function(amount){
```

```
    this.balance -= amount;
    this.emit('balanceChanged');
  };
}
Account.prototype.__proto__ = events.EventEmitter.prototype;
function displayBalance(){
  console.log("Account balance: $%d", this.balance);
}
function checkOverdraw(){
  if (this.balance < 0){
    console.log("Account overdrawn!!!");
  }
}
function checkGoal(acc, goal){
  if (acc.balance > goal){
    console.log("Goal Achieved!!!");
  }
}
var account = new Account();
account.on("balanceChanged", displayBalance);
account.on("balanceChanged", checkOverdraw);
account.on("balanceChanged", function(){
  checkGoal(this, 1000);
});
account.deposit(220);
account.deposit(320);
account.deposit(600);
account.withdraw(1200);
```

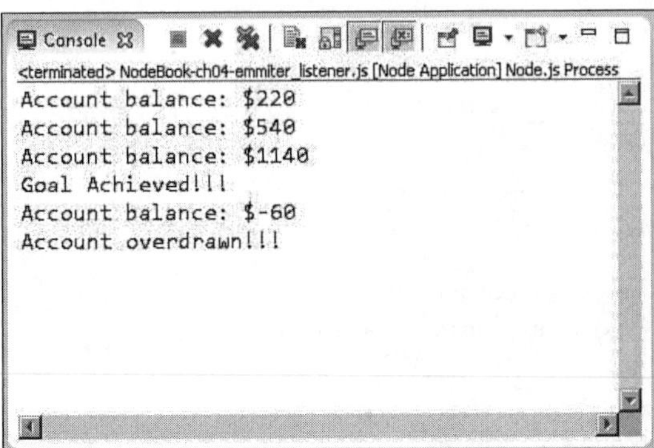

Figure 4.7 Output of `emitter_listener.js`, showing the account statements output by the listener callback functions.

Implementing Callbacks

As you have seen in previous sections, the Node.js event-driven model relies heavily on callback functions. Callback functions can be a bit difficult to understand at first, especially if you want to depart from implementing a basic anonymous function. This section deals with three specific implementations of callbacks: passing parameters to a callback function, handling callback function parameters inside a loop, and nesting callbacks.

Passing Additional Parameters to Callbacks

Most callbacks have automatic parameters passed to them, such as an error or a result buffer. A common question when working with callbacks is how to pass additional parameters to them from the calling function. The way to do this is to implement the parameter in an anonymous function and then call the callback with parameters from the anonymous function.

The code in Listing 4.5 shows how to implement callback parameters. There are two `sawCar` event handlers. Note that the `sawCar` event only emits the `make` parameter. The first event handler, on line 16, implements the `logCar(make)` callback handler. To add a color for `logColorCar()`, an anonymous function is used in the event handler defined in lines 17–21. A randomly selected color is passed to the call `logColorCar(make, color)`. Figure 4.8 shows the output from Listing 4.5.

Listing 4.5 `callback_parameter.js`: **Creating an anonymous function to add additional parameters that are not emitted by the event**

```
01 var events = require('events');
02 function CarShow() {
03   events.EventEmitter.call(this);
04   this.seeCar = function(make){
05     this.emit('sawCar', make);
06   };
07 }
08 CarShow.prototype.__proto__ = events.EventEmitter.prototype;
09 var show = new CarShow();
10 function logCar(make){
11   console.log("Saw a " + make);
12 }
13 function logColorCar(make, color){
14   console.log("Saw a %s %s", color, make);
15 }
16 show.on("sawCar", logCar);
17 show.on("sawCar", function(make){
18   var colors = ['red', 'blue', 'black'];
19   var color = colors[Math.floor(Math.random()*3)];
20   logColorCar(make, color);
21 });
```

```
show.seeCar("Ferrari");
show.seeCar("Porsche");
show.seeCar("Bugatti");
show.seeCar("Lamborghini");
show.seeCar("Aston Martin");
```

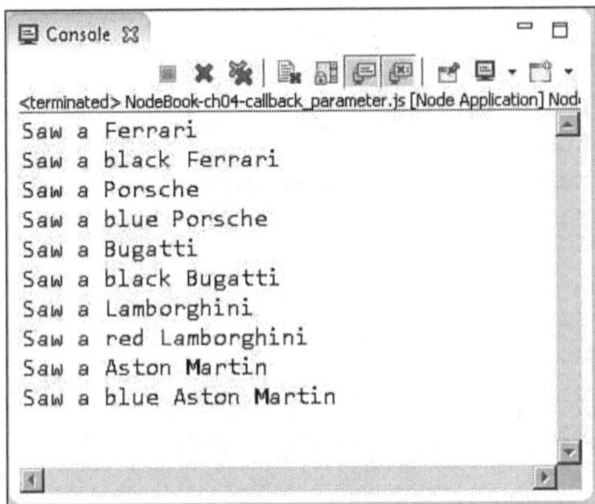

Figure 4.8 Output of `callback_parameter.js`, showing the results of adding a color parameter to the callback.

Implementing Closure in Callbacks

An interesting problem related to asynchronous callbacks is closure. *Closure* is a JavaScript term that indicates that variables are bound to a function's scope and not to the parent function's scope. When you execute an asynchronous callback, the parent function's scope may have changed (for example, when iterating through a list and altering values each iteration).

If a callback needs access to variables in the parent function's scope, you need to provide closure so that those values are available when the callback is pulled off the event queue. A basic way of doing this is to encapsulate an asynchronous call inside a function block and pass in the variables that are needed.

The code in Listing 4.6 illustrates implementing a wrapper function that provides closure to the `logCar()` asynchronous function. Notice that the loop in lines 7–12 implements a basic callback. However, the output shown in Figure 4.9 shows that the car name is always the last item read because the value of `message` changes each time through the loop.

The loop in lines 13–20 implements a wrapper function that is passed `message` as the `msg` parameter, and the `msg` value sticks with the callback. Thus the closure output shown in Figure 4.9 displays the correct message. To make the callback truly asynchronous, you use the `process.nextTick()` method to schedule the callback.

Listing 4.6 `callback_closure.js`: **Creating a wrapper function to provide closure for variables needed in the asynchronous callback**

```
function logCar(logMsg, callback){
  process.nextTick(function() {
    callback(logMsg);
  });
}
var cars = ["Ferrari", "Porsche", "Bugatti"];
for (var idx in cars){
  var message = "Saw a " + cars[idx];
  logCar(message, function(){
    console.log("Normal Callback: " + message);
  });
}
for (var idx in cars){
  var message = "Saw a " + cars[idx];
  (function(msg){
    logCar(msg, function(){
      console.log("Closure Callback: " + msg);
    });
  })(message);
}
```

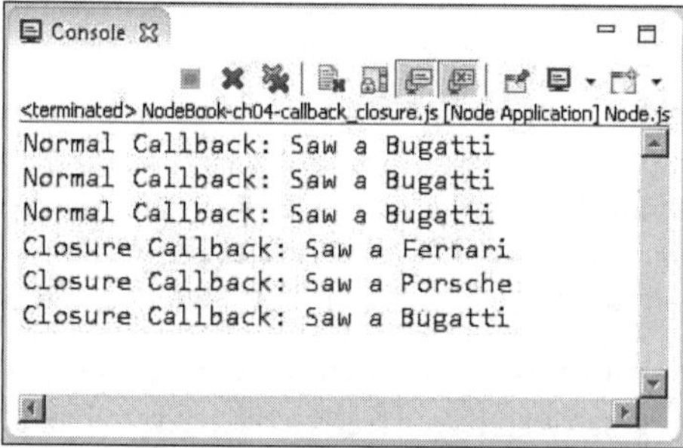

Figure 4.9 Output of `callback_closure.js`, showing how adding a closure wrapper function allows the asynchronous callback to access necessary variables.

Chaining Callbacks

With asynchronous functions, you are not guaranteed the order in which they will run if two are placed on the event queue. The best way to resolve this is to implement callback chaining by having the callback from the asynchronous function call the function again until there is no more work to do. That way, the asynchronous function is never on the event queue more than once.

The code in Listing 4.7 implements a very basic example of callback chaining. A list of items is passed into the function `logCars()`, and then the asynchronous function `logCar()` is called, and the `logCars()` function is used as the callback when `logCar()` completes. Thus only one version of `logCar()` is on the event queue at a time. Figure 4.10 shows the output of iterating though the list.

Listing 4.7 `callback_chain.js`: **Implementing a callback chain where the callback from an anonymous function calls back into the initial function to iterate through a list**

```
function logCar(car, callback){
  console.log("Saw a %s", car);
  if(cars.length){
    process.nextTick(function(){
      callback();
    });
  }
}
function logCars(cars){
  var car = cars.pop();
  logCar(car, function(){
    logCars(cars);
  });
}
var cars = ["Ferrari", "Porsche", "Bugatti",
            "Lamborghini", "Aston Martin"];
logCars(cars);
```

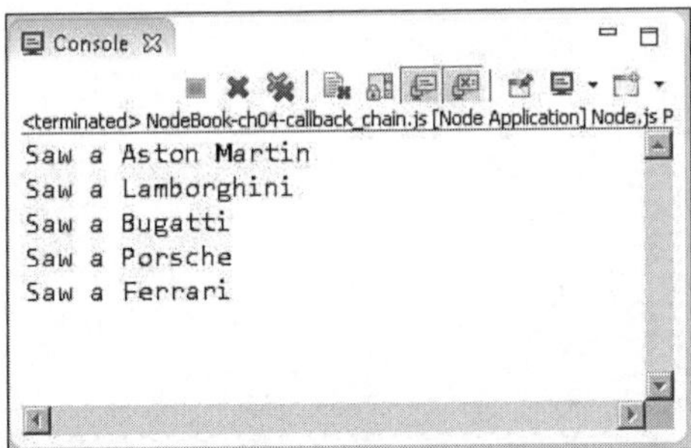

Figure 4.10 Output of `callback_chain.js`, showing how to use an asynchronous callback chain to iterate through a list.

Summary

The event-driven model that Node.js uses provides scalability and performance. In this chapter, you have learned the difference between the event-driven model and the traditional threaded model for webservers. You've also learned that you can add events to the event queue when blocking I/O is called, and you can use events, timers, or the `nextTick()` method to schedule events.

You've seen that there are three types of timer events: timeout, interval, and immediate. You can use each of these events to delay the execution of work for a period of time. You've also seen how to implement your own custom event emitters and add listener functions to them.

Up Next

In the next chapter, you'll get a chance to see how to manage data I/O by using streams and buffers. Also, you'll learn about Node.js functionality that allows you to manipulate JSON, string, and compressed forms of data.

5

Handling Data I/O in Node.js

Most active web applications and services have a lot of data flowing through them—in the form of text, JSON strings, binary buffers, and data streams. Therefore, Node.js has a lot of mechanisms built into it to support handling the data I/O from system to system. It is important to understand the mechanisms that Node.js provides to implement effective and efficient web applications and services.

This chapter focuses on manipulating JSON data, managing binary data buffers, and implementing readable and writable streams and data compression/decompression. You will learn how to leverage the Node.js functionality to work with different I/O requirements.

Working with JSON

One of the data types that you will most commonly work with when implementing Node.js web applications and services is JSON (JavaScript Object Notation). JSON is a very lightweight method to convert JavaScript objects into a string form and then back again. It works well when you need to serialize data objects when passing them from client to server, process to process, or stream to stream or when you're storing them in a database.

There are several reasons to use JSON to serialize your JavaScript objects instead of using XML:

- JSON is much more efficient and takes fewer characters.
- Serializing/deserializing JSON is faster than serializing/deserializing XML.
- JSON is easier to read from a developer's perspective because its syntax is similar to that of JavaScript.

You might want to use XML instead of JSON for extremely complex objects or if you have XML/XSLT transforms already in place.

Converting JSON to JavaScript Objects

A JSON string represents a JavaScript object in string form. The string syntax is very similar to code, so it's easy to understand. You can use the `JSON.parse(string)` method to convert a string that is properly formatted with JSON into a JavaScript object.

For example, in the following code snippet, notice that `accountStr` is defined as a formatted JSON string, then converted to a JavaScript object using `JSON.parse()` and then member properties can be accessed via dot notation:

```
var accountStr = '{"name":"Jedi", "members":["Yoda","Obi Wan"], \
                   "number":34512, "location": "A galaxy far, far away"}';
var accountObj = JSON.parse(accountStr);
console.log(accountObj.name);
console.log(accountObj.members);
```

This is the output from the code above:

```
Jedi
[ 'Yoda', 'Obi Wan' ]
```

Converting JavaScript Objects to JSON

Node allows you to convert a JavaScript object into a properly formatted JSON string. Thus you can store the string form in a file or database, send it across an HTTP connection, or write it to a stream or buffer. You use the `JSON.stringify(object)` method to parse a JavaScript object and generate a JSON string. For example, the following code defines a JavaScript object that includes string, numeric, and array properties. `JSON.stringify()` converts it to a JSON string:

```
var accountObj = {
  name: "Baggins",
  number: 10645,
  members: ["Frodo, Bilbo"],
  location: "Shire"
};
var accountStr = JSON.stringify(accountObj);
console.log(accountStr);
```

The above snippet outputs the following:

```
{"name":"Baggins","number":10645,"members":["Frodo, Bilbo"],"location":"Shire"}
```

Using the `Buffer` Module to Buffer Data

While JavaScript may be extremely Unicode friendly, it is not very good at managing binary data. However, binary data is extremely useful when implementing some web applications and services, such as:

- Transferring compressed files
- Generating dynamic images
- Sending serialized binary data

Understanding Buffered Data

Buffered data is made up of a series of octets in big-endian or little-endian format. That means they take up considerably less space than text data. Therefore, Node.js provides the `Buffer` module, which allows you to create, read, write, and manipulate binary data in a buffer structure. The `Buffer` module is global, so you do not need to use the `require()` function to access it.

Buffered data is stored in a structure similar to that of an array, but it is stored outside the normal V8 heap in raw memory allocations. Therefore, a buffer cannot be resized.

When converting buffers to and from strings, you need to specify the explicit encoding method to be used. Table 5.1 lists the various encoding methods supported.

Table 5.1 **Methods of encoding between strings and binary buffers**

Method	Description
`utf8`	Multi-byte encoded Unicode characters; the standard in most documents and webpages.
`utf16le`	Little-endian encoded Unicode characters of 2 or 4 bytes.
`ucs2`	Little-endian encoded Unicode characters of 2 or 4 bytes.
`base64`	Base-64 string encoding.
`Hex`	Each byte encoded as two hexadecimal characters.

Big Endian and Little Endian

Binary data in buffers is stored as a series of octets or a sequence of eight 0s and 1s that can be a hexadecimal value of 0x00 to 0xFF. It can be read as a single byte or as a word containing multiple bytes. *Endian* defines the ordering of significant bits when defining the word. Big endian stores the least significant word first, and little endian stores the least significant word last. For example, `0x0A 0x0B 0x0C 0x0D` would be stored in the buffer as `[0x0A, 0x0B, 0x0C, 0x0D]` in big endian but as `[0x0D, 0x0C, 0x0B, 0x0A]` in little endian.

Creating Buffers

Buffer objects are actually raw memory allocations. Therefore, you must determine their sizes when you create them. There are three methods for creating Buffer objects using the new keyword:

```
new Buffer(sizeInBytes)
new Buffer(octetArray)
new Buffer(string, [encoding])
```

For example, the following lines of code define buffers using a byte size, an octet buffer, and a UTF8 string:

```
var buf256 = new Buffer(256);
var bufOctets = new Buffer([0x6f, 0x63, 0x74, 0x65, 0x74, 0x73]);
var bufUTF8 = new Buffer("Some UTF8 Text \u00b6 \u30c6 \u20ac", 'utf8');
```

Writing to Buffers

You cannot extend the size of a Buffer object after it has been created, but you can write data to any location in the buffer. As described in Table 5.2, there are several methods you can use when writing to buffers.

Table 5.2 **Methods for writing to Buffer objects**

Method	Description
`buffer.write(string, [offset], [length], [encoding])`	Writes `length` number of bytes from the `string`, starting at the `offset` index inside the buffer using encoding.
`buffer[offset] = value`	Replaces the data at index `offset` with the `value` specified.
`buffer.fill(value, [offset], [end])`	Writes the `value` to every byte in the buffer, starting at the `offset` index and ending with the `end` index.

`writeInt8(value, offset, [noAssert])`
`writeInt16LE(value, offset, [noAssert])`
`writeInt16BE(value, offset, [noAssert])`
`...`
	There is a wide range of methods for `Buffer` objects to write integers, unsigned integers, doubles, floats of various sizes, and using little endian or big endian. `value` specifies the `value` to write, `offset` specifies the index to write to, and `noAssert` specifies whether to skip validation of the `value` and `offset`. `noAssert` should be left at the default `false` unless you are absolutely certain of correctness.

To illustrate writing to buffers, the code in Listing 5.1 defines a buffer, fills it with zeros, writes some text at the beginning using `write()` at line 4, and adds some additional text that alters part of the existing buffer via `write(string, offset, length)` at line 6. Then in line 8 it adds a + to the end by directly setting the value of an index. Figure 5.1 shows the output of this code. Notice that the `buf256.write("more text", 9, 9)` statement writes to the middle of the buffer, and `buf256[18] = 43` changes a single byte.

Listing 5.1 `buffer_write.js`: **Various ways to write to a `Buffer` object**

```
1 buf256 = new Buffer(256);
2 buf256.fill(0);
3 buf256.write("add some text");
4 console.log(buf256.toString());
5 buf256.write("more text", 9, 9);
6 console.log(buf256.toString());
7 buf256[18] = 43;
8 console.log(buf256.toString());
```

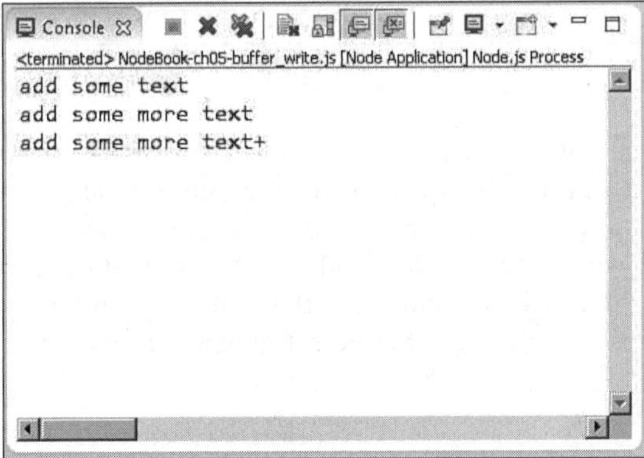

Figure 5.1 Output of `buffer_copy.js`, writing data to a `Buffer` object.

Reading from Buffers

There are several methods for reading from buffers. The simplest is to use the `toString()` method to convert all or part of a buffer to a string. However, you can also access specific indexes in the buffer directly or by using `read()`. Also, Node.js provides a `StringDecoder` object that has a `write(buffer)` method that decodes and writes buffered data using the specified encoding. Table 5.3 describes these methods for reading `Buffer` objects.

Table 5.3 **Methods of reading to `Buffer` objects**

Method	Description
`buffer.toString([encoding], [start], [end])`	Returns a string containing the decoded characters specified by encoding from the `start` index to the `end` index of the buffer. If `start` or `end` is not specified, then `toString()` uses the beginning or end of the buffer.
`stringDecoder.write(buffer)`	Returns a decoded string version of the buffer.
`buffer[offset]`	Returns the octet value in the buffer at the specified `offset`.

`readInt8(offset, [noAssert])`
`readInt16LE(offset, [noAssert])`
`readInt16BE(offset, [noAssert])`
`...`
	There is a wide range of methods for `Buffer` objects to read integers, unsigned integers, doubles, floats of various sizes, and using little endian or big endian. These functions accept the offset to read from and an optional `noAssert` Boolean value that specifies whether to skip validation of the offset. `noAssert` should be left at the default `false` unless you are absolutely certain of correctness.

To illustrate reading from buffers, the code in Listing 5.2 defines a buffer with `UTF8` encoded characters and then uses `toString()` without parameters to read all the buffer and then with the `encoding`, `start`, and `end` parameters to read part of the buffer. Then in lines 4 and 5, it creates `StringDecoder` with `UTF8` encoding and uses it to write the contents of the buffer out to the console. Next, a direct access method gets the value of the octet at index 18, and then on line 8, `readUInt32BE()` reads a 32-bit integer. Figure 5.2 shows the output of the code in Listing 5.2.

Listing 5.2 `buffer_read.js`: **Various ways to read from a `Buffer` object**

```
1 bufUTF8 = new Buffer("Some UTF8 Text \u00b6 \u30c6 \u20ac", 'utf8');
2 console.log(bufUTF8.toString());
3 console.log(bufUTF8.toString('utf8', 5, 9));
4 var StringDecoder = require('string_decoder').StringDecoder;
5 var decoder = new StringDecoder('utf8');
6 console.log(decoder.write(bufUTF8));
7 console.log(bufUTF8[18].toString(16));
8 console.log(bufUTF8.readUInt32BE(18).toString(16));
```

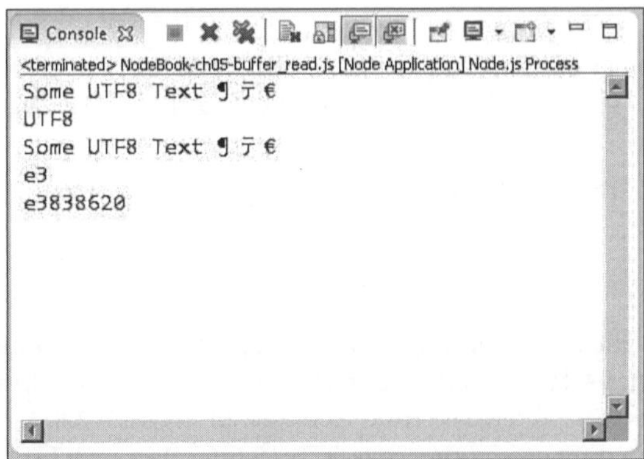

Figure 5.2 Output of `buffer_read.js`, reading data from a `Buffer` object.

Determining Buffer Length

A common task when dealing with buffers is determining the length, especially when you create a buffer dynamically from a string. You can determine the length of a buffer by calling `.length` on the `Buffer` object. To determine the byte length that a string will take up in a buffer, you cannot use the `.length` property. Instead, you need to use `Buffer.byteLength(string, [encoding])`. It is important to note that there is a difference between the string length and byte length of a buffer. To illustrate this, consider the following statements:

```
"UTF8 text \u00b6".length;
//evaluates to 11
Buffer.byteLength("UTF8 text \u00b6", 'utf8');
//evaluates to 12
Buffer("UTF8 text \u00b6").length;
//evaluates to 12
```

Notice that the same string evaluates to `11`, but because it contains a double-byte character, the `byteLength` is `12`. Also note that `Buffer("UTF8 text \u00b6").length` evaluates to `12` also. This is because `.length` on a buffer returns the byte length.

Copying Buffers

An important part of working with buffers is the ability to copy data from one buffer into another buffer. Node.js provides the `copy(targetBuffer, [targetStart], [sourceStart], [sourceIndex])` function for `Buffer` objects. The `targetBuffer` parameter is another `Buffer` object, and `targetStart`, `sourceStart` and `sourceEnd` are indexes inside the source and target buffers.

> **Note**
>
> To copy string data from one buffer to another, make sure that both buffers use the same encoding, or you may get unexpected results when decoding the resulting buffer.

You can also copy data from one buffer to the other by indexing them directly, as in this example:

```
sourceBuffer[index] = destinationBuffer[index]
```

The code in Listing 5.3 illustrates three examples of copying data from one buffer to another. The first method, in lines 4–8, copies the full buffer. The next method, in lines 10–14, copies only the middle 5 bytes of a buffer. The third example, in lines 15–22, iterates through the source buffer and copies only every other byte in the buffer. Figure 5.3 shows the results.

Listing 5.3 `buffer_copy.js`: **Various ways to copy data from one** `Buffer` **object to another**

```
01 var alphabet = new Buffer('abcdefghijklmnopqrstuvwxyz');
02 console.log(alphabet.toString());
03 // copy full buffer
04 var blank = new Buffer(26);
05 blank.fill();
06 console.log("Blank: " + blank.toString());
07 alphabet.copy(blank);
08 console.log("Blank: " + blank.toString());
09 // copy part of buffer
10 var dashes = new Buffer(26);
11 dashes.fill('-');
12 console.log("Dashes: " + dashes.toString());
13 alphabet.copy(dashes, 10, 10, 15);
14 console.log("Dashes: " + dashes.toString());
15 // copy to and from direct indexes of buffers
16 var dots = new Buffer('------------------------');
17 dots.fill('.');
18 console.log("dots: " + dots.toString());
19 for (var i=0; i < dots.length; i++){
20   if (i % 2) { dots[i] = alphabet[i]; }
21 }
22 console.log("dots: " + dots.toString());
```

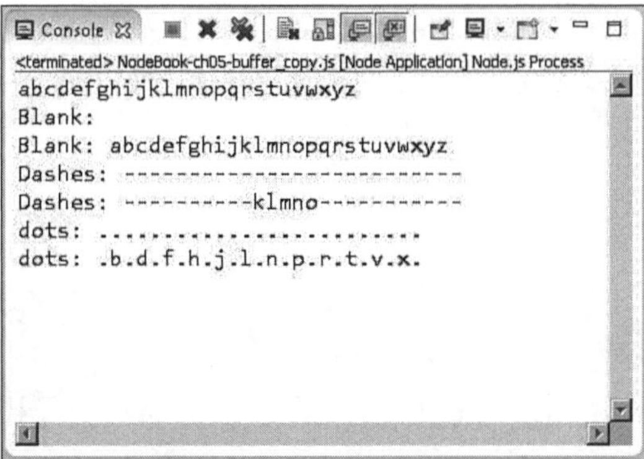

Figure 5.3 Output of `buffer_copy.js`, copying data from one `Buffer` object to another.

Slicing Buffers

Another important aspect of working with buffers is the ability to divide them into slices. A *slice* is a section of a buffer between a starting index and an ending index. Slicing a buffer allows you to manipulate a specific chunk.

You create slices by using `slice([start], [end])`, which returns a `Buffer` object that points to the `start` index of the original buffer and has a length of `end – start`. Keep in mind that a slice is different from a copy. If you edit a copy, the original does not change. However, if you edit a slice, the original does change.

The code in Listing 5.4 illustrates using slices. The important thing to note is that when the slice is altered in lines 5 and 6, it also alters the original buffer, as shown in Figure 5.4.

Listing 5.4 `buffer_slice.js`: **Creating and manipulating slices of a `Buffer` object**

```
1 var numbers = new Buffer("123456789");
2 console.log(numbers.toString());
3 var slice = numbers.slice(3, 6);
4 console.log(slice.toString());
5 slice[0] = '#'.charCodeAt(0);
6 slice[slice.length-1] = '#'.charCodeAt(0);
7 console.log(slice.toString());
8 console.log(numbers.toString());
```

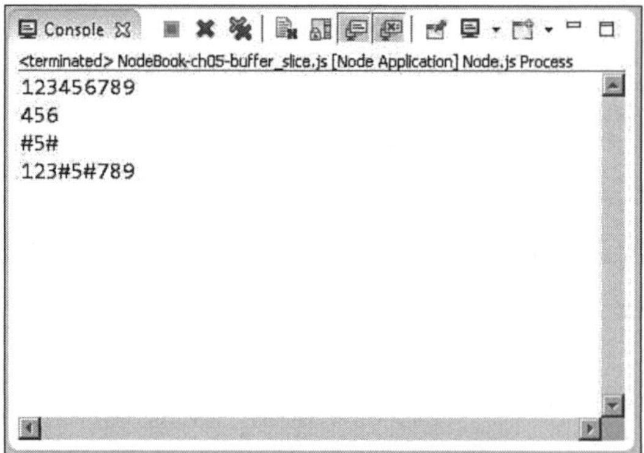

Figure 5.4 Output of `buffer_slice.js`, slicing and modifying a `Buffer` object.

Concatenating Buffers

You can concatenate two or more `Buffer` objects together to form a new buffer. The `concat(list, [totalLength])` method accepts an array of `Buffer` objects as the first parameter and `totalLength`, defining the maximum bytes in the buffer, as an optional second argument. The `Buffer` objects are concatenated in the order in which they appear in the list, and a new `Buffer` object is returned, containing the contents of the original buffers up to `totalLength` bytes.

If you do not provide a `totalLength` parameter, `concat()` figures out the total length for you. However, it has to iterate through the list, so providing a `totalLength` value is a bit faster.

The code in Listing 5.5 illustrates concatenation by concatenating a base `Buffer` object with one buffer and then another. Figure 5.5 shows the output.

Listing 5.5 `buffer_concat.js`: **Concatenating `Buffer` objects**

```
var af = new Buffer("African Swallow?");
var eu = new Buffer("European Swallow?");
var question = new Buffer("Air Speed Velocity of an ");
console.log(Buffer.concat([question, af]).toString());
console.log(Buffer.concat([question, eu]).toString());
```

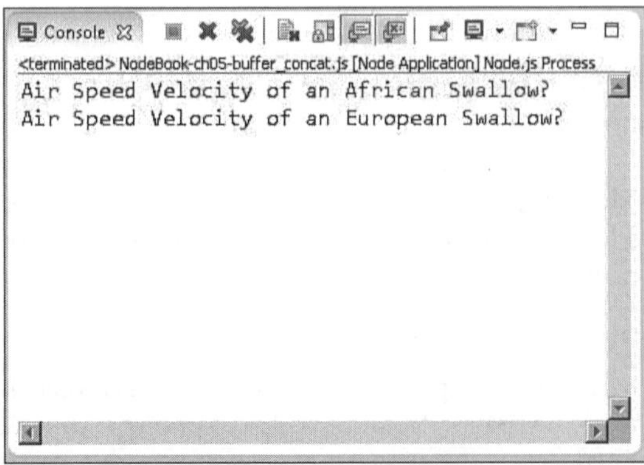

Figure 5.5 Output of `buffer_concat.js`, concatenating `Buffer` objects.

Using the `Stream` Module to Stream Data

An important module in Node.js is the `stream` module. Data streams are memory structures that are readable, writable, or both. Streams are used all over in Node.js, when accessing files, when reading data from HTTP requests, and in several other areas. This section covers using the `Stream` module to create streams as well as to read and write data from them.

The purpose of streams is to provide a common mechanism to transfer data from one location to another. They also expose events such as `data` when data is available to be read, `error` when an error occurs, and so forth so that you can register listeners to handle the data when it becomes available in a stream or is ready to be written to.

Streams are commonly used for HTTP data and files. You can open a file as a readable stream or access the data from an HTTP request as a readable stream and read bytes out as needed. In addition, you can create your own custom streams. The following sections describe the processes of creating and using `Readable`, `Writable`, `Duplex`, and `Transform` streams.

`Readable` Streams

`Readable` streams are designed to provide a mechanism to easily read data coming into an application from another source. Some common examples of readable streams are:

- HTTP responses on the client
- HTTP requests on the server
- `fs` read streams
- `zlib` streams
- `crypto` streams

- TCP sockets
- Child processes `stdout` and `stderr`
- `process.stdin`

`Readable` streams provide the `read([size])` method to read data, where `size` specifies the number of bytes to read from the stream. `read()` can return a `String` object, `Buffer` object or `null`. `Readable` streams also expose the following events:

- **`readable`:** Emitted when a chunk of data can be read from the stream.
- **`data`:** Similar to `readable`, except that when `data` event handlers are attached, the stream is turned into flowing mode, and the `data` handler is called continuously until all data has been drained.
- **`end`:** Emitted by the stream when data will no longer be provided.
- **`close`:** Emitted when the underlying resource, such as a file, has been closed.
- **`error`:** Emitted when an error occurs in receiving data.

`Readable` stream objects also provide a number of functions that allow you to read and manipulate them. Table 5.4 lists the methods available on `Readable` stream objects.

Table 5.4 **Methods available on `Readable` stream objects**

Method	Description
`read([size])`	Reads data from the stream. The data can be a `String`, `Buffer`, or `null`. (`null` means there is no more data left.) If a `size` argument is read, then the data is limited to that number of bytes.
`setEncoding(encoding)`	Sets the encoding to use when returning `String` in the `read()` request.
`pause()`	Pauses `data` events from being emitted by the object.
`resume()`	Resumes `data` events being emitted by the object.
`pipe(destination, [options])`	Pipes the output of this stream into a `Writable` stream object specified by `destination`. `options` is a JavaScript object. For example, `{end:true}` ends the `Writable` destination when `Readable` ends.
`unpipe([destination])`	Disconnects this object from the `Writable` destination.

To implement your own custom `Readable` stream object, you need to first inherit the functionality for `Readable` streams. The simplest way to do this is to use the following code, which uses the `util` module's `inherits()` method:

```
var util = require('util');
```

```
util.inherits(MyReadableStream, stream.Readable);
```

Then you create an instance of the object call:

```
stream.Readable.call(this, opt);
```

You will also need to implement a `_read()` method that calls `push()` to output the data from the `Readable` object. The `push()` call should push either a `String`, `Buffer`, or `null`.

The code in Listing 5.6 illustrates the basics of implementing and reading from a `Readable` stream. Notice that the `Answers()` class inherits from `Readable` and then implements the `Answers.prototye._read()` function to handle pushing data out. Also notice that on line 18, a direct `read()` call reads the first item from the stream, and then the `data` event handler defined on lines 19–21 reads the rest of the items. Figure 5.6 shows the output for Listing 5.6.

Listing 5.6 `stream_read.js`: **Implementing a `Readable` stream object**

```
01 var stream = require('stream');
02 var util = require('util');
03 util.inherits(Answers, stream.Readable);
04 function Answers(opt) {
05   stream.Readable.call(this, opt);
06   this.quotes = ["yes", "no", "maybe"];
07   this._index = 0;
08 }
09 Answers.prototype._read = function() {
10   if (this._index > this.quotes.length){
11     this.push(null);
12   } else {
13     this.push(this.quotes[this._index]);
14     this._index += 1;
15   }
16 };
17 var r = new Answers();
18 console.log("Direct read: " + r.read().toString());
19 r.on('data', function(data){
20   console.log("Callback read: " + data.toString());
21 });
22 r.on('end', function(data){
23   console.log("No more answers.");
24 });
```

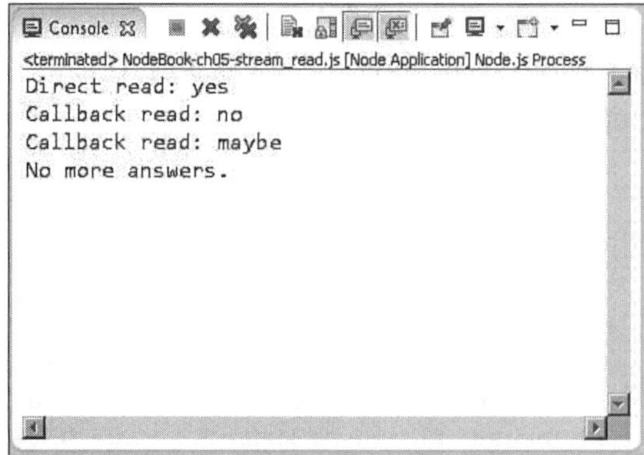

Figure 5.6 Output of `stream_read.js`, implementing a custom `Readable` object.

`Writable` Streams

`Writable` streams are designed to provide a mechanism to write data into a form that can easily be consumed in another area of code. Some common examples of `Writable` streams are:

- HTTP requests on the client
- HTTP responses on the server
- `fs` write streams
- `zlib` streams
- `crypto` streams
- TCP sockets
- Child process `stdin`
- `process.stdout` and `process.stderr`

`Writable` streams provide the `write(chunk, [encoding], [callback])` method to write data into the stream, where `chunk` contains the data to write; `encoding` specifies the string encoding, if necessary; and `callback` specifies a callback function to execute when the data has been fully flushed. The `write()` function returns `true` if the data was written successfully. `Writable` streams also expose the following events:

- **`drain`:** After a `write()` call returns `false`, emitted to notify listeners when it is okay to begin writing more data.
- **`finish`:** Emitted when `end()` is called on the `Writable` object, all data is flushed, and no more data will be accepted.

- **pipe:** Emitted when the `pipe()` method is called on a `Readable` stream to add this `Writable` as a destination.
- **unpipe:** Emitted when the `unpipe()` method is called on a `Readable` stream to remove this `Writable` as a destination.

`Writable` stream objects also provide a number of methods that you can write and manipulate. Table 5.5 lists the methods available on `Writable` stream objects.

Table 5.5 **Methods available on `Writable` stream objects**

Method	Description
`write(chunk, [encoding], [callback])`	Writes the data chuck to the stream object's data location. The data can be a `String` or `Buffer`. If `encoding` is specified, then it is used to encode string data. If `callback` is specified, then it is called after the data has been flushed.
`end([chunk], [encoding], [callback])`	Same as `write()` except it puts the `Writable` into a state where it no longer accepts data and sends the `finish` event.

To implement your own custom `Writable` stream object, you need to first inherit the functionality for `Writable` streams. The simplest way to do this is to use the following code, which uses the `util` module's `inherits()` method:

```
var util = require('util');
util.inherits(MyWritableStream, stream.Writable);
```

Then you create an instance of the object call:

```
stream.Writable.call(this, opt);
```

You also need to implement a `_write(data, encoding, callback)` method that stores the data for the `Writable` object. The code in Listing 5.7 illustrates the basics of implementing and writing to a `Writable` stream. Figure 5.7 shows the output for Listing 5.7.

Listing 5.7 `stream_write.js`: **Implementing a `Writable` stream object**

```
var stream = require('stream');
var util = require('util');
util.inherits(Writer, stream.Writable);
function Writer(opt) {
  stream.Writable.call(this, opt);
  this.data = new Array();
}
Writer.prototype._write = function(data, encoding, callback) {
  this.data.push(data.toString('utf8'));
  console.log("Adding: " + data);
```

```
  callback();
};
var w = new Writer();
for (var i=1; i<=5; i++){
  w.write("Item" + i, 'utf8');
}
w.end("ItemLast");
console.log(w.data);
```

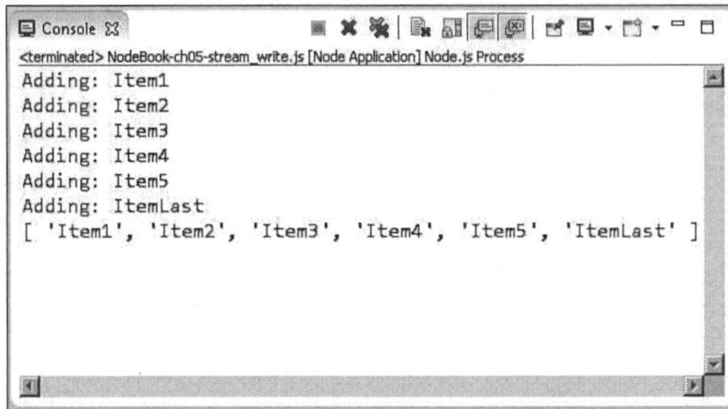

Figure 5.7 Output of `stream_write.js`, implementing a custom `Writable` object.

`Duplex` Streams

A `Duplex` stream is a stream that combines `Readable` and `Writable` functionality. A good example of a `Duplex` stream is a TCP socket connection. You can read and write from the socket connection after it has been created.

To implement your own custom `Duplex` stream object, you need to first inherit the functionality for `Duplex` streams. The simplest way to do this is to use the following code, which uses the `util` module's `inherits()` method:

```
var util = require('util');
util.inherits(MyDuplexStream, stream.Duplex);
```

Then you create an instance of the object call:

```
stream.Duplex.call(this, opt);
```

The `opt` parameter with creation of a `Duplex` stream accepts an object with the property `allowHalfOpen` set to `true` or `false`. If this option is `true`, then the readable side stays open even after the writable side has ended and vice versa. If this option is set to `false`, then ending the writable side also ends the readable side and vice versa.

When you implement a `Duplex` stream, you need to implement both a `_read(size)` and `_write(data, encoding, callback)` method when prototyping your `Duplex` class.

The code in Listing 5.8 illustrates the basics of implementing, writing to, and reading from a `Duplex` stream. The example is very basic but shows the main concepts. The `Duplexer()` class inherits from the `Duplex` stream and implements a rudimentary `_write()` function that stores data in an array in the object. The `_read()` function uses `shift()` to get the first item in the array and then pushes `null` if it is equal to `"stop"`, pushes it if there is a value, or sets a timeout timer to call back to the `_read()` function if there is no value.

Figure 5.8 shows the output for Listing 5.8. Notice that the first two writes (`"I think, "` and `"therefore"`) are read together. This is because both were pushed to `Readable` before the `data` event was triggered.

Listing 5.8 `stream_duplex.js`: **Implementing a `Duplex` stream object**

```
var stream = require('stream');
var util = require('util');
util.inherits(Duplexer, stream.Duplex);
function Duplexer(opt) {
  stream.Duplex.call(this, opt);
  this.data = [];
}
Duplexer.prototype._read = function readItem(size) {
  var chunk = this.data.shift();
  if (chunk == "stop"){
    this.push(null);
  } else{
    if(chunk){
      this.push(chunk);
    } else {
      setTimeout(readItem.bind(this), 500, size);
    }
  }
};
Duplexer.prototype._write = function(data, encoding, callback) {
  this.data.push(data);
  callback();
};
var d = new Duplexer();
d.on('data', function(chunk){
  console.log('read: ', chunk.toString());
});
d.on('end', function(){
  console.log('Message Complete');
});
d.write("I think, ");
```

```
d.write("therefore ");
d.write("I am.");
d.write("Rene Descartes");
d.write("stop");
```

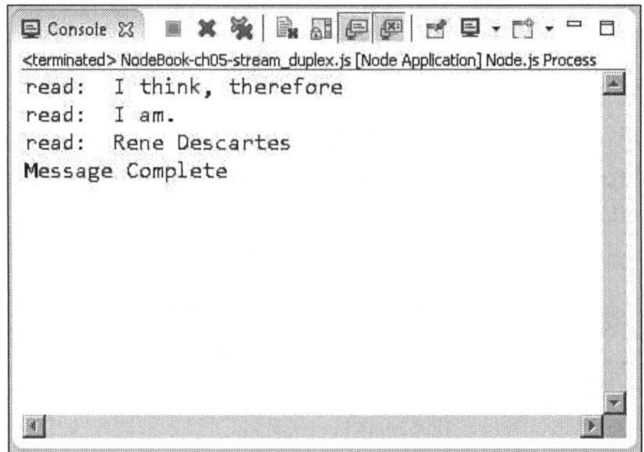

Figure 5.8 Output of `stream_duplex.js`, implementing a custom `Duplex` object.

`Transform` Streams

A `Transform` stream extends the `Duplex` stream but modifies the data between the `Writable` stream and the `Readable` stream. This stream type can be extremely useful when you need to modify data from one system to another. Some examples of `Transform` streams are:

- `zlib` stream
- `crypto` streams

A major difference between the `Duplex` and the `Transform` streams is that for `Transform` streams, you do not need to implement the `_read()` and `_write()` prototype methods. These are provided as pass-through functions. Instead, you implement the `_transform(chunk, encoding, callback)` and `_flush(callback)` methods. The `_transform()` method should accept the data from `write()` requests, modify it, and push out the modified data.

The code in Listing 5.9 illustrates the basics of implementing a `Transform` stream. The stream accepts JSON strings, converts them to objects, and then emits a custom event named `object` that sends the object to any listeners. The `_transform()` function also modifies the object to include a `handled` property and then sends on a string form. Notice that lines 18–21 implement the `object` event handler function, which displays certain attributes. Figure 5.9 shows the output for Listing 5.9. Notice that the JSON strings now include the `handled` property.

Listing 5.9 `stream_transform.js`: **Implementing a `Transform` stream object**

```
var stream = require("stream");
var util = require("util");
util.inherits(JSONObjectStream, stream.Transform);
function JSONObjectStream (opt) {
  stream.Transform.call(this, opt);
};
JSONObjectStream.prototype._transform = function (data, encoding, callback) {
  object = data ? JSON.parse(data.toString()) : "";
  this.emit("object", object);
  object.handled = true;
  this.push(JSON.stringify(object));
  callback();
};
JSONObjectStream.prototype._flush = function(cb) {
  cb();
};
var tc = new JSONObjectStream();
tc.on("object", function(object){
  console.log("Name: %s", object.name);
  console.log("Color: %s", object.color);
});
tc.on("data", function(data){
  console.log("Data: %s", data.toString());
});
tc.write('{"name":"Carolinus", "color": "Green"}');
tc.write('{"name":"Solarius", "color": "Blue"}');
tc.write('{"name":"Lo Tae Zhao", "color": "Gold"}');
tc.write('{"name":"Ommadon", "color": "Red"}');
```

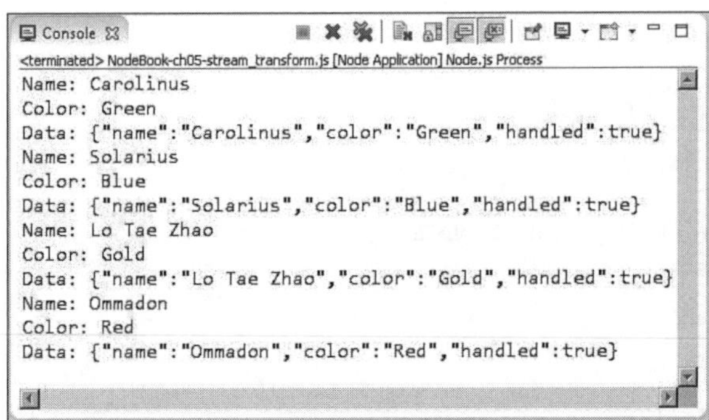

Figure 5.9 Output of `stream_transform.js`, implementing a custom `Transform` object.

Piping Readable Streams to Writable Streams

One of the coolest things you can do with stream objects is chain `Readable` streams to `Writable` streams by using the `pipe(writableStream, [options])` function. This does exactly what the name implies: It inputs the output from the `Readable` stream directly into the `Writable` stream. The `options` parameter accepts an object with the `end` property set to `true` or `false`. When `end` is `true`, the `Writable` stream ends when the `Readable` stream ends. This is the default behavior. For example:

```
readStream.pipe(writeStream, {end:true});
```

You can also break the pipe programmatically by using the `unpipe(destinationStream)` option. The code in Listing 5.10 implements a `Readable` stream and a `Writable` stream and then uses the `pipe()` function to chain them together. To show you the basic process, the data input from the `_write()` method is output to the console in Figure 5.10.

Listing 5.10 `stream_piped.js`**: Piping a** `Readable` **stream into a** `Writable` **stream**

```
var stream = require('stream');
var util = require('util');
util.inherits(Reader, stream.Readable);
util.inherits(Writer, stream.Writable);
function Reader(opt) {
  stream.Readable.call(this, opt);
  this._index = 1;
}
Reader.prototype._read = function(size) {
  var i = this._index++;
  if (i > 10){
    this.push(null);
  } else {
    this.push("Item " + i.toString());
  }
};
function Writer(opt) {
  stream.Writable.call(this, opt);
  this._index = 1;
}
Writer.prototype._write = function(data, encoding, callback) {
  console.log(data.toString());
  callback();
};
var r = new Reader();
var w = new Writer();
r.pipe(w);
```

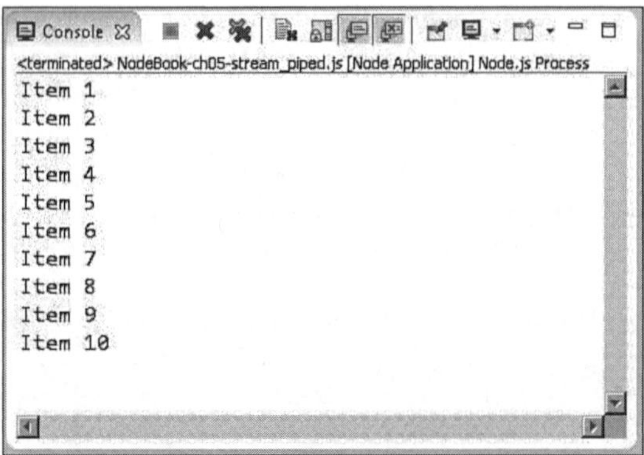

Figure 5.10 Output of `stream_piped.js`, implementing stream piping.

Compressing and Decompressing Data with `Zlib`

When working with large systems or moving large amounts of data around, it is extremely helpful to be able to compress/decompress the data. Node.js provides an excellent library in the `Zlib` module that allows you to compress and decompress data in buffers very easily and efficiently.

You need to keep in mind that compressing data takes CPU cycles, so you should be certain of the benefits of compressing data before you incur the compression/decompression cost. `Zlib` supports these compression methods:

- **`gzip/gunzip`:** Standard `gzip` compression.
- **`deflate/inflate`:** Standard deflate compression algorithm, based on Huffman coding.
- **`deflateRaw/inflateRaw`:** Deflate compression algorithm on a raw buffer.

Compressing and Decompressing Buffers

The `Zlib` module provides several helper functions that make it easy to compress/decompress data buffers. They all use the same basic format of *`function`*(*`buffer`*, *`callback`*), where *`function`* is the compression/decompression method, *`buffer`* is the buffer to be compressed/decompressed, and *`callback`* is the callback function that is executed after the compression/decompression occurs.

The simplest way to illustrate buffer compression/decompression is to show you some examples. The code in Listing 5.11 provides several compression/decompression examples and outputs the size results of each as shown in Figure 5.11.

Listing 5.11 `zlib_buffers.js`: **Compressing/decompressing buffers using the `zlib` module**

```
var zlib = require("zlib");
var input = '..............text..............';
zlib.deflate(input, function(err, buffer) {
  if (!err) {
    console.log("deflate (%s): ", buffer.length, buffer.toString('base64'));
    zlib.inflate(buffer, function(err, buffer) {
      if (!err) {
        console.log("inflate (%s): ", buffer.length, buffer.toString());
      }
    });
    zlib.unzip(buffer, function(err, buffer) {
      if (!err) {
        console.log("unzip deflate (%s): ", buffer.length, buffer.toString());
      }
    });
  }
});

zlib.deflateRaw(input, function(err, buffer) {
  if (!err) {
    console.log("deflateRaw (%s): ", buffer.length, buffer.toString('base64'));
    zlib.inflateRaw(buffer, function(err, buffer) {
      if (!err) {
        console.log("inflateRaw (%s): ", buffer.length, buffer.toString());
      }
    });
  }
});

zlib.gzip(input, function(err, buffer) {
  if (!err) {
    console.log("gzip (%s): ", buffer.length, buffer.toString('base64'));
    zlib.gunzip(buffer, function(err, buffer) {
      if (!err) {
        console.log("gunzip (%s): ", buffer.length, buffer.toString());
      }
    });
    zlib.unzip(buffer, function(err, buffer) {
      if (!err) {
        console.log("unzip gzip (%s): ", buffer.length, buffer.toString());
      }
    });
  }
});
```

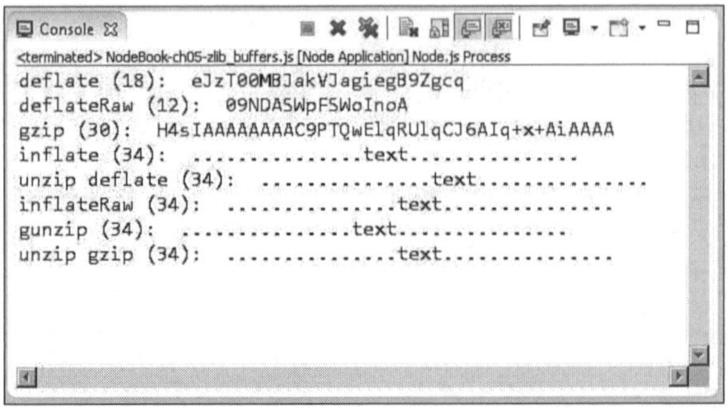

```
Console
<terminated> NodeBook-ch05-zlib_buffers.js [Node Application] Node.js Process
deflate (18):  eJzT00MBJakVJagiegB9Zgcq
deflateRaw (12):  09NDASWpFSWoInoA
gzip (30):  H4sIAAAAAAAAC9PTQwElqRUlqCJ6AIq+x+AiAAAA
inflate (34):  ...............text...............
unzip deflate (34):  ...............text...............
inflateRaw (34):  ...............text...............
gunzip (34):  ...............text...............
unzip gzip (34):  ...............text...............
```

Figure 5.11 Output of `zilb_buffers.js`, compressing/decompressing buffers.

Compressing/Decompressing Streams

Compressing/decompressing streams using `Zlib` is slightly different from compressing/decompressing buffers. Instead, you use the `pipe()` function to pipe the data from one stream through the compression/decompression object into another stream. This can apply to compressing any `Readable` streams into `Writable` streams.

A good example of doing this is compressing the contents of a file by using `fs.ReadStream` and `fs.WriteStream`. The code in Listing 5.12 shows an example of compressing the contents of one file by using a `zlib.Gzip()` object and then decompressing it by using a `zlib.Gunzip()` object. Notice that there is a 5 second timeout delay before trying to decompress the file to allow the data to be flushed to disk.

Listing 5.12 `zlib_file.js`: **Compressing/decompressing a file stream using the `Zlib` module**

```
var zlib = require("zlib");
var gzip = zlib.createGzip();
var fs = require('fs');
var inFile = fs.createReadStream('zlib_file.js');
var outFile = fs.createWriteStream('zlib_file.gz');
inFile.pipe(gzip).pipe(outFile);
setTimeout(function(){
  var gunzip = zlib.createUnzip({flush: zlib.Z_FULL_FLUSH});
  var inFile = fs.createReadStream('zlib_file.gz');
  var outFile = fs.createWriteStream('zlib_file.unzipped');
  inFile.pipe(gunzip).pipe(outFile);
}, 3000);
```

Summary

At the heart of most intense web applications and services is a lot of data streaming from one system to another. In this chapter you have learned how to use functionality built into Node.js to work with JSON data, manipulate binary buffer data, and utilize data streams. You've also had a chance to play around with compression in compressing buffered data as well as running data streams through compression/decompression.

Up Next

In the next chapter, you'll see how to interact with the file system from Node.js. You will read/write files, create directories, and read file system information.

6

Accessing the File System from Node.js

Interacting with the file system in Node.js is extremely important, especially if you need to manage dynamic files to support a web application or service. Node.js provides a good interface for interacting with the file system in the `fs` module. This module provides the standard file access APIs that are available in most languages to open, read, write, and interact with files.

This chapter explains the fundamentals of accessing the file system from Node.js applications. You should come away with the ability to create, read, and modify files as well as navigate the directory structure. You will also be able to access file and folder information and delete, truncate, and rename files and folders.

For all the file system calls discussed in this chapter, you need to have loaded the `fs` module, for example:

```
var fs  = require('fs');
```

Synchronous Versus Asynchronous File System Calls

The `fs` module provided in Node.js makes almost all functionality available in two forms: asynchronous and synchronous. For example, it offers the asynchronous form `write()` and the synchronous form `writeSync()`. It is important to understand the difference when you are implementing code.

Synchronous file system calls block until a call completes and then control is released back to the thread. This has advantages but can also cause severe performance issues in Node.js if synchronous calls block the main event thread or too many of the background thread pool threads. Therefore, you should limit the use of synchronous file system calls when possible.

Asynchronous calls are placed on the event queue to be run later. This allows the calls to fit into the Node.js event model, but it can be a bit tricky when executing your code because the calling thread continues to run before the asynchronous call gets picked up by the event loop.

For the most part, the underlying functionality of both synchronous and asynchronous file system calls is exactly the same. Both synchronous and asynchronous file system calls accept the same parameters, with one exception: All asynchronous calls require an extra parameter at the end, a callback function to execute when the file system call completes.

The following list describes the important differences between synchronous and asynchronous file system calls in Node.js:

- Asynchronous calls require a callback function as an extra parameter. The callback function is executed when the file system request completes and typically contains an error as its first parameter.
- Asynchronous calls automatically handle exceptions and pass an error object as the first parameter if an exception occurs. To handle exceptions in synchronous calls, you must use `try/catch` blocks.
- Synchronous calls run immediately, and execution does not return to the current thread until they complete. Asynchronous calls are placed on the event queue, and execution returns to the running thread code, but the actual call does not execute until it is picked up by the event loop.

Opening and Closing Files

Node.js provides synchronous and asynchronous methods for opening files. Once a file is opened, you can read data from it or write data to it, depending on the flags used to open the file. To open files in a Node.js app, use one of the following statements for asynchronous or synchronous:

```
fs.open(path, flags, [mode], callback)
fs.openSync(path, flags, [mode])
```

The `path` parameter specifies a standard path string for your file system. The `flags` parameter specifies what mode to open the file in—read, write, append, etc., as described in Table 6.1. The optional `mode` parameter sets the file access mode and defaults to `0666`, which is readable and writable.

Table 6.1 **Flags that define how files are opened**

Mode	Description
`r`	Open file for reading. An exception occurs if the file does not exist.
`r+`	Open file for reading and writing. An exception occurs if the file does not exist.
`rs`	Open file for reading in synchronous mode. This is not the same as forcing `fs.openSync()`. When used, the operating system bypasses the local file system cache. This is useful on NFS mounts because it lets you skip the potentially stale local cache. You should use this flag only if necessary because it can have a negative impact on performance.

Mode	Description
`rs+`	Same as `rs` except the file is open for both reading and writing.
`w`	Open file for writing. The file is created if it does not exist or is truncated if it does exist.
`wx`	Same as `w` but fails if the path exists.
`w+`	Open file for reading and writing. The file is created if it does not exist or is truncated if it does exist.
`wx+`	Same as `w+` but fails if the path exists.
`a`	Open file for appending. The file is created if it does not exist.
`ax`	Same as `a` but fails if the path exists.
`a+`	Open file for reading and appending. The file is created if it does not exist.
`ax+`	Same as `a+` but fails if the path exists.

Once a file has been opened, you need to close it to force flushing changes to disk and release the operating system lock. You close a file by using one of the following methods and passing the file descriptor to it. In the case of the asynchronous `close()` call, you also need to specify a callback function:

```
fs.close(fd, callback)
fs.closeSync(fd)
```

The following is an example of opening and closing a file in asynchronous mode. Notice that a callback function is specified and receives an `err` and an `fd` parameter. The `fd` parameter is the file descriptor that you can use to read or write to the file:

```
fs.open("myFile", 'w', function(err, fd){
  if (!err){
    fs.close(fd);
  }
});
```

The following is an example of opening and closing a file in synchronous mode. Notice that there is no callback function and that the file descriptor used to read and write to the file is returned directly from `fs.openSync()`:

```
var fd = fs.openSync("myFile", 'w');
fs.closeSync(fd);
```

Writing Files

The `fs` module provides four different ways to write data to files. You can write data to a file in a single call, write chunks using synchronous writes, write chunks using asynchronous writes, or stream writes through a `Writable` stream. Each of these methods accepts either a `String` or `Buffer` object as input. The following sections describe how to use these methods.

Simple File Writing

The simplest method for writing data to a file is to use one of the `writeFile()` methods. These methods write the full contents of a string or buffer to a file. The following is the syntax for `writeFile()` methods:

```
fs.writeFile(path, data, [options], callback)
fs.writeFileSync(path, data, [options])
```

The `path` parameter specifies the path to the file, which can be relative or absolute. The `data` parameter specifies the `String` or `Buffer` object that will be written to the file. The optional `options` parameter is an object that can contain `encoding`, `mode`, and `flag` properties that define the string encoding as well as the mode and flags used when opening the file. The asynchronous method also requires the `callback` parameter, which will be called when the file write has been completed.

The code in Listing 6.1 shows how to implement a simple asynchronous `fileWrite()` request to store a JSON string of a `config` object in a file. Figure 6.1 shows the output of the code in Listing 6.1.

Listing 6.1 `file_write.js`: **Writing a JSON string to a file**

```
var fs = require('fs');
var config = {
  maxFiles: 20,
  maxConnections: 15,
  rootPath: "/webroot"
};
var configTxt = JSON.stringify(config);
var options = {encoding:'utf8', flag:'w'};
fs.writeFile('config.txt', configTxt, options, function(err){
  if (err){
    console.log("Config Write Failed.");
  } else {
    console.log("Config Saved.");
  }
});
```

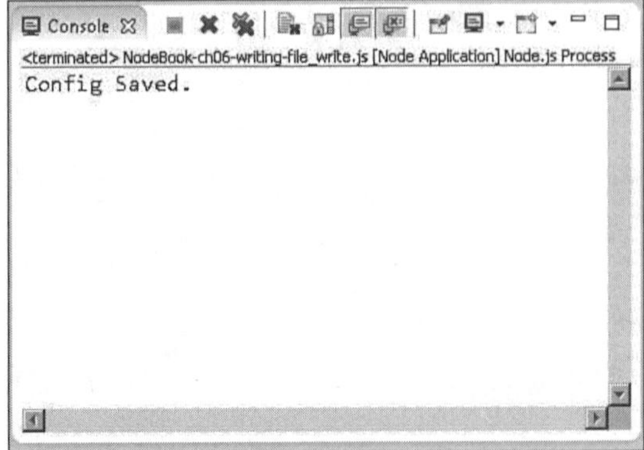

Figure 6.1 Output of `file_write.js`, writing to a configuration file.

Synchronous File Writing

The synchronous method of file writing involves writing data to a file before returning execution to the running thread. This provides the advantage of allowing you to write multiple times in the same section of code, but it can be a disadvantage if the file writes hold up other threads, as discussed earlier.

To write to a file synchronously, first open it using `openSync()` to get a file descriptor and then use `fs.writeSync()` to write data to the file. The following is the syntax for `fs.writeSync()`:

```
fs.writeSync(fd, data, offset, length, position)
```

The `fd` parameter is the file descriptor that `openSync()` returns. The `data` parameter specifies the `String` or `Buffer` object that will be written to the file. The `offset` parameter specifies the index in the `data` parameter to begin reading from. If you want to begin at the current index in the string or buffer, this value should be `null`. The `length` parameter specifies the number of bytes to write; you can specify `null` to write until the end of the `data` buffer. The `position` argument specifies the position in the file to begin writing; to use the current file position, specify `null` for this value.

The code in Listing 6.2 shows how to implement basic synchronous writing to store a series of string data in a file. Figure 6.2 shows the output of the code in Listing 6.2.

Listing 6.2 `file_write_sync.js`: **Performing synchronous writes to a file**

```
var fs = require('fs');
var veggieTray = ['carrots', 'celery', 'olives'];
fd = fs.openSync('veggie.txt', 'w');
while (veggieTray.length){
  veggie = veggieTray.pop() + " ";
  var bytes = fs.writeSync(fd, veggie, null, null);
```

```
  console.log("Wrote %s %dbytes", veggie, bytes);
}
fs.closeSync(fd);
```

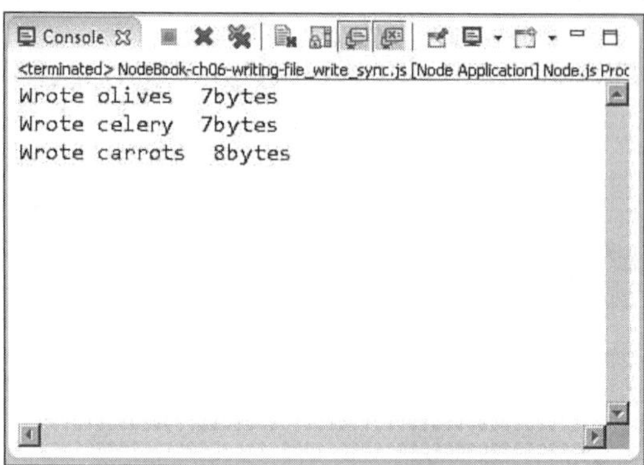

Figure 6.2 Output of `file_write_sync.js`, writing synchronously to a file.

Asynchronous File Writing

The asynchronous method of file writing puts a write request on the event queue and then returns control back to the calling code. The actual write does not take place until the event loop picks up the write request and executes it. You need to be careful when performing multiple asynchronous write requests on the same file because you cannot guarantee the execution order unless you wait for the first write callback before executing the next one. Typically the simplest way to do this is to nest writes inside the callback from the previous write. The code in Listing 6.3 illustrates this process.

To write to a file asynchronously, first open it using `open()` and then after the callback from the open request has executed, use `fs.write()` to write data to the file. The following is the syntax for `fs.write()`:

```
fs.write(fd, data, offset, length, position, callback)
```

The `fd` parameter is the file descriptor that `openSync()` returns. The `data` parameter specifies the `String` or `Buffer` object that will be written to the file. The `offset` parameter specifies the index in the input data to begin reading data. If you want to begin at the current index in the string or buffer, this value should be `null`. The `length` parameter specifies the number of bytes to write; if you want to write at the end of the buffer, specify `null` for this parameter. The `position` argument specifies the position in the file to begin writing. To use the current file position, specify `null` for this value.

The `callback` argument must be a function that can accept two parameters, `error` and `bytes`, where `error` is an error that occurred during the write and `bytes` specifies the number of bytes written.

The code in Listing 6.3 shows how to implement basic asynchronous writing to store a series of string data in a file. Notice that the callback specified in lines 18–20 in the `open()` callback calls the `writeFruit()` function and passes the file descriptor. Also notice that the `write()` callback specified in lines 6–13 also calls `writeFruit()` and passes the file descriptor. This ensures that the asynchronous write completes before another executes. Figure 6.3 shows the output of the code in Listing 6.3.

Listing 6.3 `file_write_async.js`: **Performing asynchronous writes to a file**

```
01 var fs = require('fs');
02 var fruitBowl = ['apple', 'orange', 'banana', 'grapes'];
03 function writeFruit(fd){
04   if (fruitBowl.length){
05     var fruit = fruitBowl.pop() + " ";
06     fs.write(fd, fruit, null, null, function(err, bytes){
07       if (err){
08         console.log("File Write Failed.");
09       } else {
10         console.log("Wrote: %s %dbytes", fruit, bytes);
11         writeFruit(fd);
12       }
13     });
14   } else {
15     fs.close(fd);
16   }
17 }
18 fs.open('fruit.txt', 'w', function(err, fd){
19   writeFruit(fd);
20 });
```

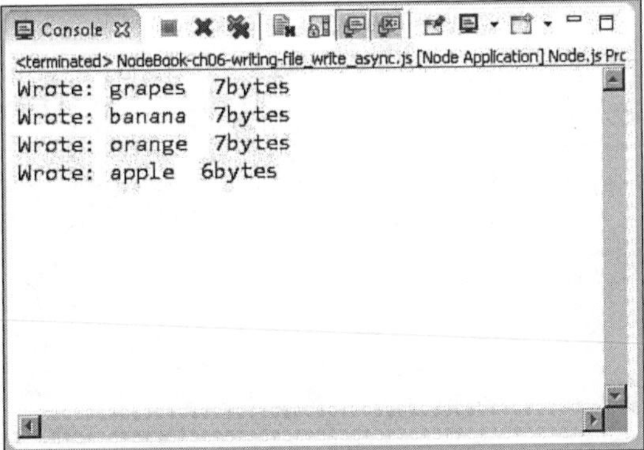

Figure 6.3 Output of `file_write_async.js`, writing asynchronously to a file.

Streaming File Writing

One of the best methods to use when writing large amounts of data to a file is streaming, which involves opening a file as a `Writable` stream. As discussed in Chapter 5, "Handling Data I/O in Node.js," `Writable` streams can easily be implemented and linked to `Readable` streams, using the `pipe()` method; this makes it very easy to write data from a `Readable` stream source such as an HTTP request.

To stream data to a file asynchronously, you first need to create a `Writable` stream object, using the following syntax:

```
fs.createWriteStream(path, [options])
```

The `path` parameter specifies the path to the file, which can be relative or absolute. The optional `options` parameter is an object that can contain `encoding`, `mode`, and `flag` properties that define the string encoding as well as the mode and flags used when opening the file.

Once you have opened the `Writable` file stream, you can write to it using the standard stream `write(buffer)` methods. When you are finished writing, call the `end()` method to close the stream.

The code in Listing 6.4 shows how to implement a basic `Writable` file stream. Notice that when the code is finished writing, the `end()` method is executed on line 13, which triggers the `close` event. Figure 6.4 shows the output of the code in Listing 6.4.

Listing 6.4 `file_write_stream.js`: Implementing a `Writable` stream to allow streaming writes to a file

```
01 var fs = require('fs');
02 var grains = ['wheat', 'rice', 'oats'];
03 var options = { encoding: 'utf8', flag: 'w' };
04 var fileWriteStream = fs.createWriteStream("grains.txt",  options);
05 fileWriteStream.on("close", function(){
06   console.log("File Closed.");
07 });
08 while (grains.length){
09   var data = grains.pop() + " ";
10   fileWriteStream.write(data);
11   console.log("Wrote: %s", data);
12 }
13 fileWriteStream.end();
```

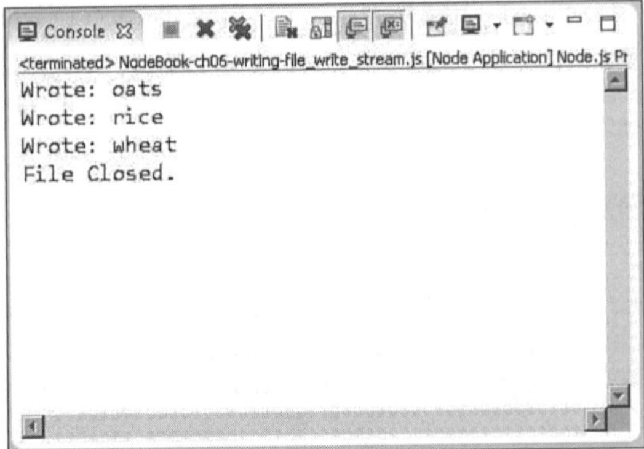

Figure 6.4 Output of `file_write_stream.js`, implementing streaming writes to a file.

Reading Files

The `fs` module provides four different ways to read data from files: in one large chunk, in chunks using synchronous writes, in chunks using asynchronous writes, or streaming through a `Readable` stream. All these methods are effective. Which one you use depends on the particular needs of your application. The following sections describe how to use and implement these methods.

Simple File Reading

The simplest method for reading data from a file is to use one of the `readFile()` methods. These methods read the full contents from a file into a data buffer. The following is the syntax for `readFile()` methods:

```
fs.readFile(path, [options], callback)
fs.readFileSync(path, [options])
```

The `path` parameter specifies the path to the file, which can be relative or absolute. The optional `options` parameter is an object that can contain `encoding`, `mode`, and `flag` properties that define the string encoding as well as the mode and flags used when opening the file. The asynchronous method also requires the `callback` parameter, which will be called when the file read has been completed.

The code in Listing 6.5 illustrates implementing a simple asynchronous `readFile()` request to read a JSON string from a configuration file and then use it to create a `config` object. Figure 6.5 shows the output of the code in Listing 6.5.

Listing 6.5 `file_read.js` code: **Reading a JSON string file to an object**

```
var fs = require('fs');
var options = {encoding:'utf8', flag:'r'};
fs.readFile('config.txt', options, function(err, data){
  if (err){
    console.log("Failed to open Config File.");
  } else {
    console.log("Config Loaded.");
    var config = JSON.parse(data);
    console.log("Max Files: " + config.maxFiles);
    console.log("Max Connections: " + config.maxConnections);
    console.log("Root Path: " + config.rootPath);
  }
});
```

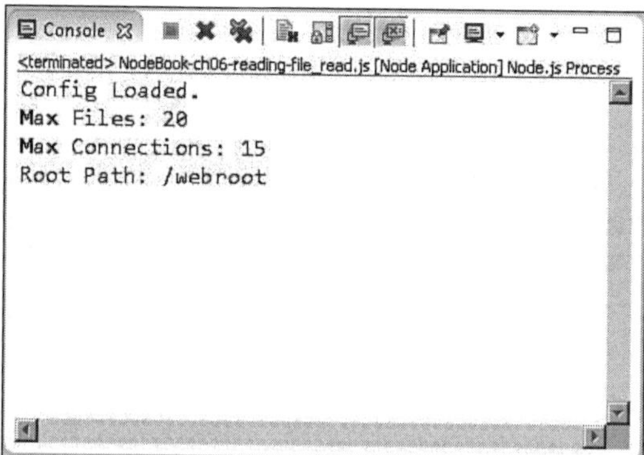

Figure 6.5 Output of `file_write.js`, reading a configuration file to an object.

Synchronous File Reading

The synchronous method of file reading involves reading the data from a file before returning execution to the running thread. This provides the advantage of allowing you to read multiple times in the same section of code, but it can be a disadvantage if the file reads hold up other threads, as discussed earlier.

To read to a file synchronously, first open it by using `openSync()` to get a file descriptor and then use `readSync()` to read data from the file. The following is the syntax for `readSync()`:

```
fs.readSync(fd, buffer, offset, length, position)
```

The `fd` parameter is the file descriptor that `openSync()` returns. The `buffer` parameter specifies the `Buffer` object that data will be read into from the file. The `offset` parameter specifies the index in the buffer to begin writing data; if you want to begin at the current index in the buffer, this value should be `null`. The `length` parameter specifies the number of bytes to read; to write until the end of the buffer, specify `null`. The `position` argument specifies the position in the file to begin reading. To use the current file position, specify `null` for this value.

The code in Listing 6.6 shows how to implement basic synchronous reading to read a chunk of string data from a file. Figure 6.6 shows the output of the code in Listing 6.6.

Listing 6.6 `file_read_sync.js`: **Performing synchronous reads from a file**

```
var fs = require('fs');
fd = fs.openSync('veggie.txt', 'r');
var veggies = "";
do {
  var buf = new Buffer(5);
  buf.fill();
  var bytes = fs.readSync(fd, buf, null, 5);
  console.log("read %dbytes", bytes);
  veggies += buf.toString();
} while (bytes > 0);
fs.closeSync(fd);
console.log("Veggies: " + veggies);
```

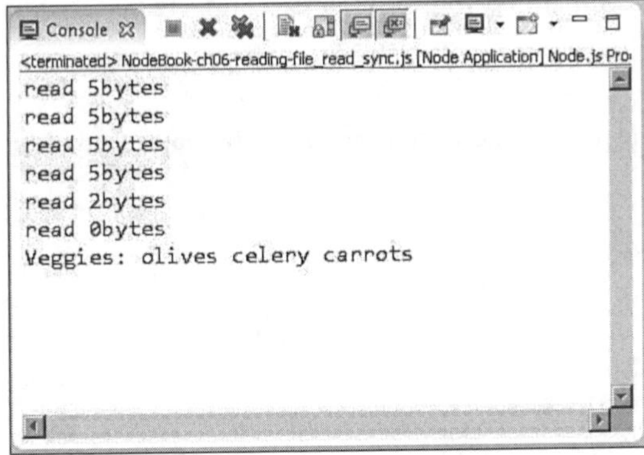

Figure 6.6 Output of `file_read_sync.js`, reading synchronously from a file.

Asynchronous File Reading

The asynchronous method of file reading puts the read request on the event queue and then returns control back to the calling code. The actual read does not take place until the event loop picks up the read request and executes it. You need to be careful when performing multiple asynchronous read requests on the same file because you cannot guarantee their execution order unless you wait for the first read callback to execute before executing the next read. Typically the simplest way to do this is to nest reads inside the callback from the previous read. The code in Listing 6.7 illustrates this process.

To read from a file asynchronously, first open it by using `open()` and then after the callback from the open request has executed, use `read()` to read data from the file. The following is the syntax for `read()`:

```
fs.read(fd, buffer, offset, length, position, callback)
```

The `fd` parameter is the file descriptor that `openSync()` returns. The `buffer` parameter specifies the `Buffer` object that data will be read into from the file. The `offset` parameter specifies the index in the buffer to begin reading data; if you want to begin at the current index in the buffer, this value should be `null`. The `length` parameter specifies the number of bytes to read; to read until the end of the buffer, specify `null`. The `position` argument specifies the position in the file to begin reading; specify `null` for this value to use the current file position.

The `callback` argument must be a function that can accept three parameters: `error`, `bytes`, and `buffer`. The `error` parameter is an error if one occurred during the read, `bytes` specifies the number of bytes read, and `buffer` is the buffer with data populated from the read request.

The code in Listing 6.7 shows how to implement basic asynchronous reading to read chunks of data from a file. Notice that the callback specified in lines 16–18 in the `open()` callback calls the `readFruit()` function and passes the file descriptor. Also notice that the `read()` callback specified in lines 5–13 also calls `readFruit()` and passes the file descriptor. This ensures that the asynchronous read completes before another executes. Figure 6.7 shows the output of the code in Listing 6.7.

Listing 6.7 `file_read_async.js`: **Performing asynchronous reads from a file**

```
01 var fs = require('fs');
02 function readFruit(fd, fruits){
03   var buf = new Buffer(5);
04   buf.fill();
05   fs.read(fd, buf, 0, 5, null, function(err, bytes, data){
06       if ( bytes > 0) {
07         console.log("read %dbytes", bytes);
08         fruits += data;
09         readFruit(fd, fruits);
10       } else {
11         fs.close(fd);
12         console.log ("Fruits: %s", fruits);
13       }
14   });
15 }
16 fs.open('fruit.txt', 'r', function(err, fd){
17   readFruit(fd, "");
18 });
```

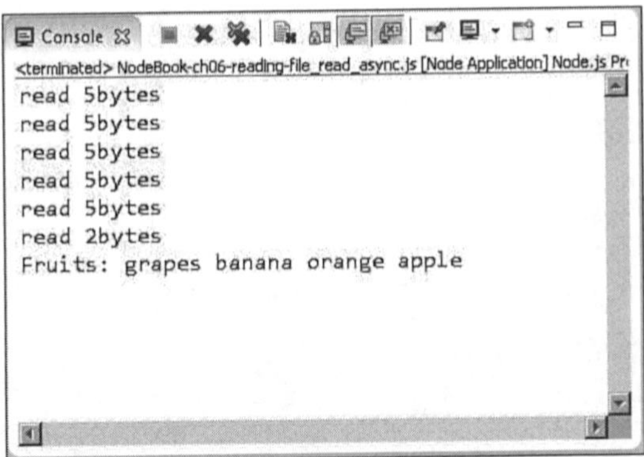

Figure 6.7 Output of `file_read_async.js`, reading asynchronously from a file.

Streaming File Reading

One of the best methods to use when reading large amounts of data from a file is streaming, which opens a file as a `Readable` stream. As discussed in Chapter 5, you can easily implement `Readable` streams and link them to `Writable` streams by using the `pipe()` method. This makes is very easy to read data from a file and inject it into a `Writable` stream source, such as an HTTP response.

To stream data from a file asynchronously, you first need to create a `Readable` stream object, using the following syntax:

```
fs.createReadStream(path, [options])
```

The `path` parameter specifies the path to the file, which can be relative or absolute. The optional `options` parameter is an object that can contain `encoding`, `mode`, and `flag` properties that define the string encoding as well as the mode and flags used when opening the file.

After you have opened the `Readable` file stream, you can easily read from it by using the readable event with `read()` requests or by implementing a data event handler, as shown in Listing 6.8.

The code in Listing 6.8 shows how to implement a basic `Readable` file stream. Notice that lines 4–7 implement a `data` event handler that continuously reads data from the stream. Figure 6.8 shows the output of the code in Listing 6.8.

Listing 6.8 `file_read_stream.js`**: Implementing a** `Readable` **stream to allow streaming reads from a file**

```
var fs = require('fs');
var options = { encoding: 'utf8', flag: 'r' };
var fileReadStream = fs.createReadStream("grains.txt",  options);
fileReadStream.on('data', function(chunk) {
  console.log('Grains: %s', chunk);
  console.log('Read %d bytes of data.', chunk.length);
});
fileReadStream.on("close", function(){
  console.log("File Closed.");
});
```

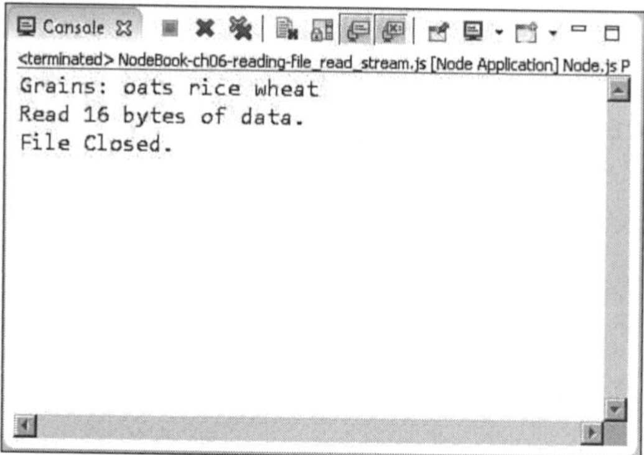

Figure 6.8 Output of `file_read_stream.js`, implementing streaming reads from a file.

Other File System Tasks

In addition to enabling you to read and write files, the `fs` module also provides additional functionality for interacting with the file system. For example, you can use it to list files in a directory, to look at file information, and much more. The following sections cover the most common file system tasks that you may need to implement when creating Node.js applications.

Verifying Path Existence

Before doing any kind of read/write operation on a file or directory, you might want to verify whether the path exists. You can easily do this by using one of the following methods:

```
fs.exists(path, callback)
fs.existsSync(path)
```

fs.existsSync(path) returns true or false, depending on whether the path exists. Just as with any other asynchronous file system call, if you use fs.exists(), you will need to implement a callback that will be executed when the call completes. The callback will be passed a Boolean value of true or false, depending on whether the path exists. For example, the following code verifies the existence of the file named filesystem.js in the current path and displays the results:

```
fs.exists('filesystem.js', function (exists) {
  console.log(exists ? "Path Exists" : "Path Does Not Exist");
});
```

Getting File Info

Another common task is to get basic information about file system objects, such as file size, mode, modification time, whether the entry is a file or folder, etc. You can obtain such information by using one of the following calls:

```
fs.stats(path, callback)
fs.statsSync(path)
```

The fsStatsSync() method returns a Stats object. The fs.stats() method is executed, and the Stats object is passed to the callback function as the second parameter. The first parameter is error if an error occurs.

Table 6.2 lists some of the most commonly used attributes and methods attached to the Stats object.

Table 6.2 **Attributes and methods of Stats objects for file system entries**

Attribute/Method	Description
isFile()	Returns true if the entry is a file.
isDirectory()	Returns true if the entry is a directory.
isSocket()	Returns true if the entry is a socket.
dev	Specifies the device ID the file is located on.
mode	Specifies the access mode of the file.
size	Specifies the number of bytes in the file.
blksize	Specifies the block size used to store the file, in bytes.
blocks	Specifies the number of blocks the file is taking on disk.
atime	Specifies the time the file was last accessed.
mtime	Specifies the time the file was last modified.
ctime	Specifies the time the file was created.

The code in Listing 6.9 illustrates the use of the `fs.stats()` call by making the call, then outputting the results of the object as a JSON string and using the `isFile()`, `isDirector()`, and `isSocket()` calls, as shown in the output in Figure 6.9.

Listing 6.9 `file_stats.js`: **Implementing an** `fs.stats()` **call to retrieve information about a file**

```
var fs = require('fs');
fs.stat('file_stats.js', function (err, stats) {
  if (!err){
    console.log('stats: ' + JSON.stringify(stats, null, '  '));
    console.log(stats.isFile() ? "Is a File" : "Is not a File");
    console.log(stats.isDirectory() ? "Is a Folder" : "Is not a Folder");
    console.log(stats.isSocket() ? "Is a Socket" : "Is not a Socket");
    stats.isDirectory();
    stats.isBlockDevice();
    stats.isCharacterDevice();
    //stats.isSymbolicLink(); //only lstat
    stats.isFIFO();
    stats.isSocket();
  }
});
```

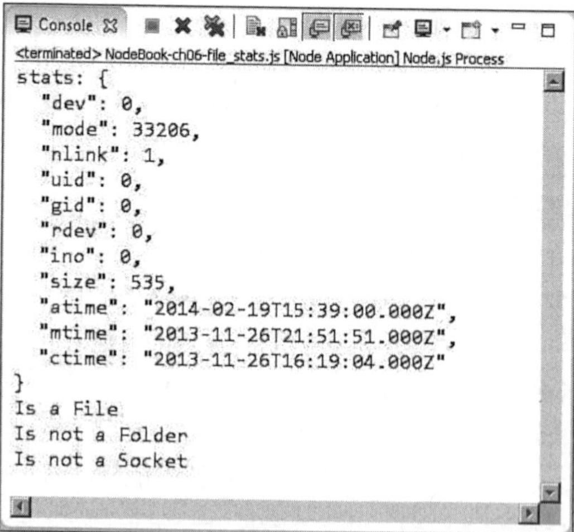

Figure 6.9 Output of `file_stats.js`, displaying information about a file.

Listing Files

Another common task when working with the file system is listing files and folders in a directory—for example, listing the files in a directory to determine whether they need to be cleaned up, to dynamically operate on the directory structure, etc.

You can access the files in the file system by using one of the following commands to read a list of entries:

```
fs.readdir(path, callback)
fs.readdirSync(path)
```

If `readdirSync()` is called, an array of strings representing the entry names in the specified `path` is returned. In the case of `readdir()`, the list is passed as the second parameter to the callback function, and an error, if there is one, is passed as the first parameter.

To illustrate the use of `readdir()`, the code in Listing 6.10 implements a nested callback chain to walk the directory structure and output the entries. Notice that the callback function implements a wrapper to provide closure for the `fullPath` variable and that the `WalkDirs()` function loops by being called by the asynchronous callback function. Figure 6.10 shows the results.

Listing 6.10 `file_readdir.js`: **Implementing a callback chain to walk down and output the contents of a directory structure**

```
var fs = require('fs');
var Path = require('path');
function WalkDirs(dirPath){
  console.log(dirPath);
  fs.readdir(dirPath, function(err, entries){
    for (var idx in entries){
      var fullPath = Path.join(dirPath, entries[idx]);
      (function(fullPath){
        fs.stat(fullPath, function (err, stats){
          if (stats && stats.isFile()){
            console.log(fullPath);
          } else if (stats && stats.isDirectory()){
            WalkDirs(fullPath);
          }
        });
      })(fullPath);
    }
  });
}
WalkDirs("../ch06");
```

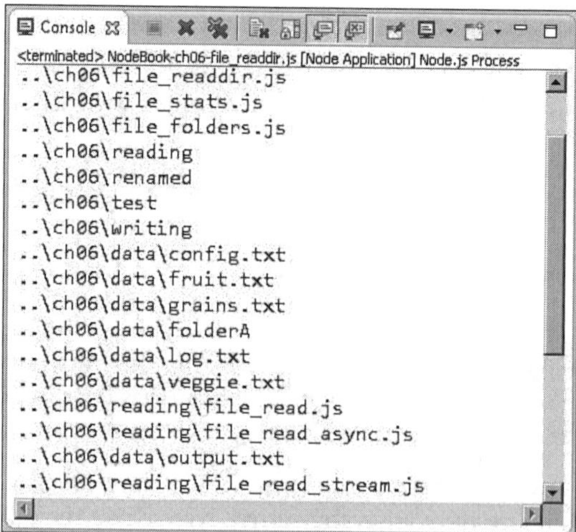

Figure 6.10 Output of `file_readdir.js`, iteratively walking the directory structure using chained asynchronous callbacks.

Deleting Files

Another common task when working with files is deleting them to clean up data or make more room on the file system. To delete a file from Node.js, use one of the following commands:

```
fs.unlink(path, callback)
fs.unlinkSync(path)
```

The `unlinkSync(path)` function returns `true` or `false`, depending on whether the delete was successful. The asynchronous `unlink()` call passes back an error value to the callback function if an error is encountered when deleting the file.

The following code snippet illustrates the process of deleting a file named `new.txt` by using the `unlink()` asynchronous `fs` call:

```
fs.unlink("new.txt", function(err){
  console.log(err ? "File Delete Failed" :  "File Deleted");
});
```

Truncating Files

Truncating a file means reducing the size of the file by setting the end to a smaller value than the current value. You may want to truncate files that grow continuously but do not contain critical data (for example, a temporary log). To truncate a file, you use one of the following `fs` calls and pass in the number of bytes you want the file to contain when the truncation completes:

```
fs.truncate(path, len, callback)
fs.truncateSync(path, len)
```

The `truncateSync(path)` function returns `true` or `false`, depending on whether the file was successfully truncated. On the other hand, an asynchronous `truncate()` call passes an error value to the callback function if an error is encountered when truncating the file.

The following code snippet illustrates the process of truncating a file named `log.txt` to zero bytes:

```
fs.truncate("new.txt", function(err){
  console.log(err ? "File Truncate Failed" :  "File Truncated");
});
```

Making and Removing Directories

At times you may need to implement a directory structure for files being stored by your Node.js application. The `fs` module provides the functionality to add and remove directories as necessary.

To add a directory from Node.js, use one of the following `fs` calls:

```
fs.mkdir(path, [mode], callback)
fs.mkdirSync(path, [mode])
```

The path can be absolute or relative. The optional `mode` parameter allows you to specify the access mode for the new directory.

The `mkdirSync(path)` function returns `true` or `false`, depending on whether the directory was successfully created. On the other hand, an asynchronous `mkdir()` call passes an error value to the callback function if an error is encountered when creating the directory.

You should keep in mind that when using the asynchronous method, you need to wait for the callback for the creation of the directory before creating a subdirectory in that directory. The following code snippet shows how to chain together the creation of a subdirectory structure:

```
fs.mkdir("./data", function(err){
  fs.mkdir("./data/folderA", function(err){
    fs.mkdir("./data/folderA/folderB", function(err){
      fs.mkdir("./data/folderA/folderB/folderD", function(err){
      });
    });
    fs.mkdir("./data/folderA/folderC", function(err){
      fs.mkdir("./data/folderA/folderC/folderE", function(err){
      });
    });
  });
});
```

To delete a directory from Node.js, use one of the following `fs` calls, with either an absolute or relative path:

```
fs.rmdir(path, callback)
fs.rmdirSync(path)
```

The `rmdirSync(path)` function returns `true` or `false`, depending on whether the directory was successfully deleted. On the other hand, an asynchronous `rmdir()` call passes an error value to the callback function if an error is encountered when deleting the directory.

Just as with the `mkdir()` calls, you should keep in mind that when using the asynchronous method, you need to wait for the callback of the deletion of the directory before deleting the parent directory. The following code snippet shows how to chain together the deletion of a subdirectory structure:

```
fs.rmdir("./data/folderA/folderB/folderC", function(err){
  fs.rmdir("./data/folderA/folderB", function(err){
    fs.rmdir("./data/folderD", function(err){
    });
  });
  fs.rmdir("./data/folderA/folderC", function(err){
    fs.rmdir("./data/folderE", function(err){
    });
  });
});
```

Renaming Files and Directories

You may need to rename files and folders in you Node.js application to make room for new data, archive old data, or apply changes made by a user. Renaming files and folders uses the following `fs` calls:

```
fs.rename(oldPath, newPath, callback)
fs.renameSync(oldPath, newPath)
```

The `oldPath` parameter specifies the existing file or directory path, and the `newPath` parameter specifies the new name. The `renameSync(path)` function returns `true` or `false`, depending on whether the file or directory was successfully renamed. On the other hand, an asynchronous `rename()` call passes an error value to the callback function if an error is encountered when renaming the file or directory.

The following code snippet illustrates how to implement `fs` calls to rename a file named `old.txt` to `new.txt` and a directory named `testDir` to `renamedDir`:

```
fs.rename("old.txt", "new.txt", function(err){
  console.log(err ? "Rename Failed" :  "File Renamed");
});
fs.rename("testDir", "renamedDir", function(err){
  console.log(err ? "Rename Failed" :  "Folder Renamed");
});
```

Watching for File Changes

Although it is not entirely stable, the fs module provides a useful tool for watching a file and executing a callback function when the file changes. This can be useful if you want to trigger events to occur when a file is modified but do not want to continually poll from your application directly. Watches do incur some overhead in the underlying operating system, so you should use them sparingly.

To implement a watch on a file, use the following command, passing the path to the file you want to watch:

```
fs.watchFile(path, [options], callback)
```

You can also pass in options, which is an object that contains persistent and interval properties. The persistent property is true if you want the process to continue to run as long as files are being watched. The interval property specifies the time, in milliseconds, that you want the file to be polled for changes.

When a file change occurs, the callback function is executed and passed current and previous Stats objects.

The following code snippet monitors a file named log.txt every 5 seconds and uses the Stats object to output the current and previous times the file was modified:

```
fs.watchFile("log.txt", {persistent:true, interval:5000}, function (curr, prev) {
  console.log("log.txt modified at: " + curr.mtime);
  console.log("Previous modification was: " + prev.mtime);
});
```

Summary

Node.js provides the fs module, which allows you to interact with the file system. The fs module allows you to create, read, and modify files. You can also use the fs module to navigate the directory structure, looking at information about files and folders, as well as change the directory structure by deleting and renaming files and folders.

Up Next

The next chapter focuses on using the http module to implement basic webservers. You will get a chance to see how to parse query strings. You will learn how to implement a basic webserver in Node.js.

7

Implementing HTTP Services in Node.js

One of the most important aspects of Node.js is the ability to implement HTTP and HTTPS servers and services very quickly. Node.js provides the `http` and `https` modules out of the box, and they give you a basic framework to do just about anything you might need to do from an HTTP and HTTPS standpoint. In fact, it is not difficult to implement a full webserver using just the `http` module.

However, the `http` module is pretty low level. You will likely use a different module, such as `express`, to implement a full-on webserver. The `http` module doesn't provide calls to handle routing, cookies, caching, etc. In Chapters 18 and 19, you will see the advantages the `express` module provides.

What you will more likely be using the `http` module for is implementing backend web services for your applications to use. This is where the `http` module is an invaluable tool in your arsenal. You can create basic HTTP servers that provide an interface for communications behind your firewall and then create basic HTTP clients that interact with those services.

This chapter focuses on the objects you use when implementing clients and servers using the `http` module. The examples in this chapter are very basic so that they will be easy to consume and expand.

Processing URLs

A uniform resource locator (URL) acts as an address label that an HTTP server uses to handle requests from the client. It provides all the information needed to get a request to the correct server on a specific port and to access the proper data.

A URL can be broken down into several different components, each providing a basic piece of information for the webserver on how to route and handle the HTTP request from the client. Figure 7.1 shows the basic structure of a URL and the components that may be included. Not all these components will be included in every HTTP request. For example, most requests do not include the auth component, and many do not include a query string or hash location.

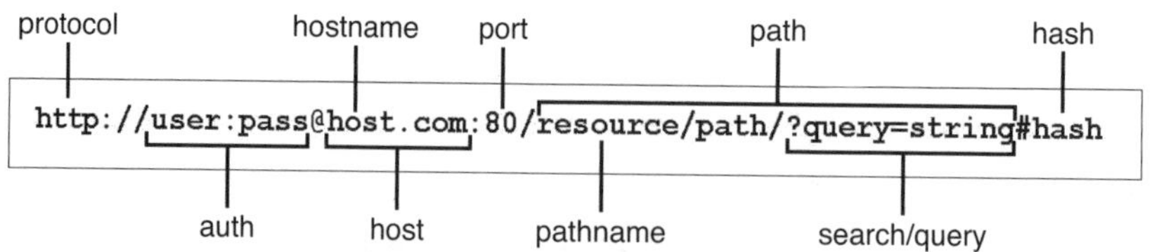

Figure 7.1 Basic components that can be included in a URL.

Understanding the `URL` Object

HTTP requests from a client include the URL string with the information shown in Figure 7.1. To be able to use the URL information more effectively, Node.js provides the `url` module, which provides functionality to convert a URL string into a `URL` object.

To create a `URL` object from a URL string, pass the URL string as the first parameter to the following method:

```
url.parse(urlStr, [parseQueryString], [slashesDenoteHost])
```

The `url.parse()` method takes the URL string as the first parameter. The `parseQueryString` parameter is a `Boolean` that when `true` also parses the query string portion of the URL into an object literal. The default is `false`. The `slashesDenoteHost` is also a `Boolean` that when `true` parses a URL with the format `//host/path` to `{host: 'host', pathname: '/path'}` instead of `{pathname: '//host/path'}`. The default is `false`.

You can also convert a `URL` object into a string form by using the `url.format()` method:

```
url.format(urlObj)
```

Table 7.1 lists the attributes of the URL objects created by `url.parse()`.

The following is an example of parsing a URL string into an object and then converting it back into a string:

```
var url = require('url');
var urlStr = 'http://user:pass@host.com:80/resource/path?query=string#hash';
var urlObj = url.parse(urlStr, true, false);
urlString = url.format(urlObj);
```

Table 7.1 **Properties of the `URL` object returned by url.parse()**

Property	Description
`href`	This is the full URL string that was originally parsed.
`protocol`	The request protocol, lowercased.
`host`	The full `host` portion of the URL, including `port` information, lowercased.
`auth`	The `authentication` information portion of a URL.

Property	Description
hostname	The hostname portion of the host, lowercased.
port	The port number portion of the host.
pathname	The path portion of the URL, including the initial slash, if present.
search	The query string portion of the URL, including the leading question mark.
path	The full path, including pathname and search.
query	This is either the parameter portion of the query string or a parsed object containing the query string parameters and values if the parseQueryString is set to true.
hash	The hash portion of the URL, including the pound sign (#).

Resolving the URL Components

A useful feature of the url module is the ability to resolve URL components in the same manner as a browser would. This allows you to manipulate URL strings on the server side to make adjustments in a URL. For example, you might want to change the URL location before processing a request because a resource has moved or changed parameters.

To resolve a URL to a new location, use the following syntax:

```
url.resolve(from, to)
```

The from parameter specifies the original base URL string. The to parameter specifies the new location to which you want the URL to resolve. The following code shows an example of resolving a URL to a new location.

```
var url = require('url');
var originalUrl = 'http://user:pass@host.com:80/resource/path?query=string#hash';
var newResource = '/another/path?querynew';
console.log(url.resolve(originalUrl, newResource));
```

The output of this code snippet is shown below:

```
http://user:pass@host.com:80/another/path?querynew
```

Notice that only the resource path and beyond are altered in the resolved URL location.

Processing Query Strings and Form Parameters

HTTP requests often include query strings in the URL or parameter data in the body for form submissions. The query string can be obtained from the URL object defined in the previous section. The parameter data sent by a form request can be read out of the body of the client request, as described later in this chapter.

The query string and form parameters are just basic key/value pairs. To actually consume these values in your Node.js webserver, you need to convert a string into a JavaScript object by using the `parse()` method from the `querystring` module:

```
querystring.parse(str, [sep], [eq], [options])
```

The `str` parameter is the query or parameter string. The `sep` parameter allows you to specify the separator character used; the default separator character is `&`. The `eq` parameter allows you to specify the assignment character to use when parsing; the default is `=`. The `options` parameter is an object with the property `maxKeys` that allows you to limit the number of keys the resulting object can contain; the default is `1000`, and if you specify `0`, there is no limit.

The following is an example of using `parse()` to parse a query string:

```
var qstring = require('querystring');
var params = qstring.parse("name=Brad&color=red&color=blue");
The params object created would be:
{name: 'Brad', color: ['red', 'blue']}
```

You can also go back the other direction and convert an object to a query string by using the `stringify()` function:

```
querystring.stringify(obj, [sep], [eq])
```

Understanding Request, Response, and Server Objects

To use the `http` module in Node.js applications, you first need to understand the request and response objects. They provide the information and much of the functionality that comes into and out of the HTTP clients and servers. Once you see the makeup of these objects—including the properties, events, and methods they provide—it will be simple to implement your own HTTP servers and clients.

The following sections cover the purposes and behaviors of the `ClientRequest`, `ServerResponse`, `IncomingMessage`, and `Server` objects. You'll learn about the most important events, properties, and methods that each provides.

The `http.ClientRequest` Object

The `ClientRequest` object is created internally when you call `http.request()` when building an HTTP client. This object is intended to represent the request while it is in progress to the server. You use the `ClientRequest` object to initiate, monitor, and handle the response from the server.

The `ClientRequest` object implements a `Writable` stream, so it provides all the functionality of a `Writable` stream object. For example, you can use the `write()` method to write to the `ClientRequest` object as well as pipe a `Readable` stream into it.

To implement a `ClientRequest` object, you use a call to `http.request()`, with the following syntax:

```
http.request(options, callback)
```

The `options` parameter is an object whose properties define how to open and send the client HTTP request to the server. Table 7.2 lists the properties that you can specify. The `callback` parameter is a callback function that is called after a request is sent to the server and that handles the response back from the server. The only parameter to the callback is an `IncomingMessage` object that is the response from the server.

The following code shows the basics of implementation of the `ClientRequest` object:

```
var http = require('http');
var options = {
  hostname: 'www.myserver.com',
  path: '/',
  port: '8080',
  method: 'POST'
};
var req = http.request(options, function(response){
  var str = ''
  response.on('data', function (chunk) {
    str += chunk;
  });
  response.on('end', function () {
    console.log(str);
  });
});
req.end();
```

Table 7.2 **Options that can be specified when creating a `ClientRequest` object**

Option	Description
`host`	The domain name or IP address of the server to issue the request to. Defaults to `localhost`.
`hostname`	Same as `host` but preferred over `host` to support `url.parse()`.
`port`	The port of the remote server. Defaults to `80`.
`localAddress`	The local interface to bind for network connections.
`socketPath`	The Unix domain socket (use either `host:port` or `socketPath`).
`method`	A string that specifies the HTTP request method. For example, `GET`, `POST`, `CONNECT`, `OPTIONS`, etc. Defaults to `GET`.
`path`	A string that specifies the requested resource path. Defaults to `/`. This should also include the query string, if any. For example: `/book.html?chapter=12`

Option	Description
`headers`	An object that contains request headers. For example: `{ 'content-length': '750', 'content-type': 'text/plain'}s`
`auth`	Basic authentication, in the form of `user:password`, used to compute an `Authorization` header.
`agent`	The definition of the `Agent` behavior. When an `Agent` is used, the request defaults to `Connection:keep-alive`. Possible values are: `undefined` (default): Uses the global `Agent`. `Agent`: Use a specific `Agent` object. `false`: Disables `Agent` behavior.

`ClientRequest` objects provide several events that enable you to handle the various states the request may experience. For example, you can add a listener that is called when the `response` event is triggered by the server's response. Table 7.3 lists the events available on `ClientResponse` objects.

Table 7.3 **Events available on `ClientRequest` objects**

Event	Description
`response`	Emitted when a response to this request is received from the server. The callback handler receives an `IncomingMessage` object as the only parameter.
`socket`	Emitted after a socket is assigned to this request.
`connect`	Emitted every time a server responds to a request that was initiated with a `CONNECT` method. If this event is not handled by the client, the connection will be closed.
`upgrade`	Emitted when the server responds to a request that included an update request in the headers.
`continue`	Emitted when the server sends a `100 Continue HTTP` response instructing the client to send the request body.

In addition to providing events, `ClientRequest` objects also provide several methods that can be used to write data to the request, abort the request, or end the request. Table 7.4 lists the methods available on `ClientRequest` objects.

Table 7.4 **Methods available on `ClientRequest` objects**

Method	Description
`write(chunk, [encoding])`	Writes a chunk—`Buffer` or `String` object—of body data into the request. This allows you to stream data into the `Writable` stream of the `ClientRequest` object. If you stream the body data, you should include the `{'Transfer-Encoding', 'chunked'}` header option when you create the request. The encoding parameter defaults to `utf8`.
`end([data], [encoding])`	Writes the optional data out to the request body and then flushes the `Writable` stream and terminates the request.
`abort()`	Aborts the current request.
`setTimeout(timeout, [callback])`	Sets the socket timeout for the request.
`setNoDelay([noDelay])`	Disables the Nagle algorithm, which buffers data before sending it. The `noDelay` argument is a `Boolean` that is `true` for immediate writes and `false` for buffered writes.
`setSocketKeepAlive ( [enable], [initialDelay])`	Enables and disables the keep-alive functionality on the client request. The `enable` parameter defaults to `false`, which is disabled. The `initialDelay` parameter specifies the delay between the last data packet and the first keep-alive request.

The `http.ServerResponse` Object

The HTTP server creates the `ServerResponse` object internally when it receives a `request` event. This object is passed to the `request` event handler as the second argument. You use the `ServerRequest` object to formulate and send a response to the client.

The `ServerResponse` object implements a `Writable` stream, so it provides all the functionality of a `Writable` stream object. For example, you can use the `write()` method to write to the `ServerResponse` object as well as pipe a `Readable` stream into it to write data back to the client.

When handling the client request, you use the properties, events, and methods of the `ServerResponse` object to build and send headers; write data; and send the response. Table 7.5 lists the event and properties available on `ServerResponse` objects. Table 7.6 lists the methods available on `ServerResponse` objects.

Table 7.5 **Events and properties available on `ServerResponse` objects**

Event or property	Description
`close`	Emitted when the connection to the client is closed prior to sending the `response.end()` to finish and flush the response.
`headersSent`	`Boolean`: `true` if headers have been sent and otherwise `false`. This is read-only.
`sendDate`	`Boolean`: When set to `true`, the `Date` header is automatically generated and sent as part of the response.
`statusCode`	Allows you to specify the response status code without having to explicitly write the headers. For example: `response.statusCode = 500;`

Table 7.6 **Methods available on `ServerResponse` objects**

Method	Description
`writeContinue()`	Sends an `HTTP/1.1 100 Continue` message to the client, requesting that the body data be sent.

`writeHead(statusCode, [reasonPhrase], [headers])`	Writes a response header to the request. The `statusCode` parameter is the three-digit HTTP response status code, such as `200`, `401`, or `500`. The optional `reasonPhrase` is a string indicating the reason for the `statusCode`. The `headers` are the response headers object. For example:
	`response.writeHead(200, 'Success', {`
	`'Content-Length': body.length,`
	`'Content-Type': 'text/plain' });`

`setTimeout(msecs, callback)`	Sets the socket timeout for the client connection, in milliseconds, along with a `callback` function to be executed if the timeout occurs.
`setHeader(name, value)`	Sets the value of a specific header, where `name` is the HTTP header name and `value` is the header value.
`getHeader(name)`	Gets the value of an HTTP header that has been set in the response.
`removeHeader(name)`	Removes an HTTP header that has been set in the response.

Method	Description
`write(chunk, [encoding])`	Writes a `chunk`, `Buffer`, or `String` object of data out to the response `Writable` stream. This only writes data to the body portion of the response. The default encoding is `utf8`. Returns `true` if the data is written successfully or `false` if the data is written to user memory. If it returns `false`, a `drain` event will be emitted by the `Writable` stream when the buffer is free again.
`addTrailers(headers)`	Adds HTTP trailing headers to the end of the response.
`end([data], [encoding])`	Writes the optional data out to the response body and then flushes the `Writable` stream and finalizes the response.

The `http.IncomingMessage` Object

Either the HTTP server or the HTTP client creates the `IncomingMessage` object. On the server side the client request is represented by an `IncomingMessage` object, and on the client side the server response is represented by an `IncomingMessage` object. The reason that the `IncomingMessage` object can be used for both is that the functionality is basically the same.

The `IncomingMessage` object implements a `Readable` stream, allowing you to read the client request or server response as a streaming source. This means that the `readable` and `data` events can be listened on and used to read data from the stream.

In addition to the functionality provided by the `Readable` class, `IncomingMessage` objects also provide the properties, events, and methods listed in Table 7.7. These allow you to access information from the client request or server response.

Table 7.7 **Events, properties, and methods available on `ServerResponse` objects**

Method, event, or property	Description
`close`	Emitted when the underlying socket is closed.
`httpVersion`	Specifies the version of HTTP used to build the client request/response.
`headers`	An object containing the headers sent with the request/response.
`trailers`	An object containing any trailer headers sent with the request/response.
`method`	Specifies the method for the request/response (for example, `GET`, `POST`, or `CONNECT`).

Method, event, or property	Description
`url`	The URL string sent to the server. This is the string that can be passed to `url.parse()`. This attribute is valid only in the HTTP server handling client requests.
`statusCode`	Specifies the three-digit status code from the server. This attribute is valid on the HTTP client only when handling server responses.
`socket`	This is a handle to the `net.Socket` object, used to communicate with the client/server.
`setTimeout(msecs, callback)`	Sets the socket timeout for the connection, in milliseconds, along with a callback function to be executed if the timeout occurs.

The HTTP `Server` Object

The Node.js HTTP `Server` object provides the fundamental framework to implement HTTP servers. It provides an underlying socket that listens on a port and handles receiving requests and then sending responses out to client connections. While the server is listening, the Node.js application does not end.

The `Server` object implements `EventEmitter` and emits the events listed in Table 7.8. As you implement an HTTP server, you need to handle at least some or all of these events. For example, at a minimum, you need an event handler to handle the `request` event that is triggered when a client request is received.

Table 7.8 **Events that can be triggered by `Server` objects**

Event	Description
`request`	Triggered each time the server receives a client request. The callback should accept two parameters. The first is an `IncomingMessage` object representing the client request, and the second is a `ServerResponse` object you use to formulate and send the response. For example: `function callback (request, response){}`
`connection`	Triggered when a new TCP stream is established. The callback receives the socket as the only parameter. For example: `function callback (socket){}`
`close`	Triggered when the server is closed. The callback receives no parameters.

Event	Description
checkContinue	Triggered when a request that includes the `Expect: 100-continue` header is received. A default event handler responds with an `HTTP/1.1 100 Continue` even if you do not handle this event. For example: `function callback (request, response){}`
connect	Emitted when an HTTP `CONNECT` request is received. `callback` receives `request`, `socket`, and `head`, which is a buffer containing the first packet of the tunneling stream. For example: `function callback (request, socket, head){}`
upgrade	Emitted when the client requests an HTTP upgrade. If this event is not handled, clients sending an upgrade request have their connections closed. `callback` receives `request`, `socket`, and `head`, which is a buffer containing the first packet of the tunneling stream. For example: `function callback (request, socket, head){}`
clientError	Emitted when the client connection socket emits an error. `callback` receives `error` as the first parameter and `socket` as the second. For example: `function callback (error, socket){}`

To start the HTTP server, you need to first create a `Server` object, using the `createServer()` method, shown below:

```
http.createServer([requestListener])
```

This method returns the `Server` object. The optional `requestListener` parameter is a callback that is executed when the request event is triggered. The callback should accept two parameters. The first is an `IncomingMessage` object representing the client request, and the second is a `ServerResponse` object you use to formulate and send the response.

Once you have created the `Server` object, you can begin listening on it by calling the `listen()` method on the `Server` object:

```
listen(port, [hostname], [backlog], [callback])
```

This is the method you are most likely to use. The following are the parameters:

- **`port`:** Specifies the port to listen on.
- **`hostname`:** Specifies when `hostname` will accept connections; if omitted, the server accepts connections directed to any IPv4 address (`INADDR_ANY`).
- **`backlog`:** Specifies the maximum number of pending connections that are allowed to be queued. The default is `511`.
- **`callback`:** Specifies the callback handler to execute when the server has begun listening on the specified port.

The following code shows an example of starting an HTTP server and listening on port 8080. Notice that a request callback handler function is passed into the `createServer()` method:

```
var http = require('http');
http.createServer(function (req, res) {
  <<handle the request and response here>>
}).listen(8080);
```

You can use two other methods to listen for connections through the file system. The first accepts a `path` to a file to listen on, and the second accepts an already open file descriptor `handle`:

```
listen(path, [callback])
listen(handle, [callback])
```

To stop the HTTP server from listening once it has started, use the following `close()` method:

```
close([callback])
```

Implementing HTTP Clients and Servers in Node.js

Now that you understand the `ClientRequest`, `ServerResponse`, and `IncomingMessage` objects, you are ready to jump in and implement some Node.js HTTP clients and servers. This section guides you through the process of implementing basic HTTP clients and servers in Node.js. You will implement a client and server in each section to see how the two interact.

The examples in the following sections are extremely basic to make it easy for you to grasp the concepts of starting the client/server and then handling the different requests and responses. The examples contain no error handling, no protection against attacks, and not much other functionality. However, these examples provide a good variety of the basic flow and structure required to handle general HTTP requests using the `http` module.

Serving Static Files

The most basic type of HTTP server is one that serves static files. To serve static files from Node.js, you need to first start the HTTP server and listen on a port. Then, in the request handler, you need to open the file locally, using the `fs` module, and then write the file contents to the response.

Listing 7.1 shows the basic implementation of a static file server. Notice that line 5 creates the server using `createServer()` and also defines the request event handler shown in lines 6–15. Also notice that the server is listening on port 8080 by calling `listen()` on the `Server` object.

Inside the request event handler on line 6, the `url.pars()` method parses the URL so that you can use the `pathname` attribute when specifying the path for the file in line 7. The static file is opened and read using `fs.readFile()`, and in the `readFile()` callback, the contents of the file are written to the response object, using `res.end(data)`, on line 14.

Listing 7.1 `http_server_static.js`: **Implementing a basic static file webserver**

```
var fs = require('fs');
var http = require('http');
var url = require('url');
var ROOT_DIR = "html/";
http.createServer(function (req, res) {
  var urlObj = url.parse(req.url, true, false);
  fs.readFile(ROOT_DIR + urlObj.pathname, function (err,data) {
    if (err) {
      res.writeHead(404);
      res.end(JSON.stringify(err));
      return;
    }
    res.writeHead(200);
    res.end(data);
  });
}).listen(8080);
```

To test the code in Listing 7.1, you can use any web browser and hit the URL localhost:8080.

Listing 7.2 shows a basic implementation of an HTTP client that sends a `GET` request to the server to retrieve the file contents. Notice that the options for the request are set in lines 2–6, and then the client request is initiated in lines 16–18.

When the request completes, the callback function uses the `on('data')` handler to read the contents of the response from the server and then the `on('end')` handler to log the file contents to a file. Figure 7.2 shows the output of the HTTP client as well as the static file being accessed from a web browser.

Listing 7.2 `http_client_static.js`: **A basic web client retrieving static files**

```
01 var http = require('http');
02 var options = {
03     hostname: 'localhost',
04     port: '8080',
05     path: '/hello.html'
06   };
07 function handleResponse(response) {
08   var serverData = '';
09   response.on('data', function (chunk) {
10     serverData += chunk;
11   });
12   response.on('end', function () {
13     console.log(serverData);
14   });
15 }
16 http.request(options, function(response){
```

```
  handleResponse(response);
}).end();
```

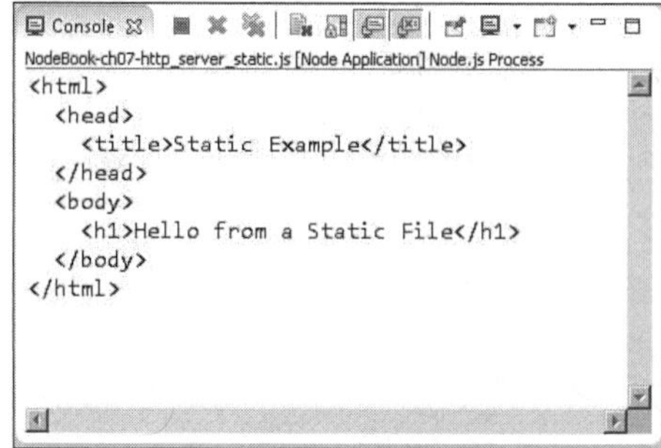

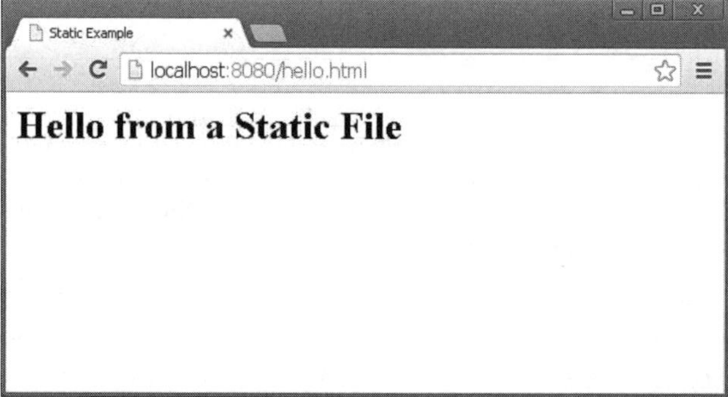

Figure 7.2 Implementing and accessing a basic static file webserver.

Implementing Dynamic `GET` Servers

You will use Node.js webservers to serve dynamic content more often than you'll use them to serve static content. This content may be dynamic HTML files or snippets, JSON data, or a number of other types of data. To serve a `GET` request dynamically, you need to implement code in the request handler that dynamically populates the data you want to send back to the client, write it out to the response, and then call `end()` to finalize the response and flush the `Writable` stream.

Listing 7.3 shows the basic implementation of a dynamic webserver. In this case, the webserver simply responds with a dynamically generated HTTP file. The example is designed to show the process of sending the headers, building the response, and then sending the data in a series of `write()` requests.

Notice that line 6 creates the server, using `createServer()`, and line 15 begins listening on port 8080, using `listen()`. Inside the request event handler defined in lines 7–15, the `Content-Type` header is set, and then the headers are sent, with a response code of `200`. In reality, you would have already done a lot of processing to prepare the data. But in this case, the data is just the `messages` array defined in lines 2–5.

Notice that in lines 11–13, the loop iterates through the messages and calls `write()` each time to stream the response to the client. Then in line 14, the response is completed with a call to `end()`.

Listing 7.3 `http_server_get.js`: **Implementing a basic `GET` webserver**

```
01 var http = require('http');
02 var messages = [
03   'Hello World',
04   'From a basic Node.js server',
05   'Take Luck'];
06 http.createServer(function (req, res) {
07   res.setHeader("Content-Type", "text/html");
08   res.writeHead(200);
09   res.write('<html><head><title>Simple HTTP Server</title></head>');
10   res.write('<body>');
11   for (var idx in  messages){
12     res.write('\n<h1>' + messages[idx] + '</h1>');
13   }
14   res.end('\n</body></html>');
15 }).listen(8080);
```

Listing 7.4 shows a basic implementation of an HTTP client that reads the response from the server in Listing 7.3. This is very similar to the example in Listing 7.2, but note that no path was specified because the service doesn't really require one. For more complex services, you would implement query strings or complex path routes to handle a variety of calls.

Note that on line 11 the `statusCode` from the response is logged to the console. Also, on line 12 the `headers` from the response are also logged. Then on line 13 the full response from the server is logged. Figure 7.3 shows the output of the HTTP client as well as the dynamic `GET` server being accessed from a web browser.

Listing 7.4 `http_client_get.js`: **A basic web client making a `GET` request to the server in Listing 7.3**

```
01 var http = require('http');
02 var options = {
03     hostname: 'localhost',
04     port: '8080',
05   };
```

```
function handleResponse(response) {
  var serverData = '';
  response.on('data', function (chunk) {
    serverData += chunk;
  });
  response.on('end', function () {
    console.log("Response Status:", response.statusCode);
    console.log("Response Headers:", response.headers);
    console.log(serverData);
  });
}
http.request(options, function(response){
  handleResponse(response);
}).end();
```

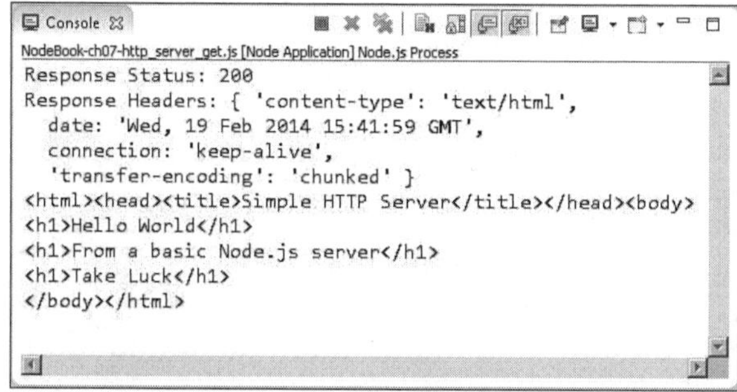

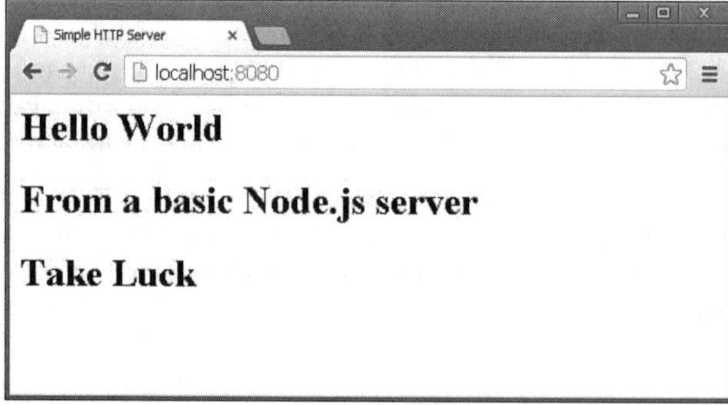

Figure 7.3 Implementing and accessing a basic HTTP GET server.

Implementing POST Servers

Implementing a POST server is similar to implementing a GET server. In fact, you may end up implementing them together in the same code for the sake of convenience. POST servers are handy if you need to send data to the server to be updated, as with form submissions. To serve a POST request, you need to implement code in the request handler that reads the contents of the post body out and processes the contents.

Once you have processed the data, you dynamically populate the data you want to send back to the client, write it out to the response, and then call end() to finalize the response and flush the Writable stream. Just as with a dynamic GET server, the output of a POST request may be a webpage, an HTTP snippet, JSON data, or some other data.

Listing 7.5 shows the basic implementation of a dynamic web service handling POST requests. In this case, the web service accepts from the client a JSON string representing an object that has name and occupation properties. The code in lines 4–6 reads the data from the request stream, and then in the event handler in lines 7–14, the data is converted to an object and used to build a new object with message and question properties. Then in lines 14 to 17 the response JSON string is converted to an object and displayed on the console.

Listing 7.5 http_server_post.js: **Implementing a basic HTTP server that handles HTTP POST requests**

```
01 var http = require('http');
02 http.createServer(function (req, res) {
03   var jsonData = "";
04   req.on('data', function (chunk) {
05     jsonData += chunk;
06   });
07   req.on('end', function () {
08     var reqObj = JSON.parse(jsonData);
09     var resObj = {
10       message: "Hello " + reqObj.name,
11       question: "Are you a good " + reqObj.occupation + "?"
12     };
13     res.writeHead(200);
14     res.end(JSON.stringify(resObj));
15   });
16 }).listen(8080);
17
18
19 var http = require('http');
20 var options = {
21   host: '127.0.0.1',
22   path: '/',
23   port: '8080',
24   method: 'POST'
```

```
};
function readJSONResponse(response) {
  var responseData = '';
  response.on('data', function (chunk) {
    responseData += chunk;
  });
  response.on('end', function () {
    var dataObj = JSON.parse(responseData);
    console.log("Raw Response: " +responseData);
    console.log("Message: " + dataObj.message);
    console.log("Question: " + dataObj.question);
  });
}
var req = http.request(options, readJSONResponse);
req.write('{"name":"Bilbo", "occupation":"Burglar"}');
req.end();
```

Listing 7.6 shows a basic implementation of an HTTP client that sends JSON data to the server as part of a `POST` request. The request starts in line 20. Then in line 21 a JSON string is written to the request stream, and line 22 finishes the request with `end()`.

When the server sends back the response, the `on('data')` handler in lines 10–12 reads the JSON response. Then the `on('end')` handler in lines 13–18 parses the response into a JSON object and outputs the raw response, message, and question. Figure 7.4 shows the output of the HTTP `POST` client.

Listing 7.6 `http_client_post.js`: **A basic HTTP client that sends JSON data to the server, using `POST`, and that handles the JSON response**

```
01 var http = require('http');
02 var options = {
03   host: '127.0.0.1',
04   path: '/',
05   port: '8080',
06   method: 'POST'
07 };
08 function readJSONResponse(response) {
09   var responseData = '';
10   response.on('data', function (chunk) {
11     responseData += chunk;
12   });
13   response.on('end', function () {
14     var dataObj = JSON.parse(responseData);
15     console.log("Raw Response: " +responseData);
16     console.log("Message: " + dataObj.message);
17     console.log("Question: " + dataObj.question);
18   });
```

```
}
var req = http.request(options, readJSONResponse);
req.write('{"name":"Bilbo", "occupation":"Burglar"}');
req.end();
```

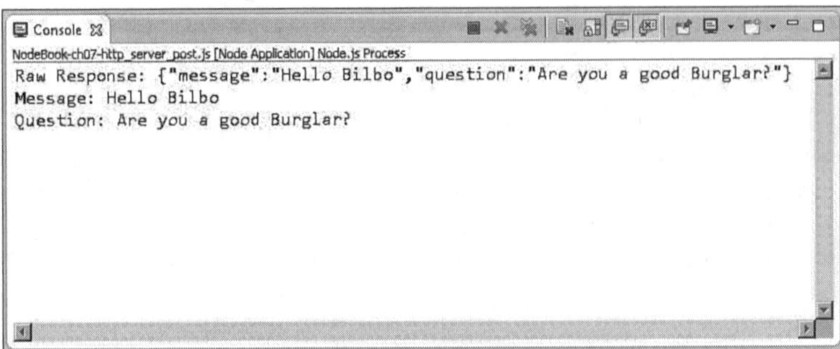

Figure 7.4 Implementing an HTTP `POST` server serving JSON data.

Interacting with External Sources

A common use of the HTTP services in Node.js is to access external systems to get data to fulfill client requests. A variety of external systems provide data that can be used in various ways. In this example, the code connects to the openweathermap.org API to retrieve weather information about a city. To keep the example simple, the output from openweathermap.org is pushed to the browser in a raw format. In reality, you would likely massage the pieces of data needed into your own pages, widgets, or data responses.

Listing 7.7 shows the implementation of a web service that accepts both `GET` and `POST` requests. For `GET` requests, a simple webpage with a form is returned that allows the user to post a city name. Then in the `POST` request, the city name is accessed, and the Node.js web client starts up and connects remotely to openweathermap.org to retrieve weather info for that city. Then that info is returned back to the server, along with the original web form.

The big difference between this example and the previous examples is that the webserver also implements a local web client to connect to the external service and get data to formulate the response. The webserver is implemented in lines 35–49. Notice that if the method is `POST`, we read the form data from the request stream and use `querystring.parse()` to get the city name and call into the `getWeather()` function.

The `getWeather()` function in lines 26–34 implements the client request to openweathermap.org. Then the `parseWeather()` request handler in lines 17–25 reads the response from openweathermap.org and passes that data to the `sendResponse()` function defined in lines 4–16, which formulates the response and sends it back to the client. Figure 7.5 shows the implementation of the external service in a web browser.

Listing 7.7 `http_server_external.js`: **Implementing an HTTP web service that connects remotely to a an external source for weather data**

```
var http = require('http');
var url = require('url');
var qstring = require('querystring');
function sendResponse(weatherData, res){
  var page = '<html><head><title>External Example</title></head>' +
    '<body>' +
    '<form method="post">' +
    'City: <input name="city"><br>' +
    '<input type="submit" value="Get Weather">' +
    '</form>';
  if(weatherData){
    page += '<h1>Weather Info</h1><p>' + weatherData +'</p>';
  }
  page += '</body></html>';
  res.end(page);
}
function parseWeather(weatherResponse, res) {
  var weatherData = '';
  weatherResponse.on('data', function (chunk) {
    weatherData += chunk;
  });
  weatherResponse.on('end', function () {
    sendResponse(weatherData, res);
  });
}
function getWeather(city, res){
  var options = {
    host: 'api.openweathermap.org',
    path: '/data/2.5/weather?q=' + city
  };
  http.request(options, function(weatherResponse){
    parseWeather(weatherResponse, res);
  }).end();
}
http.createServer(function (req, res) {
  console.log(req.method);
  if (req.method == "POST"){
    var reqData = '';
    req.on('data', function (chunk) {
      reqData += chunk;
    });
    req.on('end', function() {
      var postParams = qstring.parse(reqData);
      getWeather(postParams.city, res);
    });
```

```
  } else{
    sendResponse(null, res);
  }
}).listen(8080);
```

Figure 7.5 Implementing an external web service that connects to a remote source for weather data.

Implementing HTTPS Servers and Clients

Hypertext Transfer Protocol Secure (HTTPS) is a communications protocol that provides secure communication between HTTP clients and servers. HTTPS is really just HTTP running on top of the Transport Layer Security/Secure Sockets Layer (TLS/SSL) protocol, which is where it gets its security capabilities. HTTPS provides security in two main ways. First, it uses long-term public and secret keys to exchange a short-term session key so that data can be encrypted between client and server. It also provides authentication so that you can ensure that the webserver you are connecting to is the one you actually think it is, thus preventing man-in-the-middle attacks, in which requests are rerouted through a third party.

The following sections discuss implementing HTTPS servers and clients in your Node.js environment, using the `https` module. Before getting started using HTTPS, you need to generate a private key and a public certificate. There are several ways to do this, depending on your platform. One of the simplest methods is to use the OpenSSL library for your platform.

To generate a private key, first execute the following OpenSSL commands to generate a private key:

```
openssl genrsa -out server.pem 2048
```

Next, use the following command to create a certificate-signing request file:

```
openssl req -new -key server.pem -out server.csr
```

> **Note**
>
> When creating the certificate-signing request file, you need to answer several questions. When prompted for the common name, you should enter in the domain name of the server you want to connect to. Otherwise, the certificate will not work. Also, you can enter additional domain names and IP addresses in the Subject Alternative Names field.

Then, to create a self-signed certificate that you can use for your own purpose or for testing, use the following command:

```
openssl x509 -req -days 365 -in server.csr -signkey server.pem -out server.crt
```

> **Note**
>
> The self-signed certificate is fine for testing purposes and internal use. However, if you are implementing an external web service that needs to be protected on the Internet, you may want to get a certificate signed by a certificate authority. If you want to create a certificate that is signed by a third-party certificate authority, you need to take additional steps.

Creating an HTTPS Client

Creating an HTTPS client is almost exactly like creating an HTTP client, discussed earlier in this chapter. The only difference is that there are additional options, shown in Table 7.9, that allow you to specify the security for the client. The most important options are `key`, `cert`, and `agent`.

The `key` option specifies the private key used for SSL. The `cert` value specifies the x509 public key to use. The global agent does not support options needed by HTTPS, so you need to disable the agent by setting the agent to `null`, as shown below:

```
var options = {
  key: fs.readFileSync('test/keys/client.pem'),
  cert: fs.readFileSync('test/keys/client.crt'),
  agent: false
};
```

You can also create your own custom Agent object, as shown below:

```
options.agent = new https.Agent(options);
```

Once you have defined the options with the cert, key, and agent settings, you can call https.request(options, [responseCallback]), and it will work exactly the same as the http.request() call. The only difference is that the data between the client and server is encrypted:

```
var options = {
  hostname: 'encrypted.mysite.com',
  port: 443,
  path: '/',
  method: 'GET',
  key: fs.readFileSync('test/keys/client.pem'),
  cert: fs.readFileSync('test/keys/client.crt),
  agent: false
};
var req = https.request(options, function(res) {
  <handle the response the same as an http.request>
}
```

Table 7.9 **Additional options for** https.request() **and** https.createServer()

Option	Description
pfx	A String or Buffer object that contains the private key, certificate, and CA certs of the server, in PFX or PKCS12 format.
key	A String or Buffer object that contains the private key to use for SSL.
passphrase	A String object that contains the passphrase for the private key or PFX.
cert	A String or Buffer object that contains the public x509 certificate to use.
ca	An Array of strings or buffers of trusted certificates, in PEM format, to check the remote host against.
ciphers	A string that describes the ciphers to use or exclude.
rejectUnauthorized	A Boolean that, when true, indicates that the server certificate is verified against the list of supplied CAs. An error event is emitted if verification fails. Verification happens at the connection level, before the HTTP request is sent. Defaults to true. Only for http.request() options.
crl	Either a string or a list of strings of PEM-encoded certificate revocation lists, only for https.createServer().
secureProtocol	The SSL method to use, such as SSLv3_method to force SSL version 3.

Creating an HTTPS Server

Creating an HTTPS server is almost exactly like creating an HTTP server, discussed earlier in this chapter. The only difference is that there are additional options that you must pass into `https.createServer()`. The options, listed in Table 7.9, allow you to specify the security for the server. The most important options are `key` and `cert`.

The `key` option specifies the private key used for SSL. The `cert` value specifies the x509 public key to use. The following is an example of creating an HTTPS server in Node.js:

```
var options = {
  key: fs.readFileSync('test/keys/server.pem'),
  cert: fs.readFileSync('test/keys/server.crt')
};
https.createServer(options, function (req, res) {
  res.writeHead(200);
  res.end("Hello Secure World\n");
}).listen(8080);
```

Once the HTTPS server has been created, the request/response handling works the same way as in HTTP servers, described earlier in this chapter.

Summary

An important aspect of Node.js is the ability to implement HTTP and HTTPS servers and services very quickly. The `http` and `https` modules provide everything you need to implement webserver basics. For your full webserver, you are still going to want to use a more extended library, such as `express`. However, the `http` and `https` modules work well for some basic web services and are super simple to implement.

The examples in this chapter cover enough HTTP basics to give you a good start on implementing your own services. You also got a chance to see how to use the `url` and `querystring` modules to parse URLs and query strings into objects and back.

Up Next

In the next chapter, you will get a chance to go a little bit deeper and learn about the `net` module. You will learn how to implement your own socket services, using TCP clients and servers.

8

Implementing Socket Services in Node.js

An important part of backend services is the ability to communicate over sockets. Sockets allow one process to communicate with another process through an IP address and port. This can be useful when you're implementing interprocess communication (IPC) for two different processes running on the same server or accessing a service running on a completely different server. Node.js provides the `net` module, which allows you to create both a socket server and clients that can connect to the socket server. For secure connections, Node.js provides the `tls` module that allows you to implement secure TLS socket servers and clients.

Understanding Network Sockets

Network sockets are endpoints of communications that flow across a computer network. Sockets live below the HTTP layer and provide the point-to-point communication between servers. Virtually all Internet communication is based on Internet sockets that flow data between two points on the Internet.

A socket works using a socket address, which is a combination of IP address and port. There are two types of points in a socket connection: a server, which listens for connections, and a client, which opens a connection to the server. Both the server and the client require a unique IP address-and-port combination.

The Node.js `net` module sockets communicate by sending raw data using Transmission Control Protocol (TCP). This protocol is responsible for packaging data and guaranteeing that it is sent from point to point successfully. Node.js sockets implement the `Duplex` stream, which allows you to read and write streamed data between the server and client.

Sockets are the underlying structure for the `http` module. If you do not need the functionality for handling web requests like `GET` and `POST` and you just need to stream data from point to point, then using sockets gives you a lighter-weight solution and a bit more control.

Sockets are also extremely handy when communicating with other processes running on the same computer. Processes cannot share memory directly, so if you want to access data in one process from another process, you can open up the same socket in each process and read and write data between the two processes.

Understanding TCP Server and Socket Objects

To begin using the `net` module in Node.js applications, you first need to understand the TCP `Server` and `Socket` objects. These objects provide the framework for starting a TCP server to handle requests and implementing TCP socket clients to make requests to the socket servers. Once you understand the events, properties, methods, and behavior of these objects, it will be simple to implement your own TCP socket servers and clients.

The following sections cover the purposes and behaviors of the `net.Socket` and `net.Server` objects. You'll learn about their most important events, properties, and methods.

The `net.Socket` Object

`Socket` objects are created on both the socket server and the socket client and allow data to be written and read back and forth between them. The `Socket` object implements the `Duplex` stream, so it provides all the functionality that `Writable` and `Readable` streams provide. For example, you can use the `write()` method to stream writes of data to the server or client and a `data` event handler to stream data from the server or client.

On the socket client, the `Socket` object is created internally when you call `net.connect()` or `net.createConnection()`. This object is intended to represent the socket connection to the server. You use the `Socket` object to monitor the connection, send data to the server, and handle the response from the server. There is no explicit client object in the Node.js `net` module because the `Socket` object acts as the full client, allowing you to send/receive data and terminate the connection.

On the socket server, the `Socket` object is created when a client connects to the server and is passed to the connection event handler. This object is intended to represent the socket connection to the client. On the server, you use the `Socket` object to monitor the client connection as well as send and receive data to and from the client.

To create a `Socket` object, you use one of the following methods:

```
net.connect(options, [connectionListener])
net.createConnection(options, [connectionListener])
net.connect(port, [host], [connectListener])
net.createConnection(port, [host], [connectListener])
net.connect(path, [connectListener])
net.createConnection(path, [connectListener])
```

All the calls will return a `Socket` object; the only difference is the first parameters they accept. The final parameter for all of them is a callback function that is executed when a connection is opened to the server. Notice that for each method, there is a `net.connect()` form and a `net.createConnection()` form. These work exactly the same way.

The first way to create a `Socket` object is to pass an `options` parameter, which is an object that contains properties that define the socket connection. Table 8.1 lists the properties that can be specified when creating the `Socket` object. The second method accepts `port` and `host` values, described in Table 8.1, as direct parameters. The third option accepts a `path` parameter that specifies a file system location that is a Unix socket to use when creating the `Socket` object.

Table 8.1 **Options that can be specified when creating a `Socket` object**

Property	Description
`port`	The port number the client should connect to. This option is required.
`host`	The domain name or IP address of the server that the client should connect to. Defaults to `localhost`.
`localAddress`	The local IP address the client should bind to for network connections.
`allowHalfOpen`	A `Boolean` that, when `true`, indicates that the socket won't automatically send a FIN packet when the other end of the socket sends a FIN packet, thus allowing half of the `Duplex` stream to remain open. Defaults to `false`.

Once the `Socket` object is created, it provides several events that are emitted during the life cycle of the connection to the server. For example, the `connect` event is triggered when the socket connects, the `data` event is emitted when there is data in the `Readable` stream ready to be read, and the `close` event is emitted when the connection to the server is closed. As you implement your socket server, you can register callbacks to be executed when these events are emitted to handle opening and closing the socket, reading and writing data, etc. Table 8.2 lists the events that can be triggered on `Socket` objects.

Table 8.2 **Events that can be triggered on `Socket` objects**

Event	Description
`connect`	Emitted when a connection is successfully established with the server. The callback function does not accept any parameters.
`data`	Emitted when data is received on the socket. If no data event handler is attached, data can be lost. The callback function must accept a parameter that is a `Buffer` object containing the chunk of data that was read from the socket. For example: `function(chunk){}`
`end`	Emitted when the server terminates the connection by sending a FIN. The callback function does not accept any parameters.
`timeout`	Emitted when the connection to the server times out due to inactivity.

Event	Description
drain	Emitted when the write buffer becomes empty. You can use this event to throttle back the data stream being written to the socket. The callback function does not accept any parameters.
error	Emitted when an error occurs on the socket connection. The callback function should accept `error` as the only argument. For example: `function(error){}`
close	Emitted when the socket has fully closed either because it was closed by an `end()` method or because an error occurred. The callback function does not accept any parameters.

The `Socket` object also includes several methods that allow you to do things like read from and write to the socket as well as pause or end data flow. Many of these are inherited from the `Duplex` stream objects, so they should be familiar to you (see Chapter 5, "Handling Data I/O in Node.js"). Table 8.3 lists the methods available on `Socket` objects.

Table 8.3 **Methods that can be called on `Socket` objects**

Method	Description
setEncoding([encoding])	When this function is called, data returned from the socket's streams is an encoded `String` instead of a `Buffer` object. Sets the default encoding that should be used when writing data to and reading data from the streams. Using this option handles multi-byte characters that might otherwise be mangled when converting a buffer to a string using `buf.toString(encoding)`. If you want to read the data as strings, always use this method.
write(data, [encoding], [callback])	Writes a data buffer or string to the `Writable` stream of the socket, using the encoding if specified. The callback function is executed as soon as the data is written.
end([data], [encoding])	Writes a data buffer or string to the `Writable` stream of the socket and then flushes the stream and closes the connection.
destroy()	Forces the socket connection to shut down. You should only need to use this in case of failures.
pause()	Pauses the `Readable` stream of a socket from emitting data events. This allows you to throttle back the upload of data to the stream.
resume()	Resumes data event emitting on the `Readable` stream of the socket.

Method	Description
`setTimeout(timeout, [callback])`	Specifies a `timeout`, in milliseconds, that the server will wait before emitting a timeout event when the socket is inactive. The callback function is triggered as a once event listener. If you want the connection to be terminated on timeout, you should do it manually in the callback function.
`setNoDelay([noDelay])`	Disables/enables the Nagle algorithm, which buffers data before sending it. Setting this to `false` disables data buffering.
`setKeepAlive([enable], [initialDelay])`	Enables/disables the keep-alive functionality on the connection. The optional `initialDelay` parameter specifies the time, in milliseconds, that the socket is idle before sending the first keep-alive packet.
`address()`	Returns the bound address, the address family name, and the port of the socket, as reported by the operating system. The return value is an object that contains the `port`, `family`, and `address` properties. For example: `{ port: 8107, family: 'IPv4', address: '127.0.0.1' }`
`unref()`	Allows the Node.js application to terminate if this socket is the only event on the event queue.
`ref()`	Re-references a socket so that if this socket is the only thing on the event queue, the Node.js application does not terminate.

`Socket` objects also provide several properties that you can access to get information about the object—for example, the address and port the socket is communicating on, the amount of data being written, and the buffer size. Table 8.4 lists the properties available on `Socket` objects.

Table 8.4 **Properties that can be accessed on `Socket` objects**

Property	Description
`bufferSize`	The number of bytes currently buffered and waiting to be written to the socket's stream.
`remoteAddress`	The IP address of the remote server that the socket is connected to.
`remotePort`	The port of the remote server that the socket is connected to.
`localAddress`	The local IP address the remote client is using for the socket connection.
`localPort`	The local port the remote client is using for the socket connection.
`bytesRead`	The number of bytes read by the socket.
`bytesWritten`	The number of bytes written by the socket.

To illustrate flowing data across a `Socket` object, the following code shows the basics of implementing the `Socket` object on a client:

```
var net = require('net');
var client = net.connect({port: 8107, host:'localhost'}, function() {
  console.log('Client connected');
  client.write('Some Data\r\n');
});
client.on('data', function(data) {
  console.log(data.toString());
  client.end();
});
client.on('end', function() {
  console.log('Client disconnected');
});
```

Notice that the `net.connect()` method is called using an optional object containing a `port` and `host` attribute. The `connect` callback function logs a message and then writes some data out to the server. To handle data coming back from the server, the `on.data()` event handler is implemented. To handle the closure of the socket, the `on('end')` event handler is implemented.

The `net.Server` Object

You use the `net.Server` object to create a TCP socket server and begin listening for connections to which you will be able to read and write data. The `Server` object is created internally when you call `net.createServer()`. This object is intended to represent the socket server and handles listening for connections and then sending and receiving data on those connections to the server.

When the server receives a connection, the server creates a `Socket` object and passes it to any connection event handlers that are listening. Because the `Socket` object implements a `Duplex` stream, you can use it with the `write()` method to stream writes of data back to the client and a `data` event handler to stream data from the client.

To create a `Server` object, you use the `net.createServer()` method:

```
net.createServer([options], [connectionListener])
```

The `options` parameter is an object that specifies options to use when creating the socket `Server` object. Table 8.5 lists the option of the `Server` object. The second parameter is the `connection` event callback function, which is executed when a connection is received. This `connectionListenter` callback function is passed the `Socket` object for the connecting client.

Table 8.5 **Option that can be specified when creating `net.Server` objects**

Option	Description
`allowHalfOpen`	A `Boolean` that, when `true`, indicates that the socket won't automatically send a FIN packet when the other end of the socket sends a FIN packet, thus allowing half of the `Duplex` stream to remain open. Defaults to `false`.

Once the `Server` object is created, it provides several events that are triggered during the life cycle of the server. For example, the `connection` event is triggered when a socket client connects, and the `close` event is triggered when the server shuts down. As you implement your socket server, you can register callbacks to be executed when these events are triggered to handle connections, errors, and shutdown. Table 8.6 lists the events that can be triggered on `Socket` objects.

Table 8.6 **Events that can be triggered on a `net.Socket` object**

Event	Description
`listening`	Emitted when the server begins listening on a port by calling the `listen()` method. The callback function does not accept any parameters.
`connection`	Emitted when a connection is received from a socket client. The callback function must accept a parameter that is a `Socket` object representing the connection to the connecting client. For example: `function(client){}`
`close`	Emitted when the server closes either normally or on error. This event is not \emitted until all client connections have ended.
`error`	Emitted when an error occurs. The `close` event is also triggered on errors.

The `Server` object also includes several methods that allow you to do things like read from and write to the socket as well as pause or end data flow. Many of these are inherited from the `Duplex` stream objects, so they should be familiar to you. Table 8.7 lists the methods available on `Socket` objects.

Table 8.7 **Methods that can be called on a `net.Server` object**

Method	Description
`listen(port, [host], [backlog], [callback])`	Opens a port on the server and begins listening for connections. `port` specifies the listening port. If you specify `0` as the `port`, a random port number is selected. `host` is the IP address to listen on; if it is omitted, the server accepts connections directed to any IPv4 address. `backlog` specifies the maximum number of pending connections the server allows. The default is `511`. The callback function is called when the server has opened the port and begins listening.
`listen(path, [callback])`	Same as above except that a Unix socket server is started, to listen for connections on the file system `path` specified.
`listen(handle, [callback])`	Same as above except that a handle to a `Server` or `Socket` object has an underlying `_handle` member that points to a file descriptor handle on the server. It assumes that the file descriptor points to a socket file that has already been bound to a port.
`getConnections(callback)`	Returns the number of connections currently connected to the server. `callback` is executed when the number of connections is calculated and accepts an `error` parameter and a `count` parameter. For example: `function(error, count)`
`close([callback])`	Stops the server from accepting new connections. Current connections are allowed to remain until they complete. The server does not truly stop until all current connections have been closed.
`address()`	Returns the bound address, the address family name, and the port of the socket, as reported by the operating system. The return value is an object that contains the `port`, `family`, and `address` properties. For example: `{ port: 8107, family: 'IPv4', address: '127.0.0.1' }`
`unref()`	Calling this method allows the Node.js application to terminate if this server is the only event on the event queue.
`ref()`	References this socket so that if this server is the only thing on the event queue, the Node.js application does not terminate.

The `Server` object also provides the `maxConnections` attribute, which allows you to set the maximum number of connections that the server accepts before rejecting them. If a process has been forked to a child for processing using `child_process.fork()`, you should not use this option.

The following code shows the basics of implementing the `Server` object:

```
var net = require('net');
var server = net.createServer(function(client) {
  console.log('Client connected');
  client.on('data', function(data) {
    console.log('Client sent ' + data.toString());
  });
  client.on('end', function() {
    console.log('Client disconnected');
  });
  client.write('Hello');
});
server.listen(8107, function() {
  console.log('Server listening for connections');
});
```

Notice that the `net.createServer()` method implements a callback that accepts the client `Socket` object. To handle data coming back from the client, the `on.data()` event handler is implemented. To handle the closure of the socket, the `on('end')` event handler is implemented. To begin listening for connections, the `listen()` method is called on port `8107`.

Implementing TCP Socket Servers and Clients

Now that you understand the `net.Server` and `net.Socket` objects, you are ready to jump in and implement some Node.js TCP clients and servers. This guides you through the process of implementing basic TCP clients and servers in Node.js.

The examples in the following sections are extremely basic, to make it easy for you to grasp the concepts of starting the TCP server listening on a port and then implementing clients that can connect. The examples are designed to help you see the interactions and event handling that need to be implemented.

Implementing a TCP Socket Client

At the most basic level, implementing a TCP socket client involves creating a `Socket` object that connects to the server and then writing data to the server and handling the data that comes back. In addition, you should build the socket so that it can also handle errors, the buffer being full, and timeouts. This section discusses the steps involved in implementing a socket client using the `Socket` object. Listing 8.1 provides the full code for the following discussion.

The first step is to create the socket client by calling `net.connect()`, as shown below. Pass in the `port` and `host` that you want to connect to as well and implement a `callback` function to handle the connect event:

```
net.connect({port: 8107, host:'localhost'}, function() {
```

```
  //handle connection
});
```

Then inside the callback, you set up the connection behavior. For example, you might want to add a timeout or set the encoding as shown below:

```
this.setTimeout(500);
this.setEncoding('utf8');
```

You also need to add handlers for the `data`, `end`, `error`, `timeout`, and `close` events that you want to handle. For example, to handle the `data` event so that you can read data coming back from the server, you might add the following handler once the connection has been established:

```
this.on('data', function(data) {
  console.log("Read from server: " + data.toString());
  //process the data
  this.end();
});
```

To write data to the server, you implement a `write()` command. If you are writing a lot of data to the server and the write fails, you might also want to implement a `drain` event handler to begin writing again when the buffer is empty. The following shows an example of implementing a drain handler because of a write failure. Notice that a closure is used to preserve the values of the socket and data variables once the function has ended:

```
function writeData(socket, data){
  var success = !socket.write(data);
  if (!success){
    (function(socket, data){
      socket.once('drain', function(){
        writeData(socket, data);
      });
    })(socket, data);
  }
}
```

Listing 8.1 shows the full implementation of a basic TCP socket client. The client just sends a bit of data to the server and receives a bit of data back; however, the example could easily be expanded to support more complex data handling across the socket. Notice that there are three separate sockets opened to the server, and they are communicating at the same time. Figure 8.1 shows the output from the code in Listing 8.1. Notice that each client that is created gets a different random port number.

Listing 8.1 `socket_client.js`: Implementing basic TCP socket clients

```
var net = require('net');
function getConnection(connName){
  var client = net.connect({port: 8107, host:'localhost'}, function() {
```

```
    console.log(connName + ' Connected: ');
    console.log('   local = %s:%s', this.localAddress, this.localPort);
    console.log('   remote = %s:%s', this.remoteAddress, this.remotePort);
    this.setTimeout(500);
    this.setEncoding('utf8');
    this.on('data', function(data) {
      console.log(connName + " From Server: " + data.toString());
      this.end();
    });
    this.on('end', function() {
      console.log(connName + ' Client disconnected');
    });
    this.on('error', function(err) {
      console.log('Socket Error: ', JSON.stringify(err));
    });
    this.on('timeout', function() {
      console.log('Socket Timed Out');
    });
    this.on('close', function() {
      console.log('Socket Closed');
    });
  });
  return client;
}
function writeData(socket, data){
  var success = !socket.write(data);
  if (!success){
    (function(socket, data){
      socket.once('drain', function(){
        writeData(socket, data);
      });
    })(socket, data);
  }
}
var Dwarves = getConnection("Dwarves");
var Elves = getConnection("Elves");
var Hobbits = getConnection("Hobbits");
writeData(Dwarves, "More Axes");
writeData(Elves, "More Arrows");
writeData(Hobbits, "More Pipe Weed");
```

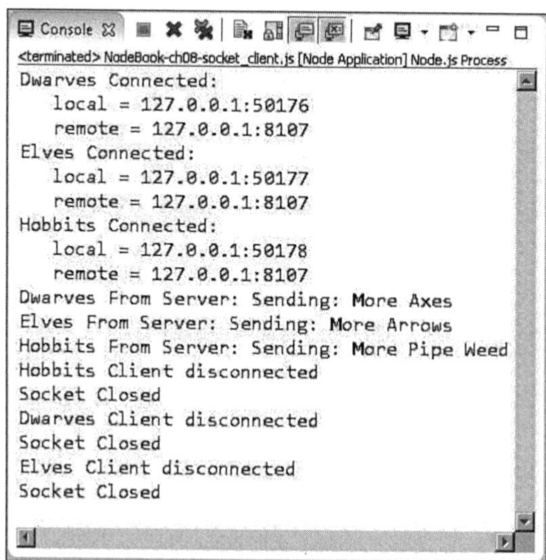

Figure 8.1 Multiple socket clients sending and receiving data from the server.

Implementing a TCP Socket Server

At the most basic level, implementing a TCP server client involves creating a `Server` object, listening on a port, and handling incoming connections, including reading and writing data to and from the connections. In addition, the socket server should handle the `close` and `error` events on the `Server` object, as well as the events that occur in the incoming client connection `Socket` object. This section discusses the steps involved in implementing a socket server using the `Server` object. Listing 8.2 provides the full code for the following discussion.

The first step is to create the socket server by calling `net.createServer()`, as shown below. You also need to provide a connection callback handler and then call `listen()` to begin listening on the port:

```
var server = net.createServer(function(client) {
  //implement the connection callback handler code here
});
server.listen(8107, function() {
 //implement the listen callback handler here.
});
```

Inside the `listen` callback handler, you also add handlers to support the `close` and `error` events on the `Server` object. These may just be log statements, or you might want to add additional code that is executed when these events occur. The following are two basic examples:

```
server.on('close', function(){
  console.log('Server Terminated');
});
server.on('error', function(err){
});
```

Inside the connection event callback, you set up the connection behavior. For example, you might want to add a timeout or set the encoding as shown below:

```
this.setTimeout(500);
this.setEncoding('utf8');
```

You also need to add handlers for the data, end, error, timeout, and close events that you want to handle on the client connection. For example, to handle the data event so that you can read data coming from the client, you might add the following handler once the connection has been established:

```
this.on('data', function(data) {
  console.log("Received from client: " + data.toString());
  //process the data
});
```

To write data to the server, you implement a write() command somewhere in your code. If you are writing a lot of data to the client, you may also want to implement a drain event handler that will begin writing again when the buffer is empty. This can help if write() returns a failure because the buffer is full or if you want to throttle back writing to the socket. The following is an example of implementing a drain handler because of a write failure. Notice that a closure is used to preserve the values of the socket and data variables once the function has ended:

```
function writeData(socket, data){
  var success = !socket.write(data);
  if (!success){
    (function(socket, data){
      socket.once('drain', function(){
        writeData(socket, data);
      });
    })(socket, data);
  }
}
```

Listing 8.2 shows the full implementation of a basic TCP socket server. The socket server accepts connections on port 8107, reads the data in, and then writes a string back to the client. Although the implementation is basic, it illustrates handling the events as well as reading and writing data in the client connection. Figure 8.2 shows the output from the code in Listing 8.2.

Listing 8.2 `socket_server.js`: **Implementing a basic TCP socket server**

```
var net = require('net');
var server = net.createServer(function(client) {
  console.log('Client connection: ');
  console.log('   local = %s:%s', client.localAddress, client.localPort);
  console.log('   remote = %s:%s', client.remoteAddress, client.remotePort);
  client.setTimeout(500);
  client.setEncoding('utf8');
  client.on('data', function(data) {
    console.log('Received data from client on port %d: %s',
                client.remotePort, data.toString());
    console.log('  Bytes received: ' + client.bytesRead);
    writeData(client, 'Sending: ' + data.toString());
    console.log('  Bytes sent: ' + client.bytesWritten);
  });
  client.on('end', function() {
    console.log('Client disconnected');
    server.getConnections(function(err, count){
      console.log('Remaining Connections: ' + count);
    });
  });
  client.on('error', function(err) {
    console.log('Socket Error: ', JSON.stringify(err));
  });
  client.on('timeout', function() {
    console.log('Socket Timed out');
  });
});
server.listen(8107, function() {
  console.log('Server listening: ' + JSON.stringify(server.address()));
  server.on('close', function(){
    console.log('Server Terminated');
  });
  server.on('error', function(err){
    console.log('Server Error: ', JSON.stringify(err));
  });
});
function writeData(socket, data){
  var success = !socket.write(data);
  if (!success){
    (function(socket, data){
      socket.once('drain', function(){
        writeData(socket, data);
      });
    })(socket, data);
  }
}
```

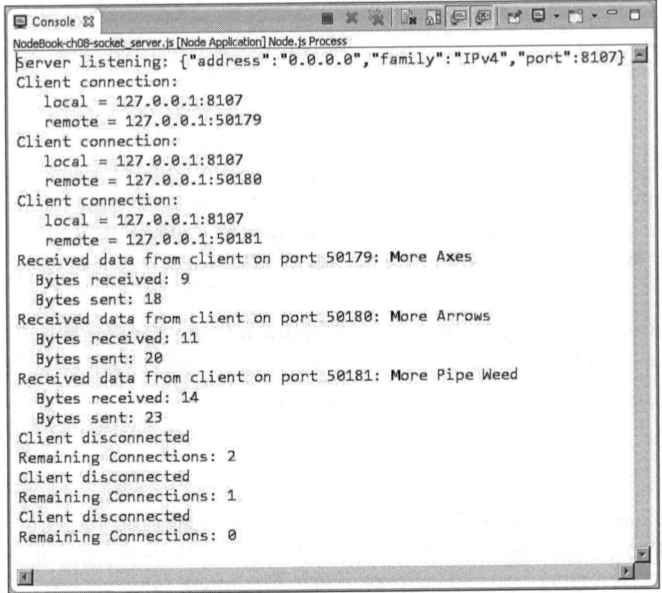

Figure 8.2 Multiple socket clients sending and receiving data from the server.

Implementing TLS Servers and Clients

Transport Layer Security/Secure Sockets Layer (TLS/SSL) is a cryptographic protocol designed to provide secure communications on the Internet. It uses X.509 certificates along with session keys to verify whether the socket server you are communicating with is the one you are intending to communicate with. TLS provides security in two main ways. First, it uses long-term public and secret keys to exchange a short-term session key so that data can be encrypted between client and server. It also provides authentication so that you can ensure that the webserver you are connecting to is the one you actually think it is, thus preventing man-in-the-middle attacks, in which requests are rerouted through a third party.

The following sections discuss implementing TLS socket servers and clients in your Node.js environment, using the `tls` module. Before getting started using TLS, you need to generate a private key and a public certificate for both your clients and your server. There are several ways to do this, depending on your platform. One of the simplest methods is to use the OpenSSL library for you platform.

To generate a private key, first execute the following OpenSSL commands to generate a private key:

```
openssl genrsa -out server.pem 2048
```

Next, use the following command to create a certificate-signing request file:

```
openssl req -new -key server.pem -out server.csr
```

> **Note**
>
> When creating the certificate-signing request file, you need to answer several questions. When prompted for the common name, you should enter in the domain name of the server you want to connect to. Otherwise, the certificate will not work. Also, you can enter additional domain names and IP addresses in the Subject Alternative Names field.

Then, to create a self-signed certificate that you can use for your own purpose or for testing, use the following command:

```
openssl x509 -req -days 365 -in server.csr -signkey server.pem -out server.crt
```

> **Note**
>
> The self-signed certificate is fine for testing purposes and internal use. However, if you are implementing an external web service that needs to be protected on the Internet, you may want to get a certificate signed by a certificate authority. If you want to create a certificate that is signed by a third-party certificate authority, you need to take additional steps.

Creating a TLS Socket Client

Creating a TLS client is almost exactly like creating a socket client, as discussed earlier in this chapter. The only difference is that there are additional options, shown in Table 8.8, that allow you to specify the security for the client. The most important options are `key`, `cert`, and `ca`.

The `key` option specifies the private key used for SSL. The `cert` value specifies the x509 public key to use. If you are using a self-signed certificate, you need to point the `ca` property at the certificate for the server:

```
var options = {
  key: fs.readFileSync('test/keys/client.pem'),
  cert: fs.readFileSync('test/keys/client.crt'),
  ca: fs.readFileSync('test/keys/server.crt')
};
```

Once you have defined the options with the `cert`, `key`, and `ca` settings, you can call `tls.connect(options, [responseCallback])`, and it will work exactly the same as the `net.connect()` call. The only difference is that the data between the client and server is encrypted:

```
var options = {
  hostname: 'encrypted.mysite.com',
  port: 8108,
  path: '/',
  method: 'GET',
```

```
  key: fs.readFileSync('test/keys/client.pem'),
  cert: fs.readFileSync('test/keys/client.crt),
  ca: fs.readFileSync('test/keys/server.crt)
};
var req = tls.connect(options, function(res) {
  <handle the connection the same as a net.connect>
}
```

Table 8.8 **Additional options for** `tls.connect()`

Event	**Description**
`pfx`	A `String` or `Buffer` object that contains the private key, certificate, and CA certs of the server, in PFX or PKCS12 format.
`key`	A `String` or `Buffer` object that contains the private key to use for SSL.
`passphrase`	A `String` object that contains the passphrase for the private key or PFX.
`cert`	A `String` or `Buffer` object that contains the public x509 certificate to use.
`ca`	An array of strings or buffers of trusted certificates, in PEM format, to check the remote host against.
`rejectUnauthorized`	A `Boolean` that, when `true`, indicates that the server certificate is verified against the list of supplied CAs. An error event is emitted if verification fails. Verification happens at the connection level, before the HTTP request is sent. Defaults to `true`.
`servername`	The server name for the Server Name Indication (SNI) TLS extension.
`secureProtocol`	The SSL method to use, such as `SSLv3_method` to force SSL version 3.

Creating a TLS Socket Server

Creating a TLS socket server is almost exactly like creating a socket server, as discussed earlier in this chapter. The only differences is that there are additional options that you must pass into `tls.createServer()`, and there are some additional events that can be triggered on the `tls.Server` object. The options, listed in Table 8.9, allow you to specify the security options for the server. Table 8.10 lists the additional events for the TLS socket server. The most important options are `key`, `cert`, and `ca`.

The `key` option specifies the private key used for SSL. The `cert` value specifies the x509 public key to use. If you are using a self-signed certificate, you need to point the `ca` property at the certificate for the client.

Table 8.9 **Additional options for `tls.createServer()`**

Option	Description
`pfx`	A `String` or `Buffer` object that contains the private key, certificate, and CA certs of the server, in PFX or PKCS12 format.
`key`	A `String` or `Buffer` object that contains the private key to use for SSL.
`passphrase`	A `String` object that contains the passphrase for the private key or PFX.
`cert`	A `String` or `Buffer` object that contains the public x509 certificate to use.
`ca`	An array of strings or buffers of trusted certificates, in PEM format, to check the remote host against.
`crl`	Either a string or list of strings of PEM-encoded certificate revocation lists.
`ciphers`	A string that describes the ciphers to use or exclude. Using this in conjunction with `honorCipherOrder` is a good way to prevent BEAST attacks.
`handshakeTimeout`	The number of milliseconds to wait before aborting the connection if the SSL/TLS handshake does not finish. If the timeout is hit, a `clientError` is emitted on `tls.Server`.
`honorCipherOrder`	A `Boolean` that, when `true`, indicates that the server honors the server's preferences over the client's when choosing a cipher.
`requestCert`	When `true`, the server requests a certificate from clients that connect and attempt to verify that certificate. Default is `false`.
`rejectUnauthorized`	When `true`, the server rejects any connection that is not authorized with the list of supplied CAs. This option has an effect only if `requestCert` is `true`. Default is `false`.
`NPNProtocols`	An array or buffer of possible NPN protocols. Protocols should be ordered by their priority.
`SNICallback`	A function that is called if the client supports the SNI TLS extension. The server name is the only argument passed to the callback.
`sessionIdContext`	A string that contains an opaque identifier for session resumption. If `requestCert` is `true`, the default is an MD5 hash value generated from the command line. Otherwise, the default is not provided.
`secureProtocol`	The SSL method to use, such as `SSLv3_method` to force SSL version 3.

The following is an example of creating a TLS socket server in Node.js:

```
var options = {
  key: fs.readFileSync('test/keys/server.pem'),
  cert: fs.readFileSync('test/keys/server.crt'),
  ca: fs.readFileSync('test/keys/client.crt')
};
tls.createServer(options, function (client) {
  client.write("Hello Secure World\r\n");
  client.end();
}).listen(8108);
```

Once the TLS socket server has been created, the request/response handling works basically the same way as for the TCP socket servers described earlier in this chapter. The server can accept connections and read and write data back to the client.

Table 8.10 **Additional events on TLS `Server` objects**

Event	Description
`secureConnection`	Emitted when a new secure connection has been successfully established. The callback accepts a single instance of a `tls.CleartextStream` streaming object that can be written to and read from. For example: `function (clearStream)`
`clientError`	Emitted when a client connection emits an error. The parameters to the callback are the error and a `tls.SecurePair` object. For example: `function (error, securePair)`
`newSession`	Emitted when a new TLS session is created. The callback is passed the `sessionId` and `sessionData` parameters, which contain the session information. For example: `function (sessionId, sessionData)`
`resumeSession`	Emitted when the client tries to resume a previous TLS session. You can store the session in external storage so you can look it up when receiving this event. The callback handler receives two parameters: a `sessionId` and a `callback` to be executed if the session cannot be established. For example: `function (sessionId, callback)`

Summary

Sockets are extremely useful when you're implementing backend services in a Node.js application. They allow a service on one system to communicate with a service on another system through an IP address and port. The also provide the ability to implement an IPC between two different processes running on the same server. The `net` module allows you to create `Server` objects that act as socket servers and `Socket` objects that act as socket clients. Because the `Socket` object extends `Duplex` streams, you can read and write data from both the server and client. For secure connections, Node.js provides the `tls` module, which allows you to implement secure TLS socket servers and clients.

Up Next

In the next chapter, you will get a chance to implement multiprocessing in a Node.js environment. This allows you to farm out work to other processes on the system and take advantage of multiprocessor servers.

9

Scaling Applications Using Multiple Processors in Node.js

In Chapter 4, "Using Events, Listeners, Timers, and Callbacks in Node.js," you learned that Node.js applications run on a single thread rather than multiple threads. Using a single thread for application processing makes Node.js processes more efficient and faster. But most servers have multiple processors, and you can scale your Node.js applications by taking advantage of them. Node.js allows you to fork work from the main application to separate processes that can then be processed in parallel with each other and the main application.

To facilitate utilizing multiple processes, Node.js provides three specific modules. The `process` module provides access to the running processes. The `child_process` module enables you to create child processes and communicate with them. The `cluster` module provides the ability to implement clustered servers that share the same port, thus allowing multiple requests to be handled simultaneously.

Understanding the `process` Module

The `process` module is a global object that can be accessed from your Node.js applications without the need to use `require()`. This module gives you access to the running processes as well as information about the underlying hardware architecture.

Understanding Process I/O Pipes

The `process` module provides access to the standard I/O pipes for the process `stdin`, `stdout`, and `stderr`. `stdin` is the standard input pipe for the process, which is typically the console. That means that you can read input from the console by using the following code:

```
process.stdin.on('data', function(data){
  console.log("Console Input: " + data);
});
```

Then when you type in data to the console and press Enter, the data is written back out. For example:

```
some data
Console Input: some data
```

The `stdout` and `stderr` attributes of the process module are `Writable` streams that can be treated accordingly.

Understanding Process Signals

A great feature of the `process` module is that it allows you to register listeners to handle signals that the operating system sends to a process. This is helpful when you need to perform certain actions such as cleanup before a process is stopped or terminated. Table 9.1 lists the process events for which you can add listeners.

To register for a process signal, simply use the `on(`*`event, callback`*`)` method. For example, to register an event handler for the `SIGBREAK` event, you would use the following code:

```
process.on('SIGBREAK', function(){
  console.log("Got a SIGBREAK");
});
```

Table 9.1 **Events that can be sent to Node.js processes**

Event	Description
`SIGUSR1`	Emitted when the Node.js debugger is started. You can add a listener, but you cannot stop the debugger from starting.
`SIGPIPE`	Emitted when the process tries to write to a pipe without a process connected on the other end.
`SIGHUP`	Emitted on Windows when the console window is closed and on other platforms under various similar conditions. Note that Windows terminates Node.js about 10 seconds after sending this event.
`SIGTERM`	Emitted when a request is made to terminate the process. This is not supported on Windows.
`SIGINT`	Emitted when a break is sent to the process, such as when Ctrl+C is pressed.
`SIGBREAK`	Emitted on Windows when Ctrl+Break is pressed.
`SIGWINCH`	Emitted when the console has been resized. On Windows, it is emitted only when you write to the console, when the cursor is being moved, or when a readable TTY is used in raw mode.
`SIGKILL`	Emitted on a process kill. Cannot have a listener installed.
`SIGSTOP`	Emitted on a process stop. Cannot have a listener installed.

Controlling Process Execution with the `process` Module

The `process` module gives you some control over the execution of processes. Specifically, it enables you to stop the current process, kill another process, or schedule work to run on the event queue. For example, to exit the current Node.js process, you would use:

```
process.exit(0)
```

Table 9.2 lists the process control methods that are available in the `process` module.

Table 9.2 **Methods that can be called on the `process` module to affect process execution**

Method	Description
`abort()`	Causes the current Node.js application to emit an `abort` event, exit, and generate a memory core.
`exit([code])`	Causes the current Node.js application to exit and return the specified `code`.
`kill(pid, [signal])`	Causes the operating system to send a kill signal to the process with the specified `pid`. The default `signal` value is `SIGTERM`, but you can specify another.
`nextTick(callback)`	Schedules the `callback` function on the Node.js application's queue.

Getting Information from the `process` Module

The `process` module has a wealth of information about the running process and the system architecture. This information can be useful when you're implementing applications. For example, the `process.pid` property gives you the process ID that you can then have your application use.

Table 9.3 lists the properties and methods that you can access from the `process` module and describes what they return.

Table 9.3 **Methods and properties of the `process` module**

Method	Description
`version`	Specifies the version of Node.js.
`versions`	Provides an object that contains the required modules and version for this Node.js application.
`config`	Contains the configuration options used to compile the current node executable.

Method	Description
`argv`	Contains the command arguments used to start the Node.js application. The first element is `node`, and the second element is the path to the main JavaScript file.
`execPath`	Specifies the absolute path from which Node.js was started.
`execArgv`	Specifies the node-specific command-line options used to start the application.
`chdir(directory)`	Changes the current working directory for the application. This can be useful if you provide a configuration file that is loaded after the application has started.
`cwd()`	Returns the current working directory for the process.
`env`	Contains the key/value pairs specified in the environment for the process.
`pid`	Specifies the current process's ID.
`title`	Specifies the title of the currently running process.
`arch`	Specifies the processor architecture the process is running on (for example, `x64`, `ia32`, or `arm`).
`platform`	Specifies the OS platform (for example, `linux`, `win32`, or `freebsd`).
`memoryUsage()`	Describes the current memory usage of the Node.js process. You need to use the `util.inspect()` method to read in the object. For example: `console.log(util.inspect(process.memoryUsage()));` `{ rss: 13946880, heapTotal: 4083456, heapUsed: 2190800 }`
`maxTickDepth`	Specifies the maximum number of events scheduled by `nextTick()` that are run before blocking I/O are processed. You should adjust this value as necessary to keep your I/O processes from being starved.
`uptime()`	Contains the number of seconds the Node.js processor has been running.
`hrtime()`	Returns a high-resolution time in the tuple `array [seconds, nanoseconds]`. Use this if you need to implement a granular timing mechanism.
`getgid()`	On POSIX platforms, returns the numerical group ID for this process.
`setgid(id)`	On POSIX platforms, sets the numerical group ID for this process.
`getuid()`	On POSIX platforms, returns the numerical or string user ID for this process.
`setuid(id)`	On POSIX platforms, sets the numerical or string user ID for this process.
`getgroups()`	On POSIX platforms, returns an array of group IDs.
`setgroups(groups)`	On POSIX platforms, sets the supplementary group IDs. Your Node.js application needs root privileges to call this method.
`initgroups(user, extra_group)`	On POSIX platforms, initializes the group access list with the information from `/etc/group`. Your Node.js application needs root privileges to call this method.

To help you understand accessing information using the `process` module, the code in Listing 9.1 makes a series of calls, and it outputs the results to the console, as shown in Figure 9.1.

Listing 9.1 `process_info.js`: **Accessing information about a process and system, using the `process` module**

```
var util = require('util');
console.log('Current directory: ' + process.cwd());
console.log('Environment Settings: ' + JSON.stringify(process.env));
console.log('Node Args: ' + process.argv);
console.log('Execution Path: ' + process.execPath);
console.log('Execution Args: ' + JSON.stringify(process.execArgv));
console.log('Node Version: ' + process.version);
console.log('Module Versions: ' +  JSON.stringify(process.versions));
//console.log(process.config);
console.log('Process ID: ' + process.pid);
console.log('Process Title: ' + process.title);
console.log('Process Platform: ' + process.platform);
console.log('Process Architecture: ' + process.arch);
console.log('Memory Usage: ' + util.inspect(process.memoryUsage()));
var start = process.hrtime();
setTimeout(function() {
  var delta = process.hrtime(start);
  console.log('High-Res timer took %d seconds and %d nanoseconds',
              delta[0], + delta[1]);
  console.log('Node has been running %d seconds', process.uptime());
}, 1000);
```

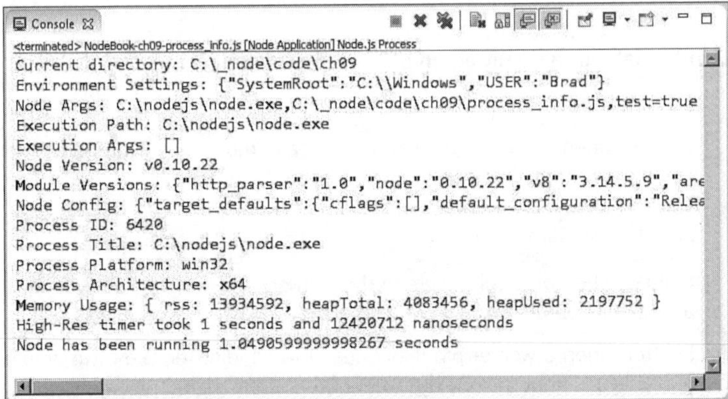

Figure 9.1 Getting information about a process and system by using the `process` module.

Implementing Child Processes

To take advantage of multiple processors in a server with your Node.js applications, you need to farm work off to child processes. The `child_process` module allows you to spawn, fork, and execute work on other processes. The following sections discuss the process of executing tasks on other processes.

> **Note**
>
> Keep in mind that child processes do not have direct access to the global memory in each other or in the parent process. Therefore, you need to design your applications to run in parallel.

Understanding the `ChildProcess` Object

The `child_process` module provides a new class called `ChildProcess` that acts as a representation of the child processes that can be accessed from the parent. This allows you to control, end, and send messages to the child processes from the parent process that started them.

Also, the `process` module is a `ChildProcess` object. This means that when you access `process` from the parent module, it is the parent `ChildProcess` object, but when you access `process` from the child process, it is the `ChildProcess` object.

In this section you will learn more about the `ChildProcess` object so that you will be able to leverage it in subsequent sections to implement multiprocess Node.js applications.

Table 9.4 lists the events that can be emitted on the `ChildProcess` object. You implement handlers for the events to handle when the child process terminates or sends messages back to the parent.

Table 9.4 **Events that can be emitted on `ChildProcess` objects**

Event	**Description**
`message`	Emitted when a `ChildProcess` object calls the `send()` method to send data. Listeners on this event implement a `callback` that can then read the data sent. For example: `child.on('send': function(message){console.log(message});`
`error`	Emitted when an error occurs in the worker. The handler receives an error object as the only parameter.
`exit`	Emitted when a worker process ends. The handler receives two arguments, `code` and `signal`, that specify the exit code and the signal passed to kill the process if it was killed by the parent.

Event	Description
`close`	Emitted when all the `stdio` streams of a worker process have terminated. It is different from `exit` because multiple processes might share the same `stdio` streams.
`disconnect`	Emitted when `disconnect()` is called on a worker.

Table 9.5 lists the methods that can be called on a child process. These methods allow you to terminate, disconnect, or send messages to the child process. For example, you can call the following code from the parent process to send an object to the child process:

```
child.send({cmd: 'command data'});
```

Table 9.5 **Methods that can be called on `ChildProcess` objects**

Method	Description
`kill([signal])`	Causes the operating system to send a kill signal to the child process. The default signal is `SIGTERM`, but you can specify another. Refer to Table 9.1 for a list of signal strings.
`send(message, [sendHandle])`	Sends a message to the handle. The message can be a string or an object. The optional `sendHandle` parameter allows you to send a TCP `Server` or `Socket` object to the client. This allows the client process to share the same port and address.
`disconnect()`	Closes the inter-process communication (or, IPC) channel between the parent and child and sets the connected flag to `false` in both the parent and child processes.

Table 9.6 lists the properties that you can access on `ChildProcess` objects.

Table 9.6 **Properties that can be accessed on `ChildProcess` objects**

Property	Description
`stdin`	An input `Writable` stream.
`stdout`	A standard output `Readable` stream.
`strerr`	A standard output `Readable` stream for errors.
`pid`	The ID of the process.
`connected`	A Boolean that is set to `false` after `disconnect()` is called. When it is `false`, you can no longer send messages to the child.

Executing a System Command on Another Process by Using exec()

The simplest way to add work to another process from a Node.js process is to execute a system command in a subshell, using the `exec()` function. The `exec()` function can execute just about anything that can be executed from a console prompt, such as a binary executable, shell script, Python script, or batch file.

When executed, the `exec()` function creates a system subshell and then executes a command string in that shell just as if you had executed it from a console prompt. This gives you the advantage of being able to leverage the capabilities of a console shell, such as accessing environment variables, on the command line.

The syntax for the `exec()` function, which returns a `ChildProcess` object, is shown below:

```
child_process.exec(command, [options], callback)
```

The `command` parameter is a string that specifies the command to execute in the subshell. The `options` parameter is an object that specifies settings to use when executing the command, such as the current working directory. Table 9.7 lists the options you can specify with the `exec()` and `execFile()` commands.

The `callback` parameter is a function that accepts three parameters: `error`, `stdout`, and `stderr`. The `error` parameter is passed an error object if an error is encountered during execution of the command. `stdout` and `stderr` are `Buffer` objects that contain the output from executing the command.

Table 9.7 **Options that can be set with the `exec()` and `execFile()` functions**

Option	Description
`cwd`	Specifies the current working directory for the child process to execute within.
`env`	Object that specifies `property:value` as environment key/value pairs.
`encoding`	Specifies the encoding to use for the output buffers when storing output from the command.
`maxBuffer`	Specifies the size of the output buffers for `stdout` and `stderr`. The default value is `200*1024`.
`timeout`	Specifies the number of milliseconds for the parent process to wait before killing the child process if it has not completed. The default is `0`, which means there is no timeout.
`killSignal`	Specifies the kill signal to use when terminating the child process. The default is `SIGTERM`.

Listing 9.2 shows an example of executing a system command using the `exec()` function. Figure 9.2 shows the output of Listing 9.2.

Listing 9.2 `child_exec.js`: **Executing a system command in another process**

```
var childProcess = require('child_process');
var options = {maxBuffer:100*1024, encoding:'utf8', timeout:5000};
var child = childProcess.exec('dir /B', options,
                              function (error, stdout, stderr) {
  if (error) {
    console.log(error.stack);
    console.log('Error Code: '+error.code);
    console.log('Error Signal: '+error.signal);
  }
  console.log('Results: \n' + stdout);
  if (stderr.length){
    console.log('Errors: ' + stderr);
  }
});
child.on('exit', function (code) {
  console.log('Completed with code: '+code);
});
```

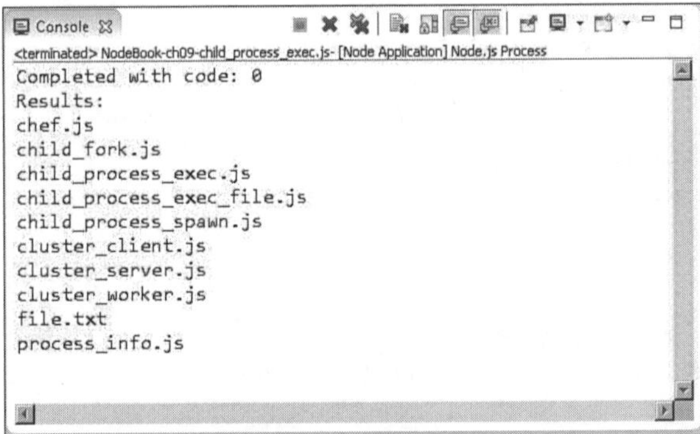

Figure 9.2 Output from executing a system command using `exec()`.

Executing an Executable File on Another Process Using `execFile()`

A simple way to add work to another process from a Node.js process is to execute an executable file on another process using the `execFile()` function. This is very similar to `exec()` except that there is no subshell used. This makes `execFile()` lighter weight, but it also means that the command to execute must be a binary executable. Shell scripts on Linux and batch files on Windows do not work with the `execFile()` function.

The syntax for the `execFile()` function, which returns a `ChildProcess` object, call is shown below:

```
child_process.execFile(file, args, options, callback)
```

The `file` parameter is a string that specifies the path to the executable file that is executed. The `args` parameter is an array that specifies command-line arguments to be passed to the executable. The `options` parameter is an object that specifies settings to use when executing the command, such as the current working directory. Table 9.7 lists the options you can specify with the `execFile()` command.

The `callback` parameter is a function that accepts three parameters: `error`, `stdout`, and `stderr`. The `error` parameter is passed an error object if an error is encountered during execution of the command. `stdout` and `stderr` are buffer objects that contain the output from executing the command.

Listing 9.3 is an example of executing a system command using the `execFile()` function. Figure 9.3 shows the output of Listing 9.3.

Listing 9.3 `child_process_exec_file.js`: **Executing an executable file in another process**

```
var childProcess = require('child_process');
var options = {maxBuffer:100*1024, encoding:'utf8', timeout:5000};
var child = childProcess.execFile('ping.exe', ['-n', '1', 'google.com'],
                                  options, function (error, stdout, stderr) {
  if (error) {
    console.log(error.stack);
    console.log('Error Code: '+error.code);
    console.log('Error Signal: '+error.signal);
  }
  console.log('Results: \n' + stdout);
  if (stderr.length){
    console.log('Errors: ' + stderr);
  }
});
child.on('exit', function (code) {
  console.log('Child completed with code: '+code);
});
```

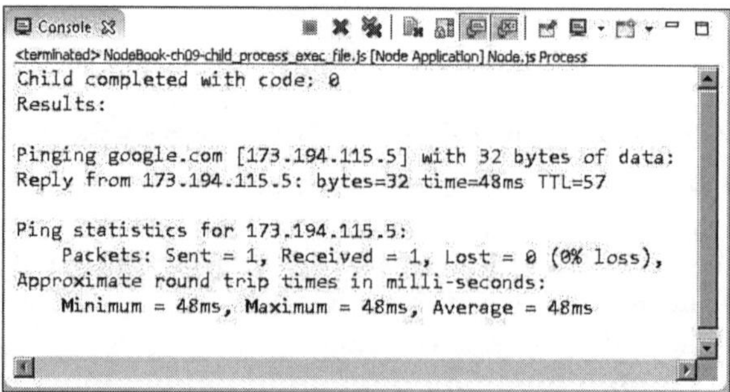

Figure 9.3 Output from executing an executable file using `execFile()`.

Spawning a Process in Another Node.js Instance Using `spawn()`

A rather complex method of adding work to another process from a Node.js process is to spawn another process; link the `stdio`, `stdout`, and `stderr` pipes between them; and then execute a file on the new process, using the `spawn()` function. This method is a bit heavier than simply using `exec()` but provides some great benefits.

The major difference between `spawn()` and `exec()`/`execFile()` is that `stdin` for the spawned process can be configured, and `stdout` and `stderr` are `Readable` streams in the parent process. This means `exec()` and `execFile()` must complete before you can read the buffer outputs. However, you can read output data from a `spawn()` process as soon as it has been written.

The syntax for the `spawn()` function, which returns a `ChildProcess` object, is shown below:

```
child_process.spawn(command, [args], [options])
```

The `command` parameter is a string that specifies the command that is executed. The `args` parameter is an array that specifies command-line arguments to be passed to the executable command. The `options` parameter is an object that specifies settings to use when executing the command, such as the current working directory. Table 9.8 lists the options you can specify with the `spawn()` command.

The `callback` parameter is a function that accepts three parameters: `error`, `stdout`, and `stderr`. The `error` parameter is passed an error object if an error is encountered during execution of the command. `stdout` and `stderr` are defined by the `stdio` option settings; by default they are `Readable` stream objects.

Table 9.8 **Options that can be set with the `spawn()` function**

Option	Description
`cwd`	Represents the current working directory of the child process.
`env`	Object that specifies `property:value` as environment key/value pairs.
`detached`	A Boolean that, when `true`, makes the child process the leader of a new process group, allowing the process to continue even when the parent exits. You should also use `child.unref()` so that the parent process will not wait for the child process before exiting.
`uid`	Specifies the user identity of the process for POSIX processes.
`gid`	Specifies the group identity of the process for POSIX processes.

Option	Description
`stdio`	Defines the child process `stdio` configuration `([stdin, stdout, stderr])`. By default, Node.js opens file descriptors `[0, 1, 2]` for `[stdin, stdout, stderr]`. The strings define the configuration of each input and output stream. For example: `['ipc', 'ipc', 'ipc']` The following options can be used: **`'pipe'`:** Creates a pipe between the child and parent process. The parent can access the pipe using `ChildProcess.stdio[fd]`, where `fd` is the file descriptors `[0, 1, 2]` for `[stdin, stdout, stderr]`. **`'ipc'`:** Creates an IPC channel for passing messages/file descriptors between the parent and child, using the `send()` method described earlier. **`'ignore'`:** Does not set up a file descriptor in the child. **`Stream`:** Specifies a `Readable` or `Writeable` stream object defined in the parent to use. `Stream`'s underlying file descriptor is duplicated in the child, and thus data can be streamed from child to parent and vice versa. **File descriptor integer:** Specifies the integer value of a file descriptor to use. **`null, undefined`:** Uses the defaults of `[0,1,2]` for the `[stdin, stdout, stderr]` values.

Listing 9.4 is an example of executing a system command using the `spawn()` function. Figure 9.4 shows the output of Listing 9.4.

Listing 9.4 `child_process_spawn_file.js`: **Spawning a command in another process**

```
var spawn = require('child_process').spawn;
var options = {
    env: {user:'brad'},
    detached:false,
    stdio: ['pipe','pipe','pipe']
};
var child = spawn('netstat', ['-e']);
child.stdout.on('data', function(data) {
  console.log(data.toString());
});
child.stderr.on('data', function(data) {
  console.log(data.toString());
});
```

```
child.on('exit', function(code) {
  console.log('Child exited with code', code);
});
```

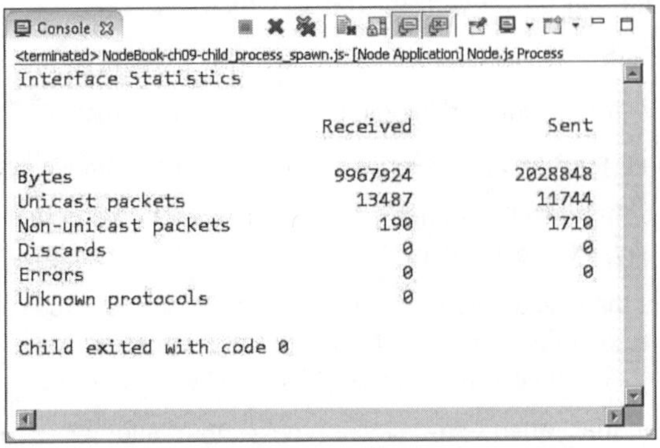

```
Console
<terminated> NodeBook-ch09-child_process_spawn.js- [Node Application] Node.js Process
Interface Statistics

                              Received            Sent

Bytes                          9967924         2028848
Unicast packets                  13487           11744
Non-unicast packets                190            1710
Discards                             0               0
Errors                               0               0
Unknown protocols                    0

Child exited with code 0
```

Figure 9.4 Output streamed from a spawned command using `spawn()`.

Implementing Child Forks

Node.js provides a specialized form of process spawning called a *fork*, which is designed to execute Node.js module code inside another V8 instance running on a separate processor. You can use a fork to run multiple services in parallel. However, it takes time to spin up a new instance of V8, and each instance takes about 10MB of memory. Therefore, you should design forked processes to be longer lived, and you shouldn't require a large number of them. Remember that you really don't get a performance benefit from creating more processes than you have CPUs in the system.

Unlike `spawn`, you cannot configure `stdio` for the child process. Instead, you use the `send()` mechanism in the `ChildProcess` object to communicate between the parent and child processes.

The syntax for the `fork()` function, which returns a `ChildProcess` object, is shown below:

`child_process.fork(`*`modulePath, [args], [options]`*`)`

The `modulePath` parameter is a string that specifies the path to the JavaScript file that is launched by the new Node.js instance. The `args` parameter is an array that specifies command-line arguments to be passed to the `node` command. The `options` parameter is an object that specifies settings to use when executing the command, such as the current working directory. Table 9.9 lists the options you can specify with the `fork()` command.

The `callback` parameter is a function that accepts three parameters: `error`, `stdout`, and `stderr`. The `error` parameter is passed an error object if an error is encountered during execution of the command. `stdout` and `stderr` are `Readable` stream objects.

Table 9.9 **Options that can be set with the `fork()` function**

Option	Description
`cwd`	Specifies the current working directory of the child process.
`env`	Object that specifies `property:value` as environment key/value pairs.
`encoding`	Specifies the encoding to use when writing data to the output streams and across the `send()` IPC mechanism.
`execPath`	Specifies the executable to use to create the spawned Node.js process. This allows you to use different versions of Node.js for different processes. However, this is not recommended in case the process functionality is different.
`silent`	A Boolean that, when `true`, causes the `stdout` and `stderror` in the forked process to not be associated with the parent process. The default is `false`.

Listing 9.5 and Listing 9.6 show examples of forking to another Node.js instance running in a separate process. The code in Listing 9.5 uses `fork()` to create three child processes that are running the code from Listing 9.6. The parent process then uses the `ChildProcess` objects to send commands to the child processes. The code in Listing 9.6 implements the `process.on('message')` callback to receive messages from the parent and the `process.send()` method to send the response back to the parent process, thus implementing the IPC mechanism between the two. Figure 9.5 shows the output of these listings.

Listing 9.5 `child_fork.js`: **A parent process that creates three child processes and sends commands to each, executing in parallel**

```
var child_process = require('child_process');
var options = {
    env:{user:'Brad'},
    encoding:'utf8'
};
function makeChild(){
  var child = child_process.fork('chef.js', [], options);
  child.on('message', function(message) {
    console.log('Served: ' + message);
  });
  return child;
}
```

```
function sendCommand(child, command){
  console.log("Requesting: " + command);
  child.send({cmd:command});
}
var child1 = makeChild();
var child2 = makeChild();
var child3 = makeChild();
sendCommand(child1, "makeBreakfast");
sendCommand(child2, "makeLunch");
sendCommand(child3, "makeDinner");
```

Listing 9.6 `chef.js`: **A child process that handles message events and sends data back to the parent process**

```
process.on('message', function(message, parent) {
  var meal = {};
  switch (message.cmd){
    case 'makeBreakfast':
      meal = ["ham", "eggs", "toast"];
      break;
    case 'makeLunch':
      meal = ["burger", "fries", "shake"];
      break;
    case 'makeDinner':
      meal = ["soup", "salad", "steak"];
      break;
  }
  process.send(meal);
});
```

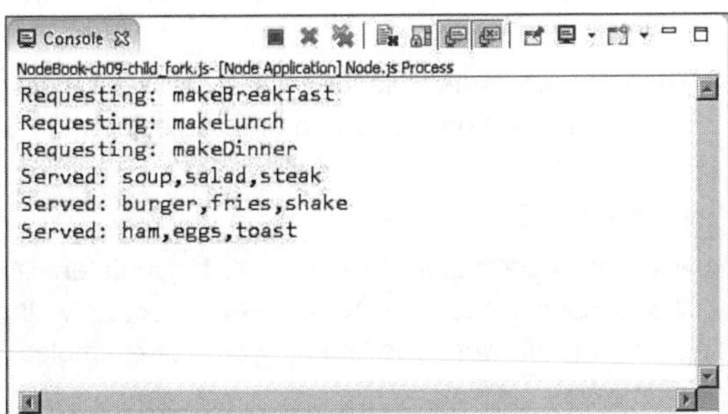

Figure 9.5 Output of executing three child processes in parallel using `fork()`.

Implementing Process Clusters

One of the coolest things you can do with Node.js is create a cluster of Node.js instances running in parallel in separate processes on the same machine. You can do this using the techniques you learned in the previous section by forking processes and then using the `send(message, serverHandle)` IPC mechanism to communicate `send()` messages and pass the underlying TCP server handles between them. However, because this is such a common task, Node.js has provided the `cluster` module, which does all that for you automatically.

> **Note**
>
> At this writing, the `cluster` module is still in an unstable state, and therefore the syntax and available options may change from what you see in this chapter. Make sure to check the syntax against the Node.js code when you decide to implement the `cluster` module.

Using the `cluster` Module

The `cluster` module lets you easily implement a cluster of TCP or HTTP servers running in different processes on the same machine but still using the same underlying socket, thus handling requests on the same IP address and port combination. The `cluster` module is simple to implement and provides several events, methods, and properties you can use to initiate and monitor a cluster of Node.js servers.

Table 9.10 lists the events that can be emitted in a `cluster` module application.

Table 9.10 **Events that can be emitted by the `cluster` module**

Event	Description
`fork`	Emitted when a new worker has been forked. The `callback` function receives a `Worker` object as the only argument. For example: `function (Worker)`
`online`	Emitted when the new worker sends back a message indicating that it has started. The `callback` function receives a `Worker` object as the only argument. For example: `function (Worker)`
`listening`	Emitted when the worker calls `listen()` to begin listening on the shared port. The `callback` handler receives the `Worker` object as well as an `address` object indicating the port the worker is listening on. For example: `function (Worker, address)`
`disconnect`	Emitted after the IPC channel has been disconnected, such as when the server calls `worker.disconnect()`. The callback function receives a `Worker` object as the only argument. For example: `function (Worker)`

Event	Description
`exit`	Emitted when the `Worker` object has disconnected. The `callback` handler receives the `worker`, `code`, and `signal` used. For example: `function (Worker, code, signal)`
`setup`	Emitted the first time `setupMaster()` is called.

Table 9.11 lists the methods and properties you can use in the `cluster` module to get information such as whether this node is a worker or the master as well as to configure and implement the forked processes.

Table 9.11 **Methods and properties of the `cluster` module**

Property	Description
`settings`	Contains the `exec`, `args`, and `silent` property values, used to set up the cluster.
`isMaster`	Is `true` if the current process is the cluster master; otherwise, it is `false`.
`isWorker`	Is `true` if the current process is a worker; otherwise, it is `false`.
`setupMaster([settings])`	Accepts an optional `settings` object that contains `exec`, `args`, and `silent` properties. The `exec` property points to the worker JavaScript file. The `args` property is an array of parameters to pass, and `silent` disconnects the IPC mechanism from the worker thread.
`disconnect([callback])`	Disconnects the IPC mechanism from the workers and closes the handles. The callback function is executed when the disconnect finishes.
`worker`	References the current `Worker` object in worker processes. This is not defined in the master process.
`workers`	Contains the `Worker` object, which you can reference by ID from the master process. For example: `cluster.workers[workerId]`

Understanding the `Worker` Object

When a worker process is forked, a new `Worker` object is created in both the master and worker processes. In the worker process, the `Worker` object is used to represent the current worker and interact with cluster events that are occurring. In the master process, the `Worker` object is used to represent child worker processes so that your master application can send messages to them, receive events on their state changes, and even kill them.

Table 9.12 lists the events that `Worker` objects can emit.

Table 9.12 **Events that can be emitted by `Worker` objects**

Event	Description
`message`	Emitted when the worker receives a new message. The callback function is passed `message` as the only parameter.
`disconnect`	Emitted after the IPC channel has been disconnected on this worker.
`exit`	Emitted when this `Worker` object has disconnected.
`error`	Emitted when an error has occurred on this worker.

Table 9.13 lists the methods and properties you can use with `Worker` objects to get information such as whether the node is a worker or the master as well as to configure and implement the forked processes.

Table 9.13 **Methods and properties of `Worker` objects**

Property	Description
`id`	Represents the unique ID of this worker.
`process`	Specifies the `ChildProcess` object this worker is running on.
`suicide`	Is set to `true` when `kill()` or `disconnect()` is called on this worker. You can use this flag to determine whether to break out of loops to try and go down gracefully.
`send(message, [sendHandle])`	Sends a message to the master process.
`kill([signal])`	Kills the current worker process by disconnecting the IPC channel and then exiting. Sets the `suicide` flag to `true`.
`disconnect()`	When called in the worker, closes all servers, waits for the close event, and disconnects the IPC channel. When called from the master, sends an internal message to the worker, causing it to disconnect itself. Sets the `suicide` flag.

Implementing an HTTP Cluster

The best way to illustrate the value of the `cluster` module is to show a basic implementation of Node.js HTTP servers. Listing 9.7 implements a basic cluster of HTTP servers. Lines 4–13 register listeners for the `fork`, `listening`, and `exit` events on cluster workers. Then the code in line 14 calls `setupMaster()` and specifies the worker executable `cluster_worker.js`. Next, lines 15–19 create the workers by calling `cluster.fork()`. Finally, on lines 20–24 the code iterates through the workers and registers an `on('message')` event handler for each one.

The code in Listing 9.8 implements the worker HTTP servers. Notice that the HTTP server sends back a response to the client and then also sends a message to the cluster master on line 7.

The code in Listing 9.9 implements a simple HTTP client that sends a series of requests to test the servers created in Listing 9.8. Figure 9.6 shows the output of the servers, and Figure 9.7 shows the output of the clients. Notice that the output in Figure 9.7 shows that the requests are being handled by different processes on the server.

Listing 9.7 `cluster_server.js`: **A master process creating up to four worker processes**

```
01 var cluster = require('cluster');
02 var http = require('http');
03 if (cluster.isMaster) {
04   cluster.on('fork', function(worker) {
05     console.log("Worker " + worker.id + " created");
06   });
07   cluster.on('listening', function(worker, address) {
08     console.log("Worker " + worker.id +" is listening on " +
09                 address.address + ":" + address.port);
10   });
11   cluster.on('exit', function(worker, code, signal) {
12     console.log("Worker " + worker.id +" Exited");
13   });
14   cluster.setupMaster({exec:'cluster_worker.js'});
15   var numCPUs = require('os').cpus().length;
16   for (var i = 0; i < numCPUs; i++) {
17     if (i>=4) break;
18     cluster.fork();
19   }
20   Object.keys(cluster.workers).forEach(function(id) {
21     cluster.workers[id].on('message', function(message){
22       console.log(message);
23     });
24   });
25 }
```

Listing 9.8 `cluster_worker.js`: **A worker process implementing an HTTP server**

```
var cluster = require('cluster');
var http = require('http');
if (cluster.isWorker) {
  http.Server(function(req, res) {
    res.writeHead(200);
    res.end("Process " + process.pid + " says hello");
    process.send("Process " + process.pid + " handled request");
  }).listen(8080, function(){
    console.log("Child Server Running on Process: " + process.pid);
  });
};
```

Listing 9.9 `cluster_client.js`: **An HTTP client sending a series of requests to test the server**

```
var http = require('http');
var options = { port: '8080'};
function sendRequest(){
  http.request(options, function(response){
    var serverData = '';
    response.on('data', function (chunk) {
      serverData += chunk;
    });
    response.on('end', function () {
      console.log(serverData);
    });
  }).end();
}
for (var i=0; i<5; i++){
  console.log("Sending Request");
  sendRequest();
}
```

```
Console
NodeBook-ch09-cluster_server.js- [Node Application] Node.js Process
Worker 1 created
Worker 2 created
Worker 3 created
Worker 4 created
Child Server Running on Process: 5068
Worker 1 is listening on 0.0.0.0:8080
Child Server Running on Process: 6744
Worker 4 is listening on 0.0.0.0:8080
Child Server Running on Process: 1744
Worker 2 is listening on 0.0.0.0:8080
Child Server Running on Process: 7288
Worker 3 is listening on 0.0.0.0:8080
Process 7288 handled request
Process 1744 handled request
Process 7288 handled request
Process 7288 handled request
Process 1744 handled request
```

Figure 9.6 Output of the cluster server, showing creation and interaction with workers.

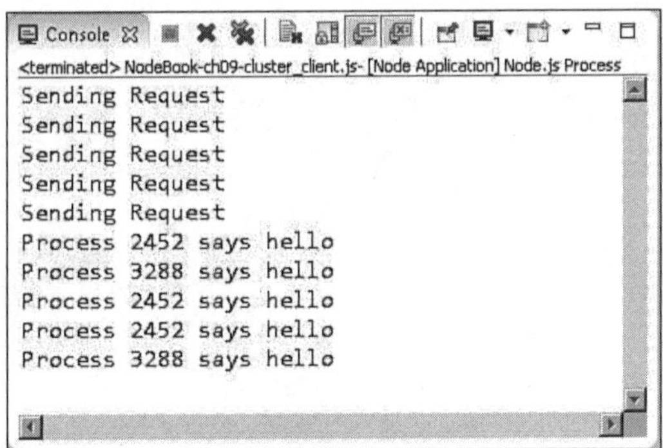

Figure 9.7 Output of the cluster client, showing results including process IDs of worker processes.

Summary

To make the most of Node.js performance on servers with multiple processors, you need to be able to farm off work to the other processes. The `process` module allows you to interact with the system process, the `child_process` module allows you to actually execute code on a separate process, and the `cluster` module allows you to create a cluster of HTTP or TCP servers.

`child_process` provides the `exec()`, `execFile()`, `spawn()`, and `fork()` functions, which start work on separate processes. The `ChildProcess` and `Worker` objects provide IPC channels that allow you to communicate between the parent and child processes.

Up Next

In the next chapter, you will see some of the other modules that Node.js provides. For example, the `os` module provides tools to interact with the operating system, and the `util` module provides useful functionality.

10

Using Additional Node.js Modules

The purpose of this chapter is to expose you to some of the additional built-in capabilities in Node.js. The `os` module exposes aspects of the operating system that can be useful when implementing applications. The `util` module provides various functionality, such as synchronous output, string formatting, and inheritance enhancements. The `dns` module enables you to perform DNS lookups and reverse lookups from a Node.js application.

The following sections describe these modules and how to utilize them in your Node.js applications. Some of the methods should already be familiar to you because you have seen them in previous chapters.

Using the `os` Module

The `os` module provides an extremely useful set of functions that allow you to get information from the operating system. For example, when accessing data from a stream that comes from the OS, you can use the `os.endianness()` function to determine whether the OS is big endian or little endian so that you can use the correct read and write methods.

Table 10.1 lists the methods provided by the `os` module and describes how you can use them.

Table 10.1 **Methods that can be called in the `os` module**

Method	Description
`tmpdir()`	Returns a string path to the default temp directory for the OS. This is useful if you need to store files temporarily and then remove them later.
`endianness()`	Returns `BE` or `LE` for big endian or little endian, depending on the architecture of the machine.
`hostname()`	Returns the hostname defined for the machine. This can be useful when implementing network services that require a hostname.

Method	Description
`type()`	Returns the OS type as a string.
`platform()`	Returns the platform as a string (for example, `win32`, `linux`, or `freeBSD`).
`arch()`	Returns back the platform architecture. For example: `x86` or `x64`.
`release()`	Returns the OS version release.
`uptime()`	Returns a timestamp, in seconds, indicating how long the OS has been running.
`loadavg()`	On UNIX-based systems, returns an array of values containing the system load value for `[1, 5, 15]` minutes.
`totalmem()`	Returns an integer specifying the system memory, in bytes.
`freemem()`	Returns an integer specifying the free system memory, in bytes.
`cpus()`	Returns an array of objects that describes the `model`, `speed`, and `times`. This array contains the amount of time the CPU has spent in `user`, `nice`, `sys`, `idle`, and `irq`.
`networkInterfaces()`	Returns an array of objects that describes the `address` and `family` of addresses bound on each network interface in your system.
`EOL`	Contains the appropriate end-of-line characters for the operating system (for example, `\n` or `\r\n`). This can be useful for making an application cross-platform compatible when processing string data.

To help you visualize using the `os` module, the code in Listing 10.1 includes each of the `os` module calls. Figure 10.1 shows the output.

Listing 10.1 `os_info.js`: **Calling methods on the `os` module**

```
var os = require('os');
console.log("tmpdir :\t" + os.tmpdir());
console.log("endianness :\t" + os.endianness());
console.log("hostname :\t" + os.hostname());
console.log("type :\t\t" + os.type());
console.log("platform :\t" + os.platform());
console.log("arch :\t\t" + os.arch());
console.log("release :\t" + os.release());
console.log("uptime :\t" + os.uptime());
console.log("loadavg :\t" + os.loadavg());
console.log("totalmem :\t" + os.totalmem());
console.log("freemem :\t" + os.freemem());
console.log("EOL :\t" + os.EOL);
```

```
console.log("cpus :\t\t" + JSON.stringify(os.cpus()));
console.log("networkInterfaces : " +
            JSON.stringify(os.networkInterfaces()));
```

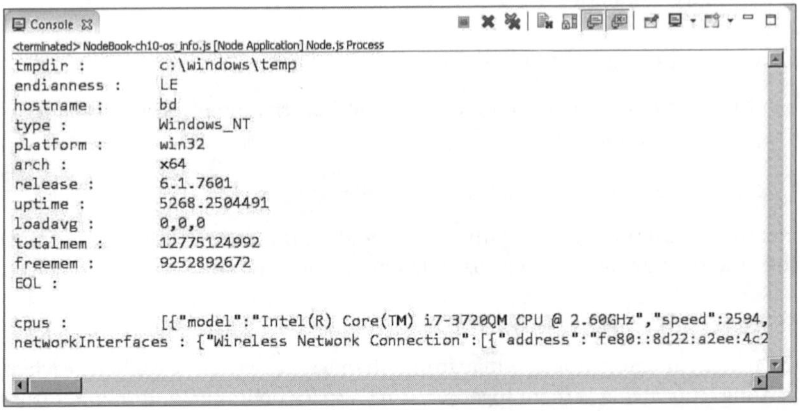

```
Console
<terminated> NodeBook-ch10-os_info.js [Node Application] Node.js Process
tmpdir :            c:\windows\temp
endianness :        LE
hostname :          bd
type :              Windows_NT
platform :          win32
arch :              x64
release :           6.1.7601
uptime :            5268.2504491
loadavg :           0,0,0
totalmem :          12775124992
freemem :           9252892672
EOL :

cpus :              [{"model":"Intel(R) Core(TM) i7-3720QM CPU @ 2.60GHz","speed":2594,
networkInterfaces : {"Wireless Network Connection":[{"address":"fe80::8d22:a2ee:4c2
```

Figure 10.1 Output from calling methods on the `os` module.

Using the `util` Module

The `util` module is kind of a catch-all module. It provides utility functions for formatting strings, converting objects to strings, checking object types, and performing synchronous writes to output streams, as well as some object inheritance enhancements.

The following sections cover most of the functionality in the `util` module. They also explain ways to use the `util` module in your Node.js applications.

Formatting Strings

When you're handling string data, you commonly need to format strings quickly. Node.js provides a rudimentary string formatting method in the `util` module that handles many string formatting needs. The `util.format()` function accepts a formatter string as the first argument and returns a formatted string. The following is the syntax for the `format()` method, where `format` is the formatter string and `[...]` represents the arguments that follow:

```
util.format(format, [...])
```

The `format` argument is a string that can contain zero or more placeholders. Each placeholder begins with a `%` character and is eventually replaced with the converted string value from its corresponding argument. The first formatter placeholder represents the second argument and so on. The following placeholders are supported:

- **%s:** Specifies a string.
- **%d:** Specifies a number (can be integer or float).
- **%j:** Specifies a JSON stringifyable object.
- **%:** If left empty, does not act as a placeholder.

Keep in mind the following when using `format()`:

- When there are not as many arguments as placeholders, the placeholders, such as `%s`, are not replaced. For example:

  ```
  util.format('%s = %s', 'Item1'); // 'Item1':%s'
  ```

- When there are more arguments than placeholders, the extra arguments are converted to strings and concatenated with a space delimiter. For example

  ```
  util.format('%s = %s', 'Item1', 'Item2', 'Item3'); // 'Item1 = Item2 Item3'
  ```

- If the first argument is not a format string, then `util.format()` converts each argument to a string, concatenates them together using a space delimiter, and then returns the concatenated string. For example:

  ```
  util.format(1, 2, 3); // '1 2 3'
  ```

Checking Object Types

It is often useful to determine whether an object you have gotten back from a command is of a certain type. You can do this in a couple different ways. For example, one way is to use the `isinstanceof` operator, which compares the object types and returns `true` or `false`. For example:

```
([1,2,3] instance of Array) //true
```

The `util` module also provides the `isArray(object)`, `isRegExp(object)`, `isDate(object)`, and `isError(object)` convenience methods to determine whether an object is an `Array`, `RexExp`, `Date`, or `Error` object. For example:

```
(util.isArray([1,2,3]) //true.
```

Synchronous Writing to Output Streams

A useful feature of the `util` module is the ability to write data out to `stdout` and `stderr` synchronously, which means blocking the process until the data is written out. This allows you to ensure that when the data is written, the system wasn't in the act of changing it.

To synchronously write data out, you can use one of the following calls, each of which blocks the process until the write completes:

- **`util.debug(string)`**: Writes the `string` out to `stderr`.
- **`util.error([...])`**: Accepts multiple arguments and writes them out to `stderr`. For example:

  ```
  util.error(errorCode, "errorname");
  ```

- **`util.puts([...])`**: Accepts multiple arguments and writes them out to `stdout`.
- **`util.print([...])`**: Accepts multiple arguments, converts each one to a string, and then writes them out to `stdout`.
- **`util.log(string)`**: Writes the `string` out to `stdout`, along with a timestamp. For example:

  ```
  util.log('Some message.');  //  30 Nov 13:26:20 - Some message.
  ```

Converting JavaScript Objects to Strings

Often, especially when debugging, you need to convert a JavaScript object into a string representation. The `util.inspect()` method allows you to inspect an object and then return a string representation of the object.

The following is the syntax for the `inspect()` method:

```
util.inspect(object, [options])
```

The `object` parameter is the JavaScript object you want to convert to a string. The `options` method allows you to control certain aspects of the formatting process. `options` can contain the following properties:

- **`showHidden`**: When set to `true`, the non-enumerable properties of the object are also converted into the string. Defaults to `false`.
- **`depth`**: Limits the number of levels deep the inspect process traverses while formatting properties that are also objects. This can prevent infinite loops and also prevent complex objects from costing a lot of CPU cycles. Defaults to `2`; if it is `null`, it can recurse forever.
- **`colors`**: When set to `true`, the output is styled with ANSI color codes. Defaults to `false`.
- **`customInspect`**: When set to `false`, any custom `inspect()` functions defined on the objects being inspected are not called. Defaults to `true`.

You can attach your own `inspect()` function to an object in order to control the output. The following code creates an object with `first` and `last` properties, and `inspect()` outputs only a `name` property:

```
var obj = { first:'Brad', last:'Dayley' };
obj.inspect = function(depth) {
  return '{ name: "' + this.first + " " + this.last + '" }';
};
console.log(util.inspect(obj));
// { name: "Brad Dayley" }
```

Inheriting Functionality from Other Objects

The `util` Module provides the `util.inherits()` method to allow you to create objects that inherit the `prototype` methods from another object. When you create a new object, the `prototype` methods are automatically used. You have already seen this in a few examples in this book—for example, when implementing your own custom `Readable` and `Writable` streams.

The following is the syntax of the `util.inherits()` method:

```
util.inherits(constructor, superConstructor)
```

The prototype `constructor` is set to the prototype `superConstructor` and is executed when a new object is created. You can access `superConstructor` from your custom object constructor by using that `constructor.super_` property.

Listing 10.2 illustrates using `inherits()` to inherit the `events.EventEmitter` object constructor to create a `Writable` stream. Notice that on line 11 the object is an instance of `events.EventEmitter`. Also notice that on line 12 the `Writer.super_` value is `eventsEmitter`. Figure 10.2 shows the results of Listing 10.2.

Listing 10.2 `util_inherit.js`: **Using** `inherits()` **to inherit the prototypes from** `event.EventEmitter`

```
01 var util = require("util");
02 var events = require("events");
03 function Writer() {
04   events.EventEmitter.call(this);
05 }
06 util.inherits(Writer, events.EventEmitter);
07 Writer.prototype.write = function(data) {
08   this.emit("data", data);
09 };
10 var w = new Writer();
11 console.log(w instanceof events.EventEmitter);
12 console.log(Writer.super_ === events.EventEmitter);
13 w.on("data", function(data) {
14     console.log('Received data: "' + data + '"');
15 });
16 w.write("Some Data!");
```

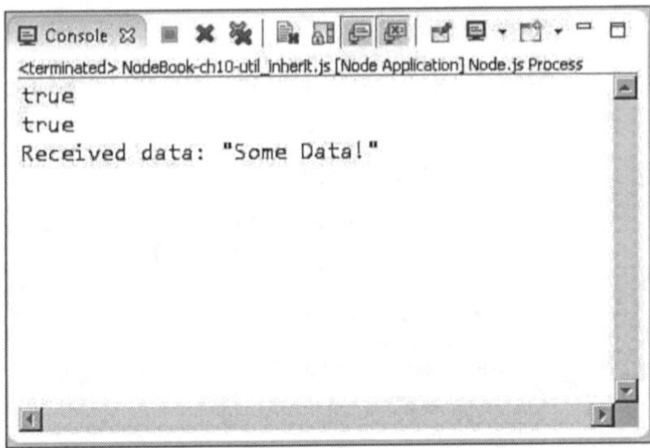

Figure 10.2 Output from implementing `inherits()` to build a `Writable` stream.

Using the `dns` Module

If you want a Node.js application to resolve DNS domain names, look up domains, or do reverse lookups, then you will find the `dns` module very helpful. A DNS lookup contacts the domain name server and requests records about a specific domain name. A reverse lookup contacts the domain name server and requests the DNS name associated with an IP address. The `dns` module provides functionality for most of the lookups you may need to perform. Table 10.2 lists the methods, their syntax, and what they do.

Table 10.2 **Methods that can be called on the `dns` module**

Method	Description
`lookup(domain, [family], callback)`	Resolves `domain`. The `family` attribute can be `4`, `6`, or `null`, where `4` resolves the first found `A` (IPv4) record, `6` resolves the first found `AAAA` (IPv6) record, and `null` resolves both. The default is `null`. The callback function receives an `error` as the first argument and an array of IP `addresses` as the second. For example: `function (error, addresses)`

Method	Description
`resolve(domain, [rrtype], callback)`	Resolves `domain` into an array of record types specified by `rrtype`. `rrtype` can be: ▪ `A`: IPv4 addresses (default) ▪ `AAAA`: IPv6 addresses ▪ `MX`: Mail Exchange records ▪ `TXT`: Text records ▪ `SRV`: SRV records ▪ `PTR`: Reverse IP lookups ▪ `NS`: Name server records ▪ `CNAME`: Canonical name records The callback function receives an `error` as the first argument and an array of IP `addresses` as the second. For example: `function (error, addresses)`
`resolve4(domain, callback)`	Same as `dns.resolve()` except only for `A` records.
`resolve6(domain, callback)`	Same as `dns.resolve()` except only for `AAAA` records.
`resolveMx(domain, callback)`	Same as `dns.resolve()` except only for `MX` records.
`resolveTxt(domain, callback)`	Same as `dns.resolve()` except only for `TXT` records.
`resolveSrv(domain, callback)`	Same as `dns.resolve()` except only for `SRV` records.
`resolveNs(domain, callback)`	Same as `dns.resolve()` except only for `NS` records.
`resolveCname(domain, callback)`	Same as `dns.resolve()` except only for `CNAME` records.
`reverse(ip, callback)`	Does a reverse lookup on the IP address. The callback function receives an `error` object if an error occurs and an array of `domains` if the lookup is successful. For example: `function (error, domains)`

Listing 10.3 shows how to perform lookups and reverse lookups. In line 3, `resolve4()` looks up the IPv4 addresses, and then in lines 5–8, `reverse()` is called on those same addresses and performs the reverse lookup. The output is shown in Figure 10.3.

Listing 10.3 `dns_lookup.js`: **Performing lookups and reverse lookups on domains and IP addresses**

```
var dns = require('dns');
console.log("Resolving www.google.com . . .");
dns.resolve4('www.google.com', function (err, addresses) {
  console.log('IPv4 addresses: ' + JSON.stringify(addresses, false, ' '));
  addresses.forEach(function (addr) {
    dns.reverse(addr, function (err, domains) {
      console.log('Reverse for ' + addr + ': ' + JSON.stringify(domains));
    });
  });
});
```

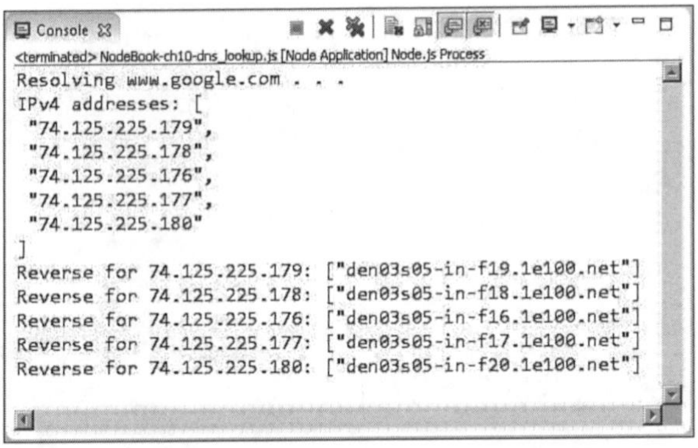

```
Console
<terminated> NodeBook-ch10-dns_lookup.js [Node Application] Node.js Process
Resolving www.google.com . . .
IPv4 addresses: [
 "74.125.225.179",
 "74.125.225.178",
 "74.125.225.176",
 "74.125.225.177",
 "74.125.225.180"
]
Reverse for 74.125.225.179: ["den03s05-in-f19.1e100.net"]
Reverse for 74.125.225.178: ["den03s05-in-f18.1e100.net"]
Reverse for 74.125.225.176: ["den03s05-in-f16.1e100.net"]
Reverse for 74.125.225.177: ["den03s05-in-f17.1e100.net"]
Reverse for 74.125.225.180: ["den03s05-in-f20.1e100.net"]
```

Figure 10.3 Output of performing lookups and DNS names when performing reverse lookups.

Summary

The `os` module allows you to get information about the system, such as the OS type and version, the platform architecture, and programming information such as the free memory, temp folder location, and end-of-line characters. The `util` module is the catch-all library for Node.js that has methods for synchronous output, string formatting, and type checking. The `dns` module enables you to perform DNS lookups and reverse lookups from a Node.js application.

Up Next

In the next chapter, you will jump into the world of MongoDB. You'll learn MongoDB basics and how to implement MongoDB in the Node.js world.

11

Understanding NoSQL and MongoDB

At the core of most large-scale web applications and services is a high-performance data storage solution. The backend data store is responsible for storing everything from user account information to shopping cart items to blog and comment data. Good web applications need to be able to store and retrieve data with accuracy, speed, and reliability. Therefore, the data storage mechanism you choose must be able to perform at a level to satisfy user demand.

Several different data storage solutions are available to store and retrieve data needed by web applications. The three most common are direct file system storage in files, relational databases, and NoSQL databases. This book focuses on the third type: a NoSQL database called MongoDB.

The following sections describe MongoDB and discuss the design considerations you need to think about before deciding how to implement the structure for your data and the configuration for your database. This chapter covers the questions to ask yourself and also the mechanisms built into MongoDB to satisfy the demands of the answers to those questions.

Why NoSQL?

NoSQL (which is short for Not Only SQL) consists of technologies that provide storage and retrieval without the tightly constrained models of traditional SQL relational databases. The main motivations behind NoSQL are simplified designs, horizontal scaling, and finer control of the availability of data.

The idea of NoSQL is to break away from the traditional structure of relational databases and allow developers to implement models in ways that more closely fit the data flow needs of their system. NoSQL databases can be implemented in ways that traditional relational databases could never be structured.

There are several different NoSQL technologies, including HBase's column structure, Redis's key/value structure, and Virtuoso's graph structure. However, this book looks at MongoDB and the document model because of the great flexibility and scalability in terms of implementing backend storage for web applications and services. Also, MongoDB is by far the most popular and well supported NoSQL database currently available.

Understanding MongoDB

MongoDB is a NoSQL database based on a document model where data objects are stored as separate documents inside a collection. You use the MongoDB database to implement a data store that provides high performance, high availability, and automatic scaling. MongoDB is extremely simple to install and implement, as you will see in the upcoming chapters.

Understanding Collections

MongoDB groups data together through the use of collections. A *collection* is simply a grouping of documents that have the same or similar purpose. A collection acts much like a table in a traditional SQL database. However, there is a major difference. In MongoDB, a collection is not enforced by a strict schema; instead, documents in a collection can have a slightly different structure from one another, if needed. This reduces the need to break items in a document into several different tables, as is often done in SQL implementations.

Understanding Documents

A *document* is a representation of a single entity of data in a MongoDB database. A *collection* is made up of one or more related objects. There is a major difference between MongoDB and SQL in that MongoDB documents are very different from SQL rows. Row data is very flat, meaning there is one column for each value in the row. However, in MongoDB, documents can contain embedded subdocuments, thus providing a much closer inherent data model to your applications.

In fact, the records in a MongoDB database that represent documents are stored as BSON, which is a lightweight binary form of JSON. In addition, MongoDB field/value pairs correspond to JavaScript property/value pairs. These field/value pairs define the values that are stored in the document. This means there is very little translation necessary to convert MongoDB records back into the JavaScript objects that you will use in your Node.js applications.

For example, a document in MongoDB may be structured like this, with `name`, `version`, `languages`, `admin`, and `paths` fields:

```
{
  name: "New Project",
  version: 1,
  languages: ["JavaScript", "HTML", "CSS"],
  admin: {name: "Brad", password: "****"},
  paths: {temp: "/tmp", project:"/opt/project", html: "/opt/project/html"}
}
```

Notice that the document structure contains fields/properties that are strings, integers, arrays, and objects, just like in a JavaScript object. Table 11.1 lists the different data types that field values can be set to in a BSON document.

The fieldnames cannot contain `null` characters, dots (.), or dollar signs (`$`). Also, the `_id` fieldname is reserved for the object ID. The `_id` field is a unique ID for the system that is made up of the following parts:

- A 4-byte value representing the seconds since the last epoch
- A 3-byte machine identifier
- A 2-byte process ID
- A 3-byte counter, starting with a random value

The maximum size of a document in MongoDB is 16MB. This prevents queries that result in an excessive amount of RAM being used or intensive hits to the file system. Although you may never come close to this number, you need to keep the maximum document size in mind when designing some complex data types that contain file data.

MongoDB Data Types

The BSON data format provides several different types that are used when storing the JavaScript objects to binary form. These types match the JavaScript types as closely as possible. It is important to understand these types because you can actually query MongoDB to find objects that have a specific property which has a value of a certain type. For example, you can look for documents in a database whose timestamp value is a `String` object or query for ones whose timestamp value is a `Date` object.

MongoDB assigns each of the data types an integer ID number from 1 to 255 that is used when querying by type. Table 11.1 shows a list of the data types that MongoDB supports, along with the numbers MongoDB uses to identify them.

Table 11.1 **MongoDB data types and corresponding ID numbers**

Type	Number
`Double`	1
`String`	2
`Object`	3
`Array`	4
`Binary data`	5
`Object id`	7
`Boolean`	8

Type	Number
`Date`	9
`Null`	10
`Regular Expression`	11
`JavaScript`	13
`Symbol`	14
`JavaScript (with scope)`	15
`32-bit integer`	16
`Timestamp`	17
`64-bit integer`	18
`Min Key`	255
`Max Key`	127

Another thing you need to be aware of when working with the different data types in MongoDB is the order in which they are compared. When comparing values of different BSON types, MongoDB uses the following comparison order, from lowest to highest:

1. `Min Key` (internal type)
2. `Null`
3. `Numbers (32-bit integer, 64-bit integer, Double)`
4. `Symbol`, `String`
5. `Object`
6. `Array`
7. `Binary Data`
8. `Object ID`
9. `Boolean`
10. `Date`, `Timestamp`
11. `Regular Expression`
12. `Max Key` (internal type)

Planning Your Data Model

Before you begin implementing a MongoDB database, you need to understand the nature of the data that is being stored, how that data is going to get stored, and how it is going to be accessed. Understanding these concepts will allow you to make determinations ahead of time and structure the data and your application for optimal performance.

Specifically, you should answer the following questions:

- What are the basic objects that the application will be using?
- What is the relationship between the different object types: one-to-one, one-to-many, or many-to-many?
- How often will new objects be added to the database?
- How often will objects be deleted from the database?
- How often will objects be changed?
- How often will objects be accessed?
- How will objects be accessed, by ID, property values, comparisons, etc.?
- How will groups of object types be accessed: by common ID, common property value, etc.?

Once you have the answers to these questions, you are ready to consider the structure of collections and documents inside the MongoDB database. The following sections discuss different methods of document, collection, and database modeling you can utilize in MongoDB to optimize data storage and access.

Normalizing Data with Document References

Data normalization is the process of organizing documents and collections to minimize redundancy and dependency. You normalize data by identifying object properties that are subobjects and that should be stored as a separate document in another collection from the object's document. Typically you do this for objects that have a one-to-many or many-to-many relationship with subobjects.

The advantage of normalizing data is that the database size will be smaller because only a single copy of each object will exist in its own collection instead of duplicated on multiple objects in a single collection. Also, if you modify the information in the subobject frequently, you only need to modify a single instance rather than every record in the object's collection that has that subobject.

A major disadvantage of normalizing data is that when you look up user objects that require the normalized subobject, a separate lookup must occur to link the subobject. This can result in a significant performance hit if you are accessing the user data frequently.

An example of when it makes sense to normalize data is a system that contains users that have a favorite store. Each `User` is an object with `name`, `phone`, and `favoriteStore` properties. The `favoriteStore` property is also a subobject that contains `name`, `street`, `city`, and `zip` properties.

However, thousands of users may have the same favorite store, so there is a high one-to-many relationship there. Therefore, it doesn't make sense to store the `FavoriteStore` object data in each `User` object because that would result in thousands of duplications. Instead, the `FavoriteStore` object should include an `_id` object property that can be referenced from documents in the user's `FavoriteStores` collection. The application can then use the reference ID `favoriteStore` to link data from the `Users` collection to `FavoriteStore` documents in the `FavoriteStores` collection.

Figure 11.1 illustrates the structure of the `Users` and `FavoriteStores` collections described above.

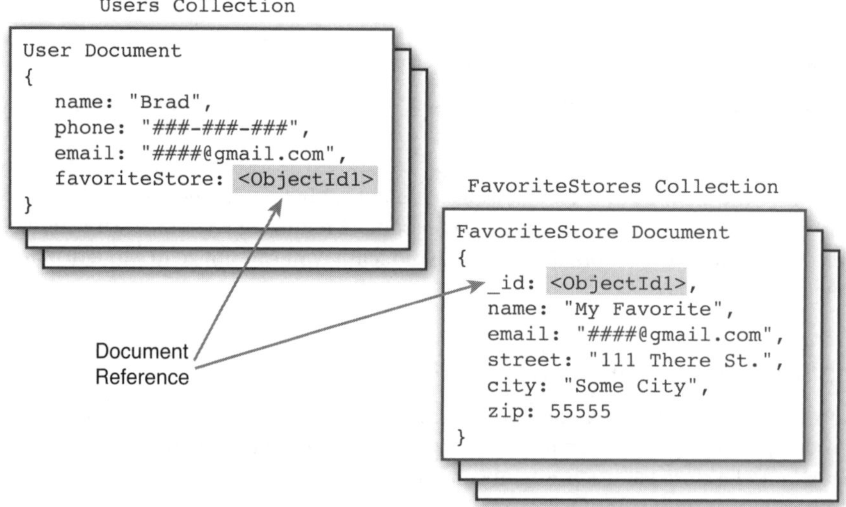

Figure 11.1 Defining normalized MongoDB documents by adding a reference to documents in another collection.

Denormalizing Data with Embedded Documents

Denormalizing data is the process of identifying subobjects of a main object that should be embedded directly into the document of the main object. Typically you do this on objects that have a mostly one-to-one relationship or are relatively small and do not get updated frequently.

The major advantage of denormalized documents is that you can get the full object back in a single lookup, without needing to do additional lookups to combine subobjects from other collections. This is a major performance enhancement. The downside is that for subobjects with a one-to-many relationship, you will be storing a separate copy in each document, which slows down insertion a bit and also takes up additional disk space.

An example of when it makes sense to denormalize data is in a system that contains users with home and work contact information. The user is an object represented by a `User` document with `name`, `home`, and `work` properties. The `home` and `work` properties are subobjects that contain `phone`, `street`, `city`, and `zip` properties.

The `home` and `work` properties do not change very often on the user. You may have multiple users from the same home, but there will not likely be a lot of them, and the actual values inside the subobjects are not really that big and will not change very often. Therefore, it makes sense to store the `home` contact information directly in the `User` object.

The `work` property takes a bit more thinking. How many people are you really going to get who have the same work contact information? If the answer is not many, then the `Work` object should be embedded with the `User` object. How often do you query the `User` object and need the `work` contact information? If the answer is very rarely, then you may want to normalize `work` into its own collection. However, if the answer is frequently or always, then you will likely want to embed `work` with the `User` object.

Figure 11.2 illustrates the structure of the `User` object with home and work contact information embedded, as described above.

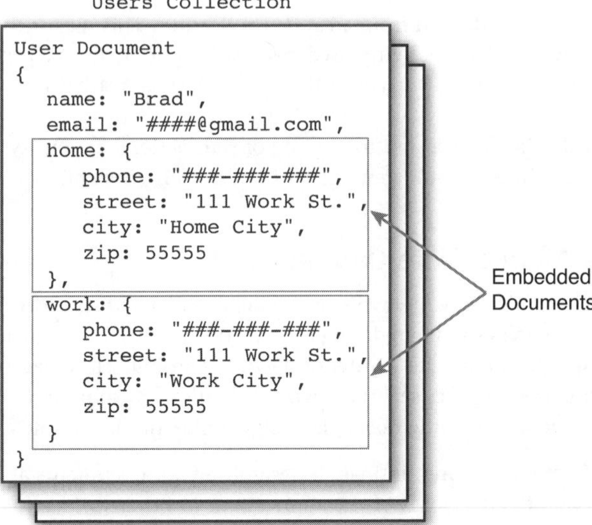

Figure 11.2 Defining denormalized MongoDB documents by implementing embedded objects inside a document.

Using Capped Collections

A great feature of MongoDB is the ability to create a capped collection. A *capped collection* is a collection that has a fixed size. When a new document needs to be written to a collection that exceeds the size of the collection, the oldest document in the collection is deleted, and the new document is inserted. Capped collections work great for objects that have a high rate of insertion, retrieval, and deletion.

The following are the benefits of using capped collections:

- They guarantee that the insert order is preserved. Thus queries do not need to utilize an index to return documents in the order in which they were stored, eliminating the indexing overhead.
- They also guarantee that the insertion order is identical to the order on disk by prohibiting updates that increase the document size. This eliminates the overhead of relocating and managing the new location of documents.
- They automatically remove the oldest documents in the collection. Therefore, you do not need to implement deletion in your application code.

You need to be careful using capped collections, though, because they are subject to the following restrictions:

- Documents cannot be updated to a larger size once they have been inserted into a capped collection. You can update them, but the data must be the same size or smaller.
- Documents cannot be deleted from a capped collection. This means the data takes up space on disk even if it is not being used. You can explicitly drop a capped collection to effectively delete all entries, but you will then need to re-create it in order to use it again.

A great use of capped collections is as a rolling log of transactions in your system. You can always access the last *X* number of log entries without needing to explicitly clean up the oldest.

Understanding Atomic Write Operations

Write operations are atomic, only one write at a time, at the document level in MongoDB. This means that only one process can be updating a single document or a single collection at a time. Therefore, writing to documents that are denormalized is atomic. However, writing to documents that are normalized requires separated write operations to subobjects in other collections, and therefore the writes of the normalized object may not be atomic as a whole.

You need to keep atomic writes in mind when designing your documents and collections to ensure that your design fits the needs of the application. In other words, if you absolutely must write all parts of an object as a whole in an atomic manner, then you need to design the object in a denormalized fashion.

Considering Document Growth

When you update a document, you need to consider what effect the new data will have on document growth. MongoDB provides some padding in documents to allow for typical growth during an update operation. However, if an update causes a document to grow until it exceeds the allocated space on disk, MongoDB has to relocate that document to a new location on the disk, incurring a performance hit on the system. Also, frequent document relocation can lead to disk fragmentation issues—for example, if a document contains an array and you add enough elements to the array.

One way to mitigate document growth is to utilize normalized objects for the properties that may grow frequently. For example, instead of using an array to store items in a `Cart` object, you could create a collection for `CartItems` and store new items that get placed in the `Cart` object as new documents in the `CartItems` collection and reference the user's `Cart` items within them.

Identifying Indexing, Sharding, and Replication Opportunities

MongoDB provides several mechanisms to optimize performance, scaling, and reliability. As you are contemplating your database design, you should consider each of the following options:

- **Indexing:** Indexes improve performance for frequent queries by building a lookup index that can be easily sorted. The `_id` property of a collection is automatically indexed on since it is a common practice to look items up by ID. However, you also need to consider what other ways users access data before you implement indexes that will enhance those lookup methods as well.
- **Sharding:** Sharding is the process of slicing up large collections of data that can be split between multiple MongoDB servers in a cluster. Each MongoDB server is considered a shard. This provides the benefit of utilizing multiple servers to support a large number of requests to a large system. It thus provides horizontal scaling to your database. You should look at the size of your data and the number of requests that will be accessing it to determine whether and how much to shard your collections.
- **Replications:** Replication is the process of duplicating data on multiple MongoDB instances in a cluster. When considering the reliability aspect of a database, you should implement replication to ensure that a backup copy of data that is critical is always readily available.

Large Collections Versus Large Numbers of Collections

Another important thing to consider when designing MongoDB documents and collections is the number of collections that the design will require. There really isn't a significant performance hit for having a large number of collections, but there is a performance hit for having large numbers of items in the same collection. You should consider ways to break up your larger collections into more consumable chunks.

Say, for example that you store a history of user transactions in a database for past purchases. You recognize that for these completed purchases, you will never need to look them up together for multiple users. You only need them available for a user to look at his or her own history. If you have thousands of users who have a lot of transactions, then it makes sense to store those histories in a separate collection for each user.

Deciding on Data Life Cycles

One of the most commonly overlooked aspects of database design is the data life cycle. How long should documents exist in a specific collection? Some collections have documents that should be indefinite—for example, active user accounts. However, keep in mind that each document in the system incurs a performance hit when querying a collection. You should define a TTL, or time-to-live, value for documents in each of your collections.

There are several ways to implement a time-to-live mechanism in MongoDB. One of them is to implement code in your application to monitor and clean up old data. Another method is to utilize the MongoDB `TTL` setting on a collection, which allows you to define a profile where documents are automatically deleted after a certain number of seconds or at a specific clock time. Another method for collections where you need only the most recent documents is to implement a capped collection that automatically keeps the size of the collection small.

Considering Data Usability and Performance

One of the most important things to consider when designing a MongoDB database is data use and how it will affect performance. The previous sections describe different methods for solving some of the complexities of data size and optimization. The final thing you should consider and even reconsider is data usability and performance. Ultimately these are the two most important aspects of any web solution and, consequently, the storage behind it.

Data usability is the ability of a database to satisfy the functionality of a website. You need to make certain that data can be accessed so that the website functions correctly. Users will not tolerate a website that simply does not do what they want it to. The accuracy of the data is also important here.

Then you can consider performance. Your database must be able to deliver the data at a reasonable rate. The previous sections of this chapter help you evaluate and design the performance factors for your database.

In some more complex circumstances, you may find it necessary to evaluate data usability and then performance and then go back to usability, through a few cycles until you get the balance correct. Also, remember that today, the usability requirements can change at any time. Remember this can influence how you design your documents and collections so that they can become more scalable in the future, if necessary.

Summary

At the core of most large-scale web applications and services is a high-performance data storage solution. The backend data store is responsible for storing everything from user account information to shopping cart items to blog and comment data. Good web applications must be able to store and retrieve data with accuracy, speed, and reliability. Therefore, the data storage mechanism you choose must be able to perform at a level that satisfies user demand.

There are several different data storage solutions available to store and retrieve data needed by your web applications. The three most common are direct file system storage in files, relational databases, and NoSQL databases. The data store this book focuses on is MongoDB, which is a NoSQL database.

In this chapter you learned about MongoDB and design considerations for the structure of data and configuration of a database. You learned about collections, documents, and the types of data that can be stored in them. You also learned how to plan your data model, what questions you need to answer, and the mechanisms built into MongoDB to satisfy the demands your database needs.

Up Next

In the next chapter, you'll get a chance to install MongoDB. You will also see how to utilize the MongoDB shell to set up user accounts and access collections and documents.

12

Getting Started with MongoDB

This chapter will get you up to speed with MongoDB. Whereas Chapter 11, "Understanding NoSQL and MongoDB," focuses on the MongoDB theory side of things, this chapter is all about practical application. You will learn what it takes to install MongoDB, start and stop the engine, and access the MongoDB shell. The MongoDB shell allows you to administer the MongoDB server as well as perform every necessary function on MongoDB databases. Using the MongoDB shell is a vital aspect of the development process as well as database administration.

This chapter covers installing MongoDB and accessing the shell. Then you'll learn some basic administrative tasks, such as setting up user accounts and authentication. The chapter wraps up with sections on how to administer databases, collections, and documents.

Building the MongoDB Environment

To get started with MongoDB, the first task is to install it on your development system. Then you can play around with its functionality, learn the MongoDB shell, and prep for Chapter 13, "Getting Started with MongoDB and Node.js," where you will begin integrating MongoDB in your Node.js applications.

The following sections cover installing, starting, and stopping the database engine and accessing the shell client. When you are able to do those things, you are ready to begin using MongoDB in your environment.

Installing MongoDB

The first step in getting MongoDB implemented in your Node.js environment is to install the MongoDB server. There is a version of MongoDB for each of the major platforms: Linux, Windows, Solaris, and OS X. There is also an enterprise version available for the Red Hat, SuSE, Ubuntu, and Amazon Linux distributions. The enterprise version of MongoDB is subscription based and provides enhanced security, management, and integration support.

For the purposes of this book and learning MongoDB, the standard edition of MongoDB is perfect. Before continuing on with this chapter, you should go to http://docs.mongodb.org/manual/installation/ and follow the instructions to download and install MongoDB in your environment. Here are the steps you need to follow:

1. Download and extract the MongoDB files.
2. Add `<mongo_install_location>/bin` to your system path.
3. Create the data files directory `<mongo_data_location>/data/db`.
4. Start MongoDB, using the following from the console prompt:

```
mongod -dbpath <mongo_data_location>/data/db
```

Starting MongoDB

Once you have installed MongoDB, you need to be able to start and stop the database engine. You start it by executing the `mongod` executable (`mongod.exe` on Windows) at `<mongo_install_location>/bin`. This executable starts MongoDB and begins listening for database requests on the configured port.

You can control the `mongod` executable by setting several different parameters. For example, you can configure the IP address and port that MongoDB listens on, as well as logging and authentication. Table 12.1 provides a list of some of the most commonly used parameters.

Here's an example of starting MongoDB with `port` and `dbpath` parameters:

```
mongod -port 28008 -dbpath <mongo_data_location>/data/db
```

Table 12.1 `mongod` **command-line parameters**

Parameter	Description
`--help, -h`	Returns basic help and usage text.
`--version`	Returns the version of MongoDB.
`--config` *<filename>*, `-f` *<filename>*	Specifies a configuration file that contains runtime configurations.
`--verbose, -v`	Increases the amount of internal reporting sent to the console and written to the log file, specified by `--logpath`.
`--quiet`	Reduces the amount of reporting sent to the console and log file.
`--port` *<port>*	Specifies a TCP port for `mongod` to listen for client connections. The default is `27017`.
`--bind_ip` *<ip address>*	Specifies the IP address to which `mongod` will bind and listen for connections. The default is `All Interfaces`.
`--maxConns` *<number>*	Specifies the maximum number of simultaneous connections that `mongod` will accept. The maximum is `20000`.

Parameter	Description
`--logpath <path>`	Specifies a path for the log file. On restart, the log file is overwritten unless you also specify `--logappend`.
`--auth`	Enables database authentication for users connecting from remote hosts.
`--dbpath <path>`	Specifies a directory for the `mongod` instance to store its data.
`--nohttpinterface`	Disables the HTTP interface.
`--nojournal`	Disables journaling.
`--noprealloc`	Disables the pre-allocation of data files, which shortens the startup time but can cause significant performance penalties during normal operations.
`--repair`	Runs a repair routine on all databases.

Stopping MongoDB

Each platform has different methods of stopping the `mongod` executable once it has started. However, one of the best methods is to do it from the shell client because that cleanly shuts down the current operations and forces `mongod` to exit.

To stop the MongoDB database you should open the shell client by executing the following command in a console window to open the MongoDB shell client:

```
mongo
```

Then from the MongoDB shell client, use the following commands to switch to the `admin` database and then shut down the database engine:

```
use admin
db.shutdownServer()
```

Accessing MongoDB from the Shell Client

Once you have installed, configured, and started MongoDB, you can access it through the MongoDB shell. The MongoDB shell is an interactive shell provided with MongoDB that allows you to access, configure, and administer MongoDB databases, users, and much more. You use the shell for everything from setting up user accounts to creating databases to querying the contents of the database.

The following sections take you through some of the most common administration tasks that you will be performing in the MongoDB shell. Here you will learn how to create user accounts, databases, and collections so that you will be able to follow the examples in the rest of the book. Also, you should be able to perform at least rudimentary queries on documents to better troubleshoot any problems with accessing data.

To start the MongoDB shell, execute the `mongo` command at the console prompt, and the shell should start up as shown in Figure 12.1.

```
MongoDB shell version: 2.4.8
connecting to: test
Welcome to the MongoDB shell.
For interactive help, type "help".
For more comprehensive documentation, see
        http://docs.mongodb.org/
Questions? Try the support group
        http://groups.google.com/group/mongodb-user
> _
```

Figure 12.1 Starting the MongoDB shell.

Once you have accessed the MongoDB shell, you will be able to administer all aspects of MongoDB. Keep in mind that when you are using the MongoDB shell, it is based on JavaScript and therefore most JavaScript syntax is available. You should also remember that the shell provides direct access to the database and collections on the server so changes you make and tasks you perform in the shell directly impact the data and performance on the server.

Understanding MongoDB Shell Commands

The MongoDB shell provides several commands that you can execute from the shell prompt. You need to be familiar with these commands because you will be using them a lot:

- **help <*option*>:** Displays syntax help for MongoDB shell commands. The `option` argument allows you to specify a specific area where you want help.
- **use <*database*>:** Changes the current `database` handle. Database operations will be processed on the current database handle.
- **show <*option*>:** Shows a list based on the `option` argument. The value of `option` can be:
  - **dbs:** Displays a list of databases.
  - **collections:** Displays a list of collections for the current database.
  - **profile:** Displays the most recent `system.profile` entries that take more than 1 millisecond.
  - **log [name]:** Displays the last segment of login memory. If nothing is specified for `name`, then `global` is used.
- **exit:** Exits the database.

Understanding MongoDB Shell Methods

The MongoDB shell provides a number of methods for performing administrative functions. You can call these methods directly from the MongoDB shell or from a script that is executed in the MongoDB shell.

You will be using a large number of methods to perform various administrative functions. Some of these are covered in later sections and chapters in this book. For now, you need to be aware of the types of shell methods and how to access them. The following list provides a few examples of shell methods:

- **`load(script)`**: Loads and runs a JavaScript file inside the shell. Using it is a great way to script operations for the database.
- **`UUID(string)`**: Converts a 32-byte hex string into a BSON UUID.
- **`db.auth(username, password)`**: Authenticates you to the current database.

There are a lot of other shell methods. Many of them are covered in subsequent sections. For a full list of the native methods, check out http://docs.mongodb.org/manual/reference/method/#native.

Understanding Command Parameters and Results

The MongoDB shell is an interactive JavaScript shell that is tightly coupled with the MongoDB data structure. This means that much of the data interaction—from parameters passed to methods to data being returned from methods—is standard MongoDB documents, which are in most respects simply JavaScript objects. For example, when creating a user, you pass in a document similar to the following to define the user:

```
db.addUser( { user: "testUser",
              userSource: "test",
              roles: [ "read" ],
              otherDBRoles: { testDB2: [ "readWrite" ] } } )
```

And when you're listing the users for a database to the shell, the users are shown as a list of documents similar to this:

```
> db.system.users.find()
{ "_id" : ObjectId("529e71927c798d1dd56a63d9"), "user" : "dbadmin",
  "pwd" : "78384f4d73368bd2d3a3e1da926dd269",
  "roles": [  "readWriteAnyDatabase",  "dbAdminAnyDatabase",  "clusterAdmin" ] }
{ "_id" : ObjectId("52a098861db41f82f6e3d489"), "user" : "useradmin",
  "pwd" : "0b4568ab22a52a6b494fd54e64fcee9f",
  "roles" : [  "userAdminAnyDatabase" ] }
```

Scripting the MongoDB Shell

As you have seen, the commands, methods, and data structure of the MongoDB shell are based on interactive JavaScript. A great method of administering MongoDB is creating scripts that can be run multiple times or that can be ready to run at specific times, such as at upgrade.

A script file can contain any number of MongoDB commands, using JavaScript code such as conditional statements and loops. There are two ways to run a MongoDB shell script. The first is from the command line, using `--eval`. The `--eval` parameter accepts a JavaScript string or a JavaScript file and launches the MongoDB shell and immediately executes the JavaScript.

For example, the following command starts the MongoDB shell and executes `db.getCollections()` on the test database. Then it outputs the JSON string results as shown in Figure 12.2:

```
mongo test --eval "printjson(db.getCollectionNames())"
```

> **Note**
>
> If are using authentication, which you should, the script may need to authenticate to perform the commands.

You can also run a MongoDB shell script by using the `load(script_path)` method. This method loads a JavaScript file and immediately executes it. For example, the following shell command loads and executes the `db_update.js` script file:

```
load("/tmp/db_update.js")
```

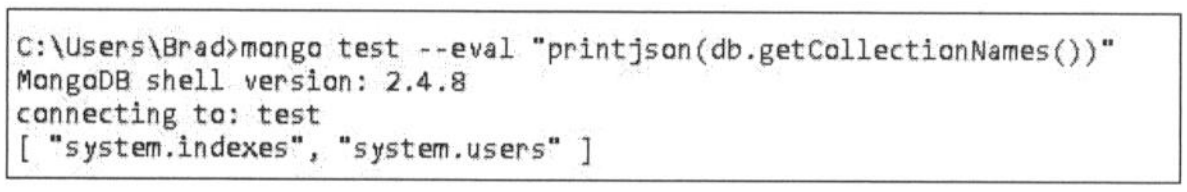

```
C:\Users\Brad>mongo test --eval "printjson(db.getCollectionNames())"
MongoDB shell version: 2.4.8
connecting to: test
[ "system.indexes", "system.users" ]
```

Figure 12.2 Executing a JavaScript file from the MongoDB shell command line.

Administering User Accounts

Once you have MongoDB up and running one of the first things you will want to do is add users to be able to access the database. MongoDB provides the ability to add, remove, and configure users from the MongoDB shell. The following sections discuss using the MongoDB shell to administer user accounts.

Listing Users

User accounts are stored in the `db.system.users` collection of each database. The `User` object contains `_id`, `user`, `pwd`, `roles`, and sometimes `otherDBRoles` fields. There are a couple different ways to get a list of user objects. The first is to change the database to the one you want to list users on and then execute the `show users` command. The following example changes to the `admin` database and lists users as shown in Figure 12.3:

```
use admin
show users
```

You can also use a query such as `find` on the `db.system.users` collection. However, `db.system.users.find()` returns a cursor object that you can use to access the `User` documents. For example, the following code gets a cursor for users in the `admin` database and returns the count of users:

```
use admin
cur = db.system.users.find()
cur.count()
```

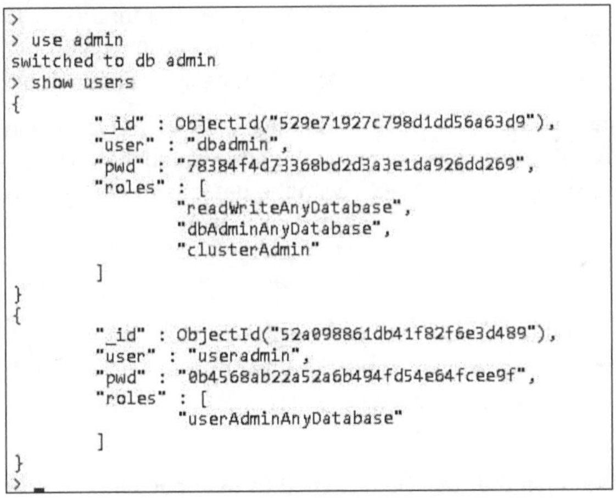

```
>
> use admin
switched to db admin
> show users
{
        "_id" : ObjectId("529e71927c798d1dd56a63d9"),
        "user" : "dbadmin",
        "pwd" : "78384f4d73368bd2d3a3e1da926dd269",
        "roles" : [
                "readWriteAnyDatabase",
                "dbAdminAnyDatabase",
                "clusterAdmin"
        ]
}
{
        "_id" : ObjectId("52a098861db41f82f6e3d489"),
        "user" : "useradmin",
        "pwd" : "0b4568ab22a52a6b494fd54e64fcee9f",
        "roles" : [
                "userAdminAnyDatabase"
        ]
}
> _
```

Figure 12.3 Listing users on the `admin` database.

Creating User Accounts

Once you have created a user administrator, you can use that account to create other user accounts that can administer, read, and write to the databases. You add user accounts by using the `addUser()` method inside the MongoDB shell. The `addUser()` method accepts a `document` object that allows you to specify the user name, roles, and passwords that apply to that user. Table 12.2 lists the fields you can specify in the `document` object.

Table 12.2 **Fields used when creating users with the `addUser()` method**

Field	Format	Description
`user`	`string`	Specifies a unique username.
`roles`	`array`	Specifies an array of user roles. MongoDB provides a large number of roles that you can assign to a user. Table 12.3 lists a few of the common roles.
`pwd`	`hashorstring`	(Optional.) Specifies a user password. When creating the user, this can be a hash or a string; however, it is stored in the database as a hash.
`userSource`	`<database>`	(Optional.) In place of the `pwd` field, points to another database that has the same user defined. The `pwd` or `userSource` of that database is then used as the credentials for the user. The `userSource` field and the `pwd` field are mutually exclusive: A document cannot contain both.
`otherDBRoles`	`{<database>: [array],<database>: [array]}`	(Optional.) Allows you to specify roles that this user has in other databases. The format is a document with the database name as the key and an array of roles in that database that applies to this user.

MongoDB provides a number of roles that you can assign to a user account. These roles enable you to implement intricate privileges and restrictions on user accounts. Table 12.3 lists some of the most common roles that can be assigned to users.

Table 12.3 **Database roles that can be assigned to user accounts**

Role	Description
`read`	Allows the user to read data from any collection in the database.
`readAnyDatabase`	Same as `read` except for all databases.
`readWrite`	Provides all the functionality of `read` and allows the user to write to any collection in the database, including inserting, removing, and updating documents as well as creating, renaming, and dropping collections.
`readWriteAnyDatabase`	Same as `readWrite` except for all databases.
`dbAdmin`	Allows the user to read from and write to the database as well as clean, modify, compact, get the statistics profile, and perform validations.
`dbAdminAnyDatabase`	Same as `dbAdmin` except for all databases.

Role	Description
`clusterAdmin`	Allows the user to generally administer MongoDB, including connections, clustering, replication, listing databases, creating databases, and deleting databases.
`userAdmin`	Allows the user to create and modify user accounts on the database.
`userAdminAnyDatabase`	Same as `userAdmin` except on all databases.

> **Note**
>
> `readAnyDatabase`, `readWriteAnyDatabase`, `dbAdminAnyDatabase`, and `userAdminAnyDatabase` can only be applied to users in the `admin` database because they must apply to all databases.

To create a user, you should switch to that database and then use the `addUser()` method to create the user object. The following MongoDB shell command illustrates creating a basic administrator user to the `test` database:

```
use test
db.addUser( { user: "testUser",
    pwd: "test",
    roles: [ "readWrite", "dbAdmin" ] } )
```

Now here's a more complex example that uses the `otherDBRoles` to add a user to multiple databases. Keep in mind that you can only use `otherDBRoles` on the `admin` database. The following commands add the same user to the `admin` database with only `read` rights and give them `readWrite` privileges to the `testDB2` database:

```
use admin
db.addUser( { user: "testUser",
    userSource: "test",
    roles: [ "read" ],
    otherDBRoles: { testDB2: [ "readWrite" ] } } )
```

Removing Users

You can remove users from MongoDB by using the `removeUser(<username>)` method. You need to first change to the database that the user is on. For example, to remove the `testUser` user from the `testDB` database, you use the following command from the MongoDB shell:

```
use testDB
db.removeUser("testUser")
```

Configuring Access Control

One of the first administration tasks that you will want to perform in the MongoDB shell is to add users to configure access control. MongoDB provides authentication and authorization at the database level, meaning that users exist in the context of a single database. For basic authentication purposes, MongoDB stores user credentials inside a collection call `system.users` in each database.

Initially, the `admin` database does not have any users assigned to it. When no users are defined in the `admin` database, MongoDB allows connections on the local host to have full administrative access to the database. Therefore, your first step in setting up a new MongoDB instance is to create user administrator and database administrator accounts. The user administrator account has the ability to create user accounts in `admin` and other databases. You also need to create a database administrator account that you can use as a superuser to manage databases, clustering, replication, and other aspects of MongoDB.

> **Note**
>
> You create the user administrator and database administrator accounts in the `admin` database. If you are using authentication for your MongoDB database, you must authenticate to the `admin` database as one of those users in order to administer users or databases. You should also create user accounts for each database for access purposes, as described in the previous section.

Creating a User Administrator Account

The first step in configuring access control is to implement a user administrator. The user administrator should only have rights to create users and not to manage the databases or other administration functions. This keeps a clean separation between database administration and user account administration.

You create a user administrator by executing the following two commands in the MongoDB shell to access the `admin` database and then add a user with `userAdminAnyDatabase` rights:

```
use admin
db.addUser( { user: "<username>",
    pwd: "<password>",
    roles: [ "userAdminAnyDatabase" ] } )
```

The user administrator account should be created with `userAdminAnyDatabase` as the only role. This gives that user the ability to create new user accounts but not to manipulate the database beyond that. The following example creates a user administrator with username `useradmin` and password `test`, as shown in Figure 12.4:

```
use admin
db.addUser( { user: "useradmin",
    pwd: "test",
    roles: [ "userAdminAnyDatabase" ] } )
```

```
> show users
> use admin
switched to db admin
> db.addUser( { user: "useradmin",
...        pwd: "test",
...        roles: [ "userAdminAnyDatabase" ] } )
{
        "user" : "useradmin",
        "pwd" : "0b4568ab22a52a6b494fd54e64fcee9f",
        "roles" : [
                "userAdminAnyDatabase"
        ],
        "_id" : ObjectId("52a0ba533120fa0d0e424dd3")
}
>
> show users
{
        "_id" : ObjectId("52a0ba533120fa0d0e424dd3"),
        "user" : "useradmin",
        "pwd" : "0b4568ab22a52a6b494fd54e64fcee9f",
        "roles" : [
                "userAdminAnyDatabase"
        ]
}
> _
```

Figure 12.4 Creating a user administrator account.

Turning on Authentication

Once the user administrator account has been created, you need to restart the MongoDB database by using the `--auth` parameter, like this:

```
mongod -dbpath <mongo_data_location>/data/db --auth
```

Clients now have to use a username and password to access the database. Also, when you access MongoDB from the shell, you need to execute the following commands to authenticate to the `admin` database so that you can add users with rights to the databases:

```
use admin
db.auth("useradmin", "test")
```

You can also authenticate to the `admin` database when you start the MongoDB shell by using the `--username` and `--password` options and specifying the `admin` database, as in this example:

```
mongo admin --username "useradmin " --password "test"
```

Creating a Database Administrator Account

You create a database administrator account by executing the `addUser` method in the MongoDB shell to access the `admin` database. Then you add a user with `readWriteAnyDatabase`, `dbAdminAnyDatabase`, and `clusterAdmin` rights. This gives that user the ability to access all databases in the system, create new databases, and manage MongoDB clusters and replicas. The following example creates a database administrator named `dbadmin`:

```
use admin
db.addUser( { user: "dbadmin",
    pwd: "test",
    roles: [ "readWriteAnyDatabase", "dbAdminAnyDatabase", "clusterAdmin" ] } )
```

You can then use that user in the MongoDB shell to administer databases. Once you have created the new administrator account, you can authenticate as that user by using the following commands:

```
use admin
db.auth("dbadmin", "test")
```

You can also authenticate to the `admin` database as the database administrator when starting the MongoDB shell by using the `--username` and `--password` options, as in this example:

```
mongo admin --username "dbadmin" --password "test"
```

Administering Databases

In order to administer databases in the MongoDB shell, you need to use a user account that has `clusterAdmin` privileges, such as the database administrator account described earlier in this chapter. Once you have such a database administrator account created, you can authenticate as that user and perform the tasks described in the following sections.

Displaying a List of Databases

Often you may need to just see a list of databases that have been created, especially if you have created a large number of database or are not the only one administering the system. To see a list of databases in a system, use the `show dbs` command:

```
show dbs
```

Changing the Current Database

You perform database operations by using the handle `db`, which is built into MongoDB. Many operations can only be applied on one database. Therefore, to perform operations on other databases, you need to change the `db` handle to point to a different database.

To switch the current database, you use the `db.getSiblingDB(database)` method or `use <database>`. For example, both of the following methods switch the current database handle to `testDB`:

```
db = db.getSiblingDB('testDB')
use testDB
```

Either one is acceptable and sets the value of `db` to the database specified. You can then use `db` to manage the new current database.

Creating Databases

MongoDB doesn't provide a command in the shell to explicitly create databases. Instead, you can simply use `use <new_database_name>` to create a new database handle. Keep in mind that the new database will not actually be saved until you add a collection to it. For example, the following commands create a new database named `newDB` and then add a collection named `newCollection` to it:

```
use newDB
db.createCollection("newCollection")
```

To verify that the new database exists, you can then use `show dbs`, as shown in Figure 12.5.

```
> show dbs
admin    0.203125GB
local    0.078125GB
test     0.203125GB
> use newDB
switched to db newDB
> db.createCollection("newCollection")
{ "ok" : 1 }
> show dbs
admin    0.203125GB
local    0.078125GB
newDB    0.203125GB
test     0.203125GB
> _
```

Figure 12.5 Creating a new database in the MongoDB shell.

Deleting Databases

Once a database has been created, it exists in MongoDB until an administrator deletes it. Deleting databases is a common task on some systems, especially when databases are created to contain temporary data. It is sometimes easier to delete databases when they become stale and simply create new ones as needed than to try to clean up the entries in a database.

To delete a database from the MongoDB shell, use the `dropDatabase()` method. For example, to delete the `newDB` database, you use the following commands to change to the `newDB` database and then delete it:

```
use newDB
db.dropDatabase()
```

You should be aware that `dropDatabase()` removes the current database, but it does not change the current database handle. This means if you drop a database and then create a collection using the handle without changing the current database first, the dropped database is re-created.

Figure 12.6 shows an example of deleting the `newDB` from MongoDB.

```
> show dbs
admin   0.203125GB
local   0.078125GB
newDB   0.203125GB
test    0.203125GB
> use newDB
switched to db newDB
> db.dropDatabase()
{ "dropped" : "newDB", "ok" : 1 }
> show dbs
admin   0.203125GB
local   0.078125GB
test    0.203125GB
> _
```

Figure 12.6 Deleting a database in the MongoDB shell.

Copying Databases

Another common task with databases is copying them. Copying a database creates a duplicate of the database that is exactly the same except for the name. There are several reasons you might want to copy a database—for example, to have a backup while you perform heavy changes or as an archive.

To create a copy of a database, you switch to that database and then use `copyDatabase(origin, destination, [hostname])` to create a copy. The `origin` parameter is a string that specifies the name of the database to copy. The `destination` parameter specifies the name of the database to create on this MongoDB server. The optional `hostname` parameter specifies a hostname of the origin database MongoDB server if you are copying a database from a different host. For example:

```
db.copyDatabase('customers', 'customers_archive')
```

Managing Collections

As a database admin, you may find yourself administering collections within a database. MongoDB provides the functionality in the MongoDB shell to create, view, and manipulate collections in a database. The following sections cover the basics you need to know to use the MongoDB shell to list collections, create new ones, and access the documents contained within them.

Displaying a List of Collections in a Database

You often need to see a list of collections contained in a database—for example, to verify that a collection exists or to find the name of a collection that you cannot remember. To see a list of collections in a database, you need to switch to that database and then use `show collections` to get the list of collections contained in the database. For example, the following commands list the collections in the `test` database:

```
use test
show collections
```

Creating Collections

You must create a collection in the MongoDB database before you can begin storing documents in it. To create a collection, you need to call `createCollection(name, [options])` on the database handle. The `name` parameter is the name of the new collection. The optional `options` parameter is an object that can have the properties listed in Table 12.4, which define the behavior of the collection.

Table 12.4 **Options that can be specified when creating a collection**

Role	Description
`capped`	A Boolean that, when `true`, indicates that the collection is a capped collection that will not grow bigger than the maximum size specified by the `size` attribute. The default is `false`.
`autoIndexID`	A Boolean that, when `true`, indicates that an `_id` field is automatically created for each document added to the collection with an index on that field implemented. This should be `false` for capped collections. The default is `true`.
`size`	The size, in bytes, for the capped collection. The oldest document is removed to make room for new documents.
`max`	The maximum number of documents allowed in a capitalized collection. The oldest document is removed to make room for new documents.

For example, the following line of code creates a new collection called `newCollection` in the `testDB` database, as shown in Figure 12.7:

```
db.createCollection("newCollection")
```

```
> use testDB
switched to db testDB
> show collections
> db.createCollection("newCollection", {capped:false})
{ "ok" : 1 }
> show collections
newCollection
system.indexes
> _
```

Figure 12.7 Creating a new collection in the MongoDB shell.

Deleting Collections

Occasionally you want to remove old collections when they are no longer needed. Removing old collections frees up disk space and eliminates any overhead, such as indexing, associated with the collection.

To delete a collection in the MongoDB shell, you need to switch to the correct database, get the collection object, and then call the `drop()` function on that object. For example, the following code deletes the `newCollection` collection from the `testDB` database, as shown in Figure 12.8:

```
use testDB
show collections
coll = db.getCollection("newCollection")
coll.drop()
show collections
```

```
> use testDB
switched to db testDB
> show collections
newCollection
system.indexes
> coll = db.getCollection("newCollection")
testDB.newCollection
> coll.drop()
true
> show collections
system.indexes
> _
```

Figure 12.8 Deleting a collection in the MongoDB shell.

Finding Documents in a Collection

Most of the time, you use a library such as the native MongoDB driver or Mongoose to access documents in a collection. However, there may be times when you need to look at documents inside the MongoDB shell.

The MongoDB shell provides full querying functionality to find documents in collections, using the `find(query)` method on the `collection` object. The optional `query` parameter specifies a query document with fields and values to match documents against in the collection. The documents that match the query are removed from the collection. Using the `find()` method with no `query` parameter returns all documents in the collection.

For example, the following lines of code first query every item in the collection and then retrieve the documents whose `speed` field is equal to `120mph` (see Figure 12.9):

```
use testDB
coll = db.getCollection("newCollection")
coll.find()
coll.find({speed:"120mph"})
```

```
> use testDB
switched to db testDB
> coll = db.getCollection("newCollection")
testDB.newCollection
> coll.find()
{ "_id" : ObjectId("52a0c65b3120fa0d0e424dd8"), "vehicle" : "plane", "speed" : "480mph" }
{ "_id" : ObjectId("52a0c65b3120fa0d0e424dd9"), "vehicle" : "car", "speed" : "120mph" }
{ "_id" : ObjectId("52a0c65b3120fa0d0e424dda"), "vehicle" : "train", "speed" : "120mph" }
> coll.find({speed:"120mph"})
{ "_id" : ObjectId("52a0c65b3120fa0d0e424dd9"), "vehicle" : "car", "speed" : "120mph" }
{ "_id" : ObjectId("52a0c65b3120fa0d0e424dda"), "vehicle" : "train", "speed" : "120mph" }
> _
```

Figure 12.9 Finding documents in a collection.

Adding Documents to a Collection

Typically, you insert documents in a collection through your Node.js application. However, there may be times when you need to manually insert a document from an administrative point of view to preload a database, fix a database, or for testing purposes.

To add documents to a collection, you need to get the `collection` object and then call the `insert(document)` or `save(document)` method on that object. The `document` parameter is a well-formatted JavaScript object that is converted to BSON and stored in the collection. For example, the following commands create three new documents inside a collection, as shown in Figure 12.10:

```
use testDB
coll = db.getCollection("newCollection")
coll.find()
coll.insert({ vehicle: "plane", speed: "480mph" })
coll.insert({ vehicle: "car", speed: "120mph" })
coll.insert({ vehicle: "train", speed: "120mph" })
coll.find()
```

```
> use testDB
switched to db testDB
> coll = db.getCollection("newCollection")
testDB.newCollection
> coll.find()
> coll.insert({ vehicle: "plane", speed: "480mph" })
> coll.insert({ vehicle: "car", speed: "120mph" })
> coll.insert({ vehicle: "train", speed: "120mph" })
> coll.find()
{ "_id" : ObjectId("52a0d2743120fa0d0e424dde"), "vehicle" : "plane", "speed" : "480mph" }
{ "_id" : ObjectId("52a0d2743120fa0d0e424ddf"), "vehicle" : "car", "speed" : "120mph" }
{ "_id" : ObjectId("52a0d2743120fa0d0e424de0"), "vehicle" : "train", "speed" : "120mph" }
> _
```

Figure 12.10 Creating documents in a collection.

Deleting Documents from a Collection

Typically you delete documents from a collection through your Node.js application. However, there may be times when you need to manually remove a document from an administrative point of view to fix a database or for testing purposes.

To remove documents from a collection, you need to get the `collection` object and then call the `remove(query)` method on that object. The optional `query` parameter specifies a query document with fields and values to match documents against in the collection. The documents that match the query are removed from the collection. Using the `remove()` method with no `query` parameter removes all documents from the collection. For example, the following commands first remove documents where `vehicle` is `plane` and then all documents from the collection, as shown in Figure 12.11:

```
use testDB
coll = db.getCollection("newCollection")
coll.find()
coll.remove({vehicle: "plane"})
coll.find()
coll.remove()
coll.find()
```

```
> use testDB
switched to db testDB
> coll = db.getCollection("newCollection")
testDB.newCollection
> coll.find()
{ "_id" : ObjectId("52a0d2743120fa0d0e424dde"), "vehicle" : "plane", "speed" : "480mph" }
{ "_id" : ObjectId("52a0d2743120fa0d0e424ddf"), "vehicle" : "car", "speed" : "120mph" }
{ "_id" : ObjectId("52a0d2743120fa0d0e424de0"), "vehicle" : "train", "speed" : "120mph" }
> coll.remove({vehicle: "plane"})
> coll.find()
{ "_id" : ObjectId("52a0d2743120fa0d0e424ddf"), "vehicle" : "car", "speed" : "120mph" }
{ "_id" : ObjectId("52a0d2743120fa0d0e424de0"), "vehicle" : "train", "speed" : "120mph" }
> coll.remove()
> coll.find()
> _
```

Figure 12.11 Deleting documents from a collection.

Updating Documents in a Collection

Typically you update documents in a collection through your Node.js application. However, at times you may need to manually update a document from an administrative point of view to fix a database or for testing purposes.

To update documents in a collection, you need to get the collection. Then you can use the `save(object)` method to save changes you have made to an object. Or you can use the `update(query, update, options)` method to query for documents in the collection and then update them as they are found.

When you use the `update()` method, the `query` parameter specifies a query document with fields and values to match documents against in the collection. The `update` parameter is an object that specifies the update operator to use when making the update. For example, `$inc` increments the value of the field, `$set` sets the value of the field, `$push` pushes an item onto an array, etc. For example, the following update object increments one field, sets another, and then renames a third:

```
{ $inc: {count: 1}, $set: {name: "New Name"}, $rename: {"nickname": "alias"} }
```

The `options` parameter of `update()` is an object that has two properties—`multi` and `upsert`—that are both `Boolean` values. If `upsert` is `true`, a new document is created if none are found. If `multi` is `true`, all documents that match the query are updated; otherwise, only the first document is updated.

For example, the following commands update documents with a `speed` of `120mph` by setting the speed to `150` and adding a new field called `updated`. Also, the `save()` method is used to save changes to the `plane` document:

```
use testDB
coll = db.getCollection("newCollection")
coll.find()
coll.update({ speed: "120mph" },
            { $set: { speed: "150mph" , updated: true } },
            { upsert: false, multi: true })
coll.save({ "_id" : ObjectId("52a0caf33120fa0d0e424ddb"),
            "vehicle" : "plane", "speed" : "500mph" })
coll.find()
```

Figure 12.12 shows the console output.

```
> use testDB
switched to db testDB
> coll = db.getCollection("newCollection")
testDB.newCollection
> coll.find()
{ "_id" : ObjectId("52a0caf33120fa0d0e424ddb"), "vehicle" : "plane", "speed" : "470mph" }
{ "_id" : ObjectId("52a0caf33120fa0d0e424ddc"), "vehicle" : "car", "speed" : "120mph" }
{ "_id" : ObjectId("52a0caf33120fa0d0e424ddd"), "vehicle" : "train", "speed" : "120mph" }
> coll.update({ speed: "120mph" },
...             { $set: { speed: "150mph" , updated: true } },
...             { upsert: false, multi: true })
> coll.save({ "_id" : ObjectId("52a0caf33120fa0d0e424ddb"),
...             "vehicle" : "plane", "speed" : "500mph" })
> coll.find()
{ "_id" : ObjectId("52a0caf33120fa0d0e424ddb"), "vehicle" : "plane", "speed" : "500mph" }
{ "_id" : ObjectId("52a0caf33120fa0d0e424ddc"), "speed" : "150mph", "updated" : true, "vehicle" : "car" }
{ "_id" : ObjectId("52a0caf33120fa0d0e424ddd"), "speed" : "150mph", "updated" : true, "vehicle" : "train" }
> _
```

Figure 12.12 Updating documents from a collection.

Summary

From a development perspective, most of the interaction you have with MongoDB is from a library such as the native MongoDB driver for Node.js. However, before you can begin implementing MongoDB in your applications, you need to install the MongoDB server and configure it to run. You should also create administrative and databases accounts and then turn on authentication to ensure security, even in your development environment.

This chapter discusses the process of installing MongoDB and accessing the MongoDB shell. You've learned how to interact with the shell to create user accounts, databases, collections, and documents.

Up Next

In the next chapter, you'll get a chance to implement MongoDB in your Node.js applications, using the native `mongodb` module. You will learn how to include this module in your applications and connect to MongoDB to perform database operations.

13

Getting Started with MongoDB and Node.js

You can use several modules to access MongoDB from your Node.js applications. The MongoDB group has adopted the MongoDB Node.js driver as the standard method. This driver provides all the functionality and is very similar to the native commands available in the MongoDB shell client.

This chapter gets you started accessing MongoDB from Node.js applications. You will learn how to install the MongoDB Node.js driver and use it to connect to MongoDB databases. Several sections also cover the process of creating, accessing, and manipulating databases and collections from your Node.js applications.

Adding the MongoDB Driver to Node.js

The first step in implementing MongoDB access from your Node.js applications is to add the MongoDB driver to your application project. The MongoDB Node.js driver is the officially supported native Node.js driver for MongoDB. It has by far the best implementation and is sponsored by MongoDB.

> **Note**
>
> This book can't cover everything about the driver. For additional information, I recommend looking at the documentation for the MongoDB Node.js driver at http://mongodb.github.io/node-mongodb-native/.

Thanks to the Node.js modular framework, adding the MongoDB Node.js driver to a project requires just a simple `npm` command. From your project root directory, execute the following commands at a console prompt to install the correct version of the MongoDB Node.js driver and the Mongoose module:

```
npm install mongodb@1.4.2
npm install mongoose@3.8.8
```

A `node_modules` directory is created if there isn't already one, and the `mongodb` driver module is installed under it. Once that is done, your Node.js application files will be able to use the `require('mongodb')` command to access the `mongodb` module functionality.

Connecting to MongoDB from Node.js

Once you have installed the `mongodb` module using the `npm` command, you can begin accessing MongoDB from your Node.js applications by opening up a connection to the MongoDB server. The connection acts as your interface to create, update, and access data in the MongoDB database.

The best way to access MongoDB is through the `MongoClient` class in the `mongodb` module. This class provides very simple ways to create connections to MongoDB. There are two main methods you can use. One is to create an instance of the `MongoClient` object and then use that object to create and manage the MongoDB connection. The other method is to use a connection string to make a connection. Both of these options work well.

Understanding the Write Concern

Before connecting to and updating data on a MongoDB server, you need to decide what level of write concern you want to implement on your connection. A write concern is the guarantee that the MongoDB connection provides when reporting on the success of a write operation. The strength of a write concern determines the level of guarantee.

The basic idea is that stronger write concerns tell MongoDB to wait until a write has successfully been written to disk before responding. On the other hand, a weaker write concern may only wait until MongoDB has successfully scheduled a change to be written before responding. The downside of stronger write concerns is that the stronger they are, the longer MongoDB waits to respond to the client connection, and thus write requests are a bit slower.

From a MongoDB driver connection perspective, the write concern can be set to one of the levels listed in Table 13.1. You set this level on the server connection, and it applies to all connections to the server. If a write error is detected, an error is returned in the callback function of the write request.

Table 13.1 **Write concern levels for MongoDB connections**

Level	Description
`-1`	Network errors are ignored.
`0`	No write acknowledgement is required.
`1`	Write acknowledgement is requested.
`2`	Write acknowledgement is requested across the primary server and one secondary server in the replica set.
`majority`	Write acknowledgement is requested from a majority of servers in the replica set.

Understanding the `Server` Object

The `MongoClient` connection utilizes a `Server` object in the background. This object defines how the MongoDB driver should connect to the server. The `Server` object contains information such as the host, port, pool size, and socket timeout values used when creating the connection.

You do not need to interact directly with the `Server` object, but you need to specify the options used to create it for the client connection. Table 13.2 lists the most important options you can set when defining the `Server` object:

Table 13.2 **Options used to create the `Server` object for a `MongoClient` connection**

Option	Description
`readPreferrnce`	Specifies which read preference to use when reading objects from a replica set. Setting the read preference allows you to optimize read operations, such as reading only from secondary servers to free up the primary server. These are the possible preferences: ▪ `ReadPreference.PRIMARY` ▪ `ReadPreference.PRIMARY_PREFERRED` ▪ `ReadPreference.SECONDARY` ▪ `ReadPreference.SECONDARY_PREFERRED` ▪ `ReadPreference.NEAREST`
`ssl`	Is a Boolean that, when set to `true`, says that the connection uses SSL. `mongod` also needs to be configured with SSL. If you are using SSL, you can also specify `sslCA`, `sslCert`, `sslKey`, and `sslPass` options to set the SSL certificate authority, certificate, key, and password.
`poolSize`	Specifies the number of connections to use in the connection pool for the server. The default is `5`, meaning there can be up to five connections to the database shared by `MongoClient`.
`socketOptions`	Defines socket creation options, including: ▪ `noDelay`: `Boolean` specifies a no-delay socket. ▪ `keepAlive`: Specifies the keep-alive time for the socket. ▪ `connectTimeoutMS`: Specifies the amount of time, in milliseconds, for the connection to wait before timing out. ▪ `socketTimeoutMS`: Specifies the amount of time, in milliseconds, for a socket send to wait before timing out.
`auto_reconnect`	Is a Boolean that, when set to `true`, says that the client will try to recreate the connection when an error is encountered.

Connecting to MongoDB via a `Client` Object

Using a `MongoClient` object to connect to MongoDB involves creating an instance of the client, opening a connection to the database, authenticating to the database if necessary, and then handling logout and closure as needed. This method has the advantage of allowing you to manipulate each step of the connection and authentication.

To connect to MongoDB via a `MongoClient` object, you need to first create an instance of the `MongoClient` object. The constructor for the `MongoClient` class takes a `Server` object as the first parameter and an object specifying the database connection options as the second parameter, as shown below:

```
MongoClient(Server, options)
```

Table 13.3 lists the most important database connection options that can be set and applied to the `MongoClient` connections:

Table 13.3 **Database connection options used to create `MongoClient` connections**

Option	Description
`w`	Specifies the write concern level for database connections. See Table 13.1 for the appropriate values.
`wtimeout`	Specifies the amount of time, in milliseconds, to wait for the write concern to finish. This value is added to the normal connection timeout value.
`fsync`	Is a Boolean that, when set to `true`, says that write requests wait for `fsync` to finish before returning.
`journal`	Is a Boolean that, when set to `true`, says that write requests wait for the journal sync to complete before returning.
`retryMilliSeconds`	Specifies the number of milliseconds to wait between connection retries. The default is `5000`.
`numberOfRetries`	Specifies the number of times to retry the connection before failing. The default is `5`.
`bufferMaxEntries`	Specifies the maximum number of operations that will be buffered waiting for a connection before failing the connection. The default is `-1`, which is unlimited.

The following example shows how to create a `MongoClient` instance. Notice that a `Server` object is created using options from Table 13.2:

```
var client = new MongoClient(new Server('localhost', 27017,  { poolSize: 5}),
                             { retryMiliSeconds: 500 }));
```

Once you have created `MongoClient`, you need to open a connection to the MongoDB server database by using the `open(callback)` method. The callback method is called with an error as the first parameter if the connection fails and a `MongoClient` object as the second parameter if the connection is successful. For example:

```
client.open(function(err, client){ . . . });
```

To connect to a specific database, you need to create an instance of the database by using the `db(databasename)` method on the `client` object. You use the database connection options to create a `Db` object instance that can be used to access collections in a specific database. If you have authentication turned on, you also need to authenticate to the database by using the `db.authenticate(username, password, callback)` method before trying to access it. For example:

```
var db = client.db("testDB");
db.authenticate("dbadmin", "test", function(err, results) { . . .});
```

To log out of the database, use the `logout()` method on the `Db` object. This closes the connection to the database, and you can no longer use the `Db` object. For example:

```
db.logout()
```

To close the connection to MongoDB, you call `close()` on the client connection as shown below:

```
client.close()
```

Listing 13.1 puts together all this connection stuff in a simple example. Notice that the code creates a client connection object on line 3 by generating a `Server` object and passing in some additional options. Also notice that the client connection is not established until line 11, when `open` is called. On line 15 a connection to the `testDB` database is made, and it's authenticated on line 18. Then inside the `authenticate()` callback function, the `db()` connection is logged out, and the client connection is closed. Figure 13.1 shows the output from Listing 13.1.

Listing 13.1 `db_connect_object.js`: **Connecting to MongoDB using a** `MongoClient` **object instance**

```
01 var MongoClient = require('mongodb').MongoClient,
02     Server = require('mongodb').Server;
03 var client = new MongoClient(new Server('localhost', 27017, {
04                                    socketOptions: { connectTimeoutMS: 500 },
05                                    poolSize: 5,
06                                    auto_reconnect: true
07                                  }, {
08                                    numberOfRetries: 3,
09                                    retryMilliSeconds: 500
10                                  }));
11 client.open(function(err, client) {
12   if(err){
13     console.log("Connection Failed Via Client Object.");
14   } else {
```

```
    var db = client.db("testDB");
    if (db){
      console.log("Connected Via Client Object . . .");
      db.authenticate("dbadmin", "test", function(err, results){
        if (err){
          console.log("Authentication failed . . .");
          client.close();
          console.log("Connection closed . . .");
        }else {
          console.log("Authenticated Via Client Object . . .");
          db.logout(function(err, result) {
            if(!err){
              console.log("Logged out Via Client Object . . .");
            }
            client.close();
            console.log("Connection closed . . .");
          });
        }
      });
    }
  }
});
```

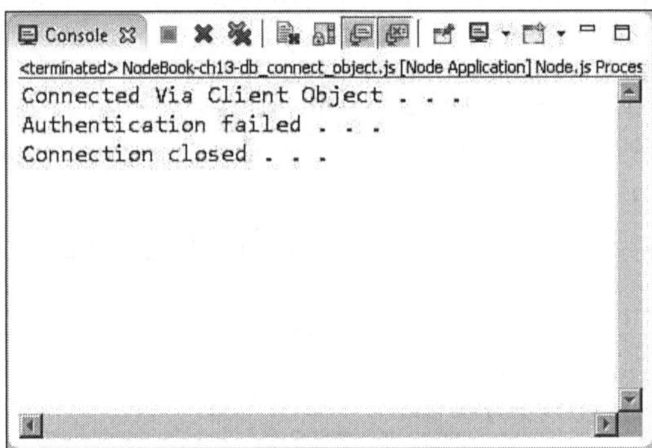

Figure 13.1 Connecting to MongoDB by using the `MongoClient` object.

Connecting to MongoDB via a Connection String

Another option for connecting to MongoDB using `MongoClient` is to use a connection string. With this option, you use a simple connection string to create, open, and authenticate a connection to the database. The `Server` and `MongoClient` options used to connect to the database are created in the background. This method has the advantage of being very simple to implement.

To connect to MongoDB via a connection string, you need to call the `connect()` method on the `MongoClient` class; no instance is required. The `connect()` method uses the following syntax:

```
MongoClient.connect(connString, options, callback)
```

The `connString` string has the following syntax (described in Table 13.4):

```
mongodb://username:password@host:port/database?options
```

The `options` parameter is an object that can contain `db`, `server`, `rplSet`, and `mongos` properties. The `db` property is an object that can contain the properties described in Table 13.3. The `server` property is an object that can contain the properties described in Table 13.2. The `replSet` property is an object that can contain options for handling connections to replica sets. The `mongos` property is also an object that can contain options for connecting to a `mongos` proxy.

The callback function accepts an error as the first parameter and a `Db` object instance as the second parameter. If an error occurs, the `Db` object instance is `null`; otherwise, you can use it to access the database because the connection has already been created and authenticated.

Table 13.4 `MongoClient` **connection string components**

Option	Description
`mongodb://`	Specifies that this string uses a MongoDB connection format.
`username`	Specifies the username to use when authenticating. Optional.
`password`	Specifies the password to use when authenticating. Optional.
`host`	Specifies the hostname or address of the MongoDB server. To connect to multiple MongoDB servers, you can specify multiple `host:port` combinations by separating them with commas. For example: `mongodb://host1:270017,host2:27017,host3:27017/testDB`
`port`	Specifies the port to use when connecting to the MongoDB server. The default is `27017`.
`database`	Specifies the name of the database to connect to. The default is `admin`.
`options`	Specifies the key/value pairs of options to use when connecting. You can also specify these options in the `dbOpt` and `serverOpt` parameters.

While in the callback function, you can access the MongoDB database by using the `Db` object passed in as the second parameter. When you are finished with the connection, you call `close()` on the `Db` object to close the connection.

Listing 13.2 is an example of using the connection string method. Line 2 specifies the connection string, and lines 3–10 specify the object that contains the `db`, `server`, `replSet`, and `mongos` properties. Lines 12–23 define the callback function. Notice that the callback function is passed a `Db` object that is already authenticated, so no authentication is necessary. Figure 13.2 shows the output from Listing 13.2.

Listing 13.2 `db_connect_string.js`: **Connecting to MongoDB using a connection string**

```
01 var MongoClient = require('mongodb').MongoClient;
02 MongoClient.connect("mongodb://dbadmin:test@localhost:27017/testDB", {
03                       db: { w: 1, native_parser: false },
04                       server: {
05                         poolSize: 5,
06                         socketOptions: { connectTimeoutMS: 500 },
07                         auto_reconnect: true
08                       },
09                       replSet: {},
10                       mongos: {}
11                     }, function(err, db) {
12   if(err){
13     console.log("Connection Failed Via Connection String.");
14   } else {
15     console.log("Connected Via Connection String . . .");
16     db.logout(function(err, result) {
17       if(!err){
18         console.log("Logged out Via Connection String . . .");
19       }
20       db.close();
21       console.log("Connection closed . . .");
22     });
23   }
24 });
```

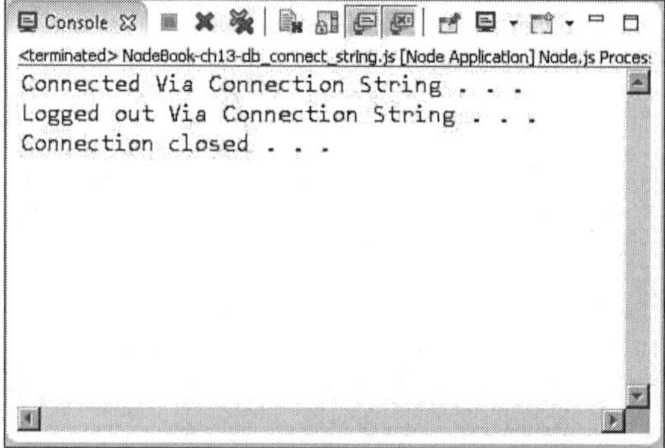

Figure 13.2 Connecting to MongoDB by using a connection string.

Understanding the Objects Used in the MongoDB Node.js Driver

The MongoDB Node.js driver makes heavy use of structured objects to interact with the database. You have already seen how the `MongoClient` object provides interactions to connect to the database. There are also objects that represent interactions with the database, collection, administrative functions, and cursors.

The following sections discuss each of these objects and provide the fundamentals of using them to implement database functionality in your Node.js applications. You will get more exposure to these objects and methods in the next few chapters as well.

Understanding the `Db` Object

The `Db` object in the MongoDB driver provides access to databases. It acts as a representation of the database, allowing you to do things like connect, add users, access collections, etc. You use `Db` objects to gain and maintain access to databases that you are interacting with in MongoDB.

A `Db` object is typically created when you connect to the database, as described in the previous section. Table 13.5 lists the methods you can call on a `Db` object.

Table 13.5 **Methods on the `Db` object**

Method	Description
`open(callback)`	Connects to the database. The `callback` function is executed after the connection has been made. The first parameter to the callback function is an error if one occurs and the second is the `Db` object. For example: `function(error, db){}`
`db(dbName)`	Creates a new instance of the `Db` object. The connection sockets are shared with the original.
`close([forceClose], callback)`	Closes the connection to the database. The `forceClose` parameter is a Boolean that, when set to `true`, forces closure of the sockets. The callback function is executed when the database is closed and accepts an `error` object and a `results` object: `function(error, results){}`
`admin()`	Returns an instance of an `Admin` object for MongoDB. See Table 13.6.
`collectionInfo([name], callback)`	Retrieves a `Cursor` object that points to collection information for the database. If `name` is specified, then only that collection is returned in the cursor. The callback function accepts `err` and `cursor` parameters: `function(err, cursor){}`

Method	Description
`collectionNames (callback )`	Returns a list of the collection names for this database. The callback function accepts `err` and `names` parameters, where `names` is an array of collection names: `function(err, names){}`
`collection(name, [options], callback)`	Retrieves information about a collection and creates an instance of a `Collection` object. The `options` parameter is an object whose properties define the access to the collection. The callback function accepts `err` and `collection` parameters: `function(err, collection){}`
`collections(callback)`	Retrieves information about all collections in this database and creates an instance of a `Collection` object for each of them. The callback function accepts `err` and `collections` as parameters, where `collections` is an array of `Collection` objects: `function(err, collections){}`
`logout(callback)`	Logs the user out from the database. The callback function accepts `error` and `results` parameters: `function(error, results){}`
`authenticate(username, password, callback)`	Authenticates as a user to this database. You can use this to switch between users while accessing the database. The callback function accepts `error` and `results` parameters: `function(error, results){}`
`addUser(username, password, callback)`	Adds a user to this database. The currently authenticated user will need user administration rights to add the user. The callback function accepts `error` and `results` parameters: `function(error, results){}`
`removeUser(username, callback)`	Removes a user from the database. The callback function accepts `error` and `results` parameters: `function(error, results){}`
`createCollection (collectionName, callback)`	Creates a new collection in the database. The callback function accepts `error` and `results` parameters: `function(error, results){}`
`dropCollection (collectionName, callback)`	Deletes the collection specified by `collectionName` from the database. The callback function accepts `error` and `results` parameters: `function(error, results){}`
`renameCollection (oldName, newName, callback)`	Renames a collection in the database. The callback function accepts `error` and `results` parameters: `function(error, results){}`
`dropDatabase(dbName, callback)`	Deletes this database from MongoDB. The callback function accepts `error` and `results` parameters: `function(error, results){}`

Understanding the Admin Object

You use the Admin object to perform certain administrative functions on a MongoDB database. The Admin object represents a connection specifically to the admin database and provides functionality not included in the Db object.

You can get the Admin object by using the admin() method on an instance of the Db object or by passing a Db object into the constructor. For example, both of the following work fine:

```
var adminDb = db.admin()
var adminDb = new Admin(db)
```

Table 13.6 lists the important methods you can call from an Admin object. These methods allow you to ping the MongoDB server, add and remove users from the admin database, list databases, etc.

Table 13.6 **Methods on the Admin object**

Method	Description
serverStatus(callback)	Retrieves status information from the MongoDB server. The callback function accepts error and status parameters: function(error, status){}
ping(callback)	Pings the MongoDB server. This is useful because you can use your Node.js apps to monitor the server connection to MongoDB. The callback function accepts error and results parameters: function(error, results){}
listDatabases(callback)	Retrieves a list of databases from the server. The callback function accepts error and results parameters: function(error, results){}
authenticate(username, password, callback)	Authenticates as a user to this database. You can use this to switch between users while accessing the database. The callback function accepts error and results parameters: function(error, results){}
logout(callback)	Logs the user out from the database. The callback function accepts error and results parameters: function(error, results){}
addUser(username, password, [options], callback)	Adds a user to this database. The currently authenticated user will need user administration rights to add the user. The callback function accepts error and results parameters: function(error, results){}
removeUser(username, callback)	Removes a user from the database. The callback function accepts error and results parameters: function(error, results){}

Understanding the `Collection` Object

The `Collection` object represents a collection in the MongoDB database. You use the `Collection` object to access items in the collection, add documents, query documents, and much more.

You can get a `Collection` object by using the `collection()` method on an instance of the `Db` object or by passing a `Db` object and collection name to the constructor. If the collection isn't already created on the MongoDB server, you can create it by using the `createCollection()` method on the `Db` object. For example, all of the following work:

```
var collection = db.collection()
var collection = new Collection(db, "myCollection")
db.createCollection("newCollection", function(err, collection){ }
```

Table 13.7 lists the basic methods you can call from a `Collection` object. These methods allow you to add and modify documents in the collection, find documents, and delete the collection.

Table 13.7 **Basic methods on the `Collection` object**

Method	Description
`insert(docs, [callback])`	Inserts one or more documents into the collection. The `docs` parameter is an object describing the documents. You must include the callback function when using a write concern. The callback function accepts `error` and `results` parameters: `function(error, results){}`
`remove([query], [options], [callback])`	Deletes documents from the collection. `query` is a parameter used to identify the documents to remove. If no `query` parameter is supplied, then all documents are deleted. If a `query` parameter is supplied, the documents that match the `query` parameter are deleted. `options` allows you to specify the write concern using `w`, `wtimeout`, `upsert`, and new options when modifying documents. You must include the callback function when using a write concern. The callback function accepts `error` and `results` parameters: `function(error, results){}`
`rename(newName, callback)`	Renames the collection `newName`. The callback function accepts `error` and `results` parameters: `function(error, results){}`

Method	Description
`save([doc],[options], [callback])`	Saves the document specified in the `doc` parameter to the database. This is useful if you are making ad hoc changes to objects and then need to save them, but it is not as efficient as `update()` or `findAndModify`. `options` allows you to specify the write concern using `w`, `wtimeout`, `upsert`, and new options when modifying documents. You must include the callback function when using a write concern. The callback function accepts `error` and `results` parameters: `function(error, results){}`
`update(query, update, [options], [callback])`	Updates the documents that match the `query` object in the database with the information specified in the `document` parameter. `options` allows you to specify the write concern by using `w`, `wtimeout`, `upsert`, and new options when modifying documents. You must include the callback function when using a write concern. The callback function accepts `error` and `results` parameters: `function(error, results){}`
`find(query, [options], callback)`	Creates a `Cursor` object that points to a set of documents that match the query. The `options` parameter allows you to specify the limit, sort, and other options to use when building the cursor on the server side. The callback function accepts `error` and `cursor` parameters: `function(error, cursor){}`
`findOne(query, [options], callback)`	Is the same as `find()` except that only the first document found is included in the `Cursor`.
`findAndModify(query, sort, update, [options], callback)`	Performs modifications on documents that match the `query` parameter. The `sort` parameter determines which objects are modified first. The `doc` parameter specifies the changes to make on the documents. `options` allows you to specify the write concern using `w`, `wtimeout`, `upsert`, and new options when modifying documents. The callback function accepts `error` and `results` objects: `function(error, results){}`
`findAndRemove(query, sort, [options], callback)`	Removes documents that match the `query` parameter. The `sort` parameter determines which objects are modified first. `options` allows you to specify the write concern `w`, `wtimeout`, `upsert`, and new options when deleting documents. The callback function accepts `error` and `results` parameters: `function(error, results){}`

Method	Description
`distinct(key, [query], callback)`	Creates a list of distinct values for a specific document `key` in the collection. If a `query` parameter is specified, then only documents that match the query are included. The callback function accepts `error` and `values` parameters, where `values` is an array of distinct values for the specified `key`: `function(error, values){}`
`count([query], callback)`	Counts the number of documents in a collection. If a `query` parameter is used, then only documents that match the query are included. The callback function accepts `error` and `count` parameters, where `count` is the number of matching documents: `function(error, count){}`
`drop(callback)`	Drops the current collection. The callback function accepts `error` and `results` parameters: `function(error, results){}`
`stats(callback)`	Retrieves the stats for the collection, including the count of items, size on disk, average object size, and much more. The callback function accepts `error` and `stats` parameters: `function(error, stats){}`

Understanding the `Cursor` Object

When you perform certain operations on MongoDB using the MongoDB Node.js driver, the result comes back as a `Cursor` object. The `Cursor` object acts as a pointer that can be iterated on to access a set of objects in the database. For example, when you use `find()`, the actual documents are not returned in the callback function; rather, a `Cursor` object is returned. You can then use the `Cursor` object to read the items in the results.

Because the `Cursor` object can be iterated on, an index to the current location is kept internally. That way, you can read items one at a time. Keep in mind that some operations only affect the current item in the `Cursor` object and increment the index. Other operations affect all items from the current index forward.

To give you an overall view of the `Cursor` object, Table 13.8 lists the basic methods you can call on the `Cursor` object. These methods allow you to add and modify documents in the collection, find documents, and delete the collection.

Table 13.8 **Basic methods on the `Cursor` object**

Method	Description
`each(callback)`	Iterates through the items in the `Cursor` object from the current cursor index and calls the callback function each time. This allows you to perform the callback function on each item represented by the cursor. The callback function accepts `err` and `item` parameters: `function(err, item){}`
`toArray(callaback)`	Iterates through the items in the `Cursor` object from the current index forward and returns an array of objects to the callback function. The callback function accepts `err` and `items` parameters: `function(err, items){}`
`nextObject(callback)`	Returns the next object in the `Cursor` object to the callback function and increments the index. The callback function accepts `err` and `items` parameters: `function(err, item){}`
`rewind()`	Resets the `Cursor` object to the initial state. This is very useful if you encounter an error and need to reset the cursor and begin processing again.
`count(callback)`	Determines the number of items represented by the cursor. The callback function accepts `err` and `count` parameters: `function(err, count){}`
`sort(keyOrList, direction, callback)`	Sorts the items represented by the `Cursor` object. The `keyOrList` parameter is a `String` or an `Array` of field keys that specifies the field(s) to sort on. The `direction` parameter is a number, with `1` indicating ascending and `-1` indicating descending. The callback function accepts `error` as the first parameter and `sortedCursor` as the second: `function(err, sortedCursor){}`
`close(callback)`	Closes the `Cursor` object, which frees up memory on the client and on the MongoDB server.
`isClosed()`	Returns `true` if the `Cursor` object has been closed; otherwise, returns `false`.

Accessing and Manipulating Databases

A great feature of the MongoDB Node.js driver is that it provides the ability to create and manage databases from your Node.js applications. For most installations, you initially design and implement your databases once and then don't touch them again. However, sometimes it is very handy to be able to dynamically create and delete databases.

Listing Databases

To list the databases in a system, you need to use the `listDatabases()` method on an `Admin` object. This means you need to create an instance of an `Admin` object first. The list of databases is returned as the second parameter to the callback function and is a simple array of database objects.

The following code shows an example of creating an `Admin` object and then using it to get a list of the databases on the MongoDB server:

```
var MongoClient = require('mongodb').MongoClient;
MongoClient.connect("mongodb://localhost/admin", function(err, db) {
  var adminDB = db.admin();
  adminDB.listDatabases(function(err, databases){
    console.log("Before Add Database List: ");
    console.log(databases);
  });
});
```

Creating a Database

Just as with the MongoDB shell, there is not an explicit method for creating databases. Databases are created automatically whenever a collection or document is added to them. Therefore, to create a new database, all you need to do is use the `db()` method on the `Db` object provided by the `MongoClient` connection to create a new `Db` object instance. Then you call `createCollection()` on the new `Db` object instance to create the database.

The following code shows an example of creating a new database named `newDB` after connecting to the server:

```
var MongoClient = require('mongodb').MongoClient;
MongoClient.connect("mongodb://localhost/", function(err, db) {
  var newDB = db.db("newDB");
  newDB.createCollection("newColleciton", function(err, collection){
    if(!err){
      console.log("New Database and Collection Created");
    }
  });
});
```

Deleting a Database

To delete a database from MongoDB, you need to get a `Db` object instance that points to that database. Then you call the `dropDatabase()` method on that object. It may take a while for MongoDB to finalize the deletion. If you need to verify that the deletion has occurred, you can use a timeout to wait for the database deletion to occur. For example:

```
newDB.dropDatabase(function(err, results){
  <handle database deletion here>
});
```

Creating, Listing, and Deleting Databases Example

To help solidify the database operations, Listing 13.3 illustrates the full process of creating, listing, and deleting databases. A connection is made to the MongoDB server, and then lines 4–7 list the current databases. Then lines 8 and 9 create a new database by calling `createCollection()`. Inside the `createCollection()` callback handler, the databases are listed again to verify creation.

Lines 15–32 delete the database by using `dropDatabase()`. Notice that inside the `dropDatabase()` callback, a `setTimeout()` timer is implemented to wait for a number of seconds before checking the list of databases to verify that the database was deleted. The output is shown in Figure 13.3.

Listing 13.3 `db_create_list_delete.js`: **Creating, listing, and deleting databases, using the MongoDB Node.js driver**

```
01 var MongoClient = require('mongodb').MongoClient;
02 MongoClient.connect("mongodb://localhost/", function(err, db) {
03   var adminDB = db.admin();
04   adminDB.listDatabases(function(err, databases){
05     console.log("Before Add Database List: ");
06     console.log(databases);
07   });
08   var newDB = db.db("newDB");
09   newDB.createCollection("newColleciton", function(err, collection){
10     if(!err){
11       console.log("New Database and Collection Created");
12       adminDB.listDatabases(function(err, databases){
13         console.log("After Add Database List: ");
14         console.log(databases);
15         db.db("newDB").dropDatabase(function(err, results){
16           if(!err){
17             console.log("Database dropped.");
18             setTimeout(function() {
19               adminDB.listDatabases(function(err, results){
20                 var found = false;
21                 for(var i = 0; i < results.databases.length; i++) {
22                   if(results.databases[i].name == "newDB") found = true;
23                 }
24                 if (!found){
25                   console.log("After Delete Database List: ");
26                   console.log(results);
```

```
                }
                db.close();
              });
            }, 15000);
          }
        });
      });
    }
  });
});
```

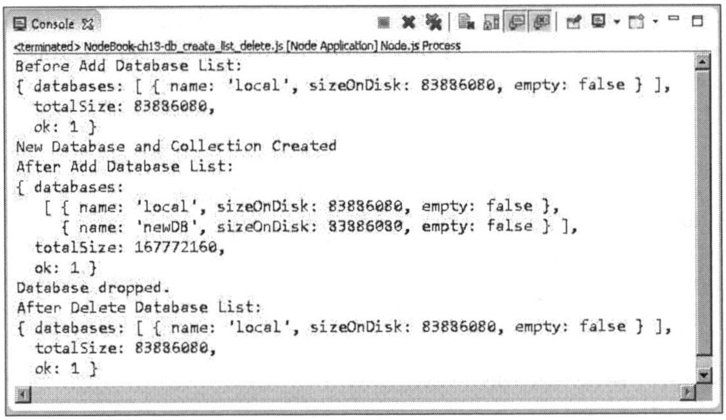

```
Console
<terminated> NodeBook-ch13-db_create_list_delete.js [Node Application] Node.js Process
Before Add Database List:
{ databases: [ { name: 'local', sizeOnDisk: 83886080, empty: false } ],
  totalSize: 83886080,
  ok: 1 }
New Database and Collection Created
After Add Database List:
{ databases:
   [ { name: 'local', sizeOnDisk: 83886080, empty: false },
     { name: 'newDB', sizeOnDisk: 83886080, empty: false } ],
  totalSize: 167772160,
  ok: 1 }
Database dropped.
After Delete Database List:
{ databases: [ { name: 'local', sizeOnDisk: 83886080, empty: false } ],
  totalSize: 83886080,
  ok: 1 }
```

Figure 13.3 Creating, listing, and deleting databases using the MongoDB Node.js driver.

Getting the Status of the MongoDB Server

Another great feature of the `Admin` object is the ability to get status information about the MongoDB server. This information includes the hostname, version, uptime, open cursors, and much more. You can use this information to determine the health and status of the MongoDB server and then make adjustments in your code to handle problem situations.

To display the status of the MongoDB server, you use the `serverStatus()` method on the `Admin` object. Listing 13.4 illustrates how to create the `Admin` object and then call `serverStatus()`. Figure 13.4 shows the results of Listing 13.4.

Listing 13.4 `db_status.js`: **Retrieving and displaying the MongoDB server status**

```
var MongoClient = require('mongodb').MongoClient;
MongoClient.connect("mongodb://localhost/test", function(err, db) {
  var adminDB = db.admin();
  adminDB.serverStatus(function(err, status){
    console.log(status);
    db.close();
  });
});
```

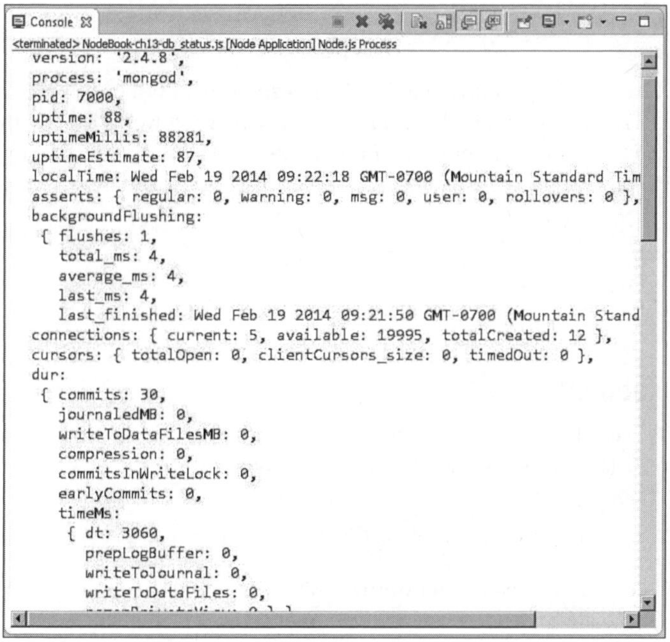

```
Console
<terminated> NodeBook-ch13-db_status.js [Node Application] Node.js Process
  version: '2.4.8',
  process: 'mongod',
  pid: 7000,
  uptime: 88,
  uptimeMillis: 88281,
  uptimeEstimate: 87,
  localTime: Wed Feb 19 2014 09:22:18 GMT-0700 (Mountain Standard Tim
  asserts: { regular: 0, warning: 0, msg: 0, user: 0, rollovers: 0 },
  backgroundFlushing:
   { flushes: 1,
     total_ms: 4,
     average_ms: 4,
     last_ms: 4,
     last_finished: Wed Feb 19 2014 09:21:50 GMT-0700 (Mountain Stand
  connections: { current: 5, available: 19995, totalCreated: 12 },
  cursors: { totalOpen: 0, clientCursors_size: 0, timedOut: 0 },
  dur:
   { commits: 30,
     journaledMB: 0,
     writeToDataFilesMB: 0,
     compression: 0,
     commitsInWriteLock: 0,
     earlyCommits: 0,
     timeMs:
      { dt: 3060,
        prepLogBuffer: 0,
        writeToJournal: 0,
        writeToDataFiles: 0,
```

Figure 13.4 Retrieving and displaying the MongoDB server status.

Accessing and Manipulating Collections

A common task for heavily used Node.js installations is dynamic manipulation of collections. For example, some larger installations give each large customer a separate collection, so as customers sign on or leave, the collections need to be added and deleted. The MongoDB Node.js driver provides very easy-to-use methods on the `Db` and `Collection` objects that allow you to easily manipulate the collections on a database.

Listing Collections

To list the collections in a database, you need to start with a `Db` object that points to the database you want to use. Then you call the `collectionNames()` method on the `Db` object. For example:

```
var newDB = db.db("newDB");
newDB.collectionNames(function(err, collectionNames)){}
```

The `collectionNames()` method returns an array of objects that contains the collection names of the collections. For example:

```
[ { name: 'newDB.system.indexes' },
  { name: 'newDB.newCollection',
    options: { create: 'newCollection' } } ]
```

You can also get back the collections of a database as an array of full `Collection` objects by using the `collections()` method. The `collections()` method works exactly the same as the `collectionNames()` method except that a fully usable `Collection` object is created for each collection. For example:

```
var newDB = db.db("newDB");
newDB.collections(function(err, collectionList){}
```

The resulting value of the `collectionList` parameter is an array of `Collection` objects.

Creating Collections

You have already seen the process of creating a collection. You simply use the `createCollection()` method on the `Db` object. For example:

```
var newDB = db.db("newDB");
newDB.createCollection("newCollection", function(err, collection){ }
```

The value of the `collection` parameter of the callback is a `Collection` object. You can use this object to manipulate the collection, add documents, etc.

Deleting Collections

There are two ways to delete collections. The first is to call `dropCollection(name)` on the `Db` object. The second is to call the `drop()` method on the `Collection` object; this is sometimes more convenient, such as when you are iterating through a list of `Collection` objects.

The following are the two methods:

```
var myDB = db.db("myDB ");
myDB.dropCollection("collectionA", function(err, results){ });
// or
myDB.collection("collectionB", function(err, collB){
  collB.drop();
});
```

Collection Creation, Listing, and Deleting Example

To illustrate the process of creating, listing, and deleting collections, Listing 13.5 makes a series of chained callbacks that list the collections, create a new collection, and then delete the new collection. The code is very basic and easy to follow. Figure 13.5 shows the output.

Listing 13.5 `collection_create_list_delete.js`: **Creating, retrieving, and deleting collections on a MongoDB database**

```
var MongoClient = require('mongodb').MongoClient;
MongoClient.connect("mongodb://localhost/", function(err, db) {
  var newDB = db.db("newDB");
  newDB.collectionNames(function(err, collectionNames){
    console.log("Initial collections: ");
    console.log(collectionNames);
    newDB.createCollection("newCollection", function(err, collection){
      newDB.collectionNames(function(err, collectionNames){
        console.log("Collections after creation: ");
        console.log(collectionNames);
        newDB.dropCollection("newCollection", function(err, results){
          newDB.collectionNames(function(err, collectionNames){
            console.log("Collections after deletion: ");
            console.log(collectionNames);
            db.close();
          });
        });
      });
    });
  });
});
```

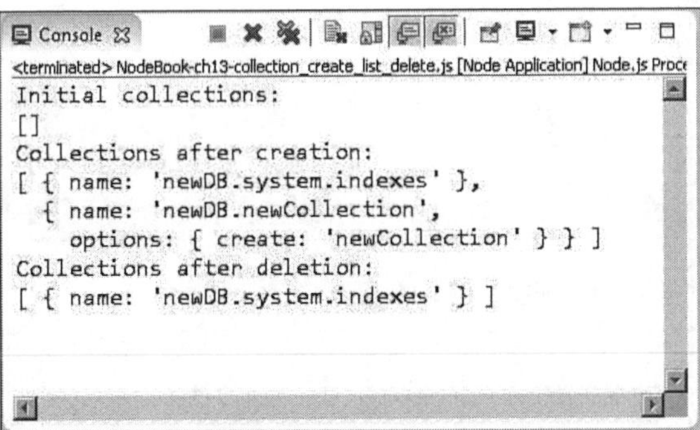

Figure 13.5 Creating, retrieving, and deleting collections on a MongoDB database.

Getting Collection Information

Another very useful feature of the `Collection` object is the ability to get the statistics for a particular collection. The statistics can give you an idea of how big the collection is, both in terms of number of documents and size on disk. You may want to add code that periodically checks the stats of your collections to determine whether they need to be cleaned up.

Listing 13.6 shows how to access the stats for a collection by calling the `stats()` method on the `Collection` object. Figure 13.6 shows the output from the `stats()` call.

Listing 13.6 `collection_stat.js`: **Retrieving and displaying the stats for a collection**

```
var MongoClient = require('mongodb').MongoClient;
MongoClient.connect("mongodb://localhost/", function(err, db) {
  var newDB = db.db("newDB");
  newDB.createCollection("newCollection", function(err, collection){
    collection.stats(function(err, stats){
      console.log(stats);
      db.close();
    });
  });
});
```

```
Console
<terminated> NodeBook-ch13-collection_stats.js [Node Application] Node.js Process
{ ns: 'newDB.newCollection',
  count: 0,
  size: 0,
  storageSize: 8192,
  numExtents: 1,
  nindexes: 1,
  lastExtentSize: 8192,
  paddingFactor: 1,
  systemFlags: 1,
  userFlags: 0,
  totalIndexSize: 8176,
  indexSizes: { _id_: 8176 },
  ok: 1 }
```

Figure 13.6 Retrieving and displaying the stats for a collection.

Summary

The MongoDB Node.js driver is the officially supported native method for accessing MongoDB from Node.js applications. It is simple to install and easy to incorporate into your Node.js applications. In this chapter you learned the various methods and options to connect to a MongoDB database using the `MongoClient` class. You also got a chance to see and work with the `Db`, `Admin`, `Collection`, and `Cursor` classes.

The examples in this chapter took you through creating, viewing, and deleting databases dynamically from your Node.js applications. You also got a chance see how to create, access, and delete collections.

Up Next

In the next chapter you will get a chance to work with MongoDB documents. You will learn the methods for inserting MongoDB documents into a collection and how to access them. You will also learn how to manipulate and delete documents in several different ways.

14

Manipulating MongoDB Documents from Node.js

In Chapter 13, "Getting Started with MongoDB and Node.js," you learned the fundamentals of using the MongoDB Node.js driver to manage and manipulate databases and collections. This chapter expands on those concepts, describing manipulation of documents within collections. As described in Chapter 13, the MongoDB Node.js driver provides a lot of functionality in the `Collection` class, which allows you to insert, access, modify, and remove documents from collections.

This chapter is broken into sections that describe the basic document management tasks you perform on collections, including insertions and deletions. This chapter introduces you to the options that control the behavior of write requests to the database. You will also learn about the update structure that MongoDB allows you to use to update documents rather than the long, complex query strings you may have seen in SQL.

Understanding Database Change Options

Several of the methods discussed in this chapter modify a MongoDB database. When you make changes to a database, the MongoDB Node.js driver needs to know how to handle the connection during the change process. For that reason, each of the methods that change the database allow you to pass in an optional `options` parameter that can specify some or all of the properties listed in Table 14.1.

Table 14.1 **Options that can be specified in the `options` parameter for database changes**

Option	Description
`w`	Specifies the write concern level for database connections. See Table 13.1 for the available values.
`wtimeout`	Specifies the amount of time, in milliseconds, to wait for the write concern to finish. This value is added to the normal connection timeout value.
`fsync`	A Boolean that, when set to `true`, indicates that write requests should wait for `fsync` to finish before returning.
`journal`	A Boolean that, when set to `true`, indicates that write requests should wait for the `journal` sync to complete before returning.
`serializeFunctions`	A Boolean that, when set to `true`, indicates that functions attached to objects should be serialized when stored in the document.
`forceServerObjectId`	A Boolean that, when set to `true`, indicates that any object ID (`_id`) value set by the client will be overridden by the server during an insertion.
`checkKeys`	A Boolean that, when set to `true`, causes the document keys to be checked when being inserted into the database. The default is `true`. Warning: Setting this to `false` can open up MongoDB for injection attacks.
`upsert`	A Boolean that, when set to `true`, indicates that if no documents match the update request, a new document will be created.
`multi`	A Boolean that, when set to `true`, indicates that if multiple documents match the query in an update request, all documents are updated. When set to `false`, only the first document found is updated.
`new`	A Boolean that, when set to `true`, indicates that the newly modified object is returned by the `findAndModify()` method instead of the pre-modified version. The default is `false`.

Understanding Database Update Operators

When performing updates on objects in MongoDB, you need to specify exactly what fields need to be changed and how they need to be changed. Unlike in SQL, where you create long query strings to define an update, in MongoDB you can implement an `update` object with operators that define exactly how to change the data in the documents.

You can include as many operators in the `update` object as you need. The format of the `update` object is shown below:

```
{
  <operator>: {<field_operation>, <field_operation>, . . .},
  <operator>: {<field_operation>, <field_operation>, . . .}
  . . .
}
```

For example, consider the following object:

```
{
  name: "myName",
  countA: 0,
  countB: 0,
  days: ["Monday", "Wednesday"],
  scores: [ {id:"test1", score:94}, {id:"test2", score:85}, {id:"test3", score:97}]
}
```

Use the following `update` object if you want to increment the `countA` field by `5`, increment `countB` by `1`, set `name` to `"New Name"`, add `Friday` to the `days` array, and sort the `scores` array by the `score` field:

```
{
  $inc:{countA:5, countB:1},
  $set:{name:"New Name"},
  $push{days:"Friday"},
  $sort:{score:1}
}
```

Table 14.2 lists the operators you can use in the `update` object to update documents.

Table 14.2 **Operators you can specify in the `update` object when performing update operations**

Operator	Description
`$inc`	Increments the value of the field by the specified amount. Operation format: `field:inc_value`
`$rename`	Renames a field. Operation format: `field:new_name`
`$setOnInsert`	Sets the value of a field when a new document is created in the update operation. Operation format: `field:value`
`$set`	Sets the value of a field in an existing document. Operation format: `field:new_value`
`$unset`	Removes the specified field from an existing document. Operation format: `field:""`
`$`	Acts as a placeholder to update the first element that matches the query condition in an update.

Operator	Description
`$addToSet`	Adds elements to an existing array only if they do not already exist in the set. Operation format: `array_field:new_value`
`$pop`	Removes the first or last item of an array. If `pop_value` is `-1`, the first element is removed. If the `pop_value` is `1`, the last element is removed. Operation format: `array_field:pop_value`
`$pullAll`	Removes multiple values from an array. The values are passed in as an array to the filedname. Operation format: `array_field:[value1, value2, ...]`
`$pull`	Removes from an array items that match a `query` statement. The `query` statement is a basic query object with fieldnames and values to match. Operation format: `array_field:[<query>]`
`$push`	Adds an item to an array. Simple array format: `array_field:new_value`; object array format: `array_field:{field:value}`
`$each`	Modifies the `$push` and `$addToSet` operators to append multiple items for array updates. Operation format: `array_field:{$each:[value1, ...]}`
`$slice`	Modifies the `$push` operator to limit the size of updated arrays.
`$sort`	Modifies the `$push` operator to reorder documents stored in an array. Operation format: `array_field:{$slice:<num> }`
`$bit`	Performs bitwise AND and OR updates of integer values. Operation format: `integer_field:{and:<integer> }` and`integer_field:{or:<integer> }`

Adding Documents to a Collection

Another common task when interacting with MongoDB databases is inserting documents into collections. To insert a document, you need to first create a JavaScript object that represents the document you want to store. You create a JavaScript object because the BSON format that MongoDB uses is based on JavaScript notation.

Once you have a JavaScript version of your new document, you can store it in the MongoDB database by using the `insert()` method on an instance of the `Collection` object that is connected to the database. The following is the syntax for the `insert()` method:

```
insert(docs, [options], callback)
```

The docs parameter can be a single document object or an array of document objects. The options parameter specifies the database change options described in Table 14.1. The callback parameter is required if you are implementing a write concern in options. The first parameter of callback is an error, and the second parameter is an array of the documents inserted into the collection.

Listing 14.1 is a basic example of inserting documents. Lines 2–9 show a function that accepts the Collection object and an object to insert. The insert() method is called, and the resulting array of inserted objects (one at a time in this case) is displayed on the console, as shown in Figure 14.1. Lines 10–13 open the connection to the MongoDB server, clear out the nebulae collection, and then re-create it to provide a clean slate. Then lines 14–19 call addObject() for a series of JavaScript objects describing nebulae.

Listing 14.1 doc_insert.js: **Inserting documents into a collection**

```
01 var MongoClient = require('mongodb').MongoClient;
02 function addObject(collection, object){
03   collection.insert(object, function(err, result){
04     if(!err){
05       console.log("Inserted : ");
06       console.log(result);
07     }
08   });
09 }
10 MongoClient.connect("mongodb://localhost/", function(err, db) {
11   var myDB = db.db("astro");
12   myDB.dropCollection("nebulae");
13   myDB.createCollection("nebulae", function(err, nebulae){
14     addObject(nebulae, {ngc:"NGC 7293", name:"Helix",
15       type:"planetary",location:"Aquila"});
16     addObject(nebulae, {ngc:"NGC 6543", name:"Cat's Eye",
17       type:"planetary",location:"Draco"});
18     addObject(nebulae, {ngc:"NGC 1952", name: "Crab",
19       type:"supernova",location:"Taurus"});
20   });
21   setTimeout(function(){ db.close(); }, 3000);
22 });
```

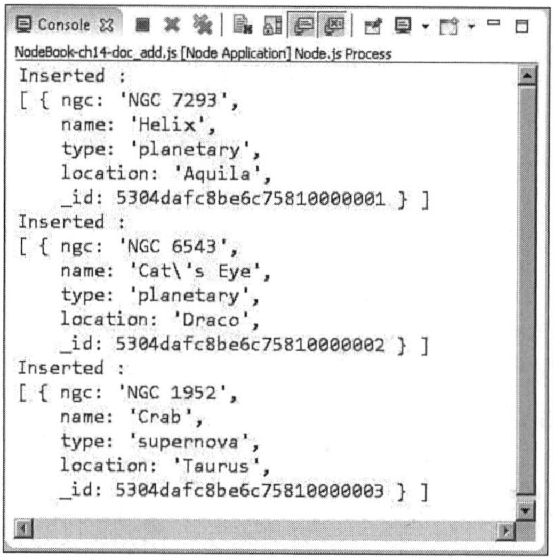
Console
NodeBook-ch14-doc_add.js [Node Application] Node.js Process
Inserted :
[{ ngc: 'NGC 7293',
name: 'Helix',
type: 'planetary',
location: 'Aquila',
_id: 5304dafc8be6c75810000001 }]
Inserted :
[{ ngc: 'NGC 6543',
name: 'Cat\'s Eye',
type: 'planetary',
location: 'Draco',
_id: 5304dafc8be6c75810000002 }]
Inserted :
[{ ngc: 'NGC 1952',
name: 'Crab',
type: 'supernova',
location: 'Taurus',
_id: 5304dafc8be6c75810000003 }]

Figure 14.1 Inserting documents into a collection.

Getting Documents from a Collection

One of the tasks that you commonly need to perform on data stored in a MongoDB database is retrieving one or more documents. For example, consider product information for products on a commercial website. The information is stored once but retrieved many times.

The retrieval of data sounds fairly simple, but it can become quite complex as you need to also filter, sort, limit, and aggregate the results. In fact, Chapter 15, "Accessing MongoDB Documents from Node.js," is devoted to the complexities of retrieving data.

This section introduces you to the simple basics of the `find()` and `findOne()` methods of the `Collection` object to make it easier to understand the code examples in this chapter. The syntax for the `find()` and `findOne()` methods is shown below:

```
find(query, [options], callback)
findOne(query, [options], callback)
```

Both `find()` and `findOne()` accept a `query` object as the first parameter. The `query` object contains properties that are matched against fields in the documents. Documents that match the `query` object are included in the list. The `options` parameter is an object that specifies everything else about the search for documents, such as the limit, sort, and what to return.

The callback function is where `find()` and `findOne()` differ. The `find()` method returns a `Cursor` object that can be iterated on to retrieve documents. On the other hand, the `findOne()` method returns a single object.

Listing 14.2 illustrates how to use `find()` and `findOne()`. Lines 5–10 implement `find()`. Notice that the result is a `Cursor` object. To display the results, the `toArray()` method iterates through the `Cursor` object and builds a basic JavaScript array of objects. This allows you to operate on the documents as you would a normal set of JavaScript objects.

Lines 11–18 use the `find()` method and also the `each()` method to iterate through the `Cursor` object. The `each()` method iterates through the documents represented in the `Cursor` object one at a time. For each iteration, a single document is retrieved from MongoDB and passed in as the second parameter to the `callback` function.

Lines 19–22 implement the `findOne()` method. Notice the simple query on the `type` field. The callback function receives the object and outputs it to the screen, as shown in Figure 14.2.

Listing 14.2 `doc_find.js`: **Finding documents in a MongoDB collection**

```
01 var MongoClient = require('mongodb').MongoClient;
02 MongoClient.connect("mongodb://localhost/", function(err, db) {
03   var myDB = db.db("astro");
04   myDB.collection("nebulae", function(err, nebulae){
05     nebulae.find(function(err, items){
06       items.toArray(function(err, itemArr){
07         console.log("Document Array: ");
08         console.log(itemArr);
09       });
10     });
11     nebulae.find(function(err, items){
12       items.each(function(err, item){
13         if(item){
14           console.log("Singular Document: ");
15           console.log(item);
16         }
17       });
18     });
19     nebulae.findOne({type:'planetary'}, function(err, item){
20       console.log("Found One: ");
21       console.log(item);
22     });
23   });
24   setTimeout(function(){ db.close(); }, 3000);
25 });
```

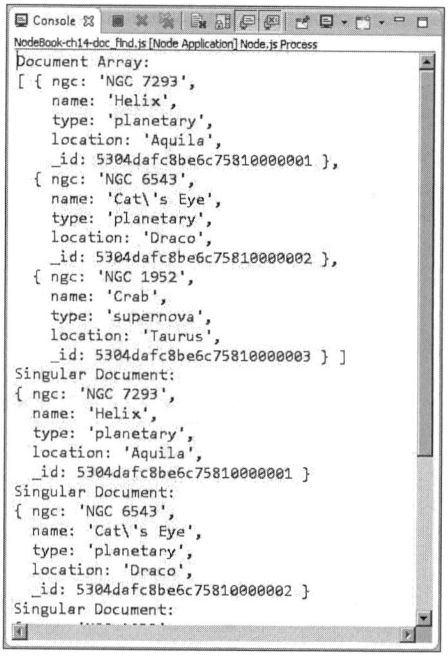
Console
NodeBook-ch14-doc_find.js [Node Application] Node.js Process
Document Array:
[{ ngc: 'NGC 7293',
name: 'Helix',
type: 'planetary',
location: 'Aquila',
_id: 5304dafc8be6c75810000001 },
{ ngc: 'NGC 6543',
name: 'Cat\'s Eye',
type: 'planetary',
location: 'Draco',
_id: 5304dafc8be6c75810000002 },
{ ngc: 'NGC 1952',
name: 'Crab',
type: 'supernova',
location: 'Taurus',
_id: 5304dafc8be6c75810000003 }]
Singular Document:
{ ngc: 'NGC 7293',
name: 'Helix',
type: 'planetary',
location: 'Aquila',
_id: 5304dafc8be6c75810000001 }
Singular Document:
{ ngc: 'NGC 6543',
name: 'Cat\'s Eye',
type: 'planetary',
location: 'Draco',
_id: 5304dafc8be6c75810000002 }
Singular Document:

Figure 14.2 Finding documents in MongoDB by using `find()` and `findOne()`.

Updating Documents in a Collection

Once objects have been inserted into a collection, you may need to update them from time to time as the data changes. The MongoDB Node.js driver provides several great methods for updating documents. The most commonly used is the `update()` method, which is versatile and yet fairly easy to implement. The following is the syntax for the `update()` method:

```
update(query, update, [options], [callback])
```

The `query` parameter is a document that is used to identify which document(s) you want to change. The request matches the properties and values in the query parameter with the fields and values of the object, and only those that match the query are updated. The `update` parameter is an object that specifies the changes to make to the documents that match the query. Table 14.2 lists the operators that can be used.

The `options` parameter specifies the database change options described in Table 14.1. The `callback` parameter is required if you are implementing a write concern in `options`. The first parameter of `callback` is an error, and the second parameter is an array of the documents inserted into the collection.

When you update multiple documents with the `update()` call, you can isolate writes to protect the documents from other writes by using the `$isolate:1` property in the `query`. This doesn't provide an all-or-nothing atomic write but simply inhibits other write processes from updating the same objects you are writing to. For example:

```
update({type:"Planetary", $isolated:1}, {updated:true}, {multi:true})
```

Listing 14.3 shows how to update multiple objects by using the `update()` method. Lines 9–19 implement the `update()` method and callback to change the type `planetary` to `Planetary` and add a new field named `updated`. Notice that the `$set` operator is used to set values. Also notice that `upsert` is `false` so that new documents will not be created, `multi` is `true` so that multiple documents will get updated, and `w` is `1` so that the request will wait for the write operation before returning (see Figure 14.3).

Listing 14.3 `doc_update.js`: **Updating multiple documents in a database**

```
01 var MongoClient = require('mongodb').MongoClient;
02 MongoClient.connect("mongodb://localhost/", function(err, db) {
03   var myDB = db.db("astro");
04   myDB.collection("nebulae", function(err, nebulae){
05     nebulae.find({type:"planetary"}, function(err, items){
06       items.toArray(function(err, itemArr){
07         console.log("Before Update: ");
08         console.log(itemArr);
09         nebulae.update({type:"planetary", $isolated:1},
10                        {$set:{type:"Planetary", updated:true}},
11                        {upsert:false, multi:true, w:1},
12                        function(err, results){
13           nebulae.find({type:"Planetary"}, function(err, items){
14             items.toArray(function(err, itemArr){
15               console.log("After Update: ");
16               console.log(itemArr);
17               db.close();
18             });
19           });
20         });
21       });
22     });
23   });
24 });
```

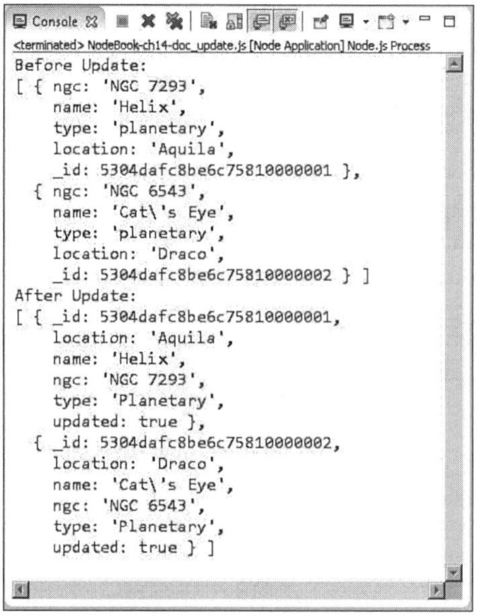
Console
<terminated> NodeBook-ch14-doc_update.js [Node Application] Node.js Process
Before Update:
[{ ngc: 'NGC 7293',
name: 'Helix',
type: 'planetary',
location: 'Aquila',
_id: 5304dafc8be6c75810000001 },
{ ngc: 'NGC 6543',
name: 'Cat\'s Eye',
type: 'planetary',
location: 'Draco',
_id: 5304dafc8be6c75810000002 }]
After Update:
[{ _id: 5304dafc8be6c75810000001,
location: 'Aquila',
name: 'Helix',
ngc: 'NGC 7293',
type: 'Planetary',
updated: true },
{ _id: 5304dafc8be6c75810000002,
location: 'Draco',
name: 'Cat\'s Eye',
ngc: 'NGC 6543',
type: 'Planetary',
updated: true }]

Figure 14.3 Updating multiple documents in a database.

Atomically Modifying Documents in a Collection

The `Collection` object provides the `findAndModify()` function, which performs an atomic write on a single document in a collection. This is extremely useful if you need to ensure that no other processes can write to your document at the same time. The following is the syntax for the `findAndModify()` method:

```
findAndModify(query, sort, update, [options], callback)
```

The `query` parameter is a document that is used to identify which document you want to modify. The request matches the properties and values in the `query` parameter with the fields and values of the object, and only those that match the query are modified.

The `sort` parameter is an array of `[field, sort_order]` pairs that specify which fields to sort on when finding the item to modify. The `sort_order` value is `1` for ascending or `-1` for descending. The `update` parameter is an object that specifies the changes to make to the documents that match the query. Table 14.2 lists the operators that can be used.

The `options` parameter specifies the database change options described in Table 14.1. The `callback` parameter is required if you are implementing a write concern in `options`. The first parameter of `callback` is an error, and the second parameter is the object that is being modified. If `new` is set to `true` in `options`, the newly modified object is returned. If `new` is set to `false`, the premodified object is returned. Getting back the premodified object can be useful if you need to verify changes or store the original somewhere else.

Listing 14.4 performs an atomic write on a single object in the MongoDB database. Lines 9–15 implement the `findAndModify()` operation. Notice that the `sort` value is `[['name', 1]]`, which indicates to sort on `name` in ascending order. Also notice that `w` is `1` to enable the write concern, and `new` is set to `true` so that the modified object is returned in the callback function and displayed on the console, as shown in Figure 14.4.

Listing 14.4 `doc_modify.js`: **Atomically modifying a document by using** `findAndModify()`

```
01 var MongoClient = require('mongodb').MongoClient;
02 MongoClient.connect("mongodb://localhost/", function(err, db) {
03   var myDB = db.db("astro");
04   myDB.collection("nebulae", function(err, nebulae){
05     nebulae.find({type:"supernova"}, function(err, items){
06       items.toArray(function(err, itemArr){
07         console.log("Before Modify: ");
08         console.log(itemArr);
09         nebulae.findAndModify({type:"supernova"}, [['name', 1]],
10             {$set: {type:"Super Nova", "updated":true}},
11             {w:1, new:true}, function(err, doc){
12           console.log("After Modify: ");
13           console.log(doc);
14           db.close();
15         });
16       });
17     });
18   });
19 });
```

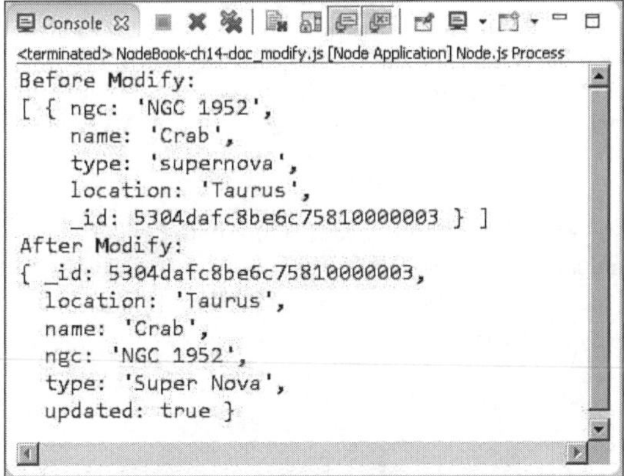

Figure 14.4 Atomically modifying a document by using `findAndModify()`.

Saving Documents in a Collection

The `save()` method on `Collection` objects is kind of interesting. You can use it to insert or update a document in a database. Although it is not as efficient as `insert()` or `update()`, the `save()` method is easier to implement in some circumstances. For example, when you are making ad hoc changes to objects already retrieved from a MongoDB database, you can use `save()` without having to implement the query and update objects of the `update()` method.

The following is the syntax of the `save()` method:

```
save(doc, [options], [callback])
```

The `doc` parameter is the document object you want to save to the collection. The `options` parameter specifies the database change options described in Table 14.1. The `callback` parameter is required if you are implementing a write concern in the options. The first parameter of the `callback` parameter is an error, and the second parameter is the object that was just saved to the collection.

Typically when you use `save()`, the `document` object is either a completely new JavaScript object that you want to add to the collection or an object you have already gotten back from the collection and made changes to, and you want to save those changes back to the database.

Listing 14.5 retrieves an object from the database, modifies it, and saves it back to the database, using the `save()` method. Lines 9–15 implement the `save()` method and `callback`. Notice that the `save()` method is much simpler to use than the `update()` and `findAndModify()` methods. Also notice that `savedItem` is returned to the callback function and displayed on the console, as shown in Figure 14.5.

Listing 14.5 `doc_save.js`**: Updating and saving an existing document by using** `save()`

```
01 var MongoClient = require('mongodb').MongoClient;
02 MongoClient.connect("mongodb://localhost/", function(err, db) {
03   var myDB = db.db("astro");
04   myDB.collection("nebulae", function(err, nebulae){
05     nebulae.findOne({type:"supernova"}, function(err, item){
06       console.log("Before Save: ");
07       console.log(item);
08       item.info = "Some New Info";
09       nebulae.save(item, {w:1}, function(err, results){
10         nebulae.findOne({_id:item._id}, function(err, savedItem){
11           console.log("After Save: ");
12           console.log(savedItem);
13           db.close();
14         });
15       });
16     });
17   });
18 });
```

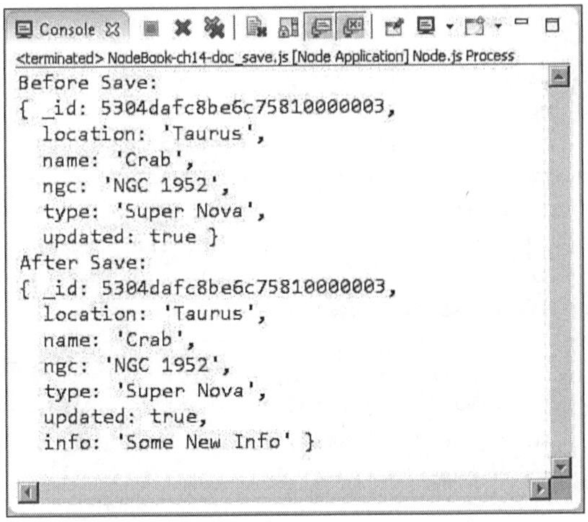

```
Console
<terminated> NodeBook-ch14-doc_save.js [Node Application] Node.js Process
Before Save:
{ _id: 5304dafc8be6c75810000003,
  location: 'Taurus',
  name: 'Crab',
  ngc: 'NGC 1952',
  type: 'Super Nova',
  updated: true }
After Save:
{ _id: 5304dafc8be6c75810000003,
  location: 'Taurus',
  name: 'Crab',
  ngc: 'NGC 1952',
  type: 'Super Nova',
  updated: true,
  info: 'Some New Info' }
```

Figure 14.5 Updating and saving an existing document by using `save()`.

Using `upsert` to Insert Documents in a Collection

Normal updates do not automatically insert objects because they incur a cost when they need to determine whether an object exists. If you know that an object exists, then a normal `update()` is efficient; `insert()` is better if you know that a document does not already exist. When you want a combination of updating an object if it exists and inserting it if it does not, you use `upsert`.

To implement `upsert`, you include the `upsert:true` option in the `update()` method's `options` parameter. This tells the request to try to update the object if it exists and to insert the object specified if it doesn't already exist.

Listing 14.6 shows how to use `upsert` with the `update()` method. The `update()` in lines 9–12 creates the object because it does not exist. Then line 17 retrieves the `_id` value of the inserted document and uses it in the query of the `update()` in lines 18–21 to ensure that an existing document will be found and updated. Figure 14.6 shows the output of the code in Listing 14.6. Notice that initially no documents match the descriptor and then after the first update, the document is inserted, and then it's modified after the second update.

Listing 14.6 `doc_upsert.js`: **Using `upsert` to Insert New Documents or Update Existing Ones**

```
01 var MongoClient = require('mongodb').MongoClient;
02 MongoClient.connect("mongodb://localhost/", function(err, db) {
03   var myDB = db.db("astro");
04   myDB.collection("nebulae", function(err, nebulae){
05     nebulae.find({type:"diffuse"}, function(err, items){
06       items.toArray(function(err, itemArr){
```

```
        console.log("Before Upsert: ");
        console.log(itemArr);
        nebulae.update({type:"diffuse"},
            {$set: {ngc:"NGC 3372", name:"Carina",
                    type:"diffuse",location:"Carina"}},
            {upsert:true, w:1,forceServerObjectId:false},
            function(err, results){
          nebulae.find({type:"diffuse"}, function(err, items){
            items.toArray(function(err, itemArr){
              console.log("After Upsert 1: ");
              console.log(itemArr);
              var itemID = itemArr[0]._id;
              nebulae.update({_id:itemID},
                  {$set: {ngc:"NGC 3372", name:"Carina",
                          type:"Diffuse",location:"Carina"}},
                  {upsert:true, w:1}, function(err, results){
                nebulae.findOne({_id:itemID}, function(err, item){
                  console.log("After Upsert 2: ");
                  console.log(item);
                  db.close();
                });
              });
            });
          });
        });
      });
    });
  });
});
```

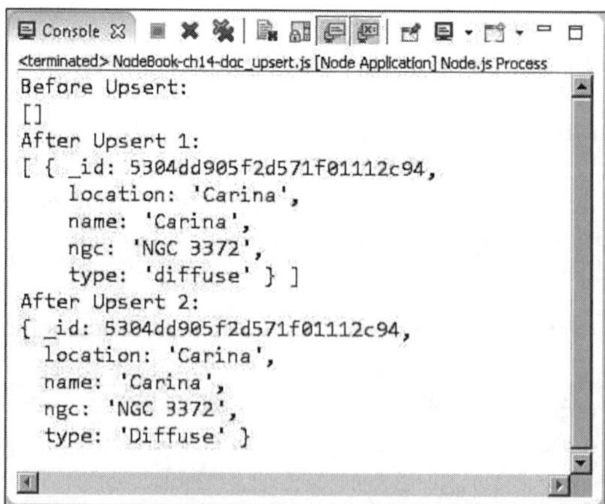

Figure 14.6 Using `upsert` to insert new documents or update existing ones.

Deleting Documents from a Collection

At times you may need to delete documents from your MongoDB collection to control space consumption, improve performance, and keep things clean. The `remove()` method on `Collection` objects makes it very simple to delete documents from a collection. The syntax for the `remove()` method is shown below:

```
remove([query], [options], [callback])
```

The `query` parameter is a document that is used to identify which document(s) you want to delete. The request matches the properties and values in `query` with the fields and values of the object, and only those that match the query are updated. If no `query` is provided, then all the documents in the collection are deleted.

The `options` parameter specifies the database change options described in Table 14.1. The `callback` parameter is required if you are implementing a write concern in `options`. The first parameter of `callback` is an error, and the second parameter is a count of the documents that were deleted.

Listing 14.7 uses the `remove()` method to delete objects from a collection. In lines 9–18, `remove()` and `callback` query the collection for documents whose `type` is `planetary` and deletes them from the collection. Notice that the `results` parameter of `callback` is the count of documents deleted. Figure 14.7 shows the output of Listing 14.7.

Listing 14.7 `doc_delete.js`: **Deleting documents from a collection**

```
01 var MongoClient = require('mongodb').MongoClient;
02 MongoClient.connect("mongodb://localhost/", function(err, db) {
03   var myDB = db.db("astro");
04   myDB.collection("nebulae", function(err, nebulae){
05     nebulae.find(function(err, items){
06       items.toArray(function(err, itemArr){
07         console.log("Before Delete: ");
08         console.log(itemArr);
09         nebulae.remove({type:"planetary"}, function(err, results){
10           console.log("Deleted " + results + " documents.");
11           nebulae.find(function(err, items){
12             items.toArray(function(err, itemArr){
13               console.log("After Delete: ");
14               console.log(itemArr);
15               db.close();
16             });
17           });
18         });
19       });
20     });
21   });
22 });
```

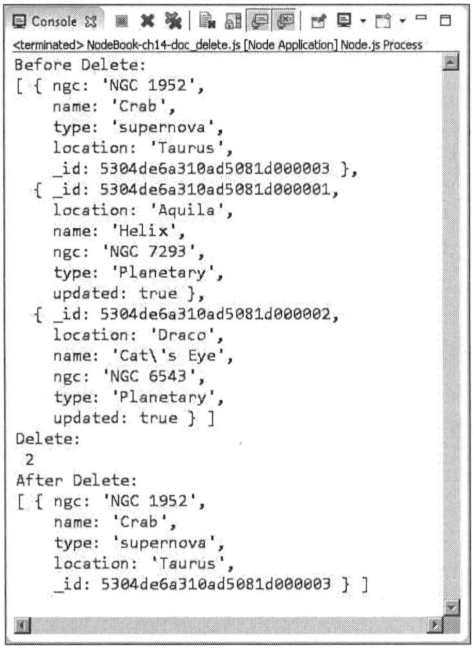

```
Console
<terminated> NodeBook-ch14-doc_delete.js [Node Application] Node.js Process
Before Delete:
[ { ngc: 'NGC 1952',
    name: 'Crab',
    type: 'supernova',
    location: 'Taurus',
    _id: 5304de6a310ad5081d000003 },
  { _id: 5304de6a310ad5081d000001,
    location: 'Aquila',
    name: 'Helix',
    ngc: 'NGC 7293',
    type: 'Planetary',
    updated: true },
  { _id: 5304de6a310ad5081d000002,
    location: 'Draco',
    name: 'Cat\'s Eye',
    ngc: 'NGC 6543',
    type: 'Planetary',
    updated: true } ]
Delete:
 2
After Delete:
[ { ngc: 'NGC 1952',
    name: 'Crab',
    type: 'supernova',
    location: 'Taurus',
    _id: 5304de6a310ad5081d000003 } ]
```

Figure 14.7 Deleting documents from a collection.

Removing a Single Document from a Collection

You can delete a single document from a database by using the `findAndRemove()` method. This is very similar to the `findAndModify()` method in syntax and application. The following is the syntax for the `findAndRemove()` method:

```
findAndRemove(query, sort, [options], callback)
```

The `query` parameter is a document that is used to identify the document to remove. The request matches the properties and values in the `query` parameter with the fields and values of the object, and only those that match the `query` parameter are modified.

The `sort` parameter is an array of `[field, sort_order]` pairs that specify which fields to sort on when finding the item to remove. `sort_order` is set to `1` for ascending and `-1` for descending. The `options` parameter specifies the database change options described in Table 14.1. The first parameter of the callback function is an error, and the second parameter is the results of the document deletion.

Listing 14.8 shows how to delete a document by using the `findAndRemove()` method. Lines 9–18 implement the `findAndRemove()` method and the callback. The code searches on the items whose `type` is `planetary`. The sort order `[['name', 1]]` specifies to sort the items by name, in ascending order. Notice in the results shown in Figure 14.8 that the `Cat's Eye` entry was deleted, but the `Helix` entry was not because of the sort order.

Listing 14.8 `doc_delete_one.js`: **Deleting single documents using** `findAndRemove()`

```
01 var MongoClient = require('mongodb').MongoClient;
02 MongoClient.connect("mongodb://localhost/", function(err, db) {
03   var myDB = db.db("astro");
04   myDB.collection("nebulae", function(err, nebulae){
05     nebulae.find(function(err, items){
06       items.toArray(function(err, itemArr){
07         console.log("Before Delete: ");
08         console.log(itemArr);
09         nebulae.findAndRemove({type:"Planetary"}, [['name', 1]],
10                               {w:1}, function(err, results){
11           console.log("Deleted:\n " + results);
12           nebulae.find(function(err, items){
13             items.toArray(function(err, itemArr){
14               console.log("After Delete: ");
15               console.log(itemArr);
16               db.close();
17             });
18           });
19         });
20       });
21     });
22   });
23 });
```

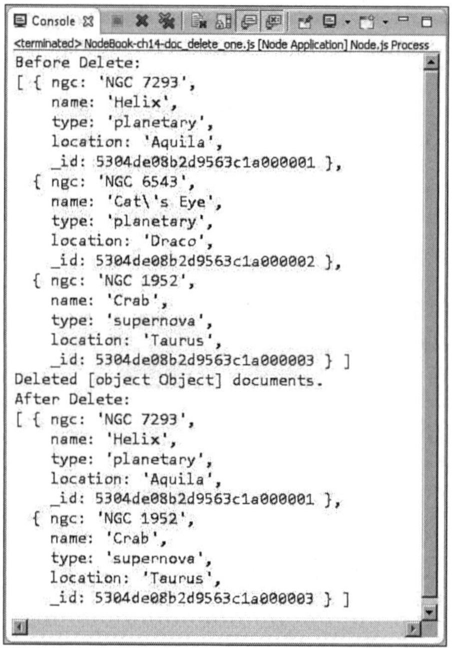

```
Console
<terminated> NodeBook-ch14-doc_delete_one.js [Node Application] Node.js Process
Before Delete:
[ { ngc: 'NGC 7293',
    name: 'Helix',
    type: 'planetary',
    location: 'Aquila',
    _id: 5304de08b2d9563c1a000001 },
  { ngc: 'NGC 6543',
    name: 'Cat\'s Eye',
    type: 'planetary',
    location: 'Draco',
    _id: 5304de08b2d9563c1a000002 },
  { ngc: 'NGC 1952',
    name: 'Crab',
    type: 'supernova',
    location: 'Taurus',
    _id: 5304de08b2d9563c1a000003 } ]
Deleted [object Object] documents.
After Delete:
[ { ngc: 'NGC 7293',
    name: 'Helix',
    type: 'planetary',
    location: 'Aquila',
    _id: 5304de08b2d9563c1a000001 },
  { ngc: 'NGC 1952',
    name: 'Crab',
    type: 'supernova',
    location: 'Taurus',
    _id: 5304de08b2d9563c1a000003 } ]
```

Figure 14.8 Deleting single documents by using `findAndRemove()`.

Summary

The MongoDB Node.js driver provides methods to insert, access, modify, and remove documents from collections. You can use `insert()`, `save()`, and even `update()` with `upsert` to insert documents into a database. You can use `update()`, `save()`, and `findAndModify()` to update existing documents. You can use the `remove()` and `findAndRemove()` methods to delete documents.

You can control changes to documents in a database in several ways, such as defining the write concern, using journaling, and using other settings to control the behavior of the write request and response. Also, the update structure that MongoDB uses to update documents is much easier to implement and maintain than the long, complex query strings in SQL.

Up Next

In this chapter you learned about using `find()` and `findOne()` to find objects in a database. The next chapter expands on those methods and provides more complex examples of how to filter, sort, and limit the results returned when finding objects in a collection.

15

Accessing MongoDB Documents from Node.js

In the previous chapter you learned how to create and manipulate documents and how to find them by using the `find()` method. This chapter takes a deeper look at accessing documents in a MongoDB collection, using the MongoDB Node.js driver module.

There is much more to accessing documents than just returning everything in a collection. This chapter covers using the `query` object to limit which documents are returned as well as methods to limit the fields and number of documents in the query results. You will also get a chance to see how to count the number of documents that match query criteria without actually retrieving them from the server. This chapter also covers some advanced aggregation techniques to group the results and even generate a new fully aggregated set of documents.

Introducing the Data Set

To introduce you to the various methods of accessing data, all the data used for examples in this chapter comes from the same data set. The data set is a collection that contains information about 5,000 words. This provides a large enough data set to implement the necessary examples.

You can create the data set on your development system by executing the ch15/generate_data.js script provided in the code archive for this book. The generate.js script is a basic JavaScript MongoDB shell script that will create a database named words and a collection named word_stats. To run the script, download the generate_data.js file from the book's code archive to your local system, start MongoDB, and execute the following command from a console prompt in the same directory as the script file:

```
mongo generate_data.js
```

The structure of objects in this data set is as follows and should be fairly intuitive (which is why it was selected):

```
{
  word: <word>,
  first: <first_letter>,
  last: <last_letter>,
  size: <character_count>,
  letters: [<array_of_characters_in_word_no_repeats>],
  stats: {
    vowels:<vowel_count>, consonants:<consonant_count>},
  charsets: [
    {
      "type": <consonants_vowels_other>,
      "chars": [<array_of_characters_of_type_in_word>]},
    . . .
  ],
}
```

This document structure includes fields that are strings, integers, arrays, subdocuments, and arrays of subdocuments.

Understanding Query Objects

Throughout this chapter, the various methods all use a `query` object of some sort or another to define which documents to retrieve from a MongoDB collection. The `query` object is a standard JavaScript object with special property names that the MongoDB Node.js driver understands. These property names closely match the native queries that you can perform inside the MongoDB client, so you can easily transfer back and forth.

The properties of the `query` object are called *operators* because they operate on the data to determine whether a document should be included in the result set. These operators match the values of fields in a document against specific criteria. For example, to find all documents with a `count` value greater than `10` and `name` value equal to `test`, you use this `query` object:

```
{count:{$gt:10}, name:'test'}
```

The operator `$gt` specifies documents with a `count` field larger than `10`. Using the standard colon syntax of `name:'test'` specifies that the `name` field must equal `test`. Notice that the `query` object has multiple operators. You can include several different operators in the same query.

When specifying fieldnames in a `query` object, you can use dot notation to specify subdocument fields. For example, consider the following object format:

```
{
  name:"test",
  stats: { height:74, eyes:'blue'}
}
```

You can query which users have blue eyes by using the following query object:

```
{stats.eyes:'blue'}
```

Table 15.1 lists the most commonly used operators.

Table 15.1 query **object operators that define the result set returned by MongoDB requests**

Operator	Description
field:value	Matches documents with fields that have a value equal to the value specified. For example: {name:"myName"}
$gt	Matches values that are greater than the value specified in the query. For example: {size:{$gt:5}}
$gte	Matches values that are equal to or greater than the value specified in the query. For example: {size:{$gte:5}}
$in	Matches any of the values that exist in an array specified in the query. For example: {name:{$in:['item1', 'item2']}}
$lt	Matches values that are less than the value specified in the query. For example: {size:{$lt:5}}
$lte	Matches values that are less than or equal to the value specified in the query. For example: {size:{$lte:5}}
$ne	Matches all values that are not equal to the value specified in the query. For example: {name:{$ne:"badName"}}
$nin	Matches values that do not exist in an array specified in the query. For example: {name:{$in:['item1', 'item2']}}
$or	Joins query clauses with a logical OR and returns all documents that match the conditions of either clause. For example: {$or:[{size:{$lt:5}}, {size:{$gt:10}}]}
$and	Joins query clauses with a logical AND and returns all documents that match the conditions of both clauses. For example: {$and:[{size:{$lt:5}}, {size:{$gt:10}}]}
$not	Inverts the effect of a query expression and returns documents that do not match the query expression. For example: {$not:{size:{$lt:5}}}}
$nor	Joins query clauses with a logical NOR and returns all documents that fail to match both clauses. For example: {$nor:{size:{$lt:5}}, {name:"myName"}}}
$exists	Matches documents that have the specified field. For example: {specialField:{$exists:true}}
$type	Selects documents if a field is of the specified BSON type number. Table 11.1 lists the different BSON type numbers. For example: {specialField:{$type:<BSONtype>}}

Operator	Description
`$mod`	Performs a modulo operation on the value of a field and selects documents with a specified result. The value for the modulo operation is specified as an array, with the first number being the number to divide by and the second being the remainder. For example: `{number:{$mod:[2,0]}}`
`$regex`	Selects documents where values match a specified regular expression. For example: `{myString:{$regex:'some.*exp'}}`
`$all`	Matches arrays that contain all elements specified in the query. For example: `{myArr:{$all:['one','two','three]}}`
`$elemMatch`	Selects documents if an element in the array of subdocuments has fields that match all the specified `$elemMatch` conditions. For example: `{myArr:{$elemMatch:{value:{$gt:5},size:{$lt:3}}}}`
`$size`	Selects documents if the array field is a specified size. For example: `{myArr:{$size:5}}`

Understanding Query `options` Objects

In addition to the `query` object, most of the methods of retrieving documents using the MongoDB Node.js driver also include an `options` object. The `options` object allows you to define the behavior of the request when retrieving documents. It allows you to limit the result set, sort items while creating the result set, and much more.

Table 15.2 lists the options that can be set on methods that retrieve documents from the MongoDB server. Not all of these methods are available on every request. For example, when counting items that match a query, it doesn't make sense to specify a limit on the result.

Table 15.2 **Options that can be specified in the `options` object when querying documents**

Option	Description
`limit`	Specifies the maximum number of documents to return.
`sort`	Specifies the sort order of documents as an array of `[field, <sort_order>]` elements, where `sort_order` is `1` for ascending and `-1` for descending. For example:`sort:[['name":1],['value':-1]]`
`fields`	Specifies an object whose fields match fields that should be included or excluded from the returned documents. A value of `1` means include, and a value of `0` means exclude. You can only include or exclude, not both. For example: `fields:{name:1,value:1}`

Option	Description
`skip`	Specifies the number of documents from the query results to skip before returning a document. Typically used when paginating result sets.
`hint`	Forces the query to use specific indexes when building the result set. For example: `hint:{'_id':1}`
`explain`	Returns an explanation of what will happen when performing the query on the server instead of actually running the query. This is essential when you're trying to debug/optimize complex queries.
`snapshot`	`Boolean`. When `true` a snapshot query is created.
`timeout`	A Boolean that, when `true`, indicates that the cursor is allowed to time out.
`maxScan`	Specifies the maximum number of documents to scan when performing a query before returning. This is useful if you have a collection that has millions of objects and you don't want queries to run forever.
`comment`	Specifies a string that will be printed out in the MongoDB logs. This can help you troubleshoot by making it easier to identify queries.
`readPreference`	Specifies whether to read from a primary server, a secondary replica, or just the nearest MongoDB server in the replica set to perform the query.
`numberOfRetries`	Specifies the number of timeout retries to perform on the query before failing. Default: `5`
`partial`	A Boolean that, when `true`, indicates that the cursor will return partial results when querying against data that is shared between sharded systems.

Finding Specific Sets of Documents

In Chapter 14, "Manipulating MongoDB Documents from Node.js," you learned about the `find()` method of the `Collection` object. This method returns a `Cursor` object to the callback function, providing access to the documents. If no query is specified, then all documents are returned, which is rarely what you want. Instead, you typically need a subset of documents that match a certain set of criteria.

To limit the number of documents the `find()` method finds, you apply a `query` object that limits the documents that will be returned in the `Cursor` object.

The code in Listing 15.1 performs a bunch of different queries against the word collection data set described earlier in this chapter. You should already recognize all the connection code as well as the code used in `displayWords()` to iterate through the cursor and display only the word names in the documents.

In line 20 the following query looks for words that start with a, b, or c:

```
{first:{$in: ['a', 'b', 'c']}}
```

In line 23 the following query looks for words longer than 12 letters:

```
{size:{$gt: 12}}
```

In line 26 the following query looks for words with an even number of letters:

```
{size:{$mod: [2,0]}}
```

In line 29 the following query looks for words with exactly 12 letters:

```
{letters:{$size: 12}}
```

In lines 32 and 33 the following query looks for words that both begin and end with a vowel:

```
{$and: [{first:{$in: ['a', 'e', 'i', 'o', 'u']}},
        {last:{$in: ['a', 'e', 'i', 'o', 'u']}}]}
```

In line 37 the following query looks for words that contain more than six vowels:

```
{"stats.vowels":{$gt:6}}
```

In line 40 the following query looks for words that contain all of the vowels:

```
{letters:{$all: ['a','e','i','o','u']}}
```

In line 44 the following query looks for words with non-alphabet characters:

```
{otherChars: {$exists:true}}
```

Line 47 uses a query that's rather challenging. It uses the `$elemMatch` operator to match the `charsets` subdocuments. The `$and` operator forces the `type` field to equal `other` and the `chars` array field to be exactly `2`:

```
{charsets:{$elemMatch:{$and:[{type:'other'},{chars:{$size:2}}]}}}
```

Figure 15.1 shows the output from Listing 15.1.

Listing 15.1 `doc_query.js`**: Finding a specific set of documents in a MongoDB collection**

```
01 var MongoClient = require('mongodb').MongoClient;
02 MongoClient.connect("mongodb://localhost/", function(err, db) {
03   var myDB = db.db("words");
04   myDB.collection("word_stats", findItems);
05   setTimeout(function(){
06     db.close();
07   }, 3000);
08 });
09 function displayWords(msg, cursor, pretty){
10   cursor.toArray(function(err, itemArr){
11     console.log("\n"+msg);
```

```
    var wordList = [];
    for(var i=0; i<itemArr.length; i++){
      wordList.push(itemArr[i].word);
    }
    console.log(JSON.stringify(wordList, null, pretty));
  });
}
function findItems(err, words){
  words.find({first:{$in: ['a', 'b', 'c']}}, function(err, cursor){
    displayWords("Words starting with a, b or c: ", cursor);
  });
  words.find({size:{$gt: 12}}, function(err, cursor){
    displayWords("Words longer than 12 characters: ", cursor);
  });
  words.find({size:{$mod: [2,0]}}, function(err, cursor){
    displayWords("Words with even Lengths: ", cursor);
  });
  words.find({letters:{$size: 12}}, function(err, cursor){
    displayWords("Words with 12 Distinct characters: ", cursor);
  });
  words.find({$and: [{first:{$in: ['a', 'e', 'i', 'o', 'u']}},
                     {last:{$in: ['a', 'e', 'i', 'o', 'u']}}]},
             function(err, cursor){
    displayWords("Words that start and end with a vowel: ", cursor);
  });
  words.find({"stats.vowels":{$gt:6}}, function(err, cursor){
    displayWords("Words containing 7 or more vowels: ", cursor);
  });
  words.find({letters:{$all: ['a','e','i','o','u']}},
             function(err, cursor){
    displayWords("Words with all 5 vowels: ", cursor);
  });
  words.find({otherChars: {$exists:true}}, function(err, cursor){
    displayWords("Words with non-alphabet characters: ", cursor);
  });
  words.find({charsets:{$elemMatch:{$and:[{type:'other'},
                                          {chars:{$size:2}}]}}},
             function(err, cursor){
    displayWords("Words with 2 non-alphabet characters: ", cursor);
  });
}
```

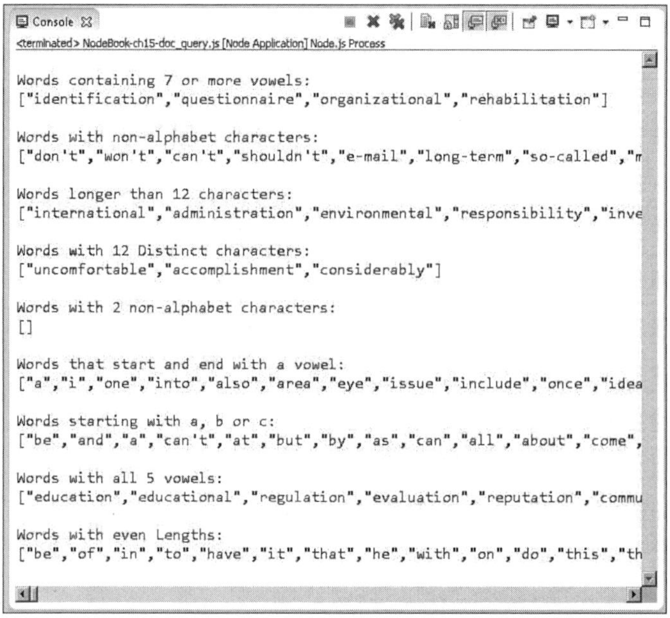

```
Console
<terminated> NodeBook-ch15-doc_query.js [Node Application] Node.js Process

Words containing 7 or more vowels:
["identification","questionnaire","organizational","rehabilitation"]

Words with non-alphabet characters:
["don't","won't","can't","shouldn't","e-mail","long-term","so-called","m

Words longer than 12 characters:
["international","administration","environmental","responsibility","inve

Words with 12 Distinct characters:
["uncomfortable","accomplishment","considerably"]

Words with 2 non-alphabet characters:
[]

Words that start and end with a vowel:
["a","i","one","into","also","area","eye","issue","include","once","idea

Words starting with a, b or c:
["be","and","a","can't","at","but","by","as","can","all","about","come",

Words with all 5 vowels:
["education","educational","regulation","evaluation","reputation","commu

Words with even Lengths:
["be","of","in","to","have","it","that","he","with","on","do","this","th
```

Figure 15.1 Finding specific documents in MongoDB by using `query` objects in `find()`.

Counting Documents

When accessing document sets in MongoDB, you might want to get a count first and then decide whether to retrieve a set of documents. There are several reasons to count specific document sets. Performing a count is much less intensive on the MongoDB side than retrieving documents using `find()` and other methods, which cause temporary objects such as `Cursor` objects to be created and maintained by the server.

When performing operations on the resulting set of documents from a `find()`, you should be aware of how many documents you are going to be dealing with, especially in larger environments. Sometimes all you want is a count. For example, if you need to know how many users are configured in your application, you could just count the number of documents in the `users` collection.

The `count()` method on the `Collection` object allows you to get a simple count of documents that match the `query` object criteria. The `count()` method is formatted exactly the same way as the `find()` method, as shown below, and it performs the `query` and `options` parameters in exactly the same manner:

```
count([query], [options], callback)
```

If no query value is specified, count() returns a count of all the documents in the database. The callback function accepts an error as the first argument and the count, as an integer, as the second.

Listing 15.2 uses the count() method with exactly the same queries performed with find() in Listing 15.1. The output in Figure 15.2 shows that instead of a Cursor object, a simple integer is returned and displayed.

Listing 15.2 doc_count.js: **Counting a specific set of documents in a MongoDB collection**

```
var MongoClient = require('mongodb').MongoClient;
MongoClient.connect("mongodb://localhost/", function(err, db) {
  var myDB = db.db("words");
  myDB.collection("word_stats", countItems);
  setTimeout(function(){
    db.close();
  }, 3000);
});
function countItems(err, words){
  words.count({first:{$in: ['a', 'b', 'c']}}, function(err, count){
    console.log("Words starting with a, b or c: " + count);
  });
  words.count({size:{$gt: 12}}, function(err, count){
    console.log("Words longer than 12 characters: " + count);
  });
  words.count({size:{$mod: [2,0]}}, function(err, count){
    console.log("Words with even Lengths: " + count);
  });
  words.count({letters:{$size: 12}}, function(err, count){
    console.log("Words with 12 Distinct characters: " + count);
  });
  words.count({$and: [{first:{$in: ['a', 'e', 'i', 'o', 'u']}},
                      {last:{$in: ['a', 'e', 'i', 'o', 'u']}}]},
              function(err, count){
    console.log("Words that start and end with a vowel: " + count);
  });
  words.count({"stats.vowels":{$gt:6}}, function(err, count){
    console.log("Words containing 7 or more vowels: " + count);
  });
  words.count({letters:{$all: ['a','e','i','o','u']}},
              function(err, count){
    console.log("Words with all 5 vowels: " + count);
  });
  words.count({otherChars: {$exists:true}}, function(err, count){
    console.log("Words with non-alphabet characters: " + count);
  });
  words.count({charsets:{$elemMatch:{$and:[{type:'other'},
```

```
                {chars:{$size:2}}]}}},
                function(err, count){
      console.log("Words with 2 non-alphabet characters: " + count);
  });
}
```

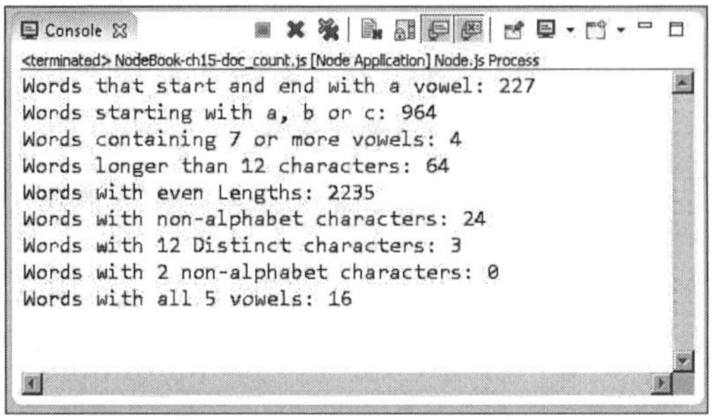

```
Console
<terminated> NodeBook-ch15-doc_count.js [Node Application] Node.js Process
Words that start and end with a vowel: 227
Words starting with a, b or c: 964
Words containing 7 or more vowels: 4
Words longer than 12 characters: 64
Words with even Lengths: 2235
Words with non-alphabet characters: 24
Words with 12 Distinct characters: 3
Words with 2 non-alphabet characters: 0
Words with all 5 vowels: 16
```

Figure 15.2 Counting specific documents in MongoDB by using `query` objects in `count()`.

Limiting Result Sets

When you're finding documents on large systems with complex documents, you often need to limit what is being returned to reduce the impact on the network, memory on both the server and client, etc. There are three ways to limit the result sets that match a specific query. You can simply accept only a limited number of documents, you can limit the fields that are returned, or you can page the results and get them in chunks.

Limiting Results by Size

The simplest way to limit the amount of data returned in a `find()` or another query request is to use the `limit` option in the `options` parameter when performing the request. The `limit` parameter, shown below, allows only a fixed number of items to be returned with the `Cursor` object. This can prevent you from accidentally retrieving more objects than your application can handle:

```
limit:<maximum_documents_to_return>
```

Listing 15.3 shows how to limit the results of a `find()` request by using the `limit:5` option in the `options` object. The output in Figure 15.3 shows that when `limit:5` is used, only five words are retrieved.

Listing 15.3 `doc_limit.js`: **Limiting a specific set of documents in a MongoDB collection**

```
var MongoClient = require('mongodb').MongoClient;
MongoClient.connect("mongodb://localhost/", function(err, db) {
  var myDB = db.db("words");
  myDB.collection("word_stats", limitFind);
  setTimeout(function(){
    db.close();
  }, 3000);
});
function displayWords(msg, cursor, pretty){
  cursor.toArray(function(err, itemArr){
    console.log("\n"+msg);
    var wordList = [];
    for(var i=0; i<itemArr.length; i++){
      wordList.push(itemArr[i].word);
    }
    console.log(JSON.stringify(wordList, null, pretty));
  });
}
function limitFind(err, words){
  words.count({first:'p'}, function(err, count){
    console.log("Count of words starting with p : " + count);
  });
  words.find({first:'p'}, function(err, cursor){
    displayWords("Words starting with p : ", cursor);
  });
  words.find({first:'p'}, {limit:5}, function(err, cursor){
    displayWords("Limiting words starting with p : ", cursor);
  });
}
```

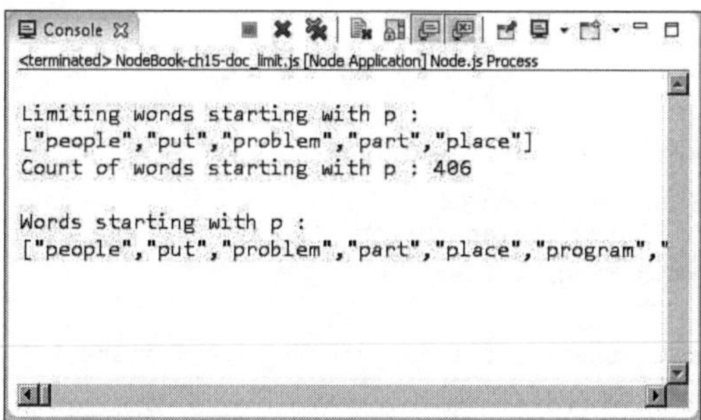

Figure 15.3 Limiting the documents returned by a `find()` request.

Limiting Fields Returned in Objects

Another extremely effective method of limiting the resulting data when retrieving documents is to limit which fields are returned. Documents may have a lot of different fields that are useful in some circumstance but not in others. You should consider which fields should be included when retrieving documents from the MongoDB server and only request the ones that are necessary.

To limit the fields returned from a server, use the `fields` option of the `options` object. The `fields` option in an object allows you to either include or exclude fields by setting the value of the `document` field to `0` for exclude or `1` for include. You cannot mix inclusions and exclusions in the same expression.

For example, to exclude the fields `stats`, `value`, and `comments` when returning a document, you use the following `fields` option:

```
{fields:{stats:0, value:0, comments:0}}
```

Often it is easier to just include a few fields. For example, if you want to include only the `name` and `value` fields of documents, you use:

```
{fields:{name:1, value:1}}
```

Listing 15.4 shows how to use the `fields` option to reduce the amount of data returned from the server by excluding fields or specifying specific fields to include. Figure 15.4 shows the output of Listing 15.4.

Listing 15.4 `doc_fields.js`: **Limiting the fields returned with a set of documents**

```
var MongoClient = require('mongodb').MongoClient;
MongoClient.connect("mongodb://localhost/", function(err, db) {
  var myDB = db.db("words");
  myDB.collection("word_stats", limitFields);
  setTimeout(function(){
    db.close();
  }, 3000);
});
function limitFields(err, words){
  words.findOne({word:'the'}, {fields:{charsets:0}},
                function(err, item){
    console.log("Excluding fields object: ");
    console.log(JSON.stringify(item, null, 2));
  });
  words.findOne({word:'the'}, {fields:{word:1,size:1,stats:1}},
                function(err, item){
    console.log("Including fields object: ");
    console.log(JSON.stringify(item, null, 2));
  });
}
```

```
Console
<terminated> NodeBook-ch15-doc_fields.js [Node Application] Node.js Process
Excluding fields object:
{
  "word": "the",
  "first": "t",
  "last": "e",
  "size": 3,
  "letters": [
    "t",
    "h",
    "e"
  ],
  "stats": {
    "vowels": 1,
    "consonants": 2
  },
  "_id": "52a639c9cc4ffbe43b000001"
}
Including fields object:
{
  "word": "the",
  "size": 3,
  "stats": {
    "vowels": 1,
    "consonants": 2
  },
  "_id": "52a639c9cc4ffbe43b000001"
}
```

Figure 15.4 Limiting the fields returned in documents by using the `fields` option.

Paging Results

A very common method of reducing the number of documents returned is paging. Paging involves specifying a number of documents to skip in the matching set as well as a limit on the documents returned. Then the skip value is incremented each time by the amount returned the previous time.

To implement paging on a set of documents, you need to implement the `limit` and `skip` options on the `options` object. The `skip` option specifies a number of documents to skip before returning documents. By moving the `skip` value each time you get another set of documents, you can effectively page through the data set. Also, you should always include a `sort` option when paging data to ensure that the order is always the same. For example, the following statements find documents 1–10, then 11–20, and then 21–30:

```
collection.find({},{sort:[['_id':1]], skip:0, limit10},
                function(err, cursor){});
collection.find({},{sort:[['_id':1]], skip:10, limit10}, function(err, cursor){});
collection.find({},{sort:[['_id':1]], skip:20, limit10}, function(err, cursor){});
```

Listing 15.5 shows how to use `limit` and `skip` to page through a specific set of documents. A new `find()` request is implemented each time, and this more closely mimics what would happen when handling paging requests from a webpage. Figure 15.5 shows the output of Listing 15.5. Notice that words are retrieved 10 at a time.

> **Warning**
>
> If the data on a system changes in such a way that it affects the results of a query, a skip may miss some items or include items again in a subsequent page request.

Listing 15.5 `doc_paging.js`: **Paging results from a specific set of documents in a MongoDB collection**

```
var util = require('util');
var MongoClient = require('mongodb').MongoClient;
var myDB;
MongoClient.connect("mongodb://localhost/", function(err, db) {
  myDB = db.db("words");
  myDB.collection("word_stats", function(err, collection){
    pagedResults(err, collection, 0, 10);
  });
});
function displayWords(msg, cursor, pretty){
  cursor.toArray(function(err, itemArr){
    console.log("\n"+msg);
    var wordList = [];
    for(var i=0; i<itemArr.length; i++){
      wordList.push(itemArr[i].word);
    }
    console.log(JSON.stringify(wordList, null, pretty));
  });
}
function pagedResults(err, words, startIndex, pageSize){
  words.find({first:'v'},
             {limit:pageSize, skip:startIndex, sort:[['word',1]]},
             function(err, cursor){
    cursor.count(true, function(err, cursorCount){
      displayWords("Page Starting at " + startIndex, cursor);
      if (cursorCount === pageSize){
        pagedResults(err, words, startIndex+pageSize, pageSize);
      } else {
        myDB.close();
      }
    });
  });
}
```

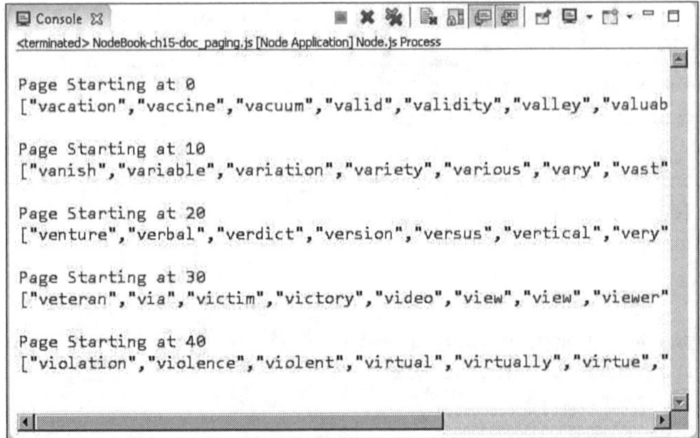

Figure 15.5 Paging the results on a specific set of documents in MongoDB by using the skip, limit, and sort options.

Sorting Result Sets

An important aspect of retrieving documents from a MongoDB database is the ability to get it in a sorted format. Sorting is especially helpful if you are only retrieving a certain number, such as the top 10, or if you are paging the requests. The options object provides the sort option, which allows you to specify the sort order and direction of one or more fields in a document.

You specify the sort option by using an array of [field,<sort_order>] pairs, where sort_order is 1 for ascending and -1 for descending. For example, to sort on the name field descending first and then on the value field ascending, you would use:

```
sort:[['name':1]['value':-1]]
```

Listing 15.6 shows how to use the sort option to find and sort lists of words in different ways. Notice that line 29 sorts the words by size first and then by last letter, whereas line 32 sorts them by last letter first and then by size. The different sort orders return different lists of words. Figure 15.6 shows the output from the code in Listing 15.6.

Listing 15.6 `doc_sort.js`**: Sorting results of a** `find()` **request for a set of documents in a MongoDB collection**

```
var MongoClient = require('mongodb').MongoClient;
MongoClient.connect("mongodb://localhost/", function(err, db) {
  var myDB = db.db("words");
  myDB.collection("word_stats", sortItems);
  setTimeout(function(){
    db.close();
  }, 3000);
});
function displayWords(msg, cursor, pretty){
  cursor.toArray(function(err, itemArr){
    console.log("\n"+msg);
    var wordList = [];
    for(var i=0; i<itemArr.length; i++){
      wordList.push(itemArr[i].word);
    }
    console.log(JSON.stringify(wordList, null, pretty));
  });
}
function sortItems(err, words){
  words.find({last:'w'}, function(err, cursor){
    displayWords("Words ending in w: ", cursor);
  });
  words.find({last:'w'}, {sort:{word:1}}, function(err, cursor){
    displayWords("Words ending in w sorted ascending: ", cursor);
  });
  words.find({last:'w'}, {sort:{word:-1}}, function(err, cursor){
    displayWords("Words ending in w sorted, descending: ", cursor);
  });
  words.find({first:'b'}, {sort:[['size',-1],['last',1]]},
              function(err, cursor){
    displayWords("B words sorted by size then by last letter: ", cursor);
  });
  words.find({first:'b'}, {sort:[['last',1],['size',-1]]},
              function(err, cursor){
    displayWords("B words sorted by last letter then by size: ", cursor);
  });
}
```

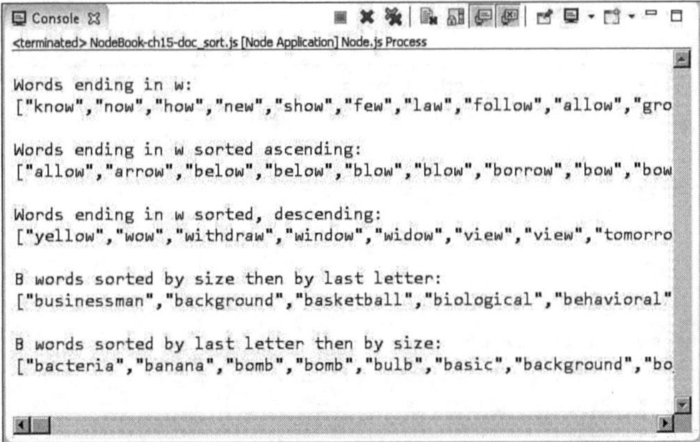

Figure 15.6 Sorting the results of a `find()` request for specific documents in a MongoDB collection.

Finding Distinct Field Values

A very useful query against a MongoDB collection is to get a list of the distinct values for a single field in a set of documents. *Distinct* in this case means that even though there are thousands of documents, you only want to know the unique values that exist.

The `distinct()` method on `Collection` objects allows you to find a list of distinct values for a specific field. The syntax for the `distinct()` method is shown below:

```
distinct(key, [query], [options],callback)
```

The `key` parameter is the string value of the fieldname you want to get values for. You can specify subdocuments by using the dot syntax—for example, `stats.count`. The `query` parameter is an object with the standard `query` object options listed in Table 15.1. The `options` parameter is an `options` object that allows you to define the `readPreference` option defined in Table 15.2. The callback function accepts an error as the first parameter and then a `results` parameter, which is an array of distinct values for the field specified in the `key` parameter.

Listing 15.7 shows how to find the distinct values in the words collection. Notice that the query in line 14 limits the words to those starting with `u`. Notice that line 18 uses dot syntax to access the `stats.vowels` field. Figure 15.7 shows the output of Listing 15.7.

Listing 15.7 `doc_distinct.js`: **Finding distinct field values in a specific set of documents in a MongoDB collection**

```
var MongoClient = require('mongodb').MongoClient;
MongoClient.connect("mongodb://localhost/", function(err, db) {
  var myDB = db.db("words");
  myDB.collection("word_stats", distinctValues);
  setTimeout(function(){
    db.close();
  }, 3000);
});
function distinctValues(err, words){
  words.distinct('size', function(err, values){
    console.log("\nSizes of words: ");
    console.log(values);
  });
  words.distinct('first', {last:'u'}, function(err, values){
    console.log("\nFirst letters of words ending in u: ");
    console.log(values);
  });
  words.distinct('stats.vowels', function(err, values){
    console.log("\nNumbers of vowels in words: ");
    console.log(values);
  });
}
```

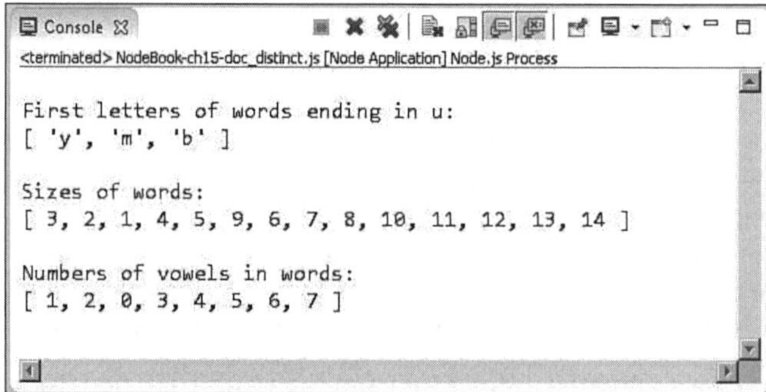

Figure 15.7 Finding distinct field values in a specific set of documents in a MongoDB collection.

Grouping Results

When performing operations on large data sets, it is often useful to group the results based on the distinct values of one or more fields in a document. You could do this in code after retrieving the documents, but it is much more efficient to have MongoDB do it for you as part of a single request that is already iterating though the documents.

To group the results of a query together, you can use the `group()` method on the `Collection` object. The `group()` request first collects all the documents that match a `query` and then adds a `group` object to an array, based on distinct values of a set of `keys`, performs operations on the `group` objects, and returns the array of `group` objects. The syntax for the `group()` methods is shown below:

```
group(keys, query, initial, reduce, finalize, command, [options], callback)
```

The parameters of the `group()` method are described in the following list:

- **`keys`:** This can be an object, an array, or a function that expresses the keys to group by. The simplest method is to specify the key(s) in an object such as `{field1:true, field2:true}` or an array such as `['first', 'last']`.
- **`query`:** The `query` object defines which documents to include in the initial set. See Table 15.1 for a list of `query` object options.
- **`initial`:** Specifies an initial `group` object to use when aggregating data while grouping. An initial `group` object is created for each distinct set of keys. The most common use is a counter that tracks the number of items that match the keys. For example:

  ```
  {"count":0}
  ```

- **`reduce`:** This function has two parameters, `obj` and `prev`. This function is executed on each document that matches the query. The `obj` parameter is the current document, and `prev` is the object that was created by the initial parameter. You can then use the `obj` object to update the `prev` object with new values such as counts or sums. For example, to increment the count value, you use:

  ```
  function(obj, prev) { prev.count++; }
  ```

- **`finalize`:** This function accepts one parameter, `obj`, which is the final object resulting from the initial parameter and is updated as `prev` in the `reduce` function. This function is called on the resulting object for each distinct key before returning the array in the response.
- **`command`:** This is a Boolean that, when `true`, indicates that the command runs using the internal `group` command instead of `eval()`. The default is `true`.
- **`options`:** This object allows you to define the `readPreference` option.
- **`callback`:** This option accepts an error as the first parameter and an array of the `results` objects as the second.

Listing 15.8 shows how to implement grouping of words based on various key sets. Lines 10–18 implement a basic grouping of words by first and last letter. The query in line 11 limits the words to those that begin with *o* and end with a vowel. The initial object for each has a `count` property only, which is updated for each matching document in the function on line 13.

Lines 19–28 sum the total vowels in the documents and group them together by incrementing `prev.totalVowels` with the `obj.stats.vowels` value in line 23. Then lines 29–40 use a `finalize` function that adds a new `obj.total` property to the `group` object that is a sum of the `obj.vowels` and `obj.consonants` properties of the object. Figure 15.8 shows the output for the code in Listing 15.8.

Listing 15.8 `doc_group.js`: **Grouping a set of documents by specific fields in a MongoDB collection**

```
var MongoClient = require('mongodb').MongoClient;
MongoClient.connect("mongodb://localhost/", function(err, db) {
  var myDB = db.db("words");
  myDB.collection("word_stats", groupItems);
  setTimeout(function(){
    db.close();
  }, 3000);
});
function groupItems(err, words){
  words.group(['first','last'],
              {first:'o',last:{$in:['a','e','i','o','u']}},
              {"count":0},
              function (obj, prev) { prev.count++; }, true,
              function(err, results){
        console.log("\n'O' words grouped by first and last" +
                    " letter that end with a vowel: ");
        console.log(results);
  });
  words.group(['first'],
              {size:{$gt:13}},
              {"count":0, "totalVowels":0},
              function (obj, prev) {
                prev.count++; prev.totalVowels += obj.stats.vowels;
              }, {}, true,
              function(err, results){
    console.log("\nWords grouped by first letter larger than 13: ");
    console.log(results);
  });
  words.group(['first'],{}, {"count":0, "vowels":0, "consonants":0},
              function (obj, prev) {
                prev.count++;
                prev.vowels += obj.stats.vowels;
                prev.consonants += obj.stats.consonants;
              },function(obj){
                obj.total = obj.vowels + obj.consonants;
              }, true,
              function(err, results){
        console.log("\nWords grouped by first letter with totals: ");
        console.log(results);
  });
}
```

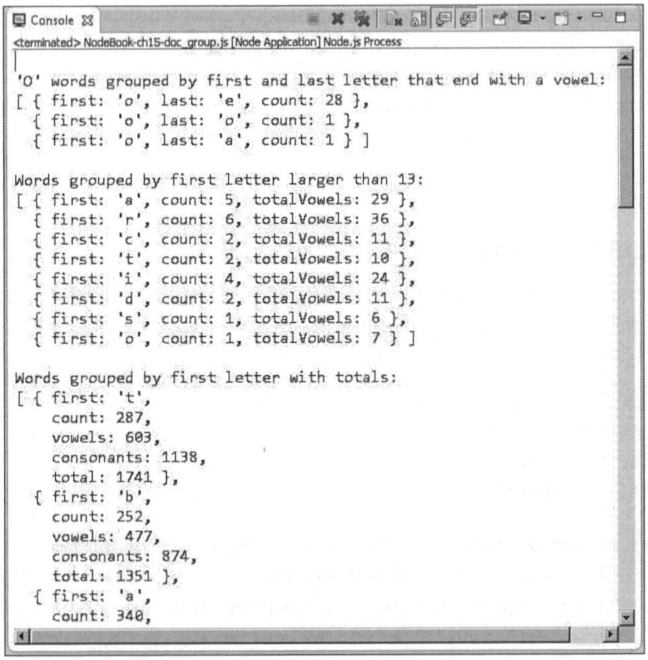

```
Console
<terminated> NodeBook-ch15-doc_group.js [Node Application] Node.js Process

'O' words grouped by first and last letter that end with a vowel:
[ { first: 'o', last: 'e', count: 28 },
  { first: 'o', last: 'o', count: 1 },
  { first: 'o', last: 'a', count: 1 } ]

Words grouped by first letter larger than 13:
[ { first: 'a', count: 5, totalVowels: 29 },
  { first: 'r', count: 6, totalVowels: 36 },
  { first: 'c', count: 2, totalVowels: 11 },
  { first: 't', count: 2, totalVowels: 10 },
  { first: 'i', count: 4, totalVowels: 24 },
  { first: 'd', count: 2, totalVowels: 11 },
  { first: 's', count: 1, totalVowels: 6 },
  { first: 'o', count: 1, totalVowels: 7 } ]

Words grouped by first letter with totals:
[ { first: 't',
    count: 287,
    vowels: 603,
    consonants: 1138,
    total: 1741 },
  { first: 'b',
    count: 252,
    vowels: 477,
    consonants: 874,
    total: 1351 },
  { first: 'a',
    count: 340,
```

Figure 15.8 Grouping documents from a MongoDB collection by specific field values.

Applying MapReduce by Aggregating Results

A great benefit of MongoDB is the ability to reduce the results of database queries into a completely different structure than the original collections by using MapReduce. MapReduce maps the values on a database lookup into a completely different form and then reduces the results to make them more consumable.

MongoDB has a MapReduce framework, and it also allows you to use aggregation to simplify the process of piping one MapReduce operation into another in a series. With MapReduce and aggregation, you can produce some extraordinary results with data. Aggregation is the concept of applying a series of operations to documents on the MongoDB server as they are being compiled into a result set. This is much more efficient than retrieving them and processing them in your Node.js application because the MongoDB server can operate on chunks of data locally.

Understanding the `aggregate()` Method

The `Collection` object provides the `aggregate()` method to perform aggregation operations on data. The syntax for the `aggregate()` method is shown below:

```
aggregate(operators, [options], callback)
```

The `operators` parameter is an array of aggregation operators, shown in Table 15.3, that allows you to define what aggregation operation to perform on the data. The `options` parameter allows you to set the `readPreference` property, which defines where to read the data from. The `callback` parameter is a function that accepts an error as the first parameter and a results array as the second parameter. The `results` parameter is a fully aggregated object set return by the aggregation.

Using Aggregation Framework Operators

MongoDB's aggregation framework is extremely powerful in that it allows you to pipe the results of one aggregation operator into another multiple times. This data set shows an example:

```
{o_id:"A", value:50, type:"X"}
{o_id:"A", value:75, type:"X"}
{o_id:"B", value:80, type:"X"}
{o_id:"C", value:45, type:"Y"}
```

The following aggregation operator set would pipeline the results of the `$match` into the `$group` operator and then return the grouped set in the `results` parameter of the callback function. Notice that when referencing the values of fields in documents, the fieldname is prefixed by a dollar sign—for example, `$o_id` and `$value`. This syntax tells the aggregate framework to treat it as a field value instead of a string.

```
aggregate([{$match:{type:"X"}},
          {$group:{set_id:"$o_id", total: {$sum: "$value"}}},
          function(err, results){});
```

After the `$match` operator completes, these documents are applied to `$group`:

```
{o_id:"A", value:50, type:"X"}
{o_id:"A", value:75, type:"X"}
{o_id:"B", value:80, type:"X"}
```

Then after the `$group` operator is applied, a new array of objects is sent to the callback function with `set_id` and `total` fields, as shown below:

```
{set_id:"A", total:"125"}
{set_id:"B", total:"80"}
```

Table 15.3 lists the aggregation commands you can include in the `operators` parameter to the `aggregate()` method.

Table 15.3 **Aggregation operators that can be used in the aggregate() method**

Operator	Description
$project	Reshapes a document by renaming, adding, or removing fields. You can also recompute values and add subdocuments. For example, the following includes title and excludes name: {$project:{title:1, name:0}} The following is an example of renaming name to title: {$project{title:"$name"}} The following is an example of adding a new field total and computing its value from price and tax fields: {$project{total:{$add:["$price", "$tax"]}}}
$match	Filters the document set by using the query object operators defined in Table 15.1. For example: {$match:{value:{$gt:50}}}
$limit	Restricts the number of documents that can be passed to the next pipe in the aggregation. For example: {$limit:5}
$skip	Specifies a number of documents to skip before processing the next pipe in the aggregation. For example: {$skip:10}
$unwind	Specifies an array field that splits, with a separate document created for each value. For example: {$unwind:"$myArr"}
$group	Groups the documents together into a new set of documents for the next level in the pipe. The fields of the new object must be defined in the $group object. You can also apply group expression operators, listed in Table 15.4, to the multiple documents in the group. For example, use this to sum the value field: {$group:{set_id:"$o_id", total: {$sum: "$value"}}}
$sort	Sorts the documents before passing them on to the next pipe in the aggregation. The sort specifies an object with field:<sort_order> properties, where <sort_order> is 1 for ascending and -1 for descending. For example: {$sort: {name:1, age:-1}}

Implementing Aggregation Expression Operators

When you implement aggregation operators, you build a new document that will be passed to the next level in the aggregation pipeline. The MongoDB aggregation framework provides a number of expression operators that help when computing values for new fields or when comparing existing fields in the documents.

When operating on a `$group` aggregation pipe, multiple documents match the defined fields in the new documents created. MongoDB provides a set of operators you can apply to those documents and use to compute values for fields in the new group document based on values of fields in the original set of documents. Table 15.4 lists the `$group` expression operators.

Table 15.4 **Aggregation `$group` expression operators**

Operator	Description
`$addToSet`	Returns an array of all the unique values for the selected field among all the documents in the group. For example: `colors: {$addToSet: "$color"}`
`$first`	Returns the first value for a field in a group of documents. For example: `firstValue:{$first: "$value"}`
`$last`	Returns the last value for a field in a group of documents. For example: `lastValue:{$last: "$value"}`
`$max`	Returns the highest value for a field in a group of documents. For example: `maxValue:{$max: "$value"}`
`$min`	Returns the lowest value for a field in a group of documents. For example: `minValue:{$min: "$value"}`
`$avg`	Returns an average of all the values for a field in a group of documents. For example: `aveValue:{$ave: "$value"}`
`$push`	Returns an array of all values for the selected field among all the documents in the group of documents. For example: `username:{$push: "$username"}`
`$sum`	Returns the sum of all the values for a field in a group of documents. For example: `total:{$sum: "$value"}`

In addition, several string and arithmetic operators can be applied when computing new field values. Table 15.5 lists some of the most common operators that can be applied when computing new field values in the aggregation operators.

Table 15.5 **String and arithmetic operators used in aggregation expressions**

Operator	Description
`$add`	Computes the sum of an array of numbers. For example: `valuePlus5:{$add:["$value", 5]}`
`$divide`	Given two numbers, divides the first number by the second. For example: `valueDividedBy5:{$divide:["$value", 5]}`
`$mod`	Given two numbers, calculates the modulo of the first number divided by the second. For example: `valueMod5:{$mod:["$value", 5]}`
`$multiply`	Computes the product of an array of numbers. For example: `valueTimes5:{$multiply:["$value", 5]}`
`$subtract`	Given two numbers, subtracts the second number from the first. For example: `valueMinus5:{$minus:["$value", 5]}`
`$concat`	Concatenates two strings. For example: `title:{$concat:["$title", " ", "$name"]}`
`$strcasecmp`	Compares two strings and returns an integer that reflects the comparison. For example: `isTest:{$strcasecmp:["$value", "test"]}`
`$substr`	Returns a portion of a string. For example: `hasTest:{$substr:["$value", "test"]}`
`$toLower`	Converts a string to lowercase. For example: `titleLower:{$toLower:"$title"}`
`$toUpper`	Converts a string to uppercase. For example: `titleUpper:{$toUpper:"$title"}`

Aggregation Examples

Listing 15.9 shows how to implement aggregation against the words collection. It includes three examples.

The first example, in lines 10–20, implements a `$match` to get words beginning in vowels, then a `$group` to calculate the largest and smallest sizes. It then sorts the results using `$sort`, as shown in Figure 15.9.

The second example, in lines 21–27, uses `$match` to limit the words to four letters. Then `$limit` is used to process only five documents in the `$project` operator.

The third example, in lines 28–34, uses `$group` to get the average size of the words and sets the `_id` value of each to that word. Then it sorts the words in descending order by average, as shown in Figure 15.9.

Listing 15.9 `doc_aggregate.js`: **Grouping a set of documents by specific fields in a MongoDB collection**

```
01 var MongoClient = require('mongodb').MongoClient;
02 MongoClient.connect("mongodb://localhost/", function(err, db) {
03   var myDB = db.db("words");
04   myDB.collection("word_stats", aggregateItems);
05   setTimeout(function(){
06     db.close();
07   }, 3000);
08 });
09 function aggregateItems(err, words){
10   words.aggregate([{$match: {first:{$in:['a','e','i','o','u']}}},
11                    {$group: {_id:"$first",
12                              largest:{$max:"$size"},
13                              smallest:{$min:"$size"},
14                              total:{$sum:1}}},
15                    {$sort: {_id:1}}],
16               function(err, results){
17     console.log("Largest and smallest word sizes for " +
18                 "words beginning with a vowel: ");
19     console.log(results);
20   });
21   words.aggregate([{$match: {size:4}},
22                    {$limit: 5},
23                    {$project: {_id:"$word", stats:1}}],
24               function(err, results){
25     console.log("Stats for 5 four letter words: ");
26     console.log(results);
27   });
28   words.aggregate([{$group: {_id:"$first", average:{$avg:"$size"}}},
29                     {$sort: {average:-1}},
30                     {$limit: 5}],
31               function(err, results){
32     console.log("Letters with largest average word size: ");
33     console.log(results);
34   });
35 }
```

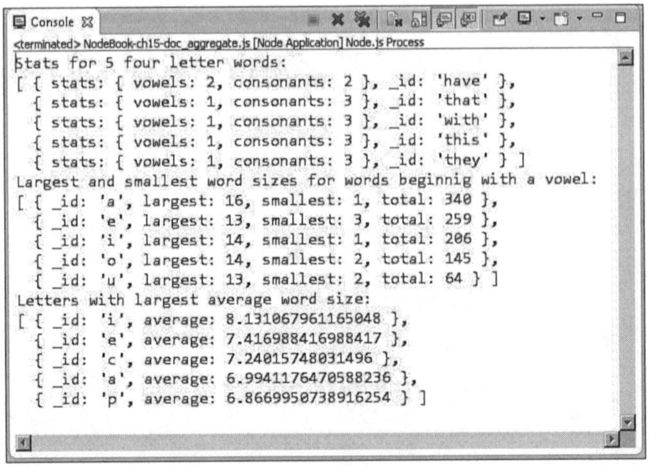

```
<terminated> NodeBook-ch15-doc_aggregate.js [Node Application] Node.js Process
Stats for 5 four letter words:
[ { stats: { vowels: 2, consonants: 2 }, _id: 'have' },
  { stats: { vowels: 1, consonants: 3 }, _id: 'that' },
  { stats: { vowels: 1, consonants: 3 }, _id: 'with' },
  { stats: { vowels: 1, consonants: 3 }, _id: 'this' },
  { stats: { vowels: 1, consonants: 3 }, _id: 'they' } ]
Largest and smallest word sizes for words beginnig with a vowel:
[ { _id: 'a', largest: 16, smallest: 1, total: 340 },
  { _id: 'e', largest: 13, smallest: 3, total: 259 },
  { _id: 'i', largest: 14, smallest: 1, total: 206 },
  { _id: 'o', largest: 14, smallest: 2, total: 145 },
  { _id: 'u', largest: 13, smallest: 2, total: 64 } ]
Letters with largest average word size:
[ { _id: 'i', average: 8.131067961165048 },
  { _id: 'e', average: 7.416988416988417 },
  { _id: 'c', average: 7.24015748031496 },
  { _id: 'a', average: 6.9941176470588236 },
  { _id: 'p', average: 6.8669950738916254 } ]
```

Figure 15.9 Grouping documents from a MongoDB collection by specific field values.

Summary

In this chapter you got a look at the `query` and `options` objects that `Collection` methods use to access documents in a database. The `query` object allows you to limit which documents are considered for operations. The `options` object allows you to control the interaction of the requests to limit the number of documents returned, which document to start on, and what fields to return.

The `distinct()`, `group()`, and `aggregate()` methods allow you to group documents based on field values. The MongoDB aggregation framework allows you to process documents on a server before returning them to a client. The aggregation framework allows you to pipe documents from one aggregation operation to the next, each time mapping and reducing to a more defined set of data.

Up Next

In the next chapter you'll get a chance to use the `mongoose` module to implement the Object Document Model (ODM), which provides a more structured approach to data modeling from Node.js.

16

Using Mongoose for Structured Schema and Validation

Now that you understand the MongoDB Node.js native driver, it won't be hard to make the jump to using Mongoose. Mongoose is an Object Document Model (ODM) library that provides additional functionality to the MongoDB Node.js native driver. For the most part, it is used to apply a structured schema to a MongoDB collection, which provides the benefits of validation and type casting.

Mongoose simplifies some of the complexities of making database calls by implementing builder objects that allow you to pipe additional commands into find, update, save, remove, aggregate, and other database operations. This can make it easier to implement your code.

This chapter discusses the `mongoose` module and how to use it to implement a structured schema and validation on your collections. You will be introduced to new objects and a new way of implementing MongoDB in your Node.js applications. Mongoose really doesn't replace the MongoDB Node.js native driver; rather, it enhances it with additional functionality.

Understanding Mongoose

Mongoose is an ODM library that wraps around the MongoDB Node.js driver. It provides a schema-based solution to model data stored in the MongoDB database.

The chief benefits of using Mongoose are:

- You can create a schema structure for you documents.
- Objects/documents in the model can be validated.
- Application data can by typecasted into the object model.

- Business logic hooks can be applied using middleware.
- Mongoose is in some ways a bit easier to use than the MongoDB Node.js native driver.

However, there are some downsides to using Mongoose as well:

- You must provide a schema, which isn't always the best option when MongoDB doesn't require it.
- It doesn't seem to perform as well at certain operations, such as storing data, as the native driver does.

Additional Objects

Mongoose sits on top of the MongoDB Node.js native driver and extends its functionality in a couple of different ways. First, it adds some new objects—`Schema`, `Model`, and `Document`—that provide the functionality necessary to implement the ODM and validation.

You use the `Schema` object to define the structured schema for documents in a collection. It allows you to define the fields and types to include, uniqueness, indexes, and validation. The `Model` object acts as a representation of all documents in a collection. The `Document` object acts as a representation of an individual document in a collection.

Mongoose also wraps the standard functionality used for implementing query and aggregation parameters into the new objects `Query` and `Aggregate` that allow you to apply the parameters of database operations in a series of method calls before finally executing them. This can make it simpler to implement code as well as reuse instances of those objects to perform multiple database operations.

Connecting to a MongoDB Database by Using Mongoose

Connecting to a MongoDB database by using Mongoose is very similar to using the connection string method discussed in Chapter 13, "Getting Started with MongoDB and Node.js." It uses the connection string format and options syntax shown below:

```
connect(uri, options, [callback])
```

> **Note**
>
> The Mongoose library must be installed using `npm install mongoose` to be able to use it in your Node.js applications.

The `connect()` method is exported at the root level of the `mongoose` module. For example the following code connects to the `words` database on the `localhost`:

```
var mongoose = require('mongoose');
mongoose.connect('mongodb://localhost/words');
```

The connection can be closed using the `disconnect()` method of the `mongoose` module. For example:

```
mongoose.disconnect();
```

Once created, the underlying `Connection` object can be accessed in the `connection` attribute of the `mongoose` module. The `Connection` object provides access to the connection, underlying `Db` object, and `Model` object that represents the collection. This gives you access to all the `Db` object functionality described in Chapter 13. For example, to list the collections on the database, you could use the following code:

```
mongoose.connection.db.collectionNames(function(err, names){
  console.log(names);
});
```

The `Connection` object emits the `open` event, which you can use to wait for the connection to open before trying to access the database. To illustrate the basic life cycle of a MongoDB connection via Mongoose, the code in Listing 16.1 imports the `mongoose` module, connects to the MongoDB database, waits for the `open` event, displays the collections in the database, and disconnects. The output is shown in Figure 16.1.

Listing 16.1 `mongoose_connect.js`: **Connecting to a MongoDB database by using Mongoose**

```
var mongoose = require('mongoose');
mongoose.connect('mongodb://localhost/words');
mongoose.connection.on('open', function(){
  console.log(mongoose.connection.collection);
  mongoose.connection.db.collectionNames(function(err, names){
    console.log(names);
    mongoose.disconnect();
  });
});
```

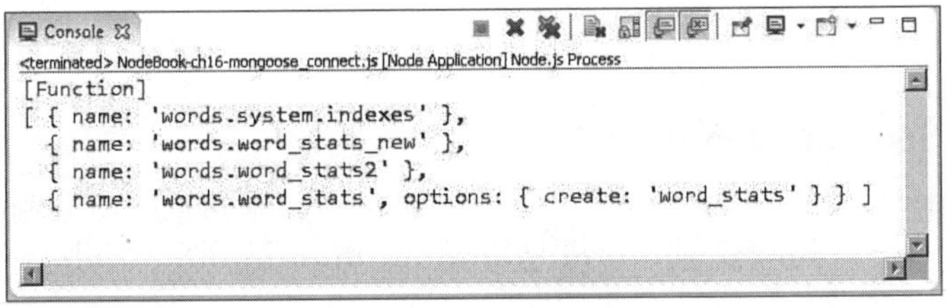

```
Console
<terminated> NodeBook-ch16-mongoose_connect.js [Node Application] Node.js Process
[Function]
[ { name: 'words.system.indexes' },
  { name: 'words.word_stats_new' },
  { name: 'words.word_stats2' },
  { name: 'words.word_stats', options: { create: 'word_stats' } } ]
```

Figure 16.1 Connecting to a MongoDB database by using Mongoose.

Defining a Schema

When you use Mongoose, you often need to implement schemas. A schema defines the fields and field types for documents in a collection. This can be very useful if your data is structured to support a schema because you can validate and typecast objects to match the requirements of the schema.

For each field in a schema, you need to define a specific value type. These value types are supported:

- `String`
- `Number`
- `Boolean` or `Bool`
- `Array`
- `Buffer`
- `Date`
- `ObjectId` or `Oid`
- `Mixed`

A schema needs to be defined for each different document type that you plan to use. Also, you should store only one document type in each collection.

Understanding Paths

Mongoose uses the term `path` to define access paths to fields in a main document as well as subdocuments. For example, if a document has a field named `name`, which is a subdocument with `title`, `first`, and `last` properties, the following are all paths:

```
name
name.title
name.first
name.last
```

Creating a Schema Definition

To define a schema for model, you need to create a new instance of a `Schema` object. The `Schema` object `definition` accepts an object that describes the schema as the first parameter and an `options` object as the second parameter:

```
new Schema(definition, options)
```

The `options` object defines the interaction with the collection on the MongoDB server. Table 16.1 lists the options that are most commonly used.

Table 16.1 **Options that can be specified when defining a `Schema` object**

Option	Description
`autoIndex`	A Boolean that, when `true`, indicates that the `autoindex` feature for the collection is turned on. The default is `true`.
`bufferCommands`	A Boolean that, when `true`, indicates that the commands that cannot be completed due to connection issues are buffered. The default is `true`.
`capped`	Specifies the maximum number of documents supported in a capped collection.
`collection`	Specifies the collection name to use for this `Schema` model. Mongoose automatically connects to this collection when compiling the schema model.
`id`	A Boolean that, when `true`, causes the documents in the model to have an `id` getter that corresponds to the `_id` value of the object. The default is `true`.
`_id`	A Boolean that, when `true`, causes Mongoose to automatically assign an `_id` field to your documents. The default is `true`.
`read`	Specifies the replica read preferences. Value can be `primary`, `primaryPreferred`, `secondary`, `secondaryPreferred`, or `nearest`.
`safe`	A Boolean that, when `true`, causes Mongoose to apply a write concern to requests that update the database. The default is `true`.
`strict`	A Boolean that, when `true`, indicates that attributes passed in the object that do not appear in the defined schema are not saved to the database. The default is `true`.

For example, to create a schema for a collection called `students`, with a `name` field that is a `String` type, an `average` field that is a `Number` type, and a `scores` field that is an `Array` of `Number` types, you use:

```
var schema = new Schema({
  name: String,
  average: Number,
  scores: [Number]
}, {collection:'students'});
```

Adding Indexes to a Schema

You might want to assign indexes to specific fields that you frequently use to find documents. You can apply indexes to a schema object when defining the schema or by using the `index(fields)` command. For example, both of the following add an `index` to the `name` field, in ascending order:

```
var schema = new Schema({
  name: {type: String, index: 1}
};
//or
var schema = new Schema({name: String)};
schema.index({name:1});
```

You can get a list of indexed fields on a schema object by using the `indexes()` method. For example:

```
schema.indexes()
```

Implementing Unique Fields

You can specify that the value of a field must be unique in a collection, meaning that no other documents can have the same value for that field. You do this by adding the `unique` property to the `Schema` object definition. For example, to add an `index` and make the `name` field `unique` in the collection, you use:

```
var schema = new Schema({
  name: {type: String, index: 1, unique: true}
};
```

Forcing Required Fields

You can specify that a field must be included when you create a new instance of a `Document` object for the model. By default, if you do not specify a field when creating a `Document` instance, the object is created without one. For fields that must exist in your model, you add the required property when defining the schema. For example, to add an index, ensure uniqueness, and force the inclusion of the `name` field in the collection, you use:

```
var schema = new Schema({
  name: {type: String, index: 1, unique: true, required: true}
};
```

You can get a list of required fields on a `Schema` object by using the `requiredPaths()` method. For example:

```
schema.requiredPaths()
```

Adding Methods to the `Schema` Object

Mongoose schemas enable you to add to the `Schema` object methods that are automatically available on document objects in the model. This allows you to call the methods by using the `Document` object.

You add methods to the `Schema` object by assigning a function to the `Schema.methods` property. The function is just a standard JavaScript function assigned to the `Document` object.

The Document object can be accessed by using the this keyword. For example, the following assigns a function named fullName to a model that returns a combination of the first and last names:

```
var schema = new Schema({
  first: String,
  last: String
});
schema.methods.fullName = function(){
  return this.first + " " + this.last;
};
```

Implementing a Schema on the Words Database

Listing 16.2 implements a schema on the word_stats collection defined in Chapter 15, "Accessing MongoDB Documents from Node.js." This schema will be used in other examples in this chapter, so it is exported in the final line of Listing 16.2. Notice that the word and first fields have an index assigned to them and that the word field is both unique and required.

For the stats subdocument, the document is defined as normal but with types specified in lines 9–11. Also notice that for the charsets field, which is an array of subdocuments, the syntax defines an array and defines the single subdocument type for the model. Lines 13–15 implement a startsWith() method that is available on Document objects in the model. Figure 16.2 shows the output of the required paths and indexes.

Listing 16.2 word_schema.js: **Defining the schema for the** word_stats **collection**

```
01 var mongoose = require('mongoose');
02 var Schema = mongoose.Schema;
03 var wordSchema = new Schema({
04   word: {type: String, index: 1, required:true, unique: true},
05   first: {type: String, index: 1},
06   last: String,
07   size: Number,
08   letters: [String],
09   stats: {
10     vowels:Number, consonants:Number},
11   charsets: [{ type: String, chars: [String]}]
12 }, {collection: 'word_stats'});
13 wordSchema.methods.startsWith = function(letter){
14   return this.first === letter;
15 };
16 exports.wordSchema = wordSchema;
17 console.log("Required Paths: ");
18 console.log(wordSchema.requiredPaths());
19 console.log("Indexes: ");
20 console.log(wordSchema.indexes());
```

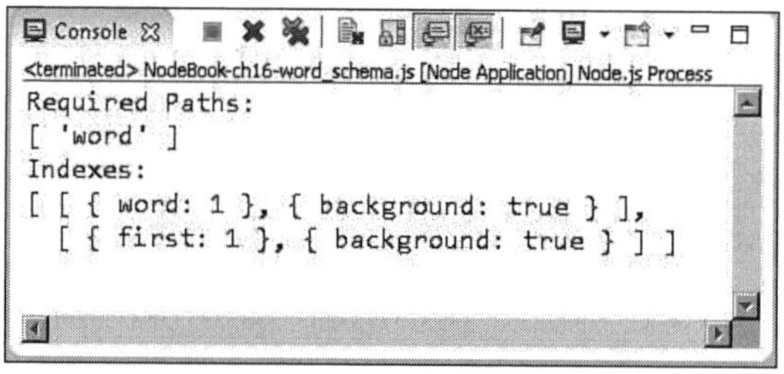

```
Console
<terminated> NodeBook-ch16-word_schema.js [Node Application] Node.js Process
Required Paths:
[ 'word' ]
Indexes:
[ [ { word: 1 }, { background: true } ],
  [ { first: 1 }, { background: true } ] ]
```

Figure 16.2 Displaying the required and indexed fields in `wordSchema`.

Compiling a Model

Once you have defined the `Schema` object for a model, you need to compile it into a `Model` object. When Mongoose compiles the model, it uses the connection to the MongoDB database established by `mongoose.connect()` to ensure that the collection is created and has the appropriate indexes, as well as required and unique settings, when applying changes.

The compiled `Model` object acts in much the same way as the `Collection` object defined in Chapter 13. It provides the functionality to access, update, and remove objects in the model and subsequently in the MongoDB collection.

To compile the model, you use the `model()` method in the `mongoose` module. The `model()` method has the following syntax:

```
model(name, [schema], [collection], [skipInit])
```

The `name` parameter is a string you can use to find the model later, using `model(name)`. The `schema` parameter is the `Schema` object discussed in the previous section. The `collection` parameter is the name of the collection to connect to if one was not specified in the `Schema` object. The `skipInit` option is a Boolean that defaults to `false`. When it is `true`, the initialization process is skipped, and a simple `Model` object with no connection to the database is created.

The following is an example of compiling the model for the `Schema` object defined in Listing 16.2:

```
var Words = mongoose.model('Words', wordSchema);
```

You can then access the compiled `Model` object at any time by using the following:

```
mongoose.model('Words')
```

Understanding the Query Object

Once you have the Schema object compiled into a Model object, you are completely ready to begin accessing, adding, updating, and deleting documents in the model, which makes the changes to the underlying MongoDB database. However, before you jump in, you need to understand the nature of the Query object provided with Mongoose.

Many of the methods in the Model object match those in the Collection object defined in Chapter 13. For example, there are find(), remove(), update(), count(), distinct(), and aggregate() methods. The parameters for these methods are for the most part exactly the same as for the Collection object, with a major difference: the callback parameter.

Using the Mongoose Model object, you can either pass in the callback function or omit it from the parameters of the method. If you pass in the callback function, the methods behave as you would expect them to. The request is made to MongoDB, and the results are returned in the callback function.

However, if you do not pass in a callback function, the MongoDB request is not sent; instead, a Query object is returned, allowing you to add additional functionality to the request before executing it. Then when you are ready to execute the database call, you use the exec(callback) method on the Query object.

To better understand this, the following example of a find() request in Mongoose uses the same syntax as in the native driver:

```
model.find({value:{$gt:5}},{sort:{[['value',-1]]}, fields:{name:1, title:1,
value:1}}},
           function(err, results){});
```

However, when you use Mongoose, you can define all the query options separately, using the following code:

```
var query = model.find({});
query.where('value').gt(5);
query.sort('-value');
query.select('name title value');
query.exec(function(err, results){});
```

The model.find() call returns a Query object instead of performing the find() because no callback is specified. Notice that the query properties and options properties are broken out in subsequent method calls on the Query object. Then, once the Query object is fully built, the exec() method is called, and the callback function is passed into that.

You can also string the Query object methods together, as in this example:

```
model.find({}).where('value').lt(5).sort('-value').select('name title value')
.exec(function(err, results){});
```

When exec() is called, the Mongoose library builds the necessary query and options parameters and then makes the native call to MongoDB. The callback function returns the results.

Setting Query Database Operation

Each `Query` object must have a database operation associated with it. The database operation determines what action to take when connecting to the database—from finding documents to storing them. There are two ways to assign a database operation to a `Query` object. One is to call the operation from the `Model` object and not specify a callback. The `Query` object returned has that operation assigned to it. For example:

```
var query = model.find();
```

Once you already have a `Query` object, you can change the operation that is applied by calling the method on the `Query` object. For example, the following code creates a `Query` object that first applies a `count()` operation and then a `find()` operation. The `where()` clause is applied to both:

```
var query = model.count();
query.where('value').lt(5);
query.exec(function(){});
query.find();
query.exec(function(){});
```

This allows you to dynamically reuse the same `Query` object to perform multiple database operations. Table 16.2 lists the methods you can call on the `Query` object. You can also use these methods on a compiled `Model` object that can return a `Query` object by omitting the callback function. Keep in mind that if you pass in a callback function to any of these methods, the operation will be executed and the callback called when finished.

Table 16.2 **Methods available on `Query` and `Model` objects to set database operation**

Method	Description
`create(objects, [callback])`	Inserts the objects specified in the `objects` parameter into the MongoDB database. The `objects` parameter can be a single JavaScript object or an array of JavaScript objects. A `Document` object instance for the model is created for each object. The callback function receives an error object as the first parameter and the saved documents as additional objects. For example: `function(err, doc1, doc2, doc3, ...)`
`count([query], [callback])`	Sets the operation to `count`. When the callback is executed, the results returned are the number of items matching `query`.
`distinct([query], [field], [callback])`	Sets the operation to `distinct`, which limits the results to an array of the distinct values of the field specified when the callback is executed.
`find([query], [options], [callback])`	Sets the operation to `find`, which returns an array of the `Document` objects that match `query`.

Method	Description
findOne([query], [options], [callback])	Sets the operation to findOne, which returns the first Document objects that match query.
findOneAndRemove([query], [options], [callback])	Sets the operation to findAndRemove, which deletes the first document in the collection that matches query.
findOneAndUpdate([query], [update], [options], [callback])	Sets the operation to findAndRemove, which updates the first document in the collection that matches query. The update operation is specified in the update parameter. See Table 14.2 for the update operators that can be used.
remove([query], [options], [callback])	Sets the operation to remove, which deletes all the documents in the collection that match query.
update([query], [update], [options], [callback])	Sets the operation to update, which updates all documents in the collection that match query. The update operation is specified in the update parameter. See Table 14.2 for the update operators that can be used.
aggregate(operators, [callback])	Applies one or more aggregate operators to the collection. The callback function accepts an error as the first parameter and an array of JavaScript objects that represents the aggregated results as the second parameter.

Setting the Query Database Operation Options

The Query object also has methods that allow you to set options such as limit, skip, and select that define how the request is processed on the server. You can set these options in the options parameter in the methods listed in Table 16.2 or by calling the methods on the Query object listed in Table 16.3.

Table 16.3 **Methods available on Query and Model objects to set database operation options**

Method	Description
setOptions(options)	Sets the options used to interact with MongoDB when performing a database request. See Table 15.2 for a description of the options that can be set.
limit(number)	Sets the maximum number of documents to include in the results.

Method	Description

`select(fields)`	Specifies the fields that should be included in each document of the result set. The `fields` parameter can be either a space-separated string or an object. When using the string method, adding a `+` to the beginning of the fieldname forces inclusion even if the field doesn't exist in the document; adding a `-` excludes the field. For example:
	`select('name +title -value');`
	`select({name:1, title:1, value:0);`

`sort(fields)`	Specifies the fields to sort on, in string form or object form. For example:
	`sort('name -value');`
	`sort({name:1, value:-1})`

`skip(number)`	Specifies the number of documents to skip at the beginning of the result set.
`read(preference)`	Allows you to set the read preference to primary, `primaryPreferred`, `secondary`, `secondaryPreferred`, or `nearest`
`snapshot(Boolean)`	Sets the query to a snapshot query when `true`.
`safe(Boolean)`	When set to `true`, the database request uses a write concern for update operations.
`hint(hints)`	Specifies the indexes to use or exclude when finding documents. Use `1` for include and `-1` for exclude. For example: `hint(name:1, title:-1);`
`comment(string)`	Adds the `string` to the MongoDB log with the query. This is useful for identifying queries in the log files.

Setting the Query Operators

The `Query` object allows you to set the operators and values used to find the document to which you want to apply the database operations. These operators define this like "field values greater than a certain amount." The operators all work off a path to the field; you can specify this path by using the `where()` method or include it in the operator method. If no operator method is specified, the last path passed to a `where()` method is used.

For example, the `gt()` operator compares against the `value` field:

```
query.where('value').gt(5)
```

However, in the statement below, the `lt()` operator compares against the `score` field:

```
query.where('value').gt(5).lt('score', 10);
```

Table 16.4 lists the most common methods that can be applied to the `Query` object.

Table 16.4 **Methods available on `Query` objects to define the query operators**

Method	Description
`where(path, [value])`	Sets the current field path for the operators. If a value is also included, then only documents where that field equals `value` are included. For example: `where('name', "myName")`

`gt([path], value)`	Matches values that are greater than the `value` setting specified in the query. For example:
	`gt('value', 5)`
	`gt(5)`

`gte([path], value)`	Matches fields that are equal to or greater than the `value` setting specified in the query.
`lt([path], value)`	Matches values that are less than the `value` setting specified in the query.
`lte([path], value)`	Matches fields that are less than or equal to the `value` setting specified in the query.
`ne([path], value)`	Matches all fields that are not equal to the `value` setting specified in the query.

`in([path], array)`	Matches any of the values that exist in an `array` setting specified in the query. For example:
	`in('name', ['item1', 'item2'])`
	`in(['item1', 'item2'])`

`nin([path], array)`	Matches values that do not exist in an `array` setting specified in the query.
`or(conditions)`	Joins query clauses with a logical OR and returns all documents that match the `conditions` setting of either clause. For example: `or([{size:{$lt:5}},{size:{$gt:10}}])`
`and(conditions)`	Joins query clauses with a logical AND and returns all documents that match the `conditions` setting of both clauses. For example: `and([{size:{$lt:5}},{size:{$gt:10}}])`
`nor(conditions)`	Joins query clauses with a logical NOR and returns all documents that fail to match both `conditions` settings. For example: `nor([{size:{$lt:5}},{name:"myName"}])`

Method	Description

`exists([path], Boolean)`	Matches documents that have the specified field. For example, the following will find documents that have a `name` field and documents that do not have a `title` field:
	`exists('name', true)`
	`exists('title', false)`

`mod([path], value, remainder)`	Performs a modulo operation on the value of a field and selects documents that have the matching remainder. For example: `mod('size', 2,0)`
`regex([path], expression)`	Selects documents where values match a specified regular expression. For example: `regex('myField', 'some.*exp')`
`all([path], array)`	Matches array fields that contain all elements specified in the `array` parameter. For example: `all('myArr', ['one','two','three'])`

`elemMatch([path], criteria)`	Selects documents if an element in the array of subdocuments has fields that match all the specified `$elemMatch` criteria. The criteria can be an object or a function. For example:
	`elemMatch('item', {value:5},size:{$lt:3}})`
	`elemMatch('item', function(elem){`
	` elem.where('value', 5);`
	` elem.where('size').gt(3);`
	`})`

`size([path], value)`	Selects documents if the array field is a specified size. For example: `size('myArr', 5)`

Understanding the `Document` Object

When you use the `Model` object to retrieve documents from a database, the documents are presented in the callback function as Mongoose `Document` objects. `Document` objects inherit from the `Model` class and represent the documents in a collection. The `Document` object allows you to interact with a document from the perspective of your schema model by providing a number of methods and extra properties that support validation, modifications, etc.

Table 16.5 lists the most useful methods and properties on the `Document` object.

Table 16.5 **Methods and properties available on `Document` objects**

Method/Property	Description
`equals(doc)`	Returns `true` if this `Document` object matches the document specified by the `doc` parameter.
`id`	Contains the `_id` value of the document.
`get(path, [type])`	Returns the value of the specified path. The `type` parameter allows you to typecast the type of value to return.
`set(path, value, [type])`	Sets the value of the field at the specified path. The `type` parameter allows you to typecast the type of value to set.
`update(update, [options], [callback])`	Updates the document in the MongoDB database. The `update` parameter specifies the `update` operators to apply to the document. See Table 14.2 for the `update` operators that can be used.
`save([callback])`	Saves to the MongoDB database changes that have been made to the `Document` object. The callback function accepts an error object as the only parameter.
`remove([callback])`	Removes the `Document` object from the MongoDB database. The callback function accepts an error object as the only parameter.
`isNew`	A Boolean that, if `true`, indicates a new object to the model that has not been stored in MongoDB.
`isInit(path)`	Returns `true` if the field at this path has been initialized.
`isSelected(path)`	Returns `true` if the field at this path was selected in the result set returned from MongoDB.
`isModified(path)`	Returns `true` if the field at this path has been modified but not yet saved to MongoDB.
`markModified(path)`	Marks the path as being modified so that it will be saved/updated to MongoDB.
`modifiedPaths()`	Returns an array of paths in the object that have been modified.
`toJSON()`	Returns a JSON string representation of the `Document` object.
`toObject()`	Returns a normal JavaScript object without the extra properties and methods of the `Document` object.
`toString()`	Returns a string representation of the `Document` object.
`validate(callback)`	Performs a validation on the document. The callback function accepts only an `error` parameter.
`invalidate(path, msg, value)`	Marks the path as invalid, causing the validation to fail. The `msg` and `value` parameters specify the error message and `value`.
`errors`	Contains a list of errors in the document.
`schema`	Links to the `Schema` object that defines the `Document` object's model.

Finding Documents by Using Mongoose

Finding documents by using the `mongoose` module is very similar to using the MongoDB Node.js native driver and yet very different in some ways. The concepts of logic operators, limit, skip, and distinct are all the same. However, there are two big differences. The first major difference is that when using Mongoose, the statements used to build the request can be piped together and reused because of the `Query` object, discussed earlier in this chapter. This allows Mongoose code to be much more dynamic and flexible when defining what documents to return and how to return them.

For example, these three queries are identical, just built in different ways:

```
var query1 = model.find({name:'test'}, {limit:10, skip:5, fields:{name:1,value:1}});
var query2 = model.find().where('name','test').limit(10).skip(5).
select({name:1,value:1});
var query3 = model.find();
query3.where('name','test');
query3.limit(10).skip(5);
query3.select({name:1,value:1});
```

A good rule to follow when building a `Query` object using Mongoose is to add only things as you know you need in your code.

The second major difference is that MongoDB operations such as `find()` and `findOne()` return `Document` objects instead of JavaScript objects. Specifically, `find()` returns an array of `Document` objects instead of a `Cursor` object, and `findOne()` returns a single `Document` object. The `Document` objects allow you to perform the operations listed in Table 16.5.

Listing 16.3 illustrates several examples of the Mongoose way of retrieving objects from a database. The example in lines 10–14 counts the number of words that begin and end with a vowel. Then in line 15, the same `Query` object is changed to a `find()` operation, and `limit()` and `sort()` are added before execution in line 16.

The example in lines 22–32 uses `mod()` to find words with an even number of letters and more than six characters. Also, the output is limited to 10 documents, and each document returns only the `word` and `size` fields. Figure 16.3 shows the output of Listing 16.3.

Listing 16.3 `mongoose_find.js`: **Finding documents in a collection by using Mongoose**

```
01 var mongoose = require('mongoose');
02 var db = mongoose.connect('mongodb://localhost/words');
03 var wordSchema = require('./word_schema.js').wordSchema;
04 var Words = mongoose.model('Words', wordSchema);
05 setTimeout(function(){
06   mongoose.disconnect();
07 }, 3000);
08 mongoose.connection.once('open', function(){
09   var query = Words.count().where('first').in(['a', 'e', 'i', 'o', 'u']);
10   query.where('last').in(['a', 'e', 'i', 'o', 'u']);
```

```
  query.exec(function(err, count){
    console.log("\nThere are " + count +
                " words that start and end with a vowel");
  });
  query.find().limit(5).sort({size:-1});
  query.exec(function(err, docs){
    console.log("\nLongest 5 words that start and end with a vowel: ");
    for (var i in docs){
      console.log(docs[i].word);
    }
  });
  query = Words.find();
  query.mod('size',2,0);
  query.where('size').gt(6);
  query.limit(10);
  query.select({word:1, size:1});
  query.exec(function(err, docs){
    console.log("\nWords with even lengths and longer than 5 letters: ");
    for (var i in docs){
      console.log(JSON.stringify(docs[i]));
    }
  });
});
```

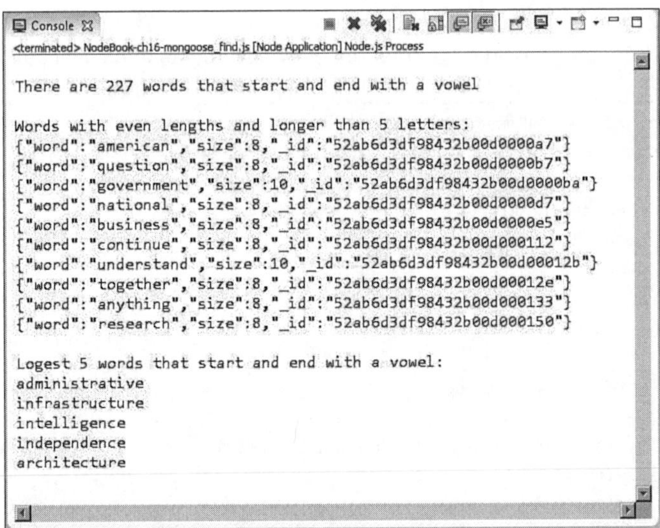

Figure 16.3 Finding documents in a collection by using Mongoose.

Adding Documents by Using Mongoose

You can add documents to the MongoDB library by using either the `create()` method on the `Model` object or the `save()` method on a newly created `Document` object. The `create()` method accepts an array of JavaScript objects and creates a `Document` instance for each JavaScript object, which applies validation and a middleware framework to them. Then the `Document` objects are saved to the database. The syntax of the `create()` method is shown below:

```
create(objects, [callback])
```

The callback function of the `create()` method receives an error for the first parameter if it occurs and then additional parameters, one for each document, saved as additional parameters. Lines 27–32 of Listing 16.4 illustrate using the `create()` method and handling the saved documents coming back. Notice that the `create()` method is called on the `Model` object `Words` and that the arguments are iterated on to display the created documents in Figure 16.4.

The `save()` method is called on a `Document` object that has already been created. It can be called even if the document has not yet been created in the MongoDB database, in which case the new document is inserted. The syntax for the `save()` method is :

```
save([callback])
```

The code in Listing 16.4 also shows the `save()` method adding documents to a collection using Mongoose. Notice that a new `Document` instance is created in lines 6–11 and that the `save()` method is called on that `Document` instance.

Listing 16.4 `mongoose_create.js`: **Creating new documents in a collection by using Mongoose**

```
01 var mongoose = require('mongoose');
02 var db = mongoose.connect('mongodb://localhost/words');
03 var wordSchema = require('./word_schema.js').wordSchema;
04 var Words = mongoose.model('Words', wordSchema);
05 mongoose.connection.once('open', function(){
06   var newWord1 = new Words({
07     word:'gratifaction',
08     first:'g', last:'n', size:12,
09     letters: ['g','r','a','t','i','f','c','o','n'],
10     stats: {vowels:5, consonants:7}
11   });
12   console.log("Is Document New? " + newWord1.isNew);
13   newWord1.save(function(err, doc){
14     console.log("\nSaved document: " + doc);
15   });
```

```
  var newWord2 = { word:'googled',
    first:'g', last:'d', size:7,
    letters: ['g','o','l','e','d'],
    stats: {vowels:3, consonants:4}
  };
  var newWord3 = {
    word:'selfie',
    first:'s', last:'e', size:6,
    letters: ['s','e','l','f','i'],
    stats: {vowels:3, consonants:3}
  };
  Words.create([newWord2, newWord3], function(err){
    for(var i=1; i<arguments.length; i++){
      console.log("\nCreated document: " + arguments[i]);
    }
    mongoose.disconnect();
  });
});
```

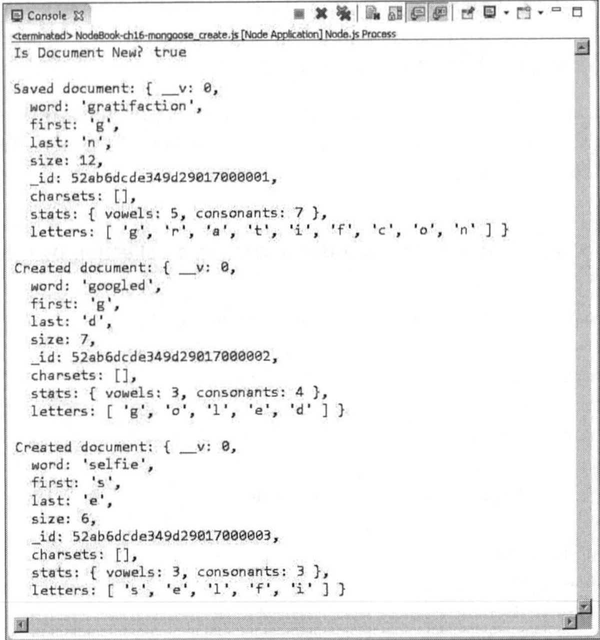

Figure 16.4 Creating new documents in a collection by using Mongoose.

Updating Documents by Using Mongoose

There are several methods for updating documents when using Mongoose. Which one you use depends on the nature of your application. One method is simply to call the `save()` function described in the previous section. You can call the `save()` method on objects already created in the database.

The other method is to use `update()` on either the `Document` object for a single update or on the `Model` object to update multiple documents in the model. The advantages of the `update()` methods are that it can be applied to multiple objects, and it provides slightly better performance. The following sections describe these methods.

Saving Document Changes

You have already seen how to use the `save()` method to add a new document to a database. You can also use it to update an existing object. Often the `save()` method is the most convenient to use when working with MongoDB because you already have an instance of the `Document` object.

The `save()` method detects whether an object is new, determines which fields have changed, and then builds a database request that updates those fields in the database. Listing 16.5 shows how to implement a `save()` request. It retrieves the word `book` from the database and capitalizes the first letter, changing the word and first fields.

Notice that `doc.isNew` in line 8 reports that the document is not new. Also, line 14 reports the modified fields to the console by using `doc.modifiedFields()`. These are the fields that will be updated. Figure 16.5 shows the full results.

Listing 16.5 `mongoose_save.js`: **Saving documents in a collection by using Mongoose**

```
01 var mongoose = require('mongoose');
02 var db = mongoose.connect('mongodb://localhost/words');
03 var wordSchema = require('./word_schema.js').wordSchema;
04 var Words = mongoose.model('Words', wordSchema);
05 mongoose.connection.once('open', function(){
06   var query = Words.findOne().where('word', 'book');
07   query.exec(function(err, doc){
08     console.log("Is Document New? " + doc.isNew);
09     console.log("\nBefore Save: ");
10     console.log(doc.toJSON());
11     doc.set('word','Book');
12     doc.set('first','B');
13     console.log("\nModified Fields: ");
14     console.log(doc.modifiedPaths());
15     doc.save(function(err){
16       Words.findOne({word:'Book'}, function(err, doc){
17         console.log("\nAfter Save: ");
```

```
            console.log(doc.toJSON());
            mongoose.disconnect();
          });
        });
      });
    });
```

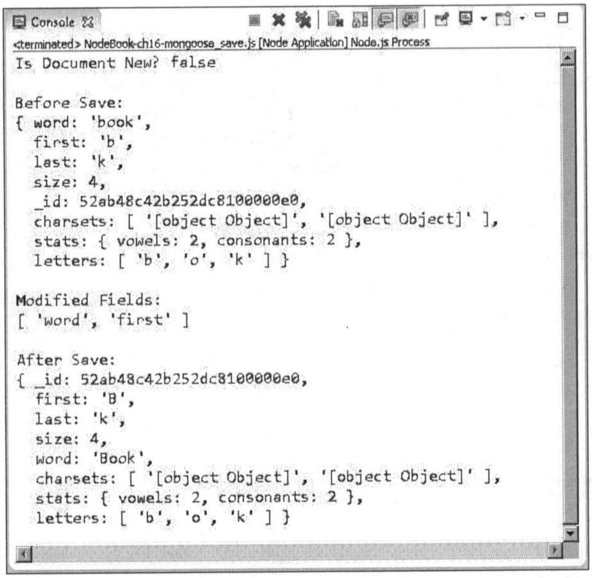

```
Console
<terminated> NodeBook-ch16-mongoose_save.js [Node Application] Node.js Process
Is Document New? false

Before Save:
{ word: 'book',
  first: 'b',
  last: 'k',
  size: 4,
  _id: 52ab48c42b252dc8100000e0,
  charsets: [ '[object Object]', '[object Object]' ],
  stats: { vowels: 2, consonants: 2 },
  letters: [ 'b', 'o', 'k' ] }

Modified Fields:
[ 'word', 'first' ]

After Save:
{ _id: 52ab48c42b252dc8100000e0,
  first: 'B',
  last: 'k',
  size: 4,
  word: 'Book',
  charsets: [ '[object Object]', '[object Object]' ],
  stats: { vowels: 2, consonants: 2 },
  letters: [ 'b', 'o', 'k' ] }
```

Figure 16.5 Saving documents in a collection by using Mongoose.

Updating a Single Document

The `Document` object provides the `update()` method, which allows you to update a single document by using the `update` operators described in Table 14.2. The syntax for the `update()` method on `Document` objects is shown below:

```
update(update, [options], [callback])
```

The `update` parameter defines the update operation to perform on the document. The `options` parameter specifies the write preferences, and the `callback` parameter accepts an error as the first argument and the number of documents updated as the second.

Listing 16.6 shows an example of using the `update()` method to update the word `gratifaction` to `gratifactions` by setting `word`, `size`, and `last` fields, using a `$set` operator as well as pushing the letter `s` on the end of `letters` by using the `$push` operator. Figure 16.6 shows the output for Listing 16.6.

Listing 16.6 `mongoose_update_one.js`: **Updating a single document in a collection by using Mongoose**

```
var mongoose = require('mongoose');
var db = mongoose.connect('mongodb://localhost/words');
var wordSchema = require('./word_schema.js').wordSchema;
var Words = mongoose.model('Words', wordSchema);
mongoose.connection.once('open', function(){
  var query = Words.findOne().where('word', 'gratifaction');
  query.exec(function(err, doc){
    console.log("Before Update: ");
    console.log(doc.toString());
    var query = doc.update({$set:{word:'gratifactions',
                                  size:13, last:'s'},
                            $push:{letters:'s'}});
    query.exec(function(err, results){
      console.log("\n%d Documents updated", results);
      Words.findOne({word:'gratifactions'}, function(err, doc){
        console.log("\nAfter Update: ");
        console.log(doc.toString());
        mongoose.disconnect();
      });
    });
  });
});
```

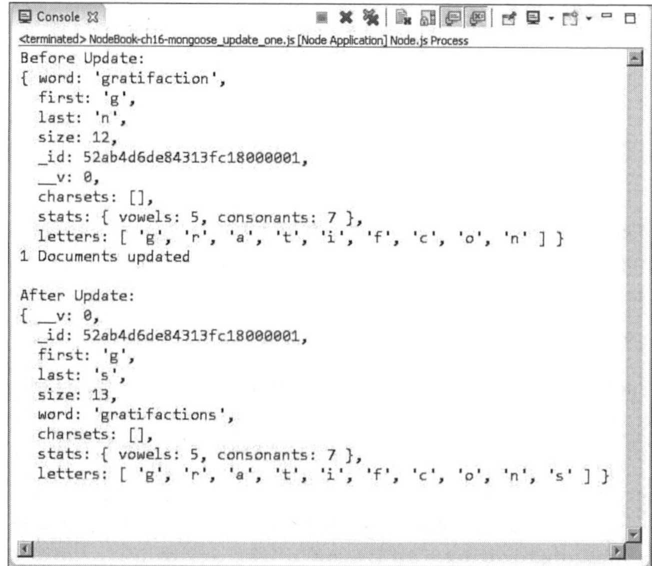

Console
<terminated> NodeBook-ch16-mongoose_update_one.js [Node Application] Node.js Process
Before Update:
{ word: 'gratifaction',
first: 'g',
last: 'n',
size: 12,
_id: 52ab4d6de84313fc18000001,
__v: 0,
charsets: [],
stats: { vowels: 5, consonants: 7 },
letters: ['g', 'r', 'a', 't', 'i', 'f', 'c', 'o', 'n'] }
1 Documents updated
After Update:
{ __v: 0,
_id: 52ab4d6de84313fc18000001,
first: 'g',
last: 's',
size: 13,
word: 'gratifactions',
charsets: [],
stats: { vowels: 5, consonants: 7 },
letters: ['g', 'r', 'a', 't', 'i', 'f', 'c', 'o', 'n', 's'] }

Figure 16.6 Updating a single document in a collection by using Mongoose.

Updating Multiple Documents

The `Model` object provides an `update()` method that allows you to update multiple documents in a collection by using the `update` operators described in Table 14.2. The syntax for the `update()` method on `Model` objects is shown below:

```
update(query, update, [options], [callback])
```

The `query` parameter defines the query used to identify which objects to update. The `update` parameter is an object that defines the update operation to perform on the document. The `options` parameter specifies the write preferences, and the `callback` parameter accepts an error as the first argument and the number of documents updated as the second.

A nice thing about updating at the model level is that you can use the `Query` object to define which objects should be updated. Listing 16.7 shows an example of using the `update()` method to update the `size` field of words that match the regex `/grati.*/` to `0`. Notice that line 11 defines an `update` object, but the code adds multiple query options onto the `Query` object before executing in line 14. Then the code makes another `find()` request, this time using the regex `/grat.*/` to show that only what matches the update query actually changes. Figure 16.7 shows the output for Listing 16.7.

Listing 16.7 `mongoose_update_many.js`: **Updating multiple documents in a collection by using Mongoose**

```
01 var mongoose = require('mongoose');
02 var db = mongoose.connect('mongodb://localhost/words');
03 var wordSchema = require('./word_schema.js').wordSchema;
04 var Words = mongoose.model('Words', wordSchema);
05 mongoose.connection.once('open', function(){
06   Words.find({word:/grati.*/}, function(err, docs){
07     console.log("Before update: ");
08     for (var i in docs){
09       console.log(docs[i].word + " : " + docs[i].size);
10     }
11     var query = Words.update({}, {$set: {size: 0}});
12     query.setOptions({multi: true});
13     query.where('word').regex(/grati.*/);
14     query.exec(function(err, results){
15       Words.find({word:/grat.*/}, function(err, docs){
16         console.log("\nAfter update: ");
17         for (var i in docs){
18           console.log(docs[i].word + " : " + docs[i].size);
19         }
20         mongoose.disconnect();
21       });
22     });
23   });
24 });
```

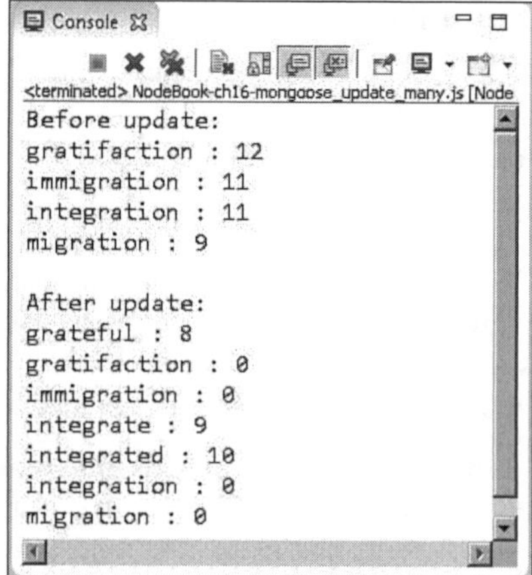

Figure 16.7 Updating multiple documents in a collection by using Mongoose.

Removing Documents by Using Mongoose

There are two main options for removing objects from a collection using Mongoose. First, you can use the `remove()` method on either the `Document` object for a single deletion or on the `Model` object to delete multiple documents in the model. Deleting a single object is often convenient if you already have a `Document` instance. However, it is often much more efficient to delete multiple documents at the same time at the model level. The following sections describe these methods.

Removing a Single Document

The `Document` object provides the `remove()` method, which allows you to delete a single document from the model. The syntax for the `remove()` method on `Document` objects is shown below:

```
remove( [callback])
```

The `callback` parameter accepts an error as the only argument if an error occurred or the deleted document as the second if the delete was successful.

Listing 16.8 shows an example of using the `remove()` method to remove the word `unhappy`. Figure 16.8 shows the output for Listing 16.8.

Listing 16.8 `mongoose_remove_one.js`: **Deleting a document from a collection by using Mongoose**

```
var mongoose = require('mongoose');
var db = mongoose.connect('mongodb://localhost/words');
var wordSchema = require('./word_schema.js').wordSchema;
var Words = mongoose.model('Words', wordSchema);
mongoose.connection.once('open', function(){
  var query = Words.findOne().where('word', 'unhappy');
  query.exec(function(err, doc){
    console.log("Before Delete: ");
    console.log(doc);
    doc.remove(function(err, deletedDoc){
      Words.findOne({word:'unhappy'}, function(err, doc){
        console.log("\nAfter Delete: ");
        console.log(doc);
        mongoose.disconnect();
      });
    });
  });
});
```

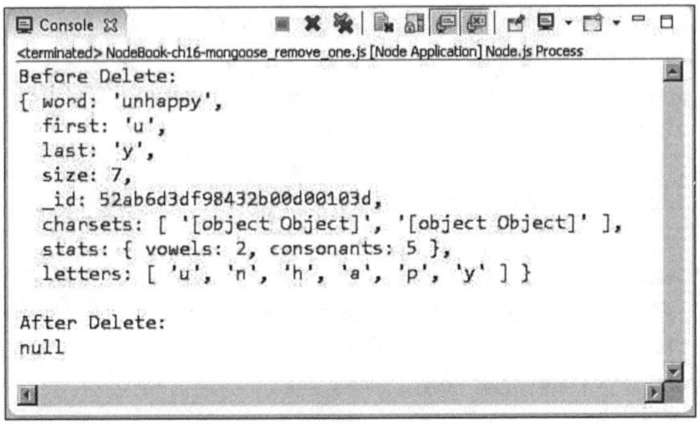

```
Console
<terminated> NodeBook-ch16-mongoose_remove_one.js [Node Application] Node.js Process
Before Delete:
{ word: 'unhappy',
  first: 'u',
  last: 'y',
  size: 7,
  _id: 52ab6d3df98432b00d00103d,
  charsets: [ '[object Object]', '[object Object]' ],
  stats: { vowels: 2, consonants: 5 },
  letters: [ 'u', 'n', 'h', 'a', 'p', 'y' ] }

After Delete:
null
```

Figure 16.8 Deleting a document from a collection by using Mongoose.

Removing Multiple Documents

The `Model` object's `remove()` method allows you to delete multiple documents in a collection by using a single call to the database. The syntax for the `remove()` method on `Model` objects is shown below:

```
update(query, [options], [callback])
```

The `query` parameter defines the query used to identify which objects to delete. The `options` parameter specifies the write preferences, and the `callback` parameter accepts an error as the first argument and the number of documents deleted as the second.

A nice thing about deleting at the model level is that you delete multiple documents in the same operation, saving the overhead of multiple requests. Also, you can use the `Query` object to define which objects to update.

Listing 16.9 shows an example of using the `remove()` method to delete words that match the regex `/grati.*/` expression. Notice that the code pipes multiple query options onto the `Query` object before line 13 executes it. The listing displays the number of documents removed, and then another `find()` request is made, this time using the regex `/grat.*/` to show that only those matching the remove query actually are deleted. Figure 16.9 shows the output for Listing 16.9.

Listing 16.9 `mongoose_remove_many.js`: **Deleting multiple documents in a collection by using Mongoose**

```
01 var mongoose = require('mongoose');
02 var db = mongoose.connect('mongodb://localhost/words');
03 var wordSchema = require('./word_schema.js').wordSchema;
04 var Words = mongoose.model('Words', wordSchema);
05 mongoose.connection.once('open', function(){
06   Words.find({word:/grat.*/}, function(err, docs){
07     console.log("Before delete: ");
08     for (var i in docs){
09       console.log(docs[i].word);
10     }
11     var query = Words.remove();
12     query.where('word').regex(/grati.*/);
13     query.exec(function(err, results){
14       console.log("\n%d Documents Deleted.", results);
15       Words.find({word:/grat.*/}, function(err, docs){
16         console.log("\nAfter delete: ");
17         for (var i in docs){
18           console.log(docs[i].word);
19         }
20         mongoose.disconnect();
21       });
22     });
23   });
24 });
```

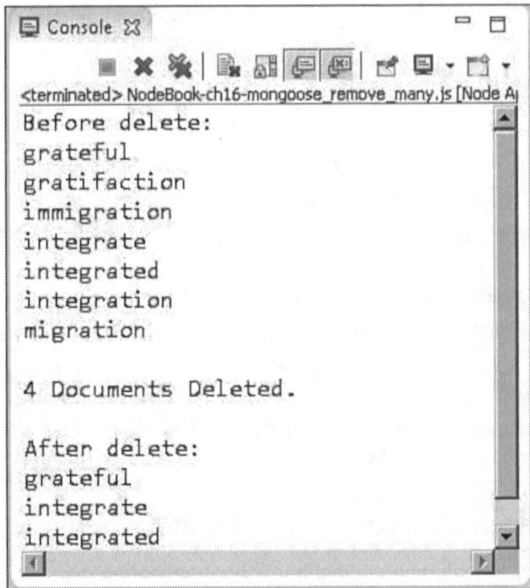

Figure 16.9 Deleting multiple documents in a collection by using Mongoose.

Aggregating Documents by Using Mongoose

The `Model` object provides an `aggregate()` method that allows you to implement the MongoDB aggregation pipeline discussed in Chapter 15. If you haven't already read the aggregation information in Chapter 15, you should read it before you read this section. It works here very similarly to the way it works in the MongoDB Node.js native driver. In fact, you can use exactly the same syntax if you want to. You also have the option of using the Mongoose `Aggregate` object to build and then execute the aggregation pipeline.

The `Aggregate` object works very similarly to the `Query` object in that if you pass in a callback function, `aggregate()` is executed immediately; if not, an `Aggregate` object is returned, and you can apply pipeline methods.

For example, the following calls the `aggregate()` method immediately:

```
model.aggregate([{$match:{value:15}}, {$group:{_id:"$name"}}],
                function(err, results) {});
```

You can also pipeline aggregation operations by using an instance of the `Aggregate` object. For example:

```
var aggregate = model.aggregate();
aggregate.match({value:15});
aggregate.group({_id:"$name"});
aggregate.exec();
```

Table 16.6 describes the methods that can be called on the `Aggregate` object.

Table 16.6 **Pipeline methods for the `Aggregate` object in Mongoose**

Method	Description
`exec(callback)`	Executes the `Aggregate` object pipeline items in the order in which they were added. The callback function receives an error as the first parameter and an array of JavaScript objects as the second, representing the aggregated results.
`append(operations)`	Appends additional operations to the `Aggregation` object pipeline. You can apply multiple operations as in this example: `append({match:{size:1}}, {$group{_id:"$title"}}, {$limit:2})`
`group(operators)`	Appends a `group` operation defined by the group operators. For example: `group({_id:"$title", largest:{$max:"$size"}})`
`limit(number)`	Appends a `limit` operation that limits the aggregated results to a specific number.
`match(operators)`	Appends a `match` operation defined by the `operators` parameter. For example: `match({value:{$gt:7, $lt:14}}, title:"new"})`
`project(operators)`	Appends a project operation defined by the `operators` parameter. For example: `project({_id:"$name", value:"$score", largest:{$max:"$size"}})`
`read(preference)`	Specifies the replica read preference use for aggregation. The value can be `primary`, `primaryPreferred`, `secondary`, `secondaryPreferred`, or `nearest`.
`skip(number)`	Appends a `skip` operation that skips the first numbered documents when applying the next operation in the aggregation pipeline.
`sort(fields)`	Appends a `sort` operation to the aggregation pipeline. The fields are specified in an object, where a value of `1` is include and a value of `-1` is exclude. For example: `sort({name:1, value:-1})`
`unwind(arrFields)`	Appends an `unwind` operation to the aggregation pipeline, which unwinds the `arrFields` parameter by creating a new document in the aggregation set for each value in the array. For example: `unwind("arrField1", "arrField2", . "arrField3")`

Listing 16.10 illustrates three examples of aggregation in Mongoose. The first example, in lines 9–19, implements aggregation in the native driver way but by using the `Model` object. The aggregated result set is the largest and smallest word sizes for words that begin with a vowel.

The next example, in lines 20–27, implements aggregation by creating an `Aggregate` object and appending operations to it by using the `match()`, `append()`, and `limit()` methods. The results are stats for the five four-letter words.

The final example, in lines 28–35, uses the `group()`, `sort()`, and `limit()` methods to build the aggregation pipeline that results in the top five letters with the largest average word size. Figure 16.10 shows the output of the code in Listing 16.10.

Listing 16.10 `mongoose_aggregate.js`: **Aggregating data from documents in a collection by using Mongoose**

```
01 var mongoose = require('mongoose');
02 var db = mongoose.connect('mongodb://localhost/words');
03 var wordSchema = require('./word_schema.js').wordSchema;
04 var Words = mongoose.model('Words', wordSchema);
05 setTimeout(function(){
06   mongoose.disconnect();
07 }, 3000);
08 mongoose.connection.once('open', function(){
09   Words.aggregate([{$match: {first:{$in:['a','e','i','o','u']}}},
10                             {$group: {_id:"$first",
11                               largest:{$max:"$size"},
12                               smallest:{$min:"$size"},
13                               total:{$sum:1}}},
14                   {$sort: {_id:1}}],
15             function(err, results){
16     console.log("\nLargest and smallest word sizes for " +
17                 "words beginning with a vowel: ");
18     console.log(results);
19   });
20   var aggregate = Words.aggregate();
21   aggregate.match({size:4});
22   aggregate.limit(5);
23   aggregate.append({$project: {_id:"$word", stats:1}});
24   aggregate.exec(function(err, results){
25     console.log("\nStats for 5 four letter words: ");
26     console.log(results);
27   });
28   var aggregate = Words.aggregate();
29   aggregate.group({_id:"$first", average:{$avg:"$size"}});
30   aggregate.sort('-average');
31   aggregate.limit(5);
32   aggregate.exec( function(err, results){
33     console.log("\nLetters with largest average word size: ");
34     console.log(results);
35  });
36 });
```

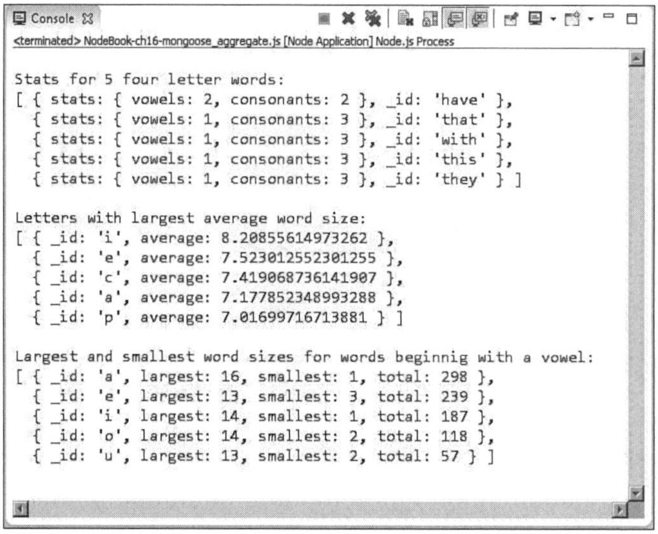

```
Console
<terminated> NodeBook-ch16-mongoose_aggregate.js [Node Application] Node.js Process

Stats for 5 four letter words:
[ { stats: { vowels: 2, consonants: 2 }, _id: 'have' },
  { stats: { vowels: 1, consonants: 3 }, _id: 'that' },
  { stats: { vowels: 1, consonants: 3 }, _id: 'with' },
  { stats: { vowels: 1, consonants: 3 }, _id: 'this' },
  { stats: { vowels: 1, consonants: 3 }, _id: 'they' } ]

Letters with largest average word size:
[ { _id: 'i', average: 8.20855614973262 },
  { _id: 'e', average: 7.523012552301255 },
  { _id: 'c', average: 7.419068736141907 },
  { _id: 'a', average: 7.177852348993288 },
  { _id: 'p', average: 7.01699716713881 } ]

Largest and smallest word sizes for words beginnig with a vowel:
[ { _id: 'a', largest: 16, smallest: 1, total: 298 },
  { _id: 'e', largest: 13, smallest: 3, total: 239 },
  { _id: 'i', largest: 14, smallest: 1, total: 187 },
  { _id: 'o', largest: 14, smallest: 2, total: 118 },
  { _id: 'u', largest: 13, smallest: 2, total: 57 } ]
```

Figure 16.10 Aggregating data from documents in a collection by using Mongoose.

Using the Validation Framework

One of the most important aspects of the mongoose module is validation against a defined model. Mongoose provides a built-in validation framework that only requires you to define validation functions to perform on specific fields that need to be validated. When you try to create a new instance of a document, read a document from the database or save a document, the validation framework calls your custom validation methods and returns an error if the validation fails.

The validation framework is actually very simple to implement. You call the validate() method on the specific path in the Model object that you want to apply validation to and pass in a validation function. The validation function accepts the value of the field and then uses that value to return true or false, depending on whether the value is valid. The second parameter to the validate() method is an error string that is applied to the error object if validation fails. For example:

```
Words.schema.path('word').validate(function(value){
  return value.length < 20;
}, "Word is Too Big");
```

The error object thrown by validation has the following fields:

- **error.errors.<field>.message:** String defined when adding the validate function
- **error.errors.<field>.type:** Type of validation error

- **error.errors.<field>.path:** Path in the object that failed validation
- **error.errors.<field>.value:** Value that failed validation
- **error.name:** Error type name
- **err.message:** Error message

Listing 16.11 shows a simple example of adding validation to the word model where a word of length 0 or greater than 20 is invalid. Notice that when the newWord is saved in line 18, an error is passed to the save() function. The output in lines 12–26 shows the various values of different parts of the error, as shown in Figure 16.11. You can use these values to determine how to handle validation failures in the code.

Listing 16.11 mongoose_validation.js: **Implementing validation of documents in the model by using Mongoose**

```
01 var mongoose = require('mongoose');
02 var db = mongoose.connect('mongodb://localhost/words');
03 var wordSchema = require('./word_schema.js').wordSchema;
04 var Words = mongoose.model('Words', wordSchema);
05 Words.schema.path('word').validate(function(value){
06   return value.length > 0;
07 }, "Word is Too Small");
08 Words.schema.path('word').validate(function(value){
09   return value.length < 20;
10 }, "Word is Too Big");
11 mongoose.connection.once('open', function(){
12   var newWord = new Words({
13     word:'supercalifragilisticexpialidocious',
14     first:'s',
15     last:'s',
16     size:'supercalifragilisticexpialidocious'.length,
17   });
18   newWord.save(function (err) {
19     console.log(err.errors.word.message);
20     console.log(String(err.errors.word));
21     console.log(err.errors.word.type);
22     console.log(err.errors.word.path);
23     console.log(err.errors.word.value);
24     console.log(err.name);
25     console.log(err.message);
26     mongoose.disconnect();
27   });
28 });
```

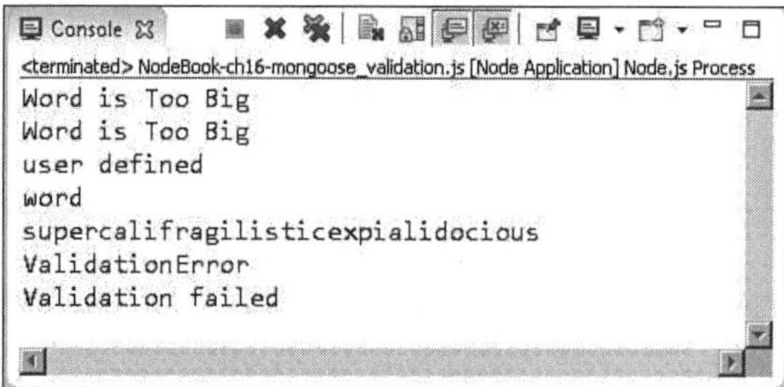

Figure 16.11 Implementing validation of documents in the model by using Mongoose.

Implementing Middleware Functions

Mongoose provides a middleware framework where `pre` and `post` functions are called before and after the `init()`, `validate()`, `save()`, and `remove()` methods on a `Document` object. A middleware framework allows you to implement functionality that should be applied before or after a specific step in a process. For example, when creating word documents using the model defined earlier in this chapter, you might want to automatically set the size to the length of the word field, as shown in the following `pre()` `save()` middleware function:

```
Words.schema.pre('save', function (next) {
  console.log('%s is about to be saved', this.word);
  console.log('Setting size to %d', this.word.length);
  this.size = this.word.length;
  next();
});
```

There are two types of middleware functions—the `pre` and `post` functions—and they are handled a bit differently. The `pre` functions receive a `next` parameter, which is the next middleware function to execute. The `pre` functions can be called asynchronously or synchronously. In the case of the asynchronous method, an additional `done` parameter is passed to the `pre` function so you can notify the asynchronous framework that you are finished. If you are applying operations that should be done in order in the middleware, you should use the synchronous method.

To apply the middleware synchronously, you simply call `next()` in the middleware function. For example:

```
shchema.pre('save', function(next)){
  next();
});
```

To apply the middleware asynchronously, add a `true` parameter to the `pre()` method to denote asynchronous behavior and then call `doAsyn(done)` inside the middleware function. For example:

```
shchema.pre('save', true, function(next, done)){
  next();
  doAsync(done);
});
```

You call the post middleware functions after the init, validate, save, or remove operation has been processed. This allows you to do any cleanup work necessary when applying the operation. For example, the following implements a simple post save method which logs that the object has been saved:

```
schema.post('save', function(doc){
  console.log("Document Saved: " + doc.toString());
});
```

Listing 16.12 illustrates the process of implementing middleware for each stage of the document life cycle. Notice that the validate and save middleware functions are executed when saving the document. You execute the init middleware functions when retrieving the document from MongoDB by using findOne().You execute the remove middleware functions when using remove() to delete a document from MongoDB.

Also notice that you can use the this keyword in all the middleware functions except pre init to access the Document object. In the case of pre init, you do not yet have a document from the database to use. Figure 16.12 shows the output of the code in Listing 16.12.

Listing 16.12 mongoose_middleware.js: **Applying a middleware framework to a model by using Mongoose**

```
var mongoose = require('mongoose');
var db = mongoose.connect('mongodb://localhost/words');
var wordSchema = require('./word_schema.js').wordSchema;
var Words = mongoose.model('Words', wordSchema);
Words.schema.pre('init', function (next) {
  console.log('a new word is about to be initialized from the db');
  next();
});
Words.schema.pre('validate', function (next) {
  console.log('%s is about to be validated', this.word);
  next();
});
Words.schema.pre('save', function (next) {
  console.log('%s is about to be saved', this.word);
  console.log('Setting size to %d', this.word.length);
  this.size = this.word.length;
  next();
});
Words.schema.pre('remove', function (next) {
  console.log('%s is about to be removed', this.word);
  next();
});
```

```
Words.schema.post('init', function (doc) {
  console.log('%s has been initialized from the db', doc.word);
});
Words.schema.post('validate', function (doc) {
  console.log('%s has been validated', doc.word);
});
Words.schema.post('save', function (doc) {
  console.log('%s has been saved', doc.word);
});
Words.schema.post('remove', function (doc) {
  console.log('%s has been removed', doc.word);
});
mongoose.connection.once('open', function(){
  var newWord = new Words({
    word:'newword',
    first:'t',
    last:'d',
    size:'newword'.length,
  });
  console.log("\nSaving: ");
  newWord.save(function (err){
    console.log("\nFinding: ");
    Words.findOne({word:'newword'}, function(err, doc){
      console.log("\nRemoving: ");
      newWord.remove(function(err){
        mongoose.disconnect();
      });
    });
  });
});
```

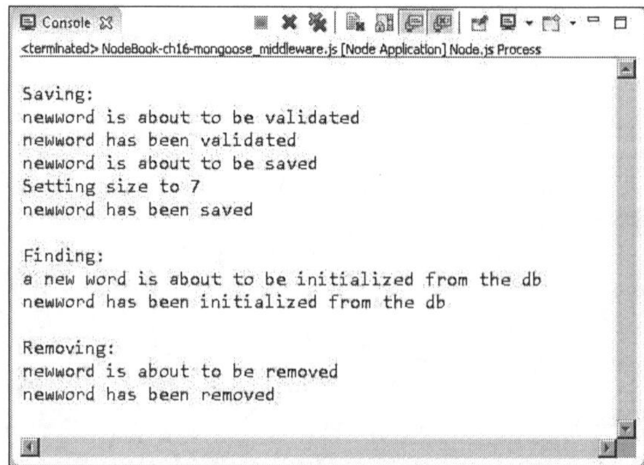

Figure 16.12 Applying a middleware framework to a model by using Mongoose.

Summary

This chapter introduces Mongoose, which provides a structured schema to a MongoDB collection that provides the benefits of validation and typecasting. You've learned about the new `Schema`, `Model`, `Query`, and `Aggregation` objects and how to use them to implement an ODM. You've also used the sometimes more friendly Mongoose methods to build a `Query` object before executing database commands.

You have also learned about the validation and middleware frameworks. The validation framework allows you to validate specific fields in the model before trying to save them to the database. The middleware framework allows you to implement functionality that happens before and/or after each `init`, `validate`, `save`, or `remove` operation.

Up Next

In the next chapter you will delve into some more advanced MongoDB topics, such as indexes, replication, and sharding.

17
Advanced MongoDB Concepts

There's a lot more to MongoDB than this book can cover. This chapter is designed to get you started with some fundamentals beyond the normal database create, access, and delete operations. Designing and implementing indexes allows you to improve database performance. Also, implementing replica sets and sharding provide additional performance improvements and high availability. When you're done with this chapter, you'll be able to implement GridFS functionality from Node.js in order to deal with extremely large files.

Adding Indexes

MongoDB allows you to index fields in your collections so that you can more quickly find documents. When you add an index in MongoDB, a special data structure is created in the background that stores a small portion of a collection's data and then optimizes the structure of that data to make it faster to find specific documents.

For example, applying an `_id` index basically creates a sorted array of `_id` values. Once the index has been created, you get these benefits:

- When looking up an object by `_id`, you can perform an optimized search on the ordered index to find the object in question.
- Say that you want objects back sorted by `_id`. The sort has already been performed on the index, so it doesn't need to be done again. MongoDB just needs to read the documents in the order in which their `_id` appears in the index.
- If you want documents 10–20 sorted by `_id`, the operation is just a matter of slicing that chunk out of the index to get the `_id` values so you can look up objects.
- Best of all, if all you need is a list of sorted `_id` values, MongoDB does not even need to read the documents at all; it can just return the values directly from the index.

You need to keep in mind, however, that those benefits come at a cost. The following are some of the costs associated with indexes:

- Indexes take up space on disk and in memory.
- Indexes take up processing time when you're inserting and updating documents. Therefore, database writes to collections with large number of indexes can suffer performance hits.
- The larger the collection, the greater the cost in terms of resources and performance. With extremely large collections, it may be impractical to apply some indexes.

Several different types of indexes can be applied to fields in a collection to support various design requirements. Table 17.1 lists the different index types.

Table 17.1 **Types of indexes supported by MongoDB**

Index	Description
`_id` (default)	All MongoDB collections have an index on `_id` by default. If applications do not specify a value for `_id`, the driver or `mongod` will create an `_id` field with an `ObjectID` value. The `_id` index is unique and prevents clients from inserting two documents with the same value for `_id`.
Single field	The most basic type of index is one on a single field. This is similar to the `_id` index but on any field that you need. The index can be sorted in ascending or descending order. The values of the fields do not necessarily need to be unique. For example: `{name: 1}`
Compound	You can specify an index on multiple fields. The index will be sorted on the first field value, then the second, and so on. You can also mix the sort direction; for example, you can have one field sort in ascending order and another sort in descending order. For example: `{name: 1, value: -1}`
Multikey	If you add a field that stores an array of items, a separate index for every element in the array will also be created. This allows you to find documents more quickly by using values contained in the index. For example, consider an array of objects named `myObjs` where each object has a `score` field: `{myObjs.score: 1}`
Geospatial	MongoDB allows you to create a geospatial index based on `2d` or `2sphere` coordinates. This allows you to more effectively store and retrieve data that has a reference to a geospatial location. For example: `{"locs":"2d"}`

Index	Description
Text	MongoDB supports adding a text index that supports faster lookup of string elements by words that are contained inside. The index does not store words like *the*, *a*, *and*, etc. For example: `{comment: "text"}`
Hashed	When using hashed base sharding, MongoDB allows you to use a hashed index, which only indexes hashed values that match those stored in a particular server. This reduces the overhead of keeping hashes around for items on other servers. For example: `{key: "hashed"}`

You can give indexes special properties to define how MongoDB will handle the index:

- **`unique`:** This property forces the index to include only a single instance of each field value, and thus MongoDB will reject adding a document that has a duplicate value to one that is already in the index.
- **`sparse`:** This property ensures that the index will contain only entries for documents that have the indexed field. The index will skip documents that do not have the indexed field.
- **`TTL`:** `TTL`, or time-to-live, indexes apply the concept of allowing documents to exist in the index only for a certain amount of time (for example, log entries or event data that should be cleaned up after a certain amount of time). The index keeps track of insertion time and removes the earliest items after they have expired.

You can combine the `unique` and `sparse` properties so that an index will reject documents that have a duplicate value for the index field and reject document that do not include the indexed field.

You can create indexes from the MongoDB shell, MongoDB Node.js native client, or Mongoose. To create an index from the MongoDB shell, you use the `ensureIndex(index, properties)` method. For example:

```
db.myCollection.ensureIndex({name:1}, {background:true, unique:true, sparse: true})
```

The `background` option specifies whether the index created should take place in the foreground of the shell or the background. Running in the foreground completes faster but takes up more system resources—so it's not a good idea on a production system during peak times.

To create an index from the MongoDB Node.js native driver, you can call the `ensureIndex(collection, index, options, callback)` method on an instance of the `Db` object. For example:

```
var MongoClient = require('mongodb').MongoClient;
MongoClient.connect("mongodb://localhost/", function(err, db) {
  db.ensureIndex('myCollection', {name: 1},
                 {background: true, unique: true, sparse: true},
                 function(err){
    if(!err) console.log("Index Created");
  });
});
```

To create an index using the `Schema` object in Mongoose, you set the index options on the field in the schema. For example:

```
var s = new Schema({ name: { type: String, index: true, unique: true, sparse: true});
```

You can also add the index to the `Schema` object later by using the `index()` method. For example:

```
s.schema.path.('some.path').index({unique: true, sparse: true});
```

Using Capped Collections

Capped collections are fixed-size collections that insert, retrieve, and delete documents based on insertion order. A capped collection can support high-throughput operations. Capped collections work much like circular buffers in that once a collection fills its allocated space, it makes room for new documents by overwriting the oldest documents in the collection.

Capped collections can also be limited based on a maximum number of documents. This is useful for reducing the indexing overhead that can occur when storing large numbers of documents in a collection.

Capped collections are extremely useful for rotating event logs or caching data because you do not need to worry about expending the overhead and effort of implementing code in your application to clean up the collection.

To create a capped collection from the MongoDB shell, you use the `createCollection()` method on the `Db` object, specify the `capped` property, and set the size, in bytes, as well as the optional maximum number of documents. For example:

```
db.createCollection("log", { capped : true, size : 5242880, max : 5000 } )
```

From the MongoDB Node.js native driver, you can also specify a capped collection in the `db.createCollection()` method, described in Chapter 13. For example:

```
db.createCollection("newCollection", { capped : true, size : 5242880, max : 5000 }
                    function(err, collection){ });
```

From Mongoose you can define the collection as capped in the `Schema` object options. For example:

```
var s = new Schema({ name:String, value:Number},
                    { capped : true, size : 5242880, max : 5000});
```

Applying Replication

One of the most critical aspects of high-performance databases is replication. *Replication* is the process of defining multiple MongoDB servers that have the same data. The MongoDB servers in the replica set will be one of three types, as illustrated in Figure 17.1:

- **Primary:** The primary server is the only server in a replica set that can be written to. This way, the primary server can ensure the data integrity during write operations. A replica set can have only one primary server.
- **Secondary:** A secondary server contains a duplicate of the data on the primary server. To ensure that the data is accurate, the replica servers apply the operations log or oplog from the primary server, ensuring that every write operation on the primary server also happens on the secondary servers, in the same order. Clients can read from secondary servers but not write to them.
- **Arbiter:** The arbiter server is kind of interesting. It does not contain a replica of the data but can be used when electing a new primary if the primary server experiences a problem. When the primary server fails, the failure is detected, and other servers in the replica set elect a new primary, using a heartbeat protocol between the primary, secondary, and arbiter servers. Figure 17.2 shows an example of the configuration using an arbiter server.

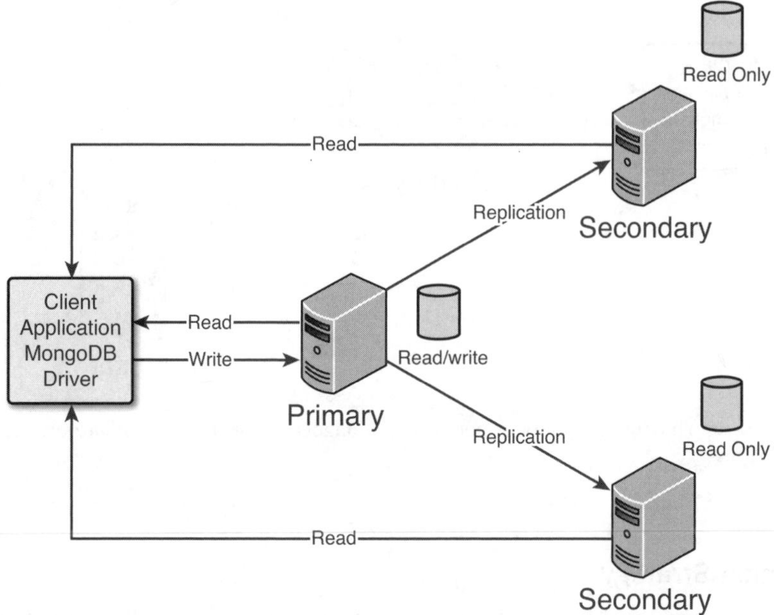

Figure 17.1 Implementing a replica set in MongoDB.

Replication provides two benefits: performance and high availability. Replica sets improve performance because although clients cannot write to secondary servers, they can read from them, which means multiple read sources for applications.

Replica sets provide high availability because if the primary server happens to fail, other servers that have a copy of the data can take over. The replica set uses a heartbeat protocol to communicate between the servers and determine whether the primary server has failed, at which point a new master is elected.

You should have at least three servers in a replica set. Also, having an odd number of servers makes it easier for the servers to elect a primary. This is where arbiter servers come in handy. They require a few resources but can save time when electing a new primary. Figure 17.2 shows the replica set configuration with an arbiter. Notice that the arbiter does not have a replica; it only participates in the heartbeat protocol.

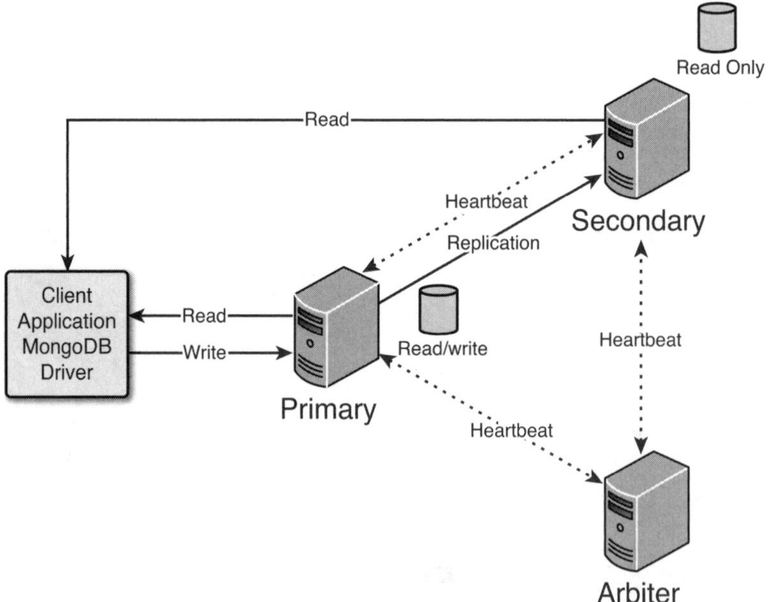

Figure 17.2 Implementing an arbiter server in a MongoDB replica set to ensure an odd number of servers.

Replication Strategy

There are a few things to think about when you are determining how to deploy a MongoDB replica set. The following sections discuss a few of the different factors you should consider before implementing a MongoDB replica set.

Number of Servers

You need to consider how many servers to include in a replica set. The number you use depends on the nature of data interaction from clients. If the data from clients is mostly writes, then you are not going to get a big benefit from having a large number of servers. However, if your data is mostly static and you have a large number of read requests, then having more secondary servers will definitely make a difference.

Number of Replica Sets

You should also consider the data. In some instances, it makes more sense to break data up into multiple replica sets, each containing a different segment of the data. This allows you to fine-tune the servers in each set to meet the data and performance needs. You should consider this only if the there is no correlation between the data such that the clients accessing the data would rarely need to connect to both replica sets at the same time.

Fault Tolerance

How important is fault tolerance to your application? It will likely be rare for your primary server to go down. If your primary server being down doesn't really affect your application too much and the data can easily be rebuilt, you may not need replication. However, if you promise your customer seven-9s availability, then any outage is extremely bad, and extended outage is unacceptable. In such cases, it makes more sense to add servers to the replica set to ensure availability.

You might also consider placing one of the secondary servers in an alternative data center for support in instances when your entire data center fails. However, for performance's sake, you should keep the majority of your secondary servers in your primary data center.

> **Note**
>
> If you are concerned about fault tolerance, you should also enable journaling, as described in Chapter 12. When you do this, transactions can be replayed even if the power fails in your data center.

Deploying a Replica Set

Implementing a replica set is very simple in MongoDB. The following steps take you through the process of prepping and deploying a replica set:

1. Ensure that all the members in the replica set are accessible to each other using DNS or hostnames. Adding a virtual private network for the replica servers to communicate on will enhance the performance of the system because the replication process will not be affected by other traffic on the network. If the servers are not behind a DMZ so the data communications are safe, then you should also configure an `auth` and a `kwFile` for the servers to communicate on for security.

2. Configure the `replSet` value, which is a unique name for the replica set either in the `mongodb.conf` file or on your command line for each server in the replica set. For example:

```
mongod --port 27017 --dbpath /srv/mongodb/db0 --replSet rs0
```

3. Start the MongoDB client, using the `mongo` command, and execute the following command on each server in the replica set to initiate the replica set operations:

```
rs.initiate()
```

4. Use the MongoDB shell to connect to the MongoDB server that will act as the primary and execute the following command for each secondary host:

```
rs.add(<secondary_host_name_or_dns>)
```

5. Use the following command to view the configuration on each server:

```
rs.conf()
```

6. Inside your application, define the read preference for reading data from the replica set. As described in earlier chapters, you do this by setting the preference to `primary`, `primaryPreferred`, `secondary`, `secondaryPreferred`, or `nearest`.

Implementing Sharding

A serious problem that many large-scale applications encounter is that the data stored in the MongoDB is so enormous that it severely impacts performance. When a single collection of data becomes too large, indexing can cause a severe performance hit, the amount of data on disk can cause a system performance hit, and the number of requests from clients can quickly overwhelm the server. The application will get increasingly slower at reading from and writing to the database.

MongoDB solves this problem through sharding. *Sharding* is the process of storing documents across multiple MongoDB servers running on different machines. This allows the MongoDB database to scale horizontally. The more MongoDB servers you add, the larger the number of documents your application can support. Figure 17.3 illustrates the concept of sharding; from the application's perspective, there is a single collection, but there are actually four MongoDB shard servers, and each contains a portion of the documents in the collections.

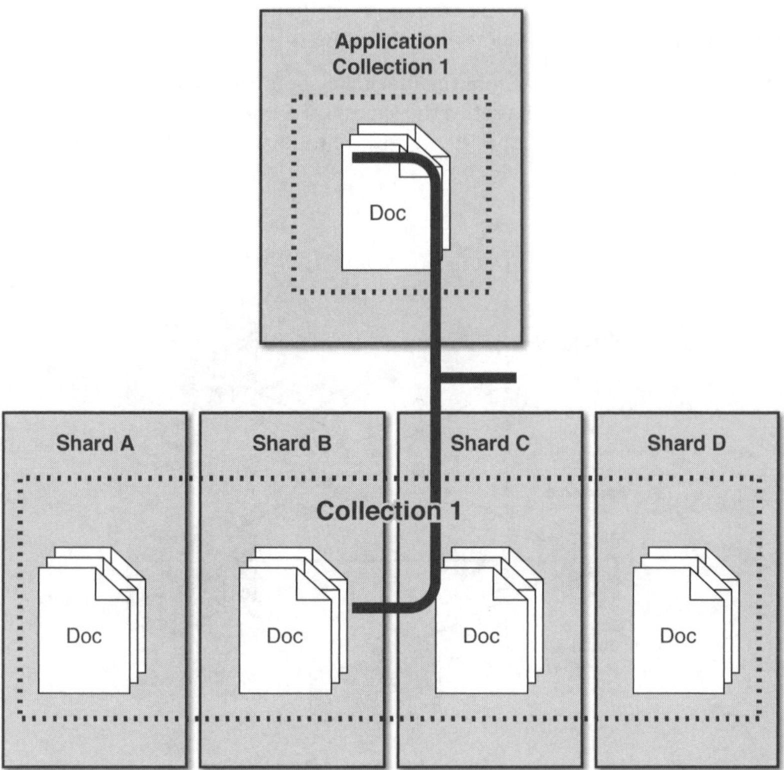

Figure 17.3 From the application's perspective, there is only a single collection to access. However, the documents for that collection are split across multiple MongoDB shard servers.

Sharding Server Types

Three types of MongoDB servers are involved in sharding data. Each of these servers plays a specific role in presenting a single unified view to the applications. The following are the server types, and Figure 17.4 illustrates the interaction between them:

- **Shard:** A shard stores the documents that make up the collection. A shard can be an individual server, but to provide high availability and data consistency in production, you should consider using a replica set that provides primary and secondary copies of the shard.
- **Query router:** A query router runs an instance of `mongos`. The query routers provide the interface for client applications to interact with the collection and obfuscate the fact that the data is in fact sharded. The query router processes a request, sends targeted operations to the shards, and then combines the shard responses into a single response

to the client. A sharded cluster can contain more than one query router, which is a great way to load balance large numbers of client requests.

- **Config server:** Config servers store the metadata about the sharded cluster that contains a mapping of the cluster's data set to the shards. The query router uses this metadata when targeting operations to specific shards. A production sharded cluster should have exactly three config servers.

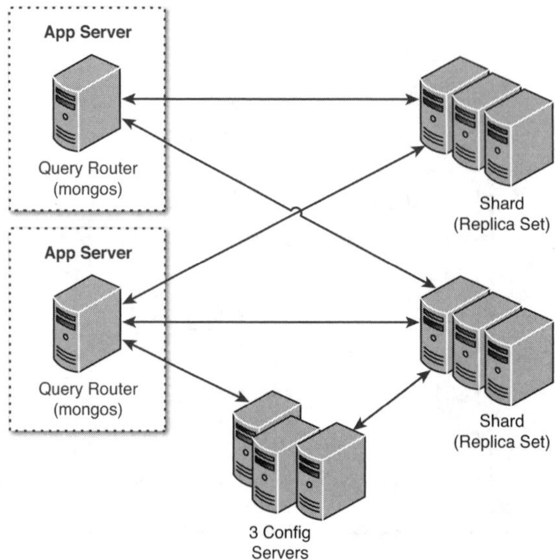

Figure 17.4 The query router servers accept requests from the MongoDB clients and then communicate with the individual shard servers to read or write data.

Choosing a Shard Key

The first step in sharding a large collection is to decide on a shard key that will be used to determine which documents should be stored in which shard. The shard key is an indexed field or an indexed compound field that must be included in every document in the collection. MongoDB uses the value of the shard key to split the collection between the shards in the cluster.

Selecting a good shard key can be critical to achieving the performance you need from MongoDB. A bad key can seriously impact the performance of the system, whereas a good key can improve performance and ensure future scalability. If a good key does not exist in your documents, you might want to consider adding a field specifically to be a sharding key.

When selecting a shard key, you should keep in mind the following considerations:

- **Easily divisible:** The shard key needs to be easily divisible into chunks.
- **Randomness:** When using range-based sharding, random keys can ensure that documents are more evenly distributed so that no one server is overloaded.
- **Compound keys:** It is best to shard using a single field when possible. However, if a good single field key doesn't exist, you can still get better performance from a good compound field than from a bad single field key.
- **Cardinality:** Cardinality defines the uniqueness of the values of a field. A field has high cardinality if it is very unique (for example, a Social Security number for a million people). A field has low cardinality if it is generally not very unique (for example, eye color for a million people). Typically fields that have high cardinality provide much better options for sharding.
- **Query targeting:** You should take a minute to look at the queries necessary in your applications. Queries will perform better if the data can be collected from a single shard in a cluster. If you can arrange for the shard key to match the most common query parameters, you will get better performance as long as all queries are not going to the same field value (for example, arranging documents based on the zip code of the user when all your queries are based on looking up users by zip code, since all the users for a given zip code will exist on the same shard server). If your queries are fairly distributed across zip codes, then a zip code key would be a good idea. However, if most of your queries are on a few zip codes, then a zip code key would be a bad idea.

To illustrate shard keys, consider the following keys:

- **`{ "zipcode": 1}`**: This shard key distributes documents based on the value of the `zipcode` field. This means that all lookups based on a specific `zipcode` will go to a single shard server.
- **`{ "zipcode": 1, "city": 1 }`**: This shard key first distributes documents by the value of the `zipcode` field. If a number of documents have the same value for `zipcode`, then they can be split off to other shards, based on the `city` field value. This means you are no longer guaranteed that a query on a single `zipcode` value will hit only one shard. However, queries based on `zipcode` and `city` will go to the same shard.
- **`{ "_id": "hashed" }`**: This shard key distributes documents based on a hash of the value of the `_id` field. This ensures a more even distribution across all shards in the cluster. However, it makes it impossible to target queries so that they will hit only a single shard server.

Selecting a Partitioning Method

The next step in sharding a large collection is to decide how to partition the documents based on the shard key. There are two methods you can use to distribute the documents into different shards, based on the shard key value. Which method you use depends on the type of shard key you select:

- **Range-based sharding:** One method is to divide the data set into specific ranges, based on the value of the shard key. This method works well for shard keys that are numeric. For example, if you have a collection of products and each product has a specific product ID from 1 to 1,000,000, you could shard the products in ranges of 1–250,000; 250,001–500,000, etc.
- **Hash-based sharding:** Another method is to use a hash function that computes a field value to create chunks. The hash function should ensure that shard keys that have a very close value should end up in different shards to ensure a good distribution.

It is vital that you select a shard key and distribution method that will distribute documents as evenly as possible across the shards. Otherwise, one server ends up overloaded while another is relatively unused.

The advantage of range-based sharding is that it is often very easy to define and implement. Also, if your queries are often range bases as well, it is more performant than hash-based sharding. However, it is very difficult to get an even distribution with range-based sharding unless you have all the data up front and the shard key values will not change in the future.

The hash-based sharding method takes more understanding of the data but typically provides the best overall approach to sharding because it ensures a much more evenly spaced distribution.

The index used when enabling sharding on the collection determines which partitioning method is used. If you have an index that is based on a value, MongoDB uses range-based sharding. For example, the following implements a range-based shard on the `zip` and `name` fields of the document:

```
db.myDB.myCollection.ensureIndex({"zip": 1, "name":1})
```

To shard using the hash-based method, you need to define the index using the hash method, as in this example:

```
db.myDB.myCollection.({"name":"hash"})
```

Deploying a Sharded MongoDB Cluster

The process of deploying a sharded MongoDB cluster involves several steps to set the different types of servers and then configuring the databases and collections. To deploy a sharded MongoDB cluster, you need to follow these basic steps:

1. Create config server database instances.
2. Start query router servers.
3. Add shards to the cluster.
4. Enable sharding on a database.
5. Enable sharding on a collection.
6. Set up shard tag ranges.

The following sections describe each of these steps in more detail.

> **Warning**
>
> All members of a sharded cluster must be able to connect to all other members of a sharded cluster, including all shards and all config servers. Ensure that your network and security systems, including all interfaces and firewalls, allow these connections.

Creating Config Server Database Instances (`mongod`)

The config server processes are simply `mongod` instances that store a cluster's metadata instead of the collections. Each config server stores a complete copy of the cluster's metadata. In production deployments, you must deploy exactly three config server instances, each running on different servers, to ensure high availability and data integrity.

To implement the config servers, you need to perform the following steps on each one:

1. Create a data directory to store the config database.
2. Start config server instances by passing the path to the data directory created in step 1 and also include the `--configsvr` option to denote that this is a config server. For example:

   ```
   mongod --configsvr --dbpath <path> --port <port>
   ```

3. Once the `mongod` instance starts up, the config server is ready.

> **Note**
>
> The default port for config servers is 27019.

Starting Query Router Servers (`mongos`)

The query router (`mongos`) servers do not require database directories because the configuration is stored on the config servers, and the data is stored on the shard server. The `mongos` servers are very lightweight, and therefore it is acceptable to have a `mongos` instance on the same system that runs your application server.

You can create multiple instances of the `mongos` servers to route requests to the sharded cluster. However, to ensure high availability, you don't want these instances running on the same system.

To start an instance of the `mongos` server, you need to pass in the `--configdb` parameter with a list of the DNS names/hostnames of the config servers you want to use for the cluster. For example:

```
mongos --configdb c1.test.net:27019,c2.test.net:27019,c3.test.net:27019
```

By default, a mongos instance runs on port 27017. However, you can also configure a different port address by using the --port <port> command-line option.

> **Tip**
>
> To avoid downtime, give each config server a logical DNS name (unrelated to the server's physical or virtual hostname). Without logical DNS names, moving or renaming a config server requires shutting down every mongod and mongos instance in the sharded cluster.

Adding Shards to the Cluster (mongod)

The shard servers in a cluster are just standard MongoDB servers loaded by the mongod command. They can be stand-alone servers or a replica set. To add the MongoDB servers as shards in the cluster, all you need to do is access the mongos server from the MongoDB shell and use the sh.addShard() command.

The syntax for the sh.addShard() command is:

```
sh.addShard(<replica_set_or_server_address>)
```

For example, to add a replica set named rs1 on a server named mgo1.test.net as a shard in the cluster server, execute the following command from the MongoDB shell on the mongos server:

```
sh.addShard( "rs1/mgo1.test.net:27017" )
```

For example, to add a server named mgo1.test.net as a shard in the cluster server, execute the following command from the MongoDB shell on the mongos server:

```
sh.addShard( "mgo1.test.net:27017" )
```

Once you have added all the shards to the replica set, the cluster will be communicating and sharding the data. However, for predefined data, it will take some time for the chunks to be fully distributed.

Enabling Sharding on a Database

Prior to sharding a collection, you need to enable sharding on the database it resides in. Enabling sharding doesn't automatically redistribute the data but just assigns a primary shard for the database and makes other configuration adjustments that make it possible to enable the collections for sharding.

To enable the database for sharding, you need to connect to a mongos instance using the MongoDB shell and issue the sh.enableSharding(database) command. For example, to enable a database named bigWords, you would use:

```
sh.enableSharding("bigWords");
```

Enabling Sharding on a Collection

Once the database has been enabled for sharding, you are ready to enable sharding at the collection level. You do not need to enable sharding for all collections in the database—just for the one that it makes sense on.

Use the following steps to enable sharding on a collection:

1. Determine which field(s) will be used for the shard key, as described above.
2. Create a unique index on the key field(s) by using `ensureIndex()`, as described earlier in this chapter:

   ```
   db.myDB.myCollection.ensureIndex( { _id : "hashed" } )
   ```

3. Enable sharding on the collection by using `sh.shardCollection(<database>.<collection>, shard_key)`. `shard_key` is the pattern used to create the index. For example:

   ```
   sh.shardCollection("myDB.myCollection", { "_id": "hashed" } )
   ```

Setting Up Shard Tag Ranges

Once you have enabled sharding on a collection, you might want to add tags to target specific ranges of the shard key values. A really good example of this is where the collection is sharded by zip codes. To improve performance, you can add tags for specific city codes, like `NYC` and `SFO`, and specify the zip code ranges for those cities. This ensures that documents for a specific city will be stored on a single shard in the cluster, which can improve query performance for queries based on multiple zip codes for the same city.

To set up shard tags, you simply need to add a tag to the shard by using the `sh.addShardTag(shard_server, tag_name)` command from a `mongos` instance. For example:

```
sh.addShardTag("shard0001", "NYC")
sh.addShardTag("shard0002", "SFO")
```

Then you specify a range for a specific tag. In this case, you would add the zip code ranges for each city tag by using the `sh.addTagRange(collection_path, startValue, endValue, tag_name)` command from the `mongos` instance. For example:

```
sh.addTagRange("records.users", { zipcode: "10001" }, { zipcode: "10281" }, "NYC")
sh.addTagRange("records.users", { zipcode: "11201" }, { zipcode: "11240" }, "NYC")
sh.addTagRange("records.users", { zipcode: "94102" }, { zipcode: "94135" }, "SFO")
```

Notice that multiple ranges are added for the `NYC`. This allows you to specify multiple ranges within the same tag that is assigned to a single shard.

If you need to remove a shard tag later, you can do so by using the `sh.removeShardTag(shard_server, tag_name)` method. For example:

```
sh.removeShardTag("shard0002", "SFO")
```

Implementing a GridFS Store

Occasionally you might want to use MongoDB to store and retrieve data that exceeds the 16MB size limit (for example, if you are storing large images, zip files, movies, etc.). To accommodate this, MongoDB provides the GridFS framework. GridFS splits large documents into chunks. The chunks are stored in one collection, and metadata that is used to access the documents is stored in another collection.

When you query GridFS for a document, the chunks are reassembled and sent back just as any other document. A great feature of GridFS is that by using `skip`, you can read from the middle of a document without needing to load the entire document from disk. This allows you to read chunks of large files without running the risk of out-of-memory conditions.

You can implement GridFS either from the MongoDB shell or by using the MongoDB Node.js driver. The MongoDB Node.js driver provides the `Grid` and `GridStore` objects, which allow you to interact with the MongoDB GridFS

Implementing a `Grid` Object from Node.js

The `Grid` object acts as a representation of GridFS. It provides a simple interface to read and write binary data to GridFS. You can instantiate the `Grid` object by calling the `Grid()` constructor from an instance of the `Db` object. For example, the following code connects to MongoDB and creates a `Grid` object attached to the `fs` collection:

```
MongoClient.connect("mongodb://localhost/", function(err, db) {
  var grid = new Grid(db, 'fs');
});
```

The `Grid` object provides several methods that allow you to put data into the grid, retrieve data in the grid, and remove data from the grid. The data stored in the grid is stored in binary format, so it must be put into the grid and read from the grid as `Buffer` objects. To put data into the grid, use the `put()` method, like this:

```
put(data, [options], callback)
```

The `put()` method writes `data`, which is a `Buffer` object to GridFS. The optional `options` parameter is an object that specifies where and how to write the data. `callback` should accept an `error` object as the first parameter and a reference to the `Grid` object as the second. You can set these options in `options`:

- **`_id`:** A unique ID for the file
- **`root`:** The name of the root collection to use
- **`content_type`:** The MIME type of the file
- **`chunk_size`:** The size of each chunk of the file, in bytes
- **`metadata`:** An object that allows you to add any additional metadata that you want

The `get()` method allows you to read data back from the `Grid` object. The `get()` method uses the following syntax:

```
get(id, callback)
```

The `id` parameter corresponds to the `_id` setting in the `options` parameter of `put()`. The callback function should accept an `error` object as the first parameter and a `Buffer` object with retrieved data as the second.

To remove data from the grid, you can use the `delete()` method:

```
delete(id, callback)
```

The `id` parameter corresponds to the `_id` setting in the `options` parameter of `put()`. The callback function should accept an `error` object as the first parameter and reference to the `Grid` object as the second.

To illustrate the use of the `Grid` object, Listing 17.1 implements a `Grid` object, writes a string to it, and then reads the string from it and deletes it. The string can be any binary data, such as an image file. Figure 17.5 shows the output of Listing 17.1.

Listing 17.1 `grid_fs.js`: **Implementing a basic `Grid` object to store data in the MongoDB GridFS**

```
var MongoClient = require('mongodb').MongoClient,
    GridStore = require('mongodb').GridStore,
    Grid = require('mongodb').Grid;
MongoClient.connect("mongodb://localhost/", function(err, db) {
  var grid = new Grid(db, 'fs');
  var data = new Buffer('Hello world');
  console.log("\nOriginal Data: ");
  console.log(data.toString());
  grid.put(data, {_id: "test.file"}, function(err, results) {
    console.log("\nPut Results: ");
    console.log(results);
    grid.get("test.file", function(err, data) {
      console.log("\nBefore Delete Get: ");
      console.log(data.toString());
      grid.delete("test.file", function(err, results) {
        console.log("\nDelete Results: ");
        console.log(results);
        db.close();
      });
    });
  });
});
```

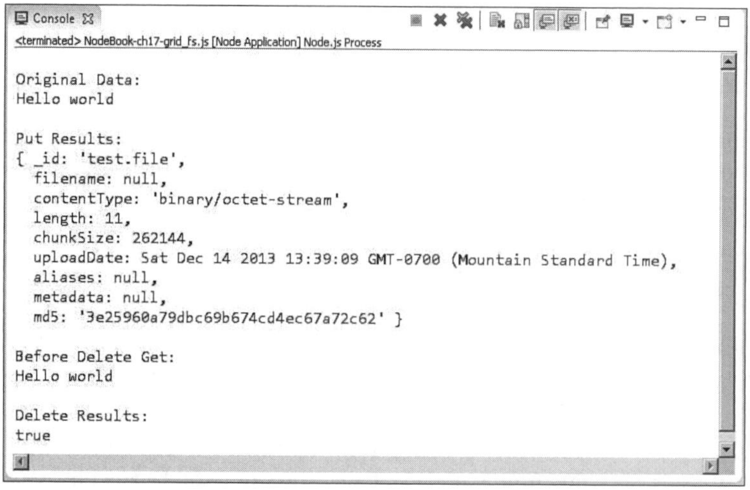

```
Console
<terminated> NodeBook-ch17-grid_fs.js [Node Application] Node.js Process

Original Data:
Hello world

Put Results:
{ _id: 'test.file',
  filename: null,
  contentType: 'binary/octet-stream',
  length: 11,
  chunkSize: 262144,
  uploadDate: Sat Dec 14 2013 13:39:09 GMT-0700 (Mountain Standard Time),
  aliases: null,
  metadata: null,
  md5: '3e25960a79dbc69b674cd4ec67a72c62' }

Before Delete Get:
Hello world

Delete Results:
true
```

Figure 17.5 Implementing a basic `Grid` object to store data in the MongoDB GridFS.

Implementing a `GridStore` Object from Node.js

The `GridStore` object acts as a representation of a binary file stored in the MongoDB GridFS. It provides the basic file interface to read and write files stored in GridFS. For example, you can stream reads and writes from GridFS, read chunks of a file without needing to read the entire file, etc. These are all things that you could do within Node.js, but without the added benefits that come with MongoDB, such as replication and high availability.

You can instantiate the `GridStore` object by calling the `GridStore()` constructor from an instance of the `Db` object. For example, the following code connects to MongoDB and creates a `GridStore` object attached to the `fs` collection:

```
MongoClient.connect("mongodb://localhost/", function(err, db) {
  var gridStore = new GridStore(db, "word_file", 'w');
});
```

Notice that the first parameter to `GridStore()` is the database. The second parameter is the unique ID for the file in GridFS, and the third is the mode with which `GridStore` is opened and corresponds to the standard file modes.

The `GridStore` object provides several methods that allow you to read, access, and write files to the MongoDB GridFS, just as if it were a normal file. Table 17.2 lists the most useful methods available on `GridStore` objects.

Table 17.2 **Methods to read and writes files from `GridStore` objects**

Method	**Description**
`Properties`	Contains the `chunkSize` and `md5` checksum for the file.
`open(callback)`	Opens the connection to the GridFS database, allowing you to read from and write to the database.
`writeFile(path, callback)`	Opens the file located at `path` and writes the contents directly to GridFS.
`close(callback)`	Flushes changes to the `GridStore` object to the database.
`chunkCollection (callback)`	Retrieves a chunk collection object from the server. The callback function gets an error as the first parameter and a `Collection` object as the second.
`unlink(callback)`	Deletes the file from GridFS.
`collection(callback)`	Retrieves the `Collection` object associated with the `GridStore` object.
`readlines([separator], callback)`	Retrieves the contents of the file as an array of strings representing the lines in the file. The `separator` parameter allows you to specify characters recognized as newlines in the file.
`rewind(callback)`	Deletes all chunks of this file in the chunks collection, essentially creating an empty file.
`read([length], [buffer], callback)`	Reads the specified `length` of bytes from the file. If no `length` is specified, the entire file is read. The `buffer` parameter allows you to pass in a `Buffer` object to write into; otherwise, a `Buffer` object is created. The `callback` function gets the bytes read as a `Buffer` object in the second parameter.
`tell(callback)`	Retrieves the current read/write position in the file.
`seek([position], [location], callback)`	Sets the current read/write location for the file. If no `position` parameter is specified, `0` is used. The `location` parameter allows you to set the seek mode.
`eof()`	Returns `true` if the current position is at the end of the file.
`getc(callback)`	Retrieves 1 byte from the current read/write position of the file and passes it as the second parameter to the callback function.
`puts(string, callback)`	Writes a string at the current read/write position of the file.
`stream(autoclose)`	Returns a `Readable` stream object representing the file in GridFS that allows you to stream reads from the database. If `autoclose` is `true`, then the `GridStore` object is closed when the end-of-file is reached.
`write(data, [close], callback)`	Writes the data parameter, which is a string, to the file at the current read/write position. If the `close` parameter is `true`, then the `GridStore` object is closed after writing.

The `GridStore` object also contains several static methods that allow you to access files in GridFS without creating an instance of a specific file. These methods allow you to determine existence, list files, and delete files. Table 17.3 describes these methods.

Table 17.3 **Static methods available in the `GridStore` class to manage GridFS files**

Method	Description
`GridStore.exist(db, name, [rootCollection], callback)`	Returns `true` in the second parameter of the callback function if the file specified by `name` exists in the GridFS store. `rootCollection` allows you to specify an alternate root collection.
`GridStore.list(db, [rootCollection], callback)`	Returns an array of filenames in the second parameter of the callback function.
`GridStore.read(db, name, [length], [offset], [options], callback)`	Reads the contents of a file specified by `name` in the GridFS store. The contents are returned in the second parameter of the callback function as a buffer. This works the same as the `read()` method on an instance of a `GridStore` object (see Table 17.2).
`GridStore.readlines(db, name, [separator], [options], callback)`	Reads the contents of a file specified by name in the GridFS store into an array of lines separated by the `separator` character. The lines are returned in the second parameter of the callback function as a string array. This works the same as the `readlines()` method on an instance of a `GridStore` object (see Table 17.2).
`GridStore.unlink(db, names, callback)`	Deletes the file(s) specified by `names` from GridFS.

For the most part, using the `GridStore` object is intuitive if you're familiar with reading from and writing to files. Listing 17.2 illustrates some of the basics of implementing a `GridStore` object in a Node.js application. The `GridStore` object is created on line 5, then opened on line 6, and the contents of a local file are written to it on line 10. Then on line 12 the full contents are read. To illustrate `seek()`, line 16 reads `50` bytes at position `100`. Then finally the file is closed on line 19 and deleted on line 20. Figure 17.6 shows the output from Listing 17.2.

Listing 17.2 `gridstore_fs.js`: **Implementing a basic `GridStore` object to store a file in the MongoDB GridFS**

```
01 var MongoClient = require('mongodb').MongoClient,
02     GridStore = require('mongodb').GridStore,
03     Grid = require('mongodb').Grid;
04 MongoClient.connect("mongodb://localhost/", function(err, db) {
05   var gridStore = new GridStore(db, "word_file", 'w');
06   gridStore.open(function(err, gridStore) {
07     GridStore.exist(db,"word_file", function(err, results) {
```

```
      console.log("File created? " + results);
    });
    gridStore.writeFile('./words.txt', function(err, results) {
      console.log("\nFile Written.");
      GridStore.read(db, "word_file", function(err, fileData) {
        console.log("\nFull Read: ");
        console.log(fileData.toString());
        gridStore.seek(100, function(err, gridStore) {
          gridStore.read(50, function(err, data) {
            console.log("\nRead 50 bytes at position 100: ");
            console.log(data.toString());
            gridStore.close();
            GridStore.unlink(db, "word_file", function(err, results){
              console.log("\nFile Deleted: " + results._id);
              db.close();
            });
          });
        });
      });
    });
  });
});
```

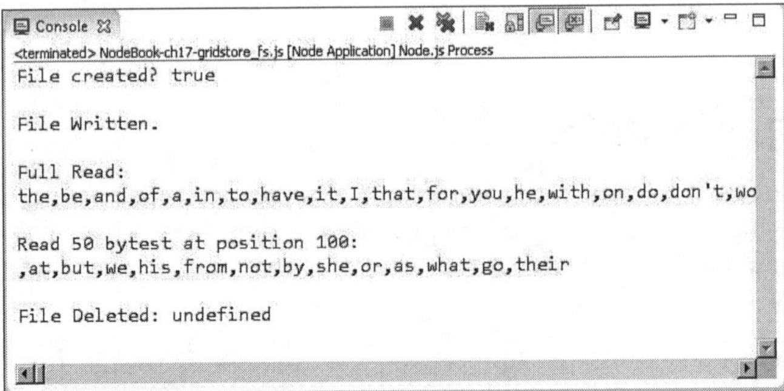

Figure 17.6 Implementing a basic `GridStore` object to store data in the MongoDB GridFS.

Repairing a MongoDB Database

There are a couple reasons to run a repair on the MongoDB database—for example, if the system crashes, or if a data integrity problem is manifested in the application, or even just to reclaim some unused disk space.

You can initiate a repair of a MongoDB database from the MongoDB shell or from the `mongod` command line. To execute a repair from the command line, use `--repair` and `--repairpath <repair_path>`. `<repair_path>` specifies the location to store temporary repair files. For example:

```
mongod --repair --repairpath /tmp/mongdb/data
```

To execute a repair from the MongoDB client, use the `db.repairDatabase(options)` command, as in this example:

```
db.repairDatabase({ repairDatabase: 1,
  preserveClonedFilesOnFailure: <boolean>,
  backupOriginalFiles: <boolean> })
```

When a repair is initiated, all collections in the database are compacted, which reduces the size on disk. Also, any invalid records in the database are deleted. Therefore, it may be better to restore from backup than to run a repair.

The time it takes to run a repair depends on the size of the data. Repairs impact the performance of systems and should be run during off-peak hours.

> **Warning**
>
> If you are trying to repair a member of a replica set and you have access to an intact copy of your data on another replica, you should restore from that intact copy because `repairDatabase` will delete the corrupt data, and it will be lost.

Backing Up MongoDB

The best backup strategy for MongoDB is to implement high availability, using a replica set. This ensures that the data is as up to date as possible and ensures that it is always available. However, you should also consider the following if your data is extremely critical and cannot be replaced:

- **What if the data center fails?** In this case, you can back up the data periodically and store it offsite, or you can add a replica somewhere offsite.
- **What if something happens to corrupt the application data that gets replicated?** This is always a concern. In such a case, the only option is to have a backup from a previous point.

If you decide that you need to implement periodic backups of data, you should also consider the impact that backups will have on the system and decide on a strategy. For example:

- **Production impact:** Backups are often intensive and need to be performed at a time when they will have a minimum impact on your environment.

- **Requirements:** If you plan on implementing something like a block-level snapshot to back up the database, you need to ensure that the system infrastructure supports it.
- **Sharding:** If you are sharding the data, all shards must be consistent; you cannot back up one without backing up all. Also, you must stop the writes to the cluster to generate the point-in-time backup.
- **Relevant data:** You can reduce the impact that backups have on your system by only backing up data that is critical to your system. For example, if a database will never change, it only needs to be backed up once, or if data in a database can easily be regenerated but is very large, it may be worth accepting the cost of regeneration rather than doing frequent backups.

There are two main approaches to backing up MongoDB. The first is to perform a binary dump of the data, using the `mongodump` command. The binary data can be stored offsite for later use. For example, you could use the following command to dump the database for a replica set named `rset1` on `host mg1.test.net` and on a stand-alone system named `mg2.test.net` to a folder called `/opt/backup/current`:

```
mongodump --host rset1/mg1.test.net:27018,mg2.test.net --out /opt/backup/current
```

The second method for backing up MongoDB databases is to use a file system snapshot. These snapshots are very quick to complete, but they are also large, and you need to have journaling enabled and the system able to support the block-level backups.

> **Note**
>
> If you are interested in implementing a snapshot method for backups, check out the guide at the following location: http://docs.mongodb.org/manual/tutorial/back-up-databases-with-filesystem-snapshots/.

Summary

This chapter finishes off the MongoDB introduction with some more advanced concepts. You've learned how to define different types of indexes to improve the speed for queries. You've also learned how to deploy a MongoDB replica set—with a read/write master and read-only replicas—to ensure high availability and improve read performance.

This chapter introduces the concept of partitioning data from extremely large collections into shards that exist on separate partitions to allow your implementation to scale horizontally. You've learned about the `Grid` and `GridStore` objects included with the MongoDB Node.js driver that allow you to interact with MongoDB's GridFS system to store extremely large files.

You've also looked at different backup strategies and options to protect the most critical data in your MongoDB databases.

Up Next

In the next chapter, you'll get back to the Node.js world with the `express` module. The `express` module allows you to more easily implement a webserver running on Node.js by supporting routes and other functionality.

18

Implementing Express in Node.js

Express provides a lightweight module that wraps the functionality of the Node.js `http` module in a simple-to-use interface. Express also extends the functionality of the `http` module by making it easy for you to handle server routes, responses, cookies, and HTTP request statuses. This chapter shows you how to implement Express as the webserver for your Node.js applications. You will learn how to configure the Express server, design routes, and utilize the `Request` and `Response` objects to send and receive HTTP requests. You will also get a look at how to implement template engines in Express.

Getting Started with Express

It is very simple to get started using Express in Node.js projects. All you need to do is add the `express` module, using the following command from the root of your project:

```
npm install express@4.0.0
```

You can also add `express` to your `package.json` module to ensure that `express` is installed when you deploy your application.

Once you have installed the `express` module, you need to create an instance of the `express` class to act as the HTTP server for your Node.js application. The following lines of code import the `express` module and create an instance of `express` that you can use:

```
var express = require('express');
var app = express();
```

Configuring Express Settings

Express provides several application settings that control the behavior of the Express server. These settings define the environment as well as how Express handles JSON parsing, routing, and views. Table 18.1 lists the settings that can be defined on an `express` object.

The express object provides the set(setting, value) and enable(setting) and disable(setting) methods to set values for the application settings. For example, the following lines of code enable the trust proxy setting and set view engine to jade:

```
app.enable('trust proxy');
app.disable('strict routing');
app.set('view engine', 'jade');
```

To get the value of a setting, you use the get(setting), enabled(setting), and disabled(setting) methods. For example:

```
app.enabled('trust proxy');  \\true
app.disabled('strict routing'); \\true
app.get('view engine'); \\jade
```

Table 18.1 **Express application settings**

Setting	Description
env	Defines the environment mode string, such as development, testing, and production. The default is process.env.NODE_ENV.
trust proxy	Enables/disables reverse proxy support. The default is disabled.
jsonp callback name	Defines the default callback name of JSONP requests. The default is ?callback=.
json replacer	Defines the JSON replacer callback function. The default is null.
json spaces	Specifies the number of spaces to use when formatting JSON response. The defaults are 2 in development and 0 in production.
case sensitive routing	Enables/disables case-sensitivity. For example, /home is not the same as /Home. The default is disabled.
strict routing	Enables/disables strict routing. For example, /home is not the same as /home/. The default is disabled.
view cache	Enables/disables view template compilation caching, which keeps the cached version of a compiled template. The default is enabled.
view engine	Specifies the default template engine extension that should be used when rendering templates if a file extension is omitted from the view.
views	Specifies the path for the template engine to look for view templates. The default is ./views.

Starting the Express Server

To implement Express as the HTTP server for a Node.js application, you need to create an instance and begin listening on a port. The following three lines of code start a very rudimentary Express server listening on port 8080:

```
var express = require('express');
var app = express();
app.listen(8080);
```

The `app.listen(port)` call binds the underlying HTTP connection to the `port` and begins listening on it. The underlying HTTP connection is the same connection produced using the `listen()` method on a `Server` object created using the `http` library discussed in Chapter 7 "Implementing HTTP Services in Node.js."

In fact, the value returned by `express()` is actually a callback function that maps to the callback function that is passed to the `http.createServer()` and `https.createServer()` methods.

Listing 18.1 shows how to implement a basic HTTP and HTTPS server using Node.js. Notice that the `app` variable that `express()` returns is passed into the `createServer()` methods. Also, notice that an `options` object is defined to set the `host`, `key`, and `cert` used to create the HTTPS server. Lines 13–15 implement a simple `get` route that handles the / path.

Listing 18.1 `express_http_https.js`: **Implementing HTTP and HTTPS servers using Express**

```
01 var express = require('express');
02 var https = require('https');
03 var http = require('http');
04 var fs = require('fs');
05 var app = express();
06 var options = {
07     host: '127.0.0.1',
08     key: fs.readFileSync('ssl/server.key'),
09     cert: fs.readFileSync('ssl/server.crt')
10   };
11 http.createServer(app).listen(80);
12 https.createServer(options, app).listen(443);
13 app.get('/', function(req, res){
14   res.send('Hello from Express');
15 });
```

Configuring Routes

The previous section discusses how to start the Express HTTP server. However, before the server can begin accepting requests, you need to define routes. A *route* is simply a definition that describes how to handle the path portion of the URI in the HTTP request to the Express server.

Implementing Routes

You define a route in two parts. First is the HTTP request method (typically GET or POST). The second part of the route definition is the path specified in the URL—for example, / for the root of a website, /login for a login page, and /cart to display a shopping cart. These methods often need to be handled completely differently.

The express module provides a series of functions that allow you to implement routes for the Express server. These functions all use the following syntax:

```
app.<method>(path, [callback . . .], callback)
```

The <method> portion of the syntax refers to the HTTP request method, such as GET or POST. For example:

```
app.get(path, [middleware, ...], callback)
app.post(path, [middleware, ...], callback)
```

path refers to the path portion of the URL that you want to be handled by the callback function. The middleware parameters are middleware functions that are applied before the callback function executes. The callback parameter is the request handler that should handle the request and send the response back to the client. The callback parameter should accept a Request object as the first parameter and a Response object as the second.

For example, the following examples implement some basic GET and POST routes:

```
app.get('/', function(req, res){
  res.send("Server Root");
});
app.get('/login', function(req, res){
  res.send("Login Page");
});
app.post('/save', function(req, res){
  res.send("Save Page");
});
```

When the Express server receives an HTTP request, it looks for a route that has been defined for the appropriate HTTP method and path. If one is found, a Request and Response object is created to manage the request and passed into the callback function(s) for the route.

Express also provides the app.all() method, which works exactly the same as the app.post() and app.get() methods. The only difference is that the callback function for app.all() is called on every request for the specified path, regardless of HTTP method. Also, the app.all() method can accept the * character as a wildcard in the path. This is a great feature for implementing request logging or other special functionality to handle requests. For example:

```
app.all('*', function(req, res){
  // global handler for all paths
});
app.all('/user/*', function(req, res){
  // global handler for /user path
});
```

Applying Parameters in Routes

As you begin implementing routes, you will quickly see that for complex systems, the number of routes can get out of hand. To reduce the number of routes, you can implement parameters within the URL. You can use parameters to use the same route for similar requests by providing unique values for different requests that define how your application handles requests and builds responses.

For example, you would not have a separate route for every user or product in your system. Instead, you would pass in a user ID or product ID as a parameter to one route, and the server code would use that ID to determine which user or product to use. There are four main methods for implementing parameters in a route:

- **Query strings:** You can use the standard `?key=value&key=value...` HTTP query string after the path in a URL. This is the most common method for implementing parameters, but the URLs can become very long and convoluted.
- **`POST` params:** When implementing a web form or another `POST` request, you can pass parameters in the body of the request.
- **Regexes:** You can define a regular expression as the path portion of the route. Express uses the regex to parse the path of the URL and stores matching expressions as an array of parameters.
- **Defined parameters:** You can define a parameter by name by using `:<parm_name>` in the path portion of the route. Express automatically assigns that parameter a name when it parses the path.

The following sections discuss all these methods except `POST` params, which are covered in Chapter 19, "Implementing Express Middleware."

Applying Route Parameters Using Query Strings

The simplest way to add parameters to a route is to pass them using the normal HTTP query string format `?key=value&key=value...` and then use the `url.parse()` method to parse the `url` attribute of the `Request` object to get the parameters.

The following code implements a basic `GET` route to `/find?author=<author>&title=<title>` that accepts `author` and `title` parameters. To actually get the value of `author` and `title`, the `url.parse()` method builds a query object:

```
var express = require('express');
var url = reauire('url');
var app = express();
app.get('/find', function(req, res){
  var url_parts = url.parse(req.url, true);
  var query = url_parts.query;
  res.send('Finding Book: Author: ' + query.author +
           ' Title: ' + query.title);
});
```

For example, consider the following URL:

```
/find?author=Brad&title=Node
```

The `res.send()` method returns:

```
Finding Book: Author: Brad Title: Node
```

Applying Route Parameters Using Regex

A great method of implementing parameters in routes is to use a regular expression to match patterns. Using regexes allows you to implement patterns that do not follow a standard / formatting for the path.

The following code implements a regex parser to generate route parameters for `GET` requests at the URL `/book/<chapter>:<page>` path:

```
app.get(/^\/book\/(\w+)\:(\w+)?$/, function(req, res){
  res.send('Get Book: Chapter: ' + req.params[0] +
           ' Page: ' + req.params[1]);
});
```

Notice that the values of the parameters are not named. Instead, `req.params` is an array of matching items in the URL path.

For example, consider the following URL:

```
/book/12:15
```

The `res.send()` method returns:

```
Get Book: Chapter: 12 Page: 15
```

Applying Route Parameters Using Defined Parameters

If your data is more structured, then instead of using regexes, you can use defined parameters. Using a defined parameter allows you to define your parameters by name within the route path. You define parameters in the path of the route by using `:<param_name>`. When using defined parameters, `req.param` is a function instead of an array, and calling `req.param(param_name)` returns the value of the parameter.

The following code implements a basic `:userid` parameter that expects a URL with a `/user/<user_id>` format:

```
app.get('/user/:userid', function (req, res) {
  res.send("Get User: " + req.param("userid"));
});
```

For example, consider the following URL:

```
/user/4983
```

The `res.send()` method returns:

```
Get User: 4983
```

Applying Callback Function for Defined Parameters

A major advantage of using defined parameters is that you can specify callback functions that are executed if the defined parameter is found in a URL. When parsing the URL, if Express finds a parameter that has a callback registered, it calls the parameter's callback function before calling the route handler. You can register more than one callback function for a route.

To register a callback function, you use the `app.param()` method. The `app.param()` method accepts the defined parameter as the first argument and then a callback function that receives the `Request`, `Response`, `next`, and `value` parameters:

```
app.param(param, function(req, res, next, value){} );
```

The `Request` and `Response` objects are the same as the objects passed to the route callback. The next parameter is a callback function for the next `app.param()` callback registered, if any. You must call `next()` somewhere in your callback function, or the callback chain will be broken. The value parameter is the value of the parameter parsed from the URL path.

For example, the following code logs every request that is received that has the `userid` parameter specified in the route. Notice the call to `next()` before leaving the callback function:

```
app.param('userid', function(req, res, next, value){
  console.log("Request with userid: " + value);
  next();
});
```

To see how this code works, consider the following URL:

```
/user/4983
```

The `userid` parameter setting of `4983` is parsed from the URL, and the `console.log()` statement displays:

```
Request with userid: 4983
```

Applying Route Parameters Example

Listing 18.2 provides an example of implementing query strings, regex, and defined parameters with Express routes. Lines 8–16 implement the query string method. Lines 17–23 implement the regex method. Lines 24–33 implement a defined parameter along with a callback function that is executed whenever the `userid` parameter is specified in the request parameters. Figure 18.1 shows the console output from the code in Listing 18.2.

Listing 18.2 `express_routes.js`: **Implementing route parameters in Express**

```
01 var express = require('express');
02 var url = require('url');
03 var app = express();
04 app.listen(80);
05 app.get('/', function (req, res) {
```

```
  res.send("Get Index");
});
app.get('/find', function(req, res){
  var url_parts = url.parse(req.url, true);
  var query = url_parts.query;
  var response = 'Finding Book: Author: ' + query.author +
                  ' Title: ' + query.title;
  console.log('\nQuery URL: ' + req.originalUrl);
  console.log(response);
  res.send(response);
});
app.get(/^\/book\/(\w+)\:(\w+)?$/, function(req, res){
  var response = 'Get Book: Chapter: ' + req.params[0] +
              ' Page: ' + req.params[1];
  console.log('\nRegex URL: ' + req.originalUrl);
  console.log(response);
  res.send(response);
});
app.get('/user/:userid', function (req, res) {
  var response = 'Get User: ' + req.param('userid');
  console.log('\nParam URL: ' + req.originalUrl);
  console.log(response);
  res.send(response);
});
app.param('userid', function(req, res, next, value){
  console.log("\nRequest received with userid: " + value);
  next();
});
```

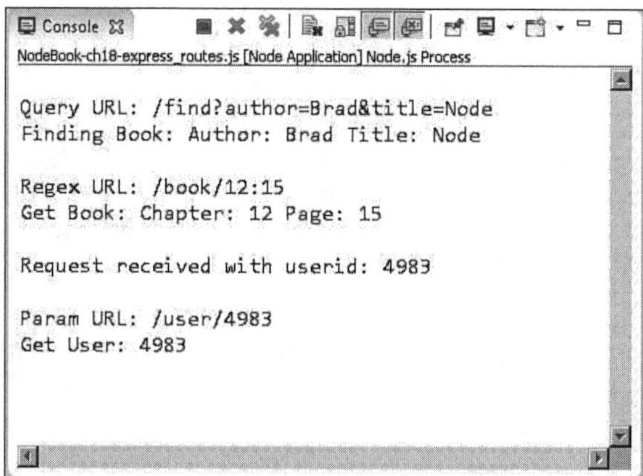

Console
NodeBook-ch18-express_routes.js [Node Application] Node.js Process
Query URL: /find?author=Brad&title=Node
Finding Book: Author: Brad Title: Node
Regex URL: /book/12:15
Get Book: Chapter: 12 Page: 15
Request received with userid: 4983
Param URL: /user/4983
Get User: 4983

Figure 18.1 Implementing route parameters using query strings, regex, and defined parameters.

Using Request Objects

You pass a Request object to a route handler as the first parameter. The Request object provides data and metadata about the request, including the URL, headers, query string, and much more. It allows you to handle a request appropriately in your code.

Table 18.2 lists some of the most commonly used properties and methods available for the Request object.

Table 18.2 **Properties and methods of the HTTP Request object**

Property or Method	Description
originalUrl	The original URL string of the request.
protocol	The protocol string—for example http or https.
ip	The IP address of the request.
path	The path portion of the request URL.
host	The hostname of the request.
method	The HTTP method: GET, POST, etc.
query	The query string portion of the request URL.
fresh	A Boolean that is true when last-modified matches the current.
stale	A Boolean that is false when last-modified matches the current.
secure	A Boolean that is true when a TLS connection is established.
acceptsCharset(charset)	A method that returns true if the character set specified by charset is supported.
get(header)	A method that returns the value of header.
headers	An object form of the request headers.

Listing 18.3 shows how to access the various parts of the Request object. The output in Figure 18.2 shows the actual values associated with a GET request.

Listing 18.3 express_request.js: **Accessing properties of the Request object in Express**

```
var express = require('express');
var app = express();
app.listen(80);
app.get('/user/:userid', function (req, res) {
  console.log("URL:\t   " + req.originalUrl);
  console.log("Protocol:  " + req.protocol);
  console.log("IP:\t    " + req.ip);
  console.log("Path:\t   " + req.path);
```

```
  console.log("Host:\t     " + req.host);
  console.log("Method:\t    " + req.method);
  console.log("Query:\t     " + JSON.stringify(req.query));
  console.log("Fresh:\t     " + req.fresh);
  console.log("Stale:\t     " + req.stale);
  console.log("Secure:\t    " + req.secure);
  console.log("UTF8:\t     " + req.acceptsCharset('utf8'));
  console.log("Connection: " + req.get('connection'));
  console.log("Headers: " + JSON.stringify(req.headers,null,2));
  res.send("User Request");
});
```

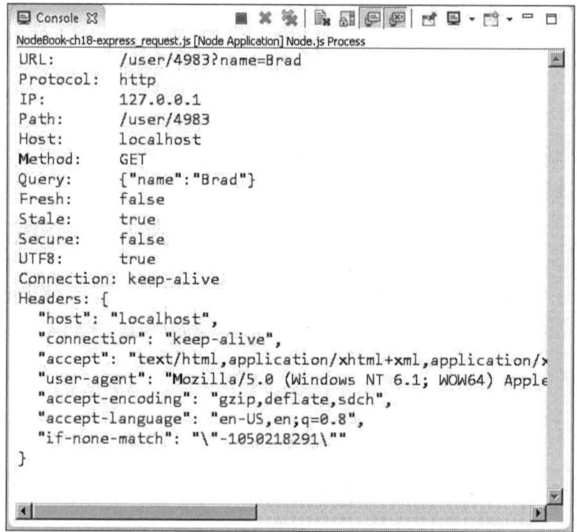

Figure 18.2 Accessing properties of the `Request` object.

Using `Response` Objects

The `Response` object passed to the route handler provides the necessary functionality to build and send a proper HTTP response. The following sections discuss using the `Response` object to set headers, set the status, and send data back to the client.

Setting Headers

An important part of formulating a proper HTTP response is to set the headers. For example, setting the `Content-Type` header tells the browser how to handle responses. The `Response` object provides several helper methods to get and set the header values that are sent with HTTP responses.

The most commonly used methods are `get(header)` and `set(header, value)`, which get and set any header value. For example, the following code first gets the `Content-Type` header and then sets it:

```
var oldType = res.get('Content-Type');
res.set('Content-Type', 'text/plain');
```

Table 18.3 describes the helper methods to get and set header values.

Table 18.3 **Methods to get and set header values on the `Response` object**

Method	Description
`get(header)`	Returns the value of the `header` parameter specified.
`set(header, value)`	Sets the value of the `header` parameter.
`set(headerObj)`	Accepts an object that contains multiple `'header':'value'` properties. Each of the headers in the `headerObj` parameter is set in the response object.
`location(path)`	Sets the location header to the `path` parameter specified. The path can be a URL path such as `/login`, a full URL such as `http://server.net/`, a relative path such as `../users`, or a browser action such as `back`.
`type(type_string)`	Sets the `Content-Type` header based on the `type_string` parameter. The `type_string` parameter can be a normal content type such as `application/json`, a partial type such as `png`, or a file extension such as `.html`.
`attachment([filepath])`	Sets the `Content-Disposition` header to `attachment`, and if `filepath` is specified, the `Content-Type` header is set based on the file extension.

Setting the Status

You need to set the HTTP status for a response if it is something other than 200. It is important to send the correct status response so that the browser or other applications can handle the HTTP response correctly. To set the status response, use the `status(number)` method, where the `number` parameter is the HTTP response status defined in the HTTP spec.

For example, the following lines set different statuses:

```
res.status(200); // OK
res.status(300); // Redirection
```

```
res.status(400); // Bad Request
res.status(401); // Unauthorized
res.status(403); // Forbidden
res.status(500); // Server Error
```

Sending Response

You have already seen the `send()` method in action, when sending simple responses in some earlier examples in this chapter. The `send()` method can use one of the following formats, where `status` is the HTTP status code and `body` is a `String` or `Buffer` object:

```
res.send(status, [body])
res.send([body])
```

If you specify a `Buffer` object, the `Content-Type` is automatically set to `application/octet-stream` unless you explicitly set it to something else. For example:

```
res.set('Content-Type', 'text/html');
res.send(new Buffer('<html><body>HTML String</body></html>'));
```

The `send()` method can really handle all the responses necessary, as long as you set the appropriate headers and status for the response. Once the `send()` method completes, it sets the value of the `res.finished` and `res.headerSent` properties. You can use these to verify that the response was sent, how much data was transferred, etc. The following is an example of the `res.headerSent` property:

```
HTTP/1.1 200 OK
X-Powered-By: Express
Content-Type: text/html
Content-Length: 92
Date: Tue, 17 Dec 2013 18:52:23 GMT
Connection: keep-alive
```

Listing 18.4 illustrates some of the basics of setting the status and headers, as well as sending a response. Notice that in lines 15–18 the route for `/error` sets the status to `400` before sending the response. Figure 18.3 shows the `res.headerSent` data in the console output on the Express server.

Listing 18.4 `express_send.js`: Sending status, headers, and response data using the `Response` object

```
01 var express = require('express');
02 var url = require('url');
03 var app = express();
04 app.listen(80);
05 app.get('/', function (req, res) {
06   var response = '<html><head><title>Simple Send</title></head>' +
07                  '<body><h1>Hello from Express</h1></body></html>';
```

```
  res.status(200);
  res.set({
    'Content-Type': 'text/html',
    'Content-Length': response.length
  });
  res.send(response);
  console.log('Response Finished? ' + res.finished);
  console.log('\nHeaders Sent: ');
  console.log(res.headerSent);
});
app.get('/error', function (req, res) {
  res.status(400);
  res.send("This is a bad request.");
});
```

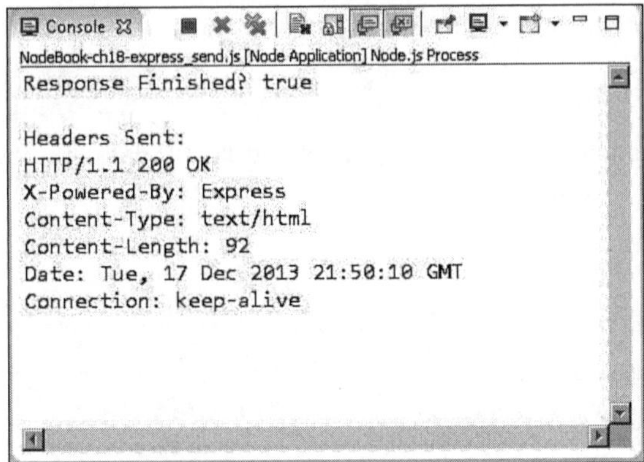

Console
NodeBook-ch18-express_send.js [Node Application] Node.js Process
Response Finished? true
Headers Sent:
HTTP/1.1 200 OK
X-Powered-By: Express
Content-Type: text/html
Content-Length: 92
Date: Tue, 17 Dec 2013 21:50:10 GMT
Connection: keep-alive

Figure 18.3 The `res.headerSent` output after a response has been sent.

Sending JSON Responses

A growing trend has been to use JSON data to transfer information from a server to a client and then have the client dynamically populate the HTML elements on the page rather than have the server build HTML documents or parts of HTML documents and send the HTML to the client. Express facilitates sending JSON very nicely by providing the `json()` and `jsonp()` methods on the `Response` object. These methods use a syntax similar to that of `send()`, except that the body is a JSON stringify JavaScript object:

```
res.json(status, [object])
res.json([body])
res.jsonp(status, [object])
res.jsonp([object])
```

The JavaScript object is converted to a JSON string and sent back to the client. In the case of jsonp(), the URL of the request object includes a ?callback=<method> parameter, and the JSON string is wrapped in a function with the method name that can be called from the browser client to support the JSONP design.

Listing 18.5 implements both json() and jsonp() to illustrate sending JSON data to the server. Notice that in line 6 the json spaces application setting is set to 4, and a basic JavaScript object is passed into the json() call on line 7. On line 12 an error code is set in the response, and the response object is a JSON object.

Lines 14–19 implement the jsonp() method. Notice that jsonp callback name is set to cb in line 15. This means that instead of passing ?callback=<function> in the URL, the client needs to pass ?cb=<function> in the URL. Figure 18.4 shows the output to the browser for each of these calls.

Listing 18.5 express_json.js: **Sending JSON and JSONP data in a response from Express**

```
01 var express = require('express');
02 var url = require('url');
03 var app = express();
04 app.listen(80);
05 app.get('/json', function (req, res) {
06   app.set('json spaces', 4);
07   res.json({name:"Smithsonian", built:'1846', items:'137M',
08             centers: ['art', 'astrophysics', 'natural history',
09                       'planetary', 'biology', 'space', 'zoo']});
10 });
11 app.get('/error', function (req, res) {
12   res.json(500, {status:false, message:"Internal Server Error"});
13 });
14 app.get('/jsonp', function (req, res) {
15   app.set('jsonp callback name', 'cb');
16   res.jsonp({name:"Smithsonian", built:'1846', items:'137M',
17             centers: ['art', 'astrophysics', 'natural history',
18                       'planetary', 'biology', 'space', 'zoo']});
19 });
```

localhost/json

```
{
    "name": "Smithsonian",
    "built": "1846",
    "items": "137M",
    "centers": [
        "art",
        "astrophysics",
        "natural history",
        "planetary",
        "biology",
        "space",
        "zoo"
    ]
}
```

localhost/jsonp?cb=handleJSONP

```
typeof handleJSONP === 'function' && handleJSONP({
    "name": "Smithsonian",
    "built": "1846",
    "items": "137M",
    "centers": [
        "art",
        "astrophysics",
        "natural history",
        "planetary",
        "biology",
        "space",
        "zoo"
    ]
});
```

Figure 18.4 Sending JSON and JSONP data to a browser.

Sending Files

A great helper method in Express is the `sendfile(filepath)` method on the `Response` object. `sendfile()` uses a single function call to do everything that needs to be done to send files to the client. Specifically, the `sendfile()` method does the following:

- Sets the `Content-Type` header to the type based on file extension.
- Sets other appropriate headers, such as `Content-Length`.
- Sets the status of the response.
- Sends the contents of the file to the client by using the connection inside the `Response` object.

The `sendfile()` method uses the following syntax:

```
res.sendfile(path, [options], [callback])
```

`path` should point to the file that you want to send to the client. The `options` parameter is an object that contains a `maxAge` property that defines the maximum age for the content and a `root` property that is a root path to support relative paths in the `path` parameter. The callback function is called when the file transfer is complete and should accept an error as the only parameter.

Listing 18.6 shows how easy it is to send the contents of a file by using the `sendfile()` command. Notice that a `root` path is specified in line 8 so only the filename is required in line 6. Also notice that the callback function has code to handle the error. This code sends an image file, and Figure 18.5 shows that image displayed in a browser.

Listing 18.6 `express_send_file.js`: **Sending files in a HTTP request from Express**

```
01 var express = require('express');
02 var url = require('url');
03 var app = express();
04 app.listen(80);
05 app.get('/image', function (req, res) {
06   res.sendfile('arch.jpg',
07                { maxAge: 1,//24*60*60*1000,
08                  root: './views/'},
09                function(err){
10     if (err){
11       console.log("Error");
12     } else {
13       console.log("Success");
14     }
15   });
16 });
```

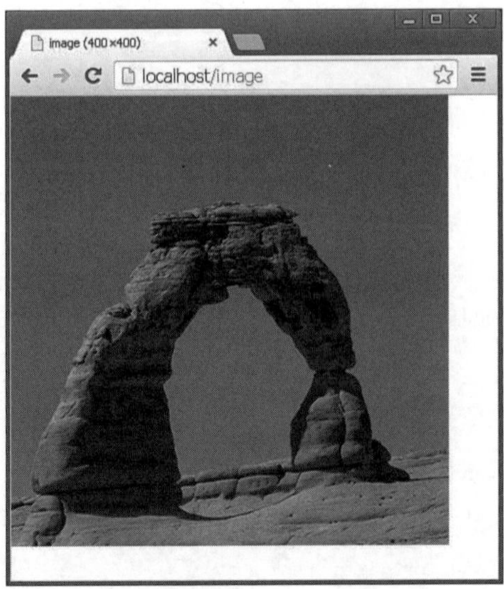

Figure 18.5 An image file sent in an HTTP response to a client.

Sending a Download Response

Express includes a `res.download()` method that works very similarly to the `res.sendfile()` method, with only a few differences. The `res.download()` method sends a file in the HTTP response as an attachment, which means the `Content-Disposition` header is set. The `res.download()` method uses the following syntax:

```
res.download(path, [filename], [callback])
```

The `path` parameter points to the file to send to the client. The `filename` parameter can specify a different filename that should be sent in the `Content-Disposition` header. The callback function is executed after the file download has completed.

Redirecting a Response

When you're implementing a webserver, you may need to redirect a request from the client to a different location on the same server or on a completely different server. The `res.redirect(path)` method handles redirection of a request to a new location.

Listing 18.7 illustrates the various redirection addressing that you can use. Line 6 redirects to a completely new domain address. Line 9 redirects to a different path on the same server, and line 15 redirects to a relative path on the same server.

Listing 18.7 `express_redirect.js`: **Redirecting requests on an Express server**

```
var express = require('express');
var url = require('url');
var app = express();
app.listen(80);
app.get('/google', function (req, res) {
  res.redirect('http://google.com');
});
app.get('/first', function (req, res) {
  res.redirect('/second');
});
app.get('/second', function (req, res) {
  res.send("Response from Second");
});
app.get('/level/A', function (req, res) {
  res.redirect("../B");
});
app.get('/level/B', function (req, res) {
  res.send("Response from Level B");
});
```

Implementing a Template Engine

A growing trend is to use a template engine to generate HTML using a template file and application data rather than build HTML files from scratch or use static files. A template engine uses the `template` object to build HTML, based on values provided by the application. Using template engines provides two benefits:

- **Simplicity:** Templates try to make it easy to generate the HTML either by a shorthand notation or by allowing JavaScript to be embedded in an HTML document directly.
- **Speed:** Template engines optimize the process of building HTML documents. Many compile a template and store the compiled version in a cache that speeds up the generation of HTML responses.

The following sections discuss implementing template engines in Express. There are several template engines available for use in Express, and this chapter focuses on two: Jade and Embedded JavaScript (EJS). These two template engines work in very different ways and should give you an idea of what is available. Jade uses a shorthand notation of HTML in the template so the template files do not look like HTML. The advantage is that the template files are very small and easy to follow. The disadvantage is that you need to learn yet another language. EJS, on the other hand, uses special notation to embed JavaScript in normal HTML documents. This makes it much easier to transition from normal HTML. The downside is that the HTML documents are even more complex than the originals and not as tidy as Jade templates.

To run the examples in this section, you need to install both the `jade` and `ejs` modules in your application, using the following commands:

```
npm install jade@1.3.1
npm install ejs@1.0.0
```

Defining a Template Engine

The first step in implementing a template engine is to define a default template engine for the Express application. You do this by setting the `view engine` setting on the `express()` application object. You also need to set the `views` setting to the location where your template files will be stored. For example, the following sets the `./views` directory as the root for template documents and `jade` as the view engine:

```
var app = express();
app.set('views', './views');
app.set('view engine', 'jade');
```

Then you need to register the template engines for the template extensions that you want them to handle by using the `app.engine(ext, callback)` method. The `ext` parameter is the file extension used for the template files, and the `callback` parameter is a function that supports Express's rendering functionality.

Many engines provide the callback functionality in an `__express` function. For example:

```
app.engine('jade', require('jade').__express)
```

The `__express` functionality often only works on the default filename extension. In that case, you can use a different function. For example, EJS provides the `renderFile` function for that purpose. You can use the following to register EJS for `ejs` extensions:

```
app.engine('ejs', require('ejs').__express)
```

However, if you want to register EJS for HTML extensions, you need to use:

```
app.engine('html', require('ejs').renderFile)
```

Once the extension is registered, the engine callback function is called to render any templates with that extension. If you choose a different engine besides Jade or EJS, you need to figure out how they expect to register with Express.

Adding Locals

When rendering a template, you may want to include dynamic data—for example, to render a page for user data just read from a database. In such a case, you can generate a `locals` object that contains properties that map to variable names defined in the templates. The `express()` app object provides the `app.locals` property to store local variables. `app.locals` is actually a function object, which means you can set variables in two different ways.

To assign a local template variable directly, you can use dot syntax. For example, the following code defines the local variables `title` and `version`:

```
app.locals.title = 'My App';
app.locals.version = 10;
```

You can also set local template variables by calling `app.locals(object)`, where `object` is a JavaScript object with variables to set. For example:

```
app.locals({title: 'My App', version:10});
```

> **Warning**
>
> Because `app.locals` is a JavaScript function object, you must not use native JavaScript names (for example, `name`, `apply`, `bind`, `call`, `arguments`, `length`, `constructor`, etc.) as properties for your own variable names.

Creating Templates

When rendering a template, you need to create template files. When creating template files, keep in mind these considerations:

- **Reusability:** Try to make your templates reusable in other parts of you application and in other applications. Most template engines cache templates to speed up performance. The more templates you have, the more caching time your engine will have to spend. Try to organize your templates so that they can be used for multiple purposes. For example, if you have several tables of data displayed in an app, make only a single template for all of them that can not only dynamically add the data but also set column headers, titles, and such.
- **Size:** As templates grow in size, they tend to become more and more unwieldy. Try to keep your templates compartmentalized to the type of data they are presenting. For example, if you have a template that has a menu bar, form, and table, you could split it into three separate templates.
- **Hierarchy:** Most websites and applications are built on some sort of hierarchy. For example, the `<head>` section as well as a banner and menu may be the same throughout a site. You should use a separate template for components that show up in multiple locations and just include those subtemplates when building your final page.

Listing 18.8 shows a basic EJS template that applies a set of local variables in a list to display user information. The EJS code is very basic and only uses the `<%= variable %>` to pull values from the Express local variables.

Listing 18.8 `user_ejs.html`: **A simple EJS template for displaying a user**

```
<!DOCTYPE html>
<html lang="en">
<head>
<title>EJS Template</title>
</head>
<body>
    <h1>User using EJS Template</h1>
    <ul>
        <li>Name: <%= uname %></li>
        <li>Vehicle: <%= vehicle %></li>
        <li>Terrain: <%= terrain %></li>
        <li>Climate: <%= climate %></li>
        <li>Location: <%= location %></li>
    </ul>
</body>
</html>
```

Listing 18.9 and Listing 18.10 show how to use Jade to implement a main template and then consume it in a subtemplate. The main template in Listing 18.9 is very basic, only implementing the `doctype`, `html`, `head`, and `title` elements. It also adds the `block content` element that is defined in Listing 18.10.

Notice that line 1 in Listing 18.10 extends `main_jade` to include those elements first and then adds the `h1`, `ul`, and `li` elements to get values from the `local` variables.

Listing 18.9 `main_jade.jade`: **A simple Jade template that defines a main webpage**

```
doctype html
html(lang="en")
  head
    title="Jade Template"
  body
    block content
```

Listing 18.10 `user_jade.jade`: **A simple Jade template that includes the** `main_jade.jade` **template and adds elements for displaying a user**

```
1 extends main_jade
2 block content
3   h1 User using Jade Template
4   ul
5     li Name: #{uname}
6     li Vehicle: #{vehicle}
7     li Terrain: #{terrain}
8     li Climate: #{climate}
9     li Location: #{location}
```

Rendering Templates in a Response

Once you have a template engine defined and configured and have created your templates, you can send a rendered template by using the Express `app` object or using the `Response` object. To render a template in the Express `app` object, you use the `app.render()` method, shown below:

```
app.render(view, [locals], callback)
```

The `view` parameter specifies the view filename in the views directory. If no extension is included on the file, the default extensions, such as `.jade` and `.ejs`, are tried. The `locals` parameter allows you to pass in a `locals` object if one has not been defined in `app.locals` already. The callback function is executed after the template has been rendered and should accept an error object for the first parameter and the string form of the rendered template as the second.

To render a template directly into a response, you can use the `res.render()` function, which works exactly the same as `app.render()` except that no callback is needed. The rendered results are automatically sent in the response.

The `app.render()` and `res.render()` methods both work well. If you do not need to do anything with the data before sending it, you can use the `res.render()` method to avoid the extra code you need in order to call `res.send()` to send the data.

Listing 18.11 puts all the template rendering concepts together in a couple of basic examples. Lines 5–8 set up the `views` directory and `view engine` and register `jade` and `ejs`. Then lines 10–16 define user information in the `app.locals` function.

Lines 17–19 handle the `/jade` route, which directly renders the `user_jade.jade` template from Listing 18.10 with the defined locals in the client response.

Lines 20–24 handle the `/ejs` route by first calling `app.render()` to render the `users_ejs.html` template defined in Listing 18.8 into the string `renderedData`. Then the `res.send()` command sends that data. Figure 18.6 shows the rendered webpages from both functions.

Listing 18.11 `express_templates.js`: **Implementing Jade and EJS templates in Express**

```
01 var express = require('express'),
02     jade = require('jade'),
03     ejs = require('ejs');
04 var app = express();
05 app.set('views', './views');
06 app.set('view engine', 'jade');
07 app.engine('jade', jade.__express);
08 app.engine('html', ejs.renderFile);
09 app.listen(80);
10 app.locals({
11   uname : 'Brad',
12   vehicle: "Jeep",
13   terrain: "Mountains",
```

```
  climate: "Desert",
  location: "Unknown"
});
app.get('/jade', function (req, res) {
  res.render('user_jade');
});
app.get('/ejs', function (req, res) {
  app.render('user_ejs.html', function(err, renderedData){
    res.send(renderedData);
  });
});
```

Figure 18.6 Webpages generated by rendering Jade and EJS templates.

Summary

This chapter focuses on the basics of getting Express installed, configured, and running for your Node.js applications. You've learned how to configure routes to handle HTTP requests and how to use the `Request` object to get information about the request. You've also seen how to configure the headers and status for the response and then send HTML strings, files, and rendered templates.

Up Next

In the next chapter you will implement some of the middleware that Express provides to extend functionality. Middleware enables you to handle cookies, sessions, and authentication, as well as control the cache.

19

Implementing Express Middleware

Much of the functionality that Express brings to the table is through middleware functions that are executed between the point where a request is received by Node.js and the point where a response is sent. Express's `connect` module provides a middleware framework that allows you to easily insert middleware functionality on a global or path level or for a single route.

The middleware supported by Express allows you to quickly serve static files, implement cookies, support sessions, process `POST` data, and much more. You can even create your own custom middleware functions and use them to preprocess requests and provide your own functionality.

This chapter focuses on the basics of implementing Express middleware. It also provides some examples of using middleware to handle `POST` requests, serve static files, and implement sessions, cookies, and authentication.

Understanding Middleware

Express provides a simple but effective middleware framework that allows you to provide additional functionality between the point where a request is received and when you actually handle the request and send the response. Middleware allows you to apply authentication, cookies, and sessions and to otherwise manipulate a request before it is passed to a handler.

Express is built on top of the `connect` NPM module and provides the underlying middleware support provided by `connect`. The following are some of the middleware components that are supported by Express:

- **`static`**: Allows the Express server to stream static file `GET` requests. This middleware is built into express and can be accessed via `express.static()`.
- **`express-logger`**: Implements a formatted request logger to track requests to the server.
- **`basic-auth-connect`**: Provides support for basic HTTP authentication.

- **cookie-parser**: Allows you to read cookies from a request and set cookies in the response.
- **cookie-session**: Provides cookie-based session support.
- **express-session**: Provides a fairly robust session implementation.
- **body-parser**: Parses JSON data in the body of POST requests into the req.body property.
- **compression**: Provides Gzip compress support for large responses to a client.
- **csurf**: Provides cross-site request forgery protection.

For the examples in this book, you will need to install the following versions of Express middleware modules using the npm install command:

```
npm install basic-auth-connect@1.0.0
npm install body-parser@1.0.2
npm install connect-mongo@0.4.0
npm install cookie-parser@1.0.1
npm install cookie-session@1.0.1
npm install express-session@1.0.3
```

You can also add express to your package.json module to ensure that these modules are installed when you deploy your application.

> **Note**
>
> Additional express middleware components are available as NPMs; just query the NPM repository. You can also create your own custom middleware.

You can apply middleware either globally to all routes under a specific path or to a specific route. The following sections describe each of these methods.

Assigning Middleware Globally to a Path

To assign middleware to all routes, you can implement the use() method on the Express app object. The use() method has the following syntax:

```
use([path], middleware)
```

The path variable is optional and defaults to /, which means all paths. The middleware parameter is a function that has the following syntax, where req is the Request object, res is the Response object, and next is the next middleware function to execute:

```
function(req, res, next)
```

Each of the middleware components has a constructor that returns the appropriate middleware function. For example, to apply the body-parser middleware to all paths with default parameters, you use the following statements:

```
var express = require('express');
var bodyParser = require('body-parser');
var app = express();
app.use('/', bodyParser());
```

Assigning Middleware to a Single Route

You can also apply `body-parser` middleware to a single route by passing it after the `path` parameter. For example, in the following code, requests to `/parsedRoute` will be logged, but requests to `/otherRoute` will not be logged:

```
var express = require('express');
var bodyParser = require('body-parser');
var app = express();
app.get('/parsedRoute', bodyParser(), function(req, res) {
  res.send('This request was logged.');
});
app.get('/otherRoute', function(req, res) {
  res.send('This request was not logged.');
});
```

Adding Multiple Middleware Functions

You can assign as many middleware functions globally and to routes as you like. For example, the following code assigns the `body-parser`, `cookie-parser` and `express-session` middleware modules:

```
var express = require('express');
var bodyParser = require('body-parser');
var cookieParser = require('cookie-parser');
var session = require('cexpress-session');
var app = express();
app.use('/', bodyParser()).
use('/', cookieParser()).
use('/', session()));
```

Keep in mind that the order in which you assign the functions is the order in which they are applied during a request. Some middleware functions need to be added before others.

Using the `query` Middleware

One of the most useful and simple middleware components is the `query` middleware. The `query` middleware converts a query string from a URL into a JavaScript object and stores it as the `query` property on the `Request` object. As of Express 4.x, the functionality exists within built-in request parser without the need for additional middleware.

The following code snippet shows the basics of utilizing the `query` middleware:

```
var express = require('express');
var app = express();
app.get('/', function(req, res) {
  var id = req.query.id;
  var score = req.query.score;
  console.log(JSON.stringify(req.query));
  res.send("done");
});
```

The query string for the request would look like `?id=10&score=95`. Notice that `JSON.stringify` can be called on `req.query` because it is a JavaScript object.

Serving Static Files

The `static` middleware is very commonly used Express middleware. The `static` middleware allows you to server static files directly from disk to the client. You can use `static` middleware to support things like JavaScript files, CSS files, image files, and HTML documents that do not change. The `static` module is extremely easy to implement and uses the following syntax:

```
express.static(path, [options])
```

The `path` parameter specifies the root path from which the static files will be referenced in the requests. The `options` parameter allows you to set the following properties:

- **`maxAge`:** The browser cache `maxAge`, in milliseconds. Defaults to `0`.
- **`hidden`:** A Boolean that, when `true`, indicates that transfer of hidden files is enabled. Defaults to `false`.
- **`redirect`:** A Boolean that, when `true`, indicates that if the request path is a directory, the request is redirected to the path with a trailing /. Defaults to `true`.
- **`index`:** The default filename for the root path. Defaults to `index.html`.

Listings 19.1 through 19.3 show the Express code, HTML, and CSS used to implement the `static` middleware to support serving static HTML, CSS, and image files. Notice that two `static` paths are implemented: one for the route / that maps to a subdirectory named `static` and the second for the route `/images` that maps to a peer directory named `images`. Figure 19.1 shows a statically served HTML document in a web browser.

Listing 19.1 `express_static.js`: **Express code that implements two static routes**

```
var express = require('express');
var app = express();
app.use('/', express.static('./static'), {maxAge:60*60*1000});
app.use('/images', express.static( '../images'));
app.listen(80);
```

Listing 19.2 `./static/index.html`: **A static HTML file that requests the CSS and image files from the server**

```
<html>
<head>
  <title>Static File</title>
  <link rel="stylesheet" type="text/css" href="css/static.css">
</head>
<body>
    <img src="/images/arch.jpg" height="200px"/>
  <img src="/images/flower.jpg" height="200px" />
    <img src="/images/bison.jpg" height="200px" />
</body>
</html>
```

Listing 19.3 `./static/css/static.css`: **A CSS file that formats the images**

```
img
{
    display:inline;
    margin:3px;
    border:5px solid #000000;
}
```

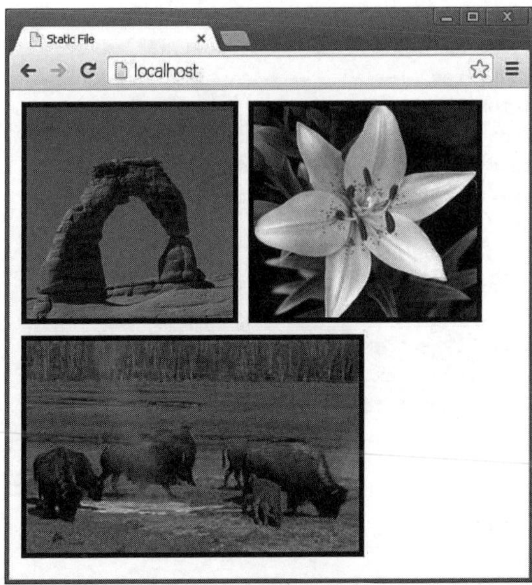

Figure 19.1 HTML, CSS, and image files served statically to a browser.

Handling POST Body Data

Another very common use for Express middleware is to handle body data inside a POST request. The data inside a request body can be in various formats, such as POST parameter strings, JSON strings, or raw data. Express's body-parser middleware attempts to parse the data in the JSON data in the body of requests and properly format them as the req.body property of the Request object.

For example, if this middleware receives POST parameters or JSON data, it converts them to a JavaScript object and stores it as the req.body property of the Request object. Listing 19.4 illustrates using the body-parser middleware to support reading form data posted to the server.

The code in lines 5–11 handles the GET request and responds with a very basic form. It is not well-formatted HTML, but it is adequate to illustrate the use of the body-parser middleware.

The code in lines 12–21 implements a POST request handler. Notice that in line 16, the first name entered in the form field is accessed using req.body.first to help build the hello message in the response. This really is it. You can handle any kind of form data in the body in this manner. Figure 19.2 shows the resulting web forms in the browser.

Listing 19.4 express_post.js: **Handling POST parameters in a request body by using the body-parser middleware**

```
01 var express = require('express');
02 var bodyParser = require('body-parser');
03 var app = express();
04 app.use(bodyParser());
05 app.get('/', function (req, res) {
06   var response = '<form method="POST">' +
07         'First: <input type="text" name="first"><br>' +
08         'Last: <input type="text" name="last"><br>' +
09         '<input type="submit" value="Submit"></form>';
10   res.send(response);
11 });
12 app.post('/',function(req, res){
13   var response = '<form method="POST">' +
14         'First: <input type="text" name="first"><br>' +
15         'Last: <input type="text" name="last"><br>' +
16         '<input type="submit" value="Submit"></form>' +
17         '<h1>Hello ' + req.body.first + '</h1>';
18   res.type('html');
19   res.end(response);
20   console.log(req.body);
21 });
22 app.listen(80);
```

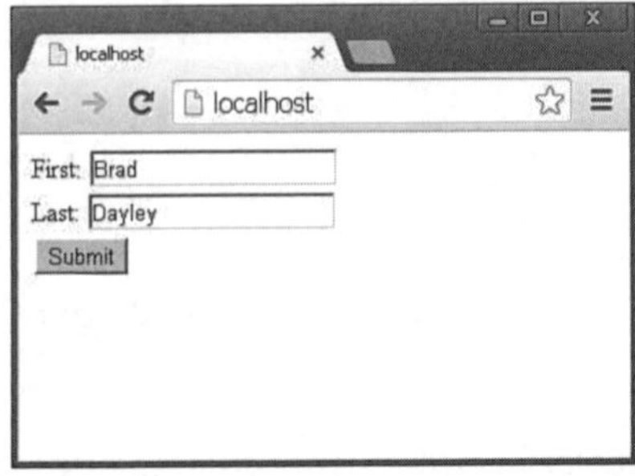

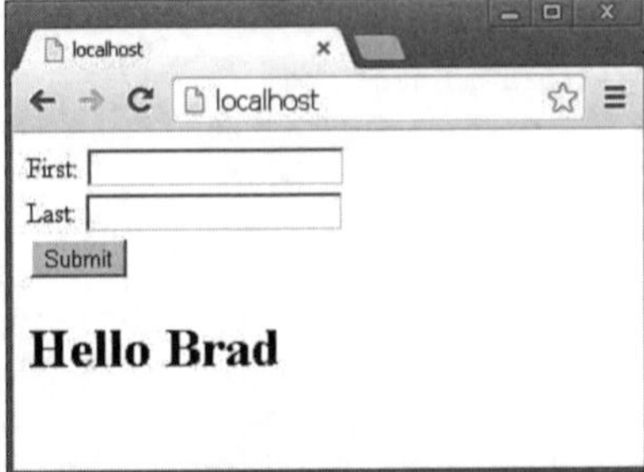

Figure 19.2 Handling `POST` parameters in a request body by using the `body-parser` middleware.

Sending and Receiving Cookies

The `cookie-parser` middleware provided in Express makes handling cookies extremely simple. The `cookie-parser` middleware parses the cookies from a request and stores them in the `req.cookies` property as a JavaScript object. The `cookie-parser` middleware uses the following syntax:

```
express.cookie-parser([secret])
```

> **Note**
>
> The `cookie-parser` middleware will be renamed `cookie` when Connect 3.0 ships. You may need to change your code to support the new name if it doesn't end up being backward compatible.

The optional `secret` string parameter prevents cookie tampering by internally signing the cookies using the `secret` string.

To set a cookie in a response, you can use the `res.cookie()` method shown below:

```
res.cookie(name, value, [options])
```

A cookie with the `name` and `value` parameters specified is added to the response. The `options` parameter allows you to set the following properties for the cookie:

- **`maxAge`:** The amount of time, in milliseconds, for a cookie to live before it expires.
- **`httpOnly`:** A Boolean that, when `true`, indicates that this cookie should only be accessed by the server and not by client-side JavaScript.
- **`signed`:** A Boolean that, when `true`, indicates that the cookie will be signed, and you need to access it using the `req.signedCookie` object instead of the `req.cookie` object.
- **`path`:** The path that the cookie applies to.

For example, the following sets a `hasVisited` cookie:

```
res.cookie('hasVisited', '1',
           { maxAge: 60*60*1000,
             httpOnly: true,
             path:'/'});
```

You can remove cookies from a client by using the `res.clearCookie()` method. For example:

```
res.clearCookie('hasVisited');
```

Listing 19.5 shows a simple example of getting a cookie named `req.cookies.hasVisited` from a request and setting it if it hasn't already been set.

Listing 19.5 `express_cookies.js`: **Sending and receiving cookies by using Express**

```
var express = require('express');
var cookieParser = require('cookie-parser');
var app = express();
app.use(cookieParser());
app.get('/', function(req, res) {
  console.log(req.cookies);
  if (!req.cookies.hasVisited){
    res.cookie('hasVisited', '1',
               { maxAge: 60*60*1000,
                 httpOnly: true,
                 path:'/'});
  }
  res.send("Sending Cookie");
});
app.listen(80);
```

Implementing Sessions

Another very common use of Express middleware is to provide session support for applications. For complex session management, you might want to implement it yourself, but for basic session support, the `cookie-session` middleware works relatively well.

The `cookie-session` middleware utilizes the `cookie-parser` middleware underneath, so you need to add `cookie-parser` prior to adding `cookie-session`. The following shows the syntax for adding the `cookie-session` middleware:

```
res.cookie([options])
```

The `options` parameter allows you to set the following properties for the cookie:

- **`key`:** The name of the cookie that identifies the session.
- **`secret`:** A string that is used to sign the session cookie to prevent cookie tampering.

- **cookie:** An object that defines the cookie's settings, including `maxAge`, `path`, `httpOnly`, and `signed`. The default is `{path:'/', httpOnly:true, maxAge:null }`.
- **proxy:** A Boolean that, when `true`, causes Express to trust the reverse proxy when setting secure cookies via `x-forwarded-proto`.

When `cookie-session` is implemented, a session is stored as an object in `req.session`. Any changes you make to `req.session` flow across multiple requests from the same browser.

Listing 19.6 shows an example of implementing a basic `cookie-session` session. Notice that `cookie-parser` is added first in line 5 and then `cookie-session` is added in line 6, with a `secret` string. There are two routes in this example. When the `/restricted` route is accessed, the `restrictedCount` value is incremented in the session, and the response is redirected to `/library`. Then in `library`, if `restrictedCount` is not `undefined`, the value is displayed; otherwise, a welcome message is displayed. Figure 19.3 shows the different outputs in a web browser.

Listing 19.6 `express_session.js`: **Implementing a basic cookie session by using Express**

```
01 var express = require('express');
02 var cookieParser = require('cookie-parser');
03 var cookieSession = require('cookie-session');
04 var app = express();
05 app.use(cookieParser());
06 app.use(cookieSession({secret: 'MAGICALEXPRESSKEY'}));
07 app.get('/library', function(req, res) {
08   console.log(req.cookies);
09   if(req.session.restricted) {
10     res.send('You have been in the restricted section ' +
11              req.session.restrictedCount + ' times.');
12   }else {
13     res.send('Welcome to the library.');
14   }
15 });
16 app.get('/restricted', function(req, res) {
17   req.session.restricted = true;
18   if(!req.session.restrictedCount){
19     req.session.restrictedCount = 1;
20   } else {
21     req.session.restrictedCount += 1;
22   }
23   res.redirect('/library');
24 });
25 app.listen(80);
```

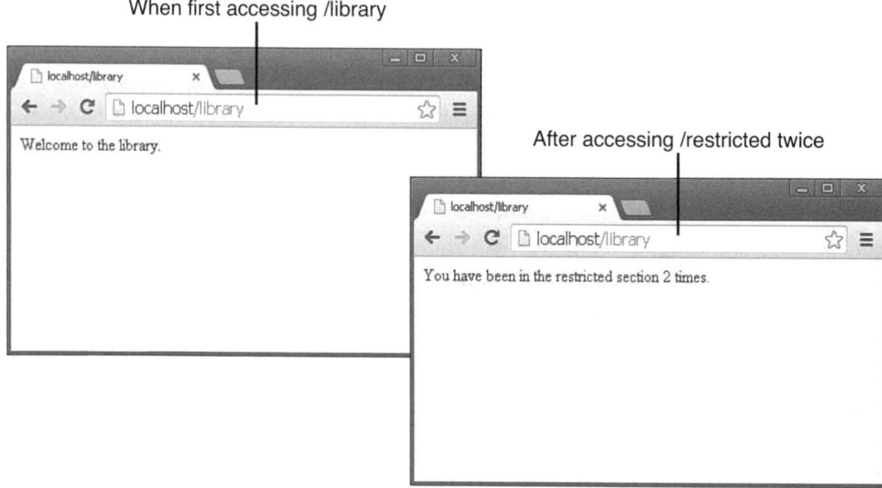

Figure 19.3 Using basic session handling to track improper access to a route.

Applying Basic HTTP Authentication

Another common use for Express middleware is to apply basic HTTP authentication. HTTP authentication uses the `Authorization` header to send an encoded username and password from a browser to a server. If no authorization information is stored in the browser for the URL, the browser launches a basic login dialog box to allow the user to enter the username and password. Basic HTTP authentication works well for basic sites that require a minimal authenticate method and is very easy to implement.

The `basic-auth-connect` middleware function in Express provides the support to handle basic HTTP authentication. The `basic-auth-connect` middleware uses the following syntax:

```
var basicAuth = require('basic-auth-connect');

express.basicAuth(function(user, pass){})
```

The function passed to `basic-auth-connect` accepts the username and password and then returns `true` if they are correct and `false` if they are not. For example:

```
app.use(express.basicAuth(function(user, password) {
  return (user === 'testuser' && pass === 'test');
}));
```

Typically you store the username and password in the database and then, inside the authentication function, you retrieve the `user` object to validate against.

Listing 19.7 and Listing 19.8 illustrate how easy it is to implement the `basic-auth-connect` middleware. Listing 19.7 implements a global authentication. Listing 19.8 implements authentication against a single route. Figure 19.4 shows the browser requesting authentication and then the authenticated webpage.

Listing 19.7 `express_auth.js`: **Implementing basic HTTP authentication globally for a site**

```
var express = require('express');
var basicAuth = require('basic-auth-connect');
var app = express();
app.listen(80);
app.use(basicAuth(function(user, pass) {
  return (user === 'testuser' && pass === 'test');
}));
app.get('/', function(req, res) {
  res.send('Successful Authentication!');
});
```

Listing 19.8 `express_auth_one.js`: **Implementing basic HTTP authentication for a single route**

```
var express = require('express');
var basicAuth = require('basic-auth-connect');
var app = express();
var auth = basicAuth(function(user, pass) {
  return (user === 'user1' && pass === 'test');
});
app.get('/library', function(req, res) {
  res.send('Welcome to the library.');
});
app.get('/restricted', auth, function(req, res) {
  res.send('Welcome to the restricted section.');
});
app.listen(80);
```

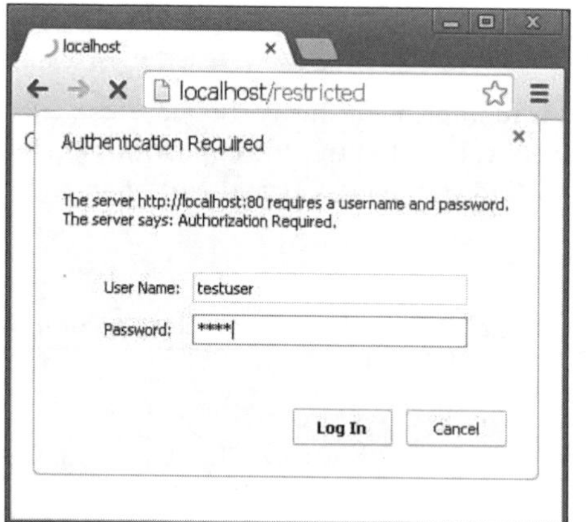

Figure 19.4 Using basic HTTP authentication.

Implementing Session Authentication

A major downside to basic HTTP authentication is that the login sticks around as long as the credentials are stored and is not very secure. A much better method is to implement your own authentication and store it in a session that you can expire whenever you want.

The `session` middleware inside Express works very well for implementing session authentication. The `session` middleware attaches a `Session` object `req.session` to the `Request` object to provide the session functionality. Table 19.1 describers the methods you can call on the `res.session` object.

Table 19.1 **Methods on the `res.session` object to manage sessions**

Method	Description
`regenerate([callback])`	Removes the `req.session` object and creates a new one, allowing you to reset the session.
`destroy([callback])`	Removes the `req.session` object.
`save([callback])`	Saves the session data.
`touch([callback])`	Resets the `maxAge` count for the session cookie.
`cookie`	Specifies the cookie object that links the session to the browser.

Listing 19.9 shows how to implement session authentication using the `crypto` module to generate secure passwords. The example is very rudimentary to keep it small enough for the book, but it contains the basic functionality so you can see how to implement session authentication.

Lines 6–9 encrypt the passwords by using the `hasPW()` function. Notice that the listing uses the `body-parser`, `cookieParser`, and `session` middleware. Lines 44 and 45 simulate getting a `user` object from the database and comparing the stored password hash with the password hash from the request body. Lines 46–50 create the session. Notice that the `regenerate()` function is used to regenerate a new session, and the callback function passed to `regenerate()` sets the `session.user` and `session.success` properties of the session. If the authentication fails, then only the `session.error` property is set for the session.

The `/login` route in lines 29–41 displays a rudimentary login to get credentials. If `session.error` is set, then it is also displayed on the login page. The `/restricted` route in lines 14–23 checks the session to see if it has a valid user, and if it does, displays a success message; otherwise, `session.error` is set, and the response is redirected to `/login`.

The `/logout` route in lines 24–28 calls `destroy()` on the session to remove the authentication. You could also have other code destroy the session, based on a timeout, a number of requests, etc. Figure 19.5 shows the browser screens forcing a login and then displaying success.

Listing 19.9 `express_auth_session.js`: Implementing session authentication in Express

```
01 var express = require('express');
02 var bodyParser = require('body-parser');
03 var cookieParser = require('cookie-parser');
04 var session = require('express-session');
05 var crypto = require('crypto');
06 function hashPW(pwd){
07   return crypto.createHash('sha256').update(pwd).
08          digest('base64').toString();
09 }
10 var app = express();
11 app.use(bodyParser());
12 app.use(cookieParser('MAGICString'));
13 app.use(session());
14 app.get('/restricted', function(req, res){
15   if (req.session.user) {
16     res.send('<h2>'+ req.session.success + '</h2>' +
17              '<p>You have entered the restricted section<p><br>' +
18              ' <a href="/logout">logout</a>');
19   } else {
20     req.session.error = 'Access denied!';
21     res.redirect('/login');
22   }
23 });
```

```
app.get('/logout', function(req, res){
  req.session.destroy(function(){
    res.redirect('/login');
  });
});
app.get('/login', function(req, res){
  var response = '<form method="POST">' +
    'Username: <input type="text" name="username"><br>' +
    'Password: <input type="password" name="password"><br>' +
    '<input type="submit" value="Submit"></form>';
  if(req.session.user){
    res.redirect('/restricted');
  }else if(req.session.error){
    response +='<h2>' + req.session.error + '<h2>';
  }
  res.type('html');
  res.send(response);
});
app.post('/login', function(req, res){
  //user should be a lookup of req.body.username in database
  var user = {name:req.body.username, password:hashPW("myPass")};
  if (user.password === hashPW(req.body.password.toString())) {
    req.session.regenerate(function(){
      req.session.user = user;
      req.session.success = 'Authenticated as ' + user.name;
      res.redirect('/restricted');
    });
  } else {
    req.session.regenerate(function(){
      req.session.error = 'Authentication failed.';
      res.redirect('/restricted');
    });
    res.redirect('/login');
  }
});
app.listen(80);
```

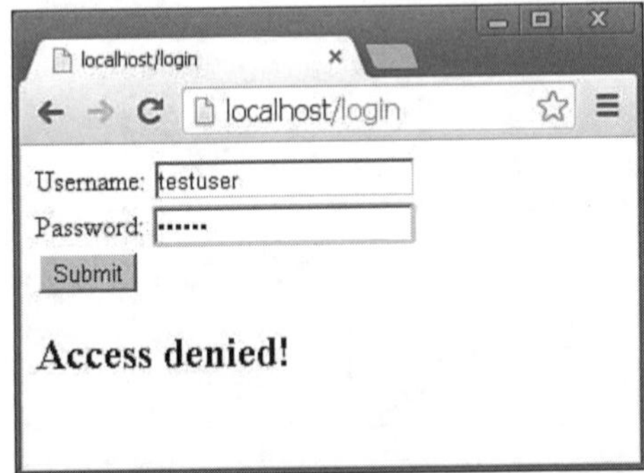

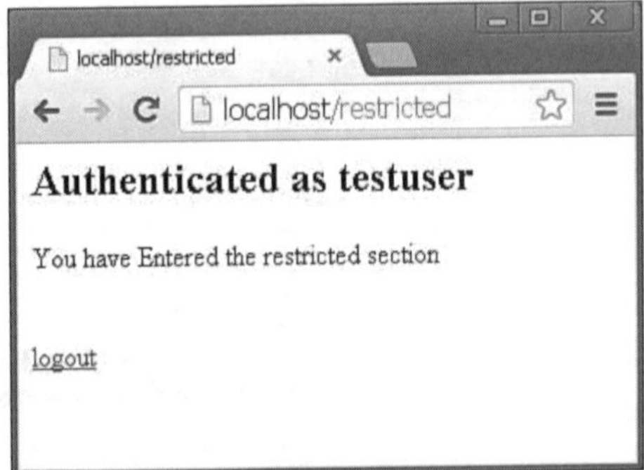

Figure 19.5 Implementing session authentication in Node.js using Express session middleware.

Creating Custom Middleware

With Express, you can create your own middleware. All you need to do is provide a function that accepts the `Request` object as the first parameter, the `Response` object as the second parameter, and `next` as the third parameter. The `next` parameter is a function passed by the middleware framework that points to the `next` middleware function to execute, so you must call `next()` prior to exiting your custom function, or the handler will never be called.

To illustrate how easy it is to implement your own custom middleware functionality in Express, Listing 19.10 implements a middleware function named `queryRemover()` that strips the query string off the URL before sending it on to the handler.

Notice that `queryRemover()` accepts the `Request` and `Response` objects as the first two parameters and `next` as the third parameter. The `next()` callback function is executed prior to leaving the middleware function, as required. Figure 19.6 displays the console output; as you can see, the query string portion of the URL has been removed.

Listing 19.10 `express_middleware.js`: Implementing custom middleware to remove the query string from the `Request` object

```
var express = require('express');
var app = express();
function queryRemover(req, res, next){
  console.log("\nBefore URL: ");
  console.log(req.url);
  req.url = req.url.split('?')[0];
  console.log("\nAfter URL: ");
  console.log(req.url);
  next();
};
```

```
app.use(queryRemover);
app.get('/no/query', function(req, res) {
  res.send("test");
});
app.listen(80);
```

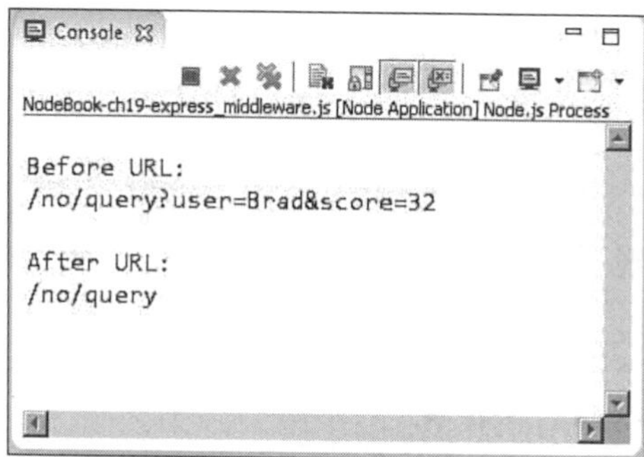

Figure 19.6 Implementing custom middleware to remove the query string from the `Request` object.

Summary

This chapter introduces the world of Express middleware. You've seen how to implement middleware in your code. The `parse-body` middleware allows you to parse `POST` parameters or JSON data in the body of the request. The `static` middleware allows you to set routes to serve static files such as JavaScript, CSS, and images. The `cookie-parser`, `cookie-session`, and `session` middleware allow you to implement cookies and sessions.

In this chapter you've also gotten a glimpse of using the middleware framework to implement basic HTTP authentication and more advanced session authentication. A great advantage of Express middleware is that it makes it extremely simple to implement your own middleware functionality.

Up Next

In the next chapter you'll jump into the world of AngularJS. You will get an overview of the design and intention of AngularJS. You'll learn where it fits in the Node.js stack and how to begin implementing it in your projects.

20

Getting Started with AngularJS

AngularJS is a JavaScript framework that provides a very structured method of creating websites and web applications. AngularJS is a JavaScript library that is built on a lightweight version of jQuery. It allows AngularJS to provide the best of JavaScript and jQuery and at the same time enforce a structured Model View Controller (MVC) framework.

AngularJS is a perfect client-side library for the Node.js stack because it provides a very clean and structured approach. With a clean, structured frontend, the Node.js backend performs much better. Also, the fact that AngularJS uses JavaScript objects as its model plays right into the Node.js and MongoDB platforms because the objects do not need to be converted to some other structure to be used in both locations.

This chapter introduces you to AngularJS as well as the major components involved in an AngularJS application. Understanding these components is critical before you try to implement an AngularJS application because the framework is different from more traditional JavaScript web application programming.

Once you have a good grasp of the components and the life cycle of an AngularJS application, you'll learn how to construct a basic AngularJS application, step by step. This should prepare you to jump into the following chapters, which provide much more detail on implementing AngularJS.

Why AngularJS?

AngularJS is an MVC framework that that is built on top of JavaScript and a lightweight version of jQuery. MVC frameworks separate the business logic in code from the view and the model. Without this separation, JavaScript-based web applications can quickly get out of hand when you are trying to manage all three together and a complex maze of functions.

Everything that AngularJS provides you could implement yourself by using JavaScript and jQuery, or you could even try using another MVC JavaScript framework. However, AngularJS has a lot of functionality, and the design of the AngularJS framework makes it easy to implement MVC in the correct manner. The following are some of the reasons to choose AngularJS:

- The AngularJS framework forces correct implementation of MVC and also makes it easy to implement MVC correctly.
- The declarative style of AngularJS HTML templates makes the intent of the HTML more intuitive and makes the HTML easier to maintain.
- The model portion of AngularJS is basic JavaScript objects, making it easy to manipulate, access, and implement.
- AngularJS uses a declarative approach to extend the functionality of HTML by having a direct link between the HTML declaratives and the JavaScript functionality behind them.
- AngularJS provides a very simple and flexible filter interface that allows you to easily format data as it passes from the model to the view.
- AngularJS applications tend to use a fraction of the code that traditional JavaScript applications use because you only need to focus on the logic and not all the little details, such as data binding.
- AngularJS requires a lot less Document Object Model (DOM) manipulation than traditional methods and guides you to put the manipulations in the correct locations in applications. It is easier to design applications based on presenting data than on DOM manipulation.
- AngularJS provides several built-in services and enables you to implement your own in a structured and reusable way. This makes your code more maintainable and easier to test.
- Due to the clean separation of responsibilities in the AngularJS framework, it is easy to test your applications and even develop them using a test-driven approach.

Understanding AngularJS

AngularJS provides a very structured framework based on an MVC model. This framework allows you to build structured applications that are robust and easily understood and maintained. To get started with AngularJS, you first need to understand the various components that you will be implementing and how they interact with each other. The following sections discuss the various components involved in an AngularJS application, their purpose, and what each is responsible for.

Modules

AngularJS introduces the concept of a module representing components in an application. The module provides a namespace that allows you to reference directives, scopes, and other components based on model name. This makes it easier to package and reuse parts of an application.

Each view or webpage in AngularJS has a single module assigned to it via the `ng-app` directive. (Directives are discussed later in this chapter.) However, you can add other modules to the main module as dependencies, which provides a very structured and componentized application.

Scopes and the Data Model

AngularJS introduces the concept of a scope. A scope is really just a JavaScript representation of data used to populate a view presented on a webpage. The data can come from any source, such as a database, a remote web service, or the client side AngularJS code, or it can be dynamically generated by the webserver.

A great feature of scopes is that they are just plain JavaScript objects, which means you can manipulate them as needed in your AngularJS code with ease. Also, you can nest scopes to organize your data to match the context that they are being used in.

Views with Templates and Directives

HTML webpages are based on a DOM where each HTML element is represented by a DOM object. A web browser reads the properties of a DOM object and knows how to render the HTML element on the webpage, based on the DOM object's properties.

Most dynamic web applications use direct JavaScript or a JavaScript-based library such as jQuery to manipulate a DOM object to change values such as adding/changing elements to a table or menu.

AngularJS introduces a new concept of combining templates with directives to build an HTML view that is presented to a user. Directives have two parts. The first part is extra attributes, elements, and CSS classes that are added to an HTML template. The second part is JavaScript code that extends the normal behavior of the DOM.

The advantage of using directives is that an HTML template indicates the intended logic with a directive. Also, the built-in AngularJS directives handle most of the necessary DOM manipulation functionality that you need to implement to bind the data in the scope to a view.

You can also create your own AngularJS directives to implement any necessary custom functionality you need in a web application. In fact, you should use your own custom directives to do any direct DOM manipulation that a web application needs.

Expressions

A great feature of AngularJS is the ability to add expressions inside the HTML template. AngularJS evaluates expressions and then dynamically adds the result to a webpage. Expressions are linked to the scope, so you can have an expression that utilizes values in the scope, and as the model changes, so does the value of the expression.

Controllers

AngularJS completes the MVC framework through the implementation of controllers. Controllers augment the scope by setting up the initial state or values in the scope and by adding behavior to the scope. For example, you can add a function that sums values in a scope to provide a total such that if the model data behind the scope changes, the total value always changes.

You add controllers to HTML elements by using a directive and then implement them as JavaScript code in the background.

Data Binding

One of the best features of AngularJS is the built-in data binding. Data binding is the process of linking data from the model with what is displayed in a webpage. AngularJS provides a very clean interface to link the model data to elements in a webpage.

In AngularJS data binding is a two-way process: When data is changed on a webpage the model is updated, and when data is changed in the model the webpage is automatically updated. This way, the model is always the only source for data represented to the user, and the view is just a projection of the model.

Services

Services are the major workhorses in the AngularJS environment. Services are singleton objects that provide functionality for a web app. For example, a common task of web applications it to perform AJAX requests to a webserver. AngularJS provides an HTTP service that houses all the functionality to access a webserver.

The service functionality is completely independent of context or state, so it can be easily consumed from the components of an application. AngularJS provides a lot of built-in service components for basic uses, such as HTTP requests, logging, parsing, animation, etc. You can also create your own services and reuse them throughout your code.

Dependency Injection

Dependency injection is a process in which a code component defines dependencies on other components. When the code is initialized, the dependent component is made available for access within the component. AngularJS applications make heavy use of dependency injection.

A common use for dependency injection is consuming services. For example, if you are defining a module that requires access to the webserver via HTTP requests, you can inject the HTTP service into the module, and the functionality is available in the module code. In addition, one AngularJS module consumes the functionality of another via dependency.

Separation of Responsibilities

An extremely important part of designing AngularJS applications is the separation of responsibilities. The whole reason you choose a structured framework is to ensure that code is well implemented, easy to follow, maintainable, and testable. Angular provides a very structured framework to work from, but you still need to ensure that you implement AngularJS in the appropriate manner.

The following are a few rules to follow when implementing AngularJS:

- The view acts as the official presentation structure for the application. Indicate any presentation logic as directives in the HTML template of the view.
- If you need to perform any DOM manipulation, do it in a built-in or your own custom directive JavaScript code—and nowhere else.
- Implement any reusable tasks as services and add them to your modules by using dependency injection.
- Ensure that the scope reflects the current state of the model and is the single source for data consumed by the view.
- Ensure that the controller code only acts to augment the scope data and doesn't include any business logic.
- Define controllers within the module namespace and not globally. This ensures that your application can be packaged easily and prevents overwhelming the global namespace.

An Overview of the AngularJS Life Cycle

Now that you understand the components involved in an AngularJS application, you need to understand what happens during the life cycle, which has three phases—bootstrap, compilation, and runtime. Understanding the life cycle of an AngularJS application makes it easier to understand how to design and implement your code.

The three phases of the life cycle of an AngularJS application happen each time a webpage is loaded in the browser. The following sections describe these phases of an AngularJS application.

The Bootstrap Phase

The first phase of the AngularJS life cycle is the bootstrap phase, which occurs when the AngularJS JavaScript library is downloaded to the browser. AngularJS initializes its own necessary components and then initializes your module, which the `ng-app` directive points to. The module is loaded, and any dependencies are injected into your module and made available to code within the module.

The Compilation Phase

The second phase of the AngularJS life cycle is the HTML compilation stage. Initially when a webpage is loaded, a static form of the DOM is loaded in the browser. During the compilation phase, the static DOM is replaced with a dynamic DOM that represents the AngularJS view.

This phase involves two parts: traversing the static DOM and collecting all the directives and then linking the directives to the appropriate JavaScript functionality in the AngularJS built-in library or custom directive code. The directives are combined with a scope to produce the dynamic or live view.

The Runtime Data Binding Phase

The final phase of the AngularJS application is the runtime phase, which exists until the user reloads or navigates away from a webpage. At that point, any changes in the scope are reflected in the view, and any changes in the view are directly updated in the scope, making the scope the single source of data for the view.

AngularJS behaves differently from traditional methods of binding data. Traditional methods combine a template with data received from the engine and then manipulate the DOM each time the data changes. AngularJS compiles the DOM only once and then links the compiled template as necessary, making it much more efficient than traditional methods.

Integrating AngularJS with Existing JavaScript and jQuery

The fact that AngularJS is based on JavaScript and jQuery makes it tempting to simply try to add it to existing applications to provide data binding or other functionality. That approach will almost always end up in problem code that is difficult to maintain. However, using AngularJS doesn't mean that you need to simply toss out your existing code either.

The following steps suggest a method to integrate AngularJS into your existing JavaScript and jQuery applications:

1. Write at least one AngularJS application from the ground up that uses a model, custom HTML directives, services, and controllers. In other words, in this application, ensure that you have a practical comprehension of the AngularJS separation of responsibilities.
2. Identify the model portion of your code. Specifically, try to separate out the code that augments the model data in the model into controller functions and code that accesses the backend model data into services.
3. Identify the code that manipulates DOM elements in the view. Try to separate out the DOM manipulation code into well-defined custom directive components and provide an HTML directive for them. Also identify any of the directives for which AngularJS already provides built-in support.
4. Identify other task-based functions and separate them out into services.

5. Isolate the directives and controllers into modules to organize your code.
6. Use dependency injection to link up your services and modules appropriately.
7. Update the HTML templates to use the new directives.

Obviously, in some instances it just doesn't make sense to use much if any of your existing code. However, by running through the above steps, you will get well into the design phase of implementing a project using AngularJS and can then make an informed decision.

Adding AngularJS to the Node.js Environment

AngularJS is a client-side JavaScript library, which means the only thing you need to do to implement AngularJS in your Node.js environment is to provide a method for the client to get the `angular.js` library file by using a `<script>` tag in the HTML templates.

The simplest method of providing the `angular.js` library is to use the Content Delivery Network (CDN), which provides a URL for downloading the library from a third party. The downside of this method is that you must rely on a third party to serve the library, and if the client cannot connect to that third-party URL, your application will not work. For example, the following `<script>` tag loads the `angular.js` library from Google APIs CDN:

```
<script src="https://ajax.googleapis.com/ajax/libs/angularjs/1.2.5/angular.min.js">
</script>
```

The other method of providing the `angular.js` library is to download it from the AngularJS website (http://angularjs.org) and use Node.js to serve the file to the client. This method takes more effort and also requires extra bandwidth on your webserver; however, it may be a better option if you want more control over how the client obtains the library.

Bootstrapping AngularJS in an HTML Document

To implement AngularJS in your webpages, you need to bootstrap the HTML document. Bootstrapping involves two parts. The first part is to define the application module by using the `ng-app` directive, and the second is to load the `angular.js` library in a `<script>` tag.

The `ng-app` directive tells the AngularJS compiler to treat that element as the root of the compilation. The `ng-app` directive is typically loaded in the `<html>` tag to ensure that the entire webpage is included; however, you could add it to another container element, and only elements inside that container would be included in the AngularJS compilation and consequently in the AngularJS application functionality.

When possible, you should include the `angular.js` library as one of the last tags, if not the last tag, inside the `<body>` of the HTML. When the `angular.js` script is loaded, the compiler kicks off and begins searching for directives. Loading `angular.js` last allows the webpage to load faster.

The following is an example of implementing the `ng-app` and `angular.js` bootstrap in an HTML document:

```
<!doctype html>
<html ng-app="myApp">
  <body>
    <script src="http://code.angularjs.org/1.2.9/angular.min.js"></script>
    <script src="/lib/myApp.js"></script>
  </body>
</html>
```

Using the Global APIs

As you are implementing AngularJS applications, you will find that there are common JavaScript tasks that you need to perform regularly, such as comparing objects, deep copying, iterating through objects, and converting JSON data. AngularJS provides a lot of this basic functionality in the global APIs.

The global APIs are available when the `angular.js` library is loaded, and you can access them by using the `angular` object. For example, to create a deep copy of an object named `myObj`, you use the following syntax:

```
var myCopy = angular.copy(myObj);
```

The following code shows an example of iterating through an array of objects by using the `forEach()` global API:

```
var objArr = [{score: 95}, {score: 98}, {score: 92}];
var scores = [];
angular.forEach(objArr, function(value, key){
  this.push(key + '=' + value);
}, scores);
// scores == ['score=95', 'score=98', 'score=92']
```

Table 20.1 lists some of the most useful utilities provided in the global APIs. You will see these used in a number of examples in this book.

Table 20.1 **Useful global API utilities provided in AngularJS**

Utility	Description
`copy(src, [dst])`	Creates a deep copy of the `src` object or array. If a `dst` parameter is supplied, it is completely overwritten by a deep copy of the source.
`element(element)`	Returns the DOM element specified as a jQuery element. If you have loaded jQuery prior to loading AngularJS, then the object is a full jQuery object; otherwise, it is only a subset of a jQuery object, using the jQuery lite version built into AngularJS.

Utility	Description
`equals(o1, o2)`	Compares `o1` with `o2` and returns `true` if they pass an `===` comparison.
`extend(dst, src)`	Copies all the properties from the `src` object to the `dst` object.
`forEach(obj, iterator, [context])`	Iterates through each object in the `obj` collection, which can be an object or an array. The iterator specifies a function to call, using the following syntax: `function(value, key)` The `context` parameter specifies a JavaScript object that acts as the context, accessible via the `this` keyword, inside the `forEach` loop.
`fromJson(json)`	Returns a JavaScript object from a JSON `string`.
`toJson(obj)`	Returns a JSON string form of the JavaScript object `obj`.
`isArray(value)`	Returns `true` if the `value` parameter passed in is an `Array` object.
`isDate(value)`	Returns `true` if the `value` parameter passed in is a `Date` object.
`isDefined(value)`	Returns `true` if the `value` parameter passed in is a defined object.
`isElement(value)`	Returns `true` if the `value` parameter passed in is a DOM element object or a jQuery element object.
`isFunction(value)`	Returns `true` if the `value` parameter passed in is a JavaScript function.
`isNumber(value)`	Returns `true` if the `value` parameter passed in is a number.
`isObject(value)`	Returns `true` if the `value` parameter passed in is a JavaScript object.
`isString(value)`	Returns `true` if the `value` parameter passed in is a `String` object.
`isUndefined(value)`	Returns `true` if the `value` parameter passed in is not defined.
`lowercase(string)`	Returns a lowercase version of the `string` parameter.
`uppercase(string)`	Returns an uppercase version of the `string` parameter.

Creating a Basic AngularJS Application

Now that you understand the basic components in the AngularJS framework, the intent and design of the AngularJS framework, and how to bootstrap AngularJS, you are ready to get started implementing AngularJS code. This section walks you through a very basic AngularJS application that implements an HTML template, AngularJS module, controller, scope, and expression.

The first step is to implement a basic Node.js webserver. The code in Listing 20.1 shows a basic Node.js webserver that serves static files that serve the following routes:

- **/static**: Maps to `./static` in the project directory and contains the HTML documents to be served statically.
- **/static/js**: Contains the necessary JavaScript for the examples.
- **/static/css**: Contains the necessary CSS for the examples.
- **/images**: Maps to `../images` from the project directory and serves any images used in examples.

The basic static server in Listing 20.1 is used in the AngularJS examples in the following chapters.

Listing 20.1 `node_server.js`: **A basic Node.js static webserver**

```
var express = require('express');
var app = express();
app.use('/', express.static('./static')).
    use('/images', express.static( '../images')).
    use('/lib', express.static( '../lib'));
app.listen(80);
```

The next step is to implement an AngularJS HTML template, such as `first.html` in Listing 20.2, and an AngularJS JavaScript module, such as `first.js` in Listing 20.3.

The following sections describe the important steps in implementing the AngularJS application and the code involved in each step. Each of these steps is described in much more detail in later chapters, so don't get bogged down in them here. What is important at this point is that you understand the process of implementing the template, module, controller, and scope and generally how they interact with each other.

The webpage defined by Listing 20.2 and 20.3 is a simple web form that allows you to type in first and last names and then click a button to display a message, as shown in Figure 20.1.

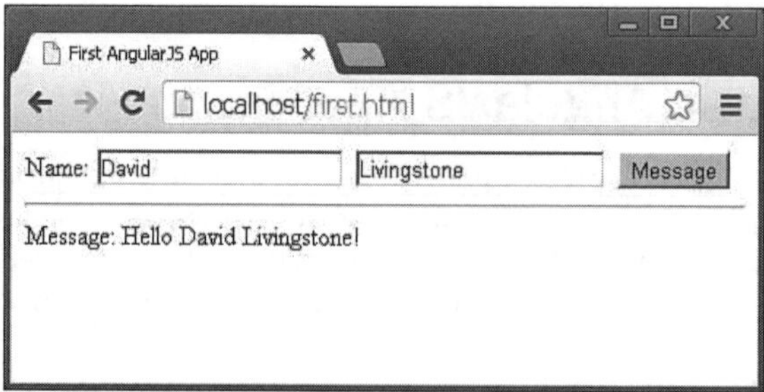

Figure 20.1 Implementing a basic AngularJS web application that uses inputs and a button to manipulate the model and consequently the view.

Loading the AngularJS Library and Your Main Module

Before you can implement an AngularJS application, you need to get the library loaded in an HTML template. The following lines in Listing 20.2 load the `angular.js` library and then load the `first.js` JavaScript custom module.

```
15      <script src="http://code.angularjs.org/1.2.9/angular.min.js"></script>
16      <script src="/js/first.js"></script>
```

Defining the AngularJS Application Root Element

The next step is to define the `ng-app` parameter in the root element so that AngularJS knows where to begin compiling the application. You should also define the module in your JavaScript code to provide a namespace to use when adding controllers, filters, and services.

Line 2 of Listing 20.2 defines the DOM root for an AngularJS module. Notice that `ng-app` is assigned the module name `firstApp`, which corresponds to the module in the JavaScript code:

```
02 <html ng-app="firstApp">
```

Line 1 in Listing 20.3 shows the `firstApp` module object being created in the JavaScript code:

```
01 var firstApp = angular.module('firstApp', []);
```

Adding a Controller to the Template

Next, you need to add a controller for HTML elements that you want the AngularJS module to control. You also need to define the controller in your module code.

Line 7 in Listing 20.2 assigns a controller named `FirstController` to a `<div>` element. This maps the element in the view to a specific controller, which contains a scope:

```
07      <div ng-controller="FirstController">
```

Line 2 in Listing 20.3 shows the `FirstController` code being added to the `firstApp` module:

```
02 firstApp.controller('FirstController', function($scope) {
```

Implementing the Scope Model

Once the controller has been defined, you can implement the scope, which involves linking HTML elements to scope variables, initializing the variables in the scope, and providing functionality to handle changes to the scope values.

Lines 9 and 10 in Listing 20.2 are `<input>` elements that are assigned to the `first` and `last` values in the scope. These elements provide a method to update the scope from the browser. If the user types in the input, the scope is also updated:

```
09        <input type="text" ng-model="first">
10        <input type="text" ng-model="last">
```

Lines 3–5 in Listing 20.3 show the initial values of the scope being defined:

```
03    $scope.first = 'Some';
04    $scope.last = 'One';
05    $scope.heading = 'Message: ';
```

Line 11 in Listing 20.2 links a click handler to the `updateMessage()` function defined in the scope:

```
11        <button ng-click='updateMessage()'>Message</button>
```

Lines 6–8 in Listing 20.3 show the `updateMessage()` definition in the scope:

```
06    $scope.updateMessage = function() {
07      $scope.message = 'Hello ' + $scope.first +' '+ $scope.last + '!';
08    };
```

Line 13 implements an expression that displays the value of the `heading` and `message` variables in the scope on the HTML page:

```
13        {{heading + message}}
```

Listing 20.2 `first.html`: **A simple AngularJS template that provides two input elements and a button to interact with the model**

```
01 <!doctype html>
02 <html ng-app="firstApp">
03   <head>
04     <title>First AngularJS App</title>
05   </head>
06   <body>
07     <div ng-controller="FirstController">
08       <span>Name:</span>
09       <input type="text" ng-model="first">
10       <input type="text" ng-model="last">
11       <button ng-click='updateMessage()'>Message</button>
12       <hr>
13       {{heading + message}}
14     </div>
15     <script src="http://code.angularjs.org/1.2.9/angular.min.js"></script>
16     <script src="/js/first.js"></script>
17   </body>
18 </html>
```

Listing 20.3 `first.js`: **A simple AngularJS module that implements a controller to support the template in Listing 20.2**

```
var firstApp = angular.module('firstApp', []);
firstApp.controller('FirstController', function($scope) {
  $scope.first = 'Some';
  $scope.last = 'One';
  $scope.heading = 'Message: ';
  $scope.updateMessage = function() {
    $scope.message = 'Hello ' + $scope.first +' '+ $scope.last + '!';
  };
});
```

Summary

AngularJS is a JavaScript library framework that provides a very structured method for creating websites and web applications. AngularJS structures a web application into a very clean MVC-styled approach. The scope acts as the model for the application and is made up of basic JavaScript objects. AngularJS utilizes templates with directives that extend HTML capabilities, allowing you to implement totally customized HTML components.

In this chapter you've looked at the different components in an AngularJS application and how they interact with each other. You've also learned about the life cycle of an AngularJS application, which involves bootstrap, compilation, and runtime phases. At the end of this chapter, you walked through a step-by-step example of implementing a basic AngularJS application, including a template, module, controller, and scope.

Up Next

In the next chapter you'll learn more about modules and dependency injection. You will learn how to define providers as part of a module and then how to inject the functionality included in a provider into other modules and AngularJS components.

21

Understanding AngularJS Modules and Dependency Injection

One of the most important aspects of AngularJS to understand is dependency injection and how it relates to modules. Dependency is a common concept across many server-side languages but has not really been implemented much in JavaScript until AngularJS.

Dependency injection allows AngularJS modules to maintain a very clean, organized form and yet more easily access functionality from other modules. When implemented correctly, it also tends to reduce the amount of code by a considerable amount.

This chapter provides a basic overview of dependency injection and then describes how to create modules that provide functionality and how to consume that functionality in other modules as well as other AngularJS components, such as controllers.

Overview of Modules and Dependency Injection

As you begin writing AngularJS applications, it is vital that you understand the basics of modules and dependency injection in the AngularJS world. This seems to be a difficult concept to grasp and implement correctly for some, especially those coming from a more open, anything-goes JavaScript background.

This section introduces you to the concepts behind AngularJS modules and dependency injection. Understanding how modules utilize dependency injection to access functionality in other modules will make it easier for you to implement your code inside the AngularJS framework.

Understanding Modules

AngularJS modules are containers that allow you to compartmentalize and organize your code into concise, clean, reusable chunks. Modules themselves do not provide direct functionality, but they contain instances of other objects, such as controllers, filters, services, animations, etc. that do.

You build a module by defining the objects it provides. Then, by linking together modules through dependency injection, you build a full application.

AngularJS is built on the module principle. Most of the functionality provided by AngularJS is built into a module named `ng`, which contains most of the directives and services used throughout this book.

Dependency Injection

Dependency injection can be a difficult concept to fully grasp. However, once you understand the basics, the AngularJS implementation becomes quite clear. Dependency injection is a well-known design pattern in many server-side languages but has not been used much in JavaScript before now.

The idea of AngularJS dependency injection is to define and dynamically inject a dependency object into another object, making available all the functionality provided by the dependency object. AngularJS provides dependency injection through the use of providers and an injector service.

A provider is essentially a definition of how to create an instance of an object with all the necessary functionality. Providers should be defined as part of an AngularJS module. A module registers the provider with the injector server. Only one instance of a provider's object is ever created in the AngularJS application.

The injector service is responsible for keeping track of instances of provider objects. An injector service instance is created for each module that registers a provider. When a dependency request is made for a provider object, the injector service first checks whether an instance already exists in the injector cache. If so, that instance is used. If no instance is found in the cache, then a new instance is created using the provider definition, stored in the cache, and then returned.

Defining AngularJS Modules

Now that you understand the relationship between modules and dependency injection, you need to look at the process of implementing AngularJS modules. AngularJS modules are implemented in two phases: the configuration phase and the run phase. The following sections discuss these phases and the basic process of adding providers to an AngularJS module.

Creating an AngularJS `Module` Object

Creating AngularJS modules is a simple process that involves calling the `angular.module()` method. This method creates an instance of a `Module` object, registers it with the injector service, and then returns an instance of the newly created `Module` object that you can use to implement provider functionality. The `angular.module()` method uses the following syntax:

```
angular.module(name, [requires], [configFn])
```

The `name` parameter is the name under which the module is registered in the injector service. The `requires` parameter is an array of names of modules that are added to the injector service for this module to use. If you need functionality from another module, you need to add it in the `requires` list. The `ng` module is automatically added to every module instantiated by default, so you have access to the AngularJS providers without explicitly specifying `ng` in the list.

Instances of all dependencies are automatically injected into an instance of a module. Dependencies can be modules, services, and any other objects registered in the injector service. The `configFn` parameter is another function that is called during the module configuration phase. Configuration functions are described in the next section.

The following is an example of creating an AngularJS module with dependencies on the `$window` and `$http` services. The definition also includes a configuration function that adds a `value` provider named `myValue`:

```
var myModule = angular.module('myModule', ['$window', '$http'], function(){
    $provide.value('myValue', 'Some Value');
});
```

If you do not specify a `requires` parameter, then instead of a `Module` object being created, the already created instance is returned. For example, the following code overwrites the instance defined above:

```
var myModule2 = angular.module('myModule', []);
```

However, the following code returns the instance created above because no dependencies are listed in the `require` array in the parameters list:

```
var myModule3 = angular.module('myModule');
```

Using Configuration Blocks

The AngularJS module configuration phase is executed when a module is being defined. During this phase, any providers are registered with the dependency injector. You should put only configuration and provider code inside the configuration block.

You implement the configuration block by calling the `config()` method on the instance of the `Module` object, using the following syntax:

```
config(function([injectable, . . .]))
```

A function with the `injectable` parameters is passed in. The `injectable` parameters are typically provider services functions such as `$provide`.

The following is an example of a basic configuration block:

```
var myModule = angular.module('myModule', []).
  config(function($provide, $filterProvider) {
    $provide.value("startTime", new Date());
    $filterProvider.register('myFilter', function(){});
});
```

Notice that the `$provide` and `$filterProvider` services are passed into the `config` function. They are used to register a value provider named `startTime` and a filter provider named `myFilter` with the injector service.

Using Run Blocks

Once an entire configuration block has finished, the run phase of an AngularJS module can execute. During this phase, you can implement any code necessary to instantiate the module. You cannot implement any provider code during the run block because the entire module should already be configured and registered with the dependency injector by this point.

The `run` block is implemented by calling the `run()` method of the `Module` object, using the following syntax:

```
run(function([injectable, . . .]))
```

A function with the instance `injectable` parameters is passed in. The `injectable` parameters should only be instances of injectors because configuration should already have been completed.

The following is a basic implementation of the `run` block continued from the example above:

```
myModule.run(function(startTime) {
  startTime.setTime((new Date()).getTime());
});
```

Notice that the `startTime` instance defined in the `config()` section above is passed into the `run()` function. This allows the `run()` function to update the `startTime` provider to a new value.

Adding Providers to AngularJS Modules

The `Module` object provides several helper methods for adding providers as an alternative to using the `config()` method. These methods are simpler to use and clearer in your code. You can add two types of provider objects to AngularJS modules. Each of these methods accepts two parameters: the name that will be registered with the dependency injector and the provider function that defines how to build the specific object. The following sections describe these methods in more detail.

Specialized AngularJS Object Providers

The `Module` object provides special constructor methods to add providers for the AngularJS objects that you need to implement in your modules. These specialized methods allow you to add definitions for the following types of objects:

- **`animation(name, animationFactory)`**
- **`controller(name, controllerFactory)`**
- **`filter(name, filterFactory)`**
- **`directive(name, directiveFactory)`**

The reason these are specialized methods is that there are corresponding `animation`, `controller`, `filter`, and `directive` objects defined in AngularJS for these provider methods.

Each of these objects is covered in more detail in later chapters. For now, here's a quick look at a basic controller definition:

```
var mod = angular.module('myMod', []);
mod.controller('myController', function($scope) {
  $scope.someValue = 'Some Value';
});
```

A simple module named `mod` is created, and then the `controller()` method is called and passed in `myController` along with a `controllerFactory` function. The `controllerFactory` function accepts the `$scope` variable as a parameter. This is because AngularJS has a built-in controller object and knows that all controller objects must receive a scope object as the first parameter.

Service Providers

The service providers are a unique category of providers because there is not already a specific format for the resulting provider objects. Instead, a provider acts as a service to provide functionality. AngularJS provides some specific creation methods for building services and exposes them through the following methods:

- **`value(name, object)`**: This is the most basic of all providers. The `object` parameter is simply assigned to `name`, so there is a direct correlation in the injector between the `name` value and the `object` value.
- **`constant(name, object)`**: This is similar to the `value()` method, but the value is not changeable. Also, `constant()` methods are applied before other provider methods.
- **`factory(name, factoryFunction)`**: This method uses the `factoryFunction` parameter to build an object that will be provided by the injector.
- **`service(name, serviceFactory)`**: This method adds the concept of implementing a more object-oriented approach to the provider object. Much of the built-in functionality of AngularJS is provided through service providers.

- **provider(name, providerFactory):** This method is the core for all the other methods. Although it provides the most functionality, it is not used frequently because the other methods are simpler.

Later chapters cover these objects in more detail. For now, here's a quick example of some basic value and constant definitions:

```
var mod = angular.module('myMod', []);
mod.constant("cID", "ABC");
mod.value('counter', 0);
mod.value('image', {name:'box.jpg', height:12, width:20});
```

A simple module named mod is created, and then the constant() and two value() providers are defined. The values defined in these methods are registered in the injector server for the myMod module and are then accessible by name.

Implementing Dependency Injection

Once you have defined a module and appropriate providers, you can add the module as a dependency to other modules, controllers, and a variety of other AngularJS objects. You need to set the value of the $inject property of the object that depends on the providers. The $inject property contains an array of provider names that should be injected into it.

For example, the following code defines a basic controller that accepts the $scope and appMsg parameters. Then the $inject property is set to an array that contains $scope, which is the AngularJS scope service that provides access to the scope and a custom appMsg. Both $scope and appMsg are injected into the myController function:

```
var myController = function($scope, appMsg) {
  $scope.message = appMsg;
};
controller['$inject'] = ['$scope', 'appMsg'];
myApp.myController('controllerA', controller);
```

This method can become a bit clumsy when you're implementing certain objects, so AngularJS also provides a bit more elegant method for injecting the dependencies, using the following syntax in place of the normal constructor function:

```
[providerA, providerB, . . ., function(objectA, objectB, . . .) {} ]
```

For example, the above code can also be written as:

```
myApp.controller('controllerA', ['$scope', 'appMsg', function($scope, appMsg) {
  $scope.message = appMsg;
}]);
```

Listing 21.1 shows how to implement dependency injection with two modules, each with a value provider and a controller. Lines 2 and 7 add the value providers. Lines 3 and 8 use dependency injection to inject the value providers into the controllers for each module.

Notice in line 6 that the definition for the `myApp` module includes the `myMod` module in its dependency list. This injects `myMod`, including the `controllerB` functionality, enclosed inside.

Listing 21.2 shows HTML that implements the `myApp` module as the AngularJS application. Notice that it uses both the `controllerA` and `controllerB` controllers. They can be used because the `myMod` module was injected into the `myApp` module. Figure 21.1 shows the resulting webpage, with a different message from each module's controller.

Listing 21.1 `injector.js`: **Implementing dependency injection in controller and module definitions**

```
01 var myMod = angular.module('myMod', []);
02 myMod.value('modMsg', 'Hello from My Module');
03 myMod.controller('controllerB', ['$scope', 'modMsg',
04                                  function($scope, msg) {
05   $scope.message = msg;
06 }]);
07 var myApp = angular.module('myApp', ['myMod']);
08 myApp.value('appMsg', 'Hello from My App');
09 myApp.controller('controllerA', ['$scope', 'appMsg',
10                                  function($scope, msg) {
11   $scope.message = msg;
12 }]);
```

Listing 21.2 `injector.html`: **Using HTML code to implement an AngularJS module that depends on another module**

```
<!doctype html>
<html ng-app="myApp">
  <head>
    <title>AngularJS Dependency Injection</title>
  </head>
  <body>
    <div ng-controller="controllerA">
      <h2>Application Message:</h2>
      {{message}}
    </div><hr>
    <div ng-controller="controllerB">
      <h2>Module Message:</h2>
      {{message}}
    </div>
    <script src="http://code.angularjs.org/1.2.9/angular.min.js"></script>
```

```
    <script src="/js/injector.js"></script>
  </body>
</html>
```

Figure 21.1 Implementing dependency injection to provide additional functionality to modules and controllers.

Summary

Dependency injection allows you to define provider functionality that can be injected into other AngularJS components. The provider functionality is contained inside modules and registered with an injector service. Providers define how to build the functionality so that when another component defines a dependency on a provider, an instance of the provider object can be created and injected.

AngularJS provides a fairly robust dependency injection model that allows you to define different types of service providers. Using dependency injection rather than global definitions makes your code more modularized and easier to maintain. In this chapter you've been introduced to the dependency injection model and have seen how to implement it in both modules and a controller component.

Up Next

In the next chapter you'll get a deeper look at scopes and how to apply events within them. You will be introduced to the controller functionality and how it relates to scopes. You'll also learn how to nest scopes to more closely match your model with your view.

22

Implementing the Scope as a Data Model

One of the most important aspects of an AngularJS application is scope. Scope not only provides the data represented in a model but also binds together all the other components of the AngularJS application, such as modules, controllers, services, and templates. This chapter explains the relationships between scope and other AngularJS components.

Scope provides the binding mechanism that allows DOM elements and other code to be updated when changes occur in the model data. In this chapter you will learn about scope hierarchies and how to communicate between them via events.

Understanding Scopes

In AngularJS, the scope acts as a data model for an application. It is one of the most critical parts of any application that relies on data in any fashion because it acts as the glue that binds together the views, business logic, and server-side data. Understanding how scopes work enables you to design your AngularJS applications to be more efficient, use less code, and be easier to follow.

The following sections discuss the relationships between scope and applications, controllers, templates, and server-side data. There is also a section that covers the life cycle of scope, to help you see how scope is built, manipulated, and updated during the application life cycle.

The Relationship Between the Root Scope and Applications

When an application is bootstrapped, a root scope is created. The root scope stores data at the application level, and you can access it by using the `$rootScope` service. The root scope data should be initialized in the `run()` block of the module, but you can also access it in components of the module. To illustrate this, the following code defines a value at the root scope level and then accesses it in a controller:

```
angular.module('myApp', [])
.run(function($rootScope) {
    $rootScope.rootValue = 5;
})
.controller('myController', function($scope, $rootScope) {
  $scope.value = 10;
  $scope.difference = function() {
        return $rootScope.rootValue - $scope.value;
    };
});
```

The Relationship Between Scopes and Controllers

Controllers are pieces of code that are intended to provide business logic by augmenting scope. You create controllers by using the `controller()` method on the `Model` object of an application. This function registers a controller as a provider in the module, but it does not create an instance of the controller. That occurs when the `ng-controller` directive is linked in an AngularJS template.

The `controller()` method accepts the controller name as the first parameter and an array of dependencies as the second parameter. For example, the following code defines a controller that uses dependency injection to access a `value` provider named `start`:

```
angular.module('myApp', []).
  value('start', 200).
  controller('Counter', ['$scope', 'start',
                        function($scope, startingValue) {
  }]);
```

When a new instance of a controller is created in AngularJS, a new child scope specific to that controller is also created and accessible via the `$scope` service that is injected into the `Counter` controller above. Also in the example above, the start provider is injected into the controller and passed to the controller function as `startingValue`.

The controller must initialize the state of a scope that is created and added to it. The controller is also responsible for any business logic attached to that scope. This can mean handling update changes to the scope, manipulating scope values, or emitting events based on the state of the scope.

Listing 22.1 shows how to implement a controller that utilizes dependency injection, initializes some values, and implements rudimentary business logic, using `inc()`, `dec()`, and `calcDiff()` functions.

Listing 22.1 **scope_controller.js: Implementing a basic controller that uses dependency injection, initializes scope values, and implements business logic**

```
angular.module('myApp', []).
  value('start', 200).
  controller('Counter', ['$scope', 'start',
                        function($scope, start) {
    $scope.start = start;
    $scope.current = start;
    $scope.difference = 0;
    $scope.change = 1;
    $scope.inc = function() {
      $scope.current += $scope.change;
      $scope.calcDiff();
    };
    $scope.dec = function() {
      $scope.current -= $scope.change;
      $scope.calcDiff();
    };
    $scope.calcDiff = function() {
      $scope.difference = $scope.current - $scope.start;
    };
  }]);
```

The Relationship Between Scopes and Templates

Templates provide the view for an AngularJS application. HTML elements are defined as controllers, using the `ng-controller` attribute. Inside a controller HTML element and its children, the scope for that controller is available for expressions and other AngularJS functionality.

Values in a scope can be directly linked to the values of `<input>`, `<select>`, and `<textarea>` elements in the template, using the `ng-model` directive. This directive links the value of an element to a property name in the scope. When the user changes the value of the input element, the scope is automatically updated. For example, the following links the value of a number of `<input>` element to the scope named `valueA`:

```
<input type="number" ng-model="valueA" />
```

You can add scope properties and even functions to expressions in a template by using the `{{expression}}` syntax. The code inside the brackets is evaluated, and the results are displayed in the rendered view. For example, if a scope contains properties named `valueA` and `valueB`, you can reference these properties in an expression in the template as shown below:

```
{{valueA + valueB}}
```

You can also use scope properties and functions when defining AngularJS directives in a template. For example, the `ng-click` directive binds the browser click event to a function in a scope named `addValues()` and passes the values of properties `valueA` and `valueB` in the scope:

```
<span ng-click="addValues(valueA, valueB")>Add Values{{valueA}} & {{valueB}}</span>
```

Notice that in this code, the `{{}}` brackets are required. However, in the `addValues()` function call they are not required. That is because `ng-click` and other AngularJS directives automatically evaluate as expressions.

The code in Listing 22.2 and Listing 22.3 puts all these concepts together in a very basic example to make it easy to understand the relationship between the model and scope. Listing 22.2 implements a controller named `SimpleTemplate` that initializes a scope with three values: `valueA`, `valueB`, and `valueC`. The scope also contains a function named `addValues()` that accepts two parameters and adds them together to set the value of `$scope.valueC`.

Listing 22.3 implements a template that initializes the `SimpleTemplate` controller defined in Listing 22.2. Lines 8 and 9 link the scope properties `valueA` and `valueB` to `<input>` elements by using `ng-model`. Line 10 adds `valueA` and `valueB` in the scope to display the added value.

Lines 11 and 12 implement an `<input>` element that uses `ng-click` to bind the browser click event to the `addValues()` function in the scope. Notice that `valueA` and `valueB` are passed in as parameters to the function.

Figure 22.1 shows this simple application in a web browser. As the two input elements are changed, the expressions change automatically. However, the `valueC` expression changes only when the `Click to Add Values` element is clicked.

Listing 22.2 **`scope_template.js`: Implementing a basic controller to support template functionality**

```
angular.module('myApp', []).
  controller('SimpleTemplate', function($scope) {
    $scope.valueA = 5;
    $scope.valueB = 7;
    $scope.valueC = 12;
    $scope.addValues = function(v1, v2) {
      var v = angular.$rootScope;
      $scope.valueC = v1 + v2;
    };
  });
```

Listing 22.3 **`scope_template.html`: HTML template code that implements a controller and various HTML fields linked to the scope**

```
<!doctype html>
<html ng-app="myApp">
  <head>
    <title>AngularJS Scope and Templates</title>
  </head>
  <body>
    <div ng-controller="SimpleTemplate">
      ValueA: <input type="number" ng-model="valueA" /><br>
      ValueB: <input type="number" ng-model="valueB" /><br><br>
      Expression Value: {{valueA + valueB}}<br><br>
      <input type="button" ng-click="addValues(valueA, valueB)"
        value ="Click to Add Values {{valueA}} & {{valueB}}" /><br>
      Clicked Value: {{valueC}}<br>
    </div>
    <script src="http://code.angularjs.org/1.2.9/angular.min.js"></script>
    <script src="/js/scope_template.js"></script>
  </body>
</html>
```

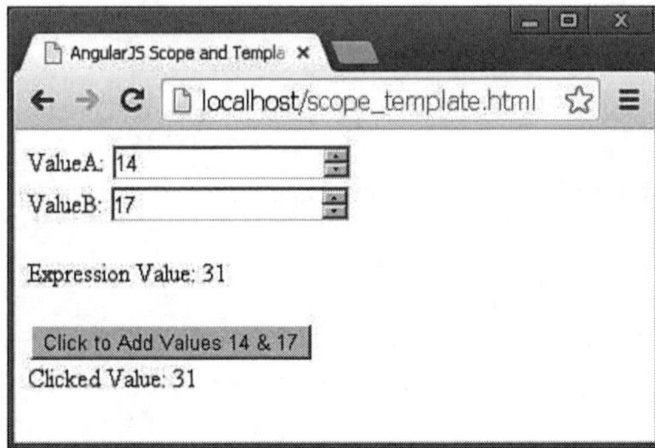

Figure 22.1 A basic AngularJS template that implements a controller and links several fields to the scope to provide both input of values and displayed results.

The Relationship Between Scope and Backend Server Data

Often data that is used for an AngularJS application comes from a backend data source such as a database. In such instances, the scope still acts as the definitive source of data for the AngularJS application. You should use the following rules when interacting with data that is coming from the server side:

- Access data from the database or other backend sources via AngularJS services, which are discussed in a later chapter. This includes both reading and updating data.
- Ensure that data read from the server updates the scope, which in turn updates the view. Avoid the temptation to manipulate the HTML values directly from the database, which can lead to the scope becoming out of sync with the view.
- Reflect changes that are made to the database or other backend source in scope as well. You can do this by first updating the scope and then updating the database using a service, or you can update the database and then use the results from the database to repopulate the appropriate values in the scope.

The Scope Life Cycle

Scope data goes through a life cycle while the application is loaded in the browser. Understanding this life cycle will help you understand the interaction between scope and other AngularJS components, especially templates.

Scope data goes through the following life cycle phases:

1. Creation
2. Watcher registration
3. Model mutation
4. Mutation observation
5. Scope destruction

These life cycle phases are described in the sections below.

The Creation Phase

The creation phase occurs when a scope is initialized. Bootstrapping the application creates a root scope. Linking the template creates child scopes when `ng-controller` or `ng-repeat` directives are encountered.

Also during the creation phase, a digest loop is created that interacts with the browser event loop. The digest loop is responsible for updating DOM elements with changes made to the model as well as executing any registered watcher functions. Although you should never need to execute a digest loop manually, you can do so by executing the `$digest()` method on the scope. For example, the following evaluates any asynchronous changes and then executes the watch functions on the scope:

```
$scope.$digest()
```

The Watcher Registration Phase

The template linking phase registers watches for values in the scope that are represented in the template. These watches propagate model changes automatically to the DOM elements.

You can also register your own watch functions on a scope value by using the `$watch()` method. This method accepts a scope property name as the first parameter and then a callback function as the second parameter. The old and new values are passed to the callback function when the property is changed in the scope.

For example, the following adds a watch to the property `watchedItem` in the scope and increments a counter each time it is changed:

```
$scope.watchedItem = 'myItem';
$scope.counter = 0;
$scope.$watch('name', function(newValue, oldValue) {
  $scope.watchedItem = $scope.counter + 1;
});
```

The Model Mutation Phase

The model mutation phase occurs when data in the scope changes. When you make changes in your AngularJS code, a scope function called `$apply()` updates the model and calls the `$digest()` function to update the DOM and watches. This is how changes made in your AngularJS controllers or by the `$http`, `$timeout`, and `$interval` services are automatically updated in the DOM.

You should always try to make changes to scope inside the AngularJS controller or those services. However, if you must make changes to the scope outside the AngularJS realm, you need to call `scope.$apply()` on the scope to force the model and DOM to be updated correctly. The `$apply()` method accepts an expression as the only parameter. The expression is evaluated and returned, and the `$digest()` method is called to update the DOM and watches.

The Mutation Observation Phase

The mutation observation phase occurs when the `$digest()` method is executed by the digest loop, an `$apply()` call, or manually. When `$digest()` executes, it evaluates all watches for changes. If a value has changed, `$digest()` calls the `$watch` listener and updates the DOM.

The Scope Destruction Phase

The `$destroy()` method removes scopes from the browser memory. The AngularJS libraries automatically call this method when child scopes are no longer needed. The `$destroy()` method stops `$digest()` calls and removes watches, allowing the memory to be reclaimed by the browser garbage collector.

Implementing Scope Hierarchy

A great feature of scopes is that they are organized in a hierarchy. The hierarchy helps you keep scopes organized and relevant to the context of the view they represent. Also, the `$digest()` method uses the scope hierarchy to propagate scope changes to the appropriate watchers and the DOM elements.

Scope hierarchies are created automatically based on the location of `ng-controller` statements in the AngularJS template. For example, the following template code defines two `<div>` elements that create instances of controllers that are siblings:

```
<div ng-controller="controllerA"> . . . </div>
<div ng-controller="controllerB"> . . . </div>
```

However, the following template code defines controllers where `controllerA` is the parent of `controllerB`:

```
<div ng-controller="controllerA">
  <div ng-controller="controllerB"> . . . </div>
</div>
```

You can access the values of parent scopes from a controller, but you can't access the values of sibling or children scopes. If you add a property name in a child scope, it does not overwrite the parent but creates a property of the same name in the child scope that has a different value from the parent.

Listings 22.4 and 22.5 implement a basic scope hierarchy to demonstrate how scopes work in a hierarchy. Listing 22.4 creates an application with three controllers, each with two scope items defined. They all share the common scope property `title` and the scope properties `valueA`, `valueB`, and `valueC`.

Listing 22.5 creates the three controllers in an AngularJS template. Figure 22.2 shows the rendered AngularJS application. Notice that the value of the `title` property in all three scopes is different. That is because a new `title` property is created for each level in the hierarchy.

Lines 17–19 display the `valueA`, `valueB`, and `valueC` properties. These values are read from three different levels in the scope hierarchy. The application shows that as you increment the value in the parent scope, a DOM element in a child controller is updated with the new value.

Listing 22.4 **`scope_hierarchy.js`: Implementing a basic scope hierarchy with access to properties at each level**

```
01 angular.module('myApp', []).
02   controller('LevelA', function($scope) {
03     $scope.title = "Level A"
04     $scope.valueA = 1;
05     $scope.inc = function() {
06       $scope.valueA++;
07     };
08   }).
09   controller('LevelB', function($scope) {
10     $scope.title = "Level B"
11     $scope.valueB = 1;
```

```
    $scope.inc = function() {
      $scope.valueB++;
    };
  }).
  controller('LevelC', function($scope) {
    $scope.title = "Level C"
    $scope.valueC = 1;
    $scope.inc = function() {
      $scope.valueC++;
    };
  });
```

Listing 22.5 **`scope_hierarchy.html`: HTML template code that implements a hierarchy of controllers and renders results from the multiple levels of scope**

```
<!doctype html>
<html ng-app="myApp">
<head>
<title>AngularJS Scope Hierarchy</title>
</head>
<body>
  <div ng-controller="LevelA">
    <h3>{{title}}</h3>
    ValueA = {{valueA}} <input type="button" ng-click="inc()" value="+" />
    <div ng-controller="LevelB"><hr>
      <h3>{{title}}</h3>
      ValueA = {{valueA}}<br>
      ValueB = {{valueB}}
      <input type="button" ng-click="inc()" value="+" />
      <div ng-controller="LevelC"><hr>
       <h3>{{title}}</h3>
        ValueA = {{valueA}}<br>
        ValueB = {{valueB}}<br>
        ValueC = {{valueC}}
        <input type="button" ng-click="inc()" value="+" />
      </div>
    </div>
  </div>
  <script src="http://code.angularjs.org/1.2.9/angular.min.js"></script>
  <script src="/js/scope_hierarchy.js"></script>
</body>
</html>
```

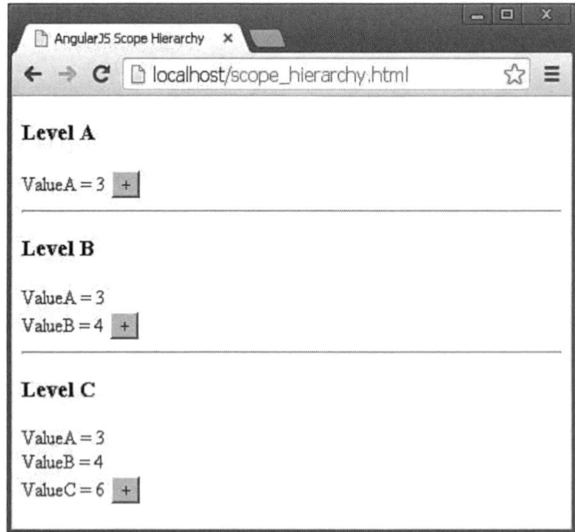

Figure 22.2 Implementing a hierarchy of controllers that render results from the multiple levels of scope.

Emitting and Broadcasting Events

A great feature of scopes is the ability to emit and broadcast events within the scope hierarchy. Events allow you to send notification to different levels in the scope that an event has occurred. Events can be anything you choose, such as a value changed or threshold reached. This is extremely useful in many situations, such as letting child scopes know that a value has changed in a parent scope or vice versa.

To emit an event from a scope, you use the `$emit()` method. This method sends an event upward through the parent scope hierarchy. Any ancestor scopes that have registered for the event are notified. The `$emit()` method uses the following syntax, where `name` is the event name and `args` is zero or more arguments to pass to the event handler functions:

```
scope.$emit(name, [args, . . .])
```

You can also broadcast an event downward through the child scope hierarchy by using the `$broadcast()` method. Any descendent scopes that have registered for the event are notified. The `$broadcast()` method uses the following syntax, where `name` is the event name and `args` is zero or more arguments to pass to the event handler functions:

```
scope.$broadcast(name, [args, . . .])
```

To handle an event that is emitted or broadcasted, you use the `$on()` method. The `$on()` method uses the following syntax, where `name` is the name of the event to listen for:

```
scope.$on(name, listener)
```

The `listener` parameter is a function that accepts the event as the first parameter and any arguments passed by the `$emit()` or `$broadcast()` method as subsequent parameters. The `event` object has the following properties:

- **targetScope:** The scope from which `$emit()` or `$broadcast()` was called.
- **currentScope:** The scope that is currently handling the event.
- **name:** The name of the event.
- **stopPropagation():** A function that stops the event from being propagated up or down the scope hierarchy.
- **preventDefault():** A function that prevents default behavior in a browser event but only executes your own custom code.
- **defaultPrevented:** A Boolean that is `true` if `event.preventDefault()` has been called.

Listings 22.6 and 22.7 illustrate the use of `$emit()`, `$broadcast()`, and `$on()` to send and handle events up and down the scope hierarchy. In Listing 22.6, lines 2–15 implement a parent scope called `Characters`, and lines 16–28 define a child scope named `Character`.

Also in Listing 22.6, `changeName()` function changes the `currentName` value and then broadcasts a `CharacterChanged` event. The `CharacterChanged` event is handled in lines 22–24, using the `$on()` method, and sets the `currentInfo` value in the scope, which will update the page elements.

Notice that line 6 of Listing 22.6 uses the `this` keyword to access the `name` property. The `name` property actually comes from a dynamic child scope that was created because the following directives were used to generate multiple elements in Listing 22.7. The child scope can be accessed from the `changeName()` method in the scope by using the `this` keyword:

```
ng-repeat="name in names"
ng-click="changeName()"
```

Lines 9–14 of Listing 22.6 implement a handler for the `CharacterDeleted` event that removes the character `name` from the `names` property. The child controller in line 27 broadcasts this event via `$broadcast()`.

The AngularJS template code in Listing 22.7 implements the nested `ng-controller` statements, which generates the scope hierarchy and displays scope values for the characters. This code also includes some very basic CSS styling to make spans look like buttons and to position elements on the page. Figure 22.3 shows the resulting webpage. As you click a character name, information about that character is displayed, and when you click the Delete button, the character is deleted from the buttons and the Info section.

Listing 22.6 **`scope_events.js`: Implementing `$emit()` and `$broadcast()` events within the scope hierarchy**

```
angular.module('myApp', []).
  controller('Characters', function($scope) {
    $scope.names = ['Frodo', 'Aragorn', 'Legolas', 'Gimli'];
    $scope.currentName = $scope.names[0];
    $scope.changeName = function() {
      $scope.currentName = this.name;
      $scope.$broadcast('CharacterChanged', this.name);
    };
    $scope.$on('CharacterDeleted', function(event, removeName){
      var i = $scope.names.indexOf(removeName);
      $scope.names.splice(i, 1);
      $scope.currentName = $scope.names[0];
      $scope.$broadcast('CharacterChanged', $scope.currentName);
    });
  }).
  controller('Character', function($scope) {
    $scope.info = {'Frodo':{weapon:'Sting', race:'Hobbit'},
                   'Aragorn':{weapon:'Sword', race:'Man'},
                   'Legolas':{weapon:'Bow', race:'Elf'},
                   'Gimli':{weapon:'Axe', race:'Dwarf'}};
    $scope.currentInfo = $scope.info['Frodo'];
    $scope.$on('CharacterChanged', function(event, newCharacter){
      $scope.currentInfo = $scope.info[newCharacter];
    });
    $scope.deleteChar = function() {
      delete $scope.info[$scope.currentName];
      $scope.$emit('CharacterDeleted', $scope.currentName);
    };
  });
```

Listing 22.7 **`scope_events.html`: HTML template code that renders the scope hierarchy for Listing 22.6 controllers**

```
<!doctype html>
<html ng-app="myApp">
  <head>
    <title>AngularJS Scope Events</title>
    <style>
      div{padding:5px; font: 18px bold;}
      span{padding:3px; margin:12px; border:5px ridge;
           cursor:pointer;}
      label{padding:2px; margin:5px; font: 15px bold;}
      p{padding-left:22px; margin:5px; }
    </style>
```

```
  </head>
  <body>
    <div ng-controller="Characters">
      <span ng-repeat="name in names"
            ng-click="changeName()">{{name}}</span>
      <div ng-controller="Character"><hr>
        <label>Name: </label><p>{{currentName}}</p>
        <label>Race: </label><p>{{currentInfo.race}}</p>
        <label>Weapon: </label><p>{{currentInfo.weapon}}</p>
        <span ng-click="deleteChar()">Delete</span>
      </div>
    </div>
    <script src="http://code.angularjs.org/1.2.9/angular.min.js"></script>
    <script src="/js/scope_events.js"></script>
  </body>
</html>
```

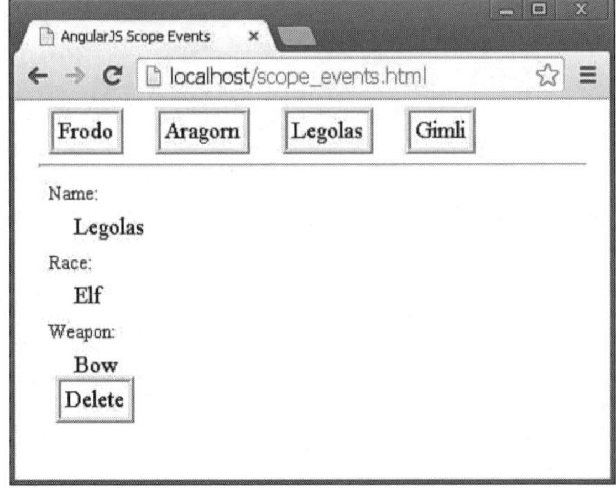

Figure 22.3 Using `$brodcast()` and `$emit()` to send change and delete events through a scope hierarchy.

Summary

A scope is the definitive source for data in AngularJS applications. A scope has direct relationships with the template views, controllers, modules, and services and acts as the glue that binds the application together. A scope also acts as a representation of a database or another server-side data source.

The scope life cycle is linked to the browser event loop so that changes in the browser can change the scope and changes in the scope are reflected in the DOM element that represent them. You can also add custom watch functions that are notified when the scope changes.

Scopes are organized into hierarchies, and the root scope is defined at that application level. Each instance of a controller also gets an instance of a child scope. You can emit or broadcast events from within a scope and then implement handlers that listen for those events and are executed when they are sent.

Up Next

In the next chapter you will get a closer look at implementing AngularJS templates to define the view for AngularJS applications. You will learn about the built-in expressions and filters, as well as how to create your own custom versions.

23

Using AngularJS Templates to Create Views

AngularJS templates provide a framework to represent the application view to the user. AngularJS templates contain expressions, filters, and directives that define additional functionality and behavior to the DOM elements. The templates are built on top of normal HTML and simply extend the functionality of HTML by adding additional elements and attributes.

This chapter focuses on AngularJS templates, as well as expressions and filters. Expressions allow you to implement JavaScript like code alongside the HTML code in a template. Filters enable you to modify data values before you display them—for example, to format text.

Understanding Templates

AngularJS templates are fairly straightforward and yet very powerful and easy to extend. Templates are based on standard HTML documents but extend the HTML functionality with three additional components:

- **Expressions:** Expressions are bits of JavaScript-like code that are evaluated within the context of a scope. Expressions are denoted by `{{}}` brackets. The results of an expression are added to a compiled HTML webpage. Expressions can be placed in normal HTML text or in the values of attributes, as shown here:

  ```
  <p>{{1+2}}</p>
  href="/myPage.html/{{hash}}"
  ```

- **Filters:** Filters transform the appearance of data that is placed on a webpage. For example, a filter can convert a number from the scope into a currency string or a time string.
- **Directives:** Directives are new HTML element names or attribute names within HTML elements. They add to and modify the behavior of HTML elements to provide data binding, event handling, and other support to an AngularJS application.

The following code snippet shows an example of implementing directives, expressions, and filters. The `ng-model="msg"` attribute is a directive that binds the value of the `<input>`

element to `msg` in the scope. The code in the `{{}}` brackets is an expression that applies the `uppercase` filter:

```
<div>
  <input ng-model="msg">
  {{msg | uppercase}}
</div>
```

When you load an AngularJS webpage into a browser, you load it in a raw state, containing template code along with HTML code. The initial DOM is built from that webpage. When the AngularJS application is bootstrapped, the AngularJS template compiles into the DOM, dynamically adjusting the values, event bindings, and other properties of the DOM elements to the directives, expressions, and filters in the template.

During compilation, HTML tags and attributes are normalized to support the fact that AngularJS is case-sensitive, whereas HTML is not. Normalization does two things:

- Strips the `x-` and `data-` prefixes from the front of elements and attributes.
- Converts names with `:` or `-` or `_` to camelCase.

For example, all of the following normalize to `ngModel`:

```
ng-model
data-ng-model
x-ng:model
ng_model
```

Using Expressions

Using expressions is the simplest way to represent data from the scope in an AngularJS view. Expressions are encapsulated blocks of code inside brackets: `{{expression}}`. The AngularJS compiler compiles an expression into HTML elements so that the results of the expression are displayed. For example, look at the following expressions:

```
{{1+5}}
{{'One' + 'Two'}}
```

Based on those expressions, the webpage displays these values:

```
6
OneTwo
```

Expressions are bound to the data model, which provides two huge benefits. First, you can use the property names and functions that are defined in the scope inside your expressions. Second, because the expressions are bound to the scope, when data in the scope changes, so do the expressions. For example, say that the scope contains the following values:

```
$scope.name='Brad';
$scope.score=95;
```

You can directly reference the name and score values in the template expressions as shown below:

```
Name: {{name}}
Score: {{score}}
Adjusted: {{score+5}}
```

AngularJS expressions are similar to JavaScript expressions in several ways, but they differ in these ways:

- **Attribute evaluation:** Property names are evaluated against the scope model instead of against the global JavaScript namespace.
- **More forgiving:** Expressions do not throw exceptions when they encounter undefined or null variable types; instead, they treat these as having no value.
- **No flow control:** Expressions do not allow JavaScript conditionals or loops. Also, you cannot throw an error inside an expression.

AngularJS evaluates the strings used to define the value of directives as expressions. This allows you to include expression-type syntax within a definition. For example, when you set the value of the `ng-click` directive in the template, you specify an expression. Inside that expression, you can reference scope variable and use other expression syntax, as shown below:

```
<span ng-click="scopeFunction()"></span>
<span ng-click="scopeFunction(scopeVariable, 'stringParameter')"></span>
<span ng-click="scopeFunction(5*scopeVariable)"></span>
```

Since the AngularJS template expressions have access to the scope, you can also make changes to the scope inside the AngularJS expression. For example, the following `ng-click` directive changes the value of `msg` inside the scope model:

```
<span ng-click="msg='clicked'"></span>
```

Listings 23.1 and 23.2 illustrate the various methods of implementing expressions in an AngularJS template that are linked to the scope. Listing 23.1 implements a simple controller named `myController` that defines `first`, `last`, `newFirst`, and `newLast` properties. Also, a `combine()` function combines two parameters and returns the results. The `setName()` function accepts two parameters and changes the values of `first` and `last`.

Listing 23.2 implements the various methods that use the scope and expressions. Line 9 adds two strings, and line 10 reads the `first` and `last` values from the scope. Lines 11 and 12 call the `combine()` function, which returns the combined string. Notice that line 12 passes `first` and `last` properties from the scope into the function.

Lines 13–16 evaluate the `ng-click` assignment as an expression. In line 13, because there are no quotes around `newFirst` and `newLast`, their values are read from the scope. However, line 15 passes the strings specified to the `setName()` function.

Figure 23.1 shows the AngularJS webpage defined by Listings 23.1 and 23.2.

Listing 23.1 `angular_expressions.js`: **Building a scope that AngularJS expressions can use**

```
angular.module('myApp', []).
  controller('myController', function($scope) {
    $scope.first = 'Thorin';
    $scope.last = 'Oakenshield';
    $scope.newFirst = 'Gandalf';
    $scope.newLast = 'Greyhame';
    $scope.combine = function(fName, lName){
      return fName + ' ' + lName;
    };
    $scope.setName = function(fName, lName){
      $scope.first = fName;
      $scope.last = lName;
    };
  });
```

Listing 23.2 `angular_expressions.html`: **An AngularJS template that uses expressions in various ways to obtain data from the scope model**

```
<!doctype html>
<html ng-app="myApp">
  <head>
    <title>AngularJS Expressions</title>
  </head>
  <body>
    <div ng-controller="myController">
      <h1>Expressions</h1>
      {{'Bilbo' + ' Baggins'}}<br>
      {{first}} {{last}}<br>
      {{combine('Bilbo', 'Baggins')}}<br>
      {{combine(first, last)}}<br>
      <p ng-click="setName(newFirst, newLast)">
        Click to Change to {{newFirst}} {{newLast}}</p>
      <p ng-click="setName('Bilbo', 'Baggins')">
        Click to Change to Bilbo Baggins</p>
    <script src="http://code.angularjs.org/1.2.9/angular.min.js"></script>
    <script src="/js/angular_expressions.js"></script>
  </body>
</html>
```

Figure 23.1 Using AngularJS expressions to represent and use scope data in the AngularJS view.

Using Filters

A great feature of AngularJS is the ability to implement filters. Filters are a type of provider that hooks into the expression parser and modifies the results of the expression for display in a view—for example to format time or currency values.

You implement filters inside expressions, using the following syntax:

```
{{ expression | filter}}
```

If you chain multiple filters together, they are executed in the order in which you specify them:

```
{{ expression | filter | filter }}
```

Some filters allow you to provide input in the form of function parameters. You add these parameters by using the following syntax:

```
{{ expression | filter:parameter1:parameter2 }}
```

Also you can add filters, which are providers, to controllers and services by using dependency injection. The filter provider name is the name of the filter plus `Filter`. For example, the currency filter provider is named `currencyFilter`. The filter provider acts as a function, with the expression as the first parameter and any additional parameters after that. The following code defines a controller that injects `currencyFilter` and uses it to format results. Notice that `currencyFilter` is added to the dependency injection for the controller and is called as a function:

```
controller('myController', ['$scope', 'currencyFilter',
                            function($scope, currencyFilter){
  $scope.getCurrencyValue = function(value){
```

```
    return currencyFilter(value, "$USD");
  };
}]);
```

Using Built-in Filters

AngularJS provides several different types of filters that enable you to easily format strings, objects, and arrays in AngularJS templates. Table 23.1 lists the built-in filters provided with AngularJS.

Table 23.1 **Filters that modify expressions in AngularJS templates**

Filter	Description
`currency[:symbol]`	Formats a number as currency, based on the `symbol` value provided. If no `symbol` value is provided, the default symbol for the locale is used. For example: `{{123.46 | currency:"$USD" }}`
`filter:exp:compare`	Filters the expression with the value of the `exp` parameter, based on the value of `compare`. The `exp` parameter can be a string, an object, or a function. The `compare` parameter can be a function that accepts expected and actual values and returns `true` or `false`. The `compare` parameter can also be a Boolean, where `true` is a strict comparison of `actual===expected` or `false` for a relaxed comparison that checks whether the value is a subset of the actual value. For example: `{{"Some Text to Compare" | filter:"text":false`
`json`	Formats a JavaScript object into a JSON string. For example: `{{ {'name':'Brad'} | json }}`
`limitTo:limit`	Limits the data represented in the expression by the `limit` amount. If the expression is a `String`, then it is limited by the number of characters. If the result of the expression is an `Array`, then it is limited by the number of elements. For example: `{{ ['a','b','c','d'] | limitTo:2 }}`
`lowercase`	Outputs the result of the expression as lowercase.
`uppercase`	Outputs the result of the expression as uppercase.
`number[:fraction]`	Formats the number as text. If a `fraction` parameter is specified, the number of decimal places displayed is limited to that size. For example: `{{ 123.4567 | number:3 }}`
`orderBy:exp:reverse`	Orders an array based on the `exp` parameter. The `exp` parameter can be a function that calculates the value of an item in the array or a string that specifies an object property in an array of objects. The `reverse` parameter is `true` for descending order or `false` for ascending.

Filter	Description
`date[:format]`	Formats a JavaScript `Date` object, timestamp, or date ISO 8601 date strings, using the `format` parameter. For example: `{{1389323623006 | date:'yyyy-MM-dd HH:mm:ss Z'}}` The `format` parameter uses the following date formatting characters: ▪ `yyyy`: Four-digit year ▪ `yy`: Two-digit year since 2000 ▪ `MMMM`: Month in year, January–December ▪ `MMM`: Month in year, Jan–Dec ▪ `MM`: Month in year, padded, 01–12 ▪ `M`: Month in year, 1–12 ▪ `dd`: Day in month, padded, 01–31 ▪ `d`: Day in month, 1–31 ▪ `EEEE`: Day in week, Sunday–Saturday ▪ `EEE`: Day in week, Sun–Sat ▪ `HH`: Hour in day, padded, 00–23 ▪ `H`: Hour in day, 0–23 ▪ `hh`: Hour in am/pm, padded, 01–12 ▪ `h`: Hour in am/pm, 1–12 ▪ `mm`: Minute in hour, padded, 00–59 ▪ `m`: Minute in hour, 0–59 ▪ `ss`: Second in minute, padded, 00–59 ▪ `s`: Second in minute, 0–59 ▪ `.sss` or `,sss`: Millisecond in second, padded, 000–999 ▪ `a`: am/pm marker ▪ `Z`: Four-digit time zone offset, -1200-+1200 The `format` string for date can also be one of the following pre-defined names. The format below is shown as `en_US` but will match the locale of the AngularJS application: ▪ `medium`: `'MMM d, y h:mm:ss a'` ▪ `short`: `'M/d/yy h:mm a'` ▪ `fullDate`: `'EEEE, MMMM d,y'` ▪ `longDate`: `'MMMM d, y'` ▪ `mediumDate`: `'MMM d, y'` ▪ `shortDate`: `'M/d/yy'` ▪ `mediumTime`: `'h:mm:ss a'` ▪ `shortTime`: `'h:mm a'`

Listings 23.3 and 23.4 show how to implement some basic filters in AngularJS. Listing 23.3 implements a controller with `JSONObj`, `word`, and `days` properties. Listing 23.4 implements `number`, `currency`, `date`, `json`, `limitTo`, `uppercase`, and `lowercase` filters directly in expressions in the template. Figure 23.2 shows the output of these listings.

Listing 23.3 `angular_filters.js`: **Building a scope that AngularJS filters can use**

```
angular.module('myApp', []).
  controller('myController', function($scope) {
    $scope.JSONObj = {title:"myTitle"};
    $scope.word="Supercalifragilisticexpialidocious";
    $scope.days=['Monday', 'Tuesday', 'Wednesday',
                 'Thursday', 'Friday'];
  });
```

Listing 23.4 `angular_filters.html`: **An AngularJS template that implements various types of filters to modify data displayed in the rendered view**

```
<!doctype html>
<html ng-app="myApp">
  <head>
    <title>AngularJS Filters</title>
  </head>
  <body>
    <div ng-controller="myController">
      <h2>Basic Filters</h2>
      Number: {{123.45678|number:3}}<br>
      Currency: {{123.45678|currency:"$"}}<br>
      Date: {{1389323623006 | date:'yyyy-MM-dd HH:mm:ss Z'}}<br>
      JSON: {{ JSONObj | json }}<br>
      Limit Array: {{ days | limitTo:3 }}<br>
      Limit String: {{ word | limitTo:10 }}<br>
      Uppercase: {{ word | uppercase | limitTo:10 }}<br>
      Lowercase: {{ word | lowercase | limitTo:10 }}
    <script src="http://code.angularjs.org/1.2.9/angular.min.js"></script>
    <script src="/js/angular_filters.js"></script>
  </body>
</html>
```

Figure 23.2 Using AngularJS filters to modify data before displaying it in the AngularJS view.

Using Filters to Implement Ordering and Filtering

A very common use of filters is to order or filter out dynamic elements built using the `ng-repeat` directive from JavaScript arrays. This section provides an example of implementing `orderBy` filters to generate a table that can be sorted by column and filtered by a string from an `<input>` element.

Listing 23.5 implements a controller that defines the `$scope.cameras` array to use as input data in the scope. Since you do not want to alter the actual model data when sorting and filtering, line 9 adds the `$scope.filteredCameras` property to store the filtered array.

Notice that line 10 sets a `$scope.reverse` value to keep track of the sort direction. Then line 11 sets a `$scope.column` value to keep track of which property name of objects in the cameras array to sort on. Lines 12–15 define the `setSort()` function, which is used to update the `column` and `reverse` values.

Line 15 defines the `$scope.filterString` property, which filters the objects to include in `filteredCameras`. Lines 17–20 define the `setFilter()` function, which calls the `filterFilter()` provider to limit the items in `filteredCameras` to the ones that loosely match `filterString`. Lines 2 and 3 inject the `filterFilter` provider into the controller.

Listing 23.6 implements a template that includes a text `<input>` that binds to the `filterString` value and a button `<input>` that calls `setFilter()` when clicked.

Notice that in lines 14–16 the table headers apply `ng-click` directives to call `setSort()` to set the sort column. Lines 18–23 implement the rows of the table by using the `ng-repeat` directive. Notice that the `ng-repeat` directive uses the `orderBy` filter to specify the column name and reverse values set by the `setSort()` function. Figure 23.3 shows the resulting webpage.

Listing 23.5 `angular_filter_sort.js`: **Building a scope that AngularJS can use and then sorting and ordering**

```
angular.module('myApp', []).
  controller('myController', ['$scope', 'filterFilter',
                              function($scope, filterFilter) {
    $scope.cameras = [
      {make:'Canon', model:'70D', mp:20.2},
      {make:'Canon', model:'6D', mp:20},
      {make:'Nikon', model:'D7100', mp:24.1},
      {make:'Nikon', model:'D5200', mp:24.1}];
    $scope.filteredCameras = $scope.cameras;
    $scope.reverse = true;
    $scope.column = 'make';
    $scope.setSort = function(column){
      $scope.column = column;
      $scope.reverse = !$scope.reverse;
    };
    $scope.filterString = '';
    $scope.setFilter = function(value){
      $scope.filteredCameras =
        filterFilter($scope.cameras, $scope.filterString);
    };
  }]);
```

Listing 23.6 `angular_filter_sort.html`: **An AngularJS template that implements** `filter` **and** `orderBy` **filters to order and filter items in a table view**

```
<!doctype html>
<html ng-app="myApp">
  <head>
    <title>AngularJS Sorting and Filtering</title>
    <style>table{text-align:center;}td,th{padding:3px;}</style>
  </head>
  <body>
    <div ng-controller="myController">
      <h2>Sorting and Filtering</h2>
      <input type="text" ng-model="filterString">
      <input type="button" ng-click="setFilter()" value="Filter">
      <table>
      <tr>
        <th ng-click="setSort('make')">Make</th>
        <th ng-click="setSort('model')">Model</th>
        <th ng-click="setSort('mp')">MegaPixel</th>
      </tr>
      <tr ng-repeat=
          "camera in filteredCameras | orderBy:column:reverse">
```

```
          <td>{{camera.make}}</td>
          <td>{{camera.model}}</td>
          <td>{{camera.mp}}</td>
        </tr>
        </table>
      <script src="http://code.angularjs.org/1.2.9/angular.min.js"></script>
      <script src="/js/angular_filter_sort.js"></script>
    </body>
</html>
```

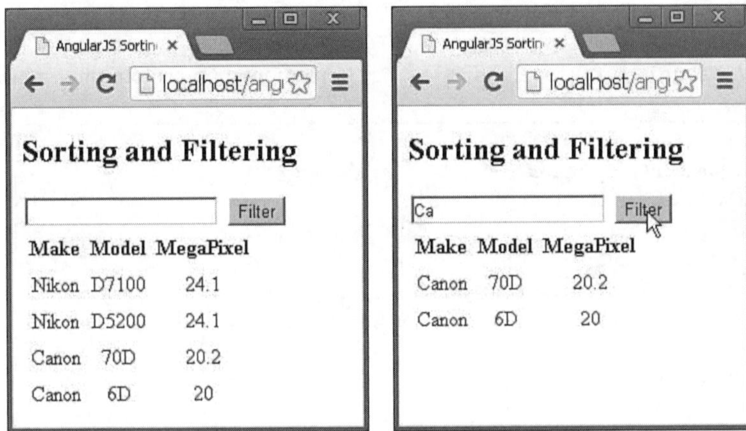

Figure 23.3 Using AngularJS filters to filter and order items in a table in the AngularJS view.

Creating Custom Filters

AngularJS allows you to create your own custom filter provider and then use it in expressions, controllers, and services as if it were a built-in filter. AngularJS provides the `filter()` method to create a filter provider and register it with the dependency injector server.

The `filter()` method accepts a name for the filter as the first argument and a function for the second argument. The filter function should accept the expression input as the first parameter and any additional parameters following that. For example:

```
filter('myFilter', function(){
  return function(input, param1, param2){
    return <<modified input>>;
  };
});
```

Inside the filter function you can change the value of the input any way you like. Whatever value is returned from the filter function is returned as the expression results.

Listings 23.7 and 23.8 create a custom filter function that censors words from a string and allows for a replacement value as an optional parameter. Listing 23.7 implements the `censor` filter provider in lines 2–10. Then in lines 12–29 the controller adds the `censorFilter` provider, using dependency injection. The `fitlerText()` function in lines 16–18 utilizes the `censorFilter` provider to censor text and replace it with <<censored>>.

The code in Listing 23.8 implements a template that utilizes the filter in a couple different ways, including calling `filterText()` based on a click event. Figure 23.4 shows the output of these listings.

Listing 23.7 `angular_filter_customer.js`: **Implementing a custom filter provider in AngularJS**

```
01 angular.module('myApp', []).
02   filter('censor', function() {
03     return function(input, replacement) {
04       var cWords = ['bad', 'evil', 'dark'];
05       var out = input;
06       for(var i=0; i<cWords.length; i++){
07         out = out.replace(cWords[i], replacement);
08       }
09       return out;
10     };
11   }).
12   controller('myController', ['$scope', 'censorFilter',
13                               function($scope, censorFilter) {
14     $scope.phrase="This is a bad phrase.";
15     $scope.txt = "Click to filter out dark and evil.";
16     $scope.filterText = function(){
17       $scope.txt = censorFilter($scope.txt, '<<censored>>');
18     };
19   }]);
```

Listing 23.8 `angular_filter_custom.html`: **An AngularJS template that uses a custom filter**

```
<!doctype html>
<html ng-app="myApp">
  <head>
    <title>AngularJS Custom Filter</title>
  </head>
  <body>
    <div ng-controller="myController">
```

```
      <h2>Sorting and Filtering</h2>
      {{phrase | censor:"***"}}<br>
      {{"This is some bad, dark evil text." | censor:"happy"}}
      <p ng-click="filterText()">{{txt}}</p>
    <script src="http://code.angularjs.org/1.2.9/angular.min.js"></script>
    <script src="/js/angular_filter_custom.js"></script>
  </body>
</html>
```

Figure 23.4 Creating and using custom filters in an AngularJS view.

Summary

AngularJS templates are simple to implement yet very powerful and extensive. This chapter discusses the components of AngularJS templates and how they work together to extend HTML DOM behavior and functionality. Expressions are bits of JavaScript code contained in `{{}}` brackets or within directive definitions in the AngularJS template. Expressions have access to the scope, so you can render scope values to the view.

Filters act as modifiers to expressions and allow you to format expression results for specific purposes. AngularJS provides several built-in filters, such as for currency and date formatting. You can also create your own custom filters that provide any formatting or modifications you want to apply before rendering data to the page. You inject filters as providers into the injector service and can therefore access them inside controllers and templates, using dependency injection. This means you have access to filters within your JavaScript code as well.

Up Next

In the next chapter you will continue learning about templates by looking at directives. Directives provide much of the extended functionality for AngularJS templates and are very powerful tools for building web applications.

24

Implementing Directives in AngularJS Views

One of the most powerful features of AngularJS is directives. Directives extend the behavior of HTML, allowing you to create custom HTML elements, attributes, and classes with functionality specific to an application. AngularJS provides several built-in directives. In fact, the majority of the AngularJS library is built-in directives. These directives provide the ability to interact with form elements, bind data in the scope to the view, and interact with browser events.

This chapter discusses the built-in directives and how to implement them in AngularJS templates. In this chapter you'll also learn how to build your own custom directives.

Understanding Directives

Directives are a combination of AngularJS template markups and supporting JavaScript code. AngularJS directive markups can be HTML attributes, element names, or CSS classes. The JavaScript directive code defines the template data and behavior of the HTML elements.

The AngularJS compiler traverses the template DOM and compiles all directives. Then it links the directives by combining a directive with a scope to produce a new live view. The live view contains the DOM elements and functionality defined in the directive.

Using Built-in Directives

Most of the AngularJS functionality that you need to implement in HTML elements is provided in the built-in directives. These directives are provided by the library and are available when the AngularJS JavaScript library is loaded.

Directives provide a wide variety of support for AngularJS applications. The following sections describe most of the AngularJS directives, which fall into the following categories:

- Directives that support AngularJS functionality
- Directives that extend form elements

- Directives that bind the scope to page elements
- Directives that bind page events to controllers

Directives That Support AngularJS Functionality

Several directives provide support for AngularJS functionality. These directives do everything from bootstrapping an application to ensuring that Boolean expressions that AngularJS requires are preserved in the DOM.

Table 24.1 lists these directives and describes the behavior and usage of each.

Table 24.1 **Directives that support AngularJS template functionality**

Directive	Description
`ngApp`	This directive is used to bootstrap an application to a root element. This attribute is set to the name of the AngularJS module to use as the application root, and the HTML element that contains it acts as the compilation root for the template. For example, the following sets module `myApp` as the application in the `<html>` element: `<html ng-app="myApp">`
`ngCloak`	When this attribute is present in an element, that element is not displayed until after the AngularJS template has been fully compiled. Otherwise, the raw form of the element with the template code is displayed.
`ngController`	This directive attaches a controller to this element in the view to create a new scope, as described in earlier chapters. For example: `<div ng-controller="myController">`
`ngHref`	This is an option you can use instead of using the `href` attribute, which may be broken if the user clicks the link before the expression has been evaluated if you include template syntax such as `{{hash}}`.
`ngInclude`	This directive automatically fetches, compiles, and includes an external HTML fragment from the server. Using it is a great way to include partial HTML data from server-side scripts. For example: `<div ng-include="/info/sidebar.html">`
`ngList`	This directive converts an `Array` object in the scope into a delimiter-separated string. (Comma is the default delimiter.) For example, if the scope contains an array named `items`, the displayed value in the following `<input>` would be `item1, item2, item3, . . . :` `<input ng-model="items" ng-list=",">`
`ngNonBindable`	When this directive is present in an element, AngularJS does not compile or bind the contents of the element during compilation. This is useful if you are trying to display code in the element. For example: `<p ng-non-bindable>Expression Syntax: {{exp}}</p>`

Directive	Description
`ngOpen`	Browsers are not required to preserve Boolean attributes of elements. If this attribute is present, then it is `true`. This directive allows you to preserve the `true/false` state of an element by testing the existence of the attribute. For example, the following applies `ngOpen` based on the `open` value in the scope: `<details ng-open="open">`

`ngPluralize`	This directive allows you to display messages according to the `en-US` localization rules bundled with AngularJS. You can configure `ngPluralize` by adding the `count` and `when` attributes, as shown below:
	`<p ng-pluralize count="itemCount"`
	`   when="{'0': 'Cart is empty.',`
	`          'one': 'Purchase 1 item.',`
	`          'other': 'Purchase {{itemCount}} items.'}">`
	`</p>`

`ngReadonly`	Similar to `ngOpen` but for the `readonly Boolean` value. For example, the following applies `ngReadonly` based on the `notChangeable` value in the scope: `<input type="text" ng-readonly="notChangeable">`
`ngRequired`	This directive is similar to `ngOpen` but for the required Boolean value. For example, the following applies `ngRequired` based on the required value in the scope: `<input type="text" ng-readonly="required">`
`ngSelected`	This directive is similar to `ngOpen` but for the selected Boolean value. For example, the following applies `ngSelected` based on the selected value in the scope: `<option id="optionA" ng-selected="selected">Option A</option>`
`ngSrc`	You can use this directive instead of using the `src` attribute, which is broken until the expression has been evaluated if you include template syntax such as `{{hash}}`.
`ngSrcset`	You can use this directive instead of using the `srcset` attribute, which is broken before the expression has been evaluated. For example: `<img ng-src="/images/{{hash}}/test.jpg 2x" />`
`ngTransclude`	This directive marks the element as the transclude point for directives that use the transclude option to wrap other elements.
`ngView`	This directive includes a rendered template of the current route into the main layout file. Routes are discussed in Chapter 25, "Implementing AngularJS Services in Web Applications."
`script`	This directive loads the content of a `script` tag with `next/ng-template` so that it can be used by `ngInclude`, `ngView`, or other template directives.

Directives That Extend Form Elements

AngularJS is heavily integrated with form elements to provide data binding and event binding for form elements in applications. In order to provide AngularJS functionality in the correct way, form elements are extended when compiled.

Table 24.2 lists the form elements that AngularJS extends.

Table 24.2 **Directives that extend form elements to support AngularJS template functionality**

Directive	Description
a	This directive modifies the default behavior to prevent the default action when the href attribute is empty. This allows you to create action links by using ngClick or other event directives. For example: <a href="" ng-click="handleClick()">Click Me</a>
form/ngForm	AngularJS allows forms to be nested for validation purposes such that a form is valid when all child forms are valid as well. However, browsers do not allow nesting of <form> elements; therefore, you should use <ng-form> instead. For example: <ng-form name="myForm> <input type="text" ng-model="myName" required> </ng-form>
input	You can modify this directive to provide the following additional AngularJS attributes: ▪ ngModel: Binds the value of this input to a variable in the scope. ▪ name: Specifies the name of the form. ▪ required: When present, a value is required for this field. ▪ ngRequired: Sets the required attribute based on the evaluation of the ngRequired expression. ▪ ngMinlenght: Sets the minlength validation error amount. ▪ ngMaxlenght: Sets the maxlength validation error amount. ▪ ngPattern: Specifies a regex pattern to match the input value against for validation. ▪ ngChange: Specifies an expression to be executed when the input changes—for example, executing a function in the scope.
input.checkbox	This directive adds the following extra AngularJS attributes in addition to those already provided with input: ▪ ngTrueValue:Sets a value in the scope when the element is checked. ▪ ngFalseValue:Sets a value in the model when the element is not checked.

Directive	Description
input.email	Same as input.
input.number	This directive adds the following extra AngularJS attributes in addition to those already provided to input: ▪ min: Sets the min validation error amount. ▪ max: Sets the max validation error amount.
input.radio	This directive adds the following extra AngularJS attribute in addition to those already provided to input: ▪ value: Sets a value in the scope when the element is selected.
input.text	This directive is the same as input.
input.url	This directive is the same as input.
select	This directive adds the additional ngOptions directive to the <select> element.
ngOptions	This directive allows you to add options based on an iterative expression. If the data source in the scope is an array, use the following expressions for ngOptions to set the label, name, and value attributes of each <option> element in the <select>: label for value in array select as label for value in array label group by group for value in array select as label group by group for value in array track by trackexpr If the source for ngOptions in the scope is a JavaScript object, use the following expression syntax: label for (key , value) in object select as label for (key , value) in object label group by group for (key, value) in object select as label group by group for (key, value) in object For example: <select ng-model="color" ng-options="c.name for c in colors"> <option value="">-- choose color --</option> </select>
textarea	This directive is the same as input.

Listings 24.1 and 24.2 implement some basic AngularJS form element integration with the scope. Listing 24.1 initializes the scope. Listing 24.2 implements several common form components, including a text box, a check box, radio buttons, and a `select` element to illustrate how they are defined in the template and interact with data in the scope. Figure 24.1 shows the resulting webpage.

Listing 24.1 `directive_form.js`: **Implementing a controller for form directives**

```
angular.module('myApp', []).
  controller('myController', function($scope) {
    $scope.cameras = [
      {make:'Canon', model:'70D', mp:20.2},
      {make:'Canon', model:'6D', mp:20},
      {make:'Nikon', model:'D7100', mp:24.1},
      {make:'Nikon', model:'D5200', mp:24.1}];
    $scope.cameraObj=$scope.cameras[0];
    $scope.cameraName = 'Canon';
    $scope.cbValue = '';
    $scope.someText = '';
  });
```

Listing 24.2 `directive_form.html`: **An AngularJS template that implements several different form element directives**

```
<!doctype html>
<html ng-app="myApp">
<head>
  <title>AngularJS Form Directives</title>
</head>
<body>
  <div ng-controller="myController">
    <h2>Forms Directives</h2>
    <input type="text" ng-model="someText"> {{someText}}<hr>
    <input type="checkbox" ng-model="cbValue"
           ng-true-value="AWESOME" ng-false-value="BUMMER">
    Checkbox: {{cbValue}}<hr>
    <input type="radio"
      ng-model="cameraName" value="Canon"> Canon<br/>
    <input type="radio"
      ng-model="cameraName" value="Nikon"> Nikon<br/>
    Selected Camera: {{cameraName}} <hr>
    <select ng-model="camera"
      ng-options="c.model group by c.make for c in cameras">
    </select>
    {{camera|json}}
  <script src="http://code.angularjs.org/1.2.9/angular.min.js"></script>
```

```
  <script src="/js/directive_form.js"></script>
</body>
</html>
```

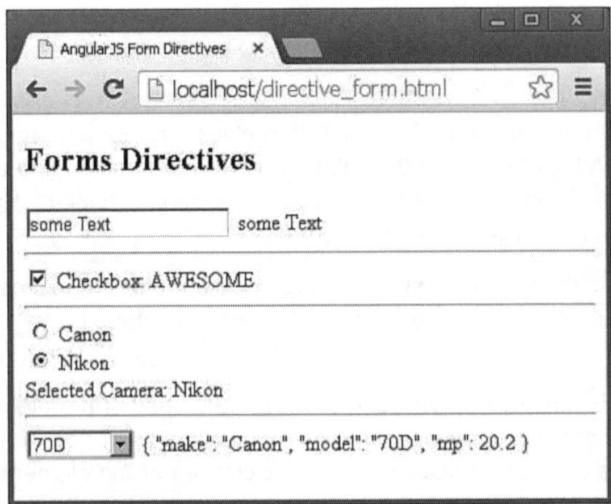

Figure 24.1 Implementing form directive elements in AngularJS template views.

Directives That Bind the Model to Page Elements

AngularJS templates enable you to bind data in the scope directly to what is displayed in HTML elements. You can bind data to the view in several different ways, including:

- **Value:** You can directly represent the value of a form element in the scope. For example, a text input can be a `String` variable in the scope, but a check box would be represented by a `Boolean` value.
- **HTML:** You can represent the value of data in the scope in the HTML output of an element by using expressions such as:

  <p>{{myTitle}}</p>
- **Attributes:** The value of HTML element attributes can reflect the data in the scope by using expressions in the definition such as:

  <a ng-href="/{{hash}}/index.html">{{hash}}</a>.
- **Visibility:** The visibility of an element can reflect the scope in the view. For example, when an expression based on the scope is `true`, the element is visible; otherwise, it is invisible.
- **Existence:** You can omit elements from the compiled DOM, based on values in the scope.

Table 24.3 lists the directives that bind the data in the scope directly to elements in the view.

Table 24.3 **Directives that bind data in the scope to the value, expressions, visibility, and existence of HTML elements**

Directive	Description
`ngBind`	This directive tells AngularJS to replace the `text` content of the HTML element with the value of a given expression and also to update the `text` content if the value in the scope changes. For example: `<span ng-bind="titleString"></span>`
`ngBindHtml`	This directive tells AngularJS to replace the `innerHTML` content of the HTML element with the value of a given expression and also to update the `innerHTML` content if the value in the scope changes. For example: `<div ng-bind="someHTML"></div>`
`ngBindTemplate`	This directive is similar to `ngBind` except that the expression can contain multiple `{{}}` expression blocks. For example: `<span ng-bind="{{aValue}} and {{anotherValue}}"></span>`
`ngClass`	This directive dynamically sets the CSS class of the element by data binding an expression that represents the classes to be added. When the value of the expression changes, the CSS classes of the element are automatically updated. For example: `<p ng-class="myPStyles"></p>`

`ngClassEven`	This directive is the same as `ngClass` except that it works with `ngRepeat` to apply the class changes only to even indexed elements in the set. For example:
	`<li ng-repeat="item in items">`
	`  <span ng-class-even="evenRowClass">{{item}}</span>`
	`</li>`

`ngClassOdd`	This directive is the same as `ngClass` except that it works with `ngRepeat` to apply the class changes only to odd indexed elements in the set. For example:
	`<li ng-repeat="item in items">`
	`  <span ng-class-odd="oddRowClass">{{item}}</span>`
	`</li>`

`ngDisabled`	This directive disables a button element if the expression evaluates to `true`.
`ngHide`	This directive shows or hides the HTML element based on the expression provided, using the `.ng-hide` CSS class provided in AngularJS. If the expression evaluates to `false` in the scope, the element is displayed; otherwise, it is hidden. For example: `<div ng-hide="myValue"></div>`
`ngShow`	This directive is the same as `ngHide` except in reverse: If the expression evaluates to `true` in the scope, the element is displayed; otherwise, it is hidden. For example: `<div ng-show="myValue"></div>`

Directive	Description
`ngIf`	This directive deletes or re-creates a portion of the DOM tree, based on the expression. This is different from `show` or `hide` because the HTML does not show up at all in the DOM. For example: `<div ng-if="present"> </div>`
`ngModel`	This directive binds the value of an `<input>`, `<select>`, or `<textarea>` element to a value in the scope model. When the user changes the value of the element, the value is automatically changed in the scope and vice versa. For example: `<input type="text" ng-model="myString">`

`ngRepeat`	This directive allows you to add multiple HTML elements based on an array in the scope. This is extremely useful for lists, tables, and menus. `ngRepeat` uses the `item in collections` style of iteration syntax. A new scope is created for each individual HTML element created. During the looping to generate the HTML elements, the following variables are visible in the scope:
	▪ `$index:` An iterator index based on 0 for the first element.
	▪ `$first:` A Boolean that is `true` if this is the first element.
	▪ `$middle:` A Boolean that is `true` if this is not the first or last element.
	▪ `$last:` A Boolean that is `true` if this is the last element.
	▪ `$even:` A Boolean that is `true` if the iterator is even.
	▪ `$odd:` A Boolean that is `true` if the iterator is odd.
	For example, the following iterates and builds a series of `<li>` elements based on an array of users with a `firstname` property:
	`<li ng-repeat="user in users">`
	`  {{$index}}: {{user.firstname}}</li>`

`ngInit`	This directive is used with `ngRepeat` to initialize a value during the iteration. For example:
	`<div ng-repeat="user in users" ng-init="offset=21">`
	`  {{$index+offset}}: {{user.firstname}}</div>`

`ngStyle`	This directive allows you to set the style dynamically, based on an object in the scope where the property names and values match CSS attributes. For example: `<span ng-style="myStyle">Stylized Text</span>`

`ngSwitch`	This directive allows you to dynamically swap which DOM element to include in the compiled template, based on a scope expression. The following is an example of the syntax used for multiple elements:
	`<div ng-switch="myLocation">`
	`  <div ng-switch-when="home">Home Info</div>`
	`  <div ng-switch-when="work">Work Info</div>`
	`  <div ng-switch-default>Default Info</div>`
	`</div>`

Directive	Description

`ngValue`	This directive binds the selected value of an `input[select]` or `input[radio]` to the expression specified in `ngModel`. For example:
	`<div ng-repeat="pizza in pizzas"`
	  `<input type="radio" name="pizza"`
	    `ng-model="myPizza" ng-value="pizza" id="{{pizza}}" >`
	`</div>`

Listings 24.3 and 24.4 provide some examples of basic AngularJS binding directives. Listing 24.3 initializes the scope values, including the `myStyle` object in line 4. Listing 24.4 provides the actual implementation of the binding directives in the template.

With only a few exceptions, the template code in Listing 24.4 is straightforward. Lines 15 and 16 bind the `radio` button `<input>` to the `myStyle['background-color']` property in the scope. This illustrates how to handle style names that do not allow the dot notation that's usually used (for example, `myStyle.color`). Also note that the value of the radio buttons is set using `ng-value` to get the color value from the `ng-repeat` scope.

Also note that when you set the class name using `ng-class-even`, the class name `even` needs to be in single quotes because it is a string. Figure 24.2 shows the resulting webpage.

Listing 24.3 `directive_bind.js`: **Implementing a controller with a scope model to support data binding directives**

```
01 angular.module('myApp', []).
02   controller('myController', function($scope) {
03     $scope.colors=['red','green','blue'];
04     $scope.myStyle = { "background-color": 'blue' };
05     $scope.days=['Monday', 'Tuesday', 'Wednesday',
06                  'Thursday', 'Friday'];
07     $scope.msg="Message from the model";
08   });
```

Listing 24.4 `directive_bind.html`: **An AngularJS template that implements several different data binding directives**

```
01 <!doctype html>
02 <html ng-app="myApp">
03 <head>
04   <title>AngularJS Data Binding Directives</title>
05   <style>
06     .even{background-color:lightgrey;}
```

```
    .rect{display:inline-block; height:40px; width:100px;}
  </style>
</head>
<body>
  <div ng-controller="myController">
    <h2>Data Binding Directives</h2>
    <label ng-repeat="color in colors">
      {{color}}
      <input type="radio" ng-model="myStyle['background-color']"
             ng-value="color" id="{{color}}" name="mColor">
    </label>
    <span class="rect" ng-style="myStyle"></span><hr>
    <li ng-repeat="day in days">
      <span ng-class-even="'even'">{{day}}</span>
    </li><hr>
    Show Message: <input type="checkbox" ng-model="checked" />
    <p ng-if="checked" ng-bind="msg"> </p>
  </div>
  <script src="http://code.angularjs.org/1.2.9/angular.min.js"></script>
  <script src="/js/directive_bind.js"></script>
</body>
</html>
```

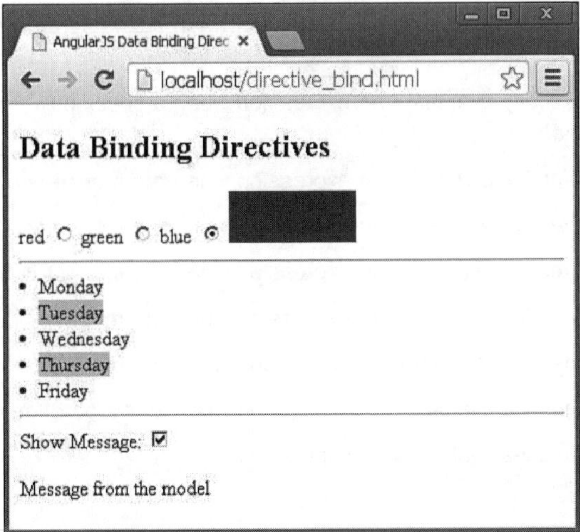

Figure 24.2 Implementing data binding directives in AngularJS template views.

Directives That Bind Page Events to Controllers

AngularJS templates enable you to bind browser events to controller code. This means you can handle user input from the scope's perspective. You can then implement handlers for browser events directly to the appropriate scope. The `event` directive works very much like the normal browser event handlers, except that they are directly linked to the scope context.

Table 24.4 lists the directive that binds page and device events to the AngularJS model. Each of these directives allows you to specify an expression, which is typically a function defined in the scope, as discussed in Chapter 23, "Using AngularJS Templates to Create Views." For example, the following is a function named `setTitle` in the scope:

```
$scope.setTitle = function(title){
  $scope.title = title;
};
```

You can bind the `setTitle()` function in the scope directly to an input button in the view by using the following `ng-click` directive:

```
<input type="button" ng-click="setTitle('New Title')">
```

Table 24.4 **Directives that bind page/device events to AngularJS model functionality**

Directive	Description
`ngBlur`	This directive evaluates an expression when the blur event is triggered.
`ngChange`	This directive evaluates an expression when the value of a form element is changed.
`ngChecked`	This directive evaluates an expression when a check box or radio element is checked.
`ngClick`	This directive evaluates an expression when the mouse is clicked.
`ngCopy`	This directive evaluates an expression when the blur copy is triggered.
`ngCut`	This directive evaluates an expression when the blur cut is triggered.
`ngDblclick`	This directive evaluates an expression when the mouse is double-clicked.
`ngFocus`	This directive evaluates an expression when the blur focus is triggered.
`ngKeydown`	This directive evaluates an expression when a keyboard key is pressed down.
`ngKeypress`	This directive evaluates an expression when a keyboard key is pressed and released.
`ngKeyup`	This directive evaluates an expression when a keyboard key is released.
`ngMousedown`	This directive evaluates an expression when a mouse key is pressed.
`ngMouseenter`	This directive evaluates an expression when the mouse enters the element.
`ngMouseleave`	This directive evaluates an expression when the mouse leaves the element.

Directive	Description
`ngMousemove`	This directive evaluates an expression when the mouse cursor moves.
`ngMouseover`	This directive evaluates an expression when the mouse hovers over an element.
`ngMouseup`	This directive evaluates an expression when the mouse button is released.
`ngPaste`	This directive evaluates an expression when the paste event is triggered.
`ngSubmit`	This directive prevents the default form submit action, which sends a request to the server and instead evaluates the specified expression.
`ngSwipeLeft`	This directive evaluates an expression when the swipe left event is triggered.
`ngSwiteRight`	This directive evaluates an expression when the swipe right event is triggered.

You can pass the JavaScript `Event` object into the event expressions by using the `$event` keyword. This allows you to access information about the event as well as stop propagation and everything else you normally can do with a JavaScript `Event` object. For example, the following `ng-click` directive passes the mouse click event to the `myClick()` handler function:

```
<input type="button" ng-click="myClick($event)">
```

Listings 24.5 and 24.6 provide some examples of basic AngularJS event directives. Listing 24.5 initializes the scope values and implements a keyboard press and mouse click event handler that collect information from the `Event` object.

Listing 24.6 implements a series of event directives on a single `<input>` element, as shown in Figure 24.3. Notice that lines 17 and 18 pass the keyboard and mouse event object into the function by using the `$event` variable name.

Listing 24.5 `directive_event.js`: **Implementing a controller with scope data and event handlers**

```
angular.module('myApp', []).
  controller('myController', function($scope) {
    $scope.keyInfo = {};
    $scope.mouseInfo = {};
    $scope.keyStroke = function(event){
      $scope.keyInfo.keyCode = event.keyCode;
    };
    $scope.mouseClick = function(event){
      $scope.mouseInfo.clientX = event.clientX;
      $scope.mouseInfo.clientY = event.clientY;
      $scope.mouseInfo.screenX = event.screenX;
      $scope.mouseInfo.screenY = event.screenY;
    };
  });
```

Listing 24.6 `directive_event.html`: **An AngularJS template that implements several different event directives**

```
<!doctype html>
<html ng-app="myApp">
<head>
  <title>AngularJS Event Directives</title>
</head>
<body>
  <div ng-controller="myController">
    <h2>Event Directives</h2>
    <input type="text"
        ng-blur="focusState='Blurred'"
        ng-focus="focusState='Focused'"
        ng-mouseenter="mouseState='Entered'"
        ng-mouseleave="mouseState='Left'"
        ng-mouseclick="mouseState='Clicked'"
        ng-mousedown="mouseState='Down'"
        ng-mouseup="mouseState='Up'"
        ng-keyup="keyStroke($event)"
        ng-click="mouseClick($event)"><hr>
    Focus State: {{focusState}}<br/>
    Mouse State: {{mouseState}}<br/>
    Key Info: {{keyInfo|json}}<br/>
    Mouse Info: {{mouseInfo|json}}<br/>
  </div>
  <script src="http://code.angularjs.org/1.2.9/angular.min.js"></script>
  <script src="/js/directive_event.js"></script>
</body>
</html>
```

Figure 24.3 Implementing event directives in AngularJS template views.

Creating Your Own Directives to Extend HTML

As with many other features of AngularJS, you can extend directive functionality by creating your own custom directives. Custom directives allow you to extend the functionality of HTML by implementing the behavior of elements yourself. If you have code that needs to manipulate the DOM, you should make this happen by using a custom directive.

You implement custom directives by calling the `directive()` method on a `Module` object. The `directive()` method accepts the name of a directive as the first parameter and a provider function that returns an object containing the necessary instructions to build the directive object. For example, the following is a basic definition for a directive:

```
angular.module('myApp', []).
  directive('myDirective', function() {
    return {
      template: 'Name: {{name}} Score: {{score}}'
    };
  });
```

The following is a list of the properties you can apply to the object returned by the directive definition as `template` is returned in the code above:

- **`template`:** Allows you to define the AngularJS template text that is inserted into the directive's element.
- **`templateUrl`:** Same as `template` except that you specify a URL at the server, and the partial template is downloaded and inserted into the directive's element.
- **`restrict`:** Allows you to specify whether the directive applies to an HTML element, an attribute, or both.
- **`replace`:** Tells the compiler to replace the element the directive is defined in with the directive's template.
- **`transclude`:** Allows you to specify whether the directive has access to scopes outside the internal scope.
- **`scope`:** Allows you to specify an internal scope for the directive.
- **`link`:** Allows you to specify a link function that has access to the scope, DOM element, and other attributes and is able to manipulate the DOM.
- **`controller`:** Allows you to define a controller within the directive to manage the directive scope and view.
- **`require`:** Allows you to specify other directives that are required to implement this directive. Providers for those directives must be available for an instance of this directive to be created.

The following sections discuss the directive options in more detail.

Defining the Directive View Template

You can include AngularJS template code to build view components that will be displayed in the HTML element that contains the directive. You can add template code directly by using the `template` property, as in this example:

```
directive('myDirective', function() {
  return {
    template: 'Name: {{name}} Score: {{score}}'
  };
});
```

You can specify a root element in the custom template—but only one element. This element acts as the root element for any child element defined in the AngularJS template to be placed inside. Also, if you are using the `transclude` flag, the element should include `ngTransclude`. For example:

```
directive('myDirective', function() {
  return {
    transclude: true,
    template: '<div ng-transclude></div>'
  };
});
```

You can also use the `templateUrl` property to specify a URL of an AngularJS template located on the webserver, as in this example:

```
directive('myDirective', function() {
  return {
    templateUrl: '/myDirective.html'
  };
});
```

The template URL can contain any standard AngularJS template code. You can therefore make your directives as simple or as complex as you need them to be.

Restricting Directive Behavior

You can apply a directive as an HTML element, an attribute, or both. The `restrict` property allows you to limit how your custom directive can be applied. The `restrict` property can be set to:

- **`A`:** Applied as an attribute name.
- **`E`:** Applied as an element name.
- **`C`:** Applied as a class name.
- **`AEC`:** Applied as an attribute, an element, or a class name. You can also use other combinations, such as `AE` or `AC`.

For example, you can apply the following directive as an attribute or an element:

```
directive('myDirective', function() {
  return {
    restrict: 'AE',
    templateUrl: '/myDirective.html'
  };
});
```

The following shows how to implement the directive as both an element and an attribute. Notice that the camelCase name is replaced by one with hyphens:

```
<my-directive></my-directive>
<div my-directive></div>
```

Replacing the Template Element

You can add a directive template as a child to the AngularJS template element where you define it, or you can replace it by using the `replace` attribute. To illustrate this, look at the following directive:

```
directive('myDirective', function() {
  return {
    replace: true,
    templateUrl: '<div>directive</div>'
  };
});
```

Then look at the following template code:

```
<div>
  <span my-directive></span>
</div>
```

The compiler sees that `replace` is `true` and replaces the inner `<span>` element as shown below:

```
<div>
  <div>directive</div>
</div>
```

Transcluding External Scopes

You can set the `transclude` option in the directive definition to `true` or `false`. If it is set to `true`, then components inside the directive have access to the scope outside the directive. You must also include the `ngTransclude` directive in elements inside your directive template. The following is an example of implementing `transclude` to access the `title` variable in the controller scope from the `myDirective` directive template:

```
angular.module('myApp', []).
  directive('myDirective', function() {
    return {
      transclude: true,
      scope: {},
      template: '<div ng-transclude>{{title}}</div>'
    };
  }).
  controller('myController', function($scope) {
    $scope.title="myApplication";
  });
```

Configuring the Directive Scope

At times you may want to separate the scope inside a directive from the scope outside the directive. Doing so prevents the possibility of the directive changing values in the local controller. The directive definition allows you to specify a `scope` that creates an isolate scope. An isolate scope isolates the directive scope from the outer scope to prevent the directive from accessing the outer scope and the controller in the outer scope from altering the directive scope. For example, the following isolates the scope of the directive from the outside scope:

```
directive('myDirective', function() {
  return {
    scope: { },
    templateUrl: '/myDirective.html'
  };
});
```

Using this code, the directive has a completely empty isolate scope. However, you might want to still map some items in the outer scope to the directive's inner scope. You can use the following prefixes to attribute names to make local scope variables available in the directive's scope:

- `@`: Binds a local scope string to the value of the DOM attribute. The value of the attribute will be available inside the directive scope.
- `=`: Creates a bidirectional binding between the local scope property and the directive scope property.
- `&`: Binds a function in the local scope to the directive scope.

If no attribute name follows the prefix, the name of the directive property is used. For example:

```
title : '@'
```

is the same as:

```
title: '@title'
```

The following code shows how to implement each of the different methods to map local values into a directive's isolate scope:

```
angular.module('myApp', []).
  controller('myController', function($scope) {
    $scope.title="myApplication";
    $scope.myFunc = function(){
      console.log("out");
    };
  }).
  directive('myDirective', function() {
    return {
      scope: {title: '=', newFunc:"&myFunc", info: '@'},
      template: '<div ng-click="newFunc()">{{title}}: {{info}}</div>'
    };
  });
```

The following code shows how to define the directive in the AngularJS template to provide the necessary attributes to map the properties:

```
<div my-directive
     my-func="myFunc()"
     title="title"
     info="SomeString"></div>
```

Manipulating the DOM with a Link Function

When the AngularJS HTML compiler encounters a directive, it runs the directive's compile function, which returns the `link()` function. The `link()` function is added to the list of AngularJS directives. Once all directives have been compiled, the HTML compiler calls the `link()` functions in order, based on priority.

If you want to modify the DOM inside a custom directive, you should use a `link()` function. The `link()` function accepts the scope, element, and attributes associated with the directive, allowing you to manipulate the DOM directly within the directive.

Inside the `link()` function, you handle the `$destroy` event on the directive element and clean up anything necessary. The `link()` function is also responsible for registering DOM listeners to handle browser events.

The `link()` function uses the following syntax:

```
link: function(scope, element, attributes, [controller])
```

The `scope` parameter is the scope of the directive, `element` is the element where the directive will be inserted, `attributes` lists the attributes declared on the element, and `controller` is the controller specified by the `require` option.

The following directive shows the implementation of a basic `link()` function that sets a scope variable, appends data to the DOM element, implements a `$destroy` event handler, and adds a `$watch` to the scope:

```
directive('myDirective', function() {
  return {
    scope: {title: '='},
    require: '^otherDirective',
    link: function (scope, elem, attr, otherController){
      scope.title = "new";
      elem.append("Linked");
      elem.on('$destroy', function() {
        //cleanup code
      });
      scope.$watch('title', function(newVal){
        //watch code
      });
    }
  };
```

Adding a Controller to a Directive

You can add a custom controller to a directive by using the `controller` property of the directive definition. This allows you to provide controller support for the directive template. For example, the following code adds a simple controller that sets up a scope value and function:

```
directive('myDirective', function() {
  return {
    scope: {title: '='},
    controller: function ($scope){
      $scope.title = "new";
      $scope.myFunction = function(){
      });
    }
  };
});
```

You can also use the `require` option to ensure that a controller is available to the directive. The `require` option uses the `require:'^controller'` syntax to instruct the injector service to look in parent contexts until it finds the controller. The following is an example of requiring the `myController` controller in a directive:

```
directive('myDirective', function() {
  return {
    require: '^myController'
  };
});
```

When you add the `require` option, the specified controller is passed as the fourth parameter of the `link()` function. If you specify the name of another directive in the `require` option, the controller for that directive is linked.

Creating a Custom Directive

The types of custom directives you can define are really limitless, and this makes AngularJS really extensible. Custom directives are the most complex portion of AngularJS to explain. The best way to get you started is to show you an example of two custom directives, to give you a feel for how to implement them and have them interact with each other.

Listing 24.7 implements two custom directives: `myPhotos` and `myPhoto`. The `myPhotos` directive is designed to be a container for the `myPhoto` directive. Notice that lines 7–18 define a controller that provides the functionality for the `myPhotos` directive, including an `addPhoto()` function. Because the code uses `require:'^myPhotos'` in the `myPhoto` directive, you can also call the `addPhoto()` method from the `link()` function by using the `photosControl` handle to the `myPhotos` controller.

Listing 24.8 implements the `myPhotos` and `myPhoto` directives in an AngularJS template. The `myPhoto` directives are nested inside the `myPhotos` directive. Notice that the `title` attribute is set on each `myPhoto` directive and linked to the scope in line 28 of Listing 24.7.

Listing 24.9 implements a partial template loaded by the `myPhotos` directive. It generates a `<div>` container and then uses the `photos` array in the `myPhotos` scope to build a list of links bound to the `select()` function, using `ng-click`. `<div ng-transclude></div>` provides the container for the `myPhoto` child elements.

Figure 24.4 shows the webpage created by Listings 24.7, 24.8, and 24.9.

Listing 24.7 `directive_custom.js`: **Implementing custom directives that interact with each other**

```
01 angular.module('myApp', [])
02   .directive('myPhotos', function() {
03     return {
04       restrict: 'E',
05       transclude: true,
06       scope: {},
07       controller: function($scope) {
08         var photos = $scope.photos = [];
09         $scope.select = function(photo) {
10           angular.forEach(photos, function(photo) {
11             photo.selected = false;
12           });
13           photo.selected = true;
14         };
15         this.addPhoto = function(photo) {
```

```
          photos.push(photo);
        };
      },
      templateUrl: 'my_photos.html'
    };
  })
  .directive('myPhoto', function() {
    return {
      require: '^myPhotos',
      restrict: 'E',
      transclude: true,
      scope: { title: '@'},
      link: function(scope, elem, attrs, photosControl) {
        photosControl.addPhoto(scope);
      },
      template: '<div ng-show="selected" ng-transclude></div>'
    };
  });
```

Listing 24.8 `directive_custom.html`: **An AngularJS template that implements nested custom directives**

```
<!doctype html>
<html ng-app="myApp">
<head>
  <title>AngularJS Custom Directive</title>
</head>
<body>
   <my-photos>
     <my-photo title="Flower">
       <img src="/images/flower.jpg" height="150px"/>
     </my-photo>
     <my-photo title="Arch">
       <img src="/images/arch.jpg" height="150px"/>
     </my-photo>
     <my-photo title="Lake">
       <img src="/images/lake.jpg" height="150px"/>
     </my-photo>
   </my-photos>
  <script src="http://code.angularjs.org/1.2.9/angular.min.js"></script>
  <script src="/js/directive_custom.js"></script>
</body>
</html>
```

Listing 24.9 `my_photos.html`: **A partial AngularJS template that provides the root element for the `myPhotos` custom directive**

```
<div>
  <span ng-repeat="photo in photos"
        ng-class="{active:photo.selected}">
    <a href="" ng-click="select(photo)">{{photo.title}}</a>
  </span>
  <div ng-transclude></div>
</div>
```

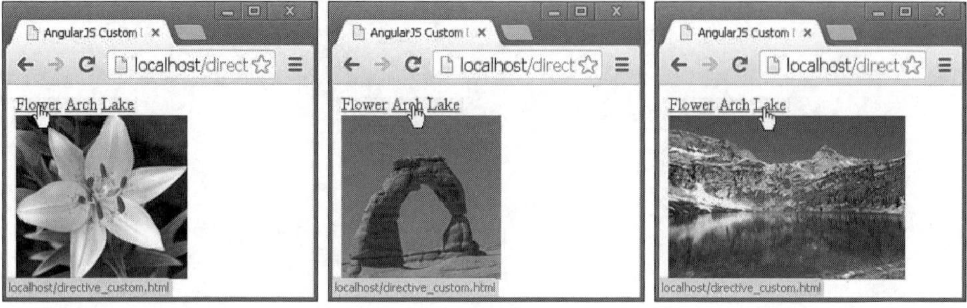

Figure 24.4 Implementing event directives in AngularJS template views.

Summary

AngularJS directives extend the behavior of HTML. You can apply directives to AngularJS templates as HTML elements, attributes, and classes. You define the functionality of directives by using JavaScript code. AngularJS provides several built-in directives that interact with form elements, bind data in the scope to the view, and interact with browser events. For example, `ngModel` binds the value of a form element directly to the scope. When the scope value changes, so does the value displayed by the element and vice versa.

One of the most powerful features of AngularJS is the ability to create your own custom directives. Implementing a custom directive in code is simple using the `directive()` method on a `Module` object. However, directives can also be very complex because of the myriad of ways they can be implemented.

Up Next

In the next chapter you'll learn about integrating AngularJS services into your web applications. AngularJS services provide component functionality that is commonly used between modules. For example, the `$http` service provides HTTP communication to a webserver.

25

Implementing AngularJS Services in Web Applications

One of the most fundamental components of AngularJS functionality is services. Services provide task-based functionality to your applications. Think about a service as a chunk of reusable code that performs one or more related tasks. AngularJS provides several built-in services and also allows you to create your own customized services.

This chapter introduces the AngularJS services. You will get a chance to see and implement some of the built-in services, such as `$http` for webserver communication. You will also learn about the different methods for creating custom services and how to implement them.

Understanding AngularJS Services

AngularJS services are singleton objects, which means only one instance is ever created. The intent of a service is to provide a concise bit of code that performs specific tasks. A service can be as simple as providing a value definition or as complex as providing full HTTP communication to a webserver.

A service provides a container for reusable functionality that is readily available to AngularJS applications. Services are defined and registered with AngularJS's dependency injection mechanism. This allows you to inject services into modules, controllers, and other services.

> **Note**
>
> Chapter 21, "Understanding AngularJS Modules and Dependency Injection," discusses dependency injection. You should read that chapter if you haven't already before continuing on with this one.

Using the Built-in Services

AngularJS provides several built-in services. These are automatically registered with the dependency injector and you can therefore easily incorporate them into your AngularJS applications by using dependency injection.

Table 25.1 describes some of the most common built-in services to give you an idea of what is available. The following sections cover some of these services in more detail.

Table 25.1 **Common services that are built in to AngularJS**

Service	Description
`$animate`	Provides animation hooks to link into both CSS- and JavaScript-based animations.
`$cacheFactory`	Provides the ability to put key/value pairs into an object cache, where they can be retrieved later by other code components using the same service.
`$compile`	Provides the ability to compile an HTML string or DOM object into a template and produce a template function that can link the scope and template together.
`$cookies`	Provides read and write access to the browser's cookies.
`$document`	Specifies a jQuery-wrapped reference to the browser's `window.document` element.
`$http`	Provides a simple-to-use functionality to send HTTP requests to the webserver or other service.
`$interval`	Provides access to a browser's `window.setInterval` functionality.
`$locale`	Provides localization rules that are consumed by various AngularJS components.
`$location`	Provides the ability to interact with a browser's `window.location` object.
`$resource`	Allows you to create an object that can interact with a RESTful server-side data source.
`$rootElement`	Provides access to the root element in the AngularJS application.
`$rootScope`	Provides access to the root scope for the AngularJS application.
`$route`	Provides deep-linking URL support for controllers and views by watching the `$location.url()` and mapping the path to existing route definitions.
`$sce`	Provides strict contextual escaping functionality when handling data from untrusted sources.
`$templateCache`	Provides the ability to read templates from a webserver into a cache for later use.
`$timeout`	Provides access to a browser's `window.setTimeout` functionality.
`$window`	Specifies a jQuery-wrapped reference to the browser's `window` element.

Sending HTTP GET and PUT Requests with the $http Service

The $http service enables you to directly interact with the webserver from your AngularJS code. The $http service uses the browser's XMLHttpRequest object underneath, but from the context of the AngularJS framework.

There are two ways to use the $http service. The simplest is to use one of the following built-in shortcut methods that correspond to standard HTTP requests:

- delete(url, [config])
- get(url, [config])
- head(url, [config])
- jsonp(url, [config])
- post(url, data, [config])
- put(url, data, [config])

In these methods, the url parameter is the URL of the web request. The optional config parameter is a JavaScript object that specifies the options to use when implementing the request. Table 25.2 lists the properties you can set in the config parameter.

You can also specify the request, URL, and data by sending the config parameter directly to the $http(config) method. For example, the following are exactly the same:

```
$http.get('/myUrl');
$http({method: 'GET', url:'/myUrl'});
```

Table 25.2 **Properties that can be defined in the config parameter for $http service requests**

Property	Description
method	An HTTP method, such as GET or POST.
url	The URL of the resource that is being requested.
params	Parameters to be sent. This can be a string in the format ?key1=value1&key2=value2&..., or it can be an object, in which case it is turned into a JSON string.
data	Data to be sent as the request message data.
headers	Headers to send with the request. You can specify an object containing the header names to be sent as properties. If a property in the object has a null value, the header is not sent.
xsrfHeaderName	The name of the HTTP header to populate with the XSRF token.
xsrfCookieName	The name of the cookie containing the XSRF token.

Property	Description
`transformRequest`	A function that is called to transform/serialize the request headers and body. The function accepts the body data as the first parameter and a getter function to get the headers by name as the second. For example: `function(data, getHeader)`
`transformResponse`	A function that is called to transform/deserialize the response headers and body. The function accepts the body data as the first parameter and a getter function to get the headers by name as the second. For example: `function(data, getHeader)`
`cache`	A Boolean that, when `true`, indicates that a default `$http` cache is used to cache `GET` responses; otherwise, if a cache instance is built with `$cacheFactory`, that cache is used for caching. If `false` and there is no `$cacheFactory` built, the responses are not cached.
`timeout`	The timeout, in milliseconds, when the request should be aborted.
`withCredentials`	A Boolean that, when `true`, indicates that the `withCredentials` flag on the `XHR` object is set.
`responseType`	The type of response to expect, such as `json` or `text`.

When you call a request method by using the `$http` object, you get back an object with the promise methods `success()` and `error()`. You can pass to these methods a callback function that is called if the request is successful or if it fails. These methods accept the following parameters:

- **`data`**: Response data.
- **`status`**: Response status.
- **`header`**: Response header.
- **`config`**: Request configuration.

The following is a simple example of implementing the `success()` and `error()` methods on a `get()` request:

```
$http({method: 'GET', url: '/myUrl'}).
  success(function(data, status, headers, config) {
    // handle success
  }).
  error(function(data, status, headers, config) {
    // handle failure
  });
```

The code in Listings 25.1 through 25.3 implements an end-to-end AngularJS/Node.js web application that allows a user to initialize a list of days and remove days from the list. The example is very rudimentary so that the code is easy to follow, but it incorporates `GET` and `POST` requests as well as error-handling examples.

Listing 25.1 implements the Node.js webserver that handles the `GET` route `/reset/days` and the `POST` route `/remove/day`. If there are fewer than two days in the list, the `/remove/day` route returns an HTTP error.

Listing 25.2 implements the AngularJS application and controller. Notice that the `removeDay()` method calls the `/remove/day POST` route on the server and places the results in the scope variable `$scope.days`. If an error occurs, the `$scope.status` variable is set to the `msg` value in the error response object. The `resetDays()` method calls the `/reset/days GET` route on the server and updates `$scope.days` with the successful response.

Listing 25.3 implements an AngularJS template that includes the `Initialize Days` button, `status` message on error, and a list of `days`. Figure 25.1 shows how the days are deleted and an error message is shown when too many days are removed.

Listing 25.1 `node_server.js`: Implementing an Express server that supports `GET` and `POST` routes for an AngularJS controller

```
var express = require('express');
var bodyParser = require('body-parser');
var app = express();
app.use('/', express.static('./static')).
    use('/images', express.static( '../images')).
    use('/lib', express.static( '../lib'));
app.use(bodyParser());
var days=['Monday', 'Tuesday', 'Wednesday',
          'Thursday', 'Friday'];
var serviceDays = days.slice(0);
app.get('/reset/days', function(req, res){
  serviceDays = days.slice(0);
  res.json(serviceDays);
});
app.post('/remove/day', function(req, res){
  if (serviceDays.length > 2){
    serviceDays.splice(serviceDays.indexOf(req.body.day), 1);
    console.log(days);
    res.json(serviceDays);
  }else {
    res.json(400, {msg:'You must leave 2 days'});
  }
});
app.listen(80);
```

Listing 25.2 `service_http.js`: **Implementing an AngularJS controller that interacts with the webserver using the `$http` service**

```
angular.module('myApp', []).
 controller('myController', ['$scope', '$http',
               function($scope, $http) {
  $scope.days=[];
  $scope.status = "";
  $scope.removeDay = function(deleteDay){
   $http.post('/remove/day', {day:deleteDay}).
    success(function(data, status, headers, config) {
     $scope.days = data;
    }).
    error(function(data, status, headers, config) {
     $scope.status = data.msg;
    });
  };
  $scope.resetDays = function(){
   $scope.status = "";
   $http.get('/reset/days')
       .success(function(data, status, headers, config) {
    $scope.days = data;
   }).
   error(function(data, status, headers, config) {
    $scope.status = data;
   });
  };
 }]);
```

Listing 25.3 `service_http.html`: **An AngularJS template that implements directives that are linked to webserver data**

```
<!doctype html>
<html ng-app="myApp">
<head>
 <title>AngularJS $http Service</title>
 <style>span{color:red;}</style>
</head>
<body>
 <div ng-controller="myController">
  <h2>$http Service</h2>
  <input type="button" ng-click="resetDays()"
      value="Initialize Days"/>
  {{status}}
  <h3>Days Available</h3>
  <div ng-repeat="day in days">
   {{day}}
```

```
          [<span ng-click="removeDay(day)">remove</span>]
        </div>
      </div>
      <script src="http://code.angularjs.org/1.2.9/angular.min.js"></script>
      <script src="/js/service_http.js"></script>
    </body>
    </html>
```

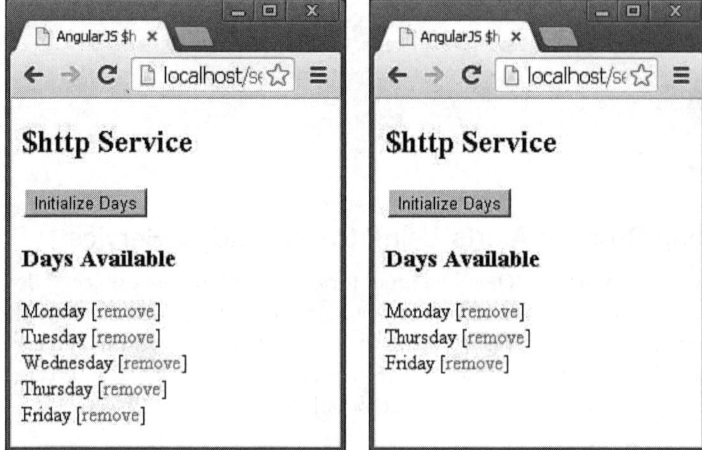

Figure 25.1 Implementing the `$http` service to allow AngularJS controllers to interact with the webserver.

Using the `$cacheFactory` Service

The `$cacheFactory` service provides a very handy repository for temporarily storing data as key/value pairs. Because `$cacheFactory` is a service, it is available to multiple controllers and other AngularJS components.

When creating the `$cacheFactory` service, you can specify an `options` object that contains the `capacity` property—for example `{capacity: 5}`. By adding this `capacity` setting, you limit the maximum number of elements in the cache to five. When a new item is added, the oldest item is removed. If no capacity is specified, the cache continues to grow.

Listing 25.4 illustrates a basic example of implementing `$cacheFactory` in a `Module` object and then accessing it from two different controllers.

Listing 25.4 `service_cache.js`: **Implementing a `$cacheFactory` service in an AngularJS application**

```
var app = angular.module('myApp', []);
app.factory('MyCache', function($cacheFactory) {
  return $cacheFactory('myCache', {capacity:5});
});
app.controller('myController', ['$scope', 'MyCache',
                               function($scope, cache) {
    cache.put('myValue', 55);
  }]);
app.controller('myController2', ['$scope', 'MyCache',
                                function($scope, cache) {
  $scope.value = cache.get('myValue');
}]);
```

Implementing Browser Alerts Using the `$window` Service

The `$window` service provides a jQuery wrapper for a browser's `window` object, allowing you to access the `window` object as you normally would from JavaScript. To illustrate this, the following code pops up a browser alert, using the `alert()` method on the `window` object. The message of the alert gets data from the `$window.screen.availWidth` and `$window.screen.availHeight` properties of the browser's `window` object:

```
var app = angular.module('myApp', []);
app.controller('myController', ['$scope', '$window',
                               function($scope, window) {
    window.alert("Your Screen is: \n" +
        window.screen.availWidth + "X" + window.screen.availHeight);
  }]);
```

Interacting with Browser Cookies Using the `$cookieStore` Service

AngularJS provides a couple services for getting and setting cookies: `$cookie` and `$cookieStore`. Cookies provide temporary storage in a browser and persist even when the user leaves the webpage or closes the browser.

The `$cookie` service allows you to get and change string cookie values by using dot notation. For example, the following retrieves the value of a cookie with the name `appCookie` and then changes it:

```
var cookie = $cookies.appCookie;
$cookies.appCookie = 'New Value';
```

The `$cookieStore` service provides `get()`, `put()`, and `remove()` functions to get, set, and remove cookies. A nice feature of the `$cookieStore` service is that it serializes JavaScript object values to a JSON string before setting them, and then it de-serializes them back to objects when getting them.

To use the `$cookie` and `$cookieStore` services, you need to do three things. First, you load the `angular-cookies.js` library in the template after `angular.js` but before `application.js`. For example:

```
<script src="http://code.angularjs.org/1.2.9/angular.min.js"></script>
<script src="http://code.angularjs.org/1.2.9/angular-cookies.min.js"></script>
```

Note

You can also download the angular-cookies.js file from the AngularJS website at http://code.angularjs.org/<version>/ where <version> is the version of AngularJS that you are using. You may also need to download the angular-cookies.min.js.map file as well depending on which version of AngularJS you are using.

Second, you to add `ngCookies` to the required list in your application `Module` definition. For example:

```
var app = angular.module('myApp', ['ngCookies']);
```

Third, you inject the `$cookies` or `$cookieStore` service into your controller. For example:

```
app.controller('myController', ['$scope', '$cookieStore',
                                 function($scope, cookieStore) {
}]);
```

Listings 25.5 and 25.6 illustrate getting and setting cookies using the `$cookie` service. Listing 25.5 loads `ngCookies` in the application, injects `$cookieStore` into the controller, and then uses the `get()`, `put()`, and `remove()` methods to interact with a cookie named `myAppCookie`.

Listing 25.6 implements a set of radio buttons that tie to the `favCookie` value in the model and use `ng-change` to call `setCookie()` when the values of the buttons change. Figure 25.2 shows the resulting webpage.

Listing 25.5 `service_cookies.js`: **Implementing an AngularJS controller that interacts with browser cookies by using the `$cookieStore` service**

```
var app = angular.module('myApp', ['ngCookies']);
app.controller('myController', ['$scope', '$cookieStore',
                                 function($scope, cookieStore) {
    $scope.favCookie = '';
    $scope.myFavCookie = '';
    $scope.setCookie = function(){
      if ($scope.favCookie === 'None'){
        cookieStore.remove('myAppCookie');
      }else{
        cookieStore.put('myAppCookie', {flavor:$scope.favCookie});
```

```
      }
      $scope.myFavCookie = cookieStore.get('myAppCookie');
    };
  }]);
```

Listing 25.6 `service_cookies.html`: **An AngularJS template that implements radio buttons to set a cookie value**

```
<!doctype html>
<html ng-app="myApp">
<head>
  <title>AngularJS $cookie Service</title>
</head>
<body>
  <div ng-controller="myController">
    <h3>Favorite Cookie:</h3>
    <input type="radio" value="Chocolate Chip" ng-model="favCookie"
           ng-change="setCookie()">Chocolate Chip</value><br/>
    <input type="radio" value="Oatmeal" ng-model="favCookie"
           ng-change="setCookie()">Oatmeal</value><br/>
    <input type="radio" value="Frosted" ng-model="favCookie"
           ng-change="setCookie()">Frosted</value>
    <input type="radio" value="None" ng-model="favCookie"
           ng-change="setCookie()">None</value>
    <hr>Cookies: {{myFavCookie}}
  </div>
  <script src="http://code.angularjs.org/1.2.9/angular.min.js"></script>
  <script src="http://code.angularjs.org/1.2.9/angular-cookies.min.js"></script>
  <script src="/js/service_cookie.js"></script>
</body>
</html>
```

Figure 25.2 Implementing the `$cookieStore` service to allow AngularJS controllers to interact with the browser cookies.

Implementing Timers with `$interval` and `$timeout` Services

AngularJS's `$interval` and `$timeout` services enable you to delay execution of code for an amount of time. These services interact with the JavaScript `setInterval` and `setTimeout` functionality—but within the AngularJS framework.

The `$interval` and `$timeout` services use the following syntax:

```
$interval(callback, delay, [count], [invokeApply]);
$timeout(callback, delay, [invokeApply]);
```

The parameters are described below:

- **`callback`:** Is executed when the delay has expired.
- **`delay`:** Specifies the number of milliseconds to wait before executing the callback function.
- **`count`:** Indicates the number of times to repeat the interval
- **`invokeApply`:** A Boolean that, if `true`, causes the function to only execute in the `$apply()` block of the AngularJS event cycle. The default is `true`.

When you call the `$interval()` and `$timeout()` methods, they return a promise object that you can use to cancel the timeout or interval. To cancel an existing `$timeout` or `$interval`, call the `cancel()` method. For example:

```
var myInterval = $interval(function(){$scope.seconds++;}, 1000, 10, true);
. . .
$interval.cancel(myInterval);
```

If you create timeouts or intervals by using `$timeout` or `$interval`, you must explicitly destroy them by using `cancel()` when the `scope` or `elements` directives are destroyed. The easiest way to do this is by adding a listener to the `$destroy` event. For example:

```
$scope.$on('$destroy', function(){
  $scope.cancel(myInterval);
});
```

Using the `$animate` Service

The `$animate` service provides animation detection hooks you can use when performing enter, leave, and move DOM operations as well as `addClass` and `removeClass` operations. You can use these hooks either through CSS classnames or through the `$animate` service in JavaScript.

To implement animation, you need to add a directive that supports animation to the element that you want to animate. Table 25.3 lists the directives that support animation and the types of animation events that they support.

Table 25.3 **AngularJS directives that support animation**

Directive	Description
ngRepeat	Supports enter, leave, and move events.
ngView	Supports enter and leave events.
ngInclude	Supports enter and leave events.
ngSwitch	Supports enter and leave events.
ngIf	Supports enter and leave events.
ngClass	Supports addClass and removeClass events.
ngShow	Supports addClass and removeClass events.
ngHide	Supports addClass and removeClass events.

Implementing Animation in CSS

To implement animation in CSS, you need to include the ngClass directive in the element that you want to animate. AngularJS uses the ngClass value as a root name for additional CSS classes that will be added and removed from the element during animation.

An animation event is called on an element with an ngClass directive defined. Table 25.4 lists the additional classes that are added and removed during the animation process.

Table 25.4 **AngularJS directives that are automatically added and removed during animation**

Class	Description
ng-animate	Added when an event is triggered.
ng-animate-active	Added when animation starts and triggers CSS transitions.
<super>-ng-move	Added when move events are triggered.
<super>-ng-move-active	Added when move animation starts and triggers CSS transitions.
<super>-ng-leave	Added when leave events are triggered.
<super>-ng-leave-active	Added when leave animation starts and triggers CSS transitions.
<super>-ng-enter	Added when enter events are triggered.
<super>-ng-enter-active	Added when enter animation starts and triggers CSS transitions.
<super>-ng-add	Added when addClass events are triggered.
<super>-ng-add-active	Added when add class animation starts and triggers CSS transitions.
<super>-ng-remove	Added when removeClass events are triggered.
<super>-ng-remove-active	Added when remove class animation starts and triggers CSS transitions.

To implement CSS-based animations, all you need to do is add the appropriate CSS transition code for the additional classes listed in Table 25.4. To illustrate this, the following snippet implements add class and remove class transitions for a user-defined class named `.img-fade` that animates changing the `opacity` of the image to `.1` for a two-second duration:

```
.img-fade-add, .img-fade-remove {
  -webkit-transition:all ease 2s;
  -moz-transition:all ease 2s;
  -o-transition:all ease 2s;
  transition:all ease 2s;
}
.img-fade, .img-fade-add.img-fade-add-active {
   opacity:.1;
}
```

Notice that the transitions are added to the `.img-fade-add` and `.img-fade-remove` classes, but the actual class definition is applied to `.img-fade`. You also need the class definition `.img-fade-add.img-fade-add-active` to set the ending state for the transition.

Implementing Animation in JavaScript

Implementing AngularJS CSS animation is very simple, but you can also implement animation in JavaScript using jQuery. JavaScript animations provide more direct control over your animations. Also, JavaScript animations do not require a browser to support CSS3.

To implement animation in JavaScript, you need to include the jQuery library in your template before the `angular.js` library is loaded. For example:

```
<script src="http://code.jquery.com/jquery-1.11.0.min.js"></script>
```

> **Note**
>
> Including the full jQuery library is necessary if you want to be able to utilize the full features of jQuery animation. If you do decide to include the jQuery library make certain that it is loaded before the AngularJS library in your HTML code. This will eliminate the risk of the jQuery library overwriting variables necessary for AngularJS to function properly.

You also need to include the `ngAnimate` dependency in your application `Module` object definition. For example:

```
var app = angular.module('myApp', ['ngAnimate']);
```

You can then use the `animate()` method on your `Module` object to implement animations. The `animate()` method returns an object that provides functions for the `enter`, `leave`, `move`, `addClass`, and `removeClass` events that you want to handle. These functions are passed the element to be animated as the first parameter. You can then use the jQuery `animate()` method to animate an element.

The jQuery `animate()` method uses the following syntax, where `cssProperties` is an object of CSS attribute changes, `duration` is specified in milliseconds, `easing` is the easing method, and `callback` is the function to execute when the animation completes:

```
animate(cssProperties, [duration], [easing], [callback])
```

For example, the following code animates adding the `fadeClass` class to an element by setting `opacity` to `0`:

```
app.animation('.fadeClass', function() {
  return {
    addClass : function(element, className, done) {
      jQuery(element).animate({ opacity: 0}, 3000);
    },
  };
});
```

Animating Elements Using AngularJS

Listings 25.7, 25.8, and 25.9 implement a basic animation example that applies a fade in/out animation to an image, using the JavaScript method, and uses CSS transition animation to animate resizing the image.

Listing 25.7 contains the AngularJS controller and animation code. Notice that the same class `.fadeOut` is used to apply both the fade in and fade out animations by hooking into the `addClass` and `removeClass` events.

Listing 25.8 implements the AngularJS template that supports the animation. Notice that line 5 loads the jQuery library to support the JavaScript animation code. Also, line 6 loads the `animate.css` script that contains the transition animations shown in Listing 25.9. The buttons simply add and remove the appropriate classes to initiate the animations.

Listing 25.9 provides the necessary transition CSS definitions for the `add` and `remove` classes that get implemented during the animation process. Figure 25.3 shows the results.

Listing 25.7 `service_animate.js`: **Implementing an AngularJS controller that implements jQuery animation using the `$animation` service**

```
var app = angular.module('myApp', ['ngAnimate']);
app.controller('myController', function($scope ) {
  $scope.myImgClass = 'start-class';
  });
app.animation('.fadeOut', function() {
  return {
    enter: function(element, parentElement, afterElement, doneCallback){},
    leave: function(element, doneCallback) {},
    move: function(element, parentElement, afterElement, doneCallback){},
    addClass: function(element, className, done) {
      jQuery(element).animate({ opacity: 0}, 3000);
```

```
    },
    removeClass : function(element, className, done) {
      jQuery(element).animate({ opacity: 1}, 3000);
    }
  };
});
```

Listing 25.8 `service_animate.html`: **An AngularJS template that implements buttons that change the class on an image to animate fading and resizing**

```
<!doctype html>
<html ng-app="myApp">
<head>
  <title>AngularJS $animate Service</title>
  <script src="http://code.jquery.com/jquery-1.11.0.min.js"></script>
  <link rel="stylesheet" href="/css/animate.css">
</head>
<body>
  <div ng-controller="myController">
    <h3>Image Animation:</h3>
    <input type="button" ng-click="myImgClass='fadeOut'" value="Fade Out"/>
    <input type="button" ng-click="myImgClass=''" value="Fade In"/>
    <input type="button" ng-click="myImgClass='shrink'" value="Small"/>
    <input type="button" ng-click="myImgClass=''" value="Big"/>
    <hr>
    <img ng-class="myImgClass" src="/images/arch.jpg" />
  </div>
  <script src="http://code.angularjs.org/1.2.9/angular.min.js"></script>
  <script src="http://code.angularjs.org/1.2.9/angular-animate.min.js"></script>
  <script src="/js/service_animate.js"></script>
</body>
</html>
```

Note

You can also download the angular-animate.js file from the AngularJS website at http://code.angularjs.org/<version>/ where <version> is the version of AngularJS that you are using. You may also need to download the angular-animate.min.js.map file as well depending on which version of AngularJS you are using.

Listing 25.9 `animate.css`: **CSS code that provides transition effects for the various class stages of the AngularJS animation code**

```
.shrink-add, .shrink-remove {
  -webkit-transition:all ease 2.5s;
  -moz-transition:all ease 2.5s;
  -o-transition:all ease 2.5s;
  transition:all ease 2.5s;
}
.shrink,
.shrink-add.shrink-add-active {
  height:100px;
}
.start-class,
.shrink-remove.shrink-remove-active {
  height:400px;
}
```

Figure 25.3 Implementing the `$animation` service in both CSS and JavaScript to animate fading and resizing an image.

Creating Custom Services

AngularJS enables you to create your own custom services to provide functionality in AngularJS components that require it. As you have seen so far in this chapter, services provide a wide variety of functionality for AngularJS applications.

There are four main types of services that you will likely be implementing in your code: `value`, `constant`, `factory`, and `service`. The following sections cover them.

Creating `value` Services

You use the very simple `value` service to define a single value that you can inject as a service provider. The `value` method uses the following syntax, where `name` is the service name and `object` is any JavaScript object you want to provide:

```
value(name, object)
```

For example:

```
var app = angular.module('myApp', []);
app.value('myValue', {color:'blue', value:'17'});
```

Creating `constant` Services

The `constant` service is basically the same as the `value` service, except that `constant` services are available in the configuration phase of building the `Module` object, whereas `value` services are not. The `constant` method uses the following syntax, where `name` is the service name and `object` is any JavaScript object you want to provide:

```
constant(name, object)
```

For example:

```
var app = angular.module('myApp', []);
app.constant('myConst', "Constant String");
```

Creating `factory` Services

The `factory` method provides the ability to implement functionality into a service. It can also be dependent on other service providers, allowing you to build up compartmentalized code. The `factory` method uses the following syntax, where `name` is the service name and `factoryProvider` is a provider function that builds the factory service:

```
factory(name, factoryProvider)
```

You can inject the `factory` method with other services, and it returns the service object with the appropriate functionality. The functionality can be a complex JavaScript service, a value, or a simple function. For example, the following code implements a `factory` service that returns a function that adds two numbers:

```
var app = angular.module('myApp', []);
app.constant('myConst', 10);
app.factory('multiplier', ['myConst', function (myConst) {
  return function(value) { return value*myConst; };
}]);
```

Creating `service` Services

The `service` method provides the ability to implement functionality into a server. However, the `service` method works slightly differently from the `factory` method. The `service` method accepts a constructor function as the second argument and uses it to create a new instance of an object. The `service` method uses the following syntax, where `name` is the service name and `constructor` is a constructor function:

```
service(name, constructor)
```

The `service` method can also accept dependency injection. The following code implements a basic service method that provides an `add()` function and a `multiply()` function:

```
var app = angular.module('myApp', []);
app.constant('myConst', 10);
function ConstMathObj(myConst) {
  this.add = function(value){ return value + myConst; };
  this.multiply = function(value){ return value * myConst; };
}
app.service('constMath', ['myConst', ConstMathObj]);
```

Notice that the `ConstMathObj` constructor is created first, and then the `service()` method calls it and uses dependency injection to insert the `myConst` service.

Integrating Services in a Module

The code in Listing 25.10 shows an example of integrating `value`, `constant`, `factory`, and `service` services into a single module. The example is very basic and easy to follow. Notice that `censorWords` and `repString` are injected into and used in the `factory` and `service` definitions.

Lines 4–13 implement a `factory` service that returns a function that censors a string. Notice that line 26 calls the `factory` directly to censor the string.

Lines 14–23 implement a `service` service by first defining an object constructor and then, on line 23, registering the service to the application. Notice that line 27 calls the `censor()` method defined in the constructor to censor the text.

Listing 25.10 `service_custom.js`: **Implementing and consuming custom services in an AngularJS controller**

```
var app = angular.module('myApp', []);
app.value('censorWords', ['bad','mad','sad']);
app.constant('repString', "****");
app.factory('censorF', ['censorWords', 'repString',
                        function (cWords, repString) {
  return function(inString) {
    var outString = inString;
    for(i in cWords){
      outString = outString.replace(cWords[i], repString);
    }
    return outString;
  };
}]);
function CensorObj(cWords, repString) {
  this.censor = function(inString){
    var outString = inString;
    for(i in cWords){
      outString = outString.replace(cWords[i], repString);
    }
    return outString;
  };
}
app.service('censorS', ['censorWords', 'repString', CensorObj]);
app.controller('myController', ['$scope', 'censorF', 'censorS',
                                function($scope, censorF, censorS) {
    $scope.censoredByFactory = censorF("mad text");
    $scope.censoredByService = censorS.censor("bad text");
  }]);
```

Summary

AngularJS services are singleton objects that you can register with the dependency injector; controllers and other AngularJS components, including other services, can consume them. AngularJS provides much of the backend functionality in services, such as `$http`, which allows you to easily integrate webserver communication into your AngularJS applications.

AngularJS provides several methods for creating custom services, with varying levels of complexity. The `value` and `constant` methods create simple services. On the other hand, the `factory` and `service` methods allow you to create much more complex services.

Up Next

In the next chapter, you'll switch gears and start looking at more practical applications of the things you have learned so far in this book. The next chapter provides an end-to-end example of adding user accounts to a website, including various methods of authentication.

26

Adding User Accounts to Your Website

In this chapter you'll see a practical example of implementing the full Node.js, MongoDB, and AngularJS stack; the example shows how to add, modify, and remove users from your website. Adding users is a common task for many websites, and there are a number of methods to do this, even within the Node.js, MongoDB, and AngularJS stack. The example in this chapter shows one of these methods to illustrate the basic principle, which you can then build upon.

Libraries Used

The project in this chapter uses the following add-on Node.js NPMs. You need to install them into your project directory in order to follow along with the code examples:

- **`express`:** Used as the main webserver for the project.
- **`ejs`:** Used to render the HTML templates.
- **`mongodb`:** Used to access the MongoDB database.
- **`mongoose`:** Used to provide the structured data model.
- **`connect-mongo`:** Provides a link between Express and MongoDB so that you can use MongoDB as the persistent store for sessions.

The code in this chapter also requires that you have the AngularJS library.

Project Directory Structure

The project is organized into the following directory structure:

- `./`: Contains the base application files and supporting folders. This is the project root.
- **`../node_modules`:** Created when the NPMs listed above are installed in the system.

- **./controllers**: Contains the Express route controllers that provide the interaction between routes and changes to the MongoDB database.
- **./models**: Contains the Mongoose model definitions for objects in the database.
- **./static**: Contains any static files that need to be sent, such as CSS and AngularJS code.
- **./views**: Contains the HTML templates that will be rendered by EJS.

This is just one method of organizing your code. You do not have to follow this directory structure, but keep in mind that directory structure should be part of the overall design of your projects so that you can easily find the code you are looking for.

In addition to the directory structure, the following code files are included. The following list is intended to give you an idea of the functionality of each file:

- **./auth_server.js**: Loads the necessary libraries, creates a connection to MongoDB, and starts the Express server. This is the main application file.
- **./routes.js**: Defines the routes for the Express server. This file handles functionality that does not apply to the database.
- **./controllers/users_controller.js**: Defines the functionality for the routes that require interaction with the MongoDB database model, including adding, retrieving, and deleting user objects.
- **./models/users_model.js**: Defines the user object model.
- **./views/index.html**: Provides the main page for the application, with links to edit the user or log out.
- **./views/login.html**: Provides the login page that authenticates the user.
- **./views/signup.html**: Provides a signup form that allows new users to create profiles.
- **./views/user.html**: Provides a form for editing a user profile.
- **./static/js/my_app.js**: Provides the AngularJS module and controller definitions to support AngularJS code in the view files already mentioned.
- **./static/css/styles.css**: Provides the CSS styling for the AngularJS HTML pages.
- **../lib**: A folder that contains the necessary AngularJS library files used in this example. This folder is a peer to the chapter folder in the book's code archive.

Defining the User Model

One of the first things that you should do when you begin implementing an application is define the model for the objects that will be stored in the database. In this case you need a `User` object. Defining the model first helps you get a better idea of how to implement the routes and controllers.

Listing 26.1 implements the `User` model for this chapter's application. It is very simple but provides a good example of what you can do. You can easily enhance this example as much as needed.

Notice that the schema defined implements a unique `username` as well as `email`, `color`, and `hashed_password` fields. The final line creates the model in Mongoose.

Listing 26.1 `users_model.js`: Implementing the `User` model for Mongoose

```
var mongoose = require('mongoose'),
    Schema = mongoose.Schema;
var UserSchema = new Schema({
    username: { type: String, unique: true },
    email: String,
    color: String,
    hashed_password: String
});
mongoose.model('User', UserSchema);
```

Creating the Server

Listing 26.2 implements the Express webserver for the application. You should recognize much of the code. The general flow of this code is to first require the necessary modules, connect to the MongoDB database, configure the Express server, and begin listening.

The following line ensures that the `User` model is registered in Mongoose:

```
require('./models/users_model.js');
```

Also, the following `require()` adds the routes from `./routes` to the Express server:

```
require('./routes')(app);
```

The following Express configuration code uses the `connect-mongo` library to register the MongoDB connection as the persistent store for the authenticated sessions. Notice that the `connect-mongo` store is passed an object with `session` set to the `express-session` module instance. Also notice that the `db` value in the `mongoStore` instance is set to the `mongoose.connection.db` database that is already connected:

```
var expressSession = require('express-session');
var mongoStore = require('connect-mongo')({session: expressSession});
app.use(expressSession({
  secret: 'SECRET',
  cookie: {maxAge: 60*60*1000},
  store: new mongoStore({
      db: mongoose.connection.db,
      collection: 'sessions'
```

```
    })
  }));
```

This code adds a `session` property to the `request` object. The `session` object is directly tied to the `sessions` collection in MongoDB so that when you make changes to the session, they are saved in the database.

Listing 26.2 `auth_server.js`: **Implementing the application database connection and Express webserver**

```
var express = require('express');
var bodyParser = require('body-parser');
var cookieParser = require('cookie-parser');
var expressSession = require('express-session');
var mongoStore = require('connect-mongo')({session: expressSession});
var mongoose = require('mongoose');
require('./models/users_model.js');
var conn = mongoose.connect('mongodb://localhost/myapp');
var app = express();
app.engine('.html', require('ejs').__express);
app.set('views', __dirname + '/views');
app.set('view engine', 'html');
app.use(bodyParser());
app.use(cookieParser());
app.use(expressSession({
  secret: 'SECRET',
  cookie: {maxAge: 60*60*1000},
  store: new mongoStore({
      db: mongoose.connection.db,
      collection: 'sessions'
    })
  }));
require('./routes')(app);
app.listen(80);
```

Implementing Routes

As part of the Express server configuration, the `./routes.js` file shown in Listing 26.3 is loaded. This file implements the routes necessary to support signup, login, editing, and user deletion. This code also implements static routes that support loading the static files.

Notice that `req.session` is used frequently throughout the routes code. This is the session created when `expressSession()` middleware was added in the previous section. Notice that the following code is called to clean up the existing session data when the user logs out or is deleted:

```
req.session.destroy(function(){});
```

The code attaches text strings to the `session.msg` variable so that they can be added to the template. (This is just for example purpose so that you can see the status of requests on the webpages.)

Notice at the bottom of Listing 26.3 that the handler function for the routes point to the functions from `users_controller`, loaded by the following statement:

```
var users = require('./controllers/users_controller');
```

Listing 26.3 provides the full route implementation, including in the application, with the exception of the routes that modify the database; that is discussed in the next section.

Listing 26.3 `routes.js`: **Implementing the Express server routes to handle web requests**

```
var crypto = require('crypto');
var express = require('express');
module.exports = function(app) {
  var users = require('./controllers/users_controller');
  app.use('/static', express.static( './static')).
      use('/lib', express.static( '../lib')
  );
  app.get('/', function(req, res){
    if (req.session.user) {
      res.render('index', {username: req.session.username,
                           msg:req.session.msg});
    } else {
      req.session.msg = 'Access denied!';
      res.redirect('/login');
    }
  });
  app.get('/user', function(req, res){
    if (req.session.user) {
      res.render('user', {msg:req.session.msg});
    } else {
      req.session.msg = 'Access denied!';
      res.redirect('/login');
    }
  });
  app.get('/signup', function(req, res){
    if(req.session.user){
      res.redirect('/');
    }
    res.render('signup', {msg:req.session.msg});
  });
  app.get('/login',  function(req, res){
    if(req.session.user){
      res.redirect('/');
    }
```

```
    res.render('login', {msg:req.session.msg});
  });
  app.get('/logout', function(req, res){
    req.session.destroy(function(){
      res.redirect('/login');
    });
  });
  app.post('/signup', users.signup);
  app.post('/user/update', users.updateUser);
  app.post('/user/delete', users.deleteUser);
  app.post('/login', users.login);
  app.get('/user/profile', users.getUserProfile);
}
```

Implementing the User Controller Routes

Now you need to implement the route code to support interaction with the MongoDB model. The code in Listing 26.9, later in this chapter, implements the database interaction routes in a separate file to keep the functionality separated from the normal routing. Due to the size of the `users_conroller.js` code, the following sections discuss each of the routes individually.

Implementing the User Signup Route

Listing 26.4 implements the `signup` route. The logic in this route first creates a new `User` object and then adds the email address and hashed password, using the `hashPW()` function defined in the same file. Then the Mongoose `save()` method is called on the object to store it in the database. On error, the user is redirected back to the signup page.

If the user saves successfully, the ID created by MongoDB is added as the `req.session.user` property, and the username is added as the `req.session.username`. The request is then directed to the index page.

Listing 26.4 `users_controller.js-signup`: **Implementing the route for user signup for the Express server**

```
exports.signup = function(req, res){
  var user = new User({username:req.body.username});
  user.set('hashed_password', hashPW(req.body.password));
  user.set('email', req.body.email);
  user.save(function(err) {
    if (err){
      res.session.error = err;
      res.redirect('/signup');
    } else {
      req.session.user = user.id;
```

```
      req.session.username = user.username;
      req.session.msg = 'Authenticated as ' + user.username;
      res.redirect('/');
    }
  });
};
```

Implementing the User Login Route

Listing 26.5 implements the `login` route. First, the handler finds the user by username, then it compares the stored hashed password with a hash of the password sent in the request. If the passwords match, the user session is regenerated using the `regenerate()` method. Notice that `req.session.user` and `req.session.username` are set in the regenerated session.

Listing 26.5 `users_controller.js-login`: **Implementing the route for user login for the Express server**

```
exports.login = function(req, res){
  User.findOne({ username: req.body.username })
  .exec(function(err, user) {
    if (!user){
      err = 'User Not Found.';
    } else if (user.hashed_password ===
             hashPW(req.body.password.toString())) {
      req.session.regenerate(function(){
        req.session.user = user.id;
        req.session.username = user.username;
        req.session.msg = 'Authenticated as ' + user.username;
        res.redirect('/');
      });
    }else{
      err = 'Authentication failed.';
    }
    if(err){
      req.session.regenerate(function(){
        req.session.msg = err;
        res.redirect('/login');
      });
    }
  });
};
```

Implementing the Get User Profile Route

Listing 26.6 implements the `getUserProfile` route. This handler finds the user by using the user `id` that is stored in `req.session.user`. If the user is found, a JSON representation of the user object is returned in the request. If the user is not found, a 404 error is sent.

Listing 26.6 `users_controller.js-getUserProfile`: **Implementing the route to get user profiles for the Express server**

```
exports.getUserProfile = function(req, res) {
  User.findOne({ _id: req.session.user })
  .exec(function(err, user) {
    if (!user){
      res.json(404, {err: 'User Not Found.'});
    } else {
      res.json(user);
    }
  });
};
```

Implementing the Update User Route

Listing 26.7 implements the `updateUser` route. This handler finds the user and then sets the values from the `req.body.email` and `req.body.color` properties that will come from the update form in the body of the `POST` request. Then the `save()` method is called on the `User` object, and the request is redirected back to the `/user` route to display the changed results.

Listing 26.7 `users_controller.js-updateUser`: **Implementing the route to update users for the Express server**

```
exports.updateUser = function(req, res){
  User.findOne({ _id: req.session.user })
  .exec(function(err, user) {
    user.set('email', req.body.email);
    user.set('color', req.body.color);
    user.save(function(err) {
      if (err){
        res.sessor.error = err;
      } else {
        req.session.msg = 'User Updated.';
      }
      res.redirect('/user');
    });
  });
};
```

Implementing the Delete User Route

The code in Listing 26.8 implements the `deleteUser` route. This route finds the user in the MongoDB database and then calls the `remove()` method on the `User` object to remove the user from the database. Also notice that `req.session.destroy()` is called to remove the session because the user no longer exists.

Listing 26.8 `users_controller.js-deleteUser`: **Implementing the route to delete users for the Express server**

```
exports.deleteUser = function(req, res){
  User.findOne({ _id: req.session.user })
  .exec(function(err, user) {
    if(user){
      user.remove(function(err){
        if (err){
          req.session.msg = err;
        }
        req.session.destroy(function(){
          res.redirect('/login');
        });
      });
    } else{
      req.session.msg = "User Not Found!";
      req.session.destroy(function(){
        res.redirect('/login');
      });
    }
  });
```

Full User Controller Code

Listing 26.9 shows the complete `users_controller.js` code. Notice that the `crypto` library is loaded and used to implement the `hashPW()` function that creates the hashed password values. Also notice that the `User` schema is loaded to provide access to the database in the route handlers.

Listing 26.9 `users_controller.js`: **Fully implementing the routes that interact with the `User` model**

```
var crypto = require('crypto');
var mongoose = require('mongoose'),
    User = mongoose.model('User');
function hashPW(pwd){
  return crypto.createHash('sha256').update(pwd).
         digest('base64').toString();
```

```
}
exports.signup = function(req, res){
  var user = new User({username:req.body.username});
  user.set('hashed_password', hashPW(req.body.password));
  user.set('email', req.body.email);
  user.save(function(err) {
    if (err){
      res.sessor.error = err;
      res.redirect('/signup');
    } else {
      req.session.user = user.id;
      req.session.username = user.username;
      req.session.msg = 'Authenticated as ' + user.username;
      res.redirect('/');
    }
  });
};
exports.login = function(req, res){
  User.findOne({ username: req.body.username })
  .exec(function(err, user) {
    if (!user){
      err = 'User Not Found.';
    } else if (user.hashed_password ===
                hashPW(req.body.password.toString())) {
      req.session.regenerate(function(){
        req.session.user = user.id;
        req.session.username = user.username;
        req.session.msg = 'Authenticated as ' + user.username;
        res.redirect('/');
      });
    }else{
      err = 'Authentication failed.';
    }
    if(err){
      req.session.regenerate(function(){
        req.session.msg = err;
        res.redirect('/login');
      });
    }
  });
};
exports.getUserProfile = function(req, res) {
  User.findOne({ _id: req.session.user })
  .exec(function(err, user) {
    if (!user){
      res.json(404, {err: 'User Not Found.'});
    } else {
```

```
      res.json(user);
    }
  });
};
exports.updateUser = function(req, res){
  User.findOne({ _id: req.session.user })
  .exec(function(err, user) {
    user.set('email', req.body.email);
    user.set('color', req.body.color);
    user.save(function(err) {
      if (err){
        res.sessor.error = err;
      } else {
        req.session.msg = 'User Updated.';
      }
      res.redirect('/user');
    });
  });
};
exports.deleteUser = function(req, res){
  User.findOne({ _id: req.session.user })
  .exec(function(err, user) {
    if(user){
      user.remove(function(err){
        if (err){
          req.session.msg = err;
        }
        req.session.destroy(function(){
          res.redirect('/login');
        });
      });
    } else{
      req.session.msg = "User Not Found!";
      req.session.destroy(function(){
        res.redirect('/login');
      });
    }
  });
};
```

Implementing the User and Authentication Views

Now that the routes are set up and configured, you are ready to implement the views that are rendered by the routes. These views are intentionally very basic to allow you to see the interaction between the EJS render engine and the AngularJS support functionality. The following sections discuss the `index`, `signup`, `login`, and `user` views.

These views are implemented as EJS templates. This chapter uses the EJS render engine because it is very similar to HTML, so you do not need to learn a new template language, such as Jade. However, you can use any template engine that is supported by Express to produce the same results.

Implementing the signup View

For the signup view, Listing 26.10 implements a simple signup form that allows you to specify a new username, password, and email address. The body contains a <div> element that acts as a container for the form for styling. The form is made up of text, password, and email <input> elements. The form method is POST, to include the username, password, and email fields in the POST body for the route. Notice that the <%=msg> EJS script element is included to display the message if one exists on the session. Figure 26.1 shows the rendered view.

Listing 26.10 signup.html: Implementing the signup EJS HTML template

```
<!doctype html>
<html>
<head>
  <title>User Login and Sessions Signup</title>
  <link rel="stylesheet" type="text/css"
      href="/static/css/styles.css" />
</head>
<body>
  <div class="form-container">
    <p class="form-header">Sign Up</p>
    <form method="POST">
      <label>Username:</label>
        <input type="text" name="username"><br>
      <label>Password:</label>
        <input type="password" name="password"><br>
      <label>Email:</label>
        <input type="email" name="email"><br>
      <input type="submit" value="Register">
    </form>
  </div>
  <hr><%= msg %>
</body>
</html>
```

Figure 26.1 The rendered `signup` view allows you to add a user.

Implementing the `index` View

For the `index` view, Listing 26.11 implements a very basic index page. The page only includes links to the logout and user views to allow you to access those views from the browser. Also, the `<%=msg>` EJS script element is included to display the message if one exists on the session. Figure 26.2 shows the rendered view.

Listing 26.11 `index.html`: **Implementing the `index` EJS HTML template**

```
<!doctype html>
<html ng-app="myApp">
<head>
  <title>User Login and Sessions</title>
  <link rel="stylesheet" type="text/css"
      href="/static/css/styles.css" />
</head>
<body>
  <div ng-controller="myController">
    <h2>Welcome. You are Logged In as <%= username %></h2>
    <a href="/logout">logout</a>
    <a href="/user">Edit User</a>
    <p>Place Your Code Here<p>
  </div>
  <hr><%= msg %>
  <script src="http://code.angularjs.org/1.2.9/angular.min.js"></script>
  <script src="/static/js/my_app.js"></script>
</body>
</html>
```

Figure 26.2 The rendered `index` view allows you to log out and edit a user.

Implementing the `login` View

For the `login` view, Listing 26.12 implements a simple login form that allows you to specify a username and password to use to create an authenticated session. The form includes text and password `<input>` elements. The form method is `POST`, to include the `username` and `password` fields in the `POST` body for the route. Notice that the `<%=msg>` EJS script element is included to display the message if one exists on the session. Figure 26.3 shows the rendered login page.

Listing 26.12 `login.html`: **Implementing the `login` EJS HTML template**

```
<!doctype html>
<html>
<head>
  <title>User Login and Sessions</title>
  <link rel="stylesheet" type="text/css"
        href="/static/css/styles.css" />
</head>
<body>
  <div class="form-container">
    <p class="form-header">Login</p>
    <form method="POST">
        <label>Username:</label>
        <input type="text" name="username"><br>
        <label>Password:</label>
        <input type="password" name="password"><br>
        <input type="submit" value="Login">
    </form>
  </div>
  <a href="/signup">Sign Up</a>
```

```
  <hr><%= msg %>
</body>
</html>
```

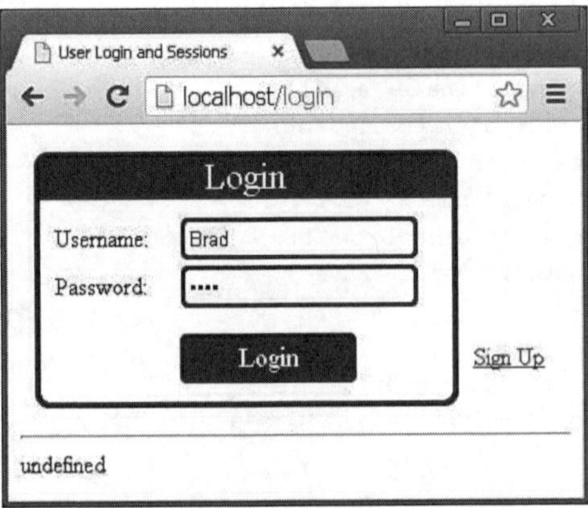

Figure 26.3 The rendered `login` view allows you to log in to the server.

Implementing the `user` View

For the `user` view, Listing 26.13 implements two simple forms. The first allows you to modify the `email` and `color` preferences of the user. The body contains a `<div>` element that creates an instance of an AngularJS controller that gets the user information from the webserver. The username `<input>` element is set to `disabled` to prevent the user from changing the username.

Notice that the inputs are bound to the `$scope.user` value in the AngularJS scope by using `ng-model`. Also notice that the form methods are `POST` but also include the `action` attribute, which specifies the route to use to save or delete the user. Remember that using the `action` attribute overrides the AngularJS suppression of the normal `<form>` functionality. This page also includes the `<%=msg>` EJS script element to display the message if one exists on the session. Figure 26.4 shows the rendered `user` view.

Listing 26.13 `user.html`: Implementing the `user` EJS HTML template

```
<!doctype html>
<html ng-app="myApp">
<head>
  <title>User Login and Sessions</title>
  <link rel="stylesheet" type="text/css"
      href="/static/css/styles.css" />
</head>
<body>
```

```
  <div class="form-container" ng-controller="myController">
    <p class="form-header">User Profile</p>
    <form method="POST" action="/user/update">
       <label>Username:</label>
         <input type="text" name="username"
                ng-model="user.username" disabled><br>
       <label>Email:</label>
         <input type="email" name="email"
                ng-model="user.email"><br>
       <label>Favorite Color:</label>
         <input type="text" name="color"
                ng-model="user.color"><br>
       <input type="submit" value="Save">
    </form>
  </div>
  <form method="POST" action="/user/delete">
    <input type="submit" value="Delete User">
  </form>
  <hr><%= msg %>
  <hr>{{error}}
  <script src="http://code.angularjs.org/1.2.9/angular.min.js"></script>
  <script src="/static/js/my_app.js"></script>
</body>
</html>
```

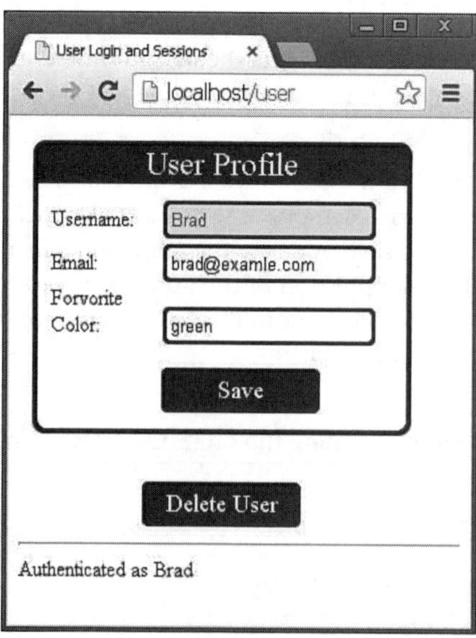

Figure 26.4 The rendered `user` view allows you to edit and delete the user.

Adding CSS Code to Style Views

Listing 26.14 shows the CSS code used to style the elements in the views. Each of the views links the `styles.css` script template in its header.

Listing 26.14 `styles.css`: **Implementing the CSS styles for the view HTML files**

```
div.form-container{
  display: inline-block;
  border: 4px ridge blue;
  width: 280px;
  border-radius:10px;
  margin:10px;
}
p.form-header{
  margin:0px;
  font: 24px bold;
  color:white;  background:blue;
  text-align:center;
}
form{
  margin:10px;
}
label{ width:80px; display: inline-block;}
input{
  border: 3px ridge blue;
  border-radius:5px;
  padding:3px;
}
input[type=submit]{
  font: 18px bold;
  width: 120px;
  color:white;  background:blue;
  margin-top:15px;
  margin-left:85px;
}
```

Implementing the AngularJS Module and Controller

With the views finished, you need to implement the AngularJS controller code to support them. Listing 26.15 implements the AngularJS controller that supports the `user` view. The controller, like the web forms, is very basic. The controller uses the `$http` service to get the user data from the `/user/profile` route and provide it to the AngularJS template in the `$scope.user` value.

Listing 26.15 `my_app.js`: Implementing an AngularJS controller to get user data by using an `$http` request

```
angular.module('myApp', []).
  controller('myController', ['$scope', '$http',
                              function($scope, $http) {
    $http.get('/user/profile')
        .success(function(data, status, headers, config) {
      $scope.user = data;
      $scope.error = "";
    }).
    error(function(data, status, headers, config) {
      $scope.user = {};
      $scope.error = data;
    });
  }]);
```

Using Social Media Accounts as Authentication Sources

At times you might want to allow users the ability to use other authentication sources to authenticate to your server. The `passport` NPM provides functionality that allows you to implement `OAuth` and `OpenID` authentication methods from social media sites such as Google, Facebook, and Twitter.

Implementing authentication using these sources can be a hassle, but the Passport NPM provides middleware that hooks into Express and obfuscates most of the complexity. The following sections take you through the process of using Passport to implement authentication using social media `OAuth` and `OpenID` sources.

Adding Passport

Before you move on, you need to add Passport to your project. You need to install the correct Passport NPM by using the following command or include the `package.json` file for the project:

```
npm install passport@0.2.0
```

Adding Authentication Strategies

Once the `passport` NPM is installed, you need to define which authentication strategies you want to implement. Authentication strategies are source specific—so Passport provides separate authentication strategies for Google, Facebook, Twitter, etc.

Each authentication strategy comes packaged in its own NPM prefixed with `passport-`. This keeps your code base small and makes it easy to implement multiple strategies. For example, the following commands install the Google, Facebook, and Twitter NPMs:

```
npm install passport-google-google@0.3.0
npm-install passport-facebook-facebook@1.0.3
npm-install passport-twitter@1.0.2
```

Now you need to use `require()` to load a strategy before you can use it in your application. For example:

```
var GoogleStrategy = require('passport-google').Strategy;
```

Then you need to add the strategy to the Passport middleware by using the `use()` function. This function accepts a new instance of the `Strategy` object for the authentication source. In the case of Google, the strategy requires a `returnURL` for the application from the Google website and also the realm or domain for which the login is valid.

For example, the following code creates an instance of the Google strategy and configures it:

```
passport.use(new GoogleStrategy({
    returnURL: 'http://localhost/auth/google/return',
    realm: 'http://localhost/'
  },
  function(identifier, profile, done) {
    process.nextTick(function () {
      profile.identifier = identifier;
      return done(null, profile);
    });
  }
));
```

The `Strategy` constructor function accepts a callback function that is executed when the authentication information is returned from Google. You use this function to add the authentication information to the database or manipulate the information, if necessary. The example above adds the identifier to the profile on the next Node.js tick. The authentication identifier that Google assigns is passed into the callback function, along with the `profile` of the Google user.

When the callback function is finished, you call the `done()` function and pass an error as the first parameter if one occurred and the user information as the second. If you use sessions, the second parameter is assigned to the `req.user` property of `Request` objects.

Each authentication source is implemented a bit differently, so you need to view the Passport documentation on the specific source configuration method.

Implementing Application Middleware

You need to register Passport in the middleware service by using the `initialize()` method of the Passport NPM. This configures the Passport strategies and hooks them into the Express middleware mechanism. For example:

```
app.use(passport.initialize());
```

If you want to store the authentication in sessions, you also need to register the `passport.session()` middleware. You must do this after the `expressSession()` middleware if you are doing both. For example:

```
app.use(expressSession({ secret: 'SECRET' }));
app.use(passport.initialize());
app.use(passport.session());
```

Adding Authenticated User Serialization and Deserialization

Typically the credentials used to authenticate are transmitted during a login request. On a successful login, a session cookie is implemented in the user's browser to verify authentication. Subsequent requests from the browser include the `session` cookie that can be used to verify the authentication.

Passport serializes and deserializes the authenticated `User` object returned from the authentication source. You need to specify how the serialization takes place. The `serializeUser()` and `deserializeUser()` methods accept the serialization functions. They accept a `user` object and modify it and pass it on by using the `done()` method. The following is an example of using the serialization method to store the `user.id` in the session rather than the entire `user` object and then uses a Mongoose call to `findByID()` in the deserialization to look up the user by the ID from the session:

```
passport.serializeUser(function(user, done) {
  done(null, user.id);
});
passport.deserializeUser(function(id, done) {
  User.findById(id, function(err, user) {
    done(err, user);
  });
});
```

Implementing Routes to Use Authentication

Passport is fully configured now, and you are ready to implement the middleware in your application's routes. The next step is to add the `passport.authenticate()` method to your authentication route. The authentication method accepts the authentication source as the first parameter and then an object that contains `successRedirect` and `failureRedirect` sources. In the case of Google, a double authentication must take place, as shown in the routes below:

```
app.get('/auth/google',
  passport.authenticate('google'));
app.get('/auth/google/return',
  passport.authenticate('google', {
    successRedirect: '/info',
    failureRedirect: '/login' }));
```

You can also use the `req.login()` method to later log in using the `user` object. For example:

```
req.login(user, function(err) {
  if (err) { return next(err); }
  return res.redirect('/users/' + req.user.username);

});
```

You can also use the `req.logout()` method to log out, which destroys the session. The actual authentication in the browser to the authentication source—Google, for example—is not terminated. You can still go to gmail.com and access your email, for instance. The following shows using `logout()` in a route:

```
app.get('/logout', function(req, res){
  req.logout();
  res.redirect('/login');

});
```

Another very helpful method is the `req.isAuthenticated()` method, which returns `true` if the current session is in an authenticated state. You can use this method to redirect to login. For example:

```
app.get('/login', function(req, res){
  if(req.isAuthenticated()){
    res.redirect('/info');
  } else{
    res.render('login', { user: req.user });
  }
});
```

Authenticating Using Google

The code in Listing 26.16 shows the basics of implementing a Google authentication strategy using Passport. The `/login` displays a login page with a simple link to log in via Google. The `/info` route displays profile information from the Google authentication.

Notice that both the `/auth/google` and `/auth/google/return` routes are implemented, and the user is redirected to `/info`. The `serializeUser()` and `deserializeUser()` methods alter the `user` object because you are not using MongoDB storage for this example.

Listing 26.17 implements the `login.html` template that is used to display the Google login link. Listing 26.18 implements the user info page, which displays the `identifier`, `displayName`, and `email` address returned from the Google login.

Figure 26.5 shows the authentication path from the login page to Google's authentication to the user info and back to login, when the user logs out.

Listing 26.16 `google_auth.js`: Implementing Google as an authentication source for an Express server

```
var express = require('express'),
    passport = require('passport'),
    GoogleStrategy = require('passport-google').Strategy;
passport.serializeUser(function(user, done) {
  done(null, user);
});
passport.deserializeUser(function(obj, done) {
  done(null, obj);
});
passport.use(new GoogleStrategy({
    returnURL: 'http://localhost/auth/google/return',
    realm: 'http://localhost/'
  },
  function(identifier, profile, done) {
    process.nextTick(function () {
      profile.identifier = identifier;
      return done(null, profile);
    });
  }
));
var app = express();
app.engine('.html', require('ejs').__express);
app.set('views', __dirname + '/views');
app.set('view engine', 'html');
app.use(express.cookieParser());
app.use(express.json()).use(express.urlencoded());
app.use(express.session({ secret: 'SECRET' }));
app.use(passport.initialize());
app.use(passport.session());
app.use(express.static(__dirname + '/static'));
app.get('/login', function(req, res){
  if(req.isAuthenticated()){
    res.redirect('/info');
  } else{
    res.render('login', { user: req.user });
  }
});
app.get('/auth/google',
```

```
  passport.authenticate('google'));
app.get('/auth/google/return',
  passport.authenticate('google', {
    successRedirect: '/info',
    failureRedirect: '/login' }));
app.get('/logout', function(req, res){
  req.logout();
  res.redirect('/login');
});
app.get('/info', function(req, res){
  if(req.isAuthenticated()){
    res.render('info', { user: req.user });
  } else {
    res.redirect('/login');
  }
});
app.listen(80);
```

Listing 26.17 `login.html`: **Implementing the Google login EJS HTML template**

```
<!doctype html>
<html>
<head>
  <title>Google Authentication</title>
</head>
<body>
  <h2>Google Authentication</h2>
  <a href="/auth/google">Sign In with Google</a>
</body>
</html>
```

Listing 26.18 `info.html`: **Implementing the Google info EJS HTML template**

```
<!doctype html>
<html>
<head>
  <title>Google Authentication</title>
</head>
<body>
  <h2>Google Authentication Info</h2>
  <p>ID: <%= user.identifier %></p>
  <p>Name: <%= user.displayName %></p>
  <p>Email: <%= user.emails[0].value %></p>
  <a href="/logout">Logout</a>
</body>
</html>
```

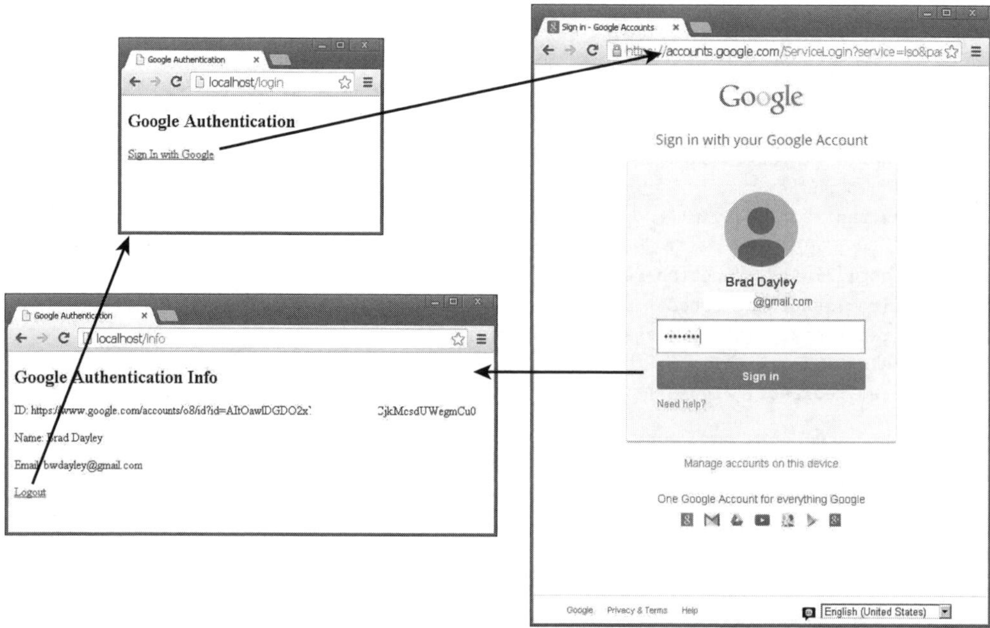

Figure 26.5 Using Google as an authentication source for Node.js Express applications.

Summary

In this chapter you've seen an end-to-end example of implementing users in a website. You set up and configured Express as the webserver. Then you connected to MongoDB and used it as the source for the `User` schema defined in Mongoose and as the persistent store for the authentication sessions. You configured the routes to allow users to sign up, log in, update their profiles, and delete their accounts. The AngularJS implementation shows how to use the `$http` service to get user data from the server.

In this chapter, you've also seen how to utilize the Passport module to implement `OAuth` and `OpenID` authentication sources such as Google in your application. Passport makes it very simple to add one or more authentication sources to your applications.

Up Next

In the next chapter you'll add comment sections to webpages. As you do that, you'll learn about the interaction between the various components in the Node.js, MongoDB, and AngularJS stack.

27

Adding Comment Threads to Pages

This chapter provides a practical example of implementing the full Node.js, MongoDB, and AngularJS stack; in it, you'll learn how to allow users to add nested comments to one or more areas of a webpage. Adding comments is a common aspect for many websites and involves a few challenges.

The example in this chapter provides a single webpage that enables comments for the whole page as well as comments for individual photos that can be loaded on the page. The code is basic and easy to follow.

The code in this example does not include user, authentication, and session management to make it easier to follow; if you want a refresher on those topics, see Chapter 26, "Adding User Accounts to Your Website." This example does, however, contain a small function that simulates having a username in a session to allow you to see comments from multiple users.

Libraries Used

The project in this chapter uses the following add-on Node.js NPMs. You need to install them into your project directory in order to follow along with the code examples:

- **`express`**: Used as the main webserver for the project.
- **`body-parser`**: Provides JSON body support for POST requests.
- **`ejs`**: Used to render the HTML templates.
- **`mongodb`**: Used to access the MongoDB database.
- **`mongoose`**: Used to provide the structured data model.

This code in this chapter also requires that you have the AngularJS library.

Project Directory Structure

The project is organized into the following directory structure:

- `./`: Contains the base application files and supporting folders. This is the project root.
- `../node_modules`: Created when the NPMs listed above are installed in the system.
- `./controllers`: Contains the Express route controllers that provide the interaction between routes and changes to the MongoDB database.
- `./models`: Contains the Mongoose model definitions for objects in the database.
- `./static`: Contains any static files that need to be sent, such as CSS and AngularJS code.
- `./views`: Contains the HTML templates that will be rendered by EJS.

> **Note**
>
> This is just one method of organizing your code. You do not have to follow this directory structure, but keep in mind that directory structure should be part of the overall design of your projects so that you can easily find the code you are looking for.

In addition to the directory structure, the following code files are included. This list is intended to give you an idea of the functionality of each file:

- `./comment_init.js`: Provides standalone initialization code for this example. It adds the initial page object and several photos to the MongoDB database to initialize the project.
- `./comment_server.js`: Loads the necessary libraries, creates a connection to MongoDB, and starts the Express server. This is the main application file.
- `./comment_routes.js`: Defines the routes for the Express server. This file handles functionality that does not apply to the database.
- `./controllers/comments_controller.js`: Defines the functionality for the routes that require interaction with the MongoDB database to get and update comments.
- `./controllers/pages_controller.js`: Defines the functionality for the routes that require interaction with the MongoDB database to get the page objects.
- `./controllers/photos_controller.js`: Defines the functionality for the routes that require interaction with the MongoDB database to get one or all of the photo objects.
- `./models/comments_model.js`: Defines the comment object model.
- `./models/page_model.js`: Defines the comment page model.
- `./models/photo_model.js`: Defines the comment photo model.
- `./views/photos.html`: Provides the main photo page for the application that will allow users to select photos and add comments to the page or to an individual photo.

- **./static/comment.html:** Allows nested comments to be displayed, using the ng-repeat directive. This is an AngularJS partial template.
- **./static/comment_thread.html:** Provides the framework for adding a comment thread to different locations on the webpage. This is an AngularJS partial template.
- **./static/js/comment_app.js:** Provides the AngularJS module and controller definitions to handle getting the page, photo, and comment objects from the servers as well as saving new comments.
- **./static/css/comment_styles.css:** Provides the CSS styling for the AngularJS HTML pages.
- **../images:** A folder that contains images used in this example. This folder is a peer to the chapter folder in the book's code archive.
- **../lib:** A folder that contains the necessary AngularJS library files used in this example. This folder is a peer to the chapter folder in the book's code archive.

Defining the Comment, Reply, Photo, and Page Models

You should always look at the object model needs as the first step in implementing an application. In this example, the goal is to allow users to add comments to webpages. To do so, you first need to identify objects that users can add comments to. This example provides a webpage that contains several photos. You will take advantage of reusability as you enable users to attach comments to both the webpage and individual photos. You need a model for the pages and a model for the photos to provide objects to attach the comments to. The following sections discuss the designs of the model schemas.

Defining the Page Model

Listing 27.1 implements the Page model schema for the application. The schema is very simple and includes only name and commentId fields. Notice that the name field is set to be unique, which is necessary to be able to look up the page by name. The main purpose of the Page model is to provide a place where you can associate a webpage with a comment thread.

Listing 27.1 page_model.js: **Implementing the Page model for Mongoose**

```
var mongoose = require('mongoose'),
    Schema = mongoose.Schema;
var PageSchema = new Schema({
    name: {type: String, unique: true},
    commentId: Schema.ObjectId
});
mongoose.model('Page', PageSchema);
```

Defining the Photo Model

Listing 27.2 implements the Photo model schema for the application. The schema is also very basic; it includes title, filename, timestamp, and commentId fields. The commentId field has the same purpose as the commentId field in the Page model. This reused field makes it easier to later add comments to any additional pages or object models that you want to add to the application.

Listing 27.2 photo_model.js: **Implementing the Photo model for Mongoose**

```
var mongoose = require('mongoose'),
    Schema = mongoose.Schema;
var PhotoSchema = new Schema({
    title: String,
    filename: String,
    timestamp: { type: Date, default: Date.now },
    commentId: Schema.ObjectId
});
mongoose.model('Photo', PhotoSchema);
```

Defining the CommentThread Model

The goal of the comments model is to support nested comments. In MongoDB there are a couple different methods to do that. You can store each comment as an individual document and provide a link to parent objects, or you can store all comments for a thread in a single document. Either way works, but they have very different implementations and consequences.

Storing the comment tree in a single document makes it simple and fast to load from MongoDB. The drawback is that because there is not a fixed depth for comments, the entire reply structure needs to be saved when new comments are added. Also, you need to get the entire document to get any of the comments.

Storing the comments as individual documents means that you can easily look up a single document, and it is simple to save any additional comments/replies because they are single documents. However, if you want to load the entire comment tree, you have to implement a complex aggregation function or do multiple lookups to build out the tree, and these approaches are both much less efficient than loading a single document.

Because comments are read very frequently but are not created very often, a good approach is to store the nested comment/reply structure in a single MongoDB document and then update the entire structure when a new comment is added.

Listing 27.3 implements the CommentThread and Reply model schemas. The CommentThread model schema is used as the root document for comments on a given object. The Reply model schema is designed to store comments/replies added to the page or photo. Notice that the `replies` field of both the `Reply` and `CommentThread` objects is an array of reply schema objects:

```
replies:[ReplySchema]
```

This setup allows the comments to be nested inside each other and for multiple comments to be created on the same level. Figure 27.1 shows the nested structure in an actual document stored in MongoDB.

Listing 27.3 `comments_model.js`: **Implementing the** `CommentThread` **model for Mongoose**

```
var mongoose = require('mongoose'),
    Schema = mongoose.Schema;
var ReplySchema = new Schema({
  username: String,
  subject: String,
  timestamp: { type: Date, default: Date.now },
  body: String,
  replies:[ReplySchema]
}, { _id: true });
  var CommentThreadSchema = new Schema({
    title: String,
    replies:[ReplySchema]
});
mongoose.model('Reply', ReplySchema);
mongoose.model('CommentThread', CommentThreadSchema);
```

```
Command Prompt - mongo
> db.commentthreads.findOne({title:'Strength Comments'})
{
        "__v" : 0,
        "_id" : ObjectId("52c56bb63a6e67681f000003"),
        "replies" : [
                {
                        "_id" : ObjectId("52c56bcc3a6e67681f000010"),
                        "body" : "Awesome location!",
                        "subject" : "Great Photo",
                        "username" : "Brendan",
                        "replies" : [
                                {
                                        "timestamp" : ISODate("2014-01-02T13:39:37.938Z"),
                                        "replies" : [ ],
                                        "_id" : ObjectId("52c56c193a6e67681f000011"),
                                        "body" : "Miss the desert.",
                                        "subject" : "Love It!!!!",
                                        "username" : "DaNae"
                                }
                        ],
                        "timestamp" : ISODate("2014-01-02T13:38:20.896Z")
                }
        ],
        "title" : "Strength Comments"
}
```

Figure 27.1 A `CommentThread` object with nested replies stored in MongoDB.

Creating the Comments Server

With the model defined, you can begin implementing the comments server. Listing 27.4 implements the Express server for the comments application. This code should be familiar to you. It includes the `express` and `mongoose` libraries and connects to MongoDB via Mongoose.

Notice that there is a `require` statement for each of the model definitions to build the `Schema` object within Mongoose. Also, the `./comment_routes` file is included to initialize the routes for the server before listening on port 80.

Listing 27.4 `comments_server.js`: **Implementing the comment application server by using Express and connecting to MongoDB**

```
var express = require('express');
var bodyParser = require('body-parser');
var mongoose = require('mongoose');
var db = mongoose.connect('mongodb://localhost/comments');
require('./models/comments_model.js');
require('./models/photo_model.js');
require('./models/page_model.js');
var app = express();
app.engine('.html', require('ejs').__express);
app.set('views', __dirname + '/views');
app.set('view engine', 'html');
app.use(bodyParser());
require('./comment_routes')(app);
app.listen(80);
```

Implementing Routes to Support Viewing and Adding Comments

As part of the Express server configuration, you load the `./comment_routes.js` file as shown in Listing 27.4. Listing 27.5 provides the routes necessary to get the page, photo, and comment data, as well as add additional comments to photos or pages.

Lines 6–9 implement the static routes to support getting the AngularJS, CSS, JavaScript, images, and AngularJS partial templates used in this example. The images and AngularJS `lib` folders are located in a sibling directory to the project. The other static files are in the `./static` folder inside the project.

Notice that when the user accesses the root location for the site, the `photos.html` template is rendered on line 9. The routes in lines 13–17 all involve interaction with the MongoDB database and are handled in the controller route handlers described in the next section.

Listing 27.5 `comments_routes.js`: **Implementing the comment application server routes for Express**

```
var express = require('express');
module.exports = function(app) {
  var photos = require('./controllers/photos_controller');
  var comments = require('./controllers/comments_controller');
  var pages = require('./controllers/pages_controller');
  app.use('/static', express.static( './static')).
      use('/images', express.static( '../images')).
      use('/lib', express.static( '../lib')
  );
  app.get('/', function(req, res){
    res.render('photos');
  });
  app.get('/photos', photos.getPhotos);
  app.get('/photo', photos.getPhoto);
  app.get('/page', pages.getPage);
  app.get('/comments/get', comments.getComment);
  app.post('/comments/add', comments.addComment);
}
```

Implementing the Model-Based Controller Routes

In addition to implementing the standard route handling, you also need to implement route handling to interact with the database. You break these route handlers out of the standard `comment_route.js` file and into their own files for each model, to keep the code clean and ensure a good division of responsibilities.

The following sections cover the implementation of the model-specific controllers for the `Page`, `Photo`, and `CommentThread` models.

Implementing the `Page` Model Controller

Listing 27.6 implements the route handling code for the `Page` model. There is only one route, the `getPage()` route, which finds the page based on the name field and returns an error or the JSON string form of the object. The name of the page to find comes in as `pageName` in the `GET` query string.

Listing 27.6 `pages_controller.js`: **Implementing the** `getPage` **route for the Express server**

```
var mongoose = require('mongoose'),
    Page = mongoose.model('Page');
exports.getPage = function(req, res) {
```

```
  Page.findOne({ name: req.query.pageName })
  .exec(function(err, page) {
    if (!page){
      res.json(404, {msg: 'Page Not Found.'});
    } else {
      res.json(page);
    }
  });
};
```

Implementing the Photo Model Controller

Listing 27.7 implements the route handling code for the `Photo` model. There are two routes handled. The `getPhoto()` route handler looks up a single `Photo` document, based on the `_id` field passed in as `photoId` in the `GET` query string. The `getPhotos()` route handler retrieves all `Photo` documents. Both handlers return a JSON string form of the results.

Listing 27.7 `photos_controller.js`: **Implementing the `getPhoto` and `getPhoto` routes in the Express server to get photos**

```
var mongoose = require('mongoose'),
    Photo = mongoose.model('Photo');
exports.getPhoto = function(req, res) {
  Photo.findOne({ _id: req.query.photoId })
  .exec(function(err, photo) {
    if (!photo){
      res.json(404, {msg: 'Photo Not Found.'});
    } else {
      res.json(photo);
    }
  });
};
exports.getPhotos = function(req, res) {
  Photo.find()
  .exec(function(err, photos) {
    if (!photos){
      res.json(404, {msg: 'Photos Not Found.'});
    } else {
      res.json(photos);
    }
  });
};
```

Implementing the `CommentThread` Model Controller

Listing 27.8 implements the route handling code for the `CommentThread` model. Two routes are handled: `getComment()` and `addComment()`. Due to the size of the file, the code for these two routes is broken down in the following sections.

Implementing the `getComment()` Route

The `getComment()` route handler looks up a single `CommentThread` document, based on the `_id` field passed in as `commentId` in the `GET` request query string.

Listing 27.8 `comments_controller.js-getComment`: **Implementing the route to get comment threads for the Express server**

```
exports.getComment = function(req, res) {
  CommentThread.findOne({ _id: req.query.commentId })
  .exec(function(err, comment) {
    if (!comment){
      res.json(404, {msg: 'CommentThread Not Found.'});
    } else {
      res.json(comment);
    }
  });
};
```

Implementing the `addComment()` Route

The `addComment()` route handler, shown in Listing 27.9, is quite a bit more complex than `getComment()` and involves a chain of functions to support updating nested comments. The logic flow for adding new comments is as follows:

1. The client sends a request that includes the `CommentThread` ID, a parent comment ID to add the new comment to, and a JSON object that represents the new comment.
2. The `/comment/add` route handler calls `addComment()`.
3. The `CommentThread` object is located using the `req.body.rootCommentId` value from the `POST` data.
4. A new `Reply` object named `newComment` object is created from the `req.body.newComment` value from the `POST` data.
5. `addComment()` is run recursively, looking through the nested comments until it finds a comment that matches the `req.body.parentCommentId` passed in from the `POST` body.
6. The new comment is pushed into the `replies` array of the parent comment.

7. The `updateCommentThread()` method uses the following `update()` operation to update the `replies` field in the `CommentThread` document with the one that now contains the updated comment:

```
CommentThread.update({ _id: commentThread.id },
                {$set:{replies:commentThread.replies}}).exec();
```

8. A success or failure response is sent back to the client.

Listing 27.9 `comments_controller.js-addComment`: **Implementing the** `addComment()` **route for the Express server**

```
exports.addComment = function(req, res) {
  CommentThread.findOne({ _id: req.body.rootCommentId })
  .exec(function(err, commentThread) {
    if (!commentThread){
      res.json(404, {msg: 'CommentThread Not Found.'});
    } else {
      var newComment = Reply(req.body.newComment);
      newComment.username = generateRandomUsername();
      addComment(req, res, commentThread, commentThread,
                 req.body.parentCommentId, newComment);
    }
  });
};
function addComment(req, res, commentThread, currentComment,
                    parentId, newComment){
  if (commentThread.id == parentId){
    commentThread.replies.push(newComment);
    updateCommentThread(req, res, commentThread);
  } else {
    for(var i=0; i< currentComment.replies.length; i++){
      var c = currentComment.replies[i];
      if (c._id == parentId){
        c.replies.push(newComment);
        var replyThread = commentThread.replies.toObject();
        updateCommentThread(req, res, commentThread);
        break;
      } else {
        addComment(req, res, commentThread, c,
                   parentId, newComment);
      }
    }
  }
};
function updateCommentThread(req, res, commentThread){
  CommentThread.update({ _id: commentThread.id },
    {$set:{replies:commentThread.replies}})
```

```
  .exec(function(err, savedComment){
    if (err){
      res.json(404, {msg: 'Failed to update CommentThread.'});
    } else {
      res.json({msg: "success"});
    }
  });
}
```

Looking at the Comment Model Route Handler

Listing 27.10 shows the full implementation of the `comments_controller.js` file that provides route handling involving the `Comment` model. The `Comment` model route handler code loads the schema for both the `CommentThread` and `Reply` models. The `CommentThread` model provides the ability to look up `CommentThread` documents as well as update them when new comments are added. The `Reply` model creates the `Reply` object when a new comment is added.

The comment controller code provides a function that randomly generates a username for testing purposes:

```
function generateRandomUsername(){
  //typically the username would come from an authenticated session
  var users=['DaNae', 'Brad', 'Brendan', 'Caleb', 'Aedan', 'Taeg'];
  return users[Math.floor((Math.random()*6))];
}
```

Typically the username would come from the session in the `Request` object, but session code is omitted from this example to keep it easier to follow.

Listing 27.10 `comments_controller.js`: **Full implementation of the `Comment` model route handlers for the Express server**

```
var mongoose = require('mongoose'),
    CommentThread = mongoose.model('CommentThread'),
    Reply = mongoose.model('Reply');
exports.getComment = function(req, res) {
  CommentThread.findOne({ _id: req.query.commentId })
  .exec(function(err, comment) {
    if (!comment){
      res.json(404, {msg: 'CommentThread Not Found.'});
    } else {
      res.json(comment);
    }
  });
};
exports.addComment = function(req, res) {
  CommentThread.findOne({ _id: req.body.rootCommentId })
```

```
  .exec(function(err, commentThread) {
    if (!commentThread){
      res.json(404, {msg: 'CommentThread Not Found.'});
    } else {
      var newComment = Reply(req.body.newComment);
      newComment.username = generateRandomUsername();
      addComment(req, res, commentThread, commentThread,
                 req.body.parentCommentId, newComment);
    }
  });
};
function addComment(req, res, commentThread, currentComment,
                    parentId, newComment){
  if (commentThread.id == parentId){
    commentThread.replies.push(newComment);
    updateCommentThread(req, res, commentThread);
  } else {
    for(var i=0; i< currentComment.replies.length; i++){
      var c = currentComment.replies[i];
      if (c._id == parentId){
        c.replies.push(newComment);
        var replyThread = commentThread.replies.toObject();
        updateCommentThread(req, res, commentThread);
        break;
      } else {
        addComment(req, res, commentThread, c,
                   parentId, newComment);
      }
    }
  }
};
function updateCommentThread(req, res, commentThread){
  CommentThread.update({ _id: commentThread.id },
      {$set:{replies:commentThread.replies}})
  .exec(function(err, savedComment){
    if (err){
     res.json(404, {msg: 'Failed to update CommentThread.'});
    } else {
     res.json({msg: "success"});
    }
  });
}
function generateRandomUsername(){
  //typically the username would come from an authenticated session
  var users=['DaNae', 'Brad', 'Brendan', 'Caleb', 'Aedan', 'Taeg'];
  return users[Math.floor((Math.random()*5))];
}
```

Implementing Photo and Comment Views

Now that the routes are set up and configured, you are ready to implement the views that are rendered by the routes and AngularJS templates. The following sections discuss the photos.html view rendered by EJS as well as the comment.html and comment_thread.html partials that are served statically.

Implementing the Photo View

The photo view, shown in Listing 27.11, is the main view for the application in this example. It is loaded at the root route, /. The header of the view registers the <html> element with the AngularJS application and loads the comment_styles.css file. The <body> element is broken down into two main sections.

The upper section initializes the AngularJS ng-controller="photoController" to provide the functionality to interact with the photos from the webserver, including comments on photos. The lower section initializes ng-controller="photoController" to provide the functionality to interact with the webpage comments. You use two controllers to keep the scope separate because both are implementing comment sections.

The following code defines the AngularJS template that renders an array of Photo documents stored in $scope.photos in the model, using the ng-repeat directive:

```
<div id="photosContainer">
  <div class="photoItem" ng-repeat="photo in photos">
    <img class="listPhoto" ng-click="setPhoto(photo._id)"
         ng-src="../images/{{photo.filename}}" />
  </div>
</div>
```

Notice that ng-click is set to the setPhoto() method in the controller code to set the current photo. Figure 27.2 shows the rendered element on the pages.

Figure 27.2 Photos rendered as <img> elements in the browser.

The following template code renders the current $scope.photo object to the screen by using photo.title for display and photo.filename to set the src attribute on the <img> element:

```
<div id="photoContainer">
  <p class="imageTitle">{{photo.title}}</p>
  <img class="mainPhoto"
       ng-src="../images/{{photo.filename}}" />
</div>
```

Figure 27.3 shows the rendered image portion of the page.

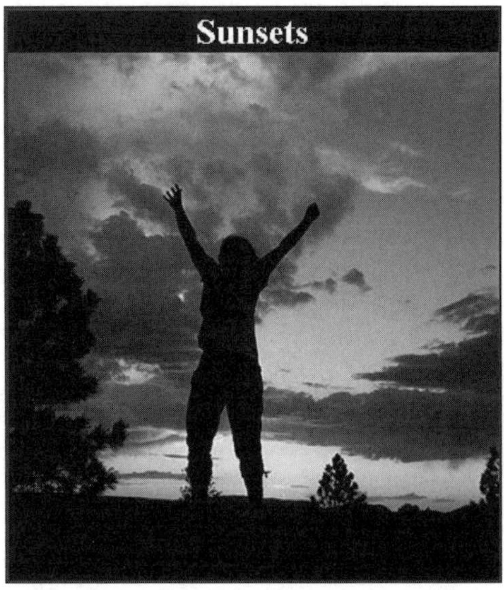

Figure 27.3 Larger view of a photo and title rendered in the browser.

You add the comments portion of the webpage by using the following code, which uses `ng-init` to initialize the `addComment`, `replySubject`, and `replyBody` values in the current scope and then `ng-include` to include the `comment_thread.html` partial template code described in the next section:

```
<div id="photoComments"
    ng-init="addComment=false;replySubject='';replyBody=''">
   <div class="comment"
        ng-include="'/static/comment_thread.html'"></div>
</div>
```

A section similar to this is added to the photo portion of the page and to the bottom of the page, allowing you to have comments in both places. You use the `addComment` value in the `comment_thread.html` template to determine whether to turn comments on or off.

Figure 27.4 shows the full application, with comments in the photo section and at the bottom for the page.

Listing 27.11 `photos.html`: **Implementing the main photo page AngularJS template code**

```
<!doctype html>
<html ng-app="myApp">
<head>
  <title>Comments</title>
  <link rel="stylesheet" type="text/css"
      href="/static/css/comment_styles.css" />
</head>
<body>
  <h2>Comments Example</h2>
  <div ng-controller="photoController">
    <div id="photosContainer">
      <div class="photoItem" ng-repeat="photo in photos">
        <img class="listPhoto" ng-click="setPhoto(photo._id)"
             ng-src="../images/{{photo.filename}}" />
      </div>
    </div>
    <div>
      <div id="photoContainer">
        <p class="imageTitle">{{photo.title}}</p>
        <img class="mainPhoto"
             ng-src="../images/{{photo.filename}}" />
      </div>
      <div id="photoComments"
          ng-init="addComment=false;replySubject='';replyBody=''">
        <div class="comment"
             ng-include="'/static/comment_thread.html'"></div>
      </div>
    </div>
  </div>
  <div ng-controller="pageController">
   <div id="pageComments"
          ng-init="addComment=false;replySubject='';replyBody=''">
     <div class="comment"
          ng-include="'/static/comment_thread.html'"></div>
   </div>
  </div>
  <script src="http://code.angularjs.org/1.2.9/angular.min.js"></script>
  <script src="/static/js/comment_app.js"></script>
</body>
</html>
```

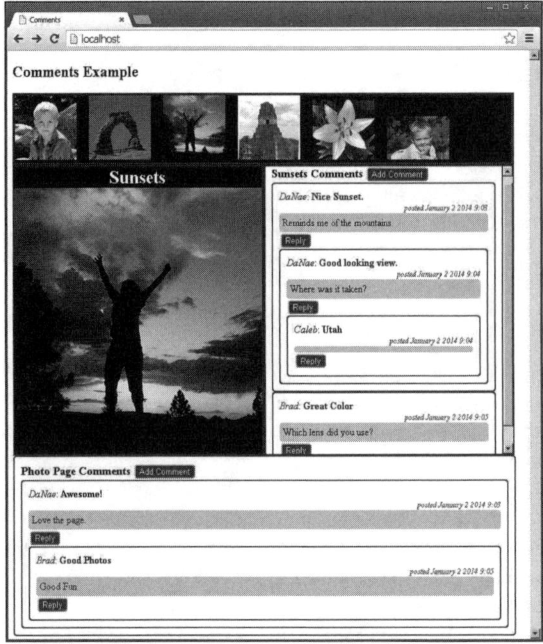

Figure 27.4 Rendered photo page with comments in both the photo area and at the bottom of the page.

Implementing the Comment Thread View

As discussed in the previous section, the photo and main mage sections of the photos page use `ng-include` to include the `comment_thread.html` partial template shown in Listing 27.12. You break out the partial template so that you can later easily include it in other pages or even additional sections of the same page.

The partial template includes the `CommentThread` title, using `{{commentThread.title}}`. An `<input>` button toggles `addComment` to `true`, allowing the reply form to be displayed. (It is currently hidden using `ng-show`.) Inside the reply form, the subject `<input>` is defined, along with a comment body `<textarea>`, as shown in Figure 27.5. The Add Comment button executes the `addReply()` method in the scope and passes `commentThread._id`, `replySubject`, and `replyBody` to the controller to send the add request to the server.

Figure 27.5 shows the rendered comment thread view before the Add Comment button is clicked and the reply form that opens after the Add Comment button is clicked.

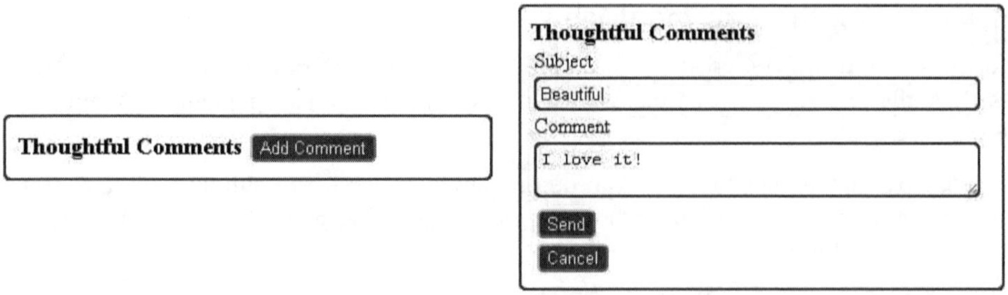

Figure 27.5 The comment thread area with the Add Comment button and a form to add a comment.

At the bottom of the comment thread template, the following lines use `ng-repeat` to load the `comment.html` partial template that renders the comment using `ng-include`. Also notice that the `reply`, `replySubject`, and `replyBody` values are initialized. Those are used in the comment template to display/hide the reply form as well as to pass data to the `addReply()` function:

```
<div ng-repeat="comment in commentThread.replies"
     ng-init="reply=false;replySubject='';replyBody=''">
  <div class="comment" ng-include="'/static/comment.html'"></div>
</div>
```

Listing 27.12 `comment_thread.html`: **Implementing the partial comment thread template**

```
<span class="commentTitle">{{commentThread.title}}</span>
<input type="button" ng-show="addComment==false"
       value="Add Comment" ng-click="addComment=true"></input>
<form ng-show="addComment==true">
  <label>Subject</label>
  <input type="text" ng-model="replySubject")></input>
  <label>Comment</label>
  <textarea ng-model="replyBody"></textarea>
  <input type="button" value="Send"
  ng-click=
  "addComment=false; addReply(commentThread._id,replySubject,replyBody)"
  ></input>
</form>
<input type="button" ng-show="addComment==true"
       value="Cancel" ng-click="addComment=false;"></input>
<div ng-repeat="comment in commentThread.replies"
     ng-init="reply=false;replySubject='';replyBody=''">
  <div class="comment" ng-include="'/static/comment.html'"></div>
</div>
```

Implementing the Comment View

As discussed in the previous section, the comment thread section of the page uses `ng-include` to include the `comment.html` partial, shown in Listing 27.13, for each reply in the comment object `replies` array.

By using a partial template here, you can nest replies inside replies by simply reading the same block, shown below, to iterate through replies using `ng-repeat` and using `ng-include` to include the same form:

```
<div ng-repeat="comment in comment.replies"
     ng-init="reply=false;replySubject='';replyBody=''">
  <div class="comment" ng-include="'/static/comment.html'"></div>
</div>
```

The `comment.html` partial template includes the comment username, subject, timestamp, and body. An `<input>` button toggles `reply` to `true`, allowing the reply form to be displayed. (It is currently hidden using `ng-show`.) The reply form, shown in Figure 27.6, is similar to the one for adding the first comment. The Reply button executes the `addReply()` method in the scope and passes `comment._id`, `replySubject`, and `replyBody` to the controller to send the add request to the server.

Figure 27.6 shows the rendered reply thread view before the Reply button is clicked and the reply form that opens after the Reply button is clicked.

Listing 27.13 `comment_thread.html`: **Implementing the partial comment template**

```
<span class="username">{{comment.username}}</span>:
<span class="subject">{{comment.subject}}</span>
<p class="timestamp"
>posted {{comment.timestamp|date:"MMMM d yyyy H:mm"}}</p>
<p class="commentBody">{{comment.body}}</p>
<input type="button" ng-show="reply==false"
       value="Reply" ng-click="reply=true"></input>
<form ng-if="reply">
  <label>Subject</label>
  <input type="text" ng-model="replySubject")></input>
  <label>Comment</label>
  <textarea ng-model="replyBody"></textarea>
  <input type="button" value="Send"
         ng-click="addReply(comment._id,replySubject,replyBody)" />
</form>
<input type="button" ng-show="reply==true"
       value="Cancel" ng-click="reply=false;"></input>
<div ng-repeat="comment in comment.replies"
     ng-init="reply=false;replySubject='';replyBody=''">
  <div class="comment" ng-include="'/static/comment.html'"></div>
</div>
```

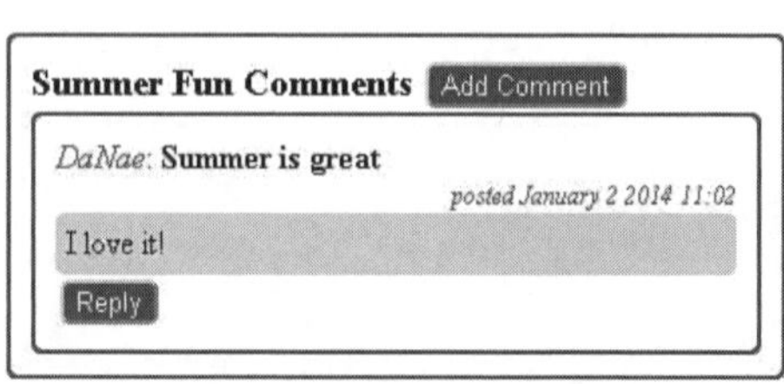

Figure 27.6 Replying to a comment already in the thread.

Adding CSS to Stylize the Views

Listing 27.14 shows the CSS code used to style the elements in the photo view as well as the AngularJS partial templates.

Listing 27.14 `comment_styles.css`: **Implementing the CSS styles for the view HTML files**

```
div#photosContainer{
  background:black; color: white;
  border: 4px ridge blue; width:800px;
}
div.photoItem{ display:inline-block; width:120px; }
div#photoContainer,
div#photoComments{
  background:black; color: white; width: 400px; height:450px;
  display: inline-block;  float:left; border: 2px ridge blue;
}
div#photoComments{ background:white; color: black;
  max-height:500px; overflow-y:scroll;
}
div#pageComments{ margin:0px; clear:both; width:810px; }
div.comment{ border: 2px ridge blue; padding:10px;
  border-radius: 5px;
}
img.listPhoto{ width:100px; }
img.mainPhoto{ width:400px; }
.commentBody{ background-color:lightgray;
  border-radius: 5px; padding: 5px; margin:0;
}
```

```
.imageTitle{ font-size: 28px; font-weight: bold;
  text-align: center; margin:0
}
.commentTitle{ font-size: 18px; font-weight: bold;}
.username{ font-style: italic; color:blue; }
.subject{ font-weight: bold;}
.timestamp{ color:#555555; font-style: italic;
  font-size: 12px; text-align: right; margin:0;
}
input[type="text"],
textarea{ border: 2px ridge blue; border-radius: 5px;
  padding:3px; width:95%;
}
input[type="button"]{ background-color:blue;color:white;
  border-radius: 5px;
}
```

Implementing the AngularJS Module and Controller to Support Comment Views

With the views finished, you need to implement the AngularJS controller code to support them. The views need the ability to get the page, photos, and comments. They also need the ability to add new comments.

You should provide two controllers: one for the photo comments and another for the comments on the full page. Because there are multiple controllers that need to interact with the server to get and add comments, it is also a good idea to create a service that handles getting and adding comments. The following sections describe the process of creating the full Angular JS code in Listing 27.18.

Creating a Comment Service

Because you know you will need a comment service to handle getting and adding comments, you need to add that first. Listing 27.15 implements a comment service that uses the service method. You need to create a function definition called `CommentObj`. The constructor function accepts the `$http` service as the only parameter.

You define a `getComment()` function that accepts `commentId` and then does a `GET` request to the `/comment/get` route to get the full comment data. Notice that this function also accepts a callback function. The callback function returns an error if `$http` reports one or the comment data from the server.

The `addComment()` function accepts `rootCommentId` for the comment thread, `parentId` for the parent comment, and a `newComment` parameter that is a JavaScript object with `subject` and `body` properties. It then does a `POST` request to `/comment/add` to add the new comment to

MongoDB. Just as with `getComment()`, a callback function is executed and returns the results. Then the service is created using the following line to inject `$http`:

```
app.service('commentSrv', ['$http', CommentObj]);
```

Then you can inject the `commentSrv` service into your controllers.

Listing 27.15 `comment_app.js-commentSrv`: **Implementing an AngularJS service that provides reusable functionality to get comments from and add new comments to the server**

```
function CommentObj($http) {
  this.getComment = function(commentId, callback){
    $http.get('/comments/get', {params: {commentId: commentId}})
      .success(function(data, status, headers, config) {
        callback(null, data);
      })
      .error(function(data, status, headers, config) {
        callback(data, {});
      });
  };
  this.addComment = function(rootCommentId, parentId,
                             newComment, callback){
    $http.post('/comments/add', { rootCommentId: rootCommentId,
                                  parentCommentId: parentId,
                                  newComment: newComment })
    .success(function(data, status, headers, config) {
      callback(null, data);
    })
    .error(function(data, status, headers, config) {
    });
  };
}
app.service('commentSrv', ['$http', CommentObj]);
```

Implementing the Photo Controller

Next, you need to implement a controller to support the photo portion of the page. Listing 27.16 shows the `photoController` code. Notice that `commentSrv` is injected into the controller, along with the `$http` service.

The controller initializes `$scope.photos` and `$scope.photo`, using an `$http GET` request to the `/photos` route. The `$scope.loadComments()` function uses the `commentSrv.getComment()` function to retrieve the comments for the current photo by passing `$scope.photo.commentId`. The callback function simply sets the `$commentThread` value that is used in the view.

The `$scope.addReply()` method is called when the user clicks Send for a comment reply in the template. Notice that it first generates a `newComment` object with the subject and body passed in from the view and then uses `commentSrv.addComment()` to send the update to the server.

The `$setPhoto()` function accepts the `photoID` from the user interface and then makes an `$http GET` request to `/photo` to retrieve the photo object. `$scope.photo` is updated with the data, and `$scope.loadComments()` is called to load the comments for the new folder.

Listing 27.16 `comment_app.js-photoController`: **Implementing an AngularJS controller that supports the photo and photo comments portions of the view**

```
app.controller('photoController', ['$scope', '$http', 'commentSrv',
                                   function($scope, $http, commentSrv) {
    $http.get('/photos')
     .success(function(data, status, headers, config) {
        $scope.photos = data;
        $scope.photo = $scope.photos[0];
        $scope.loadComments();
      })
      .error(function(data, status, headers, config) {
        $scope.photos = [];
      });
    $scope.loadComments = function(){
      commentSrv.getComment($scope.photo.commentId,
                                 function(err, comment){
        if(err){
          $srope.commentThread = {};
        } else {
          $scope.commentThread = comment;
        }
      });
    };
    $scope.addReply = function(parentCommentId, subject, body){
      var newComment = {subject:subject, body:body};
      commentSrv.addComment($scope.commentThread._id,
                                parentCommentId,
                                newComment, function(err, comment){
          $scope.loadComments();
        });
    };
    $scope.setPhoto = function(photoId){
      $http.get('/photo', {params: {photoId: photoId}})
        .success(function(data, status, headers, config) {
            $scope.photo = data;
            $scope.loadComments();
          })
```

```
        .error(function(data, status, headers, config) {
          $scope.photo = {};
        });
    };
  }]);
```

Implementing the Page AngularJS Controller

Next, you need to implement a controller to support the webpage comments. Listing 27.17 shows the `pageController` code. Notice that `commentSrv` is also injected into this controller, along with the `$http` service.

The controller initializes `$scope.page`, makes an `$http GET` request to `/pages`, and passes the hard-coded `"Photos Page"` name as a parameter. The `$scope.loadComments()` function calls the `commentSrv.getComment()` function to retrieve the comments for the page by `$scope.page.commentId`. The callback function simply sets the `$commentThread` value that is used in the view.

The `$scope.addReply()` method is called when the user clicks Send in the page comments template. Notice that it first generates a `newComment` object with the subject and body passed in from the view and then uses `commentSrv.addComment()` to send the update to the server.

Listing 27.17 `comment_app.js-pageController`: **Implementing an AngularJS controller that supports the page comments portion of the view**

```
app.controller('pageController', ['$scope', '$http','commentSrv',
                              function($scope, $http, commentSrv) {
    $http.get('/page', {params:{pageName:"Photos Page"}})
      .success(function(data, status, headers, config) {
        $scope.page = data;
        $scope.loadComments();
      })
      .error(function(data, status, headers, config) {
        $scope.Page = {};
      });
    $scope.addReply = function(parentCommentId, subject, body){
      var newComment = {subject:subject, body:body};
      commentSrv.addComment($scope.commentThread._id,
                            parentCommentId,
                            newComment, function(err, comment){
        $scope.loadComments();
      });
    };
    $scope.loadComments = function(){
      commentSrv.getComment($scope.page.commentId,
                            function(err, comment){
```

```
      if(err){
        $srope.commentThread = {};
      } else {
        $scope.commentThread = comment;
      }
    });
  };
}]);
```

The Full AngularJS Application

Listing 27.18 shows the full AngularJS application code all together. Notice that line 1 defines the application and then the following code adds the `commentSrv` service, `photoController`, and `pageController` controllers.

Listing 27.18 `comment_app.js`: **Implementing an AngularJS application that supports comments on webpages**

```
01 var app = angular.module('myApp', []);
02 function CommentObj($http) {
03   this.getComment = function(commentId, callback){
04     $http.get('/comments/get', {params: {commentId: commentId}})
05       .success(function(data, status, headers, config) {
06         callback(null, data);
07       })
08       .error(function(data, status, headers, config) {
09         callback(data, {});
10       });
11   };
12   this.addComment = function(rootCommentId, parentId,
13                              newComment, callback){
14     $http.post('/comments/add', { rootCommentId: rootCommentId,
15                                   parentCommentId: parentId,
16                                   newComment: newComment })
17     .success(function(data, status, headers, config) {
18       callback(null, data);
19     })
20     .error(function(data, status, headers, config) {
21     });
22   };
23 }
24 app.service('commentSrv', ['$http', CommentObj]);
25 app.controller('photoController', ['$scope', '$http', 'commentSrv',
26                                  function($scope, $http, commentSrv) {
27     $http.get('/photos')
28      .success(function(data, status, headers, config) {
```

```
        $scope.photos = data;
        $scope.photo = $scope.photos[0];
        $scope.loadComments();
      })
      .error(function(data, status, headers, config) {
        $scope.photos = [];
      });
    $scope.loadComments = function(){
      commentSrv.getComment($scope.photo.commentId,
                            function(err, comment){
        if(err){
          $srope.commentThread = {};
        } else {
          $scope.commentThread = comment;
        }
      });
    };
    $scope.addReply = function(parentCommentId, subject, body){
      var newComment = {subject:subject, body:body};
      commentSrv.addComment($scope.commentThread._id,
                            parentCommentId,
                            newComment, function(err, comment){
          $scope.loadComments();
        });
    };
    $scope.setPhoto = function(photoId){
      $http.get('/photo', {params: {photoId: photoId}})
        .success(function(data, status, headers, config) {
            $scope.photo = data;
            $scope.loadComments();
          })
        .error(function(data, status, headers, config) {
            $scope.photo = {};
          });
    };
  }]);
app.controller('pageController', ['$scope', '$http','commentSrv',
                            function($scope, $http, commentSrv) {
     $http.get('/page', {params:{pageName:"Photos Page"}})
       .success(function(data, status, headers, config) {
          $scope.page = data;
          $scope.loadComments();
        })
        .error(function(data, status, headers, config) {
          $scope.Page = {};
        });
     $scope.addReply = function(parentCommentId, subject, body){
```

```
    var newComment = {subject:subject, body:body};
    commentSrv.addComment($scope.commentThread._id,
                          parentCommentId,
                          newComment, function(err, comment){
      $scope.loadComments();
    });
  };
  $scope.loadComments = function(){
    commentSrv.getComment($scope.page.commentId,
                          function(err, comment){
      if(err){
        $srope.commentThread = {};
      } else {
        $scope.commentThread = comment;
      }
    });
  };
}]);
```

Initializing the Application

Now that the application is created, you need to also create the `Page` and `Photo` documents in the database. You can do this in several different ways. For example, you can add this ability directly to your application, which is a good way to go if you need it there later. Or you can use a JavaScript script directly in the MongoDB shell that includes the appropriate commands to create the documents. Or you can write a simple script in Node.js or some other language that supports accessing MongoDB.

Listing 27.19 shows a basic script that creates the `Page` document and adds several `Photo` documents as well. Each `Page` and `Photo` document also has a `CommentThread` document created and associated with the `commentId` reference.

Listing 27.19 `comment_init.js`: **Implementing a Node.js script that initializes the data for the application**

```
var mongoose = require('mongoose');
var db = mongoose.connect('mongodb://localhost/comments');
require('./models/comments_model.js');
require('./models/photo_model.js');
require('./models/page_model.js');
var CommentThread = mongoose.model('CommentThread');
var Reply = mongoose.model('Reply');
var Photo = mongoose.model('Photo');
var Page = mongoose.model('Page');
function addPhoto(title, filename){
```

```
  var comment = new CommentThread({title: title +" Comments"});
  comment.save(function(err, comment){
    var photo = new Photo({title:title, filename:filename});
    photo.commentId = comment.id;
    photo.save(function(){
      console.log(title + " Saved.");
    });
  });
}
CommentThread.remove().exec(function(){
  Photo.remove().exec(function(){
    Page.remove().exec(function(){
      var comment = new CommentThread({title:"Photo Page Comments"});
      comment.save(function(err, comment){
        var page = new Page({name:"Photos Page"});
        page.commentId = comment.id;
        page.save();
      });
      addPhoto('Strength', 'arch.jpg');
      addPhoto('Power', 'pyramid.jpg');
      addPhoto('Beauty', 'flower.jpg');
      addPhoto('Thoughtful', 'boy.jpg');
      addPhoto('Summer Fun', 'boy2.jpg');
      addPhoto('Sunsets', 'jump.jpg');
    });
  });
});;
```

Summary

In this chapter you've learned how to define a model to store and retrieve nested comments. The model in this chapter stores a full comment thread as a single document rather than storing a document for each comment; this makes it simpler to read the full thread.

In this chapter you've also implemented a basic model for a webpage and for photos, and you've integrated multiple models into the Express route handlers, AngularJS templates, and AngularJS application.

Up Next

In the next chapter you'll work through another practical example of adding products and a shopping cart to a website.

28

Creating Your Own Shopping Cart

This chapter provides a practical example of implementing a shopping cart. This chapter uses a shopping cart example because shopping carts are very common and familiar, so the concepts will be easy to pick up throughout the chapter. Also, this example allows you to look at one way to take advantage of the ability to switch between views in AngularJS as you navigate through the checkout process.

The shopping cart you will create in this chapter provides most of the necessary functionality, but it is not intended for production. It is missing validation and error handling to keep the example a reasonable length. However, you will learn the basic steps of creating a shopping cart and develop a fundamental understanding of how the Node.js, MongoDB, and AngularJS stack operates.

Project Description

The implementation in this chapter is a fairly basic shopping cart that allows you to add items, remove items, go through the checkout process, and view your orders. The example provides most of the basic functionality that is required for a shopping cart. Keep in mind, though, that it is not intended for production use but rather as a teaching aid. Also keep in mind that the cart does not actually link to a credit card verification service to process payments. That would be beyond the scope of the project. You would need to do a fair amount of further work to make this project into something that could be used in production.

In addition, this example does not include login, authentication, and session management; if you want a refresher on those topics, see Chapter 26, "Adding User Accounts to Your Website." The example in this chapter is hard-coded to a user with a `userid` of `customerA`. Therefore, in places where the authenticated user would be, you'll see `customerA` hard coded in the example.

The general logic flow of the example is as follows:

1. The root page contains a list of prints that can be purchased.
2. The user clicks a print to view details and add it to the cart. The user can add multiple items. The top link to the cart shows the number of items in the cart.
3. The user clicks the cart to see the items. The user can then change the quantity of items, remove items, continue shopping, or check out.
4. At checkout, the customer sees a shipping information page.
5. The customer then sees billing information, including the billing address and credit card data.
6. When the customer clicks to submit the billing information, a review of the validated transaction is displayed, and the user can select to make the final purchase.
7. After the user makes the final purchase, he or she sees a list of orders, including the recently completed one.

Libraries Used

The project in this chapter uses the following add-on Node.js NPMs. You need to install them into your project directory in order to follow along with the code examples:

- **`express`**: Used as the main webserver for the project.
- **`body-parser`**: Provides JSON body support for POST requests.
- **`ejs`**: Used to render the HTML templates.
- **`mongodb`**: Used to access the MongoDB database.
- **`mongoose`**: Used to provide the structured data model.

The code in this chapter also requires that you have the AngularJS library.

Project Directory Structure

The project is organized into the following directory structure:

- `./`: Contains the base application files and supporting folders. This is the project root.
- **`./npm_modules`**: Created when the NPMs listed above are installed in the system.
- **`./controllers`**: Contains the Express route controllers that provide the interaction between routes and changes to the MongoDB database.
- **`./models`**: Contains the Mongoose model definitions for objects in the database.
- **`./static`**: Contains any static files that need to be sent, such as CSS and AngularJS code.

- **./views**: Contains the HTML templates that will be rendered by EJS.
- **../images**: Contains any images for the project. This is at a peer level to the project so that multiple projects can use the same images.
- **../lib**: Contains the AngularJS libraries so that multiple projects can load them locally. In production, you may want to use a CDN delivery address instead.

> **Note**
>
> This is just one method of organizing your code. You do not have to follow this directory structure, but keep in mind that directory structure should be part of the overall design of your projects so that you can easily find the code you are looking for.

In addition to the directory structure, the following code files are included. This list is intended to give you an idea of the functionality of each file:

- **./cart_init.js**: Provides standalone initialization code for this example. It creates a single customer named `customerA` and adds several products to use in the example.
- **./cart_server.js**: Loads the necessary libraries, creates a connection to MongoDB, and starts the Express server. This is the main application file.
- **./cart_routes.js**: Defines the routes for the Express server. This file handles functionality that does not interact with the database.
- **./controllers/customers_controller.js**: Defines the functionality for the routes that require interaction with the MongoDB database to get and update customer data, such as cart, shipping, and billing information.
- **./controllers/orders_controller.js**: Defines the functionality for the routes that require interaction with the MongoDB database to get the order objects.
- **./controllers/products_controller.js**: Defines the functionality for the routes that require interaction with the MongoDB database to get one or all of the product objects.
- **./models/cart_model.js**: Defines the customer, product, order, and supporting models for the cart example.
- **./views/shopping.html**: Provides the main shopping page for the application, which allows the user to view products and place them into the cart.
- **./static/billing.html**: Implements the billing information view. This is an AngularJS partial template.
- **./static/cart.html**: Implements the shopping cart view. This is an AngularJS partial template.
- **./static/orders.html**: Implements a view with a list of orders. This is an AngularJS partial template.
- **./static/products.html**: Implements a list of products view. This is an AngularJS partial template.

- **./static/product.html**: Implements a view for a single product with an Add to Cart button. This is an AngularJS partial template.
- **./static/review.html**: Implements a view to allow the user to review the order before placing it. This is an AngularJS partial template.
- **./static/shipping.html**: Implements the shipping information view. This is an AngularJS partial template.
- **./static/js/cart_app.js**: Provides the AngularJS module and controller definitions to handle all the shopping cart interaction between the AngularJS code and the webserver.
- **./static/css/cart_styles.css**: Provides the CSS styling for the AngularJS HTML pages.

Defining the Customer, Product, and Orders Models

You should always look at the object model needs as the first step in implementing an application. In this example, the goal is to provide a shopping cart. To do so, you need a customer model as a container for the shopping cart. Also, you need products to place into the shopping cart. To check out, you need billing information and shipping information, and then once the order is placed, you need a way to store the order. Therefore, you need a model for the customer, product, order billing, and shipping data to support the shopping cart.

The following sections discuss the design of each of the model schemas implemented in the project. The schemas are all contained in a file named `cart_model.js` that implements all the schemas. You need to load the `mongoose` library's `Schema` object:

```
var mongoose = require('mongoose'),
    Schema = mongoose.Schema;
```

The following sections describe the rest of the code you need to use to implement this example. The full schema definition can be viewed in Listing 28.7.

Defining the Address Schema

You begin by defining an address schema that will be generic so that it can be used in the shipping information and as part of the billing information. Listing 28.1 implements `AddressSchema`, which contains the standard address information. Notice that the following code is used to disable the `_id` property since you do not need to look up addresses by ID:

```
{ _id: false }
```

Listing 28.1 `cart_model.js-AddressSchema`: **Defining a schema for shipping and billing addresses**

```
var AddressSchema = new Schema({
  name: String,
  address: String,
  city: String,
  state: String,
  zip: String
}, { _id: false });
mongoose.model('Address', AddressSchema);
```

Defining the Billing Schema

With the `AddressSchema` defined, you can now define the billing schema to keep track of credit card information as well as billing information. Listing 28.2 implements `BillingSchema`, which contains standard credit card data. Notice that the following implementation for `cardtype` requires entry of `Visa`, `MasterCard`, or `Amex` (not any other values):

```
cardtype: { type: String, enum: ['Visa', 'MasterCard', 'Amex'] },
```

Also notice that the `address` field is assigned the `AddressSchema` object type. Mongoose requires you to include nesting schemas in an array. You'll see this in several places in this example, and you'll see that through the example, that the address is accessed by using `address[0]` to get the first item in the array.

Listing 28.2 `cart_model.js-BillingSchema`: **Defining a schema for billing credit card and address**

```
var BillingSchema = new Schema({
  cardtype: { type: String, enum: ['Visa', 'MasterCard', 'Amex'] },
  name: String,
  number: String,
  expiremonth: Number,
  expireyear: Number,
  address: [AddressSchema]
}, { _id: false });
mongoose.model('Billing', BillingSchema);
```

Defining the Product Schema

Next, you define the schema to store product information. The product model for this example is a print with `name`, `imagefile`, `description`, `price`, and `instock` counters. Listing 28.3 shows the full definition of `ProductSchema`.

Listing 28.3 `cart_model.js-ProductSchema`: **Defining a basic product schema for prints**

```
var ProductSchema = new Schema({
  name: String,
  imagefile: String,
  description: String,
  price: Number,
  instock: Number
});
mongoose.model('Product', ProductSchema);
```

Defining the Quantity Schema

For orders and the shopping cart, you can include the products in an array. However, you also need to be able to store a quantity. One method of doing this is to define a quantity schema with quantity and product fields. Listing 28.4 implements `ProductQantitySchema`, which does just that. Notice that because you are embedding `ProductSchema`, you include it as an array, and throughout the example, you access it by using `product[0]`.

Listing 28.4 `cart_model.js-QuantitySchema`: **Defining a basic quantity schema for quantity of products in orders and the cart**

```
var ProductQuantitySchema = new Schema({
  quantity: Number,
  product: [ProductSchema]
}, { _id: false });
mongoose.model('ProductQuantity', ProductQuantitySchema);
```

Defining the Order Schema

Next, you need to create the order schema to keep track of the items ordered, shipping information, and billing information. Listing 28.5 implements the `OrderSchema` model, which stores the necessary information about the order. Notice that a `Date` type is assigned to the `timestamp` field to keep track of when the order was placed. Also, the `items` field is an array of `QuantitySchema` subdocuments.

Listing 28.5 `cart_model.js-OrderSchema`: **Defining the order schema to store the order information**

```
var OrderSchema = new Schema({
  userid: String,
  items: [ProductQuantitySchema],
  shipping: [AddressSchema],
  billing: [BillingSchema],
  status: {type: String, default: "Pending"},
```

```
  timestamp: { type: Date, default: Date.now }
});
mongoose.model('Order', OrderSchema);
```

Defining the Customer Schema

The final schema is the customer schema. Listing 28.6 shows the full application schema including the `CustomerSchema` on lines 42-48. The `CustomerSchema` contains a unique `userid` field to identify the customer and associate orders with the customer. This field would normally map to an authenticated session `userid`.

Notice that the shipping, billing, and cart are all nested schemas. That makes it simple to define the model. You will see that each of these is accessed in the JavaScript, using `shipping[0]`, `billing[0]`, and `cart[0]` array indexing. No cart object schema is necessary because it is inherently implemented by the array of `ProductQuantitySchema` subdocuments.

Listing 28.6 `cart_model.js`: **Full application schema including the customer schema to store the shipping, billing, and cart**

```
01 var mongoose = require('mongoose'),
02     Schema = mongoose.Schema;
03 var AddressSchema = new Schema({
04   name: String,
05   address: String,
06   city: String,
07   state: String,
08   zip: String
09 }, { _id: false });
10 mongoose.model('Address', AddressSchema);
11 var BillingSchema = new Schema({
12   cardtype: { type: String, enum: ['Visa', 'MasterCard', 'Amex'] },
13   name: String,
14   number: String,
15   expiremonth: Number,
16   expireyear: Number,
17   address: [AddressSchema]
18 }, { _id: false });
19 mongoose.model('Billing', BillingSchema);
20 var ProductSchema = new Schema({
21   name: String,
22   imagefile: String,
23   description: String,
24   price: Number,
25   instock: Number
26 });
27 mongoose.model('Product', ProductSchema);
```

```
var ProductQuantitySchema = new Schema({
  quantity: Number,
  product: [ProductSchema]
}, { _id: false });
mongoose.model('ProductQuantity', ProductQuantitySchema);
var OrderSchema = new Schema({
  userid: String,
  items: [ProductQuantitySchema],
  shipping: [AddressSchema],
  billing: [BillingSchema],
  status: {type: String, default: "Pending"},
  timestamp: { type: Date, default: Date.now }
});
mongoose.model('Order', OrderSchema);
var CustomerSchema = new Schema({
  userid: { type: String, unique: true, required: true },
  shipping: [AddressSchema],
  billing: [BillingSchema],
  cart: [ProductQuantitySchema]
});
mongoose.model('Customer', CustomerSchema);
```

Creating the Shopping Cart Server

With the model defined, you can begin implementing the shopping cart server. Listing 28.7 implements the Express server for the shopping cart application. This code should be familiar to you. It includes the `express` and `mongoose` libraries and connects to MongoDB via Mongoose.

Notice that there is a `require` statement for the model definition to build the `Schema` object within Mongoose. Also, the `./cart_routes` file is included to initialize the routes for the server before listening on port 80.

Listing 28.7 `cart_server.js`: **Implementing the shopping cart application server using Express and connecting to MongoDB**

```
var express = require('express');
var bodyParser = require('body-parser');
var mongoose = require('mongoose');
var db = mongoose.connect('mongodb://localhost/cart');
require('./models/cart_model.js');
var app = express();
app.engine('.html', require('ejs').__express);
app.set('views', __dirname + '/views');
app.set('view engine', 'html');
```

```
app.use(bodyParser());
require('./cart_routes')(app);
app.listen(80);
```

Implementing Routes to Support Product, Cart, and Order Requests

As part of the Express server configuration, you load the `./cart_routes.js` file shown in Listing 28.7. Listing 28.8 provides the routes necessary to get the customer, product, and order objects. It also provides routes to add orders to the database and update the customer shipping, billing, and cart information.

Lines 6–9 implement the static routes to support getting the AngularJS, CSS, JavaScript, images, and AngularJS partial templates used in this example. The images and AngularJS `lib` folders are located in a sibling directory to the project. The other static files are in the `./static` folder inside the project.

Notice that when the user accesses the root location for the site (/), the `shopping.html` template is rendered on line 11. The remaining routes on lines 13–19 all involve interaction with the MongoDB database and are handled in the controller route handlers described in the next section.

Listing 28.8 `cart_routes.js`: **Implementing routes for shopping cart web requests from the client**

```
01 var express = require('express');
02 module.exports = function(app) {
03   var customers = require('./controllers/customers_controller');
04   var products = require('./controllers/products_controller');
05   var orders = require('./controllers/orders_controller');
06   app.use('/static', express.static( './static')).
07       use('/images', express.static( '../images')).
08       use('/lib', express.static( '../lib')
09   );
10   app.get('/', function(req, res){
11     res.render('shopping');
12   });
13   app.get('/products/get', products.getProducts);
14   app.get('/orders/get', orders.getOrders);
15   app.post('/orders/add', orders.addOrder);
16   app.get('/customers/get', customers.getCustomer);
17   app.post('/customers/update/shipping', customers.updateShipping);
18   app.post('/customers/update/billing', customers.updateBilling);
19   app.post('/customers/update/cart', customers.updateCart);
20 }
```

Implementing the Model-Based Controller Routes

In addition to implementing the standard route handling, you also need to implement route handling to interact with the database. You break these route handlers out of the standard `cart_route.js` file and into their own files for each model, to keep the code clean and ensure a good division of responsibilities.

The following sections cover the implementation of the model-specific controllers for the `Customer`, `Order`, and `Product` models.

Implementing the Product Model Controller

Listing 28.9 implements the route handling code for the `Product` model. There are only two routes. The `getProduct()` route finds a single product, based on the `productId` included in the query. The `getProducts()` route finds all products. If the requests are successful, the product or all products are returned to the client as JSON strings. If the requests fail, a 404 error is returned.

Listing 28.9 `products_controller.js`: **Implementing routes to get products for the Express server**

```
var mongoose = require('mongoose'),
    Product = mongoose.model('Product');
exports.getProduct = function(req, res) {
  Product.findOne({ _id: req.query.productId })
  .exec(function(err, product) {
    if (!product){
      res.json(404, {msg: 'Photo Not Found.'});
    } else {
      res.json(product);
    }
  });
};
exports.getProducts = function(req, res) {
  Product.find()
  .exec(function(err, products) {
    if (!products){
      res.json(404, {msg: 'Products Not Found.'});
    } else {
      res.json(products);
    }
  });
};
```

Implementing the Order Model Controller

Listing 28.10 implements the route handling code for the `Order` model. There are three routes. The `getOrder()` route finds a single order, based on the `orderId` included in the query. The `getOrders()` route finds all orders that belong to the current user. In this example, `userid` is hard-coded `customerA`. If the requests are successful, the order or all of this customer's orders are returned to the client as JSON strings. If the requests fails, a 404 error is returned.

The `addOrder()` route handler builds a new `Order` object by getting the `updatedShipping`, `updatedBilling`, and `orderItems` parameters from the `POST` request. If the order saves successfully, the cart field in the `Customer` object is reset to empty, using the following code, and a success is returned; otherwise, a 500 or 404 error is returned.

```
      Customer.update({ userid: 'customerA' },
          {$set:{cart:[]}})
```

Listing 28.10 `orders_controller.js`: **Implementing routes to get and add orders for the Express server**

```
var mongoose = require('mongoose'),
    Customer = mongoose.model('Customer'),
    Order = mongoose.model('Order'),
    Address = mongoose.model('Address'),
    Billing = mongoose.model('Billing');
exports.getOrder = function(req, res) {
  Order.findOne({ _id: req.query.orderId })
  .exec(function(err, order) {
    if (!order){
      res.json(404, {msg: 'Order Not Found.'});
    } else {
      res.json(order);
    }
  });
};
exports.getOrders = function(req, res) {
  Order.find({userid: 'customerA'})
  .exec(function(err, orders) {
    if (!orders){
      res.json(404, {msg: 'Orders Not Found.'});
    } else {
      res.json(orders);
    }
  });
};
exports.addOrder = function(req, res){
  var orderShipping = new Address(req.body.updatedShipping);
  var orderBilling = new Billing(req.body.updatedBilling);
  var orderItems = req.body.orderItems;
```

```
  var newOrder = new Order({userid: 'customerA',
                      items: orderItems, shipping: orderShipping,
                      billing: orderBilling});
  newOrder.save(function(err, results){
    if(err){
      res.json(500, "Failed to save Order.");
    } else {
      Customer.update({ userid: 'customerA' },
          {$set:{cart:[]}})
      .exec(function(err, results){
        if (err || results < 1){
         res.json(404, {msg: 'Failed to update Cart.'});
        } else {
         res.json({msg: "Order Saved."});
        }
      });
    }
  });
};
```

Implementing the Customer Model Controller

Listing 28.11 implements the route handling code for the `Customer` model. There are four routes. The `getCustomer()` route finds a customer order, based on the hard-coded `customerA` value. If it is successful, the `Customer` object is returned to the client as JSON strings. If the request fails, a 404 error is returned. The `updateShipping()` route creates a new `Address` object from the `updatedShipping` parameter in the `POST` request and then uses an `update()` method to update the `Customer` object with the new shipping data. If it is successful, a success message is returned; if it fails, a 404 error is returned.

The `updateBilling()` route creates a new `Billing` object from the `updatedBilling` parameter in the `POST` request and then uses an `update()` method to update the `Customer` object with the new billing data. If it is successful, a success message is returned; if it fails, a 404 error is returned. The `updateCart()` route uses the `update()` method to update the cart field of the `Customer` object with the `updatedCart` object sent in the `POST` request. If it is successful, a success message is returned. If it fails, a 404 error is returned.

Listing 28.11 `customers_controller.js`: **Implementing routes to get and update customers for the Express server**

```
var mongoose = require('mongoose'),
    Customer = mongoose.model('Customer'),
    Address = mongoose.model('Address'),
    Billing = mongoose.model('Billing');
exports.getCustomer = function(req, res) {
  Customer.findOne({ userid: 'customerA' })
```

```
  .exec(function(err, customer) {
    if (!customer){
      res.json(404, {msg: 'Customer Not Found.'});
    } else {
      res.json(customer);
    }
  });
};
exports.updateShipping = function(req, res){
  var newShipping = new Address(req.body.updatedShipping);
  Customer.update({ userid: 'customerA' },
      {$set:{shipping:[newShipping.toObject()]}})
  .exec(function(err, results){
    if (err || results < 1){
     res.json(404, {msg: 'Failed to update Shipping.'});
    } else {
     res.json({msg: "Customer Shipping Updated"});
    }
  });
};
exports.updateBilling = function(req, res){
  // This is where you could verify the credit card information
  // and halt the checkout if it is invalid.
  var newBilling = new Billing(req.body.updatedBilling);
  Customer.update({ userid: 'customerA' },
      {$set:{billing:[newBilling.toObject()]}})
  .exec(function(err, results){
    if (err || results < 1){
     res.json(404, {msg: 'Failed to update Billing.'});
    } else {
     res.json({msg: "Customer Billing Updated"});
    }
  });
};
exports.updateCart = function(req, res){
  Customer.update({ userid: 'customerA' },
      {$set:{cart:req.body.updatedCart}})
  .exec(function(err, results){
    if (err || results < 1){
     res.json(404, {msg: 'Failed to update Cart.'});
    } else {
     res.json({msg: "Customer Cart Updated"});
    }
  });
};
```

Implementing Shopping Cart and Checkout Views

Now that the routes are set up and configured, you are ready to implement the views that are rendered by the routes and AngularJS templates. The following sections discuss the main `shopping.html` view rendered by EJS as well as the various partial views that make up the `cart`, `shipping`, `billing`, `review`, and `orders` pages.

Implementing the Shopping View

The shopping view shown in Listing 28.12 is the main view for the shopping application. In fact, the user never actually leaves this page; rather, the content changes, based on the partial views described in the following sections.

The header of the view registers the `<html ng-app="myApp">` element with the AngularJS `myApp` application and loads the `cart_styles.css` file. The `<body>` element initializes the AngularJS `ng-controller="shoppingController"` to provide the functionality to interact with the products, shopping cart, checkout, and orders.

The page content changes using the following `ng-include` directive that maps to `$scope.content`, and the `content` variable in the scope can be set to any template file on the server:

```
<div ng-include="content"></div>
```

For an example, see the orders and shopping cart clickable links, shown below, which call `setContent()` with the name of the template file to load:

```
<span class="orders"
   ng-click="setContent('orders.html')">Orders</span>
<span id="cartLink" ng-click="setContent('cart.html')">
  {{customer.cart.length}} items
  <img src="/images/cart.png" />
</span>
```

Also notice that the number of items in the cart is taken directly from the scope variable `customer.cart.length`. The `Customer` object in the scope is downloaded directly from the webserver when the controller is initialized. Figure 28.1 shows the fully rendered `shopping.html` page.

Listing 28.12 `shopping.html`: **Implementing the main shopping page AngularJS 'template code**

```
<!doctype html>
<html ng-app="myApp">
<head>
  <title>Shopping Cart</title>
  <link rel="stylesheet" type="text/css"
      href="/static/css/cart_styles.css" />
</head>
```

```
<body>
  <div ng-controller="shoppingController">
    <div id="banner">
      <div id="title">My Store</div>
      <div id="bar">
        <span class="orders"
          ng-click="setContent('orders.html')">Orders</span>
        <span id="cartLink" ng-click="setContent('cart.html')">
            {{customer.cart.length}} items
            <img src="/images/cart.png" />
        </span>
      </div>
    </div>
    <div id="main">
      <div ng-include="content"></div>
    </div>
  </div>
  <script src="http://code.angularjs.org/1.2.9/angular.min.js"></script>
  <script src="/static/js/cart_app.js"></script>
</body>
</html>
```

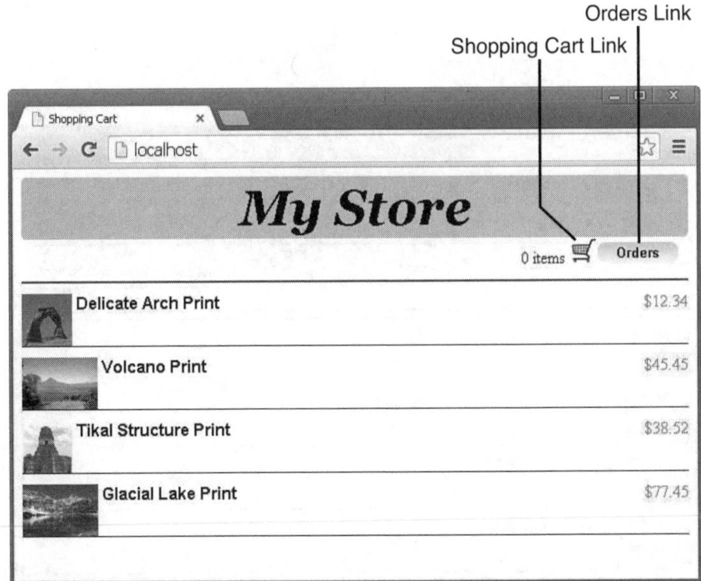

Figure 28.1 The rendered shopping page with the shopping cart link and Orders button, as well as a list of prints to shop for.

Implementing the Products View

Next, you implement the products view to provide the user with a list of products to choose from. In this example, the shopping page is very basic: only a single page with a list of prints to buy. Although it is basic, it is enough to demonstrate the implementation of the shopping cart and keeps the code simple.

Listing 28.13 is an AngularJS partial that is loaded into the view when `$scope.content` is set to `products.html`. The code uses `ng-repeat` on the products that are initialized when `shoppingController` is initialized. Notice that the product information is displayed on the page by using expressions such as `{{product.name}}`.

Also notice that when the user clicks the `<img>` element, the `setProduct()` function is called in the controller. That function sets the current `$scope.product` value and changes the `$scope.content` value to `product.html`. Figure 28.2 shows the rendered products view.

Listing 28.13 `products.html`: **Implementing the partial product listing template**

```
<div id="productsContainer">
  <div class="listItem" ng-repeat="product in products">
    <img class="listImg" ng-click="setProduct(product._id)"
         ng-src="../images/{{product.imagefile}}" />
    <span class="prodName">{{product.name}}</span>
    <span class="price">{{product.price|currency}}</span>
  </div>
</div>
```

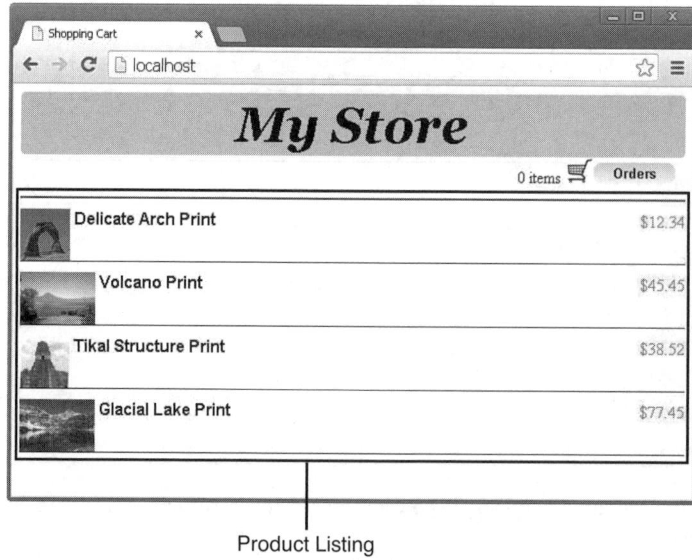

Figure 28.2 The products view, showing the prints available.

Implementing the Product Page View

When the user clicks an image in the products list, the product page view is rendered. Listing 28.14 shows the AngularJS code used for the product page view. Notice that the product information is displayed using AngularJS expressions that access the `$scope.product` value. The Add to Cart button sends `product._id` to the `addToCart()` function in the controller, which adds the print to the cart. Figure 28.3 shows the rendered product page view, which shows the image, name, description, quantity, and price, as well as the Add to Cart button.

Listing 28.14 `product.html`: **Implementing the partial product details template with an Add to Cart button**

```
<div id="productContainer">
  <img class="fullImg"
       ng-src="../images/{{product.imagefile}}" />
  <div class="prodInfo">
      <p class="itemTitle">{{product.name}}</p>
    <p class="prodDesc">{{product.description}}</p>
    <p class="fullPrice">{{product.price|currency}}</p>
      <p class="status">{{product.instock}} available</p>
      <p class="cartButton" ng-click="addToCart(product._id)">
        Add to Cart
        <img src="/images/cart.png" />
      </p>
  </div>
</div>
```

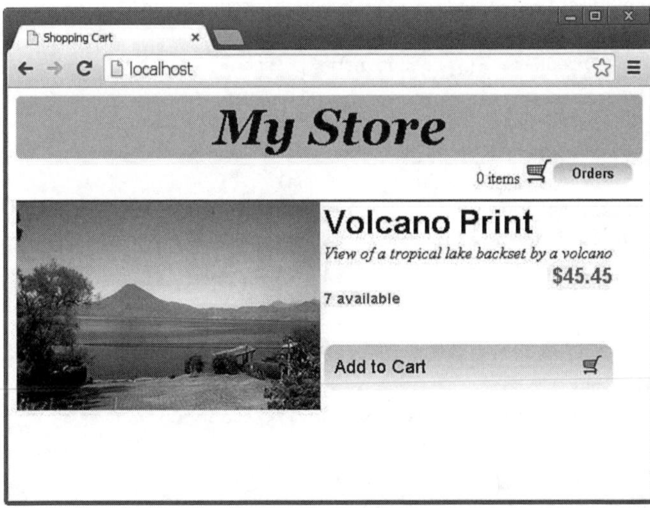

Figure 28.3 The product page view, showing the description, availability, and the Add to Cart button.

Implementing the Cart View

Once the user clicks the Add to Cart button, the item is added to the cart, and the view changes to the cart view. The cart view, shown in Listing 28.15, provides a list of products that currently exist in the cart, a price total, and buttons to check out or go back to shopping.

The following code implements a delete link in the cart to remove an item. It calls the function `deleteFromCart()`, located in the controller, and passes `product._id` to identify which item to delete:

```
<span class="delete"
      ng-click="deleteFromCart(product._id)">Remove</span>
```

Also, a quantity field links directly to the `item.quantity` element, where an item comes from the `ng-repeat` of the `customer.shopping` cart array.

A controller function calculates the shipping value and total value; it is linked by the following expression code, where the `|currency` filter formats the values of price, shipping, and total:

```
<span class="price">{{cartTotal()|currency}}</span>
```

The cool part about AngularJS is that because the `quantity` fields are linked directly to the scope, as you change them, the shipping and total values change as well. Figure 28.4 shows the rendered cart view.

Listing 28.15 `cart.html`: **Implementing the partial shopping cart template**

```
<div id="cartsContainer">
  <div class="listItem" ng-repeat="item in customer.cart"
    ng-init="product=item.product[0]">
    <img class="listImg" ng-click="setProduct(product._id)"
         ng-src="../images/{{product.imagefile}}" />
    <span class="prodName">{{product.name}}</span>
    <span >
      <span class="price">{{product.price|currency}}</span>
      <input class="quantity" type="text" ng-model="item.quantity" />
      <label class="quantity">Quantity</label>
      <span class="delete"
            ng-click="deleteFromCart(product._id)">Remove</span>
    </span>
  </div>
  <hr>
  <div>
    <span>Shipping</span>
    <span class="price">{{shipping|currency}}</span>
  </div>
  <hr>
  <div>
    <span>Total</span>
    <span class="price">{{cartTotal()|currency}}</span>
   </div>
```

```
   <hr>
  <div>
      <span class="button" ng-click="checkout()"
            ng-hide="customer.cart.length==0">
        Checkout
      </span>
      <span class="button" ng-click="setContent('products.html')">
        Continue Shopping
      </span>
  </div>
</div>
```

Figure 28.4 The cart view allows the customer to change the quantity of items, remove items, and check out.

Implementing the Shipping View

When the user clicks the Checkout button in the shopping cart, the shipping view appears, allowing the user to enter shipping information. The shipping view, shown in Listing 28.16, provides a series of input fields to input the shipping information.

The shipping template code is very straightforward. There are a series of text inputs with labels for each shipping field value. The fields are linked to the `customer.shipping[0]` object in the scope model, using the `ng-model` directive. When the user changes the field, the scope changes automatically. This is very useful when sending customer changes back to the database. When the user clicks the Continue to Billing button, the shipping data is updated on the server as well, and the user is taken to the billing view. Figure 28.5 shows the rendered shipping view.

Listing 28.16 `shipping.html`: **Implementing the partial shipping template**

```
<div id="shippingContainer">
  <h2>Ship To:</h2>
  <label>Name</label>
  <input type="text" ng-model="customer.shipping[0].name" /><br>
  <label>Address</label>
  <input type="text" ng-model="customer.shipping[0].address" /><br>
  <label>City</label>
  <input type="text" ng-model="customer.shipping[0].city" /><br>
  <label>State</label>
  <input type="text" ng-model="customer.shipping[0].state" /><br>
  <label>Zipcode</label>
  <input type="text" ng-model="customer.shipping[0].zip" />
  <hr>
  <div>
    <span class="button" ng-click="setShipping()">
      Continue to Billing
    </span>
    <span class="button" ng-click="setContent('products.html')">
      Continue Shopping
    </span>
  </div>
</div>
```

Figure 28.5 The shipping view allows the user to enter the address to ship the prints to.

Implementing the Billing View

When the user clicks the Continue to Billing button in the shipping view, the billing view appears, allowing the user to then enter billing information. The billing view, shown in Listing 28.17, provides a series of input fields to input the billing information.

The billing template code is similar to the shipping template code, with the addition of a few new fields. The Card radio buttons to select the credit card are bound to the customer.billing[0].cardtype value in the scope. When you change the radio button selection, the model also changes.

The values for the <select> drop-down options come from simple arrays defined in the scope and are bound to the customer.billing[0] data as well. For example, the following lines use an array of number-named months in the scope and bind the <select> value to the customer.billing[0].expiremonth value in the scope:

```
<select ng-model="customer.billing[0].expiremonth"
        ng-options="m for m in months"></select>
```

One other thing to note is that the CCV value is passed to the verifyBilling(ccv) function for verifying the credit card. The CCV number is not supposed to be stored locally on the customer site, so it is kept separate here and passed as its own parameter. Figure 28.6 shows the rendered billing view.

Listing 28.17 billing.html: Implementing the partial billing template

```
<div id="shippingContainer">
  <h2>Card Info: </h2>
  <label>Card</label>
  <input type="radio" ng-model="customer.billing[0].cardtype"
         value="Visa">  Visa
  <input type="radio" ng-model="customer.billing[0].cardtype"
         value="Amex"> Amex
  <input type="radio" ng-model="customer.billing[0].cardtype"
         value="MasterCard"> MasterCard
  <br><label>Name on Card</label>
  <input type="text" ng-model="customer.billing[0].name" />
  <br><label>Card Number</label>
  <input type="text" ng-model="customer.billing[0].number" />
  <br><label>Expires</label>
  <select ng-model="customer.billing[0].expiremonth"
          ng-options="m for m in months"></select>
  <select ng-model="customer.billing[0].expireyear"
          ng-options="m for m in years"></select>
  <label>Card CCV</label>
  <input class="security" type=text ng-model="ccv" />
```

```
  <h2>Billing Address:</h2>
  <label>Name</label>
  <input type="text"
         ng-model="customer.billing[0].address[0].name" />
  <br><label>Address</label>
  <input type="text"
         ng-model="customer.billing[0].address[0].address" />
  <br><label>City</label>
  <input type="text"
         ng-model="customer.billing[0].address[0].city" />
  <br><label>State</label>
  <input type="text"
         ng-model="customer.billing[0].address[0].state" />
  <br><label>Zipcode</label>
  <input type="text"
         ng-model="customer.billing[0].address[0].zip" />
  <hr>
  <div>
    <span class="button" ng-click="verifyBilling(ccv)">
      Verify Billing
    </span>
    <span class="button" ng-click="setContent('products.html')">
      Continue Shopping
    </span>
  </div>
</div>
```

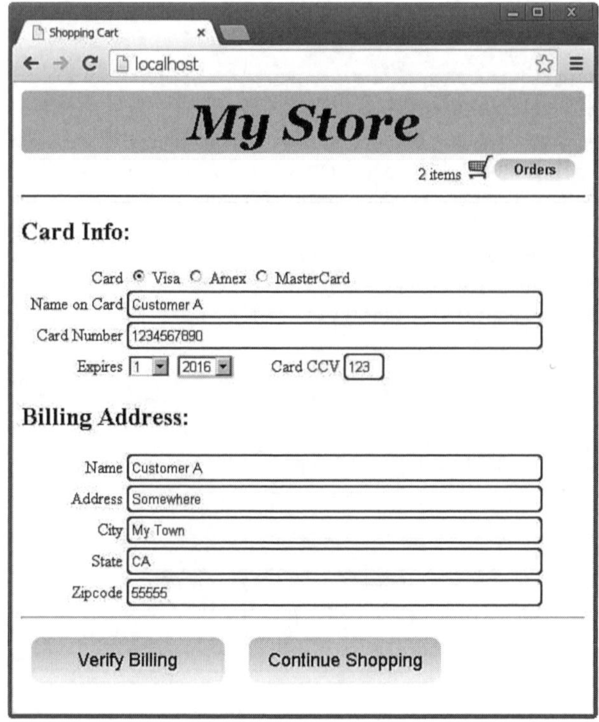

Figure 28.6 The billing view allows the user to enter credit card information and a billing address.

Implementing the Review View

When the user clicks the Verify Billing button in the billing view, the review view appears, where the user can review the order, including the shipping and billing information. The review view, shown in Listing 28.18, shows the ordered items with totals as well as the shipping and billing information. Figure 28.7 shows the rendered review view.

Notice that all the information displayed is still coming from the `Customer` object inside the scope. The shipping information comes from `customer.shipping[0]`, the billing information comes from `customer.billing[0]`, and the product list comes from `customer.cart`. When the customer clicks the Make Purchase button, this information is sent to the webserver, and a new order object is created. The view then changes to the orders view.

Listing 28.18 `review.html`: **Implementing the partial order review template**

```
<div id="reviewContainer">
  <div class="listItem" ng-repeat="item in customer.cart"
    ng-init="product=item.product[0]">
    <img class="listImg" ng-click="setProduct(product._id)"
         ng-src="../images/{{product.imagefile}}" />
    <span class="prodName">{{product.name}}</span>
    <span >
      <span class="price">{{product.price|currency}}</span>
      <label class="quantity">{{item.quantity}}</label>
      <label class="quantity">Quantity</label>
    </span>
  </div><hr>
  <div>
    <span>Shipping</span>
    <span class="price">{{shipping|currency}}</span>
  </div><hr>
  <div>
    <span>Total</span>
    <span class="price">{{cartTotal()|currency}}</span>
  </div><hr>
  <div>
    <div class="review">
      Shipping:<br>
      {{customer.shipping[0].name}}<br>
      {{customer.shipping[0].address}}<br>
      {{customer.shipping[0].city}},
      {{customer.shipping[0].state}}
      {{customer.shipping[0].zip}}<br>
    </div>
    <div class="review">
      Billing:<br>
      {{customer.billing[0].cardtype}} ending in
      {{customer.billing[0].number.slice(-5,-1)}}<br>
      {{customer.billing[0].address[0].name}}<br>
      {{customer.billing[0].address[0].address}}<br>
      {{customer.billing[0].address[0].city}},
      {{customer.billing[0].address[0].state}}
      {{customer.billing[0].address[0].zip}}<br>
    </div>
  </div>
```

```
  <div>
    <span class="button" ng-click="makePurchase()">
      Make Purchase
    </span>
    <span class="button" ng-click="setContent('products.html')">
      Continue Shopping
    </span>
  </div>
</div>
```

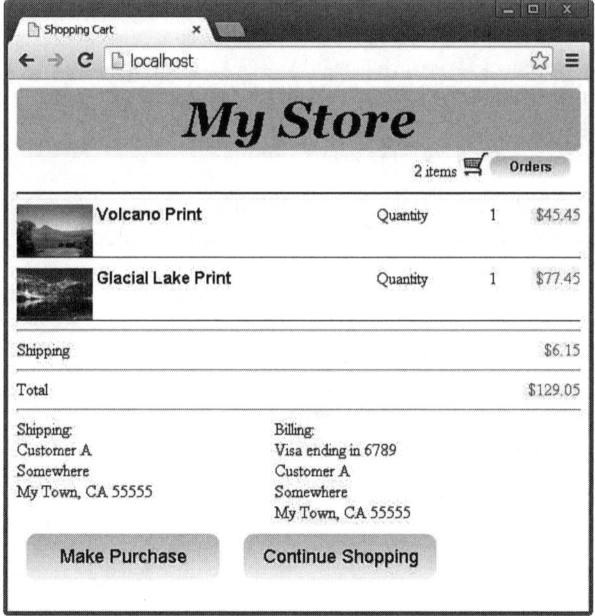

Figure 28.7 The review view allows the customer to review the order.

Implementing the Orders View

When the order is complete, the user sees the orders view, which shows the user's completed purchases. (There are other ways you can handle this part of the process. For example, you could add another page to display the completed order, or you could just send the user back to the shopping page.)

The orders view, shown in Listing 28.19, displays a list of orders that this customer has completed. The list comes from an `ng-repeat` directive on the `$scope.orders` value. The `ng-repeat` iteration lists the date the order was placed, the status, and the items bought, as shown in Figure 28.8.

Listing 28.19 `orders.html`: **Implementing the partial orders view template**

```
<div id="reviewContainer">
  <div class="listItem" ng-repeat="order in orders">
    <p class="itemTitle">Order #{{$index+1}}</p>
    <p class="prodDesc">Placed {{order.timestamp|date}}</p>
    <p class="status">{{order.status}}</p>
      <div class="listItem" ng-repeat="item in order.items"
        ng-init="product=item.product[0]">
        <img class="listImg" ng-click="setProduct(product._id)"
             ng-src="../images/{{product.imagefile}}" />
        <span class="prodName">{{product.name}}</span>
        <span >
          <span class="price">{{product.price|currency}}</span>
          <label class="quantity">{{item.quantity}}</label>
          <label class="quantity">Quantity</label>
        </span>
      </div>
  </div>
  <div>
    <span class="button" ng-click="setContent('products.html')">
      Continue Shopping
    </span>
  </div>
</div>
```

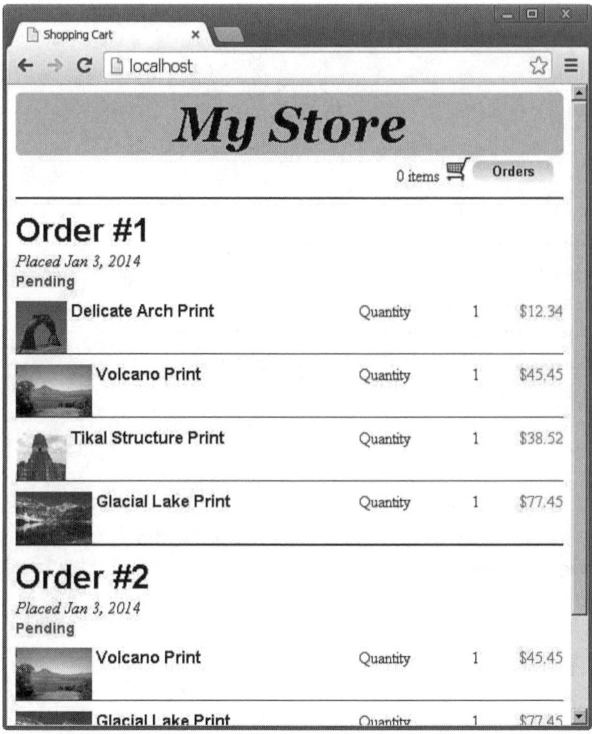

Figure 28.8 The orders view shows a list of orders that this customer has placed.

Adding CSS to Stylize the Views

Listing 28.20 shows the CSS code you use to style the elements in the shopping cart so that you can see why things look and act as they do. The CSS is condensed as much as possible to make it fit into the book. Also, the titles, buttons, and such here are large, so that they display clearly in the book's figures.

Listing 28.20 `cart_styles.css`: **Implementing the CSS styles for the view HTML files**

```
p{margin:0}
label {width:100px; display:inline-block; text-align:right; }
input[type="text"]{ border: 2px ridge blue; padding:3px;
  border-radius:5px; width:400px; }
#banner{ border-bottom: 2px blue ridge; height:100px }
#title { text-align:center; background-color:#a0d0ff;
  font:italic bold 48px/60px Georgia, serif; border-radius: 5px }
#bar { background-color:#a0d0ff; }
```

```
#cartLink { float:right; text-align:right; cursor:pointer }
#cartLink img { height:25px; }
#main {clear:both;}
.listItem{border-bottom: 1px solid black; clear:both;
  margin-top:10px }
.listImg { height:50px; vertical-align:top }
.fullImg { width:300px; vertical-align:top }
.prodName {font: bold 16px/20px Arial, Sans-serif; }
.price{ float:right; color:red; width:75px; text-align:right;
  display:inline-block}
.prodInfo{ display:inline-block; }
.itemTitle {font: bold 32px/40px Arial, Sans-serif; }
.fullPrice { color:red; font: bold 20px/24px Arial, Sans-serif;
  text-align:right}
.status {color:green; font: bold 14px/18px Arial, Sans-serif;}
.prodDesc { font-style: italic; }
.button,
.cartButton{ font: 18px/24px Arial, Sans-serif; border-radius: 10px;
  padding:10px; margin-top:35px; cursor: pointer; width:170px;
  background-image: -webkit-linear-gradient(top, #FFCC66, #FFFF99);
  text-align:center}
.cartButton img { height:20px; float:right}
.button{ display:inline-block; margin:10px;}
input.quantity { display:inline-block; float:right; width:30px; }
label.quantity { display:inline-block; float:right; width:60px;
  margin-right:8px; }
span.orders,
span.delete { cursor:pointer; display:inline-block; float:right;
  background-color:#FF5858;  border-radius: 8px; text-align:center;
  font: bold 13px/20px Arial, Sans-serif;
  margin-right:20px; width:80px; }
span.orders{ margin-top:5px; margin-right:10px;
  background-image: -webkit-linear-gradient(top, #FFCC66, #FFFF99);}
input.security { width:30px }
div.review{ display:inline-block; width:45%; vertical-align:top; }
```

Implementing the AngularJS Module and Controller to Support Shopping Cart Views

With the views finished, you need to implement AngularJS controller code to support them. The views need to be able to get the customer, product, and order documents from the webserver. They also need to be able to update the customer shipping, billing, and cart, and they need to be able to process new orders.

In the shopping cart example, everything is built into a single module and controller. The controller code is a bit long for a single section in the book, so the following sections break down the various components of the controller code and describe smaller code chunks. The full Angular JS code for the controller is shown later on, in Listing 28.29.

Initializing the Shopping Scope

To implement `shoppingController`, you need to initialize the scope values that you need. The code in Listing 28.21 initializes the shopping scope. The `$scope.months` and `$scope.years` arrays populate the credit card form. `$scope.content` determines which AngularJS partial is rendered in the view. It is initialized to `products.html` so the user can begin shopping.

Next, there are three `$http` requests that get the products, customer, and orders and use the results to set the `$scope.products`, `$scope.product`, `$scope.customer`, and `$scope.orders` objects that are utilized in the AngularJS views.

Listing 28.21 `cart_app.js-initialize`: **Initializing the scope for the shopping controller**

```
    $scope.months = [1,2,3,4,5,6,7,8,9,10,11,12];
    $scope.years = [2014,2015,2016,2017,2018,2019,2020];
    $scope.content = '/static/products.html';
    $http.get('/products/get')
     .success(function(data, status, headers, config) {
        $scope.products = data;
        $scope.product = data[0];
      })
      .error(function(data, status, headers, config) {
        $scope.products = [];
      });
    $http.get('/customers/get')
     .success(function(data, status, headers, config) {
       $scope.customer = data;
      })
     .error(function(data, status, headers, config) {
       $scope.customer = [];
     });
    $http.get('/orders/get')
     .success(function(data, status, headers, config) {
       $scope.orders = data;
     })
     .error(function(data, status, headers, config) {
       $scope.orders = [];
     });
```

Implementing Helper Functions

Next, you add the helper functions, shown in Listing 28.22, to provide functionality for the AngularJS templates. The `setContent()` function sets the `$scope.content` value, effectively changing the view. The `setProduct()` function is called when a user clicks a print image and sets the `$scope.product` used in the product view. The `cartTotal()` function iterates through the products in the user's cart, updates `$scope.shipping`, and returns a total that is then used in the cart and review views.

Listing 28.22 `cart_app.js-helpers`: **Adding helper functions to set the content, total, and shipping values**

```
    $scope.setContent = function(filename){
      $scope.content = '/static/'+ filename;
    };
    $scope.setProduct = function(productId){
      $scope.product = this.product;
      $scope.content = '/static/product.html';
    };
    $scope.cartTotal = function(){
      var total = 0;
      for(var i=0; i<$scope.customer.cart.length; i++){
        var item = $scope.customer.cart[i];
        total += item.quantity * item.product[0].price;
      }
      $scope.shipping = total*.05;
      return total+$scope.shipping;
    };
```

Adding Items to the Cart

You call the `addToCart()` function, shown in Listing 28.23, from the template when the user clicks the Add to Cart button. It iterates through the items in the `customer.cart`, and if it finds that the item is there, it increments the quantity; otherwise, it adds the item to the `customer.cart` array with a quantity of `1`.

Once `$scope.customer` is updated, you call an `$http POST` to the `/customers/update/cart` route to update the cart. This way, the cart is persistent and will be there even if the user closes the browser or navigates away. On success, the view switches to `cart.html`. On failure, an alert window appears.

Listing 28.23 `cart_app.js-addToCart`: **Adding controller functions to handle adding and removing products from the cart**

```
    $scope.addToCart = function(productId){
      var found = false;
      for(var i=0; i<$scope.customer.cart.length; i++){
        var item = $scope.customer.cart[i];
        if (item.product[0]._id == productId){
          item.quantity += 1;
          found = true;
        }
      }
      if (!found){
        $scope.customer.cart.push({quantity: 1,
                                   product: [this.product]});
      }
      $http.post('/customers/update/cart',
                 { updatedCart: $scope.customer.cart })
       .success(function(data, status, headers, config) {
         $scope.content = '/static/cart.html';
       })
       .error(function(data, status, headers, config) {
         $window.alert(data);
       });
    };
```

Deleting Items from the Cart

You call the `deleteFromCart()` function, shown in Listing 28.24, from the cart template when the user clicks the Remove button. It iterates through the items in `customer.cart`, and if it finds the item, it uses the `array.slice(index,1)` method to delete it from the array.

Once the item is removed from `$scope.customer.cart`, you call an `$http POST` to the `/customers/update/cart` route to update the cart. This way, the cart is persistent and will be there even if the user closes the browser or navigates away. On success, this switches to `cart.html`; on failure, an alert window appears.

Listing 28.24 `cart_app.js-deleteFromCart`: **Adding the delete function to handle deleting items from the cart**

```
    $scope.deleteFromCart = function(productId){
      for(var i=0; i<$scope.customer.cart.length; i++){
        var item = $scope.customer.cart[i];
        if (item.product[0]._id == productId){
          $scope.customer.cart.splice(i,1);
          break;
```

```
      }
    }
    $http.post('/customers/update/cart',
               { updatedCart: $scope.customer.cart })
     .success(function(data, status, headers, config) {
       $scope.content = '/static/cart.html';
     })
     .error(function(data, status, headers, config) {
       $window.alert(data);
     });
  };
```

Checking Out

You call the checkout() function, shown in Listing 28.25, when the user clicks the Checkout button in the cart view. This illustrates how useful AngularJS data binding really is: Because the customer information is always kept up-to-date, all that is necessary is to send an $http POST request with the parameter {updatedCart:$scope.customer.cart} to update the cart.

The cart is updated to ensure that any quantity changes made in the cart page are also persistent later on, if the user backs out of the purchase. If the request is successful, the view switches to shipping.html otherwise it stays on the checkout page.

Listing 28.25 cart_app.js-checkout: **Implementing the checkout function in the controller**

```
  $scope.checkout = function(){
    $http.post('/customers/update/cart',
               { updatedCart: $scope.customer.cart })
     .success(function(data, status, headers, config) {
       $scope.content = '/static/shipping.html';
     })
     .error(function(data, status, headers, config) {
       $window.alert(data);
     });
  };
```

Setting Shipping Information

You call the setShipping() function, shown in Listing 28.26, when the user clicks the Continue to Billing button in the cart view. The shipping information needs to be updated in the database to ensure that it is persistent when the customer leaves the website. You call an $http POST method to the /customers/update/shipping route. The POST includes the parameter {updatedShipping:$scope.customer.shipping[0]} in the body. If the request is successful, the view switches to billing.html; otherwise, an alert appears.

Listing 28.26 `cart_app.js-setShipping`: **Implementing the shipping function in the controller**

```
$scope.setShipping = function(){
  $http.post('/customers/update/shipping',
      { updatedShipping: $scope.customer.shipping[0] })
    .success(function(data, status, headers, config) {
      $scope.content = '/static/billing.html';
    })
    .error(function(data, status, headers, config) {
      $window.alert(data);
    });
};
```

Verifying Billing

You call the `verifyBilling()` function, shown in Listing 28.27, when the user clicks the Verify Billing button in the shipping view. The billing information needs to be updated in the database to ensure that it is persistent when the customer leaves the website. Also, the credit card information can be validated on the server at this point. You call an `$http POST` method to the `/customers/update/billing` route. If the request is successful, the view switches to `review.html`; otherwise, an alert appears.

Listing 28.27 `cart_app.js-verifyBilling`: **Implementing the billing function in the controller**

```
$scope.verifyBilling = function(ccv){
  $scope.ccv = ccv;
  $http.post('/customers/update/billing',
      { updatedBilling: $scope.customer.billing[0], ccv: ccv})
    .success(function(data, status, headers, config) {
      $scope.content = '/static/review.html';
    })
    .error(function(data, status, headers, config) {
      $window.alert(data);
    });
};
```

Making the Purchase

You call the `makePurchase()` function, shown in Listing 28.28, when a user clicks the Make Purchase button in the billing view. This method sends an `$http POST` method to the `/orders/add` route on the server. The `POST` request contains `orderBilling`, `orderShipping`, and `orderItems` parameters. If the request is successful, the `$scope.customer.cart` is initialized to `[]` to match the empty array value that will be set in the customer document in MongoDB.

Also, if the request is successful, a new order document will have been created in the MongoDB database. Therefore, you make another `$http` request, this time to `/orders/get`, to get the full list of orders, including the new one. Then the view switches to `orders.html`.

Listing 28.28 `cart_app.js-makePurchase`: **Implementing the purchase function in the controller**

```
$scope.makePurchase = function(){
  $http.post('/orders/add',
      { orderBilling: $scope.customer.billing[0],
        orderShipping: $scope.customer.shipping[0],
        orderItems: $scope.customer.cart })
    .success(function(data, status, headers, config) {
      $scope.customer.cart = [];
      $http.get('/orders/get')
      .success(function(data, status, headers, config) {
         $scope.orders = data;
         $scope.content = '/static/orders.html';
       })
       .error(function(data, status, headers, config) {
         $scope.orders = [];
       });
    })
    .error(function(data, status, headers, config) {
      $window.alert(data);
    });
};
```

The Full Controller

Listing 28.29 shows the full `myApp` code, with the `shoppingController` initialization and all the controller code together so you can see how everything fits together. Notice that the `shoppingController` definition includes dependencies on `$scope`, `$http`, and `$window`. The `$window` dependency allows you to add the browser alert message when errors occur.

Listing 28.29 `cart_app.js-full`: **Implementing an application that supports keeping track of items in a shopping cart and handling the checkout process**

```
var app = angular.module('myApp', []);
app.controller('shoppingController', ['$scope', '$http', '$window',
                              function($scope, $http, $window) {
    $scope.months = [1,2,3,4,5,6,7,8,9,10,11,12];
    $scope.years = [2014,2015,2016,2017,2018,2019,2020];
    $scope.content = '/static/products.html';
    $http.get('/products/get')
     .success(function(data, status, headers, config) {
        $scope.products = data;
```

```
          $scope.product = data[0];
        })
        .error(function(data, status, headers, config) {
          $scope.products = [];
        });
      $http.get('/customers/get')
       .success(function(data, status, headers, config) {
         $scope.customer = data;
        })
       .error(function(data, status, headers, config) {
         $scope.customer = [];
       });
      $http.get('/orders/get')
      .success(function(data, status, headers, config) {
         $scope.orders = data;
       })
       .error(function(data, status, headers, config) {
         $scope.orders = [];
       });
      $scope.setContent = function(filename){
        $scope.content = '/static/'+ filename;
      };
      $scope.setProduct = function(productId){
        $scope.product = this.product;
        $scope.content = '/static/product.html';
      };
      $scope.cartTotal = function(){
        var total = 0;
        for(var i=0; i<$scope.customer.cart.length; i++){
          var item = $scope.customer.cart[i];
          total += item.quantity * item.product[0].price;
        }
        $scope.shipping = total*.05;
        return total+$scope.shipping;
      };
      $scope.addToCart = function(productId){
        var found = false;
        for(var i=0; i<$scope.customer.cart.length; i++){
          var item = $scope.customer.cart[i];
          if (item.product[0]._id == productId){
            item.quantity += 1;
            found = true;
          }
        }
        if (!found){
          $scope.customer.cart.push({quantity: 1,
                                     product: [this.product]});
        }
```

```
      $http.post('/customers/update/cart',
                 { updatedCart: $scope.customer.cart })
       .success(function(data, status, headers, config) {
         $scope.content = '/static/cart.html';
       })
       .error(function(data, status, headers, config) {
         $window.alert(data);
       });
    };
    $scope.deleteFromCart = function(productId){
      for(var i=0; i<$scope.customer.cart.length; i++){
        var item = $scope.customer.cart[i];
        if (item.product[0]._id == productId){
          $scope.customer.cart.splice(i,1);
          break;
        }
      }
      $http.post('/customers/update/cart',
                 { updatedCart: $scope.customer.cart })
       .success(function(data, status, headers, config) {
         $scope.content = '/static/cart.html';
       })
       .error(function(data, status, headers, config) {
         $window.alert(data);
       });
    };
    $scope.checkout = function(){
      $http.post('/customers/update/cart',
                 { updatedCart: $scope.customer.cart })
       .success(function(data, status, headers, config) {
         $scope.content = '/static/shipping.html';
       })
       .error(function(data, status, headers, config) {
         $window.alert(data);
       });
    };
    $scope.setShipping = function(){
      $http.post('/customers/update/shipping',
          { updatedShipping :$scope.customer.shipping[0] })
        .success(function(data, status, headers, config) {
          $scope.content = '/static/billing.html';
        })
        .error(function(data, status, headers, config) {
          $window.alert(data);
        });
    };
```

```
    $scope.verifyBilling = function(ccv){
      $scope.ccv = ccv;
      $http.post('/customers/update/billing',
          { updatedBilling: $scope.customer.billing[0], ccv: ccv})
        .success(function(data, status, headers, config) {
          $scope.content = '/static/review.html';
        })
        .error(function(data, status, headers, config) {
          $window.alert(data);
        });
    };
    $scope.makePurchase = function(){
      $http.post('/orders/add',
          { orderBilling: $scope.customer.billing[0],
            orderShipping: $scope.customer.shipping[0],
            orderItems: $scope.customer.cart })
        .success(function(data, status, headers, config) {
          $scope.customer.cart = [];
          $http.get('/orders/get')
          .success(function(data, status, headers, config) {
             $scope.orders = data;
             $scope.content = '/static/orders.html';
          })
          .error(function(data, status, headers, config) {
             $scope.orders = [];
          });
        })
        .error(function(data, status, headers, config) {
          $window.alert(data);
        });
    };
  }]);
```

Initializing the Application

Now that the application is done, you need to create the initial `Customer`, `Order`, and `Product` documents in the database. There are several different ways to do this, such as using a database script or creating an admin interface for you application. To make it simple, this example includes a basic Node.js script to generate the data you've seen so far.

The code in Listing 28.30 shows a basic Node.js script that first cleans up, removing the customers, orders, and products collections. It then creates a `Customer` document and an `Order` document and then adds several `Product` documents. It adds the `Product` documents to the `Customer` document's cart and the `Order` document's items.

Listing 28.30 `cart_init.js`: **Initializing the shopping cart application data in MongoDB**

```
var mongoose = require('mongoose');
var db = mongoose.connect('mongodb://localhost/cart');
require('./models/cart_model.js');
var Address = mongoose.model('Address');
var Billing = mongoose.model('Billing');
var Product = mongoose.model('Product');
var ProductQuantity = mongoose.model('ProductQuantity');
var Order = mongoose.model('Order');
var Customer = mongoose.model('Customer');
function addProduct(customer, order, name, imagefile,
                    price, description, instock){
  var product = new Product({name:name, imagefile:imagefile,
                             price:price, description:description,
                             instock:instock});
  product.save(function(err, results){
    order.items.push(new ProductQuantity({quantity: 1,
                                          product: [product]}));
    order.save();
    customer.save();
    console.log("Product " + name + " Saved.");
  });
}
Product.remove().exec(function(){
  Order.remove().exec(function(){
    Customer.remove().exec(function(){
      var shipping = new Address({
        name: 'Customer A',
        address: 'Somewhere',
        city: 'My Town',
        state: 'CA',
        zip: '55555'
      });
      var billing = new Billing({
        cardtype: 'Visa',
        name: 'Customer A',
        number: '1234567890',
        expiremonth: 1,
        expireyear: 2020,
        address: shipping
      });
      var customer = new Customer({
        userid: 'customerA',
        shipping: shipping,
        billing: billing,
        cart: []
      });
      customer.save(function(err, result){
```

```
      var order = new Order({
        userid: customer.userid,
        items: [],
        shipping: customer.shipping,
        billing: customer.billing
      });
      order.save(function(err, result){
        addProduct(customer, order, 'Delicate Arch Print',
            'arch.jpg', 12.34,
            'View of the breathtaking Delicate Arch in Utah',
            Math.floor((Math.random()*10)+1));
        addProduct(customer, order, 'Volcano Print',
            'volcano.jpg', 45.45,
            'View of a tropical lake backset by a volcano',
            Math.floor((Math.random()*10)+1));
        addProduct(customer, order, 'Tikal Structure Print',
            'pyramid.jpg', 38.52,
            'Look at the amazing architecture of early America.',
            Math.floor((Math.random()*10)+1));
        addProduct(customer, order, 'Glacial Lake Print',
            'lake.jpg', 77.45,
            'Vivid color, crystal clear water from glacial runoff.',
            Math.floor((Math.random()*10)+1));
      });
    });
  });
 });
});;
```

Summary

In this chapter you've gone through the process of implementing a basic shopping cart by using the Node.js, MongoDB, and AngularJS web application stack. You've defined a solid model in Mongoose to support customers, products, and orders—the full checkout process.

Also in this chapter you've glimpsed the benefits of being able to easily switch between HTML template views in AngularJS and yet have all your data bound to a page automatically. You've also seen the value of data binding in this chapter: You were able to update the MongoDB database with only a simple function call because the `$scope` data was consistently kept up-to-data as you added items to the cart and changed shipping and billing information.

Up Next

In the next chapter you'll learn about some rich Internet application concepts.

29

Building Interactive Web 2.0 Application Components

This chapter will give you some practical experience with implementing Web 2.0 components. The terms *Web 2.0* and *rich Internet applications* (*RIAs*) have been around for a while and have been interpreted many different ways. The opening statement on Wikipedia describes it well: "Web 2.0 describes web sites that use technology beyond the static pages of earlier web sites." The Node.js-to-AngularJS stack fits well into this definition because of how easy it is to integrate services on both the server and client that interact with each other, without the need to page around in the browser.

The chapter takes you through the process of implementing tabbed views, a weather gadget, draggable components, and interactive table data to give you a sampling of the spectrum of Web 2.0 and RIA components. The projects in this chapter are basic enough to make them easy to follow but should provide you with some good ideas about how to leverage the Node.js-to-AngularJS stack to implement Web 2.0 and RIA applications.

Project Description

The project in this chapter takes you through the process of implementing tabbed views, a weather service view, draggable components, and interactive table data. These components use different types of component interaction:

- The tabbed view allows you to easily integrate tabbed views that are hidden and yet still gives the user the ability to access the views quickly in an obvious way.
- The weather gadget hooks into a backend remote weather service to get weather information. This allows you to see how to implement services on the backend that support views on the frontend.
- The draggable view is a basic page with images and text elements that you can drag and reposition. It illustrates the concept of component interactions beyond the standard web elements.

- The tables view implements a frontend for the words database used in Chapters 13–16. There are controls that allow you to sort, filter, and page through the results without reloading the page. The tables view illustrates how tabular data can be interactive.

Libraries Used

The project in this chapter uses the following add-on Node.js NPMs. You need to install them into your project directory in order to follow along with the code examples:

- **`express`**: Used as the main webserver for the project.
- **`body-parser`**: Provides JSON body support for POST requests.
- **`ejs`**: Used to render the HTML templates.
- **`mongodb`**: Used to access the MongoDB database.
- **`mongoose`**: Used to provide the structured data model.

The code in this chapter also requires that you have the AngularJS library.

Project Directory Structure

The project is organized into the following directory structure:

- **`./`**: Contains the base application files and supporting folders. This is the project root.
- **`./npm_modules`**: Created when the NPMs listed above are installed in the system.
- **`./controllers`**: Contains the Express route controllers that provide the interaction between routes and changes to the MongoDB database.
- **`./models`**: Contains the Mongoose model definitions for objects in the database.
- **`./static`**: Contains any static files that need to be sent, such as CSS and AngularJS code.
- **`./views`**: Contains the HTML templates that will be rendered by EJS.
- **`../images`**: Contains any images for the project. This is at a peer level to the project so that multiple projects can use the same images.
- **`../lib`**: Contains the AngularJS libraries so that multiple projects can load them locally. In production, you may want to use a CDN delivery address instead.

> **Note**
>
> This is just one method of organizing your code. You do not have to follow this directory structure, but keep in mind that directory structure should be part of the overall design of your projects so that you can easily find the code you are looking for.

In addition to the directory structure, the following code files are included. This list is intended to give you an idea of the functionality of each file:

- **`./word_init.js`**: Provides standalone initialization code that generates a words database used for the tabular view. You need to run this to test the tables view.
- **`./rich_ui_server.js`**: Loads the necessary libraries, creates a connection to MongoDB, and starts the Express server. This is the main application file.
- **`./rich_ui_routes.js`**: Defines the routes for the Express server. This file handles functionality that does not interact with the database.
- **`./controllers/weather_controller.js`**: Defines the functionality for the routes to access the remote weather service.
- **`./controllers/words_controller.js`**: Defines the functionality for the routes that require interaction with the MongoDB database to get the word objects.
- **`./models/word_model.js`**: Defines the word object structure used for the table example.
- **`./views/rich_ui.html`**: Provides the main example page that implements the tabbed view elements to support the other views.
- **`./static/rich_tabs.html`**: Acts as the container object for multiple tabbed views. This is an AngularJS partial template.
- **`./static/rich_pane.html`**: Houses the individual tabbed view. This is an AngularJS partial template.
- **`./static/draggable.html`**: Implements the draggable example view. This is an AngularJS partial template.
- **`./static/tables.html`**: Implements the interactive tabular view. This is an AngularJS partial template.
- **`./static/weather.html`**: Implements a simple weather widget. This is an AngularJS partial template.
- **`./static/js/rich_ui_app.js`**: Provides the AngularJS module and controller definitions to handle all of the example code.
- **`./static/css/draggable_styles.css`**: Provides the CSS styling for the draggable AngularJS HTML partial.
- **`./static/css/rich_ui_styles.css`**: Provides the CSS styling for the tabbed views.
- **`./static/css/table_styles.css`**: Provides the CSS styling for the tables AngularJS HTML partial.
- **`./static/css/weather_styles.css`**: Provides the CSS styling for the weather AngularJS HTML partial.

Defining the Project Model

For this example, you only need to implement the schema for the words database to store words for the tables example. Listing 29.1 shows the `WordSchema` model. You should already be familiar with this schema from Chapters 13–16.

Listing 29.1 `word_model.js`: **Defining a schema for the words database**

```
var mongoose = require('mongoose');
var Schema = mongoose.Schema;
var WordSchema = new Schema({
  word: {type: String, index: 1, required:true, unique: true},
  first: {type: String, index: 1},
  last: String,
  size: Number,
  letters: [String],
  stats: {
    vowels:Number, consonants:Number},
  charsets: [{ type: String, chars: [String]}]
});
mongoose.model('Word', WordSchema);
```

Creating the Application Server

With the model defined, you can begin implementing the web application server. Listing 29.2 implements the Express server for the web application. This code should be familiar to you. It includes the `express` and `mongoose` libraries and connects to the MongoDB `words` database via Mongoose.

Notice that there is a `require('./models/word_model.js')` statement for the model definition to build the `Schema` object within Mongoose. Also, the `./rich_ui_routes` files initialize the routes for the server before listening on port 80.

Listing 29.2 `rich_ui_server.js`: **Implementing the web application server using Express and connecting to MongoDB**

```
var express = require('express');
var bodyParser = require('body-parser');
var mongoose = require('mongoose');
var db = mongoose.connect('mongodb://localhost/words');
require('./models/word_model.js');
var app = express();
app.engine('.html', require('ejs').__express);
app.set('views', __dirname + '/views');
app.set('view engine', 'html');
```

```
app.use(bodyParser());
require('./rich_ui_routes')(app);
app.listen(80);
```

Implementing Routes to Support the Views

As part of the Express server configuration, you load the `./rich_ui_routes.js` file shown in Listing 29.2. Listing 29.3 provides the routes necessary to load the tabbed view, access the words database, access the backend weather service, and get the necessary static files.

Lines 6–9 implement the static routes to support getting the AngularJS, CSS, JavaScript, images, and AngularJS partial templates used in this example. The images and AngularJS `lib` folders are located in a sibling directory to the project. The other static files are in the `./static` folder inside the project.

Notice that when the user accesses the root location for the site (/), the `rich_ui.html` template is rendered on line 11. The `/weather` route gets data through the `getWeather()` handler in `weather_controller.js`. The `/words` route provides interaction with the MongoDB database through the `words_controller.js` controller.

Listing 29.3 `rich_ui_routes.js`: **Implementing the routes for web application requests from the client**

```
01 var express = require('express');
02 module.exports = function(app) {
03   var weather = require('./controllers/weather_controller');
04   var words = require('./controllers/words_controller');
05   app.use('/static', express.static( './static')).
06       use('/images', express.static( '../images')).
07       use('/lib', express.static( '../lib')
08   );
09   app.get('/', function(req, res){
10     res.render('rich_ui');
11   });
12   app.get('/weather', weather.getWeather);
13   app.get('/words', words.getWords);
14 };
```

Implementing a Tabbed View

With the server and routes configured, you are ready to implement the examples. You'll start with the tabbed view since the other parts of the example are implemented as tabs inside it. You create the tabbed view entirely with custom AngularJS template directives, and it is based on an example that is provided on the AngularJS documentation website.

The directive has two components: the templates that use the directive and the JavaScript code that implements the directive. The following sections describe implementing the templates first and then the JavaScript `Module` object code.

Creating the AngularJS Tabbed View Templates

You need to implement three templates to support the tabbed views. The first supports the pane, the second supports tabs by supporting multiple panes, and the third actually implements the tabbed directives in a standard AngularJS template.

Defining the Pane Template

You need to define a template to act as the pane for the tabbed view. The pane is just a container that can hold whatever content you want to add. Listing 29.4 shows the basic pane template with a single `<div>` element.

You assign a `pane` class to an element for styling, and you use the `ng-show` directive to show the pane only when `selected` is `true`, and you use the `ng-transclude` directive to allow wrapping of content.

Listing 29.4 `rich_pane.html`: **Implementing the pane template view for the tabbed view**

```
<div class="pane"
     ng-show="selected"
     ng-transclude>
</div>
```

Defining the Tabs Template

Next, you need to define a template to act as the container for the pane elements to support multiple panes in the tabbed view. The tabs container needs to support defining multiple pane elements. Listing 29.5 shows the tabs template code.

You assign a `tabs` class to an element for styling. To implement multiple panes, you define a `<span>` element that implements the `ng-repeat` directive on a panes array defined in the custom directive code. Notice that the `ng-click` directive calls `select(pane)` to select the pane and make it visible.

Also, you use the `ng-class` directive to add the `activeTab` class if `pane.selected` is `true`. Line 8 defines the `<div>` element, where the pane content is transcluded.

Listing 29.5 `rich_tabs.html`: **Implementing the tabs template view for the tabbed view**

```
<div class="tabbable">
  <div class="tabs">
    <span class="tab" ng-repeat="pane in panes"
        ng-class="{activeTab:pane.selected}"
        ng-click="select(pane)">{{pane.title}}
    </span>
  </div>
  <div class="tabcontent" ng-transclude></div>
</div>
```

Implementing the Tabbed View

With the pane and tabs templates defined, you can add the new custom directives to your AngularJS templates. The format for adding multiple tabs for the new directives is as follows, with `title` set to the value that will be rendered in the template code:

```
<rich_tabs>
  <rich_pane title="Tab 1">
Your Content
  </rich_pane>
  <rich_pane title="Tab 2">
Your Content
  </rich_pane>
</rich_tabs>
```

Listing 29.6 shows the full application view defined for all three projects and implements separate tabs for the weather, draggable, and tables examples. It also loads the CSS code and the `rich_ui_app.js` file that will house the JavaScript supporting code for the tabs and pane directives. Notice that you use the `ng-include` directive to link to the AngularJS partial files, which makes the template very clean.

Listing 29.6 `rich_ui.html`: **Implementing the AngularJS template that uses a tabbed view**

```
<!doctype html>
<html ng-app="richApp">
<head>
  <title>Rich UI</title>
  <link rel="stylesheet" type="text/css"
      href="/static/css/rich_ui_styles.css" />
  <link rel="stylesheet" type="text/css"
      href="/static/css/draggable_styles.css" />
  <link rel="stylesheet" type="text/css"
      href="/static/css/weather_styles.css" />
  <link rel="stylesheet" type="text/css"
      href="/static/css/table_styles.css" />
```

```
</head>
<body>
  <rich_tabs>
    <rich_pane title="Weather">
      <div ng-include="'/static/weather.html'"></div>
    </rich_pane>
    <rich_pane title="Draggable">
      <div ng-include="'/static/draggable.html'"></div>
    </rich_pane>
    <rich_pane title="Tables">
      <div ng-include="'/static/tables.html'"></div>
    </rich_pane>
  </rich_tabs>
  <script src="http://code.angularjs.org/1.2.9/angular.min.js"></script>
  <script src="/static/js/rich_ui_app.js"></script>
</body>
</html>
```

Implementing the AngularJS Custom Directives

You now need to implement the custom directive code to support the `richTabs` and `richPane` directive templates. Listing 29.7 shows the portion of `rich_ui_app.js` that implements the backend code necessary to support the `richTabs` and `richPane` directive templates.

The `richTabs` directive defines the controller function that contains the panes array used to populate the tabs. Also, the `select()` function sets the `select` value of all the panes in the array to `false` and then the current pane to `true`, which hides all the panes except the selected one. The `addPane()` function is called from the `richPane` directive and adds the pane to the panes list in `richTabs`. Notice that `tempalteUrl` points to the `rich_tabs.html` template defined above.

`richPane` defines a directive and specifies the `rich_pane.html file` as the template source. It defines the `title` in the scope such that it will be available to be displayed in the tabs. Notice that `richTabs` is required to provide access from this directive via `tabsCtrl`. Then in the `link` function, a call can be made to `addPane()` to add the pane to the panes array.

Listing 29.7 `rich_ui_app.js-richPane/richTabs`: **Implementing the AngularJS directive code for pane and tabs directives**

```
var app = angular.module('richApp', []);
. . .
app.directive('richTabs', function() {
  return { restrict: 'E', transclude: true,
    scope: {},
    controller: function($scope) {
      var panes = $scope.panes = [];
```

```
      $scope.select = function(pane) {
        angular.forEach(panes, function(pane) {
          pane.selected = false;
        });
        pane.selected = true;
      };
      this.addPane = function(pane) {
        if (panes.length == 0) {
          $scope.select(pane);
        }
        panes.push(pane);
      };
    },
    templateUrl: '/static/rich_tabs.html'
  };
});
app.directive('richPane', function() {
  return { require: '^richTabs', restrict: 'E',
    templateUrl: '/static/rich_pane.html',
    transclude: true, scope: { title: '@' },
    link: function(scope, element, attrs, tabsCtrl) {
      tabsCtrl.addPane(scope);
    }
  };
});
```

Styling the Tabs View

Listing 29.8 shows the CSS code that is used to style the tabbed views defined in the sections above so that you can see why things look and act as they do. The code is compact to fit in the book. Notice that as you click on different tabs, the view changes. Figure 29.1 shows the different rendered views and gives you a preview of what is to come.

Listing 29.8 `rich_ui_styles.css`: **Implementing the CSS styles for the tabbed views**

```
.tab{display:inline-block; width:100px; cursor: pointer;
  border-radius: .5em .5em 0 0; border:1px solid black;
  text-align:center; font: 15px/28px Helvetica, sans-serif;
  background-image: -webkit-linear-gradient(top, #CCCCCC, #EEEEEE) }
.activeTab{border-bottom:none;
  background-image: -webkit-linear-gradient(top, #66CCFF, #CCFFFF) }
.pane{border:1px solid black; margin-top:-2px;
  background-color:#CCFFFF; height:450px; width:700px;
  padding:10px; }
```

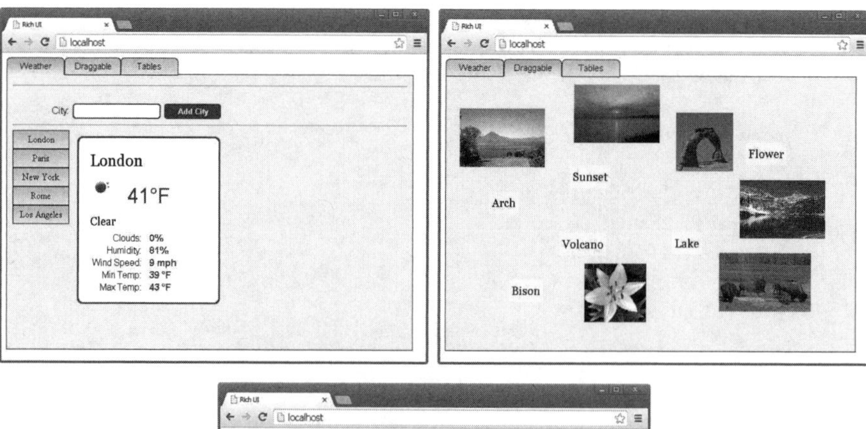

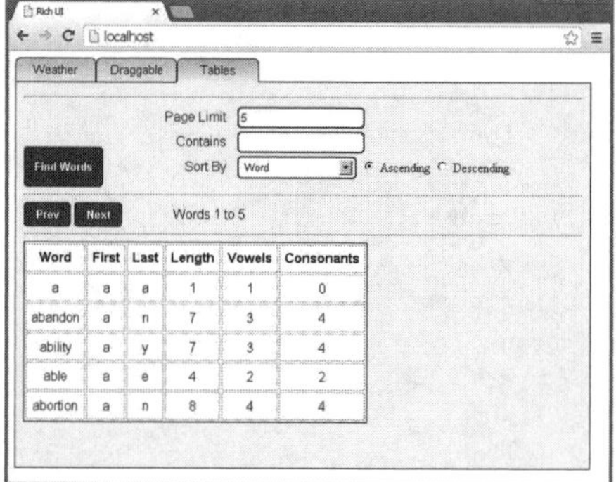

Word	First	Last	Length	Vowels	Consonants
a	a	a	1	1	0
abandon	a	n	7	3	4
ability	a	y	7	3	4
able	a	e	4	2	2
abortion	a	n	8	4	4

Figure 29.1 The tabbed views allow you to quickly change content without reloading from the server.

Implementing a Weather Service View

With the tabbed views in place, you can begin implementing the other components, starting with the weather view. The weather view part of this example illustrates using a backend service to connect to the openweathermap.com website and retrieve weather for a specific city. Using the backend server to access remote sites can be useful if there are cross-domain issues with the browser, to format the remote data before sending it to the client, etc.

The following sections take you through the process of implementing the backend server, the AngularJS controller to connect to the backend server, and the actual HTML view.

Creating the Backend Weather Service

Listing 29.9 implements the backend web service on the Node.js server. The service exports the `getWeather()` route handler to handle the `/weather` route in Express. When this code receives the request, it pulls the city name from `req.query.city` and uses it to make the remote web request on the server. The `parseWeather()` function handles the request.

The `parseWeather()` function reads the data and formats it into a JavaScript object that the client can more easily consume. `res.json()` returns the results.

Listing 29.9 `weather_controller.js`: **Implementing the backend weather service on the Node.js server**

```
var http = require('http');
function toFahrenheit(temp){
  return Math.round((temp-273.15)*9/5+32);
}
function parseWeather(req, res, weatherResponse) {
  var weatherData = '';
  weatherResponse.on('data', function (chunk) {
    weatherData += chunk;
  });
  weatherResponse.on('end', function () {
    var wObj = JSON.parse(weatherData);
    if (wObj.name){
      var wData = {
        name: wObj.name,
        temp: toFahrenheit(wObj.main.temp),
        tempMin: toFahrenheit(wObj.main.temp_min),
        tempMax: toFahrenheit(wObj.main.temp_max),
        humidity: wObj.main.humidity,
        wind: Math.round(wObj.wind.speed*2.23694), //mph
        clouds: wObj.clouds.all,
        description: wObj.weather[0].main,
        icon: wObj.weather[0].icon
      };
    } else {
      wObj = {name: "Not Found"};
    }
    res.json(wData);
  });
}
exports.getWeather = function(req, res){
  var city = req.query.city;
  var options = {
    host: 'api.openweathermap.org',
    path: '/data/2.5/weather?q=' + city
  };
  http.request(options, function(weatherResponse){
    parseWeather(req, res, weatherResponse);
  }).end();
}
```

Defining the Weather AngularJS Controller

With the weather service and route defined on the Node.js server side, you can implement a controller that accesses the route to get weather data. Listing 29.10 implements `weatherController` in the AngularJS application `Module` object. The scope contains a list of cities and the location or city name used when getting weather data. Also, a `locationIn` value is defined to provide a model for a text input to add new city names.

The `getWeather()` function makes an `$http GET` request, passing the city parameter from `$scope.location`, and sets the `$scope.weather` value that will be bound to the view.

The `addCity()` function uses `locationIn` to add new cities to the cities array. If a city already exists, then it is not added. The location is set to the new city, and `getWeather()` retrieves the weather data.

Listing 29.10 `rich_ui_app.js-weatherController`: **Implementing the AngularJS controller to interact with the view and backend service**

```
var app = angular.module('richApp', []);
. . .
app.controller('weatherController', function($scope, $http) {
  $scope.cities = ['London', 'Paris', 'New York',
                   'Rome', 'Los Angeles'];
  $scope.location = $scope.cities[0];
  $scope.locationIn = '';
  $scope.getWeather = function(){
    $http({url: '/weather', method: "GET",
           params:{city:$scope.location}})
    .success(function(data, status, headers, config) {
      $scope.weather = data;
     })
     .error(function(data, status, headers, config) {
      $scope.weather = data;
     });
  };
  $scope.addCity = function(){
    if ($scope.cities.indexOf($scope.locationIn) != 0){
      $scope.cities.push($scope.locationIn);
    }
    $scope.location = $scope.locationIn;
    $scope.getWeather();
  };
  $scope.setLocation = function(city){
    $scope.location = city;
    $scope.getWeather();
  };
  $scope.getWeather('London');
});
```

Defining the Weather AngularJS View

With the controller in place, you can define the view to consume the weather data. Listing 29.11 shows the basic template that consumes the weather data from the scope and renders it as shown in Figure 29.2.

A text input at the top accepts the new city name and binds it to `locationIn` and a button that calls `addCity()` in the controller when clicked. Notice that all the weather data comes from the `$scope.weather` variable and is rendered using AngularJS expressions.

Listing 29.11 `weather.html`: **Implementing AngularJS template for the weather view**

```
<div ng-controller="weatherController"><hr>
  <br><label class="weatherInfo">City:</label>
  <input class="weatherInput" type="text" ng-model="locationIn" />
  <input class="weatherButton" type="button"
         ng-click="addCity()" value="Add City"/><hr>
  <div class="cities">
      <div class="city" ng-repeat="city in cities"
           ng-click="setLocation(city)">
        {{city}}
      </div>
  </div>
  <div class="weatherData">
    <p class="weatherCity">{{weather.name}}</p>
    <img
    ng-src="http://openweathermap.org/img/w/{{weather.icon}}.png" />
    <span class="weatherTemp">{{weather.temp}}&deg;F</span>
    <p class="weatherDesc">{{weather.description}}</p>
    <label class="weatherInfo">Clouds:</label>
    <span class="weatherInfo">{{weather.clouds}}%</span>
    <label class="weatherInfo">Humidity:</label>
    <span class="weatherInfo">{{weather.humidity}}%</span>
    <label class="weatherInfo">Wind Speed:</label>
    <span class="weatherInfo">{{weather.wind}} mph</span>
    <label class="weatherInfo">Min Temp:</label>
    <span class="weatherInfo">{{weather.tempMin}} &deg;F</span>
    <label class="weatherInfo">Max Temp:</label>
    <span class="weatherInfo">{{weather.tempMax}} &deg;F</span>
  </div>
</div>
```

Styling the Weather View

Listing 29.12 shows the CSS code you use to style the weather view defined in the sections above so that you can see why things look and act as they do. Once again, the code is compact to fit better in the book. Figure 29.2 shows the rendered weather view with the CSS styling applied.

Listing 29.12 `weather_styles.css`: **Implementing the CSS styles for the weather view**

```
.cities { display:inline-block; width:100px; vertical-align: top; }
.city{ border: 1px solid black; cursor: pointer; padding: 5px;
  text-align: center;
  background-image: -webkit-linear-gradient(top, #CCCCCC, #EEEEEE); }
.weatherData { display:inline-block; width:220px;
  background-color:white; border:3px ridge blue; margin:10px;
  padding:15px; border-radius:10px; }
.weatherInfo { display:inline-block; width:100px;
  font: 16px/20px Helvetica, sans-serif; }
label.weatherInfo{ text-align: right; }
span.weatherInfo{ padding-left: 10px; color: blue;
  font-weight: bold; }
.weatherTemp { font: 36px/48px Helvetica, sans-serif;
  padding-left:20px; color:blue }
.weatherCity { font: 28px/36px Georgia, serif;
  padding:5px; margin:0}
.weatherDesc { font: 20px/28px Georgia, serif;
  padding:5px; margin:0}
.weatherInput { padding:3px; border:2px ridge blue;
  border-radius: 5px; }
.weatherButton { padding:3px; width:100px; border:2px ridge blue;
  border-radius: 5px; background-color: blue; color: white;
  font-weight: bold; }
```

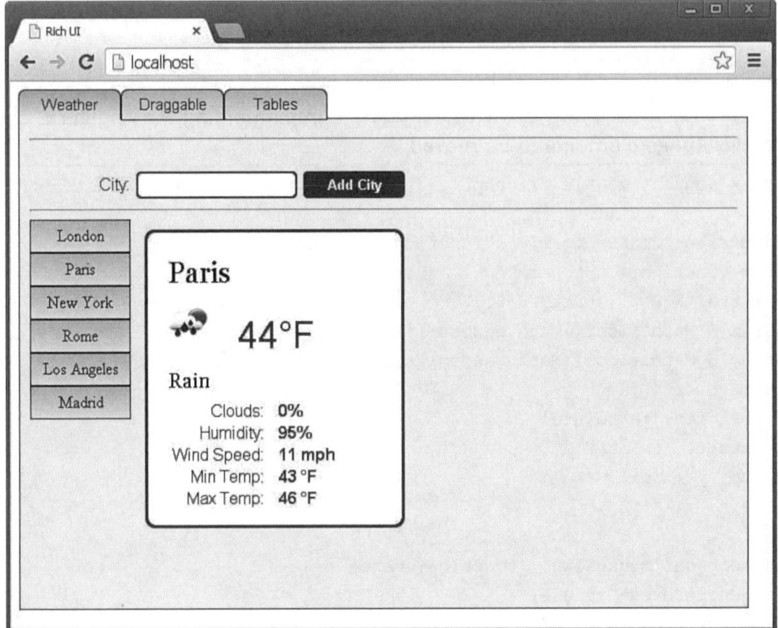

Figure 29.2 The weather view allows you to quickly see the weather in a list of cities and add additional cities.

Implementing Draggable Elements

With the weather view complete, you can move on to the draggable view. The draggable view illustrates using web elements in unconventional ways. The actual implementation is simple. A custom AngularJS directive allows you to make elements draggable by hooking into the mouse events and changing relative CSS position of the element.

In this example, you make several images and words draggable. You can drag them around the screen as much as you like. This example could make a good teaching aid for a small child but can be utilized in many other creative ways as well.

Defining the Draggable Custom AngularJS Directive

Listing 29.13 defines a custom directive named `richDraggable`. This directive stores the initial position of the element passed in when the template is compiled and then registers a handler with the `mousedown` event on the element.

When the mouse is pressed, the handler adds events for `mousemove` and `mouseup`. The `mousemove` handler adjusts the `top` and `left` CSS attributes to move the element around the screen.

The mouseup event handler unbinds the mousemove and mouseup event handlers to stop dragging.

Listing 29.13 rich_ui_app.js-richDraggable: **Implementing the AngularJS custom directive to allow page elements to be moved**

```
var app = angular.module('richApp', []);
. . .
app.directive('richDraggable', function($document, $window) {
  return function(scope, element, attr) {
    var startX = 0, startY = 0;
    var x = Math.floor((Math.random()*500)+40);
    var y = Math.floor((Math.random()*360)+40);
    element.css({
      position: 'absolute',
      cursor: 'pointer',
      top: y + 'px',
      left: x + 'px'
    });
    element.on('mousedown', function(event) {
      event.preventDefault();
      startX = event.pageX - x;
      startY = event.pageY - y;
      $document.on('mousemove', mousemove);
      $document.on('mouseup', mouseup);
    });
    function mousemove(event) {
      y = event.pageY - startY;
      x = event.pageX - startX;
      element.css({
        top: y + 'px',
        left:  x + 'px'
      });
    }
    function mouseup() {
      $document.unbind('mousemove', mousemove);
      $document.unbind('mouseup', mouseup);
    }
  };
});
```

Implementing the Draggable Directive in an AngularJS View

With the draggable directive defined in the AngularJS `Module` object, you can implement it in your views by simply including the `rich-draggable` directive in the HTML element definition. For example, to drag a paragraph around, you could use:

```
<p rich-draggable>My draggable paragraph.</p>
```

Listing 29.14 shows the implementation used in the example shown in Figure 29.3. It is very basic—just a series of `<img>` and `<span>` elements that use the `rich-draggable` directive.

Listing 29.14 `draggable.html`: **Implementing an AngularJS template for the draggable view**

```
<img class="dragImage" rich-draggable src="/images/arch.jpg" />
<img class="dragImage" rich-draggable src="/images/flower.jpg" />
<img class="dragImage" rich-draggable src="/images/lake.jpg" />
<img class="dragImage" rich-draggable src="/images/volcano.jpg" />
<img class="dragImage" rich-draggable src="/images/sunset2.jpg" />
<img class="dragImage" rich-draggable src="/images/bison.jpg" />
<span class="dragLabel" rich-draggable>Lake</span>
<span class="dragLabel" rich-draggable>Volcano</span>
<span class="dragLabel" rich-draggable>Sunset</span>
<span class="dragLabel" rich-draggable>Bison</span>
<span class="dragLabel" rich-draggable>Flower</span>
<span class="dragLabel" rich-draggable>Arch</span>
```

Styling the Draggable View

Listing 29.15 shows the CSS code you use to style the draggable view defined in the sections above so that you can see why things look and act as they do. Figure 29.3 shows the rendered draggable view with the CSS styling applied.

Listing 29.15 `draggable_styles.css`: **Implementing the CSS styles for the draggable view**

```
.dragImage{
    height:100px;
}
.dragLabel{
    background-color:rgba(255, 255, 255, 0.5);
    display:inline-block;
    font: 20px/28px Georgia, serif;
    padding:5px;
}
```

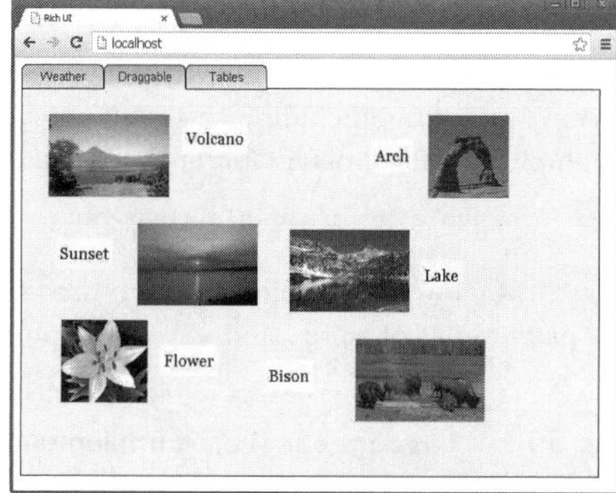

Figure 29.3 The draggable view allows you to drag images and words around the browser window by using the mouse.

Implementing Dynamic Data Access

The final example in this chapter involves a words database to illustrate implementing interactive tables. Using tables is a great way to display large amounts of data from the server in an easy-to-read form. By using the interactive techniques you have already learned in this book, you can make the tables come alive for users, allowing them to sort data, set the size of that table, page through large amounts of data, and even filter the data in the table.

The following sections show you how to implement a basic interactive table that allows you to set the limit, filter, and sort criteria for MongoDB queries that provide the data for the table.

Creating the Express Route Controller for the `/words` Route

First, you need to implement the route handler that will interact with the `Word` model to retrieve the words from MongoDB. Listing 29.16 implements the `getWords()` route handler for the `/words` route. This handler reads the `limit`, `skip`, `sort`, and `direction` parameters from the query and uses them to query the MongoDB database.

The `getSortObj()` function transforms the sort fields and direction into the sort object that will be used in the `.sort()` method on the `Query` object.

Listing 29.16 `words_controller.js`: **Implementing the backend word route controller to support the `/words` route**

```
var mongoose = require('mongoose'),
    Word = mongoose.model('Word');
exports.getWords = function(req, res) {
  var sort = getSortObj(req);
```

```
  var query = Word.find();
  if(req.query.contains.length > 0){
    query.find({'word' : new RegExp(req.query.contains, 'i')});
  }
  query.sort(sort)
  .limit(req.query.limit)
  .skip(req.query.skip)
  .exec(function(err, word) {
    if (!word){
      res.json(404, {msg: 'Word Not Found.'});
    } else {
      res.json(word);
    }
  });
};
function getSortObj(req){
  var field = "word";
  if(req.query.sort == 'Vowels'){
    field = 'stats.vowels';
  } else if(req.query.sort == 'Consonants'){
    field = 'stats.consonants';
  } else if(req.query.sort == 'Length'){
    field = 'size';
  }else{
    field = req.query.sort.toLowerCase();
  }
  var sort = new Object();
  sort[field] = req.query.direction;
  return sort;
};
```

Defining the Table AngularJS Controller

With the `/word` route handler in place, you can implement the AngularJS controller that accesses the list of words displayed in the table. Listing 29.17 implements `tableController` in the AngularJS application `Module` object.

The first few lines define the words array, which contains the data for the table as well as the `contains`, `limit`, `skip`, and `direction` values used in the `$http GET` request to retrieve the set of words. The `sortFields` array provides data to select which field to sort on.

The `getWords()` function makes an `$http GET` request to the `/words` route and populates the `$scope.words` array that is bound to the table data with the results. Notice that the `limit`, `skip`, `sort`, `direction`, and `contains` fields are sent with the request to support sorting, paging, and filtering.

The `find()` method reinitializes the `skip` value and then calls `getWords()` to perform a new search. The `next()` and `prev()` methods adjust the `skip` value to page the results from the words database.

Listing 29.17 `rich_ui_app.js-tableController`: **Implementing the AngularJS controller to interact with the `Word` model on the server**

```
var app = angular.module('richApp', []);
app.controller('tableController', function($scope, $http) {
  $scope.words = [];
  $scope.contains = '';
  $scope.limit = 5;
  $scope.skip = 0;
  $scope.skipEnd = 0;
  $scope.sortFields = ['Word', 'First', 'Last', 'Length',
                       'Vowels', 'Consonants'];
  $scope.sortField ="Word";
  $scope.direction = "asc";
  $scope.getWords = function(){
    $http({url: '/words', method: "GET",
           params:{ limit:$scope.limit,
                    skip:$scope.skip,
                    sort:$scope.sortField,
                    direction:$scope.direction,
                    contains:$scope.contains }})
    .success(function(data, status, headers, config) {
       $scope.words = data;
       $scope.skipEnd = $scope.skip + $scope.words.length;
     })
     .error(function(data, status, headers, config) {
       $scope.words = [];
       $scope.skipEnd = $scope.skip + $scope.words.length;
     });
  };
  $scope.find = function(){
    $scope.skip = 0;
    $scope.getWords();
  };
  $scope.next = function(){
    if($scope.words.length == $scope.limit){
      $scope.skip += parseInt($scope.limit);
      $scope.getWords();
    }
  };
  $scope.prev = function(){
```

```
    if($scope.skip > 0){
      if($scope.skip >= parseInt($scope.limit)){
        $scope.skip -= parseInt($scope.limit);
      } else{
        $scope.skip = 0;
      }
      $scope.getWords();
    }
  };
  $scope.getWords();
});
```

Implementing the Tables AngularJS View

With `tableController` implemented, you can implement the AngularJS view that utilizes the words data in table form. Listing 29.18 implements a simple template to provide controls to filter, sort, and page the words, as well as display the words in a table.

Note that you populate `<select>` by using `ng-options` on the `sortFields` array. Also, you use the `ng-repeat` on the `<tr>` element to implement the rows in the table. The individual values for the words data are rendered to the page by using AngularJS expressions.

The `limit` field sets the number of rows returned, the `contains` field sets the filter for words that contain the text, and `sort by` allows you to select a field and direction for sorting. Figure 29.4 shows a couple different views of the rendered template.

Listing 29.18 `tables.html`: **Implementing the AngularJS template for the tables view**

```
<div ng-controller="tableController"><hr>
<input class="findButton" type="button"
       value="Find Words" ng-click="find()" />
<div id="sortOptions">
  <label class="tableLabel">Page Limit</label>
  <input class="tableInput" type="text" ng-model="limit" /><br>
  <label class="tableLabel">Contains</label>
  <input class="tableInput" type="text" ng-model="contains" /><br>
  <label class="tableLabel">Sort By</label>
  <select class="tableInput" ng-model="sortField"
          ng-options="field for field in sortFields"></select>
  <input type="radio" ng-model="direction" value="asc"> Ascending
  <input type="radio" ng-model="direction" value="desc"> Descending
</div>
<hr>
<div>
  <input class="pageButton" type="button" value="Prev"
         ng-click="prev()" />
```

```
  <input class="pageButton" type="button" value="Next"
         ng-click="next()" />
  <label class="tableLabel">Words {{skip+1}} to {{skipEnd}}</label>
  <hr>
  <div id="tableContainer">
    <table>
      <tr><th>Word</th><th>First</th><th>Last</th><th>Length</th>
      <th>Vowels</th><th>Consonants</th></tr>
      <tr ng-repeat="word in words">
        <td>{{word.word}}</td>
        <td>{{word.first}}</td>
        <td>{{word.last}}</td>
        <td>{{word.size}}</td>
        <td>{{word.stats.vowels}}</td>
        <td>{{word.stats.consonants}}</td>
      </tr>
    </table>
  </div>
</div>
</div>
```

Styling the Tables View

Listing 29.19 shows the CSS code you use to style the tables view defined in the sections above so that you can see why things look and act as they do. Figure 29.4 shows the rendered tables view with the CSS styling applied.

Listing 29.19 `table_styles.css`: **Implementing the CSS styles for the tables view**

```
#tableContainer{ display: inline-block;
  max-height:270px; overflow-y:auto; }
#sortOptions{ display:inline-block; }
.pageButton,
.findButton { padding:3px; width:100px; height:50px;
  border:2px ridge blue; border-radius: 5px;
  background-color: blue; color: white;
  font-weight: bold; cursor: pointer; }
.pageButton { width: 60px; height:50px; height:30px; }
.tableLabel { display: inline-block; width:150px;
  text-align:right; margin-right:10px;
  font: 16px/20px Helvetica, sans-serif; }
.tableInput { padding:3px; border:2px ridge blue;
  border-radius: 5px; width: 150px}
table { border:1px solid black; background-color:white;
  padding:0px; margin-right:20px; }
```

```
td, th { text-align:center; padding: 6px; border: .1em dotted grey;
  font: 16px/20px Helvetica, sans-serif; }
th {font-weight: bold; }
tr {padding:0px; }
```

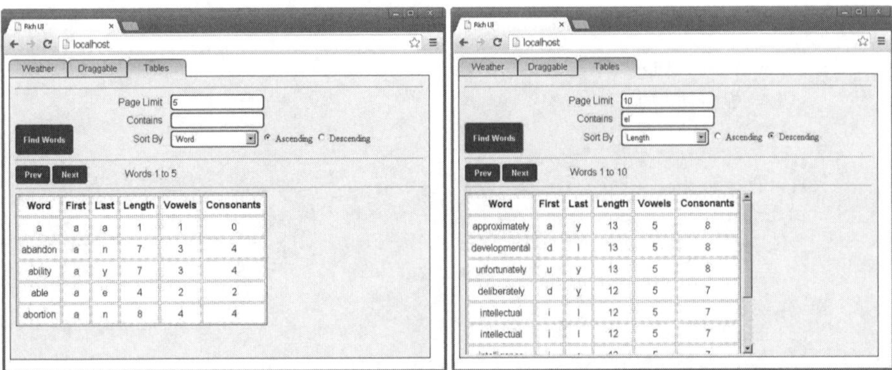

Figure 29.4 The tables view allows you to dynamically adjust which words are displayed by using filtering, sorting, and paging.

Initializing the Application

To implement the tables view, you need a database of words. Listing 29.20 provides a basic Node.js application that implements the words database used in this chapter. You need to run this before you can test the tables view defined in the previous sections. You need to modify the `words` variable on line 3 to include the words you want in the database. The example on the book's website includes about 5,000 words.

Listing 29.20 `word_init.js`: **Initializing the words database for the tables view**

```
01 var vowelArr = "aeiou";
02 var consenantArr = "bcdfghjklmnpqrstvwxyz";
03 var words = "the,be,and,of,a,in ... ,middle-class,apology,till";
04 var wordArr = words.split(",");
05 var wordObjArr = new Array();
06 for (var i=0; i<wordArr.length; i++){
07   try{
08     var word = wordArr[i].toLowerCase();
09     var vowelCnt = ("|"+word+"|").split(/[aeiou]/i).length-1;
10     var consonantCnt =
11       ("|"+word+"|").split(/[bcdfghjklmnpqrstvwxyz]/i).length-1;
12     var letters = [];
```

```
    var vowels = [];
    var consonants = [];
    var other = [];
    for (var j=0; j<word.length; j++){
      var ch = word[j];
      if (letters.indexOf(ch) === -1){
        letters.push(ch);
      }
      if (vowelArr.indexOf(ch) !== -1){
        if(vowels.indexOf(ch) === -1){
          vowels.push(ch);
        }
      }else if (consenantArr.indexOf(ch) !== -1){
        if(consonants.indexOf(ch) === -1){
          consonants.push(ch);
        }
      }else{
        if(other.indexOf(ch) === -1){
          other.push(ch);
        }
      }
    }
    var charsets = [];
    if(consonants.length){
      charsets.push({type:"consonants", chars:consonants});
    }
    if(vowels.length){
      charsets.push({type:"vowels", chars:vowels});
    }
    if(other.length){
      charsets.push({type:"other", chars:other});
    }
    var wordObj = {
      word: word,
      first: word[0],
      last: word[word.length-1],
      size: word.length,
      letters: letters,
      stats: { vowels: vowelCnt, consonants: consonantCnt },
      charsets: charsets
    };
    if(other.length){
      wordObj.otherChars = other;
    }
    wordObjArr.push(wordObj);
  } catch (e){
    console.log(e);
```

```
    console.log(word);
  }
}
var MongoClient = require('mongodb').MongoClient;
MongoClient.connect("mongodb://localhost/", function(err, db) {
  var myDB = db.db("words");
  myDB.dropCollection("words");
  myDB.createCollection("words", function(err, wordCollection){
    wordCollection.insert(wordObjArr, function(err, result){
      console.log(result);
      db.close();
    });
  });
});
```

Summary

In this chapter, you looked at some of the ways to implement interactive Web 2.0 components in a web application. The tabbed view example shows one way to allow users to switch between unrelated views without having to navigate away from the page they are on. The weather example shows you how you can implement backend services to support views with data from external sources.

The draggable view illustrates the web components you can extend with behavior that is not native to the browser, providing more of an application experience. The tables view provides an example of allowing the user to dynamically modify the data in a view by setting parameters used to query the MongoDB database.

As you have seen in the exercises in these past few chapters, Node.js, MongoDB, Express, and AngularJS provide an extremely powerful and yet easy-to-use web application stack from the server up to the client.

You started your journey learning about how Node.js can be used for all things server-side, including server-side scripts, communication with external services and databases, as well as the webserver itself. Then you got a chance to learn how to incorporate MongoDB as the data store for your applications and access it directly from Node.js using the Mongoose library. Next you learned how to utilize the power of Express to build out robust webserver features very rapidly.

With the server-side stuff learned, you then moved onto using AngularJS as the framework for your client applications. You learned how AngularJS allows you to create and build custom HTML elements that fit the exact needs of your applications and how to implement services to provide the communication to and from your applications.

One of the best aspects that you should have noticed is that the entire stack uses the JavaScript language. That means that you can use the same JavaScript objects in JavaScript format in the client, server, and stored in the database with no translation other than object to JSON and back. That also means that you can easily migrate your JavaScript code between the server and client with little or no changes.

Node.js, AngularJS, and MongoDB are some of the most exciting technologies available today. They are simple to use and to integrate with each other and provide robust features that allow you to build enterprise-ready websites and applications. I hope you have enjoyed this book and love these technologies as much as I do.

Thanks and enjoy.

Index

Symbols

A

B

D

E

J

K

L

M

N

O

P

Q

R

U

W

X-Y-Z

Brad Dayley

Node.js, MongoDB and AngularJS Web Development

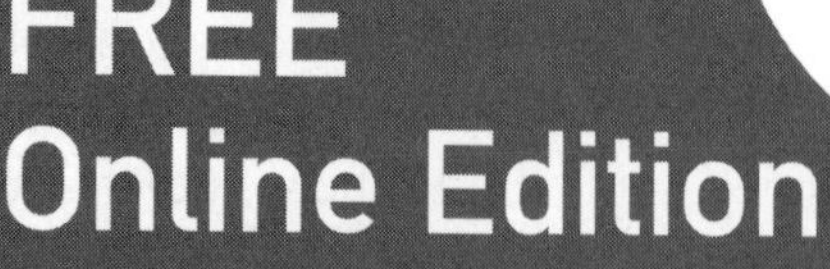

Your purchase of ***Node.js, MongoDB and AngularJS Web Development*** includes access to a free online edition for 45 days through the **Safari Books Online** subscription service. Nearly every Addison-Wesley Professional book is available online through **Safari Books Online**, along with thousands of books and videos from publishers such as Cisco Press, Exam Cram, IBM Press, O'Reilly Media, Prentice Hall, Que, Sams, and VMware Press.

Safari Books Online is a digital library providing searchable, on-demand access to thousands of technology, digital media, and professional development books and videos from leading publishers. With one monthly or yearly subscription price, you get unlimited access to learning tools and information on topics including mobile app and software development, tips and tricks on using your favorite gadgets, networking, project management, graphic design, and much more.

Activate your FREE Online Edition at informit.com/safarifree

STEP 1: Enter the coupon code: HHLDKFH.

STEP 2: New Safari users, complete the brief registration form. Safari subscribers, just log in.

If you have difficulty registering on Safari or accessing the online edition, please e-mail customer-service@safaribooksonline.com

Cisco Press